File System Forensics

File System Forensics

Fergus Toolan
Norwegian Police University College
Ballina, Tipperary

WILEY

Published by John Wiley & Sons, Inc., Hoboken, New Jersey.
Published simultaneously in Canada.

Library of Congress Cataloging-in-Publication Applied for:

Hardback ISBN: 9781394289790

Cover Design: Wiley
Cover Image: © aleksandarvelasevic/Getty Images

Set in 9.5/12.5pt STIXTwoText by Straive, Chennai, India

To Helen
Thanks for everything!

Contents

Preface *xvii*
Acknowledgements *xxi*

Part I Preliminaries *1*

1 **Introduction** *3*
1.1 What is Digital Forensics? *4*
1.2 File System Forensics *5*
1.3 Digital Forensic Principles *5*
1.4 Digital Forensic Methodology *7*
1.4.1 Preparation *8*
1.4.2 Localisation/Preservation *8*
1.4.3 Acquisition *8*
1.4.4 Processing *9*
1.4.5 Analysis *9*
1.4.6 Reporting *9*
1.4.7 Quality Assurance *10*
1.4.8 Evidence Return *10*
1.5 About This Book *10*
1.5.1 Who Should Read This Book? *11*
1.6 Book Structure *12*
1.7 Summary *13*
Exercises *13*
Bibliography *14*

2 **Linux as a Forensic Platform** *17*
2.1 Open-Source Software *17*
2.1.1 Advantages of Open-Source Software *19*
2.1.2 Open Source ≠ Free *20*
2.2 Open-Source Software in Digital Forensics *20*
2.3 What is Linux? *21*
2.3.1 The Anatomy of the Linux OS *22*
2.3.2 Linux Distributions *27*

2.3.3 A (very) Brief History of Linux *28*
2.4 Using Linux *29*
2.4.1 User Accounts *30*
2.4.2 Basic Linux Commands *32*
2.4.2.1 Navigating the File System *32*
2.4.2.2 Getting Help *34*
2.4.2.3 Viewing/Editing Text Files *34*
2.4.2.4 Managing Directories *35*
2.4.2.5 Redirection and Pipes *35*
2.5 Linux as a Forensic Platform *36*
2.5.1 Commands for Digital Forensics *36*
2.5.1.1 Hashing *36*
2.5.1.2 Hex Viewers *38*
2.5.1.3 Archiving/Compression *39*
2.5.1.4 The file Command *40*
2.5.1.5 The strings Command *40*
2.5.1.6 Text Searching with (e)grep *41*
2.6 Summary *42*
Exercises/Discussion Topics *42*
Bibliography *43*

3 Mathematical Preliminaries *45*
3.1 Bits and Bytes *45*
3.2 Number Systems *48*
3.2.1 Notational Conventions *48*
3.2.2 Decimal *48*
3.2.3 Binary *49*
3.2.4 Hexadecimal *50*
3.2.5 Number Conversions *51*
3.2.6 Number Conversion with Bash *51*
3.2.7 Negative Numbers *53*
3.2.8 Floating-Point Numbers *53*
3.3 Representing Text *56*
3.3.1 ASCII *56*
3.3.2 ISO-8859 *57*
3.3.3 Unicode *59*
3.3.4 UTF-8 *60*
3.3.5 UTF-16 *61*
3.4 Representing Time *62*
3.4.1 Unix Time *63*
3.4.2 The Linux date Command *64*
3.5 Endianness and Raw Data *64*
3.6 Summary *66*
Exercises *67*
Bibliography *68*

4 Disks, Partitions and File Systems *69*
4.1 Disk Storage *70*
4.1.1 Traditional Rotational Hard Drives *71*
4.1.1.1 Optical Media *72*
4.1.2 Flash Drives *73*
4.1.3 Solid-State Drives *73*
4.2 Partitions *74*
4.2.1 Creating Partitions/File Systems on Linux *74*
4.2.1.1 Mounting File Systems on Linux *77*
4.2.2 Master Boot Record *78*
4.2.3 GUID Partition Table *80*
4.3 File Systems *83*
4.3.1 File System Concepts *83*
4.3.2 Comparison of File Systems *86*
4.4 Acquisition of File System Data *88*
4.4.1 Logical vs Physical Acquisition *88*
4.4.2 Acquisition Under Linux *88*
4.4.2.1 The dd Family *89*
4.4.2.2 Expert Witness Format (EWF) *90*
4.4.2.3 guymager *91*
4.5 Analysis of File Systems *92*
4.5.1 The Sleuth Kit *92*
4.5.1.1 Determine the Partition Layout *93*
4.5.1.2 Determine the File System Type *93*
4.5.1.3 List the Files *94*
4.5.1.4 Recover File Metadata *95*
4.5.1.5 Recover File Content *95*
4.5.1.6 Other TSK Commands *95*
4.5.2 Data Carving *96*
4.6 Summary *97*
Exercises *97*
Bibliography *98*

Part II Windows File Systems *99*

5 The FAT File System *101*
5.1 On-Disk Structures *101*
5.1.1 Layout *102*
5.1.2 Volume Boot Record *102*
5.1.3 File System Information (FSINFO) *102*
5.1.4 File Allocation Table *104*
5.1.5 Directory Entries *105*
5.1.6 FAT Date and Time *108*
5.1.7 Mapping Clusters to Sectors *109*
5.2 Analysis of FAT32 *109*

5.2.1 Creating FAT32 File Systems *109*
5.2.2 Supplied FAT32 Image Files *110*
5.2.3 FAT32 Manual Analysis *110*
5.2.3.1 Process the VBR *111*
5.2.3.2 Process the Root Directory *112*
5.2.3.3 Process Sub-directories *113*
5.2.3.4 Recover Metadata/Content *113*
5.3 FAT32 Advanced Analysis *115*
5.3.1 Deleted Files *116*
5.3.2 The Volume Label *117*
5.4 Summary *117*
Exercises *118*
Bibliography *118*

6 The ExFAT File System *121*
6.1 On-Disk Structures *121*
6.1.1 Volume Boot Record *122*
6.1.2 File Allocation Table *123*
6.1.3 Directory Entries *125*
6.1.3.1 Allocation Bitmap (Type: 0x81) *127*
6.1.3.2 Up-Case Table (Type: 0x82) *128*
6.1.3.3 Volume Label (Type: 0x83) *128*
6.1.3.4 File (Type: 0x85) *129*
6.1.3.5 Volume GUID (Type: 0xA0) *130*
6.1.3.6 Stream Extension (Type: 0xC0) *130*
6.1.3.7 Filename Extension *131*
6.1.3.8 Other Directory Entries *132*
6.2 Analysis of ExFAT *132*
6.2.1 Creating ExFAT File Systems *132*
6.2.2 Supplied ExFAT Image Files *132*
6.2.3 ExFAT Manual Analysis *132*
6.2.3.1 Step 1: Process the VBR *133*
6.2.3.2 Step 2: Process the Root Directory *133*
6.2.3.3 Step 3: Process Subdirectories *136*
6.2.3.4 Step 4: Recover Metadata *137*
6.2.3.5 Step 5: Recover Content *137*
6.3 ExFAT Advanced Analysis *139*
6.3.1 Long File Names *139*
6.3.2 Deleted Files *140*
6.3.3 Fragmented Files and Large Directories *141*
6.4 Summary *142*
Exercises *143*
Bibliography *143*

7 The NTFS File System *145*
7.1 On-Disk Structures *146*
7.1.1 $Boot *146*

7.1.2 Indexes 147
7.1.3 Fixup Arrays 149
7.1.4 Time in NTFS 150
7.1.5 Master File Table 151
7.1.6 MFT Record Structure 152
7.1.6.1 MFT Record Header 152
7.1.6.2 Browsing Attributes 155
7.1.6.3 $STANDARD_INFORMATION (0x10) 155
7.1.6.4 $ATTRIBUTE_LIST (0x20) 156
7.1.6.5 $FILENAME (0x30) 156
7.1.6.6 $OBJECT_ID (0x40) 157
7.1.6.7 $SECURITY_DESCRIPTOR (0x50) 159
7.1.6.8 $VOLUME_NAME (0x60) 162
7.1.6.9 $VOLUME_INFORMATION (0x70) 162
7.1.6.10 $DATA (0x80) 163
7.1.6.11 $INDEX_ROOT (0x90) 163
7.1.6.12 $INDEX_ALLOCATION (0xA0) 165
7.1.6.13 $BITMAP (0xB0) 165
7.1.6.14 $REPARSE_POINT (0xC0) 166
7.1.6.15 $EA_INFORMATION (0xD0) and $EA (0xE0) 167
7.2 Analysis of NTFS 167
7.2.1 Creating NTFS File Systems 168
7.2.2 Supplied NTFS Image Files 168
7.2.3 NTFS Manual Analysis 168
7.2.3.1 Process $Boot 169
7.2.3.2 Recover $MFT 171
7.2.3.3 Process Directories 173
7.2.3.4 Recover File Metadata 177
7.2.3.5 Recover File Content 182
7.3 NTFS Advanced Analysis 185
7.3.1 Further File System Information 185
7.3.2 Deleted Files 186
7.3.3 Fragmented Files 187
7.3.4 Alternate Data Streams 190
7.3.5 Large MFT Records 191
7.4 Summary 194
Exercises 194
Bibliography 195

Part III Linux File Systems 197

8 The EXT2 File System 199
8.1 On-Disk Structures 200
8.1.1 The Superblock 201
8.1.2 The Block Group Descriptor Table 204
8.1.3 The Inode Table 205

8.1.3.1 Mode/Permissions *207*
8.1.3.2 Inode Flags *208*
8.1.3.3 Block Pointers *208*
8.1.4 The Data and Inode Bitmaps *209*
8.1.5 Locating an Inode *209*
8.2 Analysis of ext2 *210*
8.2.1 Creating ext2 File Systems *210*
8.2.2 Supplied ext2 Image Files *210*
8.2.3 Ext2 Manual Analysis *211*
8.2.3.1 Process the Superblock *211*
8.2.3.2 Map the Block Groups *213*
8.2.3.3 Process Root Directory Inode *216*
8.2.3.4 Process the Root Directory *217*
8.2.3.5 Process Directories *219*
8.2.3.6 Process Files *219*
8.3 Ext2 Advanced Analysis *222*
8.3.1 Fragmented Files *222*
8.3.2 Links *223*
8.3.3 Deleted Files *225*
8.4 Summary *226*
Exercises *226*
Bibliography *227*

9 The EXT3/EXT4 File Systems *229*
9.1 Supplied Image Files *229*
9.2 The ext3 File System *229*
9.2.1 The Ext Journal *230*
9.2.2 HTree Directory Indexing *237*
9.3 The Ext4 File System *241*
9.3.1 Large Inodes *241*
9.3.1.1 Timestamps *241*
9.3.2 Ext4 Data Storage *244*
9.3.2.1 Extent-Based Storage *244*
9.3.2.2 Inline Storage *248*
9.3.2.3 Symbolic Links *248*
9.3.3 File Deletion in Ext4 *249*
9.3.4 Extended Attributes *252*
9.3.5 Ext4 Block Group Descriptors *255*
9.3.6 Flexible Block Groups *255*
9.4 Summary *258*
Exercises *259*
Bibliography *260*

10 The XFS File System *263*
10.1 On-Disk Structures *264*
10.1.1 Allocation Groups *264*
10.1.2 Addressing *266*

10.1.2.1 Inode Addressing *266*
10.1.3 XFS B+ Trees *267*
10.1.4 The Superblock *268*
10.1.4.1 Locating Superblocks *268*
10.1.5 XFS Signatures *271*
10.1.6 XFS Inodes *271*
10.1.7 Directories *273*
10.1.8 Extents *274*
10.1.9 Time in XFS *275*
10.2 Analysis of XFS *275*
10.2.1 Creating XFS File Systems *275*
10.2.2 Supplied XFS Image Files *275*
10.2.3 XFS Manual Analysis *276*
10.2.3.1 Process the Superblock *276*
10.2.3.2 Locate the Root Directory *277*
10.2.3.3 Process the Root Directory *279*
10.2.3.4 Process the Subdirectories *281*
10.2.3.5 Recover File Content/Metadata *281*
10.3 XFS Advanced Analysis *282*
10.3.1 AG Free Space Management *283*
10.3.1.1 AG Free List *285*
10.3.2 AG Inode Management *286*
10.3.3 Deleted Files *289*
10.3.4 Extended Attributes *290*
10.3.5 Links *291*
10.3.6 The XFS Journal *292*
10.4 Summary *300*
Exercises *301*
Bibliography *301*

11 The Btrfs File System *303*
11.1 On-Disk Structures *304*
11.1.1 The Superblock *305*
11.1.2 Btrfs Trees *305*
11.1.3 Btrfs Tree Structure *307*
11.1.3.1 Node Header Structure *307*
11.1.3.2 Internal Node Structure *309*
11.1.4 Btrfs Keys *309*
11.1.5 Btrfs Items *310*
11.1.6 Time in Btrfs *315*
11.1.7 Logical and Physical Addressing *315*
11.2 Analysis of Btrfs *317*
11.2.1 Creating Btrfs File Systems *317*
11.2.2 Supplied Btrfs Image Files *318*
11.2.3 Btrfs Analysis Methodology *318*
11.2.4 Manual Analysis of a Single Device File System *320*
11.2.4.1 Process the Superblock *320*

11.2.4.2 Process the CHUNK_ARRAY *321*
11.2.4.3 Locate the CHUNK_TREE *322*
11.2.4.4 Process the CHUNK_TREE *323*
11.2.4.5 Locate the Root Tree *326*
11.2.4.6 Locate the FS_TREE *327*
11.2.4.7 Processing the FS_TREE *328*
11.2.4.8 Process Directories *329*
11.2.4.9 Recovering Metadata *335*
11.2.4.10 Recovering File Contents *336*
11.3 Btrfs Advanced Analysis *338*
11.3.1 File Deletion *338*
11.3.2 Analysis of Internal Nodes *342*
11.3.3 Multiple Device Configuration *343*
11.3.4 Subvolumes and Snapshots *346*
11.4 Summary *350*
Exercises *350*
Bibliography *351*

Part IV Apple File Systems *353*

12 The HFS+ File System *355*
12.1 On-Disk Structures *355*
12.1.1 Forks *357*
12.1.2 Time in HFS+ *357*
12.1.3 Volume Header *358*
12.1.4 B-Trees *358*
12.1.5 Catalog File *362*
12.1.6 HFS+ Permissions *363*
12.1.7 Text Encoding *365*
12.1.8 Extents Overflow File *365*
12.1.9 Allocation File *366*
12.1.10 HFS+ Journal *367*
12.2 Analysis of HFS+ *369*
12.2.1 Creating HFS+ File Systems *369*
12.2.2 Supplied HFS+ Image Files *370*
12.2.3 HFS+ Manual Analysis *370*
12.2.3.1 Process the Volume Header *370*
12.2.3.2 Locate the Catalog File *371*
12.2.3.3 Process the Catalog B-Tree *373*
12.2.3.4 Gather Metadata *377*
12.2.3.5 Recover File Content *377*
12.3 HFS+ Advanced Analysis *380*
12.3.1 Deleted Files *380*
12.3.2 Index Nodes *381*
12.3.3 Fragmented Files *383*
12.3.4 Links *387*

12.4 Summary *390*
Exercises *391*
Bibliography *391*

13 The APFS File System *393*
13.1 On-Disk Structures *394*
13.1.1 Time in APFS *394*
13.1.2 Objects *394*
13.1.3 B-Trees *396*
13.1.4 Containers and Volumes *399*
13.1.5 Container Superblock *400*
13.1.6 Volume Superblock *402*
13.1.7 Object Maps *404*
13.1.8 File-Related Structures *405*
13.1.8.1 File System Keys *406*
13.1.8.2 Inode *407*
13.1.8.3 Directory Record *408*
13.1.8.4 Extent *410*
13.1.9 Checkpoints *410*
13.1.10 Other APFS Structures *412*
13.2 Analysis of APFS *412*
13.2.1 Creating APFS File Systems *412*
13.2.2 Supplied APFS Image Files *413*
13.2.3 APFS Manual Analysis *413*
13.2.3.1 Process the Container Superblock *414*
13.2.3.2 Process the Container Object Map *415*
13.2.3.3 Process the Volume Superblock *418*
13.2.3.4 Process the Volume Object Map *418*
13.2.3.5 Process the File System Tree *419*
13.3 APFS Advanced Analysis *425*
13.3.1 Deleted Files *425*
13.3.2 Checkpoint Recovery *426*
13.3.3 Multi-Level B-Trees *427*
13.3.4 Multiple Volumes *429*
13.3.5 Extended Attributes *430*
13.3.6 Links *431*
13.4 Summary *433*
Exercises *433*
Bibliography *434*

Part V The Future *435*

14 Future Challenges in Digital Forensics *437*
14.1 Challenges in Digital Forensics *437*
14.1.1 Data Volume *438*
14.1.2 Multi-Source Correlation *439*

14.1.3 New File Systems *440*
14.1.4 Encryption *440*
14.1.5 Cloud Storage *441*
14.1.6 Lack of Resources *441*
14.1.6.1 Human Resources *441*
14.1.6.2 Software Resources *442*
14.1.6.3 Hardware Resources *442*
14.1.7 Tool Validation/Datasets *443*
14.1.8 Lack of Standardisation *444*
14.1.9 Legal/Scientific Challenges *444*
14.1.10 Presentation of Evidence *445*
14.1.11 Human Error/Bias *446*
14.2 Where Do We Go from Here? *447*
14.2.1 Training/Education *448*
14.2.2 Free Open-Source Software (FOSS) *448*
14.2.3 Triage *449*
14.2.4 Artificial Intelligence (AI) *449*
14.2.5 Live Data Forensics *450*
14.2.6 Legal Solutions *451*
14.2.7 Data Set Development/Tool Testing *452*
14.2.8 Standardisation *452*
14.2.9 Information Sharing *453*
14.2.10 Virtualisation *453*
14.3 Summary *454*
Bibliography *454*

Index *457*

Preface

The prevalence of digital evidence in modern investigation has led to the need for more skilled analysts who can interpret digital evidence in a meaningful manner. Much digital evidence is stored in a file system and the correct recovery of this information is crucial to investigation. While there exist many tools that automate the recovery of data from file systems, there is a need for greater understanding of what these tools do. This allows the expert to verify the findings of file system forensic tools leading to greater trust in the recovered evidence.

The target audience of this title is anyone with an interest in digital investigation, who wishes to know how evidence is recovered from file systems. This includes University students taking modules or even entire programmes in the digital forensics and cybersecurity domains and law enforcement agents (or other investigators) who are tasked with recovering information from file systems and explaining its relevance. For both audiences the aim of this book is to provide an in-depth understanding of how information is recovered from common file systems.

Structure

This book is organised in five distinct parts. Part I provides the preliminaries that all digital forensic experts require. Parts II–IV provide the technical meat of the title. These parts focus on the common file systems for each of the most popular operating systems (Windows, Linux and macOS). Part V discusses the future of file system forensics and what new (and some old) challenges are ahead for the discipline.

Part I, Preliminaries, begins with an introduction to digital forensics in general and discusses some of the principles that govern the area. This chapter also introduces the reader to digital forensic methodologies and how they are used to streamline investigation. Chapter 2 describes the Linux operating system and how it can be used for file system forensics. Throughout the remainder of the text the examples will be given using the Linux command line, but there is no requirement for readers to follow this. Chapter 2 provides an introduction to Linux for those that wish to use it going forward. For those who do not intend to use (or already use) it, this chapter can be skipped. Chapter 3 discusses the topic of information representation. Computers are capable of processing and storing only binary data (ones and zeros). How these ones and zeros are interpreted as meaningful information is of vital importance. This chapter shows how numbers, text and time are represented in computing systems and how we interpret the raw hex data that we will encounter during file system forensics. The final chapter in this part introduces the reader to disk storage, partitions and file systems. This chapter describes the common partitioning schemes in use today and shows how they can be located. It then introduces the file system and shows the various concepts that exist within this organisational structure. The chapter finishes with an introduction to disk acquisition – how we acquire the file systems that we will later process – and the analysis of these file systems.

Part II introduces the Windows family of file systems, although more accurately this might be called the Microsoft family. This includes FAT (Chapter 5), ExFAT (Chapter 6) and NTFS (Chapter 7). For many years FAT file system variants were the standard for removable media. While this is changing as ExFAT becomes dominant a large volume of devices with the FAT file system are still found during investigation. This, coupled with the relative simplicity of the FAT file system, means that it is an ideal choice for the first file system to be studied in this book. Subsequently the ExFAT file system is introduced. While some consider this to be another variant of the FAT file system, it is sufficiently more advanced to be deserving of its own chapter. This is the most common file system found on removable media today. Both FAT and ExFAT are supported by all major operating systems and, as such, can be found in many cases. The final Windows file system in this text is that of NTFS. The New Technology File System is the default on all Windows systems and as such is very commonly encountered in digital investigation.

Part III introduces the Linux file systems. This begins with the ext family of filesystems (Chapters 8 and 9). Many might wonder how important these chapters are as Linux is rarely encountered in digital investigation. However, these are some of the most important file systems in use today. The ext family are one of the default file systems found in Android phones, and as such, one of the most commonly encountered file systems in investigation. Knowledge of these file systems is of vital importance to all file system forensic investigators. File systems of the ext family are commonly encountered in many IoT devices. So while true to say that they are not commonly encountered in the home computer area, they are very important file systems for the analyst. This part of the book also introduces two less common Linux file systems: XFS (Chapter 10) and BtrFS (Chapter 11). These file systems are encountered in some Linux distributions, and are also found in large scale storage applications such as data centres. As device storage capacity increases these file systems will become more common in the home market.

Part IV examines the Apple file systems. For many years Apple devices utilised the HFS+ file system (Chapter 12). Since late 2017 Apple devices have begun to use the APFS file system (Chapter 13). This is a modern file system which can scale to modern device sizes in an efficient manner. Due to the popularlity of Apple devices (phones, tablets, computers etc.) this file system is encountered very frequently in modern digital investigation. The final part of this book looks to the future and in particular examines the challenges that will face the community over the next number of years.

Each file system chapter (Chapters 5–13) is organised in a similar manner. Initially a description of the general layout and the actual structures present in the file system is provided for each file system. This is followed by a manual analysis in which the reader can see all steps required to recover file content and metadata. Finally each chapter finishes with advanced topics for each file system. This always includes topics such as deleted and fragmented files along with topics specific to each file system.

Resources

Throughout this book example file systems are used to demonstrate the manual analysis and more advanced topics. Each file system generally has between three to five different image files that are used. All of this data is available to the user through the book's supporting website. This data can be found at: https://www.fsforensics.com/book.

Please email any corrections to me at fergus@fsforensics.com.

Ireland, June 2024

FERGUS TOOLAN

Acknowledgements

When I began this project I never realised how difficult it would be to complete. It would never have been completed without the support of many people. To everyone who had any part in this thank you all very much! There are some who must be mentioned directly!

Firstly those that proof read the document itself. Thank you! To my technical proof readers Ray Genoe, Alan Browne, Ivar Friheim and Ulf Bergum who between them checked the code listings and exercises in the book. Many thanks for that! My father Dónal read every single word of the manuscript and offered countless corrections and suggestions for improvement.

Many thanks to the editorial team at John Wiley & Sons Ltd. Victoria Bradshaw, Vishal Paduchuru, and Aileen Storry for all of your help throughout the publication process.

Over the years I have been very fortunate to work with some amazing people in the area of digital forensics. In my current role I am part of an amazing team of academics and law enforcement officers. Thanks to Carlota, Georgina, Nina, Rune, Sara and Ulf. Also past colleagues including Ray, Cormac, Gerry, Kurt-Helge, Yves, Jørn Helge and Alexander. I thank the wonderful heads of the investigation section in the Norwegian Police University College: Ivar, John Ståle, Dag and Inger. All of you gave me the freedom to explore the topics that I was most interested in.

This book started as a resource for my students. I thank all of you that I taught over the years. Much of the information presented in this book is based on the challenging questions that you have asked me. Hopefully this book will answer some of them!

During my own formative years I had some wonderful teachers in University College Dublin. Special mention to Joe Carthy, John Dunnion, Nick Kushmerick and Henry McLoughlin. I would not have had the ability or the confidence to attempt this project without your inspirational teaching over the years.

This project would never have been completed without the constant belief and support of my family. Thanks to my parents, Dónal and Anna, who always encouraged me to pursue my dreams and supported me throughout.

Finally when I thought about giving up on this project, it was my partner Helen who encouraged me to keep going. She always believed that I could do this even on the days when I didn't believe that myself. Thank you!

Fergus Toolan

Part I

Preliminaries

1

Introduction

In recent years the volume of digital evidence in criminal investigations has increased dramatically. Consider the situation at the turn of the century when the standard computer was the desktop computer a device that resided on, as the name suggests, the desk. The majority of crime scenes did not involve a computer. When computers were involved they were generally relevant only in specific case types such as hacking/cybercrime; child abuse material; and fraud. Returning to the present, there is digital evidence in almost every case![1] The majority of people carry smartphones on their person at all times. Cars contain navigation, entertainment and camera systems. Homes and businesses have digital CCTV systems that run continuously. People communicate through social media. The end result for investigators[2] is that there has been a vast increase in the quantity of digital evidence encountered during investigation.

Almost all data in electronic storage media is held in files. A file is an object on a computing device that stores data, information, settings or applications. Every document, picture, spreadsheet, database, etc. on a computer system is composed of one or more files. Every computer system therefore needs a method of managing files. This is generally achieved through the use of a file system. File systems exist on every electronic storage device and provide a method of locating the actual file's content and also provide information about the file itself. An ability to access these files is of vital importance during investigation.

Investigators have many tools at their disposal which allow them to access this information. However, these tools suffer certain limitations including:

- **Unsupported File Systems:** There are many different file systems in existence. File system forensic tools generally support only the most common file systems, those that are found on the most common operating systems. However, there are many more that are sometimes encountered during an investigation. These might be impossible to process without knowledge of how file systems function.
- **Undisclosed Methods:** Most file system forensic tools are closed source[3] meaning users are unable to see exactly what actions are being performed. A knowledge of file system structures will allow the investigator to show how data is stored in a file system and therefore show possible means of recovering said data. It also supports verification of the results of closed-source tools.
- **Cost:** The majority of these tools are commercial tools with associated cost implications for users. Knowledge of how file systems function could ultimately allow an investigator to create their own tools.

1 The UK's National Police Chief's Council estimate that over 90% of crimes involved a digital element in 2020.
2 Investigator is used throughout this book to signify any party involved in criminal or corporate investigations.
3 One exception to this is the Sleuth Kit which will be used throughout this book to validate results when possible.

File System Forensics, First Edition. Fergus Toolan.

Hence it is necessary that investigators understand the structures that are utilised by file systems. This not only allows the investigator to analyse file systems which are not supported by the current tool but also allows them to explain possible means by which these tools work. Digital forensic analysts are often considered 'experts' in their field. Knowledge of file systems and their underlying structures will allow these analysts to more validly claim this title and stand over the evidence generated by file system forensic tools.

1.1 What is Digital Forensics?

In recent years the term digital forensics has become more familiar to all, especially anyone involved in investigation. Digital evidence is seen in TV shows on a regular basis. Numerous jobs are available in many areas which require skills in digital forensics, from e-discovery to incident response and cybersecurity. But what is digital forensics? That's a difficult question to answer!

There is no single accepted definition of digital forensics. In this section a number of definitions are presented and the common elements identified. This process will eventually culminate in the definition that is used throughout this book.

Interpol defines digital forensics as:

> ... a branch of forensic science that focuses on identifying, acquiring, processing, analysing, and reporting on data stored electronically.
>
> ***Interpol (n.d.)***

Lang et al define digital forensics as:

> ... the science of identifying, collecting, preserving, documenting, examining, analyzing and presenting evidence from computers, networks, and other electronic devices.
>
> ***Lang et al. (2014)***

Techopedia defines digital forensics as:

> ... the process of uncovering and interpreting electronic data. The goal of the process is to preserve any evidence in its most original form while performing a structured investigation by collecting, identifying and validating the digital information for the purpose of reconstructing past events.
>
> ***Techopedia (n.d.)***

These, and the many other definitions that can be found, all share some common traits. For instance all of them mention electronic devices/data. All evidence in digital forensics is generated from electronic traces. These traces may be found on storage media, in network traffic, online, etc. Hence digital forensics is forensic analysis performed on electronically stored/transmitted information. Additionally both Lang et al. (2014) and Interpol mention science. Digital forensics is a branch of forensic science and as such should be based on scientific principles.

All of the above definitions attempt to define the process that is followed. Many definitions use similar wording to describe these processes. For instance words such as identifying, collecting (or acquiring), preserving, presenting (or reporting) or analysing (or interpreting) are used in the majority of definitions.

Hence, for the purposes of this book the following definition will be adopted.

> Digital forensics is the application of **scientific principles** to the **identification**, **preservation**, **collection**, **analysis** and **presentation** of evidence obtained from **electronic media**.

1.2 File System Forensics

File system forensics is a particular branch of digital forensics in which the electronic medium in question is the actual storage device (i.e. the disk). File systems are structures which organise information on disk. The file system is the structure that allows saved information to be retrieved at a later date. When a file is saved, not only is the content saved but information about the content (metadata) is also saved. This metadata provides much necessary information about the file content such as timestamps and file size, but also provides information on how to locate the content on disk.

Techopedia defines a file system as:

> ... a process that manages how and where data on a storage disk, typically a hard disk drive (HDD), is stored, accessed and managed. It is a logical disk component that manages a disk's internal operations as it relates to a computer and is abstract to a human user.
>
> ***Techopedia (n.d.)***

File system forensics therefore involves the application of the scientific method to identify, preserve, collect, analyse and present evidence recovered from a file system. In order to be able to perform these tasks the analyst (whether human or software) must fully understand the structures on which the file system in question is based. Different file systems result in very different structures and hence different analysis methods.

For instance compare two commonly encountered file systems in digital forensics: The File Allocation Table (FAT) and the new Apple File System (APFS). FAT is an old file system and in comparison to modern file systems such as APFS it is very simple. Generally older file systems allow for the storage/retrieval of information from them and very little else. FAT contains three structures that are of interest to forensic examiners (the volume boot record, the file allocation table and directory entries) meaning that only a small amount of knowledge is required to analyse this file system effectively. Now compare this to APFS. APFS is a modern file system. It provides much more functionality than an older system such as FAT. This includes encryption, snapshots, compression, etc. The underlying structures are inherently more complex meaning that this file system is much more difficult to examine effectively.

1.3 Digital Forensic Principles

The United Kingdom's Association of Chief Police Officers[4] (ACPO) drafted the Good Practice Guide for Digital Evidence. Version 5 (released in 2012) is the latest version of this document. This document contains a set of four principles for the effective handling of digital evidence.

---

4 This organisation was dissolved in 2015 and replaced by the National Police Chief's Council (NPCC).

These ACPO principles, as they are often called, are based on the UK legal system and the rules of evidence in that system. However, the principles are almost universal and have been adopted in many countries over recent years. These principles are:

- **Principle 1:** No action taken by law enforcement agencies, persons employed within these agencies or their agents should change data which may subsequently be relied upon in court.
- **Principle 2:** In circumstances where a person finds it necessary to access original data, that person must be competent to do so and be able to give evidence explaining the relevance and the implications of their actions.
- **Principle 3:** An audit trail or other record of all processes applied to digital evidence should be created and preserved. An independent third party should be able to examine those processes and achieve the same result.
- **Principle 4:** The person in charge of the investigation has overall responsibility for ensuring that the law and these principles are adhered to.

These principles were originally drafted in the early days of digital evidence. At that stage most digital evidence resided on computer storage devices. The standard method was to power off the device, create an image and analyse that image. As the area of digital forensics has developed over the years this standard method of operation has also developed. Now it is no longer always advised to switch off the computer. Instead it is sometimes recommended to analyse running machines. Not all information is now stored locally, some will be stored remotely, even the crime scene itself may be remote. However, while some argue that the principles need to be updated, they are still fit for purpose.

The overall aim of these principles is to ensure that all digital evidence accessed during a criminal investigation is handled in such a manner that it can be used in court. Hence the first principle states that no changes should be made to the original data. The second principle ensures that only trained personnel will ever access original data and the third principle ensures that others will be able to recreate and validate the analysis of the evidential material. For traditional computer forensics these three principles are sufficient.

Now consider a modern scenario. First responders arrive at the home of a suspected cybercriminal. They use a warrant to enter the premises and seize all electronic evidence that is encountered. Upon entering the premises they discover a running computer. The traditional advice was to 'pull-the-plug'; however, with modern computers this might lose evidence. Most modern operating systems allow options for encrypted storage. If power is removed the data on the device will become inaccessible due to its encryption. Additionally many users use remote storage resources for files, emails, profiles, etc. Connections to these sites (and potentially access to the data they contain) will be lost if the power is removed. Hence live data forensics (LDF) is conducted, in which the running computer is analysed to determine if there is anything of evidential value present.

Returning to ACPO Principle 1 which states 'no action taken by law enforcement agencies … should change data which may subsequently be relied upon in court'. LDF immediately breaks this principle. Every action performed on a running computer system will leave traces in memory and on disk. Even the simple act of moving the mouse will have consequences, as it will change certain parts of the computer system. This has led to some researchers suggesting that the ACPO principles should be rewritten. However, they are still fit for purpose as while LDF breaks principle 1, combining this with principles 2 (competence) and 3 (audit trail), the *altered* data collected from the LDF process can still be used in a court setting.

1.4 Digital Forensic Methodology

From the early days of digital forensics it has long been recognised that there is no standard methodology for obtaining results. As, in an ideal world, digital forensics is 'based on scientific principles' it is necessary that there should be one agreed-upon methodology.

Table 1.1 summarises the phases in a number of competing methodologies for digital forensics. These include O'Ciarduin's Extended Model of Cybercrime Investigation, the Digital Forensics Research Workshop Model, Reith Carr and Gunsch's model and the Nordic Computer Forensic Investigators model.[5] Table 1.1 presents each of these methodologies grouped to show similar phases.

Combining the methodologies shown in Table 1.1 leads to the methodology that will be used throughout this book. This consists of eight phases: Preparation; Localisation/Preservation; Acquisition; Processing; Analysis; Reporting; Quality Assurance and Evidence Return. The following sections describe these phases of the proposed digital forensics methodology.

Table 1.1 Competing digital forensic methodologies. Similar phases are grouped.

DFRWS	Reith, Carr, Gunsch	O'Ciarduin	NCFI
	Identification Preparation Authorisation	Awareness Authorisation Planning Notification	Initiation Strategy Development
Identification Preservation	Preservation	Search	Localisation Preservation
Collection	Collection	Collection Transport Storage	Acquisition
Examination	Examination	Examination	Processing
Analysis	Analysis	Hypothesis Hypothesis Presentation Hypothesis Proof	Analysis
Presentation	Presentation	Dissemination	Reporting
Decision			QA/Evaluation
	Evidence Return		

5 The Nordic Computer Forensic Investigators (NCFI) methodology is used in the author's institution.

1.4.1 Preparation

The preparation phase consists of a number of tasks that must be completed in order for the digital forensic process to succeed. O'Ciarduin's extended model of cybercrime investigation subdivides this phase into four distinct phases. Common tasks in the preparation phase include:

- **Crime Identification:** Part of preparation involves identifying that a crime/incident has taken place and determining what laws have been broken. This will determine some of the hypotheses that will be developed in subsequent phases.
- **Authorisation:** Ensuring that the relevant parties have the correct authorisation to investigate/prosecute the crime in question. In certain jurisdictions the suspect must also be notified that the investigation is to take place.
- **Planning:** The investigation is planned at this stage. Necessary warrants must be obtained and initial roles are allocated to the investigative team.
- **Resource Allocation:** It is necessary to ensure that all relevant resources (hardware, software, personnel, etc.) are in place prior to commencing the investigation.
- **Training:** All members of the investigative team must have received all necessary training/education. This is directly related to the ACPO principles which require all agents handling original material to be competent to do so.

1.4.2 Localisation/Preservation

The purpose of this phase is to locate sources of potential digital evidence and to preserve these in such a way that they are not altered (or are altered as little as possible) so that they can be relied upon in court.

Traditionally this phase took place at a physical crime scene, for instance a house search. The first response team attempt to locate all sources of digital evidence at the scene. This might include traditional devices such as computers, tablets, smartphones and USB keys. It also includes less common items such as smart appliances, networking technology, vehicles and drones. In modern digital investigation the focus is shifting from the physical to the virtual. Hence localisation is also concerned with finding relevant online sources (open-source intelligence – OSINT – gathering), log files and external sources of digital evidence such as CCTV and access logs.

Once sources of potential evidence are located the next part of this phase is to preserve them. Traditionally this involved pulling the plug and then bagging and tagging the physical device. With the advent of LDF this phase sometimes involves preserving a running computer by preventing it from locking or, if battery powered, from dying. With the modern networked age another vital step at this stage is to prevent remote access to the device as a person could remotely delete evidence from the device. In the online environment preservation is often more complex. Generally the potential evidence will not be present at the crime scene indeed it may exist in a different jurisdiction to that of the investigator. Preservation of these online items might be achieved through court orders. Preservation of external records such as call data records (CDR) can also be achieved through a court order.

1.4.3 Acquisition

Acquisition is the process where a forensically sound copy of the potential evidence is created. Once this step is completed there should never be a need to return to the original source. All of the subsequent stages should be performed on the copy. With electronic storage media this stage involves the creation of an *image*, an exact bit by bit copy, of a storage device. This means not only will the live files on the device be copied, but also deleted files, slack space, unallocated space, etc. These concepts will be explained in Chapter 4.

For online resources this phase involves the acquisition of a copy of the web resource. This can be done through a browser (using the save functionality) or by taking screenshots or videos of the site. In certain cases, acquisition can be performed by the site administrator and the resulting evidence files delivered to the investigator.

1.4.4 Processing

Processing involves getting the acquired evidence file ready for analysis by investigators. This is the phase in which file system forensic analysis resides. With a traditional electronic storage device processing involves extracting all live and deleted files from the image along with the unallocated space and slack space from the device. Processing involves carving in unallocated space to recover files which are no longer part of a file system (Section 4.5.2). This stage also involves processing certain artefacts that have been recovered. This might include rebuilding browser history, extracting individual chat messages from a database, expanding archive files and so forth. In the online environment processing involves the extraction of relevant components of the online artefact such as contacts, images, email addresses and comments.

The information generated by processing is passed to the analyst to determine if the information is relevant to the investigation and if that evidence supports or refutes the investigative hypotheses.

1.4.5 Analysis

The analysis phase of the digital forensic methodology requires knowledge of the actual case being investigated. In this stage investigative hypotheses are generated and the analyst uses the evidence provided by the processing phase to prove or disprove these hypotheses. This phase is very much dependent on the case in question.

1.4.6 Reporting

The dissemination of results is one of the most important stages in any investigation. This phase covers a multitude of reporting types. The most iconic is that of the final report which is submitted to the court. This document shows all the evidence that has been discovered throughout the investigation, the relevance of this evidence to the hypotheses under investigation and the methods used to recover the evidence.

However, this phase is much more than a mere final report. Many digital forensic methodologies are described in a linear fashion, implying that one phase follows another. This is not strictly speaking correct, no more so than in the case of reporting. Firstly it is not common to find only a single final report. Generally there will be reports made at the end of most phases of the methodology. For instance a report will be written in relation to localisation/preservation (the report about the crime scene search). Another report will be written about the acquisition process and another relating to processing. All of these intermediate reports will be used to help create the final report.

The dissemination of results involves more than written reports. There are other forms of dissemination of information that are vital to the correct application of the digital forensic methodology. One example of this is the use of contemporaneous notes. It is recommended that all actors in the digital forensic process maintain their own personal notes about the case and the tasks that are performed during the case. This can act as another aid to the creation of a final report but can also be used as an audit trail (ACPO 3) allowing third parties to recreate the actions of investigators.

A final part of this phase is that of internal presentation of results. The digital forensic process may involve multiple actors (first responders, analysts, investigators, etc.). It is necessary during the process to ensure that all parties are conversant with the actions that have been taken by other parties in the handling of digital evidence in the case. This type of reporting is often achieved through briefings throughout the investigation.

The final task in some instances is the presentation of evidence in court. Generally this presentation will be based on the final report and will be directed by the prosecution while subject to cross-examination by the defence.

1.4.7 Quality Assurance

Many commentators have said that the digital forensic process is prone to error and therefore quality must be assured throughout the process. On a case-by-case basis this can be achieved using methods such as peer review in which an independent party validates the result of a forensic process. This is directly related to the ACPO principles which require that this recreation of results be possible (ACPO 3). There are different levels of peer review as proposed by Horsman and Sunde (2020), from very simple administrative checks all the way through to complete reexamination of the device(s).

While in an ideal world all cases would be subject to complete reexamination, generally the resources are not present to do this. Instead only certain cases are selected for complete examination. A complete reexamination might be required when:

- The investigator encounters a new case type or one of which they have limited knowledge of the case or data type;
- novel techniques are to be employed in the case/analysis;
- the prosecution's case revolves largely around digital evidence;
- the crime type is of a serious nature and may lead to severe sentencing; or
- the case is more complex than normal (i.e. more exhibits than usual).

Cases that meet the above criteria should be fully reexamined along with a sample of randomly chosen cases.

1.4.8 Evidence Return

Certain methodologies also include an evidence return phase, in which evidence is returned to the suspect/victim. This phase is more complex than it might at first appear as not all evidence can be returned. For instance child sexual abuse material is illegal and cannot be returned to the suspect. The devices/evidence must be evaluated and decisions made on what should legally be returned to the victim/suspect and what should be retained/destroyed.

1.5 About This Book

This book began as a series of notes created for classes given by the author throughout his career. The author has been teaching digital forensics (with a special interest in file system forensics) for over 15 years. Over that time the author has taught/analysed many different file systems. This book is a result of this work over the years.

This book is also written to pay homage to one of the greatest books in digital forensics, Brian Carrier's *File System Forensic Analysis*. This book was the author's introduction to the area of file system forensics and in the author's opinion is one of the best books on digital forensics available to this day. However, it has been many years since the publication of this book. File systems have developed in the intervening years. For instance Carrier only considered Ext 2 and 3, Ext 4 had not been released at the time of that book's publication. However, Ext 4 is now the default on the overwhelming majority of Linux installations and is also encountered on all Android devices. Hence it is a vital file system to understand. Carrier's book did not cover any Apple file systems; however, Apple devices are a large and growing part of the file system forensic analyst's workload. Older devices will use the HFS+ file systems while newer devices use APFS. Even in the world of the traditional Windows file systems times are changing. Since the publication of Carrier's book there have been two new Windows file systems, ExFAT and Refs. All of these reasons have led to a need for a new resource.

The aim of this book is to provide the reader with knowledge of how file systems function and, more importantly, how digital forensic tools function. Many digital forensic analysts rely upon their chosen file system forensic tool(s) to gather evidence that they require for court, without ever understanding what processes are being performed by that tool. This opens these analysts to challenges. In today's increasingly technical world, with the explosion in digital forensic/cybersecurity positions these challenges are more likely to occur. In order to stand over the evidence produced by a file system forensic tool the analyst should fully understand the workings of the file system and the workings of the tool used to recover the evidence.

1.5.1 Who Should Read This Book?

There are two audiences for this book, both based on the author's working experience. The author has long taught at University level in the area of digital forensics. During this time the author has taught most of the file systems in this book, so this book is written for students. The book will suit both undergraduate and graduate-level students of digital forensics.

An undergraduate course might focus on the preliminary part of this book and the manual analysis of one or two of the windows file systems (ExFAT and NTFS would be the author's recommendation). An advanced graduate-level course would focus on more file systems and include the advanced topics related to each file system. Some graduate courses may specialise in Windows/Apple/Linux system forensics. In these cases the file systems used by each OS will be important to the course. Hence each of Parts II, III and IV is independent of each other. It is assumed that the reader will understand the preliminaries but the parts stand on their own to be used as an instructor sees fit.

The second audience for this book is law enforcement or more correctly any digital forensic analyst who is required to testify in courts. Too often analysts rely on the tool to interpret complex structures without fully understanding the underlying structure. There is a potential risk in this approach. If evidence is challenged an inability to explain what the forensic tools are doing might count against the evidence provided. Hence this audience can use this book as a resource to understand how file systems function and how our forensic tools might work on particular file systems.[6]

6 The author does not claim that the tools work in an identical manner to those shown in the book, merely that it is a method which these tools might use!

Additionally knowledge of file systems at this level will leave the analyst in a position to verify the results of their forensic tools. Do these tools perform as expected? Do they recover all of the information that is present? Do they recover the information correctly? Answers to these questions are of vital importance to ensure correctness of digital evidence and everyone's right to a fair trial.

1.6 Book Structure

This book is divided into five parts. The first part is entitled Preliminaries and is just that! It reviews the basic material that is required for file system forensics. One of the topics covered in this section is the use of Linux as an investigative platform. Linux is an open-source operating system which provides great support for many file systems by default (more than Windows/macOS). This makes it an ideal forensic workstation. Chapter 2 provides information about the installation and usage of the Linux OS. Those of you that use Linux regularly may skip this section (although if you don't use Linux for file system forensics there might be some useful information in Section 2.5).

In order to fully understand a file system it is necessary that we understand how information is represented in a computer system. Remember that only ones and zeros can be stored on a disk. It is therefore necessary to understand how a sequence of ones and zeros may represent all forms of information (numbers, text, time, etc.). The mathematical preliminaries necessary for this book are introduced in Chapter 3. File Systems are generally found on disks, Chapter 4 describes the traditional hard drive structure and also newer solid-state drives. This chapter will describe partitioning and introduce the most commonly encountered partitioning schemes. Finally the chapter introduces the file system. What is a file system? What does it do? In doing this many concepts important to file system forensics will be introduced. These concepts will help the reader gain a fuller understanding of what their tools are doing.

The following parts introduce various file systems. These parts are divided into the major operating systems. For instance Part II introduces the file systems that are most often encountered on Windows systems, FAT[7] (Chapter 5), ExFAT (Chapter 6) and NTFS (Chapter 7).

Part III introduces the Linux file systems which, while not as commonly encountered as Windows/Mac file systems, are found more frequently in server-level machines. However, at the other end of the scale, the Linux OS is also regularly found on small-scale devices (Android is a form of Linux) and even on embedded devices. Linux file systems are often found accompanying the Linux OS, so a knowledge of these file systems is often important. The Linux file systems are not generally as well supported by the digital forensic tools as the Windows/macOS file systems. This part of the book covers the Ext family of file systems (Chapters 8 and 9), the XFS file system (Chapter 10) and finally the modern BtrFS file system (Chapter 11).

Part IV introduces the Apple file systems. There are two that are most likely to be encountered in modern macOS systems. Systems, both phone and computer, prior to 2017 were shipped with the Hierarchical File System, HFS+, while newer systems use the Apple File System (APFS). These two file systems are covered in Part 4 (Chapters 12 and 13).

---

7 While FAT (and ExFAT) are more commonly associated with removable media than any particular operating system, the original FAT specification was created by Microsoft and as such it is included in the Windows file systems section.

Finally Part V (Chapter 14) looks to the future. What challenges will be faced in the area of file system forensics in the years to come? Also, more importantly, it covers possible methods to overcome these potential challenges!

1.7 Summary

This chapter introduced the concept of digital forensics and its importance in modern investigation. In recent years the volume of digital evidence has increased dramatically leading to a need for more digital forensic analysts to handle the ever-growing volume of information. Consider a family home. In the 1990s this would have contained one or two computers and some external storage media (floppy disks; CD's; etc.). Now this same home will contain multiple computers/laptops; tablets; smartphones; games consoles; smart TVs; etc. The sheer volume of devices has increased over the years leading to a need for more skilled people in this area.

In order to commence working in this area the analyst must be conversant with the principles and methodologies that underpin the discipline. This chapter proceeded to introduce the ACPO principles which have formed the bedrock of digital forensic analysis over a number of years. All analysts should keep these principles in mind when handling digital evidence. Correctly adhering to these principles provides a much greater chance of digital evidence being accepted in the court.

Methodology adds structure to our activities. Methodologies ensure that vital steps are not forgotten. This chapter compares a number of methodologies proposed over the years and shows how similar all of these are to each other. The chapter then describes an eight-step methodology which contains all the various steps in the other methodologies. However, the key point is that all methodologies are very similar. Which methodology is used is not important, what is important is that a methodology is followed throughout the analysis.

The remainder of the preliminary section of this book will introduce the reader firstly to the Linux operating system and specifically its use as a forensic workstation. This is followed by the mathematical fundamentals necessary for digital forensics and an introduction to disk/file system storage.

Exercises

The following list suggests a number of topics which may be used in essay-style questions or as classroom discussion topics.

1. The necessity for digital forensics in criminal investigation has grown in recent years. What effects might this have on the quality of digital forensics?

2. Compare and contrast any two digital forensic methodologies (DFRWS, Reith, Carr and Gunsch, O'Ciarduin and NCFI are mentioned in this chapter). Are there any abstract differences between them?

3. Consider situations where it is recommended to run a full reexamination in the quality assurance phase of the digital forensic methodology. Do you consider this list to be sufficient? Should more/less situations be included?

4. Are the ACPO principles still fit-for-purpose?

Bibliography

ACPO (2011). ACPO Good Practice Guide for Digital Evidence [Internet]. [cited 2024 February 20]. https://npcc.police.uk/documents/crime/2014/Revised%20Good%20Practice%20Guide%20for%20Digital%20Evidence:Vers%205_Oct%202011_Website.pdf (accessed 12 August 2024).

Baryamureeba, V. and Tushabe, F. (2004). *The Enhanced Digital Investigation Process Model*. Digital Investigation.

Brighi, R. and Ferrazzano, M. (2021). Digital forensics: best practices and perspective. *Collezione Di Giustizia Penale* 7: 13–48.

Carrier, B. (2005). *File System Forensic Analysis*. Boston, MA; London: Addison-Wesley.

Ferguson, R.I., Renaud, K., Wilford, S., and Irons, A. (2020). PRECEPT: a framework for ethical digital forensics investigations. *Journal of Intellectual Capital* 21 (2): 257–290.

Gogolin, G. (2021). *Digital Forensics Explained*. CRC Press.

Guide, N.I. (2001). *A Guide for First Responders*, 4. National Institute of Justice.

Horsman, G. (2020). ACPO principles for digital evidence: time for an update? *Forensic Science International: Reports* 2: 100076.

Horsman, G. (2022). Defining principles for preserving privacy in digital forensic examinations. *Forensic Science International: Digital Investigation* 40: 301350.

Horsman, G. and Sunde, N. (2020). Part 1: The need for peer review in digital forensics. *Forensic Science International: Digital Investigation* 35: 301062.

INTERPOL (2022). Digital Forensics [Internet]. INTERPOL [cited 2024 February 20]. https://www.interpol.int/en/How-we-work/Innovation/Digital-forensics (accessed 12 August 2024).

Jones, A. and Vidalis, S. (2019). Rethinking digital forensics. *Annals of Emerging Technologies in Computing (AETiC)*, Print ISSN: 2516–0281.

Lang, A., Bashir, M., Campbell, R., and DeStefano, L. (2014). Developing a new digital forensics curriculum. *Digital Investigation* 11: S76–S84.

Marshall, A.M. (2010). Quality standards and regulation: challenges for digital forensics. *Measurement and Control* 43 (8): 243–247.

Nance, K., Hay, B., and Bishop, M. (2009). Digital forensics: defining a research agenda. In: *2009 42nd Hawaii International Conference on System Sciences* (5 January 2009), 1–6. IEEE.

National Police Chief's Council (2020). Digital Forensic Science Strategy [Internet]. [cited 2024 April 3]. https://www.npcc.police.uk/SysSiteAssets/media/downloads/publications/publications-log/2020/national-digital-forensic-science-strategy.pdf (accessed 12 August 2024).

Ó'Ciardhuáin, S. (2004). An extended model of cybercrime investigations. *International Journal of Digital Evidence* 3 (1): 1–22.

Pollitt, M. (2010). A history of digital forensics. In: *Advances in Digital Forensics VI: Sixth IFIP WG 11.9 International Conference on Digital Forensics*, Hong Kong, China (4–6 January 2010), Revised Selected Papers 6 2010, 3–15. Berlin, Heidelberg: Springer-Verlag.

Reith, M., Carr, C., and Gunsch, G. (2002). An examination of digital forensic models. *International Journal of Digital Evidence* 1 (3): 1–2.

Saleem, S., Popov, O., and Bagilli, I. (2014). Extended abstract digital forensics model with preservation and protection as umbrella principles. *Procedia Computer Science* 35: 812–821.

Sharevski, F. (2015). Rules of professional responsibility in digital forensics: a comparative analysis. *Journal of Digital Forensics, Security, and Law* 10 (2): 3.

Stoykova, R. (2021). The presumption of innocence as a source for universal rules on digital evidence –the guiding principle for digital forensics in producing digital evidence for criminal investigations. *Computer Law Review International* 22 (3): 74–82.

Sunde, N. and Horsman, G. (2021). Part 2: The Phase-oriented Advice and Review Structure (PARS) for digital forensic investigations. *Forensic Science International: Digital Investigation* 36: 301074.

Techopedia (2019). What is a File System? - Definition from Techopedia [Internet]. Techopedia.com. [cited 2024 April 23]. https://www.techopedia.com/definition/5510/file-system (accessed 12 August 2024).

Yeboah-Ofori, A. and Brown, A.D. (2020). Digital forensics investigation jurisprudence: issues of admissibility of digital evidence. *Journal of Forensic, Legal & Investigative Sciences* 6 (1): 1–8.

2

Linux as a Forensic Platform

This chapter examines the Linux operating system and discusses the concepts inherent in open-source software and the importance of this software in digital investigation. Why concentrate on Linux as a forensic platform? Why not use MS Windows for that? The reason is simple. The Linux platform supports many file systems by default, with the possibility to add others easily. This is not the case with MS Windows or macOS.

This chapter begins with an introduction to open-source software and discusses the advantages/disadvantages of using this during investigation. It then introduces the Linux operating system and provides a brief overview of its history and usage. The chapter then proceeds to discuss the use of Linux as a digital forensics platform, in particular a platform for analysing file systems. In order to follow the exercises in this book the reader should be proficient in the use of the Linux operating system. Hence the remainder of this chapter will describe the Linux installation process and also some of the standard tools that are available in Linux that might aid the digital forensic process.

2.1 Open-Source Software

One of the first things that everyone learns about the Linux operating system is that it is an example of open-source software. But what does this mean? In order to truly understand the benefits of Linux it is necessary to understand the concepts inherent in open-source software. This section describes the open-source movement and the general advantages of using this type of software. It then examines the specific case of digital forensics and evaluates the utility of open-source software in this arena. However, before beginning that discussion it is necessary to determine '*what software is*'?

Software is a collection of commands that tell a computer what to do! Software is generally written in a programming language of which there are many.[1] Programming languages are a particular type of language that allow communication with a computer system. Notable programming languages include C, C++, Java and Python to name a few.

The source code for a piece of software is the actual program written in the programming language, in other words the exact set of instructions that the software is passing to the computer.

1 As to the number of programming languages that exist, nobody is certain! There are various lists of languages available, of which the smallest contains only the 150 most commonly encountered languages, to the largest which contains almost 9000 languages.

File System Forensics, First Edition. Fergus Toolan.

Listing 2.1 shows example source code in the C programming language. This source code is for one of the simplest programs that can be written, Hello World.[2]

```
#include <stdio.h>
int main()
{
  printf("Hello World");
}
```

Listing 2.1 The 'simple' Hello World source code in C.

While non-programmers may struggle to understand the code in Listing 2.1 for a programmer it is (in this example) a trivial task to understand exactly what actions the code will perform. However, the computer does not directly understand the code shown in Listing 2.1. Instead the code is translated to a lower level (often called machine code) which the computer is able to understand. This translation process is known as compiling. Compiling results in an executable file (a .exe in the Windows environment). This file cannot be opened in a text editor as it is a binary file. Instead only the raw data contained in this file can be scrutinised. Listing 2.2 shows an excerpt from the raw data resulting from the compilation of the code in Listing 2.1.

```
0000: 7f45 4c46 0201 0100 0000 0000 0000 0000 .ELF............
0010: 0300 3e00 0100 0000 6010 0000 0000 0000 ..>.....`.......
0020: 4000 0000 0000 0000 7839 0000 0000 0000 @.......x9......
0030: 0000 0000 4000 3800 0d00 4000 1f00 1e00 ....@.8...@.....
0040: 0600 0000 0400 0000 4000 0000 0000 0000 ........@.......
0050: 4000 0000 0000 0000 4000 0000 0000 0000 @.......@.......
...[snip]...
```

Listing 2.2 Excerpt from the 'simple' Hello World program after compilation.

I think that everyone will agree that the compiled executable file is much more difficult for anyone to understand.[3] Now consider the scenario in which I wish to share my wonderful Hello World program with the world. There are two available options as to how I might do this. Firstly I can do what many commercial companies do, I can give them the executable file. People will be able to use my software but they will never be able to alter it (or even to read the actual code that I wrote). This is known as closed-source software: while the software is distributed the source code remains a secret. The second option is that I provide people with the actual C program file shown in Listing 2.1. Users of my software have to do a little more work – they have to compile the program themselves – however, they will also know exactly what that program is doing, as they can read the program code, if needed they can even alter the program code. This approach is known as open-source code. The actual programming language code is available to the user.

2 Generally the first program that everyone writes when learning to code is Hello World. The origins of this are uncertain but they are linked to the very early days of the C programming language in 1974, although some claim that its origins were earlier than this, either with the B programming language in 1972 or BCPL in 1967. While the exact origin is unclear every programmer has written multiple Hello World programs during their career!

3 It is possible to decompile an executable file. However, with the possible complexities inherent in programs it is unlikely that the resulting source code will be identical to that written by the programmer, although it should be functionally equivalent.

The open-source movement defines open-source software as 'software with source code that anyone can inspect, modify and enhance'.[4] It is often provided under a copyleft licence. Traditionally the purpose of copyright is to protect the author. It enforces the author's rights to the material in question. Copyleft, on the other hand, requires that the rights associated with the material are maintained even if the material is reused. If open-source software was released without a licence, anyone could use this software and convert it to proprietary software. Hence the copyleft licence protects the software, people can still use (and alter) the software but the resulting copies must continue to use the same licence agreement. In order to copyleft a piece of software it is first copyrighted and then distribution terms are added which give everyone the right to use, modify and distribute the software, or any software derived from it, as long as the distribution terms are unchanged.

Open-source software is used in countless areas in computing. Indeed without being aware of it, you use open-source software on a daily basis. For instance both the Google Chrome and Microsoft Edge browsers are based on the Chromium project – a free, open-source minimalist web browser developed by Chrome – while Mozilla Firefox is a purely open-source browser. Remaining in the web sphere over 65% of web servers are powered by the Nginx or Apache Web Servers[5] both of which are open-source products. Hence at least two-thirds of web sites are powered by open-source technology! When writing documents you may have used the Apache OpenOffice or LibreOffice suites, both of which are open-source projects. The ClamAV project provides an open-source anti-virus program. OpenSSH and PuTTY are two open-source projects that provide for secure shell (SSH) remote access. There are also developer websites solely focused on the development and distribution of open-source software such as Source Forge and Github.

2.1.1 Advantages of Open-Source Software

There are a number of reasons why many people find open-source preferable to closed-source software. The following list provides a non-exhaustive number of reasons to use open-source over closed-source software.

- **Transparency:** The user can see what they are getting! This means they can determine exactly what code is doing (if they possess the skills) something that is impossible to achieve with closed-source code. Development of the application over time is evident either based on the availability of past versions or on comments included in the source code. This transparency allows for a better informed decision-making process when selecting an open rather than closed-source solution.
- **Community:** One of the largest selling points of open-source software is the large community of users, developers and testers that exist for most popular open-source software solutions. These communities are the driving force that lead to the introduction of new features in a faster and more effective way than small teams working on closed-source proprietary software are able to achieve. The community will often also resolve issues quicker than the dedicated team due to the size of the community and the interest and enthusiasm of the members.
- **Training:** Studying open-source code can be a great method of learning to program. It is also a great way for students of programming to gather feedback on their coding efforts. In the digital forensic domain studying open-source code leads to a better understanding of the underlying structures of various artefacts.

4 https://opensource.com/resources/what-open-source.
5 Figures current as of March 2023. Source: https://w3techs.com/technologies/overview/web_server.

- **Security:** Many argue that open-source software is by its very nature less secure than closed-source software. The argument is that the hacker can read the source code and discover vulnerabilities. The open-source community take the alternative approach: software is more secure when the code is available to everyone as anyone with an interest can read the code and fix any security issues that might exist. This position is supported by the numbers of commercial companies moving towards open-source solutions.
- **Reliability:** Due to the large community of developers/testers/users etc. code tends to be more reliable when released as an open-source project rather than a closed-source one.
- **Stability:** As access to the source code is provided the user can take over in the unlikely event that the community ceases development. This is not the same with commercial closed-source software.

Notice that one reason that is not referred to in this section is cost. Many consider open-source software to be free, but while often true, it is not always the case. This will be discussed in more detail in Section 2.1.2.

2.1.2 Open Source ≠ Free

One of the most common arguments made in favour of open-source software is that it is free. However, this argument is not always correct. Richard Stallman, the founder of the Free Software Foundation, intended code to be free, not necessarily in terms of cost, but in terms of our ability to do whatever we wished with code. He famously stated that free referred to '*free as in free speech, not free as in free beer*'. The distinction is that with 'free' software users are at liberty to change anything they wish, but it does not imply there should be no cost for the software. On saying that, open-source software is often free of cost also. This is due to the copyleft licensing requirements that are enforced upon it. It is very difficult to sell open-source software as the licence says that anyone can distribute it. Hence if one person bought it they could provide it to anyone else free of charge.

Corporate entities can, and do, make money from the provision of open-source software. These entities provide source code free of charge to anyone who wishes to use it. As with all open-source projects anyone can access and modify the source code itself in order to tailor the system for their exact demands. While the source code is free of charge the company earns money by providing training courses, customisation, installation and hosting services, etc. So while the software is open-source and free, these corporate entities are still on a sound financial footing!

2.2 Open-Source Software in Digital Forensics

The methods employed in digital investigation must be beyond reproach. Errors in investigation can lead to miscarriages of justice in which the wrong person may be punished for a crime, or punished more severely than they deserve. These miscarriages of justice must be avoided at all costs. The transparency provided by open-source software provides a level of confidence in the results of the digital investigation tasks that are not present when we utilise closed-source software.

With closed-source software users rely on trust that the developers of the software performed their tasks correctly. While most people tend to trust these commercial software packages many people have encountered errors in them. Consider the infamous blue screen of death in the Windows operating system. This error was so commonplace that it even earned its own acronym, BSoD!

With an open-source solution it is no longer necessary to trust a small group of developers, instead trust is placed in the community. This provides more confidence in the correctness of open-source tools as the community can review (and fix) them at any point. Indeed if the end user has the skills to do so, they can review open-source software before utilising it in cases. This leads to increased trust in the software tools that are being used.

Additionally in investigation, and particularly in the court proceedings which may follow investigation, the notion of disclosure is of vital importance. Disclosure is the '*process of revealing evidence held by one party to an action or a prosecution to the other party*'.[6] It is the process by which each party '*puts their cards on the table*'.[7] While in the majority of jurisdictions disclosure refers to documents and testimony, i.e. the evidence that will be presented, it can also be interpreted to mean the methods by which the evidence was obtained. Where this is the case, the use of open-source software aids the disclosure process. By using open-source tools the investigator can stand over the evidence they present in court as anyone can check that the tools, and hence the evidence, are correct.

On a related note digital evidence is often considered scientific or technical evidence. Members of the courts are not expected to be experts in this area and as such guidelines are used to determine if technical or scientific evidence should be admitted to the court proceedings. In the United States these rules have been codified, initially as the Frye Standard which is gradually being replaced by the Daubert Standard. These 'tests' are used to determine the validity of scientific/technical evidence. In both cases these standards refer to the 'general acceptance of the technique' by the relevant scientific community. Software is the implementation of that technique; it is therefore not only vital that the technique can be checked, but that the implementation can also be checked. While techniques may be published and subject to review, it is only open-source implementations that are subject to any form of review. With a closed-source approach it is never entirely certain as to what the software actually does.

In summary, while maybe not (yet) essential for digital investigation and the presentation of technical evidence in court I would argue that the use of open-source software tools will greatly improve the reliability and transparency of evidence presented in court. Doing this ensures that less errors are made in the investigation process.

2.3 What is Linux?

Opensource.com defines Linux as 'the best-known and most-used open source operating system'. Many years ago people predicted that Linux would overtake Windows in the desktop OS market. Now, while we might see the beginning of the predicted revolution, it has certainly not been at the expense of Windows as a desktop OS. Even with the success of the Linux distribution, Ubuntu, Linux has not affected the Windows market share. However, its success is seen in other areas such as embedded systems; GPS systems; Android phone OS; and web servers; ... etc.

One of the main reasons for using Linux is that it is open source. As stated previously it is possibly the most used open-source software available. However, there are a number of other reasons that its use should be more common in digital forensics/investigation:

- **File System Support:** Linux provides in-built support for a large number of file systems. File system forensics is a large part of digital forensics and as such this fact is very beneficial.

6 https://legal-dictionary.thefreedictionary.com/disclosure.
7 https://www.pinsentmasons.com/out-law/guides/disclosure-and-privilege.

- **Servers Use Linux/Unix:** The majority of servers use Linux/Unix. Therefore familiarity with these operating systems can be of benefit in terms of cybercrime investigation.
- **Linux Tools Are Less Abstract:** Linux command line tools often force us to work at a lower level than with graphical tools. This provides a better understanding of what all tools (including more abstract graphical tools) are actually doing. This knowledge can be vital if questioned in court!
- **Full OS:** Linux is a full operating system. There is nothing that can be done in Windows/Mac that can't be done on Linux. You can perform your investigation, write your report, answer your email, etc. all on the same machine.
- **Linux Is Free:** Cost is not a driving force behind the selection of Linux in this book; however, this might be important to managers. All of the digital forensic tools mentioned in this book are also free.

2.3.1 The Anatomy of the Linux OS

There are a multitude of different Linux versions, many of which are specialised for particular tasks. Linux can be used as a full operating system for desktop and server-level computers, or can be used as a minimal install for IoT and embedded devices. However, each Linux distribution, regardless of how different the end result is, shares a similar anatomy. There are four main parts to Linux systems, which are:

- **Kernel:** The core of Linux providing hardware and software control.
- **GNU Utilities:** Standard utility programs to perform standard functions such as controlling files.
- **Graphical Desktop Environment:** The GUI for Linux (unlike other operating systems there is great choice of GUI with Linux).
- **Application Software:** These are the applications that are found on the system. These include browsers; office software; forensic tools; etc. This is the software that end users are most familiar with.

The smallest of distributions might only have a kernel (and probably some specialised applications), while a desktop distribution will have all four levels. Figure 2.1 shows how these various parts fit together.

The kernel is responsible for controlling all hardware and software on the computer system. While Linus Torvalds is regarded as the creator of Linux, strictly speaking it is the kernel that he

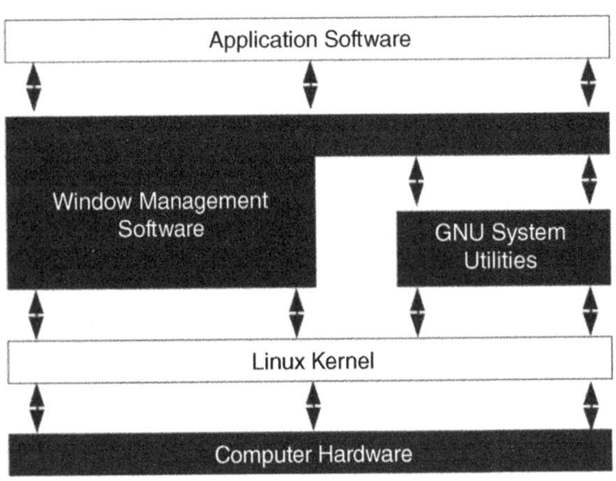

Figure 2.1 Interactions between the various layers in the Linux OS.

created (with help from others nowadays). The Linux kernel is responsible for four main functions which are:

- **Memory Management:** Computer memory consists of two types, physical and virtual memory. Computers have a limited amount of physical memory but can use hard drive space to (seemingly) increase this value. This 'extra' memory is called virtual memory. The kernel is responsible for the management of both physical and virtual memory. It attempts to ensure that the required information is in the physical memory before it is actually needed. This is done through a system called paging in which pages of memory are swapped between virtual and physical memory. The Linux OS considers the entire virtual memory space to be available as RAM however, in reality it is only the physical space that is actually available. Figure 2.2 provides a logical view of the Linux memory system.
- **Software (Process) Management:** The kernel is also responsible for the management of all software on the running Linux machine. Strictly speaking this means the management of all of the processes that are executing on the machine, ensuring that they get the resources that they require and that they do not interfere with other processes on the system. Traditionally the very first process started on a Linux system is **initd** which has a process ID of 1. In modern Linux systems this is more likely to be called **systemd** (but it still has PID 1!). All subsequent processes on the system will be children of this initialisation process.
- **Hardware Management:** Hardware devices are also managed by the kernel. This management involves loading the correct driver code for a particular device. The driver acts as a *translator* between the operating system and the device itself. Historically drivers could only be compiled into the kernel, meaning that when new hardware was released the entire kernel had to be updated (and then recompiled) to support the device. However, with the advent of kernel modules it is no longer necessary to recompile; instead the kernel merely loads the new module supplied by the hardware manufacturer (or the Linux community). This notion of kernel modules removed one of the biggest obstacles to adopting Linux as the main OS, the difficulty in configuring new hardware for Linux. Even though one of the selling points of Linux was that it could run on almost all hardware it was sometimes difficult to get it working.

  You might have heard the expression that 'everything is a file in Linux'. This includes devices themselves. Each device is accessed as if it were a file. Devices are categorised as being character,

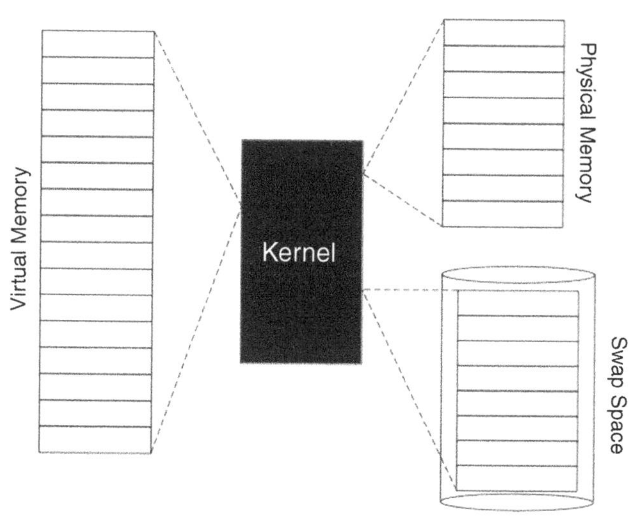

Figure 2.2 Logical view of Linux memory.

block or network devices. The categorisation is based on how communication occurs. Character devices transmit data one character at a time. These include modems, keyboards, mice, etc. Block devices handle chunks of data in one go. These chunks are often called blocks. These devices include disk drives, CD Rom, RAM, etc. Block devices generally allow faster access to data than character devices do. Network devices use packets to send and receive data. Listing 2.3 shows an example of character and block devices found in the **/dev** directory on a Linux Mint system. Note that **sdaX** refers to disk partitions and **ttyX** refers to terminals.

```
$ ls -l /dev/sda /dev/sda1 /dev/tty0 /dev/tty1
brw-rw---- 1 root disk 8, 0 Mar 23 05:33 /dev/sda
brw-rw---- 1 root disk 8, 1 Mar 23 05:33 /dev/sda1
crw--w---- 1 root tty  4, 0 Mar 23 05:33 /dev/tty0
crw--w---- 1 root tty  4, 1 Mar 23 05:33 /dev/tty1
```

Listing 2.3 Listing certain devices in the **/dev** directory showing character (**ttyX**) and block (**sdaX**) devices.

From Listing 2.3 the first character in the permission string is c (character device) or b (block device). Additionally there is a pair of numbers underlined for each device (8, 0 for **/dev/sda**). This pair of numbers allows the kernel to identify the device. Generally the major number (8) will be used by all devices of this type, while the minor number (0) represents a specific device of that type. In this case all disk drives/partitions will have a major number of 8 (as seen in Listing 2.3).

- **File System Management:** The final major duty of the kernel is file system management. As with hardware, file system support can be compiled into the kernel or can be achieved through external modules. One of the main reasons to consider using Linux for digital forensics is the vast number of file systems that are supported *out-of-the-box* by Linux systems. Consider the Windows OS, it can support the FAT family of file systems, along with ExFAT and NTFS. Some of the Windows Server versions will also support ReFS by default. Table 2.1 shows the list of file systems that are commonly supported by Linux. Support for others can be added as required.
  While the benefits to digital forensics of being able to access numerous file systems are obvious, it is also the case that the in-built support provides the analyst with much flexibility in how case files are stored. For instance a modern file system with full RAID support, such as BtrFS, can be used to store the case information for added redundancy and resilience.

The next layer in the Linux operating system are the GNU utilities. Utilities are programs which sit above the kernel and allow the user (and system) to control files and programs. The original kernel, created by Linus Torvalds, was merely a kernel. It handled all of the management, but there were no utilities to run on the kernel. In other words we couldn't do anything with the OS. However, the GNU (GNU not Unix) organisation was independently developing a set of Unix-like utility programs. The GNU utilities were developed using an open-source model (championed by Richard Stallman), and as such could be easily used with the Linux kernel. The combination of the Linux kernel and the GNU utilities led to a functioning operating system.

Aside: It's all in the name!: Strictly speaking Linux refers only to the kernel. However, when we say Linux we generally mean GNU/Linux, which is the combination of the Linux kernel and the GNU utilities. You can read a little more on the naming controversy at https://en.wikipedia.org/wiki/GNU/Linux_naming_controversy.

Table 2.1 A selection of the file systems supported in the Linux kernel. Note that not all are enabled in every distribution.

File System	Description
ext	The original Linux extended file system (early 1990s). This FS is no longer frequently encountered.
ext2	The second extended file system, providing some advanced features above and beyond ext. This was created in the early 1990s and is still used today!
ext3	The third extended file system which added support for a journal structure.
ext4	The fourth extended file system (and the default on most modern Linux systems).
hpfs	OS/2 high-performance file system.
jfs	IBM's journaled file system.
iso9660	ISO 9660 file system (CD-Rom).
minix	The MINIX file system (used with the MINIX operating system).
msdos	FAT 16.
ncp	Novell netware file system.
nfs	The network file system.
ntfs	Microsoft's new technology file system.
Reiser FS	An advanced Linux file system for better recovery and performance.
smb	The samba network sharing file system (compatible with Windows file sharing).
sysv	An old Unix file system.
ufs	BSD Unix file system.
umsdos	Unix-like file system as an overlay to msdos.
vfat	FAT 32.
exFat	The extended FAT file system.
xfs	A high-performance 64-bit journaled file system.

Generally when the term Linux is used it refers to GNU/Linux!

The Linux **coreutils** package is available for all flavours of Linux and contains many of the utility programs. Listing 2.4 shows an excerpt from the output of **apt-cache show coreutils**, showing that this package is installed and also showing the standard commands that are included here.

Shells are also considered part of the GNU utilities. A shell is merely a command line interface (CLI). It is a program which waits for the user (or another program) to input a command and then executes the command. The default shell on many modern Linux systems is Bash, but there are many others available. Most have similar features (e.g. command history, auto-completion, selection statements and iterative statements.) but there are differences between them. Bash is a replacement for the standard Unix Shell and is a play on words standing for the Bourne Again Shell (the original Unix shell was often called the Bourne shell after its creator!). Bash is compatible with the Unix shell but has more features. Other common shells include:

- **ash:** A lightweight shell that is compatible with Bash, but can run in low-resource environments.

```
Description-en: GNU core utilities
This package contains the basic file, shell and text manipulation
utilities which are expected to exist on every operating system.
.
Specifically, this package includes:
 arch base64 basename cat chcon chgrp chmod chown chroot cksum
 comm cp csplit cut date dd df dir dircolors dirname du echo
 env expand expr factor false flock fmt fold groups head hostid
 id install join link ln logname ls md5sum mkdir mkfifo mknod
 mktemp mv nice nl nohup nproc numfmt od paste pathchk pinky pr
 printenv printf ptx pwd readlink realpath rm rmdir runcon
 sha*sum seq shred sleep sort split stat stty sum sync tac tail
 tee test timeout touch tr true truncate tsort tty uname
 unexpand uniq unlink users vdir wc who whoami yes
```

Listing 2.4 Detailed information about the GNU coreutils package on Linux Mint.

- **korn:** korn is a programming shell compatible with Bash but providing support for more advanced programming constructs than Bash (e.g. associative arrays and floating point arithmetic).
- **tcsh:** A shell that provides elements of the C programming language.
- **zsh:** An advanced shell combining elements from Bash, korn and tcsh.

Throughout this book commands will be executed in the Bash shell.

The third major component of a Linux system is the graphical desktop environment. This is the first component that is not required. Many small devices (IoT for instance) do not use a graphical component as it is not necessary and only wastes resources. For similar reasons many servers do not use graphical desktop environments either, preferring to save as many resources for serving client requests rather than running computationally expensive graphical processes. On those Linux systems that have graphical desktop environments, they are actually composed of two subsystems: The X Window System and the graphical desktop environment.

The X Windows System is responsible for communication with the video card and monitor on a computer system. The name is derived from the most popular X Windows System produced by X.org. There are now multiple packages that implement this behaviour including Wayland (Fedora) and Mir (Ubuntu). When Linux is installed the X Windows System will query your display hardware and determine what devices are connected. Configuration files for these devices will be automatically created. During installation you sometimes notice flickering on-screen (or even the screen going black for a few seconds). This is often the X Window System attempting to determine the installed display hardware. While X allows for graphics, it does not allow for the full desktop experience. For that a graphical desktop environment is required.

There are many desktop environments available for Linux. Two of the most well known are KDE and Gnome. For instance Linux Mint uses Mate (based on Gnome 2) or Cinnamon (based on Gnome 3) desktop environments. There are also desktop environments such as XFCE, Openbox and LXQt which are specifically designed to be lightweight. By the way these desktop environments make Linux the perfect OS for older hardware. Imagine trying to run Windows 11 with only 1 GB RAM! It will be really slow. Use a Linux distro with XFCE or Openbox and you will get reasonably fast performance!

The final piece of the jigsaw is the application software that is installed on the distribution. This software can be terminal level (i.e. command line) or graphical applications. Application software makes the distribution. Most distros will include standard applications such as web browsers, email clients and office software. while specialist distributions will include specialist software.

2.3.2 Linux Distributions

A Linux distribution (generally abbreviated to distro) is an operating system composed of a collection of software that is based on the Linux kernel. Section 2.3.1 described the major components of the Linux operating system. Distros use different combinations of software in each of these layers to create unique operating systems. There are hundreds of Linux distributions in active use at any one time. DistroWatch provides a summary of distro popularity. Table 2.2 summarises the most popular Linux distros in recent years.

As can be seen in Table 2.2 there are lots of distros and it is important to understand their specific features before using them. In this section, some of the main components of distros that must be considered when choosing which one to use are discussed.

Linux distributions are more than just the look and feel of the desktop. Linux distros are customisable. Any software can generally be installed on any distro. However, how close the original distro is to our end requirements should be one of our main concerns. Finding the right distro saves time and user effort. Some of the issues to be considered in identifying a distribution are:

- **Package Managers:** Different distros have different package managers. For example, APT is used in Debian-based distros such as Ubuntu, Mint, CAInE, Backtrack and of course Debian whereas Fedora/Red Hat uses YUM (or dnf) for package management. It is not that difficult to build a program from scratch, but doing so does not allow automatic updates of that program when new versions are released. Therefore, the availability of utilities and the ease of using package managers is very important when selecting a distro.
- **Desktop Environment:** Some graphical desktop environments that can be used with Linux distributions have already been mentioned. The choice of distro should be based on the desktop

Table 2.2 Distro popularity based on Distro Watch page views (April 2024).

	April 2020	April 2021	April 2023	April 2024
1	MX Linux	MX Linux	MX Linux	MX Linux
2	Manjaro	Manjaro	EndeavourOS	Mint
3	Linux Mint	Linux Mint	Linux Mint	EndeavourOS
4	Ubuntu	Pop!_OS	Manjaro	Debian
5	Debian	Ubuntu	Pop!_OS	Manjaro
6	Elementary	EndeavourOS	Ubuntu	Ubuntu
7	Solus	Debian	Fedora	Fedora
8	Zorin	Elementary	Debian	Pop!_OS
9	Fedora	Fedora	Elementary	openSuse
10	Deepin	Open Suse	Lite	Zorin

environment (while the default can be changed it is often easier to find a distro that uses the favoured desktop system).

- **Stability vs Cutting Edge:** Some distros focus on providing up-to-date versions of packages as quickly as possible whereas others focus on stability first and only then do they update the packages.
- **Hardware Compatibility:** Drivers in the installer may vary with different distros making them more or less compatible with the computer hardware. This is no longer the arduous task that it once was. Linux support for hardware has improved greatly in recent years (mainly due to the kernel modules mentioned earlier). Most of the distributions on the top 10 list (Table 2.2) would provide plug-and-play support for most major hardware manufacturers.
- **Community Support:** Community support is very useful when troubleshooting. Distros with larger communities often provide quicker support when needed.

But which distro should you choose for digital forensics? There are two main options. You can go for a general-purpose distribution in which you can install all of the required forensic tools, or you can opt for a digital forensic distribution. These distributions have many forensic tools pre-installed and are also configured specifically for digital investigation/forensics. For instance when removable media are inserted into the system, the system will not automount said media. Indeed all mounting, when done, is read-only by default. Some examples of forensic/cybersecurity distros include:

- **Caine:** The **C**omputer-**A**ided **IN**vestigative **E**nvironment. Forensics, OSINT and Pen Testing tools are pre-installed.
- **Tsurugi:** A DFIR (Digital Forensics Incident Response) distro which has a number of OSINT/ Pen Testing tools also installed along with many digital forensic tools.
- **Kali:** A distro specifically focused on penetration testing which also contains open-source intelligence and digital forensic tools.
- **Backbox:** An Ubuntu-based penetration testing distro.
- **BlackArch:** A penetration testing distro based on Arch Linux.
- **Pentoo:** A penetration testing distro based on Gentoo Linux.
- **Parrot Security:** A penetration testing distro that also contains tools for other areas of digital investigation.

The choice of distro is yours to make. If you want a ready made forensic distribution then by all means choose one of the above distros. If you want to learn more about Linux then choose a general-purpose distribution such as Ubuntu, Fedora or Open Suse. What's my choice? Mostly I use a general-purpose distribution which is configured for digital investigation. Over the years I have used all of the major distributions (Debian, Red Hat, Suse, etc.) but my favourites are generally Debian based. For those reasons I currently use Linux Mint regularly. The desktop environment is nice and simple (not too many bells and whistles!), the Apt package manager is used (which is very easy to use – either through the GUI or directly from the terminal), the OS is stable and there is great support if something goes wrong. Examples that you will see in this book have all been created using Linux Mint (indeed this book was originally typeset using latex running on Linux Mint!).

2.3.3 A (very) Brief History of Linux

The first public indication that Linux was on the way came in August 1991 when a Finnish student, Linus Torvalds, posted on the Minix OS usenet group the following message:

> Hello everybody out there using minix -
>
> I'm doing a (free) operating system (just a hobby, won't be big and professional like gnu) for 386(486) AT clones. This has been brewing since April, and is starting to get ready. I'd like any feedback on things people like/dislike in minix, as my OS resembles it somewhat (same physical layout of the file-system (due to practical reasons) among other things).
>
> I've currently ported bash(1.08) and gcc(1.40), and things seem to work. This implies that I'll get something practical within a few months, and I'd like to know what features most people would want. Any suggestions are welcome, but I won't promise I'll implement them:-)
>
> Linus (torvalds@kruuna.helsinki.fi)
>
> PS. Yes – it's free of any minix code, and it has a multi-threaded fs. It is NOT portable (uses 386 task switching etc.), and it probably never will support anything other than AT-harddisks, as that's all I have:-(.

Torvalds had begun the creation of the Linux kernel as a personal project in April 1991. There were a number of reasons for this. To that point the main operating systems available were Unix and Minix. Unix was considered the best OS at the time but the licensing costs were prohibitive, certainly for home users. Andrew Tannenbaum, the noted computer scientist, had created a *Mini-Unix* (a.k.a. Minix). The cost of this was still prohibitive (although not nearly as bad as Unix) and it also lacked some of the desired Unix functionality. Linus Torvalds set out to write a version of Minix that was as complete as Unix and could be distributed to anyone!

As seen from Torvald's initial usenet posting in August 1991, Linux was originally just aimed at the 386 architecture and nothing more. Torvalds never thought that Linux would run on everything! Now Linux runs on almost every piece of hardware in use!

Linux kernel version 0.01 was released on 17 September 1991 but had limited functionality. Indeed Torvalds never publicised the fact that this version was available. Version 0.02 was very quickly released (5 October 1991). This version included a ported version of GNU **Bash** (the terminal interface) and GNU **gcc** (the C compiler). The addition of these two utilities meant that there was now a usable operating system available. People could install Linux and actually do something with it! Very quickly all of the GNU utilities were ported to the new Linux kernel and it began to be used more frequently.

Interest in Linux exploded in the early 1990s. The first distributions appeared in 1992, with most of the modern distribution families present by 1996 (Slackware and Debian - 1993, Red Hat - 1994, and Suse - 1996). Many of these distros included the X Window System allowing for simple graphical interfaces to the Linux kernel.

The mid-1990s saw the development of more feature-rich graphical environments such as KDE (1996) and Gnome (1997). These two systems are still in common use today. They have also both led to numerous forks over the years meaning that most Linux graphical systems can trace their roots to one of these competing systems.

The next section provides a brief tour of Linux Mint. Note for those of you that are familiar with Linux you should skip ahead to Section 2.4.2. If you are also familiar with the Linux terminal interface then you should skip directly to Section 2.5.

2.4 Using Linux

Figure 2.3 shows a running Linux Mint system. Linux Mint uses a Windows-like desktop metaphor in which files/folders can be stored directly on the desktop. The Linux Mint system also provides a

Figure 2.3 The Linux Mint desktop immediately after login.

Start Menu-like system in the bottom left of the screen. Adjacent to this is a task bar, showing the running applications. The bottom right corner of the screen shows the system tray icons.

As with Windows the system tray will show the status of various components in the Linux Mint OS. This includes the current network and battery status, information about software upgrades, date and time, etc. The Linux Mint menu is shown in Figure 2.4, again this is similar to the Windows start menu, providing search functionality and also access to all the installed applications.

One of the most commonly used applications in this book is the Linux terminal (also called the shell). The terminal is an application which allows interaction with the system through a command-line interface. Most of the examples that are encountered in this book are generated from the Linux terminal.

The terminal provides a prompt at which the user can input a command. Once the user has input the command it is parsed by the shell (e.g. Bash), the shell displays the output on screen and then presents the prompt to the user as it awaits the next command. The terminal in Linux Mint can be accessed through the main menu under *Administration | Terminal*. Figure 2.5 shows the Linux terminal awaiting input.

2.4.1 User Accounts

One of the most important concepts in Linux is that of the user account, and specifically the root user. The root user in a Linux system has the rights to perform any action on the system (this includes some pretty terminal actions such as deleting ALL files on the system). Generally in most Linux systems the first user account that is created (during the installation process) is a member of a special group that allow these users to become the root user. In general all actions in Linux should be performed from a normal user account except when it is necessary to perform an action as root. For instance to access a physical disk when acquiring an image requires root access. Root access, for a single command, can be achieved using **sudo**. Listing 2.5 shows the means by which root access is gained. Note in this example the command **whoami** is used from the Linux terminal.

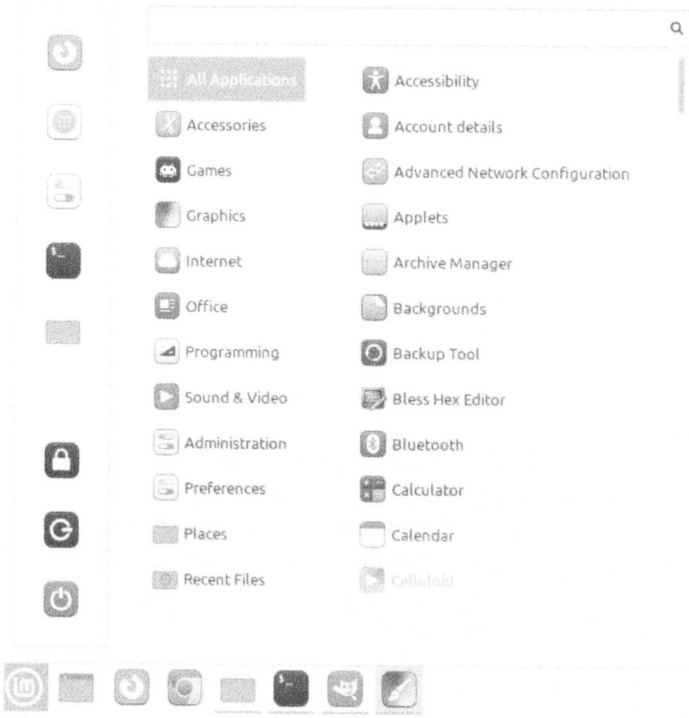

Figure 2.4 The Linux Mint Menu showing the various application categories.

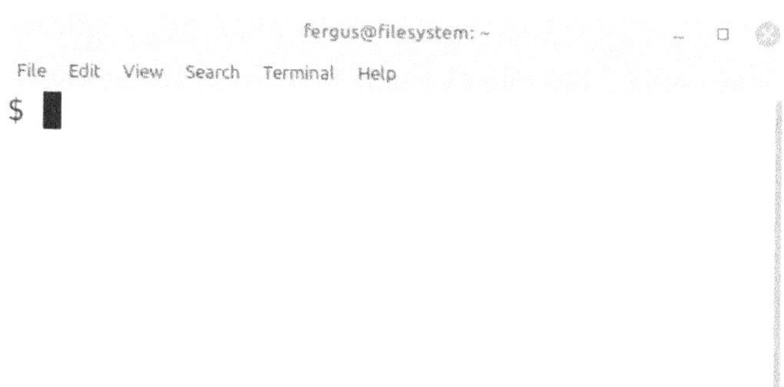

Figure 2.5 The Linux Mint terminal application.

This command merely prints the current username. Best practice in Linux usage would advise that users use the root account only when absolutely essential.

In order to gain temporary root access the command **whoami** is prefixed with another command **sudo** – sometimes called super user do! Upon executing this command the Linux system will check if the user account that is running the command (**fergus** in Listing 2.5) is a member of the **sudo** group. If so the user is prompted for their password. Once authenticated the command is executed with root privileges. This is often necessary for certain digital forensic tasks, in particular when accessing a physical device, for instance when creating a forensic image of a storage device.

```
$ whoami
fergus
$ sudo whoami
[sudo] password for fergus: ********************
root
```

Listing 2.5 Using **sudo** to access the root account.

2.4.2 Basic Linux Commands

This section provides an overview of the basic Linux commands. These commands are broken into common tasks such as navigating the file system and getting help. In each section a number of commands are provided that the reader should further explore.

2.4.2.1 Navigating the File System

One of the difficulties that many Linux newcomers face is the simple act of navigating the file system. It is first necessary to determine our current location in the file system. Generally when a terminal is executed the session will begin in the user's home directory. Consider a user named *fergus*. The default home directory for this user is **/home/fergus**. Listing 2.6 shows the command used to determine the present working directory immediately after running the terminal application. As expected this shows that the user is in **/home/fergus**.

```
$ pwd
/home/fergus
$
```

Listing 2.6 Using **pwd** to determine file system location.

Once the location is determined it is necessary to determine what files/directories are present in that location. The basic command to list files/folders is **ls**. Listing 2.7 shows the output of **ls** in the current directory.[8]

```
$ ls
dates.txt  Documents  Music    Pictures  Templates
Desktop    Downloads  perl5    Public    Videos
$
```

Listing 2.7 Using **ls** to list the files/folders in the current directory.

The general terminal command structure is:

command [options] [arguments]

When arguments are provided to a command the command will be run upon those arguments. In Listing 2.7 no arguments are provided to the **ls** command. Arguments are not necessary for this command as, by default, it operates in the current directory. Options are not provided for the

8 The output that you see will be similar but not identical to the output shown in this example.

command in this case although the **ls** command can take both arguments and options. Listing 2.8 shows an example of the **ls** command in which both options and arguments are provided to the command.

```
$ ls -lh Downloads/
total 13G
-rw-rw-r-- 1 fergus fergus 2.4M May 11  2021 01.jpg
-rw-rw-r-- 1 fergus fergus 295K Aug 26 09:43 0306511.pdf
...[snip]...
$
```

Listing 2.8 Using options and arguments with the **ls** command.

Instead of listing the contents of the current directory the argument *Downloads/*[9] is provided to the **ls** command. This has the effect of listing the contents of the **Downloads** directory rather than the current directory. Additionally the options **-lh** are provided to the command. These have the effect of listing the files in a long format (which provides the permissions, owner, group, size, modification date, etc.) for the file (-l) and providing the file size in a human-readable format (-h). Most Linux commands can take options/arguments.

But how does a user traverse the file system? The way to achieve this is through the **cd** command. The **cd** command takes as argument the directory to which the user wishes to change. For instance in Listing 2.9 the user changes to the **Downloads** directory, back up to the home directory (**..** is a special directory name for the parent directory) and then into **Documents**.

```
$ cd Downloads/
$ pwd
/home/fergus/Downloads
$ cd ..
$ pwd
/home/fergus
$ cd Documents/
$ pwd
/home/fergus/Documents
```

Listing 2.9 Using the **cd** command to change directory.

The combination of **cd** and **pwd** allows the user to navigate the file system. Note that the directory names that have been presented to this point are relative to the current directory. It is possible to provide absolute directory names also. Consider the command in Listing 2.10. This takes the user immediately to a directory called **/etc**.

```
$ cd /etc
$ pwd
/etc
```

Listing 2.10 Using the **cd** command with absolute paths.

9 The Linux terminal is case sensitive meaning that **ls Downloads/** and **ls downloads/** are different commands.

As with the **ls** command the **cd** command has a default argument if none is provided. In the case of running the **cd** command without an argument the user is immediately returned to their home directory. This is shown in Listing 2.11.

```
$ pwd
/etc
$ cd
$ pwd
/home/fergus
$
```

Listing 2.11 Using the **cd** command with no arguments to return to the home directory.

2.4.2.2 Getting Help

As one becomes more familiar with the terminal it quickly becomes clear how complex the environment is. There are many commands, each of which can have many options. How is it possible to remember all of these? The answer to this (for most people) is that it is not! Instead Linux provides a help system called the manual system. This is access through the **man** command.

```
PWD(1)                      User Commands                      PWD(1)

NAME
     pwd - print name of current/working directory

SYNOPSIS
     pwd [OPTION]...

DESCRIPTION
     Print the full filename of the current working directory.

     -L, --logical
          use PWD from environment, even if it contains ...

     -P, --physical
          avoid all symlinks
```

Listing 2.12 The manual page for the **pwd** command.

Most commands have a help or manual page. Listing 2.12 shows part of the manual page for the **pwd** command. The space bar is used to move through the manual page. Use 'q' to exit the manual system.

2.4.2.3 Viewing/Editing Text Files

Files can be created using any text editor. All of the graphical distros provide a graphical text editor from the main menu (similar to Notepad on Windows) but there are also text editors available at the terminal. These include **nano** (sometimes called **pico**), **emacs** and **vi**. The **nano** editor is by far the simplest of these.

Text files can also be viewed from the terminal. There are a number of tools that can do this including:

- **cat:** The **cat** command will display the entire contents of a file. Multiple files can be provided as argument and the **cat** command will display them all. Strictly speaking the **cat** command is used to concatenate files, taking multiple files as input and creating a new file containing the contents of all input files as output. When provided with a single input file and as the output is displayed on the terminal by default it has the effect of displaying the file's content to the user.
- **more:** The **more** command is a pager, showing a file one page at a time. Pages are advanced using the space bar (the command can be exited at any stage using 'q').
- **less:** The **less** command is another pager that is very similar to **more**. Historically there were differences in them but over time these have been reduced.
- **head:** The **head** command will display the first 10 lines of a text file by default. This behaviour can be changed using **head -n 5** for instance to display the first five lines of the file.
- **tail:** The **tail** command by default displays the last 10 lines of a text file. Similar to the **head** command the number of lines can be modified using **-n x** where **x** is the number of lines to be displayed.

2.4.2.4 Managing Directories

The **mkdir** command is used to create a directory. For instance in the home directory a directory called **Files** is created using the command shown in Listing 2.13. Note that the **cd** command is first issued to ensure that the home directory is the current directory.

```
$ cd
$ mkdir Files
$ ls
dates.txt  Documents  Files  perl5     Public     Videos
Desktop    Downloads  Music  Pictures  Templates  vmware
$
```

Listing 2.13 Using the **mkdir** command to create a directory.

2.4.2.5 Redirection and Pipes

All of the commands introduced to this point have displayed their output on the terminal itself. There are two output streams by default in Linux, STDOUT (Standard Output) and STDERR (Standard Error). By default most output is sent to STDOUT; however, error messages are often sent to STDERR. By default both of these streams default to the terminal but they can be redirected. Consider the simple **pwd** command shown in Listing 2.6. In this the command's result was displayed on the terminal screen itself. What actually happened was that the command printed information to STDOUT which was directed to the terminal. It is possible to redirect these output streams. Consider the command in Listing 2.14.

```
$ pwd > directory.txt
$ cat directory.txt
/home/fergus
```

Listing 2.14 Redirecting STDOUT to a text file.

The redirection of STDOUT is performed using the > operator. This has the effect of saving the output from the command in the specified filename (**directory.txt** in this case). This can prove invaluable during forensic analysis as it provides a quick means of saving output for further analysis or reporting. The STDERR stream can also be redirected using 2>.

There is also an input stream called STDIN (Standard Input). This can also be redirected using <. Additionally the shell provides one more redirect effect called a pipe. In this the output of one command is used as the input to another command. Later in this book pipes will be used extensively, especially to filter output from commands. At this stage the considered example is trivial.

Consider the effect of the command **cat /etc/passwd**. This displays the contents of the **/etc/-passwd** file in the terminal. However, this file is generally too large to be seen on a single screen. Instead of allowing the output to be sent to the screen, it can be piped to the **more** command to allow the output to be viewed one page at a time. This is shown in Listing 2.15.[10]

```
$ cat /etc/passwd | more
root:x:0:0:root:/root:/bin/bash
daemon:x:1:1:daemon:/usr/sbin:/usr/sbin/nologin
...[snip]...
```

Listing 2.15 Piping output from one command to input to the next.

2.5 Linux as a Forensic Platform

The Linux OS can be used very effectively as a digital forensic platform. As shown in Section 2.1.1 Linux has a number of advantages over traditional closed-source software. In terms of digital forensics and specifically file system forensics, Linux supports a large number of file systems. Support for others can be added very quickly. The open-source nature of the Linux OS (and most of the software available for the Linux OS) means that analysts can have more confidence in the results achieved in digital forensic analysis. This is of vital importance as people's lives often depend on the outcome of these tools.

2.5.1 Commands for Digital Forensics

Another benefit of using Linux as a forensic platform is the number of in-built tools which are of direct benefit to file system forensics. This section examines some of these tools. Linux provides as standard tools for calculating hash values, viewing hex, etc. (see below). Each of these (and many more) is of direct benefit to file system forensics.

In addition to the inbuilt Linux commands that are of use in file system forensics, there are also a number of tools written specifically for file system forensics that are available on the Linux system. These include tools for disk imaging, data carving and file system forensic analysis. Some of these tools will be covered in Chapter 4.

2.5.1.1 Hashing

A hash (also called a message digest) is a fixed length number representing a piece of data. It can also be considered a function which maps arbitrarily sized data to a fixed length. Generally the hash is a one-way function, meaning that it is very easy to calculate the hash value from the data, but

10 As stated earlier this example is trivial. The exact same functionality could be achieved using **more /etc/passwd**.

impossible to reverse the process and generate the data from the hash. Hashes are used in digital investigation for a number of reasons:

1) **To ensure evidential integrity:** When digital evidence is acquired a hash of that value is taken. This hash is maintained (and checked) throughout the investigation. Once the hash value matches it is certain that the content of the evidence has not changed during our analysis.
2) **To eliminate known good files from an investigation:** There are many files that are encountered regularly in investigation that are of no interest. For instance every Windows 10 computer has the same Windows logo image, every Facebook page has the same logos, etc. These are known good files, files which have been encountered previously and are known to be of no interest. By maintaining a list of hash values for these files they can be automatically eliminated from the investigation.
3) **To identify known bad files:** There are also files that have been encountered previously that contain illegal material. These are known bad files. A list of their hash values can be used to automatically identify them in a new case. Note that technically this process is identical to eliminating known good files, the only difference is that a different action is performed with bad and good files when they are identified.

From the above uses it is clear that hashing is most definitely an important tool for digital forensics. There are a number of hashing algorithm choices available which are generally divided into two **families**, Message Digest and Secure Hash Algorithm hashes.

The MD5 algorithm is the only member of the Message Digest family that is still in common usage. It produces a 128 bit hash value. Every Linux distro provides the **md5sum** command to generate an MD5 hash value. Listing 2.16 shows an example of this hash in use. This begins by calculating the MD5 hash value for the text *"Hello World"*. The second version of the command calculated the MD5 for the text *"Hello world"*, in which the case of a single character has been changed. Notice that the resulting hash value is completely different to the original.

```
$ echo "Hello World" | md5sum
e59ff97941044f85df5297e1c302d260 -
$ echo "Hello world" | md5sum
f0ef7081e1539ac00ef5b761b4fb01b3 -
$
```

Listing 2.16 Using **md5sum** to calculate the MD5 value for a piece of text. The second example shows the change in MD5 after a minor change to the text.

Generally this command is run on a file rather than STDIN. To do this merely run the command with the filename provided as an argument. For instance **md5sum river.jpg** will calculate the MD5 value for the file called **river.jpg**.

The Secure Hash Algorithm is a more recent version of hashing algorithm designed to replace MD5. There are four versions of SHA:

- **SHA-0:** A flaw was discovered very early in this and it is no longer used.
- **SHA-1:** Produces a 160 bit hash (compared to MD5's 128 bit). Some weaknesses are present in this algorithm.
- **SHA-2:** Consists of two hashing algorithms (SHA256 and SHA512) which have 256/512 bit hash values.

- **SHA-3:** The previous variants are all designed by NSA (US National Security Agency). SHA-3 algorithms were designed by others, but generally produce 256+ bit hash values.

Listing 2.17 shows the SHA1, SHA256 and SHA512 values for "Hello World".

```
$ echo "Hello World" | sha1sum
648a6a6ffffdaa0badb23b8baf90b6168dd16b3a  -
$ echo "Hello World" | sha256sum
d2a84f4b8b650937ec8f73cd8be2c74add5a911ba64df27458ed8229da804a26  -
$ echo "Hello World" | sha512sum
e1c112ff908febc3b98b1693a6cd3564eaf8e5e6ca629d084d9f0eba99247cacdd
72e369ff8941397c2807409ff66be64be908da17ad7b8a49a2a26c0e8086aa  -
$
```

Listing 2.17 Examples of the SHA family of hashing algorithms.

One caveat with the use of hashing algorithms is that hash collisions can occur. A hash collision occurs when two (or more) distinct items have the same hash value. You might ask how this can occur as a hash is meant to be unique. Well, yes, but there is only a finite set of hash values. Consider the case of using MD5. MD5 generates 128 bit hash values. That means there are 2^{128} possible hash values. Now imagine that in a (very) large investigation $2^{128} + 1$ files have been encountered. Mathematically it is now guaranteed that there exists a hash collision, in other words two files will have the same hash value. In mathematics this is known as the Pigeon Hole Principle. Probability would state that the collision would occur long before arriving at $2^{128} + 1$ files, but at that point it is guaranteed.

Smaller hash values lead to a higher probability of collision; hence, MD5 is considered the least secure (i.e. most likely to have collisions) of the hashing algorithms introduced in this lesson. Hash collisions can be demonstrated using a simple hashing algorithm called **crc32** as shown in Listing 2.18.

```
$ echo -n "plumless" > one
$ echo -n "buckeroo" > two
$ crc32 one two
4ddb0c25 one
4ddb0c25 two
$
```

Listing 2.18 An example of a hash collision using **crc32**.

In order to avoid (or at least reduce the probability of) a hash collision it is better to use the hashing algorithm with the largest output (e.g. SHA512); however, for most uses any of the hashing algorithms presented in this section (except **crc32**) are suitable for use. To further reduce the probability of collision multiple hashing algorithms can be used. For instance both MD5 and SHA1 can be used which greatly reduce the probability of collision.

2.5.1.2 Hex Viewers

There are a number of hex viewers available for Linux, both at the command line level and also using graphical interfaces. Most Linux distributions will provide **hexdump** and **xxd** by default.

These are both terminal-based commands. There are also a number of graphical hex editors available such as **bless**, **okteta** and **wxHexEditor**.

Listing 2.19 shows the **xxd** command being used to view the partition table from the second hard drive on a Linux system (**/dev/sdb**). Note that it is necessary to have root access to perform this operation (hence **sudo** is used). The partition table structure is covered in Section 4.2. Two options are provided to **xxd** in this example. The first is **-s** which provides the number of bytes which should be skipped. In other words instead of beginning the hex dump at byte zero it will begin at byte 446_d. The second option (**-l**) specifies the number of bytes that should be displayed (64_d in this case).

```
$ sudo xxd -s 446 -l 64 /dev/sdb
001be: 003c 0900 8379 463c 0008 0000 0000 2000.<...yF<...... .
001ce: 005c c533 8357 8664 0008 2000 0000 2000.\.3.W.d.. ... .
001de: 0000 0101 833f 2000 0008 4000 0000 2000 .....? ...@... .
001ee: 0000 0101 053f e05f 0008 6000 00f8 7a01 .....?._..'...z.
$
```

Listing 2.19 Using **xxd** to view the partition table on **/dev/sdb**.

Without any options the **xxd** command will begin at the first byte in the input file (i.e. **-s 0**) and will display the entire file content.

2.5.1.3 Archiving/Compression

Digital forensics involves handling large volumes of data. As such the ability to compress data is of vital importance. Linux provides support for most common archive/compression formats. One of the most common linux archiving formats is that of **tar**, the tape archive. Obviously tapes are a thing of the past, but the name has remained. The **tar** command is merely an archiving command that gathers multiple files together in one single archive. Hence the resulting file is generally larger than all of the input files combined. However, the tar command can be combined with a number of compression programs (this includes **gzip** and **bzip**). Listing 2.20 shows the creation of a compressed archive, while Listing 2.21 shows the extraction of said archive.

```
$ tar -czvf archive.tar.gz file1 file2 file3
```

Listing 2.20 Using **tar** to create a gzipped archive called **archive.tar.gz** containing three files: **file1**, **file2** and **file3**.

```
$ tar -xzvf archive.tar.gz
```

Listing 2.21 Using **tar** to extract the contents of the compressed archive, **archive.tar.gz**.

The **tar** command allows for a number of actions. Listing 2.20 shows **-c** being used to create an archive while Listing 2.21 shows **-x** used to extract that artefact. The **-z** option shows that **gzip** compression should be used.

Other compression options are available including ZIP archives. This can be created using: **zip archive.zip file1 file2 file3**, which creates an archive (**archive.zip**) containing three files: **file1**, **file2** and **file3**. ZIP archives can be extracted using **unzip archive.zip**.

2.5.1.4 The file Command

One of the most commonly encountered anti-forensic techniques is that of extension hiding. Consider a JPEG image file which a suspect wishes to *hide* from forensic analysis. The suspect might change the name of this from **picture.jpg** to **text.txt**. Most operating systems would determine this to be a text file (based on the .txt extension) and not a picture as it actually is.

The Linux system provides the **file** command which can determine the actual type of a file by reading the file's contents. Listing 2.22 shows the file command being used on a file called **text.txt**.

```
$ file text.txt
text.txt: PNG image data, 1267 x 850, 8-bit/color RGBA, non-
interlaced
$
```

Listing 2.22 Using **file** to determine file type.

The **file** command analyses the actual raw file content. Consider a JPEG image file. The JPEG standard specifies that all files must begin with the hex values 0xFFD8[11] and end with the hex values 0xFFD9. This can be seen in Listing 2.23.

```
$ xxd picture.jpg | head -n1
00000: ffd8 ffe0 0010 4a46 4946 0001 0101 0048 ......JFIF.....H
$ xxd picture.jpg | tail -n1
4e230: 086f 2f8e f426 80ff d9                  .o/..&...
```

Listing 2.23 Using **xxd** to show the header (0xFFD8) and footer (0xFFD9) values in a JPEG file.

The majority of digital forensic platforms provide functionality to determine extension mismatches where the file extension is different to that expected by the file content, e.g. if a file's content begins with 0xFFD8 and yet its file extension is **txt**. In Linux this behaviour is in-built in all distributions through the **file** command.

2.5.1.5 The strings Command

In many cases textual information is of vital importance. The **strings** command displays all printable characters (ASCII) found in a file, regardless of file type. Even binary data can be provided to strings and it will display the printable characters in the file.

The **strings** command is invoked using: **strings [options] filename** where filename can be any file type. The command can also be used on a disk image to search for particular pieces of text in the image. When **strings** is combined with **egrep** it results in a very powerful forensic tool, allowing for all instances of particular text (and textual patterns) to be located.

Listing 2.24, shows the basic use of **strings**. In this, **strings** is run on **/dev/sda2** (note the output has been truncated), a partition which contains an NTFS file system.

The output immediately hints that there is an NTFS file system present (bytes 3–6 in an NTFS file system contain the OEM name which is NTFS). The information presented in Listing 2.24 shows

11 The standard defines a larger starting signature dependent on the actual version of JPEG and the features that are supported; however, all JPEG files will begin with 0xFFD8.

```
$ sudo strings /dev/sda2
NTFS
NTFSu
TCPAu
fSfSfU
fY[ZfYfY
A disk read error occurred
BOOTMGR is missing
...[snip]...
```

Listing 2.24 Excerpt from the output of the **strings** command.

only that the information is present. Imagine that **/dev/sda2** is 1 TB in size and it is necessary to locate this text. The **strings** command tells only that it is present, not where it is located.

Like most Linux commands the behaviour of **strings** can be altered with options. The first of these is **-t** which allows the specification of a radix (base) in which we wish the output reported. This option will produce the same as before but each string will have a byte offset showing where exactly it occurred in the input file. Now, when searching for a particular piece of text it is possible to go directly to the point in the disk at which that text was found. Listing 2.25 shows the same data as Listing 2.24, but this time using **-td** to display the location of the discovered strings. The **-td** options will display the byte offset as decimal.

```
$ sudo strings -td /dev/sda2
      3 NTFS
    111 NTFSu
    227 TCPAu
    251 fSfSfU
    327 fY[ZfYfY
    398 A disk read error occurred
    427 BOOTMGR is missing
    ...[snip]...
```

Listing 2.25 Excerpt from the output of the strings command on **/dev/sda2** displaying the decimal offset at which strings are discovered.

As expected the first NTFS string occurs at offset 3. A hex viewer could now be used to jump directly to this point of interest in the device.

2.5.1.6 Text Searching with (e)grep

The **grep** family of commands allows the user to locate certain textual patterns in large volumes of data. The general regular expression parser (**grep**) searches textual data for regular expressions, patterns that express the textual properties that are sought. When **grep** finds a match to the pattern the entire line of output in which that match occurs is displayed to the user. This can be used to filter uninteresting textual data from analysis. The simplest regular expressions merely involve actual text. For instance Listing 2.26 shows searching for *root* in the **/etc/passwd** file.

However, regular expressions can be used for much more than merely searching for exact text. They can be used for searching for email addresses, IP addresses, credit card numbers, etc. Indeed any structured textual information can be sought using a regular expression. Most digital forensic tools utilise these in string searching modules that are included by default.

```
$ grep root /etc/passwd
root:x:0:0:root:/root:/bin/bash
$
```

Listing 2.26 Using **grep** to search for the text *root* in **/etc/passwd**.

A complete introduction to **grep** and regular expressions is beyond the scope of this book. However, it is a topic that can be of great utility and it is worth pursuing in further detail.

2.6 Summary

This chapter examined the Linux operating system and more generally the nature of open-source software. In digital forensics the use of open-source software allows for validation of the techniques that are being used and as such increases the confidence in the results of said tools. This increased confidence means that there is less chance of miscarriages of justice.

The GNU/Linux OS is considered the classic example of open-source software. The Linux kernel supports many file systems which make it an ideal system to use for file system forensics. GNU/Linux also provides a host of tools that can be of use in digital forensics. This includes tools for hashing, text searching, information presentation, etc. In addition to these in-built tools there are also a number of specific tools available for digital forensics. These include file system forensic and data carving tools. These will be introduced in Chapter 4. These facts make GNU/Linux an ideal candidate for use as a digital forensics workstation.

Exercises/Discussion Topics

The following are suggested topics for discussion in relation to Linux as a forensic platform and open-source software. Students are expected to research the topics more thoroughly in order to discuss them.

1 Describe the advantages of open-source software when compared with closed-source software.

2 Why is open-source software particularly good for file system forensics (and digital forensics in general)?

3 In your opinion what is the main reason for using open-source software during an investigation?

4 In relation to digital investigation does closed-source software provide any advantages over open-source software? If so what do you consider these advantages to be?

5 What specific advantages does Linux have over other operating systems in relation to file system forensic analysis?

6 If the digital forensic community were to adopt Linux as a 'standard' operating system, what challenges would you foresee?

7 Digital forensic distributions such as Deft and Caine have many advantages for the digital investigator. Can you see any disadvantages in using these specialist distributions rather than a general-purpose distribution for file system forensics?

8 Use Linux! As a final 'exercise' in this chapter it is recommended that you begin to use the Linux OS (if you don't already do so). All examples presented in the remainder of this book will be done through the Linux terminal. Therefore knowledge of the OS will make it much easier to follow the book... also I am convinced that you will fall in love with the OS once you become more familiar with it.

Bibliography

Altheide, C. and Carvey, H.A. (2011). *Digital Forensics with Open Source Tools: Using Open Source Platform Tools for Performing Computer Forensics on Target Systems: Windows, Mac, Linux, UNIX, etc.* Rockland, MA: Syngress; Oxford.

Ashawa, M.A. and Ntonja, M. (2019). Design and implementation of Linux based workflow for digital forensics investigation. *International Journal of Computer Applications* 181 (49): 40–46.

Bresnahan, R. (2021). *Linux Command Line and Shell Scripting Bible.* SL, Hoboken, NJ: Wiley.

Bromhead, B. (2017). 10 advantages of open source for the enterprise [Internet]. Opensource.com. [updated 2017; cited 2024 April 3]. https://opensource.com/article/17/8/enterprise-open-source-advantages (accessed 12 August 2024).

Carrier, B. (2002). Open source digital forensics tools: the legal argument [Internet]. [updated 2002; cited 2024 April 3]. https://www.engineering.iastate.edu/guan/course/backup-0982/CprE-592-YG-Fall-2002/paper/atstakeopensourceforensics.pdf (accessed 12 August 2024).

Citizensinformation.ie (2024). Disclosure in criminal cases [Internet]. www.citizensinformation.ie [cited 2024 April 3]. https://www.citizensinformation.ie/en/justice/criminal_law/criminal_trial/disclosure_in_criminal_cases.html (accessed 12 August 2024).

Free Software Foundation (2019). Working Together for Free Software [Internet]. Fsf.org. [cited 2024 April 3]. https://www.fsf.org/ (accessed 12 August 2024).

Garda Ombudsman (2024). Non-party disclosure [cited 2024 April 3]. https://www.gardaombudsman.ie/about-gsoc/non-party-disclosure/ (accessed 16 December 2024).

GeeksforGeeks (2021). Top 10 Hex Editors for Linux [Internet]. GeeksforGeeks [cited 2024 April 3]. https://www.geeksforgeeks.org/top-10-hex-editors-for-linux/ (accessed 12 August 2024).

GeeksforGeeks (2023). History of Linux [Internet]. GeeksforGeeks [cited 2024 April 3]. https://www.geeksforgeeks.org/linux-history/ (accessed 12 August 2024).

gnu.org (2024). What is Copyleft? - gnu.org [Internet]. www.gnu.org [cited 2024 April 3]. https://www.gnu.org/licenses/copyleft.en.html (accessed 12 August 2024).

Gupta, S., Goyal, N., and Aggarwal, K. (2014). A review of comparative study of MD5 and SSH security algorithm. *International Journal of Computers and Applications* 104 (14): 1–4.

Hayward, D. (2012). The history of Linux: how time has shaped the penguin [Internet]. TechRadar [cited 2024 April 3]. https://www.techradar.com/news/software/operating-systems/the-history-of-linux-how-time-has-shaped-the-penguin-1113914 (accessed 12 August 2024).

Lestal, J. (2020). How many programming languages are there? –DevSkiller [Internet]. DevSkiller - Powerful tool to test developers skills [cited 2024 April 3]. https://devskiller.com/how-many-programming-languages/ (accessed 12 August 2024).

Manson, D., Carlin, A., Ramos, S. et al. (2007). Is the open way a better way? Digital forensics using open source tools. In: *2007 40th Annual Hawaii International Conference on System Sciences (HICSS'07)*, –266b. IEEE.

Matthias, K.D. and Welsh, M. (2006). *Running Linux*. Sebastopol, CA: O'Reilly.

Negus, C. (2020). *Linux Bible*. John Wiley & Sons Canada, Limited.

Nemeth, E., Snyder, G., Hein, T.R. et al. (2017). *Unix and Linux System Administration Handbook*. Prentice Hall.

Nikkel, B. (2016). *Practical Forensic Imaging: Securing Digital Evidence with Linux Tools*. San Francisco, CA: No Starch Press.

OpenSource (2019). What is open source? [Internet]. Opensource.com. [cited 2024 April 3]. https://opensource.com/resources/what-open-source (accessed 12 August 2024).

Sachdeva, S., Raina, B.L., and Sharma, A. (2020). Analysis of digital forensic tools. *Journal of Computational and Theoretical Nanoscience* 17 (6): 2459–2467.

Santoshi, D., Pulgam, N., and Mane, V. (2022). Analysis and Simulation of Kali Linux Digital Forensic Tools. Available at SSRN 4111750.

UpCounsel (2024). What Does Disclosure Mean in Law? [Internet]. UpCounsel [cited 2024 April 3]. https://www.upcounsel.com/what-does-disclosure-mean-in-law (accessed 12 August 2024).

Vaughan-Nichols, S.J. (2024). Linux turns 30: the biggest events in its history so far [Internet]. ZDNET [cited 2024 April 3]. https://www.zdnet.com/pictures/linux-turns-30-the-biggest-events-in-its-history-so-far/ (accessed 12 August 2024).

Williams, R. (2024). A basic guide to disclosure [Internet]. Weightmans [cited 2024 April 3, 4]. https://www.weightmans.com/insights/a-basic-guide-to-disclosure/ (accessed 12 August 2024).

3

Mathematical Preliminaries

In order to understand how any file system functions it is first necessary to understand how information is represented in a computer system. Computers and indeed all electronic digital devices are binary in nature meaning that they are capable only of handling 0's and 1's. The interpretation of long sequences of 0's and 1's leads to all the information that is found in computer systems: numbers; text; pictures; audio; spreadsheets; databases; etc.

In order to conduct digital forensic analysis and, more importantly, to understand the results of digital forensic analysis it is necessary to first understand the underlying storage schema used for all types of data.

This chapter examines how numbers, text and time are represented in computing systems. It examines number systems, showing how decimal is related to binary and hexadecimal and also how to convert between these number systems. The various encoding schemes that are used to represent text are introduced, in particular those that are most often encountered such as ASCII, ISO-8859, UTF-8 and UTF-16. Time is of vital importance in any investigation and computer systems generally provide a wealth of time information. As such this chapter discusses how time is represented in various operating and file systems. Finally this chapter will show how information is actually stored on a hard drive either in big- or little-endian formats. In little-endian the byte order is reversed meaning little-endian data must be converted to a big-endian format before interpretation begins. The ultimate aim of this chapter is to provide the reader with the skills to manually interpret raw data when encountered during an investigation.

3.1 Bits and Bytes

In order to effectively communicate about information representation in computing systems it is first necessary to understand certain terminology. When speaking about storage capacity/size the most fundamental unit is the bit, one single binary digit. Hence a bit has the value 0 or 1.

Computers gather bits together into larger, more complex structures. Table 3.1 summarises these structural units. How many values can be stored by each of the structures? The method of calculating the number of possible values that can be represented by a particular number of bits is quite simple. Merely raise 2 to the power of the number of bits. Table 3.2 summarises this.

This knowledge provides clues as to how information is stored in computers and also why certain limitations exist! Consider the Internet Protocol Version 4 (IPv4) addresses. Networking knowledge informs us that these addresses consist of four decimal numbers between 0 and 255, separated by dots. For instance 192.168.1.12 is a valid IP address. But many people ask, why the strange maximum number, why not 999?

File System Forensics, First Edition. Fergus Toolan.

Table 3.1 Group names for binary digits.

Number of Bits	Term(s)
1	Bit
4	Nibble
8	Byte
16	Word
32	Long (or Double Word)
64	Very Long

Table 3.2 Number of values for each of the common powers of two!

Number of Bits	Number of Values
1	$2^1 = 2_d$
4	$2^4 = 16_d$
8	$2^8 = 256_d$
16	$2^{16} = 65,536_d$
32	$2^{32} = 4,294,967,296_d$
64	$2^{64} = 18,446,744,073,709,551,616_d$

The reason for this limitation is based on Table 3.2. If the possible values for each number are 0 to 255, then there are a total of 256 possible values for each number in the IPv4 IP address. A single byte (eight bits) also allows for 256 values. IP addresses are limited to numbers between 0 and 255 as they are using four individual bytes to represent these numbers. You might also have heard that there are just over four billion IPv4 addresses. Consider the theory that an IP address consists of four bytes, this means the entire IP address is a 32 bit structure. Hence the limitation of just over four billion addresses. Table 3.2 shows that 32 bits can represent $4{,}294{,}967{,}296_d$ possible values, which is exactly the number of possible IPv4 addresses!

But what about larger values? One of the largest problems in computer forensics is the sheer volume of information that requires handling. We don't refer to a disk as having a capacity of $1{,}099{,}511{,}627{,}776_d$ bytes: instead we say 1 terabyte (although this is incorrect as will be shown in a moment!).

Before proceeding to consider larger groups of bytes it is necessary to determine if they will be measured in a decimal- or binary-based system. Traditionally larger units of storage can be measured as 1000x bytes or as 1024x bytes. The first case is a decimal (base 10) multiple, also called the SI (International System of Units) system, while the second case is the binary system. When people refer to large collections of bytes there is often confusion as to exactly what is meant. Table 3.3 summarises the larger byte collections and the names/notation that will be used in this book.

Table 3.3 shows that a kilobyte means 1000 bytes while a kibibyte represents 1024 bytes. These values are often incorrectly used synonymously in common conversation but also by disk vendors on occasion!

Table 3.3 Decimal/binary prefixes and values.

Decimal			Binary		
Symbol	**Prefix**	**Meaning**	**Symbol**	**Prefix**	**Meaning**
K	Kilo	$10^3 = 1000^1$	Ki	Kibi	$2^{10} = 1024^1$
M	Mega	$10^6 = 1000^2$	Mi	Mebi	$2^{20} = 1024^2$
G	Giga	$10^9 = 1000^3$	Gi	Gibi	$2^{30} = 1024^3$
T	Tera	$10^{12} = 1000^4$	Ti	Tebi	$2^{40} = 1024^4$
P	Peta	$10^{15} = 1000^5$	Pi	Pebi	$2^{50} = 1024^5$
E	Exa	$10^{18} = 1000^6$	Ei	Exbi	$2^{60} = 1024^6$
Z	Zetta	$10^{21} = 1000^7$	Zi	Zebi	$2^{70} = 1024^7$
Y	Yotta	$10^{24} = 1000^8$	Yi	Yobi	$2^{80} = 1024^8$

The structures examined to this point are based on multiples of the byte but what about smaller structures? Bytes can be broken into smaller components, where groups of particular bits represent certain pieces of information. These are called bit fields. To demonstrate bit fields we introduce a classic example, the FAT date and time values.

FAT Date and Time are encountered in FAT file systems for metadata storage. The FAT file system records the Modified, Accessed and Created Dates, along with the Modified and Created times. All of these values are stored as FAT Date/Time values which are two byte values composed of bit fields. Figures 3.1 and 3.2 show the structure of the FAT Date and Time, respectively.

In the FAT Date value the five least significant bits represent the day. Five bits allow for 2^5 (32_d) possible values, enough to store the values between 1 and 31 to represent all of the valid days of the month. The next four bits represent the month, four bits allowing for 2^4 (16_d) values. This leaves seven bits to represent the year. Seven bits allows for 2^7 (128_d) possible values or the years 0–127 AD! Obviously computers weren't very common in 127 AD, so the FAT Date actually begins in 1980. The value that is encountered in the seven-bit bit field is added to 1980 to give the correct year. Hence if the value 41_d is discovered in this bit field, it represents the year 2021.

The FAT Time stores information in a similar manner. The five most significant bits represent the hour. Five bits provide 32_d possible values, enough to represent the numbers 0–23_d. The subsequent six bits represent the minutes, six bits allow for 64_d values in total. This leaves five bits to represent the seconds. However, five bits only allow for 32_d possible values (0–31_d), meaning it is not possible to represent all values. Instead the FAT time represents the number of seconds

Figure 3.1 FAT date bit field structure.

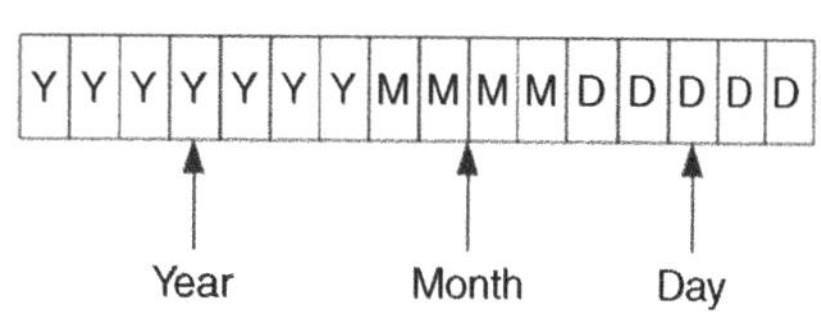

Figure 3.2 FAT time bit field structure.

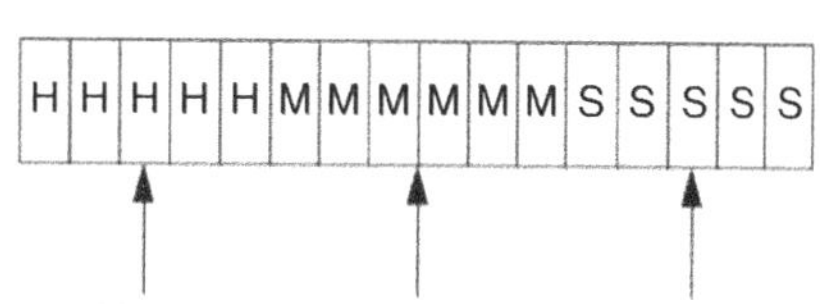

divided by 2, rather than the actual number of seconds. This means that the FAT file system can only distinguish between actions which happen more than two seconds apart.

Bit fields (an older form of storage technology) are rarely used in modern systems. This is due to the cost of storage space in the early days of computing. Each byte was valuable, so space was never wasted. The cost of storage space has decreased so much in recent years that this limitation no longer applies. Therefore modern systems are less likely to use bit fields, although as we will see they are occasionally still encountered.

3.2 Number Systems

One of the first things necessary to represent (and interpret) is numeric data. Computers use the binary number system to store numeric data. This section examines number systems in general before proceeding to look at the most commonly encountered number systems in computing, being decimal (as that is what humans understand), binary (as computers can only use ones and zeros) and hexadecimal (as hexadecimal is an easier method of representing binary data). The difference between number systems is in their *base*, the number of unique digits that the number system contains. The base of binary is 2 (the digits are 0 and 1), the base of decimal is 10 (digits 0–9) and the hexadecimal base is 16 (digits 0–9 along with A–F).

Once the number systems have been described this section proceeds to show how to convert between number systems. The basic number systems allow only the natural numbers (i.e. the non-negative integers: 0, 1, 2, 3, …) to be represented. Computers need to represent more than just these values; hence, the final topics in this section examine how computers represent negative and floating-point numbers also. However, before proceeding it is necessary to introduce the notational conventions that will be used in the remainder of this book.

3.2.1 Notational Conventions

When humans see a number such as 100 the assumption is that this is a decimal number with the value one hundred. As forensic analysts this number could be in any number system (most likely one of binary, decimal or hexadecimal). Therefore a notational convention is used which displays the number along with the number system so that the value can be correctly interpreted. There are a number of ways this can be achieved. For instance to write 100 as a decimal number any of the following notations might be used:

- 0d100
- 100_d
- 100_{10}

In each case it is clear that the number 100_d is in the decimal number system, thereby allowing analysts to correctly interpret the value. Generally a letter is used to represent the base, *d* for decimal, *b* for binary, *x* (or *h*) for hex and *o* for octal (base 8). The actual numeric base itself can also be used as seen in the final example, i.e. 100_{10}. This is particularly useful if using a non-standard number system. For instance, a value in a base 5 number system might be written as 123_5. Throughout this book the above conventions will be used for representing all numbers!

3.2.2 Decimal

The decimal number system is the *de facto* standard in daily life. Much of the world uses decimal as standard. Historically there were some famous exceptions to this. For instance the Sumerian and Babylonian civilisations used a base 60 number system, while many South American cultures (e.g. Aztec and Mayan.) used a base 20 number system. Indeed many of the Inuit peoples of North America use a base 20 number system to this day (Kaktovik numerals).

The decimal number system is an example of a place-value system. In a place-value system the value of a digit is a combination of the digit itself and also the place that it appears in the number. Consider the decimal number 333_d. This number is composed of multiple instances of one single digit, each occurrence of which has a different value due to its position. If you remember your elementary school education you most likely learnt that 333_d was three hundreds, three tens and three ones (also called units). This is the basis of the place-value system. All modern number systems (regardless of their base) operate in this fashion.

More correctly the place-value system assigns an exponent to each place. Beginning at the least significant place (i.e. the rightmost position) with an exponent of zero and increasing by 1 for each place to the left. To get the value of a digit in a particular place the base is raised to the power of the exponent which is then multiplied by the digit. This is demonstrated below for 333_d. As this is a decimal number the base is 10.

333_d

Digits	3	3	3
Exponents	2	1	0
Values	$3 * 10^2$	$3 * 10^1$	$3 * 10^0$
=	$3 * 100$	$3 * 10$	$3 * 1$
=	300_d	30_d	3_d

Total $300 + 30 + 3 = 333_d$

The above result appears to be trivial, merely showing that $333_d = 333_d$. However, it is much more fundamental than it might first appear. All modern number systems use the place-value system, meaning that the above system holds true in each case. Once a number's base is known the corresponding decimal value can be easily calculated using the above system.

3.2.3 Binary

The binary number system uses a base of two, meaning there are only two valid digits (generally called bits) which are 0 and 1. Binary is vital to our understanding of information as it is how all information is represented in an electronic storage device. Binary again uses a place-value system in which the base is 2. Consider the number 1011_b. In order to convert this number to decimal the place-value system is used. This is shown below.

1011_b

Digits	1	0	1	1
Exponents	3	2	1	0
Values	$1 * 2^3$	$0 * 2^2$	$1 * 2^1$	$1 * 2^0$
=	$1 * 8$	$0 * 4$	$1 * 2$	$1 * 1$
=	8_d	0_d	2_d	1_d

Total $8 + 0 + 2 + 1 = 11_d$

Hence the binary number 1011_b is the equivalent of 11_d.

3.2.4 Hexadecimal

Hexadecimal is a base 16 number system commonly encountered in digital forensics. Hexadecimal uses the decimal digits 0–9 alongside the letters *A*–*F* where *A* is 10, *B* is 11, *C* is 12 and so on. Hexadecimal again uses the place-value system meaning that the conversion of these values to decimal is trivial. Consider the number $1AE_x$. The conversion of this number to decimal gives:

	$1AE_x$		
Digits	1	A	E
Exponents	2	1	0
Values	$1 * 16^2$	$A(10) * 16^1$	$E(14) * 16^0$
=	$1 * 256$	$10 * 16$	$14 * 1$
=	256_d	160_d	14_d
Total	$256 + 160 + 14 = 430_d$		

Hexadecimal is frequently used in digital forensics for ease of viewing raw data. While it has been stressed on a number of occasions that raw data is found only in binary format in an electronic storage system, this is not necessarily the best way to view this raw data. The reason for this is complexity. Consider the data shown in Figures 3.3 and 3.4. Figure 3.3 shows a binary representation of raw data, while Figure 3.4 shows the same data in a hexadecimal form. While you may not yet fully understand binary or hexadecimal I am certain you will agree that the hexadecimal data looks a little easier to understand (if only for the reduced volume of data).

The reason that hexadecimal is so commonly encountered is due to the relationship between binary and hexadecimal. Binary is a base 2 number system while hexadecimal is base 16 or 2^4. This relationship means that four bits can be represented with one hexadecimal digit and a byte can be represented with two hexadecimal digits. In order to convert between the two number systems values need only to be located in Table 3.4.

```
00000000: 11101011 01010010 10010000 01001110 01010100 01000110
00000006: 01010011 00100000 00100000 00100000 00100000 00000000
0000000c: 00000010 00001000 00000000 00000000
```

Figure 3.3 Raw binary data displayed using the **xxd** command.

```
00000000: eb52 904e 5446 5320 2020 2000 0208 0000
```

Figure 3.4 Raw hexadecimal data displayed using the **xxd** command.

Table 3.4 Binary/hexadecimal conversion table.

Binary	Hex	Binary	Hex	Binary	Hex	Binary	Hex
0000	0	0100	4	1000	8	1100	C
0001	1	0101	5	1001	9	1101	D
0010	2	0110	6	1010	A	1110	E
0011	3	0111	7	1011	B	1111	F

Consider the hexadecimal number $1AE_x$. This can be converted to binary using Table 3.4. Each individual hexadecimal digit is converted to the corresponding binary value to give: 0b0001 1010 1110. The leading zeros can be removed resulting in 0b1 1010 1110.

Reversing this process is just as easy. Binary digits can be grouped in fours and replaced with the corresponding hexadecimal values. The grouping process starts at the **right-hand side** of the binary number. Consider the binary number 0b1111000110. Grouping this from the right results in three individual numbers: 11, 1100 and 0110. Converting these using Table 3.4 results in a hex value of 0x3C6.

3.2.5 Number Conversions

Using the place-value system, a number in any base can be converted to decimal. The final question to ask is how can a decimal number be converted to another base? The easiest way to do this is through repeated division. In repeated division the number to be converted is repeatedly divided by the desired base. The remainders of this division process are recorded which then result in the value. Consider the number 100_d. What is the value of this in binary? The application of repeated division results in:

$$
\begin{aligned}
100/2 &== 50 && R.0 \quad \uparrow \\
50/2 &== 25 && R.0 \quad \uparrow \\
25/2 &== 12 && R.1 \quad \uparrow \\
12/2 &== 6 && R.0 \quad \uparrow \\
6/2 &== 3 && R.0 \quad \uparrow \\
3/2 &== 1 && R.1 \quad \uparrow \\
1/2 &== 0 && R.1 \quad \uparrow
\end{aligned}
$$

The repeated division process terminates when the result is 0. The remainders are then read from *bottom up* to give the answer, in this case: 1100100_b. The result of any number conversion can always be confirmed by reversing the process. Converting 1100100_b to decimal should result in 100_d.

The same process is used to convert from decimal to hexadecimal. The value is repeatedly divided by the base to which we wish to convert (16_d) and the remainders are recorded. This process results in:

$$
\begin{aligned}
100/16 &== 6 && R.4 \quad \uparrow \\
6/16 &== 0 && R.6 \quad \uparrow
\end{aligned}
$$

Reading the remainders from bottom to top gives 0x64. Again this result can be confirmed by reversing the process!

3.2.6 Number Conversion with Bash

The Bash terminal can be used in a number of ways to perform number conversions. One of the simplest means of converting any number to decimal is through the use of the arithmetic substitution operator $((…)). Listing 3.1 shows two methods of converting the number $1AC_{16}$ to decimal.

```
$ echo $((16#1AC))
428
$ echo $((0x1AC))
428
```

Listing 3.1 Using arithmetic substitution to convert numbers to decimal in Bash.

The base is specified as 16# (or 0x) followed immediately by the number to be converted. The result is the decimal value of this hexadecimal number. The same can be done for any base number in order to convert it to decimal. For instance Listing 3.2 shows the conversion of 10101100_b to decimal.

```
$ echo $((2#10101100))
172
```

Listing 3.2 Converting binary numbers to decimal using arithmetic substitution.

To convert from decimal to other number systems requires an external program called **bc**. The use of **bc** is shown in Listing 3.3.

```
$ echo "obase=16; ibase=10; 428" | bc
1AC
```

Listing 3.3 The use of **bc** to convert to other number systems.

In Listing 3.3 the input (**ibase**) and output (**obase**) bases are specified in advance. Finally the number, in the input base, is provided. All of this is piped to **bc** which performs the conversion. Note that the default value for bases, both input and output, is 10, so the command: **echo "obase=16; 428" | bc** would have the same effect as that shown in Listing 3.3. However, the general format (i.e. specifying both input and output bases) can be used to convert any pair of number system. Listing 3.4 shows a binary to hexadecimal conversion, while Listing 3.5 shows a hexadecimal to base 5 conversion.

```
$ echo "obase=16; ibase=2; 101010" | bc
2A
```

Listing 3.4 The use of **bc** to convert from binary to hex.

```
$ echo "obase=5; ibase=16; C" | bc
22
```

Listing 3.5 The use of **bc** to convert from hex to base 5.

Of course if an even easier way of converting between the standard number systems is required the GUI's in-built calculator can be used as shown in Figure 3.5. The in-built calculator in Linux Mint (shown in Figure 3.5) allows for the selection of a Programming Mode. In this mode the user can choose the input base (decimal is selected in Figure 3.5). Any value input will be displayed in the three other number systems (the calculator supports four number system bases, 2 (binary), 8 (octal), 10 (decimal) and 16 (hexadecimal)).

Figure 3.5 The in-built calculator showing the conversion of a decimal number.

3.2.7 Negative Numbers

Up to this point only the natural (i.e. non-negative integer) numbers and their representation in computing systems have been examined. What about negative non-integer numbers? This section examines two's complement one of the most common methods of representing negative integers.

Table 3.2 showed that an 8-bit number can represent 256_d (2^8) distinct unsigned (positive) values. In an 8-bit two's complement number the most significant (left-most) bit represents the sign. If the most significant bit is zero then the number is positive, but if the most significant bit is one the number is negative. In the case of a positive number the value is merely calculated as it would be with an unsigned number; however, in the case of a negative number extra steps must be performed. Given that the number 0xA7 is an 8-bit signed two's complement number it is necessary to calculate its value. To do this begin by converting the number to binary resulting in 0b1010 0111.

From this the most significant bit is one, meaning that this is a negative number. The inverse of each individual bit is then obtained and one is added to the result. This value is known as the complement. This complement is then converted to decimal to get the absolute value of the number. This process is seen below:

Number:	0b10100111
Inverse:	0b01011000
Complement:	0b01011001
Absolute Value:	89_d
Decimal:	-89_d

With two's complement numbers it is necessary to know the number of bits used to represent the number in order to determine which is the most significant bit that represents the sign of the number.

There are alternative means of representing negative numbers in computing systems such as one's complement, sign-and-magnitude and offset binary. However, while not the simplest, two's complement is the most commonly encountered form. This is due to the ease with which mathematical operations can be performed using two's complement numbers at the CPU level.

3.2.8 Floating-Point Numbers

Real numbers are another form of data that are sometimes required in computing. The most common form of storage is as a floating-point number. In this, the decimal point can *float*; in other words, its position is not set, but can move to allow for larger numbers to be expressed with a lack of precision or to allow smaller numbers to be expressed with much greater precision. To demonstrate this concept let us briefly look at the decimal number system.

If 10 digits are permitted to represent a number then a choice must be made. If the decimal point is placed after the eighth digit the numbers from 0 to 99,999,999, quite a substantial range, can be represented but the number's precision is limited to two decimal places (10^{-2}). If on the other hand the decimal point is placed after the second digit the whole numbers 0–99, a much smaller range, can be represented, but with eight places available after the decimal for greater precision (10^{-8}). This is the trade-off made when using a floating-point number: either the number has a very large range with limited precision or greater precision with less range.

Before introducing binary floating-point numbers binary fixed-point numbers must be examined. Assume that a real number is represented using a single byte in which the four most significant bits represent the whole number part and the four least significant bits represent the fractional part of the number. Consider a byte that contains 01101010_b, in reality this is 0110.1010_b as it is a fixed-point number. Table 3.5 can be used to calculate the value of this number. Note how similar the process is for a fixed-point number as it was for an integer. The place-value system still applies, but using different place values (some of the powers are now negative!).

As with a standard binary integer the decimal value is obtained by multiplying the final two rows in Table 3.5 and adding the results to give:

$$(1 * 4) + (1 * 2) + (1 * 1/2) + (1 * 1/8)$$
$$= 4 + 2 + 0.5 + 0.125$$
$$= 6.625_d$$

Hence the fixed-point binary number 0110.1010_b has the decimal value 6.625_d.

As described earlier, fixed-point numbers have limitations. For instance in the single byte scheme shown above only 2^4 whole numbers ($0–15_d$) can be represented, along with 2^4 fractional parts. If it was desired to represent numbers such as 24.0_d or 1.234_d it is impossible to do so. With a floating-point numbering scheme both of these values can be represented.

In mathematics numbers are often represented in scientific notation such as $3.1 * 10_d^{-3}$. This has the value 0.0031_d. The number is divided into two parts in this scientific notation: the first, 3.1, is called the mantissa (m), while the second, 10^{-3}, is the base (10_d) raised to the power of the exponent (e). Generally all decimal numbers can be represented in the form shown in Equation 3.1.

$$m * 10^e \tag{3.1}$$

The principle is identical in binary. A real binary number can be represented using the notation shown in Equation 3.2.

$$m * 2^e \tag{3.2}$$

Table 3.5 Converting a fixed-point binary number to decimal.

2^3	2^2	2^1	2^0	2^{-1}	2^{-2}	2^{-3}	2^{-4}
8	**4**	**2**	**1**	**1/2**	**1/4**	**1/8**	**1/16**
0	1	1	0	1	0	1	0

Table 3.6 Calculating the value of the 12-bit floating-point binary number 011010000011_b.

	Sign	Mantissa							Exponent			
Value		1/2	1/4	1/8	1/16	1/32	1/64	1/128	8	4	2	1
Digit	0 (+)	1	1	0	1	0	0	0	0	0	1	1

in which the only change is the base used for calculation purposes. Hence floating-point numbers consist of a combination of mantissa and exponent. Consider an example in which the value $1.1101_b * 2^3$ is to be stored in a floating-point format of 12 bits, in which one bit is reserved for the sign, seven bits are reserved for the mantissa and four are used to store the exponent. The fractional part of the mantissa itself is stored, while the exponent is generally stored as a two's complement number. This is represented as: 0110 1000 0011

The above binary floating-point number can be converted to decimal using the place-value system as shown in Table 3.6. The most significant bit is zero meaning that this number is positive.

From Table 3.6 the fractional part of the mantissa is determined to be 1.1101_b (allowing for the omitted whole number component) which has the decimal value $1 + 0.5 + 0.25 + 0.0625 = 1.8125_d$. The decimal value of the exponent is 3_d. Hence the decimal value of the floating-point number is given by:

$$1.8125 * 2^3 = 14.5_d$$

The above floating-point scheme is not a commonly encountered one. A size (12 bits) was arbitrarily chosen. The most common format used in computing systems to store floating-point numbers is based on IEEE 754 (the latest version of which was released in 2019) which defines two standards for floating-point numbers, a 32-bit single precision format and a 64-bit double precision format. Each of these formats is divided into three distinct parts, the sign, the mantissa and the exponent. Both the 32- and 64-bit formats use the most significant bit to represent the sign. The 32-bit format uses the next 8 bits to represent the biased exponent and the remaining 23 bits for the fractional part of the mantissa. The 64-bit format uses 11 bits for the biased exponent and 52 bits for the fractional part of the mantissa. Instead of the exponent, a biased exponent is stored. This bias means that 127_d must be subtracted from the biased exponent in order to get the *real* value for the exponent. This allows for negative numbers even though the exponent is unsigned. This is different to the simple scheme that we proposed in which a signed value was used. Similarly the mantissa generally excludes the leading 1, this is implied. In other words it is the fractional component of the mantissa which is stored. This will be demonstrated subsequently. Both formats use the exact same method to store the data. For simplicity the 32-bit format is used in this section.

An example of a 32-bit floating-point number is:

0100 0001 0101 1010 0000 0000 0000 0000$_b$

Alternate fields are underlined in this example. From this it is clear that the sign bit is zero meaning that this is a positive number. The exponent is represented as 10000010_b which is 130_d; however, this is a biased exponent so 127_d must be subtracted from this giving an exponent value of 3_d. The mantissa is given as .101101; however, the leading 1 has been omitted meaning that the mantissa value is 1.101101_b. The mantissa value is then shifted based on the exponent value (3_d) giving a final binary value of 1101.101_b which can then be converted to decimal to get 13.625_d.

Both IEEE 754 formats function in the same manner. However, there are limitations in the representation of real numbers in a computer system. Only those numbers that are considered 'round' in binary (i.e. those that are composed of sums of $1/2$, $1/4$, $1/8$, … – or more generally $1/2^x$) can be accurately represented in binary. For instance consider the number 0.2_d, this can't be represented in IEEE 754 format exactly. The closest representations (for the 32-bit format) are 0.19999998_d and 0.200000002_d. Hence, while computers are regarded as being wonderful tools for performing mathematics, they do suffer from certain limitations. These limitations are often based on how the underlying information is represented.

3.3 Representing Text

Basic textual information is often of interest in investigation. How this is represented can be of importance to the investigator in order to ensure that their interpretation of the textual data is correct. Text is represented through the use of character encodings. In computing these encodings generally assign a number to each character. This number is then used to represent the character. The earliest examples of character encoding existed before the advent of the digital computing device. One of the most famous of these is Morse Code in which combinations of short and long signals are used to represent characters. These pre-computing encodings often made no distinction between upper and lower case letters, only providing a single encoding for each letter. Computer-based encoding schemes provide for many, many more characters than did these pre-computer encodings. This section examines some of the more commonly encountered encodings including ASCII, ISO-8859 and unicode.

3.3.1 ASCII

The American Standard Code for Information Interchange (ASCII) was developed originally in the 1960s. ASCII is a seven bit encoding scheme, allowing for the possibility to represent a maximum of 128 (2^7) characters. The ASCII scheme represents the English alphabet, numerals and punctuation characters. In total there are 95 printable characters represented in ASCII (52 of which are letters as both uppercase and lowercase letters require different encodings). The remaining 33 characters are termed control characters. These are non-printing characters which originated with the old teletype machines. Many of these control codes are now obsolete, with only a small number being used regularly such as carriage return, line feed and tab.

Each character is assigned a unique code. For instance the letter 'b' is 0b1100010 = 0d98 = 0x62. The ASCII table is shown in its entirety in Table 3.7.

In order to use the ASCII table shown in Table 3.7 one merely needs to look up the hex value in the table. Consider the ASCII value 0x5D. Find the cell at the intersection of the column beginning with 5_ and the row ending with _D. The value in this cell is the required character, ']' in the case of 0x5D.

Listing 3.6 shows a sample of ASCII encoded text. It is possible to process this using Table 3.7 to get the text 'ASCII Encoding.\n'. This text contains two *special characters*. The first is 0x20 which represents a space, while the second is 0x0A which represents a line feed.[1]

1 For those that remember the old typewriters, when the end of line was reached, the drum was pushed back to the left. This caused two actions to occur: the carriage returned to the left side of the page and the paper moved on one line. For use with teletype machines both of these characters were included in ASCII as 0x0D (carriage return) and 0x0A (line feed). Either (or both) of these characters can now be used to represent a new line in electronic text.

Table 3.7 ASCII table.

	0_	1_	2_	3_	4_	5_	6_	7_
_0	NUL	DLE	sp.	0	@	P	‘	p
_1	SOH	DC1	!	1	A	Q	a	q
_2	STX	DC2	”	2	B	R	b	r
_3	ETX	DC3	#	3	C	S	c	s
_4	EOT	DC4	$	4	D	T	d	t
_5	ENQ	NAK	%	5	E	U	e	u
_6	ACK	SYN	&	6	F	V	f	v
_7	BEL	ETB	’	7	G	W	g	w
_8	BS	CAN	(	8	H	X	h	x
_9	HT	EM	)	9	I	Y	i	y
_A	LF	SUB	*	:	J	Z	j	z
_B	VT	ESC	+	;	K	[	k	{
_C	FF	FS	,	<	L	\	l	|
_D	CR	GS	-	=	M	]	m	}
_E	SO	RS	.	>	N	^	n	~
_F	SI	US	/	?	O	_	o	DEL

```
4153 4349 4920 456e 636f 6469 6e67 2e0a
```

Listing 3.6 Sample ASCII encoded text. When decoded the text reads "ASCII Encoding.\n".

Each byte in Listing 3.6 is read individually and decoded (i.e. 0x41 is 'A', 0x53 is 'S', etc.). Note the final byte 0x0A, looking this up in Table 3.7 gives the LF control character. This is the Line Feed (newline) character. Note that Linux systems by default use only 0x0A to represent a newline. Windows/Dos-based systems generally use two bytes to represent newlines, Carriage Return and Line Feed, 0x0D0A.

3.3.2 ISO-8859

ASCII is limited to the English language. Indeed some argue that ASCII is limited to countries in which English is the main language and the dollar is the currency! Examining Table 3.7 shows that there is only a single currency symbol present in ASCII, the dollar ($). There are no pound (£) or Euro (€) symbols meaning that ASCII cannot be used in English-speaking countries using these currencies.

Then consider non-English languages. For instance in Irish the phrase '*tá Linux go hiontach*' means Linux is great but this phrase is not possible to represent in ASCII (there is no á character). Furthermore the Irish language contains é, ó, í and ú characters also, along with the corresponding uppercase characters, Á, É, Ó, Í and Ú and of course that is only one extra language. All languages must be considered.

Hence ASCII cannot be used to represent all Western European languages. Indeed the situation becomes much worse moving further East, as different alphabets such Cyrillic, Greek and Arabic are encountered.

The solution to this is to use the eighth bit in the byte to provide for more characters (128 more to be precise) than that provided by ASCII. This was originally known as Extended ASCII, the first 128 code points are identical to that of ASCII and the extra 128 could be used for other characters. Numerous extended ASCII encodings were devised for different countries, tasks, etc. Finally the International Standards Organisation defined their own extended ASCII standard, releasing this as ISO 8859.

There are a number of variants of ISO 8859. The first is called ISO 8859-1 which contains the characters required to represent most Western European languages. This is known as ISO Latin 1. In total there exist 15 ISO 8859 variants from ISO 8859-1 to ISO 8859-16 (ISO 8859-12 was discontinued during development and was never released, but the 8859-12 designation was never reused). Table 3.8 provides a summary of the ISO 8859 variants. Note that in all of the ISO 8859 variants the first 128 characters are identical to those of basic ASCII.

The number of variants of ISO 8859 means that it is necessary to ensure the correct encoding is being used before attempting to decode any textual data. Consider the Irish message, '*tá Linux go*

Table 3.8 ISO-8859 variants.

Part	Name	Description
ISO-8859-1	Latin-1 Western Europe	Western European languages including English, Irish, Norwegian, German, Italian, Portuguese and Spanish
ISO-8859-2	Latin-2 Central Europe	Central and Eastern European languages using the Latin alphabet, e.g. Bosnian, Polish, Croatian, Czech and Slovak
ISO-8859-3	Latin-3 South European	Turkish, Maltese and Esperanto (generally replaced by 8859-5).
ISO-8859-4	Latin-4 North European	Estonian, Latvian, Lithuanian, Greenlandic and Sami.
ISO-8859-5	Latin/Cyrillic	Cyrillic alphabet languages, e.g. Belarusian, Bulgarian and Russian.
ISO-8859-6	Latin/Arabic	Arabic characters.
ISO-8859-7	Latin/Greek	Modern Greek alphabet.
ISO-8859-8	Latin/Hebrew	Modern Hebrew alphabet.
ISO-8859-9	Latin-5 Turkish	The same as Latin-1 but some rarely used characters are replaced by Turkish characters.
ISO-8859-10	Latin-6 Nordic	Rearrangement of Latin-4 for Nordic languages. Baltic languages still use Latin-4.
ISO-8859-11	Latin-Thai	Thai alphabet characters.
ISO-8859-12	Latin/Devanagari	Work abandoned.
ISO-8859-13	Latin-7 Basic Rim	Extra characters for Baltic languages that were not present in Latin 4/6.
ISO-8859-14	Latin-8 Celtic	Gaelic and Breton languages.
ISO-8859-15	Latin-9	Provides full support for French, Finnish and Estonian.
ISO-8859-16	Latin-10 SE Europe	Complete support for south eastern European Latin alphabets.

Table 3.9 Interpretation of 0xE1 in all ISO-8859 variants.

ISO-8859-1	á	**ISO-8859-9**	á
ISO-8859-2	á	**ISO-8859-10**	á
ISO-8859-3	á	**ISO-8859-11**	แ
ISO-8859-4	á	**ISO-8859-13**	į
ISO-8859-5	с	**ISO-8859-14**	á
ISO-8859-6	ف	**ISO-8859-15**	á
ISO-8859-7	α	**ISO-8859-16**	á
ISO-8859-8	ב		

hiontach', in particular consider the first word *tá*. It is impossible to represent this word in ASCII as there is no *á*. Hence one of the ISO 8859 variants (for instance ISO 8859-1) must be used. The code for á in ISO 8859-1 is 0xE1. Table 3.9 summarises the meaning of 0xE1 in all of the ISO 8859 encoding schemes.

Hence the word *tá* could be decoded in numerous different ways depending on the variant of ISO 8859 that is being used. This is the reason investigators must ensure they firstly determine the correct encoding before attempting to decode text; otherwise, the result may be very different from the original intended meaning.

3.3.3 Unicode

The ISO 8859 standard was introduced to overcome the 128 character limitation of ASCII but it did not go far enough. The previous section showed how ISO 8859 can be used to represent the European languages (and a little further East). However, Oriental languages introduce further difficulties. Consider the Chinese language, the Chart of Generally Utilised Characters of Modern Chinese defines 7000 characters, while the Great Compendium of Chinese characters defines 54,678 characters.[2] Even the lower of these two numbers is vastly greater than the 256_d characters available in any of the ISO-8859 encodings. For Oriental languages the ISO-8859 system is not sufficient to represent the languages. Something larger is required. This came about in the form of unicode.

The unicode encoding aims to combine all of the previous encodings and add support for all languages, mathematics, emojis, etc. At the time of writing there are almost 150,000 unicode code points defined. The maximum number of possible unicode code points is 0x10FFFF ($1,114,111_d$). The initial version of unicode, released in October 1991, defined a little over 7000_d characters. Unicode code points provide a unique numeric identifier for each of the characters that are defined. Regardless of the OS, language, etc., the unique identifier (also called the code point) will be constant. This should have solved all of the problems of communication encoding, but unfortunately it introduced another problem.

Listing 3.7 shows a possible encoding of the word Hello in unicode.

```
0000: 0000 4800 0065 0000 6C00 006C 0000 6F ..H..e..l..l..o
```

Listing 3.7 Possible encoding of Hello in unicode, using three bytes for each character.

2 https://www.hutong-school.com/how-many-chinese-characters-are-there.

From Listing 3.7 we see an immediate problem in the unicode encoding scheme, for many characters (all English alphabet characters, some European alphabet characters, all punctuation, numbers, etc.) only one single byte is required, but three bytes are being stored. The example in Listing 3.7 requires 15_d bytes of storage space, in which only 5_d of these are non-zero. While storage space is not at the premium that it was in the early days of computing, this is still a very inefficient use of space. To alleviate this problem unicode transform functions were introduced. These take the unicode code point and transform it in such a way that it (generally) uses less storage space than merely using the code point. The two most commonly encountered transform functions are UTF-8 (commonly encountered on the web) and UTF-16 (commonly encountered in Microsoft products). The next two sections will examine these transform functions in more detail. Other transform functions include UTF-32 in which every character is represented by four bytes! It is this inefficiency that means that UTF-32 is not very commonly encountered. Another transform function is called UCS-2 (Universal Coded Character Set) which is a two byte encoding that can represent the first $65,535_d$ unicode Code Points. Again the inability to represent the entire code point range is the main reason that UCS-2 is no longer commonly encountered.

3.3.4 UTF-8

UTF-8 is a variable-width character encoding scheme which transforms unicode code points into values of one to four bytes in size. It is capable of representing all 0x10FFFF possible unicode code points (CPs) and has become the *de facto* standard for web page encoding. One of the benefits of UTF-8 is that the basic ASCII characters are represented in the same manner in UTF-8 as they are in ASCII – this is the reason that so much of the web is considered to be in UTF-8 encoding as it includes ASCII only pages also.

Table 3.10 shows how unicode code points are encoded using UTF-8. The x's represent the bits in the actual unicode Code Point. A single byte can be used to represent the first 128_d characters (i.e. the ASCII characters). The next 1920_d characters can be represented using two bytes and so on. Probably the easiest way to explain Table 3.10 is through an example. Consider the unicode code point 0xE1 (the á character) the following steps show how this is represented in UTF-8.

1. Convert 0xE1 to binary: 0b1110 0001.
2. The resulting binary value has 8_d bits and therefore row 2 of Table 3.10 is required (maximum code point length is 11_d bits whereas it is only 7_d bits on the first row).
3. Pad the binary value so that it contains the maximum bit length bits (11_d in this case) giving: 0b000 1110 0001.
4. Fit the padded binary value into the byte pattern specified in Table 3.10. This byte pattern is **110**x xxxx **10**xx xxxx. The x's are replaced by the values in Step 3 giving: 0b**110**0 0011 **10**10 0001.
5. Convert the UTF-8 encoded binary value to hexadecimal giving: 0xC3A1.

Table 3.10 UTF-8 structure.

Max. CP Length	Num. Bytes	Byte 1	Byte 2	Byte 3	Byte 4
7 bits	1	**0**xxx xxxx			
11 bits	2	**110**x xxxx	**10**xx xxxx		
16 bits	3	**1110** xxxx	**10**xx xxxx	**10**xx xxxx	
21 bits	4	**1111 0**xxx	**10**xx xxxx	**10**xx xxxx	**10**xx xxxx

In order to get the unicode code point from a UTF-8 encoded value the above process is reversed. For instance if the UTF-8 encoded value was: 0xC3B8 then the unicode Code Point would be found using the following method:

1. Convert the UTF-8 value to binary: 0b1100 0011 1011 1000.
2. From Table 3.10 the binary value fits the pattern in row 2: 0b**1100** 0011 **10**11 1000.
3. Remove the pattern bits giving: 0b000 1111 1000.
4. Remove the leading zeros giving: 0b1111 1000.
5. Convert to hexadecimal (0xF8) and look up in a Code Point table giving the character: ø.

While knowledge of UTF-8 encoded data is vital for any work on the web, it is also the standard encoding used in most Linux versions (and many file systems) and hence is vital for Linux Forensic Analysis.

3.3.5 UTF-16

UTF-16 is another transform function which, like UTF-8, is capable of representing all valid unicode code points. This uses one or two 16 bit (two byte) code units to represent a character encoding. The first $65,536_d$ characters are trivial to represent, it is merely the two byte representation of their unicode code point value.[3] Consider the two characters demonstrated in the previous section, á and ø, with code points, 0xE1 and 0xF8, respectively, their UTF-16 representations are 0x00E1 and 0x00F8, respectively. Remember that UTF-16 must use two or four bytes for character representation.

But what happens in the case of a character in which the code point is greater than two bytes in length (i.e. greater than 0xFFFF)? In this case two 16-bit code units are used, which together are referred to as a surrogate pair. In order to represent a code point such as 0x1F5A5 (a desktop computer) the following method is used:

1. Subtract the value 0x10000 from the unicode Code Point (0x1F5A5) 0xF5A5.
2. Convert this to binary, 0b1111 0101 1010 0101, and pad to 20 bits if needed: 0b0000 1111 0101 1010 0101.
3. Take the 10 most significant bits (0b00 0011 1101) and convert to hexadecimal (0x3D) and add this to 0xD800 giving 0xD83D. This is the first code unit, also known as the high surrogate (W1) which is always in the range 0xD800–0xDBFF.
4. Take the 10 least significant bits (0b01 1010 0101) and convert this to hexadecimal (0x1A5) and add this to 0xDC00 giving 0xDDA5. This is the second code unit, also known as the low surrogate (W2) which is always in the range (0xDC00–0xDFFF).
5. Combine the high and low surrogate (W1 and W2) to get the result: 0xD83D DDA5.

As with UTF-8, if an already-encoded UTF-16 value is encountered the above process is merely reversed. Consider the UTF-16 encoding 0xD83C DFC9, the following method is used to determine the code point:

1. Split the high and low surrogates to give 0xD83C (high) and 0xDFC9 (low).
2. Subtract 0xDC00 from the low surrogate to give 0x3C9 and convert this to binary (10 bits) giving: 0b11 1100 1001.
3. Subtract 0xD800 from the high surrogate to give 0x3C and convert this to binary (10 bits) giving 0b00 0011 1100.

3 The code point values in the range 0xD800–0xDFFF are not representable in UTF-16, because these are used in the representation of code points requiring more than two bytes. However, the code points 0xD800–0xDFFF are not used as unicode Code Points (and never will be) due to their use in the UTF-16 encoding scheme.

4. Combine these values to give: 0b0000 1111 0011 1100 1001 and convert to hex giving: 0xF3C9.
5. Add 0x10000 to 0xF3C9 to give 0x1F3C9 which is the unicode code point for a rugby football.

While not directly relevant to every case (in the same way that UTF-8 is based on its penetration of web-based text encoding) UTF-16 is encountered often in the Microsoft product family (and due to the prevalence of Office documents in particular it can be encountered on any OS), and as the default encoding used in some programming languages such as Python (certain versions) and Java. Hence UTF-16 data might be encountered in any system under analysis.

3.4 Representing Time

Time is a fundamental concept in all investigation. On TV detectives are seen trying to establish the time of death for a murder victim. They ask suspects 'where were you at midnight'? Traditionally time information was obtained from clocks and watches, interpreted by people and provided to law enforcement as part of a witness statement.

A computer system has a vast array of time data available to an investigator. To process this information correctly a complete understanding of how time is represented in a computer system is required along with the skills to interpret this information.

When introducing the concept of bit fields the FAT Date and Time were introduced. This is an older time representation system which is no longer used in modern systems.[4] Modern systems generally use epoch-based time values.

Epoch-based systems are merely counters. They count in defined time intervals from a particular point in time. In order to interpret them the epoch from which the count begins (i.e. time zero) and the frequency of counts (sometimes referred to as the granularity) must be known. Table 3.11 summarises some of the more common epoch-based timestamp systems in use in modern computing systems.

Unix time is commonly encountered in Unix/Linux systems (including file systems) but also throughout the computing world, being also encountered in some Apple file systems and some applications on other operating systems. Hence the Unix time format will be covered in detail in the next section.

Table 3.11 Common epoch-based time formats.

Time	Epoch	Granularity	Notes
Windows/NTFS	01.01.1601	10^{-7} s	Used in the Windows OS and the NTFS file system. This is one of the most commonly encountered time formats in digital forensics.
Unix Time	01.01.1970	1 s	Used in all Unix systems/file systems. Encountered in some browser artefacts and other applications.
Web-kit/Chrome	01.01.1601	10^{-6} s	Used in the Google Chrome browser.
Mac/HFS+ Time	01.01.1904	1 s	Used in Apple's HFS+ file system.

4 This does not mean that knowledge of FAT Date and Time is no longer required. While most modern systems no longer use this style of time representation, the FAT file system is still very commonly encountered in investigation. Many removable devices still use this system to store time information. The latest file system for removable media, ExFAT, also uses this system although it does include both millisecond and timezone components.

3.4.1 Unix Time

As stated in Table 3.11 the Unix time is based on an epoch of 1 January 1970 at 00:00:00 UTC. This is time zero for Unix time. The counter is advanced every second. Hence, in reality, Unix time measures the number of seconds that have elapsed since 1 January 1970. Unix time is a UTC time, the Unix time value is always stored as UTC. The OS will then apply local settings to the UTC time to display it in the system's timezone.

From an investigative point of view the granularity of the basic Unix timestamp is important. The counter is updated once every second. This means that two operations which occur at the same second will have the same timestamp. While this is not a major issue for files accessed directly by a human user (humans can only open a small number of files in a 1 second period) automated processes can access many files in a one second timeframe. These actions cannot be ordered. Note that most modern implementations of Unix Time include a nano-second subcomponent to allow for improved granularity. This can be seen in Listing 3.8.

```
EXT 2
Inode Times:
Accessed: 2021-01-12 10:19:52 (GMT)
File Modified: 2021-01-12 09:48:43 (GMT)
Inode Modified: 2021-01-12 09:53:03 (GMT)

EXT 4
Inode Times:
Accessed: 2021-06-06 08:17:02.191048178 (IST)
File Modified: 2021-05-21 06:29:30.037357544 (IST)
Inode Modified: 2021-05-21 06:29:30.037357544 (IST)
File Created: 2021-05-21 06:23:31.291162553 (IST)
```

Listing 3.8 Output from the **istat** command for EXT2 and EXT4 file systems.

Listing 3.8 shows the difference in the granularity of timestamps from an older Linux filesystem (ext2) when compared with a newer file system (ext4). In ext2 traditional Unix time values are used, meaning that the granularity is one second. In ext4, there is an added nano-second component which the forensic tools also process. This means the order of operations can be better determined in this file system.[5]

Unix time is traditionally stored as a 32-bit signed quantity. This means that the largest possible time that can be represented is $2^{31} - 1$. This value, $2,147,483,647_d$, represents a time of 2038-01-19 03:14:07 UTC. This is the last possible time that can be represented by a traditional Unix timestamp value. When the computer attempts to increase the counter it will 'wrap around' resulting in a time of 1901-12-13 20:45:52 UTC. This problem is often called the Y2038 problem (and sometimes the Epochalypse!). In recent years many systems are beginning to use a 64-bit signed integer to represent the Unix time value. This means that the largest possible value is $2^{63} - 1$ which is $9,223,372,036,854,775,807_d$. This will not expire until 11 April 2262 at 23:47:16 (UTC). Safe to say that I will certainly not be here to see the expiration of 64-bit Unix time!

5 You might also notice that there is a difference in the recorded timestamps. Ext2 records Modification, Access and Inode Change times. Ext4 records these three timestamps and also a Creation timestamp. Both file systems also record a Deleted timestamp but this is only set if the file has been deleted.

3.4.2 The Linux date Command

The Linux shell provides the **date** command to allow us to process Unix epoch time values. Listing 3.9 shows the command to determine the current Unix epoch time value.

```
$ date '+%s'
1623060055
```

Listing 3.9 Using the **date** command to display the current Unix time.

Listing 3.10 shows how the **date** command is used to convert a unix timestamp into a human-readable format.

```
$ date -d @1623060055
Mon 07 Jun 2021 11:00:55 IST
```

Listing 3.10 Using the **date** command to convert a Unix time to a human-readable format.

Notice in Listing 3.10 that the time is given in IST (Irish Summer Time). This is applied by the OS using the current locale settings of the machine on which the command is executed. Listing 3.11 shows the **date** command being used to display the time value in UTC (being the exact data that is stored on the file system).

```
$ date -ud @1623060055
Mon 07 Jun 2021 10:00:55 UTC
```

Listing 3.11 Using **date** to display a Unix time in UTC.

During an investigation it is often necessary to display times in other timezones. This can be achieved using TZ= as shown in Listing 3.12 where the **TZ=US/Eastern** directive prior to the date command alters the displayed timezone.

```
$ TZ=US/Eastern date -d @1623060055
Mon 07 Jun 2021 06:00:55 EDT
```

Listing 3.12 Specifying the timezone for the **date** command's result.

3.5 Endianness and Raw Data

This chapter has examined how data is represented in computer systems, but the overall aim of this chapter is to allow for the interpretation of raw data. While it is vital to understand how information is represented in ones and zeros it is also necessary to understand how it is stored in computer systems before being able to interpret data accurately.

Generally there are two methods used by computers to store information either in a big- or little-endian format. This endianness describes how the information should be read. Consider the natural languages of English and Arabic, English is read from left to right while Arabic is read from right to left. These languages could be considered to have a different endianness.

In a big-endian format the most significant byte is stored first, then the next most significant and so on until the final least significant byte is reached. In a little-endian scheme the least significant byte is stored first, followed by the second least significant and so on, all the way to the final byte which is the most significant byte. In this chapter, up to this point, all data that we have encountered has been in a big-endian format.

Consider the number $56,000_d$. When converted to hexadecimal this is 0xDAC0. This is automatically a big-endian value. The byte 0xDA is the most significant byte and is stored first, the byte 0xC0 is the least significant and is stored last. If the storage method used was little-endian this would be reversed, meaning that in the raw data we would encounter the values 0xC0DA. Now consider the value $400,000,000_d$. In hex this value is: 0x17D78400. This is a big-endian value. Converting this to little-endian results in the following (note that spaces are added for clarity):

Big-Endian	**17**	**D7**	**84**	**00**
Little-Endian	**00**	**84**	**D7**	**17**

This is the final piece of information needed in order to interpret raw data. Consider the hex dump shown in Listing 3.13. This shows the Master Boot Record (MBR) partition table for a physical disk and the Linux command used to extract this information. The partition table consists of four 16-byte entries, each of which is displayed on one line below.

```
# xxd -s 446 -l 64 /dev/sda
001be: 8020 2100 07df 130c 0008 0000 0020 0300  . !.........  ..
001ce: 00df 140c 07fe ffff 0028 0300 c296 ce22  .........(....."
001de: 00fe ffff 27fe ffff 00c0 d122 0098 1100  ....'......"....
001ee: 00fe ffff 05fe ffff fe67 e322 0200 8d51  .........g."...Q
```

Listing 3.13 Displaying the contents of the partition table on the primary hard drive (**/dev/sda**).

However, like all raw data, without knowledge of the underlying structures it is almost impossible to interpret this data. The structure for a partition table entry is shown in Table 3.12. Note that all multi-byte values are stored in little-endian format!

Table 3.12 Structure of the MBR partition table entry.

Offset	Size	Description
0x00	0x01	Bootable Status – 0x00 for non-bootable partition, 0x80 for bootable partition.
0x01	0x03	Cylinder-head-sector (CHS) of the first absolute sector in the partition. This is an old form of addressing that has been replaced by the logical address and size.
0x04	0x01	Partition Type Identifier – 0x07 is NTFS; 0x0B is FAT 32; 0x83 is Linux, etc. Complete lists of these codes are available online.
0x05	0x03	CHS of the last absolute sector in the partition. This is an old form of addressing that has been replaced by the logical address and size.
0x08	0x04	Logical block address (LBA) of the first absolute sector in the partition. This is the modern form of addressing which should be used instead of the CHS addresses.
0x0C	0x04	Number of sectors in the partition.

Listing 3.14 shows the first partition table entry with alternate fields underlined. These fields are based on the offset/size combination from Table 3.12. For instance the LBA for the partition begins at offset 0x08 and is 0x04 bytes in size. This means that the raw data stored at this point is: 0x0008 0000.

```
# xxd -s 446 -l 64 /dev/sda
001be: 8020 2100 07df 130c 0008 0000 0020 0300 . !.......... ..
```

Listing 3.14 The first partition table entry from Listing 3.13 with alternate fields highlighted.

From Listing 3.14 it is clear that the partition is bootable (0x01 byte at offset 0x00) and is of type 0x07 (0x01 byte at offset 0x04), in other words an NTFS file system.[6] The LBA starting address is given by 0x04 bytes at offset 0x08, which has the value 0x0008 0000; however, this is little-endian, meaning that the least significant byte is stored first. This needs to be converted to big endian before proceeding to convert to decimal.

Little-Endian	**00**	**08**	**00**	**00**
Big-Endian	**00**	**00**	**08**	**00**

This means that the actual LBA value is 0x800 or 2048_d. A similar process is performed for the size of the partition. This is found in the four bytes at offset 0x0C which have the little-endian value 0x00 20 03 00. Converting this to big-endian gives 0x00 03 20 00 which is $204,800_d$ sectors in size. Hence the partition table entry has been manually interpreted, discovering that the partition begins at sector 2048_d and is $204,800_d$ sectors in size. This is the method used by file system forensic tools when they read the partition table. Consider the output from a file system forensic tool called **mmls** (which is covered in Chapter 4) shown in Listing 3.15. Identical information is produced by that tool as the manual interpretation of the data performed above.

```
# mmls /dev/sda
     Slot        Start      End        Length     Description
...[snip]...
002: 000:000     00002048 00206847 00204800 NTFS / exFAT (0x07)
...[snip]...
```

Listing 3.15 Using **mmls** to confirm the manual interpretation of the partition table entry from Listing 3.14. Only the relevant entry is shown, the remaining **mmls** output is omitted.

3.6 Summary

This chapter has introduced the mathematical preliminaries that are essential for digital forensics. It assumes that the reader is familiar with these concepts and serves merely as a reminder. The basic data type in the computer, and in electronic storage/transmission systems, is the bit. The single binary digit can take the values zero or one, from which all of the complex types that we encounter in the computer system are composed.

6 Note that in forensic analysis the value reported for file system type in the partition table entry is not reliable. It is necessary to examine the contents of the partition to determine the exact file system type.

In terms of interpreting raw data it is generally most important that numeric, textual and temporal data can be interpreted accurately. This is of special importance in the Linux file systems where there are not necessarily tools available for processing these. Hence it is sometimes necessary to perform manual analysis as shown with the Master Boot Record Partition Table Entries (Section 3.5). For instance only the ext Linux File System is supported by any forensic tools but other file systems such as XFS, BtrFS and ReiserFS are sometimes encountered on Linux systems. At the time of writing there are no forensic tools that fully support these file systems.

Exercises

1 Convert the following numbers to decimal:
  a) 0x4A
  b) 0x1CD
  c) 0b101101
  d) 0b11001001

2 Convert the following numbers to binary:
  a) 0x3D1
  b) 0xBAD
  c) 0d123
  d) 0d42

3 Convert the following numbers to hexadecimal
  a) 0b01011010
  b) 0b1100011
  c) 0d193
  d) 0d72

4 What are the decimal values of the following 8-bit two's complement numbers?
  a) 0b01101100
  b) 0b11100100
  c) 0b11001111
  d) 0b10011000

5 The following hexadecimal sequences represent ASCII text. What are their meanings?
  a) 4865 6C6C 6F20 576F 726C 64
  b) 4C69 6E75 7820 466F 7265 6E73 6963 730A

6 Encode the following unicode Code Points as (i) UTF-8; (ii) UTF-16
  a) Code Point: 0x0398 – Greek Capital Letter Theta
  b) Code Point: 0x1F3A7 – Headphone Emoji
  c) Code Point: 0x1F415 – Dog Emoji

7 What characters are represented by the following big-endian UTF-8 encoded values?
  a) 0xCE94
  b) 0xE29A99
  c) 0xF09FA68D

8 What characters are represented by the following big-endian UTF-16 encoded values?
a) 0x03A3
b) 0xD83CDF40
c) 0xD83CDF69

9 In Section 3.5 the first of four partition table entries were interpreted. Interpret the three remaining partition table entries.

Bibliography

Carrier, B. (2005). *File System Forensic Analysis*. Boston, MA, London: Addison-Wesley.

Chalk, B.S., Carter, A., and Hind, R. (2017). *Computer Organisation and Architecture*. Bloomsbury Publishing.

Goldberg, D. (1991). What every computer scientist should know about floating-point arithmetic. *ACM Computing Surveys (CSUR)* 23 (1): 5–48.

Harris, S.L. and Harris, D.M. (2016). *Digital Design and Computer Architecture*. Amsterdam, Paris: Elsevier, Cop.

Hough, D.G. (2019). The IEEE Standard 754: one for the history books. *Computer* 52 (12): 109–112.

IEEE STD 754-2019 (2019). *IEEE Standard for Floating-Point Arithmetic*. IEEE Computer Society, pp. 1–84. https://doi.org/10.1109/IEEESTD.2019.8766229.

International Standards Organization (1991). *ISO/IEC 646:1991 Information Technology - ISO 7-Bit Coded Character Set for Information Interchange*. Geneva, Switzerland: International Standards Organization.

International Standards Organization (1997). *ISO/IEC 8859-1 Information Technology - 8-Bit Single Byte Coded Graphic Character Sets*. Geneva, Switzerland: International Standards Organization.

International Standards Organization (2020). *ISO/IEC 10646:2020 Information Technology - Universal Coded Character Sets*, 6e. Geneva, Switzerland: International Standards Organization.

Kahan, W. (1996). Lecture Notes on the Status of IEEE Standard 754 for Binary Floating-Point Arithmetic.

Knuth, D.E. (2014). *Art of Computer Programming*, vol. 2. Addison-Wesley Professional.

Muller, J.M. (2018). *Handbook of Floating-Point Arithmetic*. Boston, MA: Birkhäuser.

Negus, C. (2020). *Linux Bible*. Wiley & Sons Canada, Limited, John.

The Unicode Consortium (2023). Unicode 15.0.0 [Internet]. www.unicode.org. [cited 2023 January 14]. https://www.unicode.org/versions/Unicode15.0.0/ (accessed 12 August 2024).

4

Disks, Partitions and File Systems

The focus of this book is file system forensics – how information can be recovered from a file system in a forensically sound manner. In order to understand file system forensics it is necessary to first understand some basic file system concepts. Knowledge of general file system concepts will aid the understanding of file/metadata recovery in particular file systems. Before it is possible to introduce these concepts it is first necessary to speak about storage technology.

This chapter focuses initially on storage media, as it is upon a storage medium that a file system will be found. Traditionally storage media referred to rotational hard drives (and also floppy drives). Over the years other forms of storage media have evolved. These have included optical media (CDs, DVDs and Blu-rays), and in more recent times flash media, which is found in most modern USB devices. Currently the ultimate in storage technology for the home market is the solid-state drive (SSD). Although often based on flash technology, SSDs add much more functionality including parallel access, caching solutions and so on, to greater increase the speed of the overall solution.

This chapter will then turn its focus to the logical aspects of storage media. There are a number of layers of abstraction between the physical storage medium and the end-user. The user views a disk as a series of partitions, logically contiguous areas, each of which appear as a single structure to the end-user. However, multiple partitions may exist on a single physical disk, or indeed a single partition might occupy multiple physical disks. There are numerous methods used to describe the partition layout on a device. During the discussion on partitions two of the more common partitioning schemes will be introduced, the master boot record (MBR) and the GUID Partition Table (GPT). The analysis of these structures is generally the first step in file system forensics. These structures tell where the partitions are located on a physical device, and as such they inform the analyst of the potential file system locations.

This chapter also describes the file system at a conceptual level, and also describes the functionality that file systems can provide to users. It is important to note that not all file systems provide all this functionality to users as some file systems are less complex than others. It is important that the analyst understands what potential information is available from the particular file system under investigation.

The final topic in this chapter is that of analysis of file systems using Linux. This is further broken into:

- **Acquisition (or imaging):** How does the analyst gain access to the data on the physical storage media in such a way that the digital forensic principles (Section 1.3) are followed. This section discusses some of the different forms of acquisition including logical and physical acquisition (Section 4.4).

File System Forensics, First Edition. Fergus Toolan.

- **File System Forensics:** Once an image has been acquired the file system forensic analysis task can begin (Section 4.5). In this, the file system contents (files/folders) are recovered along with their associated metadata. Open source tools such as the Sleuth Kit (Section 4.5.1) are available to automate this process.
- **Data Carving:** Occasionally file content exists in a disk image for which no file system information is available. In this case the data must be carved. This is achieved by searching for known file signatures (those same values that the **file** command exploits – Section 2.4.2). One of the most effective tools for achieving data carving in Linux is Photorec (Section 4.5.2).

4.1 Disk Storage

Computer storage mechanisms are classified into a four-layer descending hierarchy consisting of primary; secondary; tertiary; and offline storage solutions. The lower the storage level, the longer it takes to access information held on that device (latency) and the slower it is to transfer information to/from the device (bandwidth). Primary storage has the best bandwidth/latency, while offline storage has the worst.

Primary storage generally refers to random-access memory (RAM). This storage is volatile; hence, all information stored in RAM is lost when power is removed. RAM is generally a form of semiconductor-based memory. Primary memory is the only form of memory that the central processing unit (CPU) can access directly. RAM alone is not sufficient to start a computer. Due to its volatility the start-up instructions would be lost when the computer is powered down. It would not be able to restart. Hence RAM is combined with a non-volatile primary memory area called read-only memory (ROM). This area maintains the information needed to start the computer. There are two other forms of primary storage in common usage. These are the processor cache and the processor's registers. Both of these are also volatile.

From a file system forensic perspective, primary memory is of little interest. While file system structures will exist on occasion in RAM (e.g. file metadata) the file system as a whole will never be held in RAM. As most primary memory is volatile (ROM is an exception, but generally ROM is not re-programmed by users and will contain only system boot information) it is not examined during file system forensics. Instead if a running machine is encountered it is analysed using live data forensics (LDF), one effect of which will generally be to acquire a copy of the volatile primary storage.

The next level encountered in the hierarchy is that of secondary storage. Secondary storage is not directly accessible from the CPU, some intermediary must be involved in the communication. Secondary storage access speed is much slower than that of primary storage[1]; however, secondary storage is non-volatile meaning that secondary storage retains data even in the absence of power. The most common forms of secondary storage in modern computer systems are hard disk drives (HDDs) and SSDs. Certain secondary storage devices are removable. These include optical media such as CDs/DVDs along with USB flash drives, floppy disks, tapes, etc. These media are considered secondary when inserted in a computer but considered offline when removed from the computer.

Tertiary storage is very infrequently encountered. Tertiary storage involves a robotic mechanism which will mount and dismount archive storage devices as needed. The devices in question are

1 Primary storage speeds are generally measured in nanoseconds while secondary storage speeds are measured in milliseconds.

generally tape (although they could use other storage technology). Tertiary storage is a form of disconnected storage which can be re-connected automatically when it is needed.

The final category is that of offline storage mechanisms. As with tertiary storage devices these are not immediately available to the computer. The distinction is that offline storage devices require human intervention to become online. Strictly speaking the USB Flash Drive is offline. There is no way to bring it online automatically; the human must insert it. As stated earlier, many offline storage devices can be considered secondary storage when they are inserted into the computer.

In the remainder of this section the physical forms of secondary/offline disk storage are briefly introduced. While the focus of this book is more towards logical storage mechanisms (i.e. file systems) than the physical, it is important to have an understanding of the physical side of the task as certain physical devices provide some issues for digital forensics. The section begins with the traditional rotational hard drive and also discusses the other forms of rotational storage devices based on optical technology such as CDs, DVDs and Blu-ray storage (Section 4.1.1.1). These rotational storage devices operate on a similar principle, the main difference being in how information is stored/read, either magnetically or optically.

Modern storage devices generally use some form of flash storage (Section 4.1.2). The key difference between the traditional rotational storage technologies and modern flash-based storage devices is that there are no moving parts in flash-based storage devices. Flash storage technology is found in most modern storage devices such as USB devices (often called flash drives), SD cards and SSD. SSDs are discussed separately in this chapter (Section 4.1.3) as, while they often use flash storage as their underlying storage mechanism, they incorporate much more functionality into the device, some of which has particular implications for digital forensics.

4.1.1 Traditional Rotational Hard Drives

The traditional HDD is still commonly encountered in digital forensics. Physically this device uses magnetic polarities to store data. Figure 4.1 shows a HDD with the cover removed. This shows the internal structure of the HDD.

The platters are the area of the HDD that store the magnetic charges. A stack of these are mounted on a spindle. These platters rotate continuously while the drive has power. Data is read/written by the read/write head. The head actually consists of multiple heads between each of the platters.

Each platter is divided into a number of areas called tracks and sectors. Tracks are circular paths that are found on both sides of the platter. Tracks are the area of the platter which store information. The track can be seen in Figure 4.2. Tracks are divided into a number of sectors. The file system groups sectors into structures called clusters which are used as the logical unit for storing data. Sectors in tracks nearer the outer rim of the platter are physically larger than those nearing the centre; in reality they each contain the same amount of information. The information density is higher in the inner tracks than the outer tracks.

As its name suggests the Read/Write Head is used to access information on a HDD. Information is read/written one sector at a time. In order to read a particular sector the read/write head aligns itself with the track on which the sector is found. The platter is constantly rotating. The read/write head waits for the platter to rotate so that the desired sector is correctly positioned. Once this happens data can be read/written.

The mechanical nature of data access in a HDD means that it is a relatively slow form of technology. There are two times to consider: the seek time and the latency. The seek time is the amount of time that it takes for the read/write head to be positioned correctly in relation to the

Figure 4.1 A traditional HDD with the cover removed showing the internal structure.

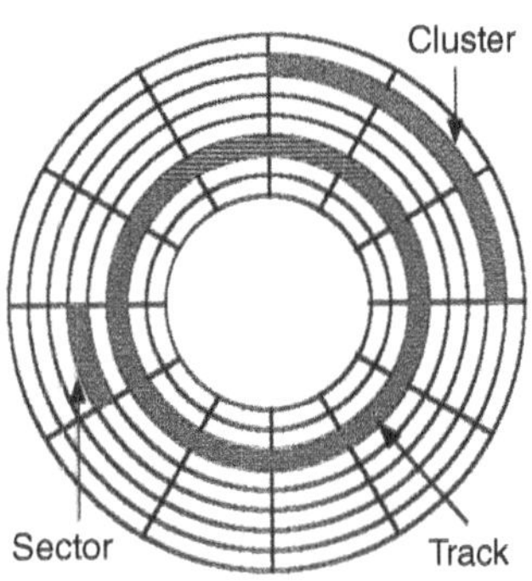

Figure 4.2 Platter structure showing the tracks, sectors and clusters.

desired track. The latency (often called rotational latency) is the time taken for the desired sector to rotate under the read/write head. This is one of the reasons that the spindle speed (RPM) is very important in HDD technology. The faster the platters rotate, the lower the latency and hence the faster that data can be accessed overall.

4.1.1.1 Optical Media

Optical disks are another form of rotational data storage technology. These include CD, DVD and Blu-ray. These are traditionally used for offline storage but have been replaced by USB devices in recent years.

Optical disks all have platters similar to those found in rotational HDDs. Unlike the HDD these use optical rather than magnetic technology. Data is encoded as a series of pits and lands on a platter. Pits are etched into the reflective surface of the platter while lands are the flat areas that occur between pits. Changes from pit to land (or vice versa) signify a bit value of 1, while no change, irrespective of whether pits or lands, signifies a bit value of zero. Data storage (and access) generally uses lasers.

4.1.2 Flash Drives

Flash memory is a form of non-volatile storage that, instead of being based on mechanical devices, is based on electronic storage means. Flash memory is a form of Electronically Erasable Programmable Read-Only Memory (EEPROM). Traditional EEPROM required the entire device to be erased in order to rewrite information. This is not suitable for hard-drives. If all information from a hard-drive needed to be erased in order to change one byte it would be an inefficient process.[2]

Flash memory allows for the erasure of data from the device at the block (or even byte) level. This means that updating a single byte requires the erasure and rewriting of a single block (or byte) of data, rather than the entire device.

Two types of flash memory are commonly used: NOR and NAND memories. The distinction is based on the type of logical circuit used to hold data. NAND-based flash storage is the most commonly encountered in investigation. This is found in phones, USB sticks and other small-scale devices.[3] NOR-based flash storage is generally more expensive and is found in smaller devices such as device controllers for instance BIOS chips.

One of the key advantages of flash memory over traditional storage technologies is that it is an electronic rather than mechanical storage system. Platter-based technology such as hard drives and optical disks requires moving parts to read/write data. These mechanical components are subject to physical damage. Electronic storage technologies are less at risk of physical failures.[4]

4.1.3 Solid-State Drives

SSD are another form of electronic non-volatile storage. These are generally based on interconnected flash memories. SSDs are much faster than traditional HDDs as there are no moving parts. This means that there is no time required to spin-up the device and that there is very little latency in seek operations. Also later in life HDDs tend to slow even further as more files are heavily fragmented. This means that read/write operations take longer. SSDs do not have an issue with fragmentation.

The nature of SSD storage leads to certain issues for digital forensics. SSD components can only be written to a certain number of times before they cease to function. Hence if a single area was written to too many times the disk would deteriorate. To combat this the SSD controller implements a technique called wear levelling. This will ensure that areas of disk are written to a similar number of times. This will occasionally cause information on disk to be moved by the controller independently of the OS.

The SSD controller also implements garbage collection. When the OS marks information as unallocated, the SSD's TRIM function will erase that area. This will allow for future information to be written back to the area of the device but it does erase the contents of the deleted files. This means that deleted files are less likely to be present on SSDs than on traditional HDDs.

SSDs also break one of the main principles of digital forensics, that no changes should be made to evidence! As with HDDs, in order to acquire a forensically sound copy of an SSD it must have power. However once power is present the SSD controller's garbage collection routines are running. This means that potentially data is changing on the device in question. These issues need to be considered when analysing SSD devices.

---

2 Not to mention the problem of where the information would be stored before it was written back to the device.
3 It is also generally found in SSDs along with more advanced controllers.
4 The lack of moving parts also means that they are much quieter than traditional mechanical storage technologies.

4.2 Partitions

A partition (also called a volume) is a sequence of consecutive sectors on a device. Each partition can be managed separately, even if all are present on the same physical device. Partitions are created before any file system is installed. The file system will be created inside a partition.

There are many reasons that partitions are used. Primarily they allow the division of a single physical disk into multiple logical areas, each of which can contain a particular file system. Partitions are used for a number of reasons, firstly most modern computer systems have multiple partitions. Generally Windows systems have a primary partition (which is mounted as C: by default) and also a system restore partition, which contains information necessary in the event of a complete system crash. The normal user never interacts with this partition. The Linux OS often has multiple partitions. This is done to separate data from operating-system-specific areas. The OS can be upgraded or even completely replaced with no risk of data loss. Secondly some users have multiple boot systems, for example having both Windows and Linux on the same computer. Each of the operating systems requires a separate partition. Windows systems need NTFS to boot correctly, while Linux systems require one of the Linux file systems (e.g. ext, BtrFS or XFS).

4.2.1 Creating Partitions/File Systems on Linux

In order to create a working file system there are two steps that need to be completed. The first is to create a partition which will contain the file system in question. This can be achieved in Linux using the **fdisk** and **gdisk** commands (or graphical tools can also be used). The second step is to create the desired file system. Note that this two-step process occurs in every operating system. It is often referred to as formatting or initialising. Most modern operating systems hide the details of the process from the user. The user will merely select a file system type with which to format the device but the tool first partitions the device (if necessary) and then creates the file system.

The remainder of this section will show how a USB device can be partitioned on a Linux system and two file systems created. For the purposes of this demonstration an ExFAT and ext2 file system will be created. The first step after inserting the USB is to identify the newly inserted device.

In Linux every device has a file in the **/dev/** directory. Hard drives (and USB drives) have the identifier **sdX**, where X is a, b, c, etc. The first (primary) hard drive will be **/dev/sda**. In a system with a single hard drive if a USB is inserted this will most likely be given the device identifier **/dev/sdb**. However, it is not guaranteed. In order to be certain of the identifier it is necessary to manually check the identifier. There are a number of ways of discovering the identifier. Two of these include the **dmesg** and **lsblk** commands.

Upon inserting a new USB device the actions are logged by the kernel. The **dmesg** command allows access to this. Immediately after the insertion of a USB key run **dmesg** and examine the final few lines. Listing 4.1 shows the output from **dmesg** after inserting a USB device. The device identifier and the partition list are underlined. From this it is clear that the device identifier is **/dev/sdb**.

Another method of determining the device identifier is to use the **lsblk** command. This will list all available block devices (e.g. disk drives). This will include all of the devices on the system. Listing 4.2 shows the output from the **lsblk** command on a machine. On this there are three devices (**/dev/sda** – the primary hard drive; **/dev/sdb** – the inserted USB key; and **/dev/sr0** – the DVD drive).

```
[ 3256.841603] usb 3-1: new high-speed USB device number 6 ...
[ 3257.080876] usb 3-1: New USB device found, idVendor=058...
[ 3257.080881] usb 3-1: New USB device strings: Mfr=1, Produc...
[ 3257.080884] usb 3-1: Product: Mass Storage
[ 3257.080886] usb 3-1: Manufacturer: Generic
[ 3257.080888] usb 3-1: SerialNumber: E8B07B49
[ 3257.081721] usb-storage 3-1:1.0: USB Mass Storage device ...
[ 3257.082005] scsi host6: usb-storage 3-1:1.0
[ 3258.103720] scsi 6:0:0:0: Direct-Access Generic Flash ...
[ 3258.104410] sd 6:0:0:0: Attached scsi generic sg2 type 0
[ 3258.105270] sd 6:0:0:0: [sdb] 31129600 512-byte logica ...
[ 3258.106061] sd 6:0:0:0: [sdb] Write Protect is off
[ 3258.106066] sd 6:0:0:0: [sdb] Mode Sense: 23 00 00 00
[ 3258.106888] sd 6:0:0:0: [sdb] Write cache: disabled, rea ...
[ 3259.129337] sdb: sdb1 sdb2 sdb3 sdb4 < sdb5 sdb6 >
[ 3259.159832] sd 6:0:0:0: [sdb] Attached SCSI removable disk
```

Listing 4.1 The output from **dmesg** after insertion of a new USB device.

```
NAME     MAJ:MIN RM   SIZE  RO TYPE MOUNTPOINT
sda        8:0    0 931.5G  0 disk
|-sda1     8:1    0   100M  0 part
|-sda2     8:2    0 278.5G  0 part
|-sda3     8:3    0   563M  0 part
|-sda4     8:4    0     1K  0 part
|-sda5     8:5    0  14.9G  0 part
|-sda6     8:6    0   512M  0 part /boot/efi
|-sda7     8:7    0   637G  0 part /
sdb        8:16   1  14.9G  0 disk
|-sdb1     8:17   1     1G  0 part
|-sdb2     8:18   1     1G  0 part
|-sdb3     8:19   1     1G  0 part
|-sdb4     8:20   1     1K  0 part
|-sdb5     8:21   1     1G  0 part
|-sdb6     8:22   1     1G  0 part
sr0       11:0    1  1024M  0 rom
```

Listing 4.2 Using **lsblk** to list the block devices connected to the system and thereby work out the device identifier.

Once the device identifier is determined it is possible to repartition the device. As shown in Listings 4.1 and 4.2 the device was identified as **/dev/sdb**. This is the identifier that will be used in the remainder of this Section. Please ensure that you are using the correct identifier on your system!

WARNING: The following steps will destroy all data on the device. Also please ensure that you are referring to the device identifier that you discover on your own machine. Do not just copy the commands here if you are on a different device!

Generally new devices will be shipped with a single partition on the device. Running the command **sudo fdisk -l /dev/sdb**[5] will list the partitions present on the device. Listing 4.3 shows the output of this command, showing the single partition.

```
Disk /dev/sdb: 3.96 GiB, 4226809856 bytes, 8255488 sectors
Disk model:
Units: sectors of 1 * 512 = 512 bytes
Sector size (logical/physical): 512 bytes / 512 bytes
I/O size (minimum/optimal): 512 bytes / 512 bytes
Disklabel type: dos
Disk identifier: 0x0bf1620a

Device     Boot Start     End Sectors Size Id Type
/dev/sdb1          2048 8255487 8253440   4G  7 HPFS/NTFS/exFAT
```

Listing 4.3 Output from the **fdisk** command on a new device. This shows one single partition.

In order to create the new partition scheme the **fdisk** command is also used. Running **fdisk** without the -l option will enter an interactive shell which can be used to partition the device. There are a number of commands which are of interest including:

- **d:** delete a partition
- **p:** print the current partition table
- **n:** create a new partition
- **t:** change the type of a partition. Note that entering **L** will list all available partition types.
- **w:** write the new partition table to disk
- **q:** quit **fdisk** without writing any changes to the device
- **m:** displays a help page

By deleting the existing partition and creating two new partitions it is possible to create the structure shown in Listing 4.4.

```
Disk /dev/sdb: 3.96 GiB, 4226809856 bytes, 8255488 sectors
Disk model:
Units: sectors of 1 * 512 = 512 bytes
Sector size (logical/physical): 512 bytes / 512 bytes
I/O size (minimum/optimal): 512 bytes / 512 bytes
Disklabel type: dos
Disk identifier: 0x0bf1620a

Device     Boot   Start End     Sectors Size Id Type
/dev/sdb1           2048 4196351 4194304 2G    7 HPFS/NTFS/exFAT
/dev/sdb2        4196352 8255487 4059136 2G   83 Linux
```

Listing 4.4 The newly created partition table showing two partitions on the device.

5 The **gdisk** command can also be used to list partitions on a device. Strictly speaking **fdisk** is for use with MBR partitioning schemes while **gdisk** is for use with GPT partitioning schemes. The differences in these schemes are introduced later in this chapter.

At this stage the partitions have been created but there is no file system present in them. Linux provides support for many file systems by default. In order to create a file system one of the **mkfs** family of commands can be used. Listing 4.5 shows an ExFAT file system being created in the first partition (**/dev/sdb1**) and an EXT file system in the second partition (**/dev/sdb2**).

```
$ sudo mkfs.exfat /dev/sdb1
mkexfatfs 1.3.0
Creating... done.
Flushing... done.
File system created successfully.

$ sudo mkfs.ext2 /dev/sdb2
mke2fs 1.45.5 (07-Jan-2020)
Creating filesystem with 507392 4k blocks and 126976 inodes
Filesystem UUID: 74b1ba39-5a2b-4913-8f3e-d94017345e91
Superblock backups stored on blocks:
      32768, 98304, 163840, 229376, 294912

Allocating group tables: done
Writing inode tables: done
Writing superblocks and filesystem accounting information: done
```

Listing 4.5 Using the **mkfs** family of commands to create file systems.

Once file systems have been created it is necessary to mount these file systems in order to use them.

4.2.1.1 Mounting File Systems on Linux

Linux provides the **mount** command which can be used to mount a file system. For this to work it is necessary to first create a mount point for the file system. This is merely a directory in the current file system. Before proceeding you can examine the currently mounted file systems using the **df** command. You might be surprised by the number that are present on a Linux system!

Assuming that directories called **fs1** and **fs2** have already been created the commands to mount the two file systems created previously are shown in Listing 4.6. Once file systems have been mounted it is possible to use them for file storage/retrieval. The remainder of this section will examine the standard partitioning schemes in more detail.

```
$ sudo mount /dev/sdb1 fs1/
FUSE exfat 1.3.0
$ sudo mount /dev/sdb2 fs2/
$ df
Filesystem 1K-blocks Used Available Use% Mounted on
...[[snip]]...
/dev/sdb1     2097152  416    2096736    1% /home/fergus/data/fs1
/dev/sdb2     1997648 2976    1893196    1% /home/fergus/data/fs2
```

Listing 4.6 Mounting the two file systems created earlier. An extract from **df** shows the two mounted file systems.

4.2.2 Master Boot Record

One method of describing partition layout that is commonly encountered is the MBR. The MBR resides on sector 0 of a storage device. It contains a number of areas. The MBR contains some bootstrap code, a disk signature, a partition table and an MBR signature. The boot code occupies the first 0x1B8 (440_d) bytes of data. This is followed by a 4_d byte disk signature. This signature should be ***unique*** to the system to which it is connected. There are then two bytes of padding, which are followed by a 64_d byte partition table. The partition table itself is composed of four 16_d byte partition entries. Finally the MBR signature of 0xAA55 is found in the final two bytes. Listing 4.7 shows the final 80_d bytes of sector 0 in an MBR formatted disk.

```
001b0: 0000 0000 0000 0000 bc50 c882 0000 003c .........P.....<
001c0: 0900 8379 463c 0008 0000 0000 2000 005c ...yF<...... ..\
001d0: c533 8357 8664 0008 2000 0000 2000 0000 .3.W.d.. ... ...
001e0: 0101 833f 2000 0008 4000 0000 2000 0000 ...? ...@... ...
001f0: 0000 0000 0000 0000 0000 0000 0000 55aa ..............U.
```

Listing 4.7 Excerpt from a sample MBR, showing the final 80_d bytes of data. Alternate partition table entries are highlighted.

Table 4.1 shows the structure of the MBR partition table entry, while Table 4.2 shows the processed values from Listing 4.7.

Table 4.3 provides a small sample of the commonly encountered MBR partition types. The values in this table cover the major file systems in this book. One of these to note is that of the extended partition (0x05). The primary MBR partition table can only hold four partitions; however, there is a special type of extended partition which can also be used. Figure 4.3 shows an MBR-partitioned disk with five partitions, three primary partitions and one extended partition containing two logical partitions. The primary and extended partition table structures are also marked.

Table 4.2 shows the processed values from the partition table in Listing 4.7. As expected there are three partitions listed in this. All three partitions have the bootable flag set to 0x00, meaning that these partitions are not bootable. Similarly all three have the partition type as Linux (0x83). One of the key things with partitions in the MBR scheme is that they are addressed in two different

Table 4.1 MBR partition table entry structure.

Offset	Size	Name	Description
0x00	0x01	Bootable	A value of 0x80 indicates the partition is bootable; otherwise, it is not bootable.
0x01	0x03	Start Sector (CHS)	A cylinder, head, sector address for the first sector in the partition. This form of addressing is no longer used.
0x04	0x01	Partition Type	Partition-type identifier. Some of the more commonly encountered partition-type identifiers are listed in Table 4.3.
0x05	0x03	End Sector (CHS)	A cylinder, head, sector address for the last sector in the partition. This form of addressing is no longer used.
0x08	0x04	Start Sector (LBA)	The logical block address for the first sector in the partition.
0x0C	0x04	# Sectors	The number of sectors in the partition.

Table 4.2 MBR partition table entry structure for Listing 4.7.

Offset	Size	Name	Entry 1	Entry 2	Entry 3
0x00	0x01	Bootable	0x00	0x00	0x00
0x01	0x03	Start Sector (CHS)	0x00093C	0x33C55C	0x010100
0x04	0x01	Partition Type	0x83	0x83	0x83
0x05	0x03	End Sector (CHS)	0x3C4679	0x648657	0x00203F
0x08	0x04	Start Sector (LBA)	0x800	0x200800	0x400800
			2048_d	$2,099,200_d$	$4,196,352_d$
0x0C	0x04	# Sectors	0x200000	0x200000	0x200000
			$2,097,152_d$	$2,097,152_d$	$2,097,152_d$

Table 4.3 Selection of values for the file system type in the MBR partitioning scheme. The complete list is available at https://en.wikipedia.org/wiki/Partition_type.

Value	File System	Value	File System
0x05	Extended partition	0x07	ExFAT/NTFS/HPFS
0x0B	FAT32	0x83	Linux file system

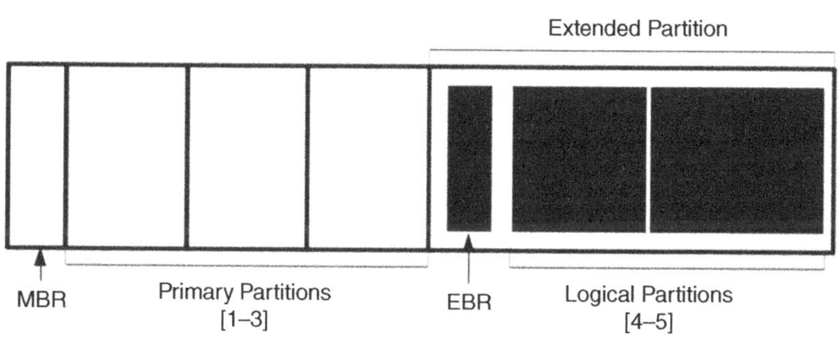

Figure 4.3 A disk with five partitions created using a primary MBR and an extended boot record (EBR).

ways. In one case they use Cylinder, Header, Sector (CHS) addressing. This is a physical address based on the actual disk geometry (hence the references to cylinders, heads and sectors). In the other case they use logical addressing. It is this logical addressing that is used most frequently in modern computer systems (and in all digital forensic tools).

The partition's location can be found using the logical block address (LBA) of the starting sector of the partition along with the number of sectors in the partition. In each of the cases in Table 4.2 the partitions occupy 2097152_d sectors with starting addresses of 2048_d, 2099200_d and 4196352_d, respectively.

Listing 4.8 shows the output from the **mmls** command when run on the device containing the partition table in Listing 4.7. Compare this to the processed values in Table 4.2 to confirm the information is correct. Note that the **mmls** tool does not list the CHS addresses.

```
$ sudo mmls /dev/sdb
[sudo] password for fergus:
DOS Partition Table
Offset Sector: 0
Units are in 512-byte sectors

      Slot     Start       End          Length       Description
000:  Meta     0000000000  0000000000   0000000001   Primary Table (#0)
001:  -------  0000000000  0000002047   0000002048   Unallocated
002:  000:000  0000002048  0002099199   0002097152   Linux (0x83)
003:  000:001  0002099200  0004196351   0002097152   Linux (0x83)
004:  000:002  0004196352  0006293503   0002097152   Linux (0x83)
005:  -------  0006293504  0031129599   0024836096   Unallocated
```

Listing 4.8 The output from Sleuthkit's **mmls** command on a disk. This disk contains the partition table in Listing 4.7.

4.2.3 GUID Partition Table

The MBR scheme does not scale well to modern devices. The logical address limit in MBR is four bytes. As each logical address is generally a 512_d byte sector this equates to a 2 TiB file system size limit. There are now devices capable of storing much greater volumes of data than 2TiB and as such MBR was no longer sufficient. The replacement structure is known as the GPT and is found in most modern devices (although MBR is still very frequently encountered). With standard sector size (512_d bytes), if it is necessary to have a partition of more than 2 TiB then GPT must be used.

Figure 4.4 shows the structure of a device that has been partitioned using the GPT scheme. The first sector of the device contains a protective MBR. This generally contains one single partition which is as large as possible (up to the device size or the MBR partition size limit). This protective

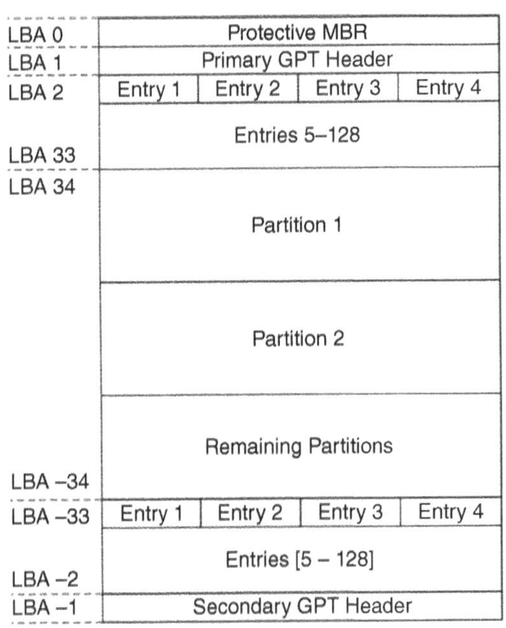

Figure 4.4 GPT-partitioned device structure.

Table 4.4 GPT header structure.

Offset	Size	Name	Description
0x00	0x08	Signature	Signature with value EFI PART.
0x08	0x04	Revision	Revision number generally 0x100.
0x0C	0x04	Header Size	The header size in bytes (Generally 0x5C).
0x10	0x04	CRC32 (Header)	CRC32 checksum for the header.
0x14	0x04	Reserved	Must be zero.
0x18	0x08	Current LBA	Location of this header sector.
0x20	0x08	Backup LBA	Location of the other header sector.
0x28	0x08	First Usable LBA	Location of the first sector available for partitions.
0x30	0x08	Last Usable LBA	Location of the last sector available for partitions.
0x38	0x10	Disk GUID	Mixed-endian disk GUID.
0x48	0x08	LBA of First Entry	The location of the first partition table entry (0x02 in primary GPT structure).
0x50	0x04	Num Entries	The number of partition table entries.
0x54	0x04	Entry Size	The size of the partition table entries in bytes (generally 0x80).
0x58	0x04	CRC32 (Entries)	CRC32 checksum values for the partition entries.
0x5C	0x1A4	Reserved	Must be zero for the remainder of this sector.

MBR will prevent older operating systems, which do not support GPT, from determining that there is no file system present and reinitialising the device.

The GPT structure itself is duplicated. The protective MBR is immediately followed by the primary GPT structure. This is a 33 sector structure. The first structure contains the Primary GPT header which provides information about the device as a whole. The structure of this is shown in Table 4.4. This is followed by 32_d sectors, each of which contains four 128_d byte partition table entries. Comparing GPT to MBR shows that there is now more space available to store information about each partition (128_d bytes as opposed to 16_d bytes) and also that there are many more partitions that can be used (128_d as opposed to 4_d). The structure of the GPT partition table entry is shown in Table 4.5.

GPT's advantage over MBR is immediately clear when examining Table 4.5 which shows the addressable space. GPT uses an 8_d byte structure to store addresses. This means that 2_d^{64} sectors

Table 4.5 GPT partition entry structure.

Offset	Size	Name	Description
0x00	0x10	Partition-Type GUID	Mixed-endian GUID representing the file system type.
0x10	0x10	Partition GUID	A unique mixed-endian GUID representing the partition itself.
0x20	0x08	First LBA	The starting sector for the partition.
0x28	0x08	Last LBA	The final sector in the partition. Note this sector is included in the partition.
0x30	0x08	Attributes	Partition attributes. See Table 4.7.
0x38	0x48	Name	36 UTF-16 characters for the partition name.

can be addressed. Compare this to MBR which uses only a 4_d byte address field (allowing for 2_d^{32} sectors). Assuming a default sector size of 512_d bytes, this means that MBR can utilise disks of up to 2^{41} bytes (i.e. 2 TiB) whereas GPT can utilise disks of up to 2^{73} bytes (i.e. 8 ZiB).

The GPT scheme also provides some identifying information which is not present in MBR. This includes a Globally Unique Identifier (GUID) to identify the partition. The GUID[6] is a 128_d bit identifier that is almost guaranteed to be unique.[7] UUIDs are generally displayed using an 8-4-4-4-12 format as shown in Listing 4.9.

```
xxxxxxxx-xxxx-Mxxx-Nxxx-xxxxxxxxxxxx
```

Listing 4.9 UUID structure showing the version nibble (M) and the variant nibble (N).

In this structure the M bit represents the UUID version. There are five valid versions (1–5) at the time of writing. The differing versions are related to how the UUID is generated. This might include using current time and Mac Address (Version 1), an identifier, time and Mac Address (Version 2), name and namespace identifier (Versions 3 and 5) and random numbers (Version 4). The variant is represented by 1–3 most significant bits in N in Listing 4.9. The possible values are:

- Variant 0 ($0xxx_2$)
- Variant 1 ($10xx_2$)
- Variant 2 ($110x_2$)

Variant 0 is now obsolete. While in textual form Variants 1 and 2 are identical (except for the contents of the variant byte) their storage is different. Variant 1 UUID's use big-endian byte ordering for all fields, while Variant 2 UUID's use little-endian byte ordering for the first three fields (8-4-4) and big-endian byte ordering for the remaining fields (4-12).

In addition to the partition's GUID there is also a GUID to represent the file system type. This is of the same structure as the partition GUID but only a limited number of values are allowed. These values summarise the file system type in the respective partition. Some of the more common values for this GUID are given in Table 4.6.[8]

Table 4.6 A selection of commonly encountered partition-type GUID values.

OS	Partition Type	GUID – Big Endian
Windows	Microsoft Reserved	E3C9E316-0B5C-4DB8-817D-F92DF00215AE
	Basic Data Partition	EBD0A0A2-B9E5-4433-87C0-68B6B72699C7
Linux	Linux File System	0FC63DAF-8483-4772-8E79-3D69D8477DE4
	Swap Partition	0657FD6D-A4AB-43C4-84E5-0933C84B4F4F
MacOS	HFS+	48465300-0000-11AA-AA11-00306543ECAC
	APFS Container	7C3457EF-0000-11AA-AA11-00306543ECAC

6 The more general term for GUID is UUID (Universally Unique Identifier), Microsoft systems tend to use GUID rather than UUID.
7 Uniqueness is not enforced; however, probability dictates that the chance of a non-unique value is so low that we can declare these to be unique.
8 For a complete list of these file system type values see: https://linux.org/attachments/guid_partition_table-pdf.5814/ – Page 8.

Table 4.7 General attribute values in GPT.

Bit	Meaning
0_d	Platform required – disk partitioning utilities must preserve this partition.
1_d	EFI Firmware should ignore this partition.
2_d	Legacy BIOS Bootable.
3_d–47_d	Reserved.
48_d–63_d	Defined by individual partition types.

Table 4.8 Attribute values specific to the Microsoft Basic Data Partition.

Bit	Meaning
60_d	Read only
61_d	Shadow copy
62_d	Hidden
63_d	No drive letter (do not automount)

The final extra functionality provided by the GPT partition scheme is the allowance of 64_d bits to store attributes. 48_d bits are general while the remaining 16_d can be used by individual file systems. Table 4.7 shows the general attribute meanings while Table 4.8 shows the Microsoft Basic Data Partition specific bit values.

4.3 File Systems

Techopedia defines a file system as 'a process that manages how and where data on a storage disk, typically a hard disk drive is stored, accessed and managed'. Brian Carrier states that 'computers need a method for the long-term storage and retrieval of data' which is achieved through the file system. The file system is a set of structures that manage how file content is stored on electronic storage media. They provide a means by which a user can organise data in a hierarchy of files and directories.

4.3.1 File System Concepts

This section introduces the general concepts which are common to many file systems. Understanding these concepts is essential in order to effectively analyse file systems. These concepts include:

- **Sector:** A sector is the basic unit of disk storage. On the majority of devices sectors are 512_d bytes in size but there are certain devices which have a larger size. Read/write operations on disk are generally conducted at the sector level. In terms of file system forensics the sector number or Logical Block Address (LBA) is used to locate structures on disk.
- **Cluster/Block:** A cluster (sometimes called a block) is a collection of sectors. This is the basic unit of storage in the file system. Files occupy clusters (or parts thereof). Consider a case in which

a file system uses eight sectors in each cluster. This results in a cluster size of 4096_d bytes. A file consisting of one single byte will occupy a single cluster. The single byte file will be of size 1_d byte but have an allocated size of 4096_d bytes; in other words, it occupies one cluster.

- **File:** Files are containers for storing information in a computer/file system. Files occupy a number of clusters/blocks in the file system. File systems also contain metadata about each file.
- **Directory:** Directories are used to organise files/directories in a hierarchical structure. File systems often treat directories as special files, in which their *content* is a list of files/directories that are contained in the directory.
- **Metadata:** Metadata is data about data. It is information that the file system maintains about each file/directory that is present on the file system. Metadata is often as important as file content during file system forensic analysis.
- **Storage Mechanisms:** In the majority of file systems the metadata allows for the content to be located. This can be achieved in a number of ways. In older file systems such as FAT and ext every cluster/block in the file system is listed. More modern file systems generally allow for extent-based storage. In this the file content location is described through a structure called an extent. This structure contains the starting cluster for the file's content along with the number of clusters in the extent. This is a more efficient way to store information about many contiguous clusters, rather than listing them all. In some file systems the content of small files may be stored in the metadata structure itself. This is known as inline storage.
- **File Deletion:** When using a standard operating system to view a file system, deleted files do not appear but the content and metadata of these files are often still present in the file system. Many file systems do not actually delete a file; instead, they mark the metadata structure as being deleted. The OS does not show these deleted files but file system forensic tools will show them. The deleted file will eventually be overwritten as the clusters occupied by that file (and the metadata structures) are marked as available and can be used for something else in the future.
- **File Fragmentation:** File fragmentation occurs when there is no single area in the file system large enough to store the entire contents of a file. The file is then split into a number of pieces each of which is stored individually. These pieces are known as fragments.
- **Unallocated Space:** Unallocated space is space in a file system that is not currently in use. It is marked as unallocated in the allocation map. When a file is deleted the clusters which contain the file's content are marked as unallocated in the allocation bitmap, meaning they become part of unallocated space; however, the file content is still present. Copying files from a file system will not include unallocated space; hence, in digital forensics a bit-by-bit image of the device is created, to ensure that unallocated space is also analysed.
- **Slack Space:** While the cluster is the basic storage unit in a file system, files do not necessarily occupy entire clusters. Consider the situation mentioned previously, a file of one single byte occupies a cluster of 4096_d bytes. The remaining 4095_d bytes in the cluster is the slack space. This may contain data from previous files that occupied this cluster.

  Figure 4.5 shows an example of this. Figure 4.5(A) shows a sequence of three clusters containing the content of a single file. If this file is deleted and another file which occupies a little more than two clusters is written to its place we see that the third cluster still retains some of the data from the first file (Figure 4.5(B)). This is the slack space.
- **Trees:** Most modern file systems use Trees as the basic storage mechanism. Generally these are self-balancing trees which allow for quick searches. Trees are composed of nodes of three types: Root node, internal (or index) nodes and leaf nodes. There are a number of types of tree that are encountered in file systems. Some use B-Trees in which all leaf nodes are at the same level but data may be found in interior nodes also. Others use B+Trees in which data is only found in

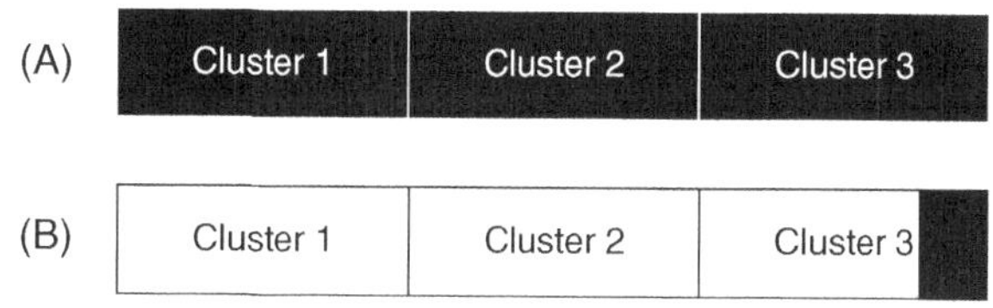

Figure 4.5 Demonstrating slack space. (A) A file that occupies three clusters on the file system. (B) This area after the original file is deleted and a new, shorter, file is written into its place. It is clear that part of the content of the original file is still present.

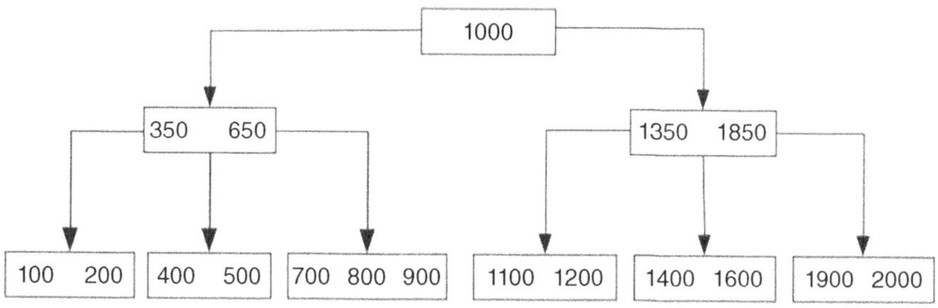

Figure 4.6 A sample B-Tree structure.

leaf nodes. Figure 4.6 shows an example B+-Tree for a directory structure. The directory contains 13_d files all consisting of numbered names. These appear in the leaf nodes.

Trees are quick structures to search as they are well organised. Consider the case of searching for the file called 1200_d in the directory structure in Figure 4.6. The root node value is 1000_d, the desired value is 1200_d which is greater than the root node value; hence, the desired file must be in the right child. The right child is an internal node. It contains pointers to three leaf nodes, one whose values are less than 1350_d, one whose values are 1350_d–1849_d, and one whose values are greater than 1850_d. The desired node, 1200_d is less than 1350_d and hence the left child is followed. This leads to a leaf node in which the desired file is found.

- **Copy on Write:** Copy-on-write (CoW) is a policy used in many modern file systems in which a copy of a resource is created when the original is modified. This means that the original is often still present on the file system. CoW is used to ensure integrity of the file system but it also gives the potential to discover earlier versions of artefacts.
- **Volume Boot Record:** Most file systems have a Volume Boot Record (VBR) structure.[9] This structure provides information about the file system as a whole. This might include labels (i.e. names), sector/cluster sizes, file system size and locations of important file system structures.
- **Allocation Maps:** The file system keeps track of all structures that it controls. These structures could be clusters, metadata structures, etc. To do this most file systems use allocation maps (also called bitmaps). These structures generally use a single bit to represent a single entity. A value of 1_b shows that the structure is currently in use, while a value of 0_b shows the structure is unused.
- **Journal:** Many modern file systems maintain a journal structure. The journal records changes to the file system before they are committed to the disk. In the event of a file system crash the journal can be used to quickly repair the file system. Most journals record only changes to metadata, not to actual content. From a forensic perspective journals provide the potential to see changes in the file system over time.
- **Snapshot:** A snapshot is a view of a file system at a particular point in time. Many modern file systems allow for snapshots to be created. This is generally achieved through copy-on-write.

9 This is sometimes called the Boot Sector, the Superblock, etc.

These snapshots are used as a backup mechanism and can therefore show the investigator older versions of the file system.

- **RAID:** A Redundant Array of Independent[10] Disks allows for multiple disks to be combined to form a single file system. This new file system can merely be used to create one single large file system (combining all drives in the array) or it can be used for redundancy purposes. Many modern file systems implement RAID in the file system itself.[11] There are a number of different RAID levels. Some of the more commonly encountered levels include: RAID 0 which is used to combine a series of disks into one large disk. There is no redundancy (although there are benefits to performance). RAID 1 is perfect mirroring. Data is written to two or more drives, giving a perfect back up solution. RAID 5 allows for full redundancy. A drive can fail in RAID 5 and the contents can still be retrieved from the other drives. RAID 5 requires at least three disks.

These concepts are present in many file systems. Simpler file systems, such as FAT, will not have many of the more advanced concepts. For instance the FAT file system does not support RAID, it has no journal, it does not use B-Trees and so forth. However, modern file systems are more likely to support all (or most) of these concepts.

4.3.2 Comparison of File Systems

There are a large number of file systems in use today, from the traditional disk-based file systems such as FAT and EXT to fault-tolerant systems such as BtrFS and ReFS. There are also distributed file systems, file systems for particular device types and so forth but only a small number of these file systems are encountered frequently in digital forensics.

The file systems that are of most interest to analysts are those that are encountered on the main operating systems (Windows, MacOS and Linux – which includes Android). The majority of file systems encountered will be traditional disk-based file systems which are commonly supported by the main operating systems.

For this reason this book will focus on the following file systems from Windows: FAT,[12] ExFAT and NTFS; from Linux: Ext,[13] XFS and BtrFS; and from MacOS: HFS+ and APFS. In this section the capabilities of each of these file systems are discussed and compared.

From Table 4.9 it is clear that as time has moved on, the capacity of file systems has increased. This is due in the main to the increasing capacity of hard drives. The early FAT 12 file system could handle only a volume of $32MiB$, tiny by today's standards. The newest file systems measure their capacities in yobibytes (2^{80} bytes).

There are some caveats to Table 4.9, for instance the filename length for all FAT file systems is given as 8.3. This refers to the 11 bytes allocated for the name, 8 of which were used for the filename and 3 for the extension. However, most variants of FAT now include support for Long File Names which provide for up 255 characters in a UTF-16 encoding. It should also be noted that the figures are based on the maximum cluster sizes, the limits might be smaller in practice.

---

10 Originally this was Inexpensive; however, later papers preferred Independent.

11 There are also hardware RAID solutions in existence but these are not the focus of this book. In the case of hardware RAID, the file system appears to exist in a traditional disk, the hardware controller handles all RAID matters. In File System RAID, it is the file system itself that controls the RAID system. This is the focus of this book.

12 There are multiple versions of the FAT file system: FAT12; FAT16; and FAT32.

13 There are multiple versions of Ext (2, 3 and 4).

Table 4.9 Comparison of the most common file systems.

File System	Year	Max. Volume Size	Max. File Size	Max. Filename Length	Filename Encoding
NTFS	1993	8_d PiB	8_d PiB	255_d	UTF-16
EXT2	1993	32_d TiB	2_d TiB	255_d	ASCII
XFS	1994	8_d EiB	8_d EiB	255_d	ASCII
FAT 32	1996	2_d TiB	4_d GB	255_d	UCS-2
HFS+	1998	8_d EiB	8_d EiB	255_d	UTF-16
EXT3	2001	32_d TiB	2_d TiB	255_d	ASCII
ExFAT	2006	128_d PiB	128_d PiB	255_d	UTF-16
EXT4	2008	1_d EiB	16_d TiB	255_d	ASCII
Btrfs	2009	16_d EiB	16_d EiB	255_d	Unicode/ASCII
APFS	2017	2^{63} blocks[a)]	8_d EiB	255_d	UTF-8

a) Assuming default block size of 2^{12} bytes this would mean that the maximum volume size is 32_d ZiB.

Table 4.10 Timestamp availability in the common file systems.

	Granularity	Modified	Accessed	Change	Creation	Other
NTFS[a)]	10^{-7} s	Yes	Yes	Yes	Yes	No
EXT2[b)]	1 s	Yes	Yes	Yes	No	Deletion
XFS	10^{-9} s	Yes	Yes	Yes	Yes	No
FAT 32	2 s	Yes	Yes[c)]	No	Yes	No
HFS+[d)]	1 s	Yes	Yes	Yes	Yes	Backup
EXT3[b)]	1 s	Yes	Yes	Yes	No	Deletion
ExFAT	10^{-2} s	Yes	Yes	No	Yes	No
EXT4[b)]	10^{-9} s	Yes	Yes	Yes	Yes	Deletion
Btrfs	10^{-9} s	Yes	Yes	Yes	Yes	No
APFS[e)]	10^{-9} s	Yes	Yes	Yes	Yes	No

a) NTFS stores times related to both file content and filename.
b) The ext2, 3 and 4 superblock contains last mount, last write and last checked times.
c) FAT32 only stores the access date not the time.
d) HFS+ stores the file system creation, modification, backup and checked timestamps in the volume header.
e) APFS stores the last modified and last unmounted times in the volume superblock.

One of the most important aspects in criminal investigation is that of time. Time can be used to support or refute a suspect's alibi. Hence it is important to understand the time values that are present in each file system. Table 4.10 shows the timestamps that are present in each of the file systems.

In relation to timestamps trends are also obvious. Modern file systems are recording timestamps with much better granularity. This is generally at the nanosecond level. Older file systems, designed for older and slower computers, did not require this level of exactness.

4.4 Acquisition of File System Data

Before file system forensic analysis can begin a disk image is required. While physically possible to run all file system forensic tools on an actual disk, any inadvertent change made to the content might invalidate all results. Hence an image of the device is acquired. In this section the types of image are described. The section then proceeds to distinguish between logical and physical acquisition. This section then describes how a Linux workstation can be configured for acquisition, ensuring that no file systems are automatically mounted before acquisition is performed. Finally some of the Linux tools that are available for performing acquisition are introduced.

4.4.1 Logical vs Physical Acquisition

Acquisition can either be logical or physical. In a physical acquisition every bit on the device is captured. This includes not only live files, but also slack space, deleted files, unallocated space, etc. This type of acquisition is the preferred method of acquisition in all cases as no potential evidence is lost. However, physical acquisition is not always possible. Sometimes there is no choice but to perform a logical acquisition.

In a logical acquisition live files, in other words those that are addressed through metadata structures and are not marked as deleted, are acquired. In certain types of device (such as some smart phones) this is the only form of acquisition that is possible. With acquisition in LDF this might also be the only form of acquisition that is possible. Consider the scenario in which a running machine contains an open encrypted container. If the machine is shutdown in order to physically acquire the device then this encrypted information will be lost, unless a key is present. Hence a logical acquisition would be performed at the scene, copying all files from the encrypted container. This, of course, will result in only live files being acquired. As this book focuses on file system forensics it is necessary to use physical acquisition. A logical acquisition would not result in the collection of file system structures. Hence, for the remainder of this section it is assumed that the reader is interested only in physical acquisition.

4.4.2 Acquisition Under Linux

Many readers may already have access to a forensic workstation which is used to acquire disk images. For those that do not have access to a workstation this section provides a brief overview of the steps in setting up a workstation using Linux.

The key point in relation to acquisition is to remember the first ACPO principle, that actions performed by the investigator may not change the underlying data. Consider the insertion of a USB key into any standard computer. The computer attempts to be helpful and mounts the device and displays the contents. This process can (and often does) change the content on the device. Now consider if this USB device was a piece of potential evidence. The simple act of plugging it into the workstation has potentially altered the content.

To combat this, best practice recommends that a write blocker be employed. These are usually hardware devices that stop all write signals being sent to the device. If no hardware write blocker is available it is possible in Linux to disable automount. In Linux Mint this is achieved through the file manager application.[14] In the Nemo file manager select Edit | Preferences. On the behavior tab find media handling and ensure that all boxes are unticked. This is shown in Figure 4.7.

14 The method of disabling automount might be different in different distributions, and even in different versions of Linux Mint. It is essential that testing is carried out to ensure that automount has been successfully disabled *before* any evidential material is inserted into the workstation.

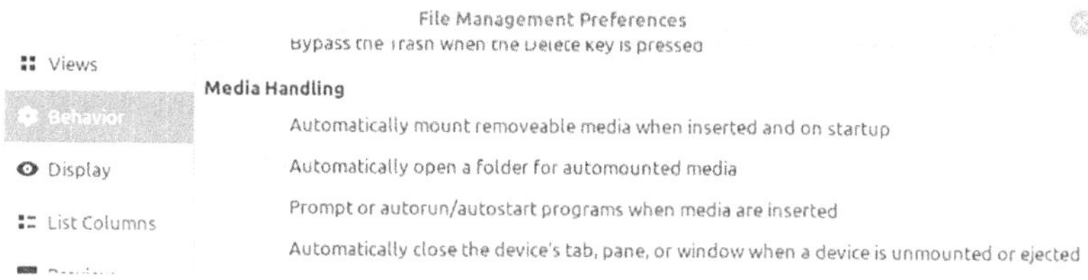

Figure 4.7 Media handling preferences in nemo file explorer when automount is disabled.

In order to acquire an image of a physical device it is necessary to discover the device identifier. This can be done in the same manner as shown in Section 4.2 either using **dmesg** or **lsblk**.

4.4.2.1 The dd Family

dd is a Linux command line utility which allows an image file to be created. Once the device has been inserted into the workstation and the identifier discovered it is a simple process to image the device using the **dd** command. For instance, Listings 4.1 and 4.2 show a device identifier of **/dev/sdb**. The command **sudo dd if=/dev/sdb of=device.dd** will take **/dev/sdb** as input file and create an image in the local file **device.dd**. The **dd** command can also be used to image a partition as shown in Listing 4.10 in which **/dev/sdb1** is imaged.

```
$ sudo dd if=/dev/sdb1 of=partition1.dd
2097152+0 records in
2097152+0 records out
1073741824 bytes (1.1 GB, 1.0 GiB) copied, 64.4124 s, 16.7 MB/s
$
```

Listing 4.10 Imaging a partition (**/dev/sdb1)** using **dd**.

From Listing 4.10 there is a discrepancy between the number of records and the number of bytes. By performing a simple calculation each record must consist of 512_d bytes. This is the default block size at which **dd** operates. The **dd** command's block size can be changed using **bs=**. Generally increasing the block size achieves the same end result as that in Listing 4.10 but results in fewer read/write operations and therefore quicker acquisition.

The starting position and the number of bytes to extract can be specified in addition to the block size. Imagine that the analyst wishes to extract the MBR from **/dev/sdb**. The MBR occupies the first sector on the device. Hence the block size should be 512_d bytes (to match the sector size), acquisition should begin at the beginning of the device (the MBR appears at the very start of the device) and only a single sector should be acquired. In this case both the block size and starting point default values (512_d and 0_d, respectively, are acceptable); however, the number of blocks to be extracted must be specified. Listing 4.11 shows how this is achieved.

```
$ sudo dd if=/dev/sdb of=mbr.dd count=1
1+0 records in
1+0 records out
512 bytes copied, 0.0017935 s, 285 kB/s
$
```

Listing 4.11 Extracting the MBR with the **count=** option for **dd**.

In Listing 4.11 only one single block is acquired. This is achieved through the **count=** option. **count=1** means that only one single block (512_d bytes) is extracted. What if only the partition table itself was required? The partition begins at byte offset 446_d and is 64_d bytes in size. In this case it is impossible to use a block size of 512_d bytes (it is too large for the desired amount of information). Instead the block size is set to 1_d byte, the count to 64_d bytes (as it is desired to extract 64_d bytes), and finally a parameter called skip is given the value 446_d. This will commence the acquisition at byte offset 446_d, reading 64_d single byte blocks. This is shown in Listing 4.12.

```
$ sudo dd if=/dev/sdb of=pt.dd bs=1 count=64 skip=446
64+0 records in
64+0 records out
64 bytes copied, 0.00377727 s, 16.9 kB/s
$
```

Listing 4.12 Extracting the partition table using **bs=**, **skip=** and **count=** to specify the exact data that is desired.

While permitting forensic acquisition the **dd** tool is not a forensic tool. For instance it does not allow for the verification of the captured data. Generally, the analyst would need to image the device and then calculate a hash over the device and over the image to ensure that the imaging process worked correctly. This process is shown in Listing 4.13.

```
$ sudo dd if=/dev/sdb1 of=partition1.dd bs=4096
262144+0 records in
262144+0 records out
1073741824 bytes (1.1 GB, 1.0 GiB) copied, 62.4354 s, 17.2 MB/s
$ sudo md5sum /dev/sdb1
7ec0ec57cb850548b7fe93e0ee13cdf1 /dev/sdb1
$ md5sum partition1.dd
7ec0ec57cb850548b7fe93e0ee13cdf1 partition1.dd
$
```

Listing 4.13 Verifying the **dd** acquisition process.

There are two common variants of **dd** that are used for forensics. Both are based on the original **dd** and as such support most of the options that have been examined previously. These are **dc3dd** and **dcfldd**. Both of these allow for hashing, logging and splitting images, etc. Both of these tools can be installed from the standard repositories.

4.4.2.2 Expert Witness Format (EWF)

The basic **dd** command creates a raw image, a bit-by-bit copy of the input device. Hence if a 1TiB hard drive is imaged the resulting file is also 1TiB in size. This can quickly lead to storage issues. The Expert Witness Format is the image format used in tools such as EnCase and is available for all major operating systems. On Linux Mint it can be installed using: **sudo apt install ewf-tools**. This package provides a number of commands related to EWF images including:

- **ewfacquire:** This command is used to image a device and create an EWF image.
- **ewfinfo:** The EWF format stores information about the image file in the image file itself. This command is used to view this information.

- **ewfverify:** The EWF format stores information about hash values of the original data and the image. This command can be run to verify that the contents of the image file are still intact.
- **ewfexport:** This is used to convert the EWF format to another format (e.g. raw).
- **ewfmount:** This is used to mount the EWF image. The mounting process creates a raw image in memory which can then be mounted as normal.

The above commands are generally self-explanatory. For instance if imaging a device with **ewfacquire** the user will be asked a series of questions related to the case and the image. Generally the default values for the image will be acceptable (the user might wish to specify best compression in order to reduce the image file size).

One command that needs a little extra information provided is that of **ewfmount**. All files supplied from this book's website are in EWF format. In order to view the hex values of these raw image files there are two options. The image can be exported to a raw format using **ewfexport** or it can be mounted which will create a raw format in memory. Listing 4.14 shows the command for mounting an image file called **FAT32_V1.E01** on a directory called **mnt**.

```
$ ewfmount FAT32_V1.E01 mnt/
ewfmount 20140807

$ ls mnt/
ewf1
```

Listing 4.14 Using **ewfmount** to mount an EWF image.

After mounting the image file the contents of the mount point directory contain the file **ewf1**. This is the raw image which can then be further analysed.

4.4.2.3 guymager

guymager is a graphical disk imaging tool which can support multiple formats. On Linux Mint it can be installed using: **sudo apt install guymager**. This tool can be executed from the command line using **sudo guymager**. Root access is required as this tool is meant to access physical disks in order to acquire an image. Figure 4.8 shows a screen shot from the **guymager** application.

Figure 4.8 The **guymager** application showing two connected disks.

Right-clicking on any device in **guymager** will allow the device to be acquired either in raw format (similar to **dd**) or in EWF format (similar to **ewfacquire**). **guymager** will also create documentation for the EWF image format. The GUI allows the user to input information such as case number and evidence number.

4.5 Analysis of File Systems

File system forensics generally involves five steps which are:

- Determine the partition layout;
- determine the file system type;
- list files in the file system;
- recover file metadata; and
- recover file content.

All digital forensic tools perform these actions. In most commercial tools an evidence item (generally a disk image) is loaded into the system and processing begins. Very quickly the analyst will see the various partitions that are on the image and also the types of file system that are contained within these partitions.

The next step performed by the tools is to provide a list of all files (and their associated directory structure) that are present in each of the file systems. These file system forensic tools not only provide the live files, in other words, those that would be seen if the file system was mounted, they also provide the deleted files where possible.

Once the digital forensic tool has listed the contents of the file system it begins to process each file (sometimes the tool will do this only at the explicit request of the user). This will gather the metadata for the particular file and also the file's content.

The above method is used by all file system forensic tools during their execution. In the next section the Sleuth Kit, a set of command line tools which can perform the above tasks, is introduced. As each individual file system is analysed in the remainder of this book it will be shown manually how forensic tools perform the above five steps.

4.5.1 The Sleuth Kit

The Sleuth Kit (TSK) provides a set of command-line utilities to perform all of the required digital forensic analysis steps. Additionally Sleuth Kit provides other *helper* commands. This section introduces the Sleuth Kit commands. Sleuth Kit was created by Brian Carrier and has become one of the most widely used file system forensic analysis toolsets in academia. There are a number of reasons for this. First and foremost the software is free! There are no licensing costs associated with Sleuth Kit. From an educational perspective, the use of the command line is better than using commercial, graphical tools. Operating at the lower, command line, level will allow investigators to better understand the individual steps that are taken by commercial forensic tools. Hence Sleuth Kit is a great introduction to the methods used by all commercial forensic tools.

The remainder of this section will demonstrate the use of the Sleuth Kit using one of the file systems available from this book's website. In this case the file **FAT32_V2.E01** is used.

As this is an EWF image file, prior to analysis the file must be mounted. Assuming that a directory called **mnt** exists in the current directory, this is achieved using the command shown in Listing 4.15.

```
$ ewfmount FAT32_V2.E01 mnt/
ewfmount 20140807

$ ls mnt/
ewf1
```

Listing 4.15 Using **ewfmount** to mount an E01 image file. The resulting **mnt/ewf1** file is the raw image.

4.5.1.1 Determine the Partition Layout

The Sleuth Kit's **mmls** command was previously introduced to show the partition layout in a device. While there are a number of Linux tools such as **fdisk** and **gdisk** that can be used to show a file system, **mmls** is specifically designed for use in file system forensics. This means that unlike the OS tools, the **mmls** command will not only display actual partitions but will also provide information about unallocated space that exists on the drive. Listing 4.8 shows the output from the **mmls** command. Note that **mmls** will not function on the disk image contained in **FAT32_V2.E01** as this image is of a partition, not of an actual disk. This means that this image contains no partition table. If the reader wishes to see **mmls** in action it can be run on the local hard drive using: **sudo mmls /dev/sda**.

4.5.1.2 Determine the File System Type

Sleuth Kit's **fsstat** tool reads the contents of the partition and checks if it follows the format of any known file system. Because **fsstat** (and many other Sleuth Kit tools) work on a file system, many of these tools require an offset to the beginning of the partition to be specified using the -o option. In the case of **FAT32_V2.E01** this is not necessary as the image is of only a partition. Listing 4.16 shows the output from **fsstat** on **FAT32_V2.E01**.

```
$ fsstat mnt/ewf1
FILE SYSTEM INFORMATION
--------------------------------------------
File System Type: FAT32

OEM Name: mkfs.fat
Volume ID: 0x2232cfe0
Volume Label (Boot Sector): FAT_FS
Volume Label (Root Directory): FAT_FS
File System Type Label: FAT32
...[snip]...
```

Listing 4.16 Using **fsstat** to determine the file system type in **mnt/ewf1** (output is truncated).

As can be seen this is a FAT32 file system. If you continue through the output of the **fsstat** command you will see that much information is provided about the file system itself. This includes the layout of the various structures (e.g. Boot Sector, FAT 1 and FAT 2, Data Area and Root Directory), device information (sector/cluster size, etc.), and, if files are present the sectors/clusters that are occupied by files. The meaning of this output will be made clear in Chapter 5.

4.5.1.3 List the Files

The basic command for listing files in the file system is **fls**. In the same manner that **fsstat** is a file system tool, **fls** is also a file system tool and as such it must be provided with the offset at which the partition starts. The command to list the files in the **FAT32_V2.E01** file is given in Listing 4.17. Remember that in this particular case no offset is necessary.

```
$ fls mnt/ewf1
r/r 3: FAT_FS (Volume Label Entry)
d/d 5: Files
r/r 7: info.txt
r/r 9: cliffs.jpg
r/r 12: thelongbridge.jpg
v/v 16743939: $MBR
v/v 16743940: $FAT1
v/v 16743941: $FAT2
V/V 16743942: $OrphanFiles
```

Listing 4.17 Basic file listing using **fls**.

Sleuth Kit tools differ from traditional file system tools in that not only do they list the live files, they also list the deleted files, and even list the file system structures. The final four entries in the output in Listing 4.17 are file system structures: $MBR, $FAT1 and $FAT2. The $OrphanFiles directory is a location used by Sleuth Kit to list deleted files in the file system for which no parent directory can found. These files cannot be placed in the file system hierarchy so are placed in this directory instead.

By default the **fls** command lists only those files in the root directory. In order to list all files the command must be made recursive. This is achieved using **-r**, the effect of which is shown in Listing 4.18.

```
$ fls -r mnt/ewf1
r/r 3: FAT_FS (Volume Label Entry)
d/d 5: Files
+ r/r * 134: delete.txt
r/r 7: info.txt
r/r 9: cliffs.jpg
r/r 12: thelongbridge.jpg
v/v 16743939: $MBR
v/v 16743940: $FAT1
v/v 16743941: $FAT2
V/V 16743942: $OrphanFiles
```

Listing 4.18 Using **fls** to recursively list all content in **FAT32_V2.E01**.

Examine the underlined entries in Listing 4.18. **Files** represents a directory (denoted by d/d) while **delete.txt** represents a file (denoted by r/r). The **delete.txt** entry is inside the **Files** directory (denoted by the + symbol). The **delete.txt** file is also deleted (denoted by *). Each of the items has a unique identifying number associated with it (**Files** is 5 and **delete.txt** is 134). How these numbers are determined is dependent on the file system in question.

By default when Sleuth Kit is run it lists the contents of the root directory. However running a command such as: **fls mnt/ewf1** 5 will list the contents of the **Files** directory. There are many further options for **fls** which can be discovered in the **man** pages.

4.5.1.4 Recover File Metadata

Metadata can be recovered using Sleuth Kit's **istat** command. The **istat** command requires the offset to the start of the file system and also the metadata address of the item in question. The output from **istat** is dependent on the file system in question.

Listing 4.19 shows the **istat** command required to view metadata for the file **delete.txt** on **FAT32_V2.E01**. The output has been truncated for presentation purposes.

```
$ istat mnt/ewf1 134
Directory Entry: 134
Not Allocated
File Attributes: File, Archive
Size: 44
Name: _ELETE.TXT

Directory Entry Times:
Written: 2023-10-27 11:45:16 (IST)
Accessed: 2023-10-27 00:00:00 (IST)
Created: 2023-10-27 11:45:16 (IST)

Sectors:
2608 0 0 0 0 0 0 0
```

Listing 4.19 The output from Sleuthkit's **istat** command when run on metadata address 134 (**delete.txt**) in **FAT32_V2.E01**.

4.5.1.5 Recover File Content

The final task that is necessary is that of file content recovery. Sleuth Kit provides the **icat** command to achieve this. The syntax is identical to that of **istat**, an offset is specified (if required), along with the metadata address. Listing 4.20 shows the recovery of **delete.txt**. Notice how the output is redirected to a local file.

```
$ icat mnt/ewf1 134 > delete.txt
$ file delete.txt
delete.txt: ASCII text
$ cat delete.txt
This file will be deleted in FAT32_V2.E01.
```

Listing 4.20 Using **icat** to recover the content of **delete.txt** (metadata address 134) in **FAT32_V2.E01**.

4.5.1.6 Other TSK Commands

Sleuth Kit provides other helpful commands for file system forensics. These include the ability to generate timelines, to extract unallocated space and to automate certain recovery tasks.

Timelines are often of vital importance in file system forensics. Sleuth Kit provides the **mactime** command which can be used to create a timeline which can be viewed in any spreadsheet application. This is achieved using: **fls -m '/' mnt/ewf1 | mactime -b - -d > timeline.csv**. The **-m** option for **fls** causes Sleuth Kit to create a body file, with each file/directory name being prefixed by /. This can then be read by the **mactime** command using **-b** - to specify that the body file should be taken from STDIN (-). The use of **-d** causes mactime to output in a format where dates can be used directly in a spreadsheet, thereby improving the analysis potential.

The **blkls** command is used to extract all unallocated sectors from an image. These sectors are not part of any file system structure; however, they may contain old files/metadata structures which may be of interest.

Finally Sleuth Kit provides a command to automate file recovery. The **icat** command used on all files would be very inefficient. TSK provides the **tsk_recover** command which, by default, will recover all deleted files in the file system. Listing 4.21 shows this command being used firstly to recover deleted files (and store them in a directory called recovered), and secondly using the **-e** option to recover all files.

```
$ tsk_recover mnt/ewf1 recovered/
Files Recovered: 1
$
$ tsk_recover -e mnt/ewf1 recovered/
Files Recovered: 4
```

Listing 4.21 Using **tsk_recover** to recover deleted files and all files.

Throughout the remainder of this book TSK will be used to confirm the results of manual analysis of those file systems that are supported by the tool. Sleuth Kit currently supports FAT (Chapter 5), ExFAT (Chapter 6), NTFS (Chapter 7), EXT (Chapters 8 and 9) and HFS+ (Chapter 12). Sleuth Kit version 4.11 (the current version at the time of writing) does not support the remaining file systems in this book.

4.5.2 Data Carving

File system forensics is the most effective means of recovering data from an electronic storage device. The main reason for this is that it recovers both the file's content and its metadata. However, in certain circumstances the file's metadata has been overwritten but the actual content is still present on the device. The lack of metadata means that the file's content can no longer be located using file system forensic tools. However, a technique called data carving may still work.

Carving exploits the structure of certain file types, searching the disk for the particular signatures of each type of file. Consider a JPEG file, the first and last bytes of which are shown in Listing 4.22.

```
[[First Line]]
00000: ffd8 ffe0 0010 4a46 4946 0001 0100 0001  ......JFIF......
[[Final Line]]
09e40: 47b7 6163 ffd9                           G.ac..
```

Listing 4.22 Raw hex representation of a JPEG file showing the start and end signatures of the file.

The signature value for JPEG files is two-fold. Every JPEG starts with the hex values 0xFFD8[15] and ends with the hex values 0xFFD9. Data carving algorithms work by scanning the disk looking

15 The signature is actually more complex than this. The subsequent bytes distinguish the exact JPEG version used but every JPEG signature begins with 0xFFD8.

for these starting signatures. Once a signature, such as 0xFFD8 is located, the carving system will read forward from that point until it encounters an 0xFFD9 value signifying the potential end of the file's contents.

Data carving is not a fully reliable technique as it results in a certain number of false-positive results. For instance it is possible to locate the hex values 0xFFD8 which are not the start of a valid JPEG file but merely random data.

Rather than searching every single byte on a drive for starting signatures, carving algorithms tend to look at sector boundaries. All file systems use the cluster (or block) as the basic storage units. The start of a file will always appear at the beginning of a cluster. While it might not be possible to determine the cluster size on a device on which carving is being performed, in all file system clusters are formed from a number of sectors. Hence examining every sector boundary for signatures is normally the preferred method. This greatly improves the efficiency of carving algorithms and limits the number of false positives.

Certain carving tools will take certain file system knowledge into account. For instance the ext family of file systems are further broken into block groups, each of which acts as a mini-file system (Chapter 8). Some carving tools (e.g. **photorec**) can exploit this structure and as such will attempt to determine if the underlying file system might be ext.

Common open source carving tools include **photorec**, **scalpel** and **foremost**. All of these can be installed from the standard Linux repositories.[16] Generally all digital forensic software suites can perform data carving.

4.6 Summary

This chapter examined some of the basic concepts that are necessary for file system forensics. In order to process a file system it is necessary to know how data is organised on disk. This organisation is both physical and logical. Physically information can be stored using magnetic charge, surface pits or electrical charge. Information can be accessed through magnetic or optical readers involving spinning platters or electronically in the case of modern storage devices.

However, the logical organisation is more important for file system forensics. This includes the partitioning structures on disk and also the file system itself. This governs how information can be located on disk and maps the logical and physical addresses, allowing forensic tools to recover information.

Subsequent sections of this book will examine actual file systems in detail. The remainder of this book is divided into three main parts covering Windows, Linux and Apple file systems.

Exercises

1 Both **mmls** and **fdisk/gdisk** display the partition table contents. In your opinion which of these is the best tool to use for digital forensics? Justify your opinion.

2 What challenges will the increased use of solid-state drives (SSDs) have for digital forensics?

3 Physical acquisition is considered best practice in digital forensics. In what situations would logical acquisition be considered?

---

16 Note that **photorec** is available as part of the **testdisk** package on Linux systems.

Bibliography

Akbal, E., Yakut, Ö.F., Dogan, S. et al. (2021). A digital forensics approach for lost secondary partition analysis using master boot record structured hard disk drives. *Sakarya University Journal of Computer and Information Sciences* 4 (3): 326–346.

Al, S.G. (2016). Analyzing master boot record for forensic investigations. *International Journal of Applied Information Systems* 10: 22–26.

Alherbawi, N., Shukur, Z., and Sulaiman, R. (2016). A survey on data carving in digital forensic. *Asian Journal of Information Technology* 15 (24): 5137–5144.

Arpaci-Dusseau, R.H. (2018). *Operating Systems: Three Easy Pieces*. Scott's Valley, CA: Createspace https://pages.cs.wisc.edu/remzi/OSTEP/.

Carrier, B. (2005). *File System Forensic Analysis*. Boston, MA; London: Addison-Wesley.

Dani, A., Mangade, S., Nimbalkar, P., and Shirwadkar, H. (2024). Next4: Snapshots in Ext4 File System. arXiv preprint arXiv:2403.06790.

Davis, K., Peabody, B., and Leach, P. (2024). RFC 9562: Universally Unique IDentifiers (UUIDs). https://doi.org/10.17487/RFC9562.

Jeong, D. and Lee, S. (2019). Forensic signature for tracking storage devices: analysis of UEFI firmware image, disk signature and windows artifacts. *Digital Investigation* 29: 21–27.

Kasampalis, S. (2010). Copy on write based file systems performance analysis and implementation. M.Sc Dissertation. Technical University of Denmark, 94p.

Nelius, J. (2020). What's the difference between flash and SSD storage? PC Gamer. https://www.pcgamer.com/whats-the-difference-between-flash-and-ssd-storage/ (accessed 12 August 2024).

Nikkel, B.J. (2009). Forensic analysis of GPT disks and GUID partition tables. *Digital Investigation* 6 (1–2): 39–47.

Nikkel, B. (2016). *Practical Forensic Imaging: Securing Digital Evidence with Linux Tools*. San Francisco, CA: No Starch Press.

Rodeh, O., Bacik, J., and Mason, C. (2013). BTRFS: The Linux B-tree filesystem. *ACM Transactions on Storage* 9 (3): 1–32.

Seppanen, E., O'Keefe, M.T., and Lilja, D.J. (2010). High performance solid state storage under Linux. In: *IEEE 26th Symposium on Mass Storage Systems and Technologies (MSST)*, 1–12. Lake Tahoe, Nevada: IEEE.

Techopedia.com (2019). What is a File System? - Definition from Techopedia [Internet]. Techopedia.com. https://www.techopedia.com/definition/5510/file-system (accessed 12 August 2024).

Vieyra, J., Scanlon, M., and Le-Khac, N.A. (2018). Solid state drive forensics: where do we stand? In: *Digital Forensics and Cyber Crime: 10th International EAI Conference*, ICDF2C 2018 (10–12 September 2018) Proceedings 10 2019, 149–164. New Orleans, LA, USA: Springer International Publishing.

Yang, X.X. (2013). Programming for I/O and storage. In: *Software Engineering for Embedded Systems*, 817–877. Elsevier B.V.

Part II

Windows File Systems

5

The FAT File System

The File Allocation Table file system, or FAT as it is more commonly known, is an old file system that still finds regular use today. The file system was named for its main organisational unit, which is also called the File Allocation Table. The original version of the FAT file system was developed for floppy disks in 1977. Since this time there have been three major versions of FAT: FAT12, FAT16 and FAT32. There have also been a number of minor variants of most of the main FAT versions. The versions differ mainly in the size of addressable space available. There are 2_d^{12} addresses in FAT12, 2_d^{16} in FAT16 and 2_d^{28} in FAT32.

FAT was commonly encountered on removable media (i.e. USB devices, cameras, etc.) and as such the file system is supported by default on all major operating systems. In recent years the ExFAT file system[1] is beginning to replace FAT as the standard on removable media but the FAT file system is still in common usage (embedded devices, UEFI boot systems, older removable media, etc.).

FAT was the traditional Windows file system before the advent of NTFS (Chapter 7). While NTFS was first released in 1993 and very soon became standard on the Windows NT family of operating systems, it was only in 2001, with the release of Windows XP, that NTFS became the standard file system on home PCs.

Traditionally FAT filenames were in the 8.3 format. That is, an eight-letter filename, followed by a three-letter extension. With the advent of long file names (LFNs), which could be overlaid on all FAT variants, filenames were limited to a much larger 255_d characters. The file system records the creation and modification dates and times and the access date by default. No access time or metadata change date or times are recorded.

Throughout this chapter the FAT32 variant is discussed but all variants are very similar in structure. The ability to analyse one will allow the analyst to very quickly analyse any of the variants. FAT32 is chosen as the target in this chapter as it is the most likely variant to be encountered.

5.1 On-Disk Structures

In this section some of the important on-disk structures in the FAT file system are analysed. The section begins with an overview of the organisation of a FAT formatted volume and what structures are expected to appear. Each of these structures is then discussed in more detail in the subsequent sections. It should be noted at this point that, unless stated otherwise, all data in the FAT file system is stored in little-endian format.

1 ExFAT is considered a variant of the FAT file system, but is sufficiently more advanced that it is discussed in a separate chapter (Chapter 6).

File System Forensics, First Edition. Fergus Toolan.

Figure 5.1 The layout of the FAT file system.

5.1.1 Layout

The FAT file system contains three main areas of interest which are summarised in Figure 5.1. The reserved area contains file system information (FSINFO). In FAT12 and FAT16 this area generally occupies only a single sector (although this should be confirmed prior to analysis). In FAT32 this area contains more information and consequently is always larger.

The reserved area in all variants of FAT contains a volume boot record (VBR) in sector 0 (Section 5.1.2). In FAT32 this is generally followed by a FSINFO structure (Section 5.1.3). FAT32 also often contains a backup of these structures. This means that the FAT32 reserved area is generally much larger than that of FAT12 and FAT16.

Following the reserved area the FAT table itself is found. Generally there are two copies of this table as it is of such great importance in the FAT file system. The FAT tables allow the file content to be recovered from disk and also allow empty clusters to be identified when allocating space for new files.

The final area of the FAT file system is that of the data area. In this area all files/directories are found. Traditionally (i.e. FAT12 and FAT16) the beginning of the data area always contains the root directory structure from which the contents of the entire file system can be listed. In FAT32 the root directory is no longer guaranteed to appear at the very beginning of the data area; instead, it can be found anywhere inside the data area. Its location is found in the VBR (although it is still commonly found at the beginning of the data area).

5.1.2 Volume Boot Record

The VBR, also called the boot sector, is contained in sector 0 of the volume. This structure contains information about the file system as a whole. The Sleuth Kit tool, **fsstat**, extensively consults this structure in order to gather information about the file system. Tables 5.1 and 5.2 provide information about this structure. Table 5.1 provides information about the first 36_d bytes in the VBR which are common to all FAT file system variants. Table 5.2 contains information about the subsequent bytes in the structure as found in a FAT32 volume. The bytes at offset 510_d and 511_d (i.e. the final two bytes in sector 0) must always have the values 0x55 and 0xAA, respectively. This is identical to the final two bytes in the master boot record (MBR) sector.

Processing the VBR allows all other structures to be located. For instance the FSINFO structure and the VBR backup are located directly from the primary VBR. FAT 0 begins after the reserved area and its size is determined from the VBR. This is followed by FAT 1 which is the same size as FAT 0. FAT 1 is followed by the data area. The root directory's starting cluster is also located in the VBR. Later the conversion of cluster to physical byte offset is shown (Section 5.1.7).

5.1.3 File System Information (FSINFO)

The FSINFO structure is an optional structure in FAT32, the location of which is found in the VBR itself. This structure is used to optimise space allocation for new files. The structure of FSINFO is provided in Table 5.3. As its purpose is space allocation the information contained in this structure is mainly related to free clusters on the device. From a file system forensics perspective the FSINFO structure is not of vital importance.

Table 5.1 Common FAT VBR structure.

Offset	Size	Name	Description
0x00	0x03	Jump	Instruction to jump to boot code.
0x03	0x08	OEM Name	The OEM Name (ASCII). This is also called the volume label.
0x0B	0x02	Sector Size	The size of each sector in bytes (must be power of 2 between 2^9 and 2^{12}).
0x0D	0x01	Cluster Size	The number of sectors in each cluster.
0x0E	0x02	Reserved Area	The size of the reserved area in sectors.
0x10	0x01	# FATs	The number of File Allocation Table (FAT) structures present in the file system.
0x11	0x02	Max. # Files	The maximum number of files allowed in the root directory in FAT12/FAT16. This value is generally 0x00 in FAT32.
0x13	0x02	# Sectors	The total number of sectors in the file system if less than 2^{16}. If larger than 2^{16} sectors the four bytes at 0x20 are used instead and this value is zero.
0x15	0x01	Media Type	0xF8 for a fixed disk, 0xF0 for a removable disk.
0x16	0x02	FAT Size	In FAT12 and FAT16 this contains the size of each FAT structure in sectors. In FAT32 this field has a value of 0x00.
0x18	0x02	Sectors/Track	The number of sectors/track on the storage device.
0x1A	0x02	# Heads	The number of heads on the underlying storage device.
0x1C	0x04	Sector Offset	The offset in sectors to the start of this file system on the device.
0x20	0x04	# Sectors	The total number of sectors on the device. Used if the two bytes at offset 0x13 are not large enough to store the value. Only one of these fields will ever be used the other will be zero.

Table 5.2 Extended FAT VBR structure (FAT32).

Offset	Size	Name	Description
0x24	0x04	FAT Size	The size of each FAT structure in sectors.
0x28	0x02	FAT Write	Describes how the FAT structures are written. If bit 7 is set then only one structure is active (bits 0–3 describe which FAT is active); otherwise, all FATS are mirrored.
0x2A	0x02	Version	The major/minor version numbers.
0x2C	0x04	Root Directory	The first cluster of the root directory structure.
0x30	0x02	FSINFO Sector	The sector at which the FSINFO structure is found. This is typically immediately after the VBR.
0x32	0x02	VBR Backup	The sector at which the backup copy of the VBR is found (typically 0x06).
0x34	0x0C	Reserved	Zero'd.
0x40	0x01	OS Specific	OS-specific field related to booting.
0x41	0x01	Unused	Unused, typically 0x00.
0x42	0x01	Signature	Signature value of 0x29, if set the next three fields are valid.
0x43	0x04	Serial Number	Volume serial number.
0x47	0x0B	Volume Label	The Volume Label in ASCII.
0x52	0x08	FS Type	The file system type (e.g. FAT32 – but nothing is required in this field).

Table 5.3 The FSINFO structure.

Offset	Size	Name	Description
0x00	0x04	Signature	0x41615252.
0x04	0x1E0	Unused	Unused.
0x1E4	0x04	Signature	0x61417272.
0x1E8	0x04	# Free Clusters	The number of free clusters on the device.
0x1EC	0x04	Next Free Cluster	The next free cluster on the device.
0x1F0	0x0C	Unused	Unused.
0x1FC	0x04	Signature	End of sector signature (0xAA550000).

5.1.4 File Allocation Table

The File Allocation Table (FAT) is of such vital importance to the FAT file system that the file system was named after this structure. The File Allocation Table serves two purposes. Firstly it acts as an allocation bitmap (although it uses more than a single bit per cluster) to allow efficient discovery of a cluster's allocation status. Secondly it allows the next allocated cluster in a file/directory to be located. The starting cluster of a file/directory is located in the directory entry (Section 5.1.5) while subsequent clusters are found in the FAT structures.

Due to its importance there are typically two FAT structures present in most FAT file systems (although this should always be confirmed in the VBR). Each cluster is represented by one entry in the FAT table. The size of each entry is dependent on the version of FAT being used. In the FAT12 file system, 12 bits are used for each entry; in FAT16, 16 bits are used; and in FAT32, 32 bits are being used.[2] The name of the file system variant is actually derived from the number of bits used to represent a cluster in the FAT table.

Each cluster in the file system is given a value in the FAT table. A value of 0x00000000 (in FAT32) means that the cluster is unallocated. Any value greater than 0x0FFFFFF8 generally signifies an end of file marker, while a value of 0x0FFFFFF7 signifies a cluster which contains one or more damaged sectors. The first cluster number in a FAT file system is 2_d. This means that the first two entries in the FAT table are not used in the same manner as the others. They can be used for other storage purposes. Officially, cluster 0_d is used to show the media type. The least significant byte is the same as that found in the boot sector while the remaining 20_d bits are set to one. This gives a value of 0x0FFFFFF8 for fixed media. The second cluster stores the end of chain marker although it would appear that any value above 0x0FFFFFF7 is accepted as the end of chain marker.

Consider a file that occupies three clusters in the file system (clusters 3, 6 and 4). Listing 5.1 shows an excerpt from this FAT structure. The three clusters of interest are underlined. In order to recover the file content the starting cluster is first determined to be 3_d from the Directory Entry (Section 5.1.5). The entry for cluster 3_d in the FAT table is then consulted. The value at this location is 0x06. This means that the next cluster in the chain is Cluster 6_d. Consulting this position in the FAT shows that the next cluster in the file's content is 4_d. When the entry for cluster 4_d is examined the end of file marker (0x0FFFFFFF) is discovered. This signifies the end of the FAT chain. Combining this information shows that the file's contents occupy clusters 3, 6 and 4.

2 Strictly speaking only 28 bits of the 32 are used for addressing in FAT32!

```
00000: f8ff ff0f ffff ff0f f8ff ff0f 0600 0000 ................
00010: ffff ff0f 0000 0000 0400 0000 0800 0000 ................
00020: 0900 0000 0a00 0000 0b00 0000 0c00 0000 ................
```

Listing 5.1 Sample FAT32 FAT table showing a file stored in clusters 3, 6 and 4.

Listing 5.1 also shows how file fragmentation is handled in FAT file systems. The fact that directory entries store only the starting cluster requires the FAT table to be consulted in every case in order to determine the subsequent clusters in the chain. Hence, in the FAT file system, there is no difference in how contiguous and fragmented files are recovered. In every case[3] the starting cluster is identified in the directory entry and the FAT chain is then extracted from the FAT table.

5.1.5 Directory Entries

Directories in the FAT file system are merely normal files which contain a sequence of directory entries as content. A directory entry is a 32_d byte structure that contains the file's name and all metadata associated with the file. The directory entry structure is of vital importance in FAT forensics. It allows the files on the volume to be listed, file metadata to be gathered and file content to be recovered.

There are two types of directory entry that are used in FAT. Every file in the FAT file system will have one of these structures. Table 5.4 shows the structure of the generic directory entry. However, this structure is limited in filename length, allowing only for 8.3 filenames. Hence there is a second type of directory entry called a LFN directory entry. This structure is shown in Table 5.6. It allows for filename length greater than the traditional 8.3 format.

There are some points to note about the FAT directory entry structure. Firstly, 32_d bytes is not much space in which to store very detailed information about a file. If you compare the output of Sleuth Kit's **istat** command when run on a FAT file system to a more modern and complex file system you will see a large difference in the volume of reported information. Listing 5.2 shows an example of this with the output from both FAT32 and ext4 file systems. It is clear that ext4 contains more metadata information than FAT. There are four timestamps for instance and not just three that are found in FAT. The timestamps are more detailed in ext4 than in FAT, although in Listing 5.2 they have been truncated, providing nanosecond granularity, as opposed to two second granularity in FAT. Ext4 also provides a generation ID, UID, GID, mode and number of links, none of which FAT provides. However, there is one piece of information that FAT provides that is not present in the ext4 filesystem, at least not in the metadata structure, that is the filename. The key realisation when performing any file system forensic task is that all file systems are different. They all store different information. It is essential that analysts fully understand the information that it is possible to obtain from a particular file system and any limitations associated with that information.

Consider the output from **istat** when run on the FAT file system (Listing 5.2). There is potential confusion in the time stamp values. The file was both created and last written at 10:46:44 (UTC) on 1 November 2021. That is understandable. It would appear from these values that the file was created and then never modified after creation. However, confusion occurs when the last access time is considered. Sleuth Kit shows that the file was last accessed at 00:00:00 on 1 November 2021. That is over 10 hours *before* the file was created! Obviously something is wrong as a file

3 In the case of small files (i.e. files that require only a single cluster) it is unnecessary to consult FAT in order to recover the file.

Table 5.4 FAT generic directory entry structure.

Offset	Len.	Name	Description
0x00	0x08	File Name	The file name (the 8 of the 8.3 naming scheme). In the case of filenames shorter than eight bytes the remaining bytes are zero filled. If the first is 0xE5 or 0x00 then the directory entry is unallocated.
0x08	0x03	File Extension	The file extension (the 3 of the 8.3 naming scheme).
0x0B	0x01	Flags	Bitmask flags representing the file attributes (see Table 5.5).
0x0C	0x01	Reserved	Reserved.
0x0D	0x01	Creation Time (10^{-1}s)	Subsecond component of the creation time. Valid values are in the range 0_d–199_d.
0x0E	0x02	Creation Time	FAT time structure representing the creation time (Section 5.1.6).
0x10	0x02	Creation Date	FAT date structure representing the creation date (Section 5.1.6).
0x12	0x02	Access Date	FAT date structure representing the last accessed date (Section 5.1.6).
0x14	0x02	First Cluster (Hi)	The high two bytes of the address of the first cluster of the file's content. In FAT12 and FAT16 these are always zero.
0x16	0x02	Modification Time	FAT time structure representing the content modification time (Section 5.1.6).
0x18	0x02	Modification Date	FAT date structure representing the content modification date (Section 5.1.6).
0x1A	0x02	First Cluster (Lo)	The low two bytes of the address of the first cluster in the file's content. In FAT12/FAT16 these two bytes are all that is required. The higher bytes are never used.
0x1C	0x04	File Size	The size of the file in bytes (0 for directories).

Table 5.5 FAT flag values.

Value	Interpretation
0x01 (00000001_b)	Read-only
0x02 (00000010_b)	Hidden
0x04 (00000100_b)	System File
0x08 (00001000_b)	Volume Label
0x0F (00001111_b)	Long File Name
0x10 (00010000_b)	Directory
0x20 (00100000_b)	Archive

can't be accessed before it is created. Examine the information that is available in the generic FAT directory entry (Table 5.4) and in particular look at the date/time values that are available. While both creation and modification have both date and time values, the access value has only a date available. There is no access time structure in the FAT directory entry! Sleuth Kit (and many other tools) choose to display a value of 00:00:00, when in reality there is no value. It is hoped the reader

```
Directory Entry: 7
Allocated
File Attributes: File, Archive
Size: 94
Name: TEST.TXT

Directory Entry Times:
Written: 2021-11-01 10:46:44 (UTC)
Accessed: 2021-11-01 00:00:00 (UTC)
Created: 2021-11-01 10:46:44 (UTC)

Sectors:
4488 0 0 0 0 0 0 0
```

```
inode: 7604675
Allocated
Group: 928
Generation Id: 1508300432
uid / gid: 0 / 0
mode: rrw-r--r--
Flags: Extents,
size: 2121728
num of links: 1

Inode Times:
Accessed: 2021-11-01 12:23:..
File Modified: 2021-11-01 11:50:..
Inode Modified: 2021-11-01 11:50:..
File Created: 2021-11-01 11:23:..

Direct Blocks:
25645056 25645057 25645058 256450..
```

Listing 5.2 Differences in **istat** output between different file systems. The output on the left is from the FAT file system, while the right is from ext4 (Chapter 9). Note the ext4 timestamps have been truncated.

can see the potential issues if asked about this in court. It is the author's belief that doubt could be cast upon an *expert's* testimony by simply asking how the file was accessed before it was created. If the analyst is unaware of the FAT file system's stored data and how forensic tools report that data, the analyst would be unable to answer the question!

The LFN directory entry allows for filenames longer than the traditional 8.3 scheme. The structure of an LFN entry is shown in Table 5.6. Generally the LFN entries are found in reverse order *before* the actual directory entry itself. The sequence number is used to confirm the order of these entries. The sequence number of the last LFN for a file (generally the first directory entry to appear

Table 5.6 FAT LFN directory entry structure.

Offset	Size	Name	Description
0x00	0x01	Sequence	Sequence number of the LFN entry. If this value is 0xE5 or 0x00 the directory entry is unallocated.
0x01	0x0A	Filename (1–5)	Characters 1–5 of the filename. Note characters are stored in UTF-16 format.
0x0B	0x01	Flags	Flag containing file attributes (see Table 5.5). The value should always be 0x0F in the case of an LFN.
0x0C	0x01	Reserved	Reserved.
0x0D	0x01	Checksum	Checksum of the short name from the subsequent generic directory entry.
0x0E	0x0C	Filename (6–11)	Characters 6–11 of the filename.
0x1A	0x02	Reserved	Reserved – must be zero.
0x1C	0x04	Filename (12–13)	Characters 12–13 of the filename.

in the sequence of directory entries) is XOR'd with 0x40. Hence to get the actual value this must be reversed, i.e. XOR'd again with 0x40. Listing 5.3 shows an example of a file with a LFN (this file is in the **FAT32_V2.E01** disk image – see Section 5.2.2).

```
1040e0: 422e 006a 0070 0067 0000 000f 0052 ffff B..j.p.g.....R..
1040f0: ffff ffff ffff ffff ffff 0000 ffff ffff ................
104100: 0174 0068 0065 006c 006f 000f 0052 6e00 .t.h.e.l.o...Rn.
104110: 6700 6200 7200 6900 6400 0000 6700 6500 g.b.r.i.d...g.e.
104120: 5448 454c 4f4e 7e31 4a50 4720 006d 9764 THELON~1JPG .m.d
104130: 5b57 5b57 0000 9764 5b57 4500 de5a 0300 [W[W...d[WE..Z..
```

Listing 5.3 Three directory entries for a file with a long file name component. The first two entries are LFNs while the final entry is the generic directory entry.

In Listing 5.3 each of the LFN directory entries has a flag value of 0x0F (underlined). In each case the checksum value is 0xA0 showing the LFNs are most likely belonging to the same file (obviously with only a single byte checksum there is a large probability of collision occurring). The first byte in each of the entries represents the sequence. These bytes are 0x42 and 0x01. As stated previously the sequence byte in the first entry is XOR'd with 0x40 giving:

$$01000010 \oplus 01000000 = 00000010 = 0x02$$

This result shows the first LFN entry is the last part of the filename, sequence number 2. The name components of each of the LFN directories can be combined to give: **thelongbridge.jpg**.

5.1.6 FAT Date and Time

Section 3.4 introduced epoch time values, in which time is implemented in a computer as a counter from a particular moment. The FAT family of file systems is the only file system that does not use an epoch-based time system. Instead FAT uses bit fields to store the date and time.

The FAT date is a two-byte structure which is divided into three separate components, year, month and day. The bit field structure is shown in Figure 5.2. In this, the most significant seven bits are used to represent the year. This allows for $2^7 = 128_d$ possible values. Hence, FAT defines year 0 to be 1980. This means that 1980 must be added to this stored value to get the actual year. The next four bits represent the month and the final five bits represent the day.

To demonstrate the FAT date consider a value of 0x5361. This value is converted as follows:

		0x5361	
Binary		$0101\ 0011\ 0110\ 0001_b$	
Group	0101001_b	1011_b	00001_b
Convert	41_d	11_d	1_d
Y + 1980	2021_d	11_d	1_d

Hence the FAT date 0x5361 is actually 1 November 2021. The FAT time uses the same method of storage (Figure 5.3). Here the five most significant bits represent the hour while the next six

Y	Y	Y	Y	Y	Y	Y	M	M	M	M	D	D	D	D	D

Figure 5.2 The FAT date bit field structure.

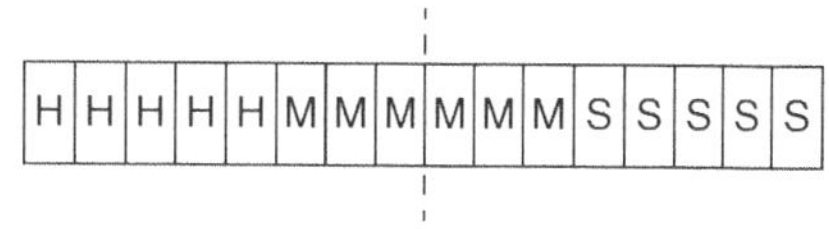

Figure 5.3 The FAT time bit field structure.

bits represent minutes. This leaves five bits to represent the seconds; however, this only provides $2^5 = 32_d$ possible values. As this is not sufficiently large to represent 60_d seconds, the FAT time actually records seconds divided by two!

Consider a recovered FAT Time value of 0x5DC5. Using the same method as shown for FAT date, this value is converted to a human-readable form.

		0x5DC5	
Binary		$0101\ 1101\ 1100\ 0101_b$	
Group	01011_b	101110_b	00101_b
Convert	11_d	46_d	5_d
S × 2	11_d	46_d	10_d

This results in a time value of 11:46:10 or 11:46:11.[4] The FAT time value that is stored in file systems is stored as local time, in other words, in the computer's timezone. This is unlike most modern file systems which generally store time as UTC.

5.1.7 Mapping Clusters to Sectors

It was mentioned previously that the clustering area in FAT begins in the data area (see Figure 5.1). The first cluster in the FAT file system is cluster 2_d. How are these cluster numbers mapped to sectors in the FAT file system? In order to determine the actual sector it is necessary to gather certain information from the VBR. This includes cluster size (C_{Size}); reserved area size (R_{Size}); FAT size (FAT_{Size}); and the number of FATs ($FAT_{\#}$).

The sector number, $S_{\#}$, corresponding to cluster number $C_{\#}$, is given by Equation 5.1.

$$S_{\#} = [(C_{\#} - 2) \times C_{Size}] + R_{Size} + (FAT_{\#} \times FAT_{Size}) \tag{5.1}$$

The value, $S_{\#}$, is the physical sector number in the file system, which is then multiplied by the sector size to obtain the actual byte offset in the file system.

5.2 Analysis of FAT32

In this section the analysis of the FAT32 file system is discussed. The section begins by providing information on how FAT32 file systems are created and is followed by a brief description of the file systems that are provided for analysis in the remainder of this chapter.

5.2.1 Creating FAT32 File Systems

A FAT32 file system can be created on all operating systems. In the Linux terminal the command to create FAT32 file systems is given in Listing 5.4 where *dev_id* is the device identifier (e.g. **/dev/sdc2**).[5]

4 There is no fractional component allowed in this value; hence, $\frac{10}{2} = \frac{11}{2} = 5$.
5 Caution: Executing this command will overwrite any previously existing file system in the partition.

```
mkfs.vfat -F 32 -n "FAT_FS" dev_id
```

Listing 5.4 Using **mkfs** to create a FAT32 file system.

The **mkfs.vfat** command creates a FAT file system. The file system type (i.e. FAT12, FAT16 or FAT32) is specified by the **-F** flag. If omitted **mkfs.vfat** will pick the variant most appropriate to the partition size. The command in Listing 5.4 also specifies the file system name (FAT_FS) using the **-n** flag.

5.2.2 Supplied FAT32 Image Files

A number of disk images are analysed during this chapter. These are available from the book's website and are summarised in Table 5.7. Listing 5.5 shows the files/directories present in **FAT32_V1.E01**. To create **FAT32_V2.E01 Files/delete.txt** was deleted, **Files/thelongbridge.jpg** was created and the file **info.txt** was replaced with an updated version.

```
/-- Files
     /-- delete.txt
/-- info.txt
/-- cliffs.jpg
```

Listing 5.5 File listing of the initial version of the FAT32 file system used in this chapter.

5.2.3 FAT32 Manual Analysis

In order to fully understand the FAT32 file system this section will introduce the reader to the manual analysis of the file system. There are a number of steps which need to be taken in order to successfully analyse a FAT32 file system. These are:

1. **Process the VBR:** The VBR is processed in order to determine the layout of the device. During this process it is necessary to determine the location of the reserved area, the FAT area and the data area. Additionally the location of the root directory is required.
2. **Process the Root Directory:** The root directory is processed beginning with the Volume Label entry and continuing with the files in the root directory itself.
3. **Process Subdirectories:** Any directories that are identified in the root directory are processed in the same manner as the root directory. Once all directories have been processed the file system's contents have been listed.

Table 5.7 Supplied image files available from the book's website.

Value	Interpretation
FAT32_V1.E01	A basic FAT32 file system with three files and one directory.
FAT32_V2.E01	This is **FAT32_V1.E01** with the file **delete.txt** deleted, and a new file called **thelongbridge.jpg** added.
FAT32_V3.E01	This file system is used in the chapter exercises.

4. **Recover Metadata/Content:** Finally the file metadata and content is recovered from the file system.

In the following sections these steps are presented in more detail using **FAT32_V1.E01** as an exemplar.

5.2.3.1 Process the VBR

Analysing a FAT file system begins by processing the VBR. The type of information that is sought is shown in the output from the Sleuth Kit's **fsstat** command. The **fsstat** tool processes more than just the VBR, it also looks at the FSINFO structure (Section 5.1.3) and the volume label in the root directory. In this section the necessary information in the VBR and FSINFO structures is processed. Listing 5.6 shows the output of **fsstat** on **FAT_V1.E01**.

```
FILE SYSTEM INFORMATION
--------------------------------------------
File System Type: FAT32

OEM Name: mkfs.fat
Volume ID: 0x2232cfe0
Volume Label (Boot Sector): FAT_FS
Volume Label (Root Directory): FAT_FS
File System Type Label: FAT32
Next Free Sector (FS Info): 2608
Free Sector Count (FS Info): 1045960

Sectors before file system: 2048

File System Layout (in sectors)
Total Range: 0 - 1048575
* Reserved: 0 - 31
** Boot Sector: 0
** FS Info Sector: 1
** Backup Boot Sector: 6
* FAT 0: 32 - 1055
* FAT 1: 1056 - 2079
* Data Area: 2080 - 1048575
** Cluster Area: 2080 - 1048575
*** Root Directory: 2080 - 2087

METADATA INFORMATION
--------------------------------------------
Range: 2 - 16743942
Root Directory: 2

CONTENT INFORMATION
--------------------------------------------
Sector Size: 512
Cluster Size: 4096
Total Cluster Range: 2 - 130813
```

Listing 5.6 Partial output from **fsstat** on **FAT32_V1.E01**.

```
000000: eb58 906d 6b66 732e 6661 7400 0208 2000 .X.mkfs.fat... .
000010: 0200 0000 00f8 0000 3f00 ff00 0008 0000 ........?.......
000020: 0000 1000 0004 0000 0000 0000 0200 0000 ................
000030: 0100 0600 0000 0000 0000 0000 0000 0000 ................
000040: 8000 29e0 cf32 2246 4154 5f46 5320 2020 ..)..2"FAT_FS
000050: 2020 4641 5433 3220 2020 0e1f be77 7cac   FAT32    ..w..
000060: 22c0 740b 56b4 0ebb 0700 cd10 5eeb f032 ".t.V.......^..2
```

Listing 5.7 Excerpt from the VBR in **FAT32_V1.E01**.

Table 5.8 Partially processed VBR from **FAT32_V1.E01**.

Offset	Size	Name	Value
0x0B	0x02	Sector Size	0x200 (512_d)
0x0D	0x01	Cluster Size	0x08 (8_d)
0x0E	0x02	Reserved Area	0x20 (32_d)
0x10	0x01	# FATS	0x02 (2_d)
0x24	0x04	FAT Size	0x400 (1024_d)
0x2C	0x04	Root Dir. Cluster	0x02 (2_d)

To perform an analysis of the FAT file system the following information must be obtained: sector size; cluster size; reserved area size; number of FATs; FAT size; and the starting cluster of the root directory.

Listing 5.7 shows the contents of the VBR in **FAT32_V1.E01**. The above values from this VBR are found in Table 5.8. The processing of the remaining VBR structure is left as an exercise for the reader.

Table 5.8 provides sufficient information to map the entire file system. The reserved area is 32_d sectors in size. This is followed by 2_d FAT tables, each of which is 1024_d sectors. The data area is found directly after this beginning at sector 2080_d (i.e. $32_d + 1024_d + 1024_d$).

The final task is to locate the root directory itself. Table 5.8 shows the starting cluster of the root directory to be cluster 2_d. Using this value, and those in Table 5.8, in Equation 5.1 gives:

$$S_{\#} = ((2-2)\times 8) + 32 + (2\times 1024) = 2080_d$$

This result means that the root directory is located at the very start of the data area, in sector 2080_d. For the purposes of analysing this file system one cluster is sufficient. It may be necessary in other file systems to follow a FAT chain in the FAT table from cluster 2_d to determine if more clusters are required.

5.2.3.2 Process the Root Directory

Once the root directory has been located the next step is to process it. Listing 5.8 shows the contents of the root directory. The first entry in the root directory is the volume label. This is followed by LFN and generic directory entries. The generic entries are underlined in Listing 5.8.

Table 5.9 shows some of the processed values of the generic directory entries in the root directory. From this it is seen that there is one directory (**Files**) and two files in the root directory of this file system. Notice that by processing the generic directory entries the file metadata is also recovered. The only structure remaining to be processed is the volume label (shown in Section 5.3.2).

```
104000: 4641 545f 4653 2020 2020 2008 0000 4d65 FAT_FS ...Me
104010: 5b57 5b57 0000 4d65 5b57 0000 0000 0000 [W[W..Me[W......
104020: 4146 0069 006c 0065 0073 000f 0079 0000 AF.i.l.e.s...y..
104030: ffff ffff ffff ffff ffff 0000 ffff ffff ................
104040: 4649 4c45 5320 2020 2020 2010 004e a85d FILES ..N.]
104050: 5b57 5b57 0000 a85d 5b57 0300 0000 0000 [W[W...][W......
104060: 4169 006e 0066 006f 002e 000f 00d8 7400 Ai.n.f.o......t.
104070: 7800 7400 0000 ffff ffff 0000 ffff ffff x.t.............
104080: 494e 464f 2020 2020 5458 5420 005e 885d INFO TXT .^.]
104090: 5b57 5b57 0000 885d 5b57 0400 8f00 0000 [W[W...][W......
1040a0: 4163 006c 0069 0066 0066 000f 00e2 7300 Ac.l.i.f.f....s.
1040b0: 2e00 6a00 7000 6700 0000 0000 ffff ffff ..j.p.g.........
1040c0: 434c 4946 4653 2020 4a50 4720 0070 985d CLIFFS JPG .p.]
1040d0: 5b57 5b57 0000 985d 5b57 0500 eae9 0300 [W[W...][W......
```

Listing 5.8 The contents of the root directory in **FAT32_V1.E01**. The first entry is the volume label, underlined entries are generic directory entries. The remaining entries are LFNs.

Table 5.9 Processed generic root directory entries in **FAT32_V1.E01**.

Offset	Size	Name	Entry 1	Entry 2	Entry 3
0x00	0x0B	File name	**FILES**	**INFO.TXT**	**CLIFFS.JPG**
0x0B	0x01	Flags	0x10	0x20	0x20
0x0C	0x01	Reserved	0x00	0x00	0x00
0x0D	0x01	Creation Time (10^{-1} s)	0x4E	0x5E	0x70
0x0E	0x02	Creation Time	0x5DA8	0x5D88	0x5D98
0x10	0x02	Creation Date	0x575B	0x575B	0x575B
0x12	0x02	Access Date	0x575B	0x575B	0x575B
0x14	0x02	First Cluster (hi)	0x00	0x00	0x00
0x16	0x02	Modification Time	0x5DA8	0x5D88	0x5D98
0x18	0x02	Modification Date	0x575B	0x575B	0x575B
0x1A	0x02	First Cluster (Lo)	0x03	0x04	0x05
0x1C	0x04	File Size	0x00	0x8F	0x3E9EA

5.2.3.3 Process Sub-directories

The next step in the analysis of the FAT file system is to process all the sub-directories. Sub-directories are identical to the root directory in structure (except that they will not have a volume label entry). Hence all sub-directories can be processed in the same manner as the root directory. Once all sub-directories have been processed the listing of all files in the file system is complete.

5.2.3.4 Recover Metadata/Content

The final step in the analysis of the FAT file system is to recover the file metadata and content. Processing directories has a very desirable side effect for metadata recovery. As all metadata is stored in the directory entries, by processing these entries metadata is also recovered. The information provided in Table 5.9 contains all of the file/directory metadata for the files/directories in the root directory.

In order to recover the file content it is also necessary to refer to Table 5.9. Consider the file **INFO.TXT**. The first cluster of this file is 0x04 (4_d) and it is 0x8F (143_d) bytes in size. Cluster 4_d is found in sector number:

$$S_{\#} = ((4 - 2) \times 8) + 32 + (2 \times 1024) = 2096_d$$

Listing 5.9 shows 0x8F bytes at sector number 2096_d.

```
$ xxd -s $((512 * 2096)) -l $((0x8F)) mnt/ewf1
106000: 5468 6973 2069 7320 6120 4641 5433 3220 This is a FAT32
106010: 6669 6c65 2073 7973 7465 6d20 636f 6e74 file system cont
106020: 6169 6e69 6e67 2074 6872 6565 2066 696c aining three fil
106030: 6573 2061 6e64 206f 6e65 2064 6972 6563 es and one direc
106040: 746f 7279 2e20 0a54 6865 2066 696c 6573 tory. .The files
106050: 2069 6e63 6c75 6465 3a0a 0a2f 2d20 4669 include:../- Fi
106060: 6c65 730a 2020 202f 2d20 6465 6c65 7465 les.   /- delete
106070: 2e74 7874 0a2f 2d20 696e 666f 2e74 7874 .txt./- info.txt
106080: 0a2f 2d20 636c 6966 6673 2e6a 7067 0a   ./- cliffs.jpg.
```

Listing 5.9 The content of sector 2096_d, i.e. **INFO.TXT**.

But what about a larger file? **INFO.TXT** was only 143_d bytes in size, much smaller than a single cluster. What about a file such as **CLIFFS.JPG** which is 0x3E9EA ($256,490_d$) bytes beginning in cluster 0x05 (5_d)? As this is much larger than the cluster size (4096_d bytes) multiple clusters must be used. The directory entry provides only the first cluster. In this case the FAT table is consulted. Listing 5.10 shows an excerpt from the FAT table for this file system. From this, the value in cluster

```
004000: f8ff ff0f ffff ff0f f8ff ff0f ffff ff0f ................
004010: ffff ff0f 0600 0000 0700 0000 0800 0000 ................
004020: 0900 0000 0a00 0000 0b00 0000 0c00 0000 ................
004030: 0d00 0000 0e00 0000 0f00 0000 1000 0000 ................
004040: 1100 0000 1200 0000 1300 0000 1400 0000 ................
004050: 1500 0000 1600 0000 1700 0000 1800 0000 ................
004060: 1900 0000 1a00 0000 1b00 0000 1c00 0000 ................
004070: 1d00 0000 1e00 0000 1f00 0000 2000 0000 ............ ...
004080: 2100 0000 2200 0000 2300 0000 2400 0000 !..."...#...$...
004090: 2500 0000 2600 0000 2700 0000 2800 0000 %...&...'...(...
0040a0: 2900 0000 2a00 0000 2b00 0000 2c00 0000 )...*...+...,...
0040b0: 2d00 0000 2e00 0000 2f00 0000 3000 0000 -......./...0...
0040c0: 3100 0000 3200 0000 3300 0000 3400 0000 1...2...3...4...
0040d0: 3500 0000 3600 0000 3700 0000 3800 0000 5...6...7...8...
0040e0: 3900 0000 3a00 0000 3b00 0000 3c00 0000 9...:...;...<...
0040f0: 3d00 0000 3e00 0000 3f00 0000 4000 0000 =...>...?...@...
004100: 4100 0000 4200 0000 4300 0000 ffff ff0f A...B...C.......
004110: ffff ff0f 0000 0000 0000 0000 0000 0000 ................
004120: 0000 0000 0000 0000 0000 0000 0000 0000 ................
```

Listing 5.10 An excerpt from the FAT table of **FAT32_V1.E01**. Clusters 5_d (first cluster) and 67_d (final cluster) are underlined.

Figure 5.4 The recovered **CLIFFS.JPG** file.

5_d's position is 0x06. This means that the second cluster is 0x06 (6_d). Reading the value here gives 0x07 and so forth. This file happens to be contiguous occupying clusters (5_d–67_d). Cluster 67_d's entry in the FAT table shows 0x0FFFFFFF, the end of chain marker.

As the file is contiguous it can be recovered in one command as shown in Listing 5.11. The starting sector for the file is 2104_d (Equation 5.1). The resulting file is shown in Figure 5.4

```
$ dd if=mnt/ewf1 of=cliffs.jpg bs=1 skip=$((2104*512))
     count=$((0x3E9EA))
256490+0 records in
256490+0 records out
256490 bytes (256 kB, 250 KiB) copied, 6.63272 s, 38.7 kB/s
$ md5sum cliffs.jpg
074a76548594690e2072fe0237042e2c cliffs.jpg
```

Listing 5.11 Command required to recover **CLIFFS.JPG** and confirm its MD5.

These methods are used to recover all files in FAT32 allowing for the verification of file system forensic tool results. It is left as an exercise for the reader to process the remaining structures in **FAT32_V1.E01**.

5.3 FAT32 Advanced Analysis

The FAT file system is the simplest of file systems that are still in regular use. Deleted files and the volume label are the only advanced topics to be considered in this section.

5.3.1 Deleted Files

Listing 5.12 shows the contents of the **Files** directory in **FAT32_V1.E01**. This directory contains a file called **delete.txt**. The generic directory entry for this file is underlined. Processing this shows that the contents of this file are located in cluster 0x44 (68_d) which is found in sector 2608_d by Equation 5.1. Listing 5.13 shows the contents of this sector, clearly showing the file's content.

```
105040: 4164 0065 006c 0065 0074 000f 009f 6500 Ad.e.l.e.t....e.
105050: 2e00 7400 7800 7400 0000 0000 ffff ffff ..t.x.t.........
105060: 4445 4c45 5445 2020 5458 5420 004e a85d DELETE TXT .N.]
105070: 5b57 5b57 0000 a85d 5b57 4400 2c00 0000 [W[W...][WD.,...
```

Listing 5.12 The directory entry for **delete.txt** in **FAT32_V1.E01**.

```
146000: 5468 6973 2066 696c 6520 7769 6c6c 2062 This file will b
146010: 6520 6465 6c65 7465 6420 696e 2046 4154 e deleted in FAT
146020: 3332 5f56 322e 4530 312e 0a0a           32_V2.E01.......
```

Listing 5.13 The contents of sector $2,608_d$ in **FAT32_V1.E01** before **delete.txt** has been deleted.

In the supplied **FAT32_V2.E01** file system this file has been deleted. Examining the content of sector $2,608_d$ in this image shows that the content of the file is still present on disk. This is shown in Listing 5.14. This means that deleting a file does not automatically overwrite the content in FAT32, the file has only been marked as deleted. Can this information be recovered using the file system structures or is it recoverable only through the use of data carving techniques?

```
146000: 5468 6973 2066 696c 6520 7769 6c6c 2062 This file will b
146010: 6520 6465 6c65 7465 6420 696e 2046 4154 e deleted in FAT
146020: 3332 5f56 322e 4530 312e 0a0a           32_V2.E01.......
```

Listing 5.14 The contents of sector $2,608_d$ in **FAT32_V2.E01** after **delete.txt** has been deleted.

Listing 5.15 shows the directory entries for the file in **FAT32_V2.E01**. Firstly we see that they are still present, both the LFN and the generic directory entry (highlighted). The first byte in each directory entry has been altered to read 0xE5, signalling that these directory entries are no longer allocated. However, the rest of the directory entry content is unchanged. This means that the file's metadata can be recovered. The filename in the generic directory entry is missing the first character; however, the LFN filename is intact. So the filename can also be recovered[6] along with the metadata.

But what about the content? The generic entry contains the starting cluster and the file size. This information is still present. Next the FAT table (Listing 5.16) is examined.

From the FAT table it is clear that the cluster which contained the file content has been marked as unallocated. This means it is impossible to guarantee correct recovery of file content, at least in the case of large files. For files smaller than a single cluster recovery is guaranteed (assuming the

6 Strictly speaking if there were multiple LFN the sequence numbers would be unknown. However, they generally appear in order from last to first so it is possible to *guess* the original LFN.

```
105040: e564 0065 006c 0065 0074 000f 009f 6500 .d.e.l.e.t....e.
105050: 2e00 7400 7800 7400 0000 0000 ffff ffff ..t.x.t.........
105060: e545 4c45 5445 2020 5458 5420 004e a85d .ELETE TXT .N.]
105070: 5b57 5b57 0000 a85d 5b57 4400 2c00 0000 [W[W...][WD.,...
```

Listing 5.15 Directory entry for deleted file **delete.txt**.

```
...[SNIP]...
004100: 4100 0000 4200 0000 4300 0000 ffff ff0f A...B...C.......
004110: 0000 0000 4600 0000 4700 0000 4800 0000 ....F...G...H...
004120: 4900 0000 4a00 0000 4b00 0000 4c00 0000 I...J...K...L...
...[SNIP]...
```

Listing 5.16 An excerpt from the FAT table in **FAT32_V2.E01**. The relevant cluster (0x44) is underlined.

file has not been overwritten in the meantime). However, recovery will work for this particular file as it occupies only a single cluster. Recovery will also work for contiguous files. Hence, in the FAT file system recovery of deleted files (which have not been overwritten) is guaranteed in the case of small files (less than a single cluster) or contiguous files, but not in the case of fragmented files as the required entries in the FAT table will be overwritten.

5.3.2 The Volume Label

The volume label is a very simple structure that is found at the beginning of the root directory. As with all directory entries it is a 32-byte structure. The volume label from **FAT32_V2.E01** is shown in Listing 5.17. Volume labels are merely generic directory entries with an attribute value of 0x08. The 'filename' in this case refers to the actual Volume Label. The value of this in Listing 5.17 is FAT_FS. The time values appear to refer to when the volume was created.

```
104000: 4641 545f 4653 2020 2020 2008 0000 4d65 FAT_FS ...Me
104010: 5b57 5b57 0000 4d65 5b57 0000 0000 0000 [W[W..Me[W......
```

Listing 5.17 The volume label from **FAT32_V2.E01**. The attribute byte is underlined.

5.4 Summary

This chapter examined the FAT file system and the forensic analysis methods used on it. The important structures such as VBR, FAT and directory entries were introduced and a method of analysis described. Additionally the effect of file deletion on analysis was discussed.

Specifically this chapter covered the FAT 32 version of the FAT file system. The analysis methods for earlier variants (FAT12 and FAT 16) are almost identical. The only change is in addressing. The FAT table uses a smaller number of bytes to represent each cluster than does FAT 32. The next chapter introduces the latest incarnation of the FAT file system, ExFAT. It is very similar to the FAT file system but is more complex and therefore deserves a separate chapter.

Exercises

1 Represent the following dates/times as FAT date/time values.
   a) 14:37:28 on 17 March 2023
   b) 07:12:57 on 25 December 2077
   c) 23:59:59 on 31 December 1999.

2 What dates/times are represented by the following FAT date/time values?
   a) Date: 0x5199; Time: 0x4CBA
   b) Date: 0x4885; Time: 0x1A3D
   c) Date: 0x4934; Time: 0x432F

3 In relation to the file system contained in **FAT32_V3.E01**, answer the following questions (note that you should use manual means to answer these and then confirm your answers using file system forensic tools):
   a) What is the volume label?
   b) In which sector does the data area commence?
   c) In which cluster/sector is the root directory located?
   d) The root directory contains a single folder. What is the complete name of this folder?
   e) In which clusters is the file **BRIDGE.JPG** located?
   f) Process the metadata structure for **BRIDGE.JPG**. In your answer all date/time values should be given in a human-readable format.

Bibliography

Altheide, C. and Carvey, H.A. (2011). *Digital Forensics with Open Source Tools: Using Open Source Platform Tools for Performing Computer Forensics on Target Systems: Windows, Mac, Linux, UNIX, etc.* Rockland, MA: Syngress; Oxford.

Bhat, W.A. and Quadri, S.M. (2010). Review of FAT data structure of FAT32 file system. *Oriental Journal of Computer Science and Technology* 3 (1): 161–164.

Buchholz, F. and Spafford, E. (2004). On the role of file system metadata in digital forensics. *Digital Investigation* 1 (4): 298–309.

Carrier, B. (2005). *File System Forensic Analysis.* Boston, MA; London: Addison-Wesley.

FAT File Systems (2024). FAT32, FAT16, FAT12 - NTFS.com [Internet]. www.ntfs.com. [cited 2024 June 1]. http://www.ntfs.com/fat\.systems.htm (accessed 13 August 2024).

GoLinuxCloud (2020). Found a swap file by the name.XXX.swp –GoLinuxCloud [Internet]. www.golinuxcloud.com. [cited 2024 June 1]. https://www.golinuxcloud.com/found-a-swap-file-by-the-name/ (accessed 13 August 2024).

Lee, W.Y., Kim, K.H., and Lee, H. (2019). Extraction of creation-time for recovered files on windows FAT32 file system. *Applied Sciences* 9 (24): 5522. https://www.mdpi.com/2076-3417/9/24/5522 (accessed 17 December 2024).

Microsoft Corporation (2024). Microsoft Extensible Firmware Initiative FAT32 File System Specification FAT: General Overview of On-Disk Format [cited 2024 March 1]. https://download.microsoft.com/download/1/6/1/161ba512-40e2-4cc9-843a-923143f3456c/fatgen103.doc (accessed 13 August 2024).

Minnaard, W. (2014). The Linux FAT32 allocator and file creation order reconstruction. *Digital Investigation* 11 (3): 224–233.

Nabity, P. and Landry, B.J. (2009). A digital forensic comparison of FAT32 and NTFS file systems using evidence eliminator [cited 2024 March 31]. https://api.semanticscholar.org/CorpusID:140112795 (accessed 13 August 2024).

Rusbarsky, K.L. (2012). A forensic comparison of NTFS and FAT32 file systems [cited 2024 March 3]. https://www.marshall.edu/forensics/files/RusbarskyKelsey_Research-Paper-Summer-2012.pdf (accessed 17 December 2024).

6

The ExFAT File System

The exFAT file system is the latest version in the File Allocation Table (FAT) family of file systems. This file system was introduced by Microsoft in 2006 with the express purpose of creating a file system that would be suitable for larger flash-based storage devices, without the high overheads that some modern file systems suffer. In doing this, exFAT overcame some of the limitations of the FAT32 file system but it is still quite similar to FAT32. An ability to analyse FAT32 will make the analysis of exFAT much easier.

One of the main developments in exFAT is the use of 8_d byte file size values as opposed to four byte values in FAT32 (and only two byte values in earlier FAT variants). This leads to support for much larger files, theoretically up to 16_d EiB. However, the maximum volume size is only 128_d PiB meaning that the largest file size must be less than this value. The maximum volume size is again theoretical. The largest recommended exFAT volume size is 512_d TiB. This is a vast increase on the 2_d TiB maximum that is available in the FAT32 file system. Other FAT32 limits such as the number of files per directory and the maximum number of files are also increased in exFAT (see Table 4.9).

All major operating systems provide native support for exFAT and as such it is replacing FAT as the standard file system on removable media. This means that knowledge of exFAT is vitally important for digital investigators.

From an investigative point of view, exFAT provides more accurate information in relation to time. Firstly the granularity of the creation and modification timestamps is 10 ms, as opposed to two seconds as found in FAT.[1] Additionally the access time granularity is now 2_d seconds. This is due to the introduction of a FAT time value for access time. Previous FAT variants maintain only an access date giving a 1_d day granularity. Finally the exFAT file system stores timezone information. As with FAT the time value recorded in the file system is a local time value but unlike FAT a timezone component is also provided. This means that more accurate information about time can be obtained from an exFAT file system than can be discovered in a FAT file system.

The remainder of this chapter will examine the on-disk structures in the exFAT file system (Section 6.1). The chapter then proceeds to manually analyse an exFAT file system (Section 6.2) before discussing some advanced topics in Section 6.3.

6.1 On-Disk Structures

The exFAT file system is, by modern standards, a simple file system. As an extension of the FAT file system, exFAT contains very similar structures. Concepts that were introduced in Chapter 5 are applicable to the exFAT file system.

1 FAT32 did employ a 10 ms granularity for the creation timestamp.

File System Forensics, First Edition. Fergus Toolan.

VBR [Sectors 0 – 11]	Backup VBR [Sectors 12 – 23]	File Allocation Table [Location in VBR]	Data Area [Location in VBR]

Figure 6.1 The layout of the exFAT file system.

The general layout of exFAT is shown in Figure 6.1. From this it is clearly similar to the FAT file system as there is a volume boot record (VBR) structure, a FAT and a data area. Where the file system differs from FAT is that a backup of the VBR structure exists and that there is generally only a single FAT.[2] The VBR backup is present due to the importance of this structure. Losing the VBR could lose access to the entire file system and as such a backup of the structure is found immediately after the original copy. Note that each VBR is 12 sectors in size. Section 6.1.1 describes the structure of the exFAT VBR. The FAT table is very similar to that found in FAT although by default only a single copy exists. The removal of the second FAT structure is designed to improve efficiency. When files are written to FAT file systems both FAT tables must be updated leading to a slower write time. In exFAT only a single FAT table needs to be updated. Also in exFAT not every file uses the FAT table as only fragmented files need to utilise the table. The FAT table is described in Section 6.1.2. The final area in the exFAT file system is the data area in which files/directories are found. ExFAT uses the same concept of directory entries that FAT used but there are many more directory entry types. Section 6.1.3 introduces the various types of directory entry that are present in the exFAT file system and explains their purpose and how they are processed.

6.1.1 Volume Boot Record

The exFAT VBR is found in the first 12_d sectors of the file system. A backup of the VBR is found immediately after the primary copy. There are a number of structures found in the VBR. The first sector contains the main boot sector, which is immediately followed by the extended boot sector. These are the two most important sectors in the VBR from an investigative perspective. Sector 9 contains OEM parameters, parameters that are specific to particular manufacturers. These parameters are defined by the individual manufacturer, not by the exFAT file system itself. The final sector contains repeating checksums of the VBR structure (excluding the percentage of the file system in use and the Volume Flags).

Listing 6.1 shows the output from the **fsstat** command on an exFAT file system. From this the similarities between exFAT and FAT are clear. The layout contains similar areas such as FAT, root directory and data area. The cluster range begins at 2_d as it does in FAT. The two largest differences are those already mentioned: exFAT contains a backup of the VBR and generally only a single copy of FAT.

The **fsstat** tool reads the VBR to generate the information in Listing 6.1. The structure of the main boot record (Sector 0) is given in Table 6.1.

From Table 6.1 it is clear that the majority of information shown in Listing 6.1 can be recreated from the volume boot record. Both sector and cluster size are given, allowing for addresses to be calculated for various structures. The sector offset to the FAT table is provided along with the size of said table. The number of FATs is also provided, although in exFAT this is 0x01 by default. The cluster number of the root directory is provided which gives the location of the root directory in

2 There may be more than one FAT structure in exFAT, but the default number is one, unlike the FAT file system which defaults to two copies of the FAT table.

the data area. This needs to be combined with cluster and sector size in order to get the actual byte offset to the root directory. The OEM Name, EXFAT, can be used to identify the file system type.

```
FILE SYSTEM INFORMATION
--------------------------------------------
File System Type: exFAT

Volume Serial Number: 212a-d518
Volume Label (from root directory): MyExFAT
File System Name (from MBR): EXFAT
File System Revision: 1.0
Partition Offset: 0
Number of FATs: 1

File System Layout (in sectors):
Range: 0 - 1048575
* Reserved: 0 - 127
** Volume Boot Record (VBR): 0 - 11
*** Boot Sector (MBR): 0
** Backup Volume Boot Record (VBR): 12 - 23
*** Backup Boot Sector (MBR): 12
** FAT alignment space: 24 - 127
* FAT 1: 128 - 255
* Data Area: 256 - 1048575
** Cluster Heap: 256 - 1048575
*** Root Directory: 384 - 447

METADATA INFORMATION
--------------------------------------------
Metadata Layout (in virtual inodes):
Range: 2 - 16773125
* Root Directory: 2

CONTENT INFORMATION
--------------------------------------------
Sector Size: 512
Cluster Size: 32768
Cluster Range: 2 - 16381
```

Listing 6.1 The output from Sleuthkit's **fsstat** command when executed on **ExFAT_V1.E01**.

6.1.2 File Allocation Table

The FAT serves the same purpose in exFAT as in the FAT file system. It allows the FAT chains to be created. When files occupy multiple clusters the first location is found in the FAT table, this then points to the next cluster in the chain, which points to the next. This process continues until an end of chain marker is discovered.

Each cluster in the FAT table is represented by a four-byte value. The first addressable cluster is cluster 2_d, as it is in the FAT file system. The first entry in the table (which could be considered the non-existent cluster 0) contains the media type in the least significant byte, with the remaining

Table 6.1 The structure of the exFAT main boot sector (sector 0).

Offset	Size	Name	Description
0x00	0x03	Jump	Jump instruction.
0x03	0x08	OEM Name	The OEM name usually *EXFAT*.
0x0B	0x35	Reserved	Zero'd.
0x40	0x08	Sector Offset	The partition sector offset, zero in the case of removable media.
0x48	0x08	Volume Size	Total volume size in sectors.
0x50	0x04	FAT Offset	Sector offset to first FAT.
0x54	0x04	FAT Size	The FAT size in sectors.
0x58	0x04	Data Region Offset	The sector offset of the data region.
0x5C	0x04	Data Region Size	The data area size in clusters.
0x60	0x04	Root Directory	Root directory cluster address.
0x64	0x04	Serial Number	The volume serial number.
0x68	0x02	Revision	The file system revision number.
0x6A	0x02	Flags	Bit field flag values: Bit 0 – currently active FAT (0 – FAT 1; 1 – FAT 2); Bit 1 – dirty flag (0 – clean; 1 – dirty); Bit 2 – media failure bit (0 – none; 1 – failure). Remaining bits are reserved.
0x6C	0x01	Bytes/Sector	The sector size in bytes is found by raising 2 to the power of this value. If the value is 0x09, then the sector size is $2^9 = 512_d$ bytes.
0x6D	0x01	Sectors/Cluster	The number of sectors per cluster is found by raising 2 to the power of this value. If the value is 0x06 then the cluster consists of $2^6 = 64_d$ sectors.
0x6E	0x01	# FATS	The number of FATs present.
0x6F	0x01	Drive #	Drive number (typically 0x80).
0x70	0x01	Used Percentage	The percentage of data area in use.
0x71	0x07	Reserved	Zero'd.

bytes containing 0xFFFFFF. The second entry in the FAT table (analogous to a non-existent cluster 1) has no meaning and is generally initialised to 0xFFFFFFFF. The subsequent four bytes refer to cluster 2, the next four bytes to cluster 3 and so forth.

Generally FAT table entries provide cluster numbers to allow the next cluster in the chain to be located. There are two special values for these entries. The first, 0xFFFFFFF7, marks a cluster as bad and as such this cluster should be unused. The second is 0xFFFFFFFF which marks the end of a FAT chain.

Unlike the FAT filesystem not all files in exFAT will have an entry in the FAT table. Only fragmented files will appear in the FAT table. Those files that are stored contiguously can be located in their entirety using the relevant directory entry for that file. As not all files will have cluster chains in the FAT Table, an allocation bitmap structure is used to record used clusters. This is described in more detail in Section 6.1.3.

6.1.3 Directory Entries

In a manner similar to that of FAT, directories in exFAT are composed of directory entries. Each directory entry is 32_d bytes. Each file/directory is represented by a number of directory entries which together are called a directory entry set. There are a total of nine directory entry types in exFAT file systems (compared to a mere three in FAT32). Directory entry types can be classified as either primary or secondary and can be further classified as critical or non-critical. Table 6.2 lists the directory entries and provides their categorisations and codes.

A directory entry set has only a single primary directory entry but can have up to 17_d secondary directory entries. The directory type is identified by the first byte in the directory entry. Regular files have at least three directory entries: a primary file directory entry which contains file metadata, a stream extension which allows the file's content to be located and a file name extension which provides the file's name.

The directory entry type is actually a bit field. Bits 0–4 provide the code in Table 6.2. Bit 5 is used to signify if an entry is critical. If set the entry is not critical, while if this bit is zero the entry is critical. Bit 6 is used to determine if it is a primary directory entry. In the case of a primary value this bit is zero, in the case of a secondary value the bit is 1. Finally, bit 7 is used to determine if a directory entry is in use. If this bit is set then the entry is in use, if it is zero the entry is not in use. Take the following directory entry type value: 0x41. This is not an entry type that appears in Table 6.2; however, it is possible to work out what this represents. The first step is to convert the value to binary giving: 0b01000001. The five least significant bits represent the code which is 0b00001 or 1_d. This means that this is either an allocation bitmap, texFAT or filename extension. Bit

Table 6.2 ExFAT directory entry types.

Name	Pri.	Crit.	Code	Type	Description
Allocation Bitmap	Yes	Yes	1	0x81	Points to the bitmap structure which maintains the allocation status of each cluster on the disk.
Up-Case Table	Yes	Yes	2	0x82	Points to the up-case table which allows for case-insensitive file name searching by mapping uppercase and lowercase characters.
Volume Label	Yes	Yes	3	0x83	Found in the root directory, containing information about the volume label (as listed in **fsstat**).
File	Yes	No	5	0x85	Main file metadata structure.
Volume GUID	Yes	Yes	0	0xA0	The GUID of the volume.
TexFAT	Yes	No	1	0xA1	Related to Transaction Safe exFAT.
Win CE ACT	Yes	No	2	0xA2	Related to Transaction Safe exFAT.
Stream Extension	No	Yes	0	0xC0	Provides the location of the file content.
Filename Extension	No	Yes	1	0xC1	The filename.

5 is zero meaning that this is a critical directory entry. Examining the three directory entries of type in Table 6.2 only the allocation bitmap and the filename extension are critical. The 0x41 type must represent one of these. Examining Bit 6 shows a value of 1. This implies that this is a non-primary directory entry. Combining this information, a code of 1, secondary, critical directory entry, means that this is a filename extension directory entry. The most significant bit is zero meaning that this is unallocated. Most likely this contains file name information for a deleted file! Hence even if the entry type code does not appear in Table 6.2 it is possible to determine its type.

Before continuing to describe each directory entry type in further detail it is necessary to describe the generic directory entry structures. Primary directory entries all follow the same structure which is shown in Table 6.3 while secondary directory entries follow the generic structure shown in Table 6.4.

The primary directory entry's generic structure records information about the directory set to which this primary entry belongs such as the number of secondary entries in the set and a checksum of the directory entry set as a whole. Note this use of checksums in exFAT means that it is a more robust file system than the earlier FAT variants as it is able to detect inconsistencies in data. The majority of data in the directory entry can be redefined by the specific directory

Table 6.3 The primary directory entry generic structure.

Offset	Size	Name	Description
0x00	0x01	Entry Type	The type identifier for the directory.
0x01	0x01	Secondary Count	The number of secondary directory entries associated with this primary entry.
0x02	0x02	Set Checksum	A checksum value for the primary entry and the set of secondary entries associated with it.
0x04	0x02	Primary Flags	Bit 0 – allocation possible; Bit 1 – no FAT Chain. The remaining bits can be defined by the specific directory entry type.
0x06	0x0E	Custom Defined	Data in this section differs for each directory entry type.
0x14	0x04	First Cluster	The first cluster at which data related to this entry is located. May be redefined by certain directory entry types.
0x18	0x08	Data Length	The size of the related data in bytes. May be redefined by certain directory entry types.

Table 6.4 The secondary directory entry generic structure.

Offset	Size	Name	Description
0x00	0x01	Entry Type	The type identifier for the directory entry.
0x01	0x01	Secondary Flags	This field is identical to the primary directory entry's flags field.
0x02	0x12	Custom Defined	Data in this section differs for each directory entry type.
0x14	0x04	First Cluster	The first cluster at which data related to this entry is located. May be redefined by certain directory entry types.
0x18	0x08	Data Length	The size of the related data in bytes. May be redefined by certain directory entry types.

entry type. The secondary entry's generic structure is similar, except that it has a larger custom defined area. This is due to the lack of necessity of recording the information about secondary entries. In the case of both the primary and secondary generic structures both contain a first cluster and a data length. Where external data is stored these are used as indicated but in certain directory entry types these can be redefined. This would allow up to 26_d bytes of custom data in a primary directory entry and up to 30_d bytes in a secondary entry.

The remainder of this section describes each of the directory entries in more detail.

6.1.3.1 Allocation Bitmap (Type: 0x81)

The allocation bitmap is a primary critical directory entry (type: 0x81) which is found in the root directory. There is one present for each copy of the FAT. The allocation bitmap is responsible for tracking used/free clusters. This is different from the other variants of the FAT file system which use the FAT table to track cluster status. In exFAT the FAT table is used only if files are fragmented. Listing 6.2 provides the allocation bitmap directory entry from the supplied file system image (**ExFAT_V1.E01**). The structure of the allocation bitmap directory entry is found in Table 6.5. This includes the interpretation of the entry in Listing 6.2.

```
0030020: 8100 0000 0000 0000 0000 0000 0000 0000 ................
0030030: 0000 0000 0200 0000 0008 0000 0000 0000 ................
```

Listing 6.2 The allocation bitmap directory entry in **ExFAT_V1.dd**

Each bit in the allocation bitmap represents a single cluster. The first bit represents cluster 2 and so on. The first bit is the least significant bit in the first byte. The location of the actual allocation bitmap is found from the directory entry.

Consider an allocation bitmap of 0xEF36. Figure 6.2 shows the binary value of this allocation bitmap and the clusters to which each individual bit refers.

Allocation Bitmap: 0xEF36

Binary	1	1	1	0	1	1	1	1	0	0	1	1	0	1	1	0
Cluster	9	8	7	6	5	4	3	2	17	16	15	14	13	12	11	10

Figure 6.2 An example allocation bitmap (0xEF36) showing the binary values of this bitmap and the cluster numbers to which each bit corresponds.

Table 6.5 The allocation bitmap directory entry structure. The values are from Listing 6.2.

Offset	Size	Name	Description	Value
0x00	0x01	Entry Type	The type identifier for the entry. 0x81 for the allocation bitmap.	0x81
0x01	0x01	Bitmap Flags	Bit 0 describes the allocation bitmap to which this entry refers. 0 represents FAT 1 and 1 represents FAT 2. Generally this is zero as there is only one FAT. The remaining bits are reserved.	0x00
0x02	0x12	Reserved	Reserved.	0x00
0x14	0x04	First Cluster	First cluster of the allocation bitmap.	0x02
0x18	0x08	Data Length	Length of the allocation bitmap (bytes).	0x800

From Figure 6.2 it is easy to determine that cluster 15_d is currently allocated. However, in the case of a larger allocation bitmap showing this for all clusters is not feasible. Instead it is necessary to calculate the exact bit for the desired cluster.

Again consider cluster 15_d's status in the allocation bitmap 0xEF36. It is necessary to determine the byte number in which this cluster will be located and also the bit number inside the byte. These calculations are:

$$byte = int((c - 2)/8)$$

$$bit = (c - 2)\%8$$

Hence cluster 15_d will be found in byte 1_d at bit position 5_d (counting from the least significant bit).[3] Byte position 1 contains the value 0x36 which in binary is 0b00**1**10110, the highlighted bit is bit position 5. This shows that cluster 15_d is allocated.

6.1.3.2 Up-Case Table (Type: 0x82)

The up-case table directory entry is a primary, critical entry with a type code value of 0x82. The up-case table entry defines the location of the up-case table which is used to allow for case-insensitive searching of file names. Listing 6.3 shows the entry from the root directory of the supplied file system image. Table 6.6 provides the structure of the up-case table directory entry and the processed values from Listing 6.3.

```
0030040: 8200 0000 0dd3 19e6 0000 0000 0000 0000  ................
0030050: 0000 0000 0300 0000 cc16 0000 0000 0000  ................
```

Listing 6.3 The up-case table directory entry in **ExFAT_V1.dd.**

6.1.3.3 Volume Label (Type: 0x83)

The volume label directory entry is a primary, critical entry with a type code of 0x83. Its purpose is identical to the volume label directory entry in FAT. It stores the actual file system label (i.e. name) that is assigned when a file system is created. This directory entry is found only in the root directory. A sample volume label is provided in Listing 6.4. The structure of this is shown in Table 6.7.

Table 6.6 The up-case table directory entry structure. The values are from Listing 6.3.

Offset	Size	Name	Description	Value
0x00	0x01	Entry Type	Type identifier (0x82).	0x82
0x01	0x03	Reserved	Reserved.	0x00
0x04	0x04	Checksum	Checksum value for the upcase table.	0xE619D30D
0x08	0x0C	Reserved	Reserved.	0x00
0x14	0x04	First Cluster	The first cluster location for the up-case table.	0x03
0x18	0x08	Data Length	The size of the up-case table in bytes.	0x16CC

3 Remember that counting begins from 0!

```
0030000: 8307 4d00 7900 4500 7800 4600 4100 5400 ..M.y.E.x.F.A.T.
0030010: 0000 0000 0000 0000 0000 0000 0000 0000 ................
```

Listing 6.4 The volume label directory entry in **ExFAT_V1.dd**.

Table 6.7 The volume label directory entry structure. The values are from Listing 6.4.

Offset	Size	Name	Description	Value
0x00	0x01	Type	Type identifier.	0x83
0x01	0x01	Name Length	The length of the name in unicode characters. Each character is 2 bytes in size.	0x07
0x02	0x16	Volume Label	Label in unicode, only 0x0E ($14_d = 7 \times 2$) bytes are used in this case.	MyExFAT
0x18	0x08	Reserved	Reserved.	0x00

6.1.3.4 File (Type: 0x85)

The file directory entry is the key metadata structure. This is a primary, critical entry with type code 0x85. Each file directory entry generally has at least two secondary entries associated with it, one stream extension which is used to locate the file's content and one filename extension which contains the file's name. Note that there may be more than two secondary entries associated with a single file entry. The structure of the file directory entry is given in Table 6.8.

The file directory entry contains the file's metadata. Often the most interesting information available to an investigator is that of time. Recall the FAT file system, this contains a FAT date and time

Table 6.8 The file directory entry structure.

Offset	Size	Name	Description
0x00	0x01	Type	Directory entry type (0x85 for File).
0x01	0x01	# Secondary Entries	The count of the number of secondary entries for this file.
0x02	0x02	Checksum	A checksum calculated for the set of directory entries for this file.
0x04	0x02	Attributes	File attributes (Bit 0: Read-Only; Bit 1: Hidden; Bit 2: System; Bit 3: Reserved; Bit 4: Directory; Bit 5: Archive).
0x06	0x02	Reserved	Reserved.
0x08	0x04	Creation	Creation timestamp.
0x0C	0x04	Last Modified	Last modification timestamp.
0x10	0x04	Last Access	Last access timestamp.
0x14	0x01	Create 10 ms	10 ms component of the creation time value.
0x15	0x01	Modification 10 ms	10 ms component of the modification time value.
0x16	0x01	Creation Timezone	Timezone offset for the creation time.
0x17	0x01	Modification Timezone	Timezone offset for the modification time.
0x18	0x01	Access Timezone	Timezone offset for the access time.
0x19	0x07	Reserved	Reserved.

structure for the creation and modification timestamps, and a FAT date for the accessed timestamp. The granularity of the access time is therefore one day, while the granularity of the creation and modification timestamps is two seconds.[4] The exFAT timestamps are composed of a FAT date and time (see Sections 3.1 and 3.2). The first two bytes of the four represent the FAT time, and the second two represent the FAT date. Consider the raw data of 0x2C783B48 (LE). The FAT Date component is 0x483B, and the FAT Time is 0x782C. These values can be converted as FAT dates and times respectively. Both the creation and modification timestamps also have a 10 ms second component. This value can be between 0x00 and 0xC7 (199_d). The value is then divided by 100_d to give the seconds to be added to the time. Consider an example in which the 10 ms component is 0x14. This is 20_d, which when divided by 100_d gives 0.2 s.

There is more time information available to the investigator in exFAT than in FAT. FAT stored local time with no reference to the actual timezone itself. Most modern file systems store time values in UTC. ExFAT still uses local time, but also stores the timezone in which the local time value was set. This allows times to be compared across devices. The timezone is stored in a single byte. The most significant bit tells if the timezone is active (1) or inactive (0). The remaining seven bits are a two's complement number (see Section 3.2.7). This is the number of 15_d minute intervals from UTC. Consider the value 0x84 (0b1000 0100). The most significant bit is 1 meaning this timezone is active. The two's complement number is 0b0000100 which is $+4_d$. This means that the UTC offset is $4 \times 15 = +60_d$ minutes. This means that the timezone for the time value is UTC+1.

6.1.3.5 Volume GUID (Type: 0xA0)

The volume GUID entry (type 0xA0) is a primary, non-critical entry which contains a GUID (Globally Unique Identifier). This GUID allows applications to distinguish between volumes based on this value. The structure of the volume GUID directory entry is shown in Table 6.9. In the case that a Volume GUID directory entry is present in the file system there should only be a single entry found in the root directory. Many file systems have no volume GUID directory entry.

6.1.3.6 Stream Extension (Type: 0xC0)

The stream extension is a critical, secondary directory entry. The stream extension is used to locate the file/directory content. The structure of the stream extension is shown in Table 6.10.

The stream extension informs the analyst whether the file is contiguous or fragmented. This is found in the secondary flags field. If the bit in position 1 has the value 1 the content is contiguous.

Table 6.9 The volume GUID directory entry structure.

Offset	Size	Name	Description
0x00	0x01	Entry Type	Type identifier (0xA0).
0x01	0x01	Secondary Count	Count of secondary directory entries.
0x02	0x02	Checksum	Checksum of the directory entry set.
0x04	0x02	Flags	Flags are all zero for this entry.
0x06	0x10	Volume GUID	The volume GUID for this file system.
0x16	0x0A	Reserved	Reserved.

4 FAT32 contains a 10 ms component for the creation time.

Table 6.10 The stream extension directory entry structure.

Offset	Size	Name	Description
0x00	0x01	Type	Type identifier (0xC0).
0x01	0x01	Flags	Secondary flags. The least significant bit is set if the record is active. Bit 1 is set in the case that the content is contiguous meaning no FAT chain is required.
0x02	0x01	Reserved	Reserved.
0x03	0x01	Name Size	Size of name (in UCS-2 encoded characters). Double this value to get the number of bytes. The name is stored in one or more file name extension entries (each entry holds 0x0F characters).
0x04	0x02	Checksum	A checksum of the name.
0x06	0x02	Reserved	Reserved.
0x08	0x08	File Size	File size.
0x10	0x04	Reserved	Reserved.
0x14	0x04	Starting Cluster	The cluster at which the file content starts. If the contiguous bit is set then clusters are stored in a single block and there is no need to consult the FAT table; otherwise, the file is fragmented and the FAT table must be consulted.
0x18	0x08	File Size	Duplicate entry for the file size.

In this case it is unnecessary to consult the FAT table to locate the content. The stream extension contains all the required information. If the value is 0 the file is fragmented. In this case the stream extension will provide the first cluster and the FAT table is then consulted to determine the remainder of the FAT chain.

6.1.3.7 Filename Extension

The filename extension directory entry is another secondary, critical directory entry, which contains the file name, or, in the case of longer filenames, a portion of the filename. Each filename extension can hold 15_d characters of the filename. The structure of the filename extension is given in Table 6.11.

In the case in which multiple filename extension entries are in use the filename is composed from all these entries in the order in which they are encountered. Any unused bytes in a filename should be zero'd. A single file directory entry can have up to 17_d filename extensions associated with it, meaning that the maximum filename length is 255_d characters (i.e. $17_d \times 15_d$).

Table 6.11 The filename extension directory entry structure.

Offset	Size	Name	Description
0x00	0x01	Type	Type identifier (0xC1).
0x01	0x01	Flags	Secondary flags.
0x02	0x1E	Filename	Null terminated file name consisting of up to 15_d UCS-2 encoded characters. Multiple filename extension attributes may be used.

6.1.3.8 Other Directory Entries

There are a number of other directory entry types but these are unlikely to be of interest in file system forensic analysis. These include the TexFAT directory entry which is used as part of the Transaction Safe exFAT system, a system which is not widely supported in current implementations. There are also two vendor-specific directory entries. These are the vendor GUID entry which is used to identify the actual vendor and the vendor extension which can contain any data that the vendor wishes. These are vendor specific and as such their definition depends solely on the vendor in question.

6.2 Analysis of ExFAT

This section introduces the analysis of the exFAT file system. It begins with instructions on how to create exFAT file systems using the Linux OS and proceeds to describe those file systems that have been supplied with this book. These are used in the remainder of this chapter. Finally this section describes the process of manually analysing an exFAT file system.

6.2.1 Creating ExFAT File Systems

ExFAT file systems, similar to FAT file systems, can be created on all major operating systems. In the Linux terminal the command to create an exFAT file system in the first partition of the second hard drive is given in Listing 6.5. This command also specifies the file system name using **-n 'MyExFAT'**.

```
mkfs.exfat -n "MyExFAT" /dev/sdb1
```

Listing 6.5 Creating an ExFAT file system in the Linux terminal.

6.2.2 Supplied ExFAT Image Files

A number of disk images are analysed during this chapter. These are available from the book's website and are summarised in Table 6.12.

6.2.3 ExFAT Manual Analysis

In this section manual analysis of the exFAT file system is performed. This allows the reader to fully understand the structures of exFAT and to see how digital forensic tools analyse the file system. For demonstration purposes **ExFAT_V1.E01** will be used throughout this section.

Table 6.12 Supplied exFAT image files available from the book's website.

Image	Description
ExFAT_V1.E01	A basic exFAT file system with four files and one directory.
ExFAT_V2.E01	This is **exFAT_V1.E01** with one file deleted and a directory added with 350_d files. This directory occupies two non-contiguous clusters.
ExFAT_V3.E01	An exFAT file system that is used in the chapter's exercises.

At an abstract level the analysis method for exFAT is almost identical to that of FAT. The necessary steps are:

1) **Process the VBR:** The VBR contains information relevant to the file system as a whole. This is the information that is seen when Sleuth Kit's **fsstat** command is used. This information is vital for all further analysis as it allows other file system structures to be located in the file system.
2) **Process the Root Directory:** The second step in analysis is to begin to list the files. This happens by firstly processing the root directory. In addition to standard user created files/directories the root directory contains some file system structure information such as the location of the allocation bitmap and up-case tables along with the volume name.
3) **Process Subdirectories:** Once the root directory is processed each discovered subdirectory is then processed. This allows all files to be listed. This process continues until there are no further files to be processed. This (combined with step 2) is equivalent to Sleuth Kit's **fls** command.
4) **Recover Metadata:** For every file/directory that is recovered the file directory entry is processed in order to gather the file's metadata (size, times, etc.)
5) **Recover Content:** The final step is to recover the file/directory content using the stream extension.

The remainder of this section examines these steps in more detail.

6.2.3.1 Step 1: Process the VBR

Listing 6.1 shows the output from the **fsstat** command when run upon the **ExFAT_V1.E01** image file. The bulk of this information is found by processing the VBR structure. Remember that in exFAT this VBR structure is 12_d sectors in size and a backup is also found on the device.

Listing 6.6 shows the first 0x80 bytes from sector 0 in **ExFAT_V1.E01**. This structure is processed in Table 6.13.

```
000: eb76 9045 5846 4154 2020 2000 0000 0000 .v.EXFAT   .....
010: 0000 0000 0000 0000 0000 0000 0000 0000 ................
020: 0000 0000 0000 0000 0000 0000 0000 0000 ................
030: 0000 0000 0000 0000 0000 0000 0000 0000 ................
040: 0000 0000 0000 0000 0000 1000 0000 0000 ................
050: 8000 0000 8000 0000 0001 0000 fc3f 0000 .............?..
060: 0400 0000 18d5 2a21 0001 0000 0906 0180 ......*!........
070: 0000 0000 0000 0000 0000 0000 0000 0000 ................
```

Listing 6.6 An excerpt from the boot sector in **ExFAT_V1.E01**.

Table 6.13 shows all the information that is available in Listing 6.1 (with the exception of the volume label which will be processed from the root directory). From the boot sector the file system structures can be mapped allowing for processing to be continued.

6.2.3.2 Step 2: Process the Root Directory

From processing the VBR the root directory is located. Table 6.13 shows that the root directory is to be found in cluster 4_d. To locate the sector number for a given cluster, n, the following formula is used:

$$[(n-2) \times sectorsPerCluster] + dataRegionOffset \tag{6.1}$$

Table 6.13 Processing the main boot sector in **ExFAT_V1.E01.**

Offset	Size	Name	Value
0x03	0x08	OEM Name	EXFAT
0x0B	0x35	Reserved	0x00
0x40	0x08	Sector Offset	0x00
0x48	0x08	Volume Size	0x100000 ($1,048,576_d$)
0x50	0x04	FAT Offset	0x80 (128_d)
0x54	0x04	FAT Size	0x80 (128_d)
0x58	0x04	Data Region Offset	0x100 (256_d)
0x5C	0x04	Data Region Size	0x3FFC ($16,380_d$)
0x60	0x04	Root Directory	0x04 (4_d)
0x64	0x04	Serial Number	0x212AD518
0x68	0x02	Revision	0x100 (i.e. 1.0)
0x6A	0x02	Flags	0x00 (FAT 1 used)
0x6C	0x01	Bytes/Sector	0x09, i.e. $2^9 = 512_d$ bytes.
0x6D	0x01	Sectors/Cluster	0x06, i.e. $2^6 = 64_d$ sectors.
0x6E	0x01	Num FATS	0x01 (1_d)
0x6F	0x01	Drive #	0x80 (128_d)
0x70	0x01	Used Percentage	0x00
0x71	0x07	Reserved	0x00

Combining this formula with the relevant values found in the VBR means that cluster 4 is located at sector $((4 - 2) * 64) + 256 = 384_d$. Extracting 64_d sectors (the sectors per cluster value) from here will extract the contents of the root directory.[5] Listing 6.7 shows the contents of this sector.

The first three directory entries are a volume label (type: 0x83), the allocation bitmap (type: 0x81) and the up-case table (type: 0x82). This is followed by four file entries (type: 0x85) each of which has a stream extension (type: 0xC0) and one or more filename extension (type: 0xC1) associated with it.

Sleuth Kit's **fsstat** command will also process the volume label directory entry. From Table 6.7 the structure of the volume label is found. This structure is very simple, a type identifier byte (0x83), followed by a single byte providing the name length (0x07 characters in this case), followed by the name itself in UTF-16 (LE) encoded unicode characters. In the example in Listing 6.7 the volume label value is MyExFAT. This can also be seen in Listing 6.1.

In the case of both the allocation bitmap and the up-case table, these directory entries are used to locate the content of these structures. Referring to Tables 6.5 and 6.6 the first cluster of both is found at offset 0x14 and the data length is found at 0x18. These values for the allocation bitmap structure are 0x02 and 0x800, respectively, meaning that the allocation bitmap will be $2,048_d$ bytes in size beginning at cluster 2_d. The values for the up-case table are 0x03 and 0x16CC, respectively.

5 This assumes that the root directory occupies only a single cluster.

```
0030000: 8307 4d00 7900 4500 7800 4600 4100 5400 ..M.y.E.x.F.A.T.
0030010: 0000 0000 0000 0000 0000 0000 0000 0000 ................
0030020: 8100 0000 0000 0000 0000 0000 0000 0000 ................
0030030: 0000 0000 0200 0000 0008 0000 0000 0000 ................
0030040: 8200 0000 0dd3 19e6 0000 0000 0000 0000 ................
0030050: 0000 0000 0300 0000 cc16 0000 0000 0000 ................
0030060: 8502 351b 1000 0000 1780 5c57 4680 5c57 ..5.......\WF.\W
0030070: 1780 5c57 6400 0000 0000 0000 0000 0000 ..\Wd...........
0030080: c003 0005 3535 0000 0080 0000 0000 0000 ....55..........
0030090: 0000 0000 0500 0000 0080 0000 0000 0000 ................
00300a0: c100 4600 6900 6c00 6500 7300 0000 0000 ..F.i.l.e.s.....
00300b0: 0000 0000 0000 0000 0000 0000 0000 0000 ................
00300c0: 8502 ba77 2000 0000 2580 5c57 6b7f 5c57 ...w ...%.\Wk.\W
00300d0: 6b7f 5c57 6464 0000 0000 0000 0000 0000 k.\Wdd..........
00300e0: c001 0009 4661 0000 299a 0800 0000 0000 ....Fa..).......
00300f0: 0000 0000 0600 0000 299a 0800 0000 0000 ........).......
0030100: c100 7400 7200 6500 6500 7300 2e00 6a00 ..t.r.e.e.s...j.
0030110: 7000 6700 0000 0000 0000 0000 0000 0000 p.g.............
0030120: 8504 fd33 2000 0000 3b80 5c57 3b80 5c57 ...3 ...;.\W;.\W
0030130: 3b80 5c57 0000 0000 0000 0000 0000 0000 ;.\W............
0030140: c003 0029 3691 0000 2500 0000 0000 0000 ...)6...%.......
0030150: 0000 0000 1800 0000 2500 0000 0000 0000 ........%.......
0030160: c100 4400 6500 6d00 6f00 6e00 7300 7400 ..D.e.m.o.n.s.t.
0030170: 7200 6100 7400 6900 6e00 6700 5600 6500 r.a.t.i.n.g.V.e.
0030180: c100 7200 7900 4c00 6f00 6e00 6700 4600 ..r.y.L.o.n.g.F.
0030190: 6900 6c00 6500 4e00 6100 6d00 6500 7300 i.l.e.N.a.m.e.s.
00301a0: c100 4900 6e00 4500 7800 4600 4100 5400 ..I.n.E.x.F.A.T.
00301b0: 2e00 7400 7800 7400 0000 0000 0000 0000 ..t.x.t.........
00301c0: 8502 c6a0 2000 0000 4480 5c57 4480 5c57 .... ...D.\WD.\W
00301d0: 4480 5c57 0000 0000 0000 0000 0000 0000 D.\W............
00301e0: c003 0008 7a2f 0000 c000 0000 0000 0000 ....z/..........
00301f0: 0000 0000 1900 0000 c000 0000 0000 0000 ................
0030200: c100 6900 6e00 6600 6f00 2e00 7400 7800 ..i.n.f.o...t.x.
0030210: 7400 0000 0000 0000 0000 0000 0000 0000 t...............
```

Listing 6.7 Contents of the root directory in **ExFAT_V1.E01**. The first byte (entry type) of each individual directory entry is highlighted.

Processing of the root directory continues with the remaining file items. Initial analysis involves file listing, as performed by **fls**. In order to do this there are two items that must be extracted, the filename and whether it represents a file/directory. The filename can be obtained from the filename extension attributes (type: 0xC1). Examining Listing 6.7 shows that there are four 'files' present called **Files**, **DemonstratingVeryLongFileNamesInExFAT.txt**, **trees.jpg** and **info.txt**, respectively. To determine if each represents a file or directory it is necessary to process the attributes in the file directory entry (type 0x85). The attributes are found in a two-byte bit field structure at offset 0x04. Bit 4 represents a directory. The values for the four discovered 'files' are: 0x10, 0x20, 0x20 and 0x20, respectively. The value 0x10 is 0b00010000. In this case bit 4 is set meaning this is a directory. In the other cases 0x20 is 0b00100000 meaning that bit 4 is not set; hence, these are files. This means that **Files** is a directory, while **DemonstratingVeryLongFileNamesInExFAT.txt**, **trees.jpeg** and **info.txt** are files. Listing 6.8 shows the output of **fls** which confirms this information.

```
$ fls mnt/ewf1
r/r 2051: MyExFAT (Volume Label Entry)
r/r 2052: $ALLOC_BITMAP
r/r 2053: $UPCASE_TABLE
d/d 2054: Files
r/r 2057: trees.jpg
r/r 2060: DemonstratingVeryLongFileNamesInExFAT.txt
r/r 2065: info.txt
v/v 16773123: $MBR
v/v 16773124: $FAT1
V/V 16773125: $OrphanFiles
```

Listing 6.8 File listing from the root directory of **ExFAT_V1.E01** using **fls**.

Notice that **fls** processes the non-file related directory entries such as the volume label, allocation bitmap and up-case table entries. Note that the virtual files/directories (v/v and V/V) are an easy way that Sleuth Kit provides to recover other file system structures.

6.2.3.3 Step 3: Process Subdirectories

In order to list all files, directories identified in the root directory must next be processed. In order to do this the directory must be located. In the previous step only one single sub-directory, **Files**, was identified. To get the content of this directory the stream extension is processed. The stream extension (type: 0xC0) is provided in Listing 6.9.

```
0030080: c003 0005 3535 0000 0080 0000 0000 0000 ....55..........
0030090: 0000 0000 0500 0000 0080 0000 0000 0000 ................
```

Listing 6.9 The stream extension directory entry for the **Files** directory showing the starting cluster and file size.

From Listing 6.9 the starting cluster is determined to be 0x05 and the file size is 0x8000 ($32,768_d$) bytes. This implies that the directory entries occupy one single cluster. Listing 6.10 shows the contents of this cluster.

```
0038000: 8502 3c31 2000 0000 4680 5c57 4680 5c57 ..<1 ...F.\WF.\W
0038010: 4680 5c57 0000 0000 0000 0000 0000 0000 F.\W............
0038020: c003 000a 232c 0000 4200 0000 0000 0000 ....#,..B.......
0038030: 0000 0000 1a00 0000 4200 0000 0000 0000 ........B.......
0038040: c100 6400 6500 6c00 6500 7400 6500 2e00 ..d.e.l.e.t.e...
0038050: 7400 7800 7400 0000 0000 0000 0000 0000 t.x.t...........
```

Listing 6.10 The contents of the **Files** sub-directory.

From Listing 6.10 the **Files** sub-directory contains a single file. Processing the file name directory entry shows this to be **delete.txt**. Examining the attributes of this shows it to be a regular file. At this stage, in this file system, all directories have been processed (and hence all files have been listed). In more complex file systems this process would continue until all directory contents had been listed.

The results obtained through manual analysis can be compared to those obtained using the **fls** command recursively. This is shown in Listing 6.11.

```
$ fls -r mnt/ewf1
r/r 2051: MyExFAT (Volume Label Entry)
r/r 2052: $ALLOC_BITMAP
r/r 2053: $UPCASE_TABLE
d/d 2054: Files
+ r/r 3075: delete.txt
r/r 2057: trees.jpg
r/r 2060: DemonstratingVeryLongFileNamesInExFAT.txt
r/r 2065: info.txt
v/v 16773123: $MBR
v/v 16773124: $FAT1
V/V 16773125: $OrphanFiles
```

Listing 6.11 The output from recursively running **fls** on **ExFAT_V1.E01**.

6.2.3.4 Step 4: Recover Metadata

Once the file list has been determined the next step is to recover the metadata in relation to every file. This is achieved using the file directory entry (type: 0x85). Listing 6.12 shows the file directory entry for the **info.txt** file in the root directory.

```
00301c0: 8502 c6a0 2000 0000 4480 5c57 4480 5c57 .... ...D.\WD.\W
00301d0: 4480 5c57 0000 0000 0000 0000 0000 0000 D.\W............
```

Listing 6.12 The file directory entry for **info.txt** in **ExFAT_V1.E01**.

Table 6.14 provides information about the file. For instance the file has two secondary entries (these are the stream and filename extension which immediately follow this file directory entry in Listing 6.7). The creation, modification and access times are FAT date/time structures. All these show times on the afternoon of 28 October 2023. The timezone for all of these structures is 0x00 (meaning that there is no offset, i.e. UTC).

6.2.3.5 Step 5: Recover Content

The final step is to recover the file content. This is achieved through the stream extension directory entry (type: 0xC0). Listing 6.13 shows the stream extension for **info.txt**. The processed values are shown in Table 6.15.

```
00301e0: c003 0008 7a2f 0000 c000 0000 0000 0000 ....z/..........
00301f0: 0000 0000 1900 0000 c000 0000 0000 0000 ................
```

Listing 6.13 The stream extension directory entry for **info.txt** in **ExFAT_V1.E01**.

Table 6.14 The file directory entry for **info.txt** in **ExFAT_V1.E01.**

Offset	Size	Name	Value
0x00	0x01	Type	0x85
0x01	0x01	# Secondary Entries	0x02
0x02	0x02	Checksum	0xA0C6
0x04	0x02	Attributes	0x20 (Archive)
0x06	0x02	Reserved	0x00
0x08	0x04	Creation	0x575C8044 2023-10-28 16:02:08
0x0C	0x04	Last Modified	0x575C8044 2023-10-28 16:02:08
0x10	0x04	Last Access	0x575C8044 2023-10-28 16:02:08
0x14	0x01	Create 10 ms	0x00
0x15	0x01	Modification 10 ms	0x00
0x16	0x01	Creation Timezone	0x00
0x17	0x01	Modification Timezone	0x00
0x18	0x01	Access Timezone	0x00
0x19	0x07	Reserved	0x00

From Table 6.15 the starting cluster is determined to be 0x19 (25_d). This is translated to a sector using the formula given in Equation 6.1.

$$[(25 - 2) \times 64] + 256 = 1728$$

The flags inform the analyst that this file is active and contiguous. The value of 0x03 means that bits 0 and 1 are set, hence determining that the file is active and contiguous, respectively. The fact

Table 6.15 The stream extension directory entry for **info.txt** in **ExFAT_V1.E01**. Values are taken from Listing 6.13.

Offset	Size	Name	Value
0x00	0x01	Type	0xC0
0x01	0x01	Flags	0x03
0x02	0x01	Reserved	0x00
0x03	0x01	Name Size	0x08 (8_d)
0x04	0x02	Checksum	0x2F7A
0x06	0x02	Reserved	0x00
0x08	0x08	File Size	0xC0 (192_d)
0x10	0x04	Reserved	0x00
0x14	0x04	Starting Cluster	0x19 (25_d)
0x18	0x08	File Size	0xC0 (192_d)

that the file is contiguous means that the FAT table is not needed in order to recover the file's content. The final piece of information required is that of the file size, which is 0xC0 in this case. Listing 6.14 shows 0xC0 bytes at cluster 25_d. Listing 6.15 compares the manual recovery of **info.txt** with that of **icat** showing both to be equivalent.

```
00d8000: 5468 6973 2069 7320 616e 2045 7846 4154 This is an ExFAT
00d8010: 2066 696c 6520 7379 7374 656d 2074 6861 file system tha
00d8020: 7420 636f 6e74 6169 6e73 2034 2066 696c t contains 4 fil
00d8030: 6573 2061 6e64 2031 2064 6972 6563 746f es and 1 directo
00d8040: 7279 2e20 0a54 6865 2073 7472 7563 7475 ry..The structu
00d8050: 7265 206f 6620 7468 6973 2069 733a 0a0a re of this is:..
00d8060: 2f2d 2046 696c 6573 0a20 2020 2f2d 2064 /- Files. /- d
00d8070: 656c 6574 652e 7478 740a 2f2d 2069 6e66 elete.txt./- inf
00d8080: 6f2e 7478 740a 2f2d 2074 7265 6573 2e6a o.txt./- trees.j
00d8090: 7067 0a2f 2d20 4465 6d6f 6e73 7472 6174 pg./- Demonstrat
00d80a0: 696e 6756 6572 794c 6f6e 6746 696c 654e ingVeryLongFileN
00d80b0: 616d 6573 496e 4578 4641 542e 7478 740a amesInExFAT.txt.
```

Listing 6.14 The contents of the **info.txt** file in **ExFAT_V1.E01**.

```
$ dd if=mnt/ewf1 bs=1 skip=$((1728*512)) count=$((0xC0)) | md5sum
192+0 records in
192+0 records out
192 bytes copied, 0.000341334 s, 562 kB/s
4bbcb05d4c32617850d2db82244b84a3  -
$ icat mnt/ewf1 2065 | md5sum
4bbcb05d4c32617850d2db82244b84a3  -
```

Listing 6.15 Comparison of manual file recovery using **dd** and automated file recovery using **icat**. The resulting MD5 sums are equal.

This technique works for contiguous files. Later the recovery of fragmented files is discussed (Section 6.3.3).

6.3 ExFAT Advanced Analysis

The basic analysis of exFAT allows for recovery of much metadata and many files. However, there are certain special cases which need further examination. In this section these cases are addressed. These include long file names, deleted files, fragmented files and large directories.

6.3.1 Long File Names

To this point all files that have been examined have had short file names. In other words they have needed only a single filename extension directory entry to store the file name. In the supplied disk image **ExFAT_V1.E01**, there is a file which requires multiple filename extensions. Listing 6.16 shows this file from **fls**.

The directory entry set for this file is shown in Listing 6.17. This directory entry set contains 4_d secondary entries. From the stream extension the name length is given as 0x29 (41_d) characters. As

```
r/r 2060: DemonstratingVeryLongFileNamesInExFAT.txt
```

Listing 6.16 A long file name found in **ExFAT_V1.E01**.

```
0030120: 8504 fd33 2000 0000 3b80 5c57 3b80 5c57 ...3 ...;.\W;.\W
0030130: 3b80 5c57 0000 0000 0000 0000 0000 0000 ;.\W............
0030140: c003 0029 3691 0000 2500 0000 0000 0000 ...)6...%.......
0030150: 0000 0000 1800 0000 2500 0000 0000 0000 ........%.......
0030160: c100 4400 6500 6d00 6f00 6e00 7300 7400 ..D.e.m.o.n.s.t.
0030170: 7200 6100 7400 6900 6e00 6700 5600 6500 r.a.t.i.n.g.V.e.
0030180: c100 7200 7900 4c00 6f00 6e00 6700 4600 ..r.y.L.o.n.g.F.
0030190: 6900 6c00 6500 4e00 6100 6d00 6500 7300 i.l.e.N.a.m.e.s.
00301a0: c100 4900 6e00 4500 7800 4600 4100 5400 ..I.n.E.x.F.A.T.
00301b0: 2e00 7400 7800 7400 0000 0000 0000 0000 ..t.x.t.........
```

Listing 6.17 A long file name directory entry set found in **ExFAT_V1.E01**.

each filename extension can store up to 15_d characters it is necessary to have 3_d filename extensions to store this filename. The directory entry type bytes for each of these are highlighted.

In order to reconstruct the filename it is necessary to process all the filename extensions in the order in which they appear in the directory entry set. Hence the first entry contains *DemonstratingVe*, the second contains *ryLongFileNames* and the final entry contains *InExFAT.txt*. Putting these together gives the filename *DemonstratingVeryLongFileNamesInExFAT.txt*.

6.3.2 Deleted Files

The disk image **ExFAT_V2.E01** contains a number of deleted files, one of which is **Files/delete.txt** which existed in **ExFAT_V1.E01**. Examining **ExFAT_V1.E01** shows the start of this file was located in cluster 0x1A (26_d) and was 0x42 (66_d) bytes. Listing 6.18 shows the contents of cluster 26_d in **ExFAT_V2.E01**, after the file was deleted. This clearly shows the file content. Hence the data has not been immediately overwritten when the file has been deleted.

```
00e0000: 5468 6973 2066 696c 6520 7769 6c6c 2062 This file will b
00e0010: 6520 6465 6c65 7465 6420 696e 2061 206c e deleted in a l
00e0020: 6174 6572 2076 6572 7369 6f6e 206f 6620 ater version of
00e0030: 7468 6973 2066 696c 6520 7379 7374 656d this file system
00e0040: 2e0a 0000 0000 0000 0000 0000 0000 0000 ................
```

Listing 6.18 An excerpt from cluster 26_d in **ExFAT_V2.E01** showing the file content still present.

Knowing the data is present after deletion is not by itself sufficient. It is also necessary to check the metadata information. Listing 6.19 shows the relevant directory entry set for the **delete.txt** file found in the **Files** directory.

In this directory entry types are underlined. These types (0x05, 0x40 and 0x41) are not types that have been encountered previously. Examining their binary values (0b00000101, 0b01000000 and 0b01000001) shows that in each case the most significant bit is 0. This means that these records are not active. This signifies that the records are deleted. However, to avoid unnecessary writes to disk the exFAT file system drivers generally leave these old entries until they require the free

```
0038000: 0502 3c31 2000 0000 4680 5c57 4680 5c57 ..<1 ...F.\WF.\W
0038010: 4680 5c57 0000 0000 0000 0000 0000 0000 F.\W............
0038020: 4003 000a 232c 0000 4200 0000 0000 0000 @...#,..B.......
0038030: 0000 0000 1a00 0000 4200 0000 0000 0000 ........B.......
0038040: 4100 6400 6500 6c00 6500 7400 6500 2e00 A.d.e.l.e.t.e...
0038050: 7400 7800 7400 0000 0000 0000 0000 0000 t.x.t...........
```

Listing 6.19 The directory entry set for **delete.txt** after deletion in **ExFAT_V2.E01**.

space. Hence it is often the case that these records will remain. The content of the deleted file can be recovered in the same manner as if the file were live, as the file (type: 0x05), stream extension (type: 0x40) and filename extension (type: 0x41) directory entries still exist.

As with the FAT file system small files and contiguous files can be recovered. Fragmented files, which require the FAT table, are not recoverable in exFAT as the FAT chain in the FAT table is generally overwritten.

6.3.3 Fragmented Files and Large Directories

In this section the concepts of file fragmentation and large directory structures are introduced. The directory used in this example is fragmented allowing both topics to be covered in a single section. The method used to locate the clusters in which these directory entries are stored is identical to those used to recover the content of a fragmented file.

In some earlier versions of the FAT file system directories were limited to one cluster in size. This is not the case in exFAT. To this point all directories that have been examined reside in one single cluster. In the image file **ExFAT_V2.E01** there is a directory in the root called **LargeDir** which contains 350_d files. From previous analysis of this file system the cluster size was determined to be 64_d sectors (i.e. 32768_d bytes). Each file requires a minimum of three directory entries (file, stream extension and file name extension). This means that each directory entry set will occupy a minimum of 96_d bytes. Dividing the cluster size by this value means that a single cluster can contain at most 341_d files. Hence by creating 350_d files it is guaranteed that more than a single cluster will be used to store the directory contents.

Listing 6.20 shows the directory entry set for **LargeDir**. In this case the stream extension marks the file as being fragmented as the flag values are 0x01 (meaning that bit 1 is not set). Hence the content's first cluster can be found at cluster 0x1B (27_d) but the FAT table must be consulted to determine the remaining content. This is also how any fragmented file, not just a directory, is located. The relevant clusters in the FAT table are shown in Listing 6.21.

```
0030220: 8502 edae 1000 0000 ba83 5c57 c283 5c57 ..........\W..\W
0030230: ba83 5c57 6464 0000 0000 0000 0000 0000 ..\Wdd..........
0030240: c001 0008 94fa 0000 0000 0100 0000 0000 ................
0030250: 0000 0000 1b00 0000 0000 0100 0000 0000 ................
0030260: c100 4c00 6100 7200 6700 6500 4400 6900 ..L.a.r.g.e.D.i.
0030270: 7200 0000 0000 0000 0000 0000 0000 0000 r...............
```

Listing 6.20 The directory entry set for the **LargeDir** directory in **ExFAT_V2.E01**.

In cluster 27_d the value 0x171 (369_d) is found. Examining that cluster information in the FAT table shows that the end of chain marker is found. Hence the **largeDir** directory is composed of

```
...[SNIP]...
0010050: 1500 0000 1600 0000 1700 0000 ffff ffff ................
0010060: 0000 0000 0000 0000 0000 0000 7101 0000 ............q...
0010070: 0000 0000 0000 0000 0000 0000 0000 0000 ................
...[SNIP]...
00105b0: 0000 0000 0000 0000 0000 0000 0000 0000 ................
00105c0: 0000 0000 ffff ffff 0000 0000 0000 0000 ................
00105d0: 0000 0000 0000 0000 0000 0000 0000 0000 ................
```

Listing 6.21 The FAT table showing the clusters used by the **LargeDir** directory in **ExFAT_V2.E01**. Some unused entries have been removed.

clusters 27_d and 369_d, meaning that large directories can be processed in an identical manner to large files. Listing 6.22 shows the first directory entry in clusters 27_d and 369_d. The byte offsets in the FAT table are computed by simply multiplying the cluster number by four. Hence cluster 27_d's FAT table entry is found at byte offset $27 * 4 = 108_d$ (0x6C) and cluster 369_d's entry is found at byte offset $369 * 4 = 1,476_d$ (0x5C4).

```
00e8000: 8502 f21d 2000 0000 c283 5c57 c283 5c57 .... .....\W..\W
00e8010: c283 5c57 6464 0000 0000 0000 0000 0000 ..\Wdd..........
...[snip]...
0b98000: c003 0009 561d 0000 0a00 0000 0000 0000 ....V...........
0b98010: 0000 0000 7201 0000 0a00 0000 0000 0000 ....r...........
```

Listing 6.22 The first directory entries from clusters 27_d and 369_d which together provide the entire content of the **LargeDir** directory in **ExFAT_V2.E01**.

6.4 Summary

This chapter has examined the exFAT file system which, while very similar to the FAT family of file systems, does provide more functionality. This is generally achieved through the use of more directory entries, in which files are not merely represented by a single directory entry but by a set of directory entries (comprising at least one file entry, one stream extension entry and one filename extension entry). While the overall structure of FAT and exFAT is similar, their uses are different. For instance the FAT table is used differently in exFAT and FAT. In FAT all files were recovered by consulting the FAT Table. In exFAT, files that are marked as contiguous (i.e. not fragmented) can be recovered without reference to the FAT table. It is only in the case of fragmented files that the FAT table is used. This means that the FAT table can no longer be used to determine the allocation status of each cluster. As such an allocation bitmap structure is also found in the root directory. This structure provides the allocation status of each cluster.

From an investigative perspective exFAT provides many advantages over the basic FAT file system. However, these advantages come with the price of a more complex file system for analysis. These advantages include:

- **Enhanced Metadata:** The exFAT file system contains more metadata information than was found in the traditional FAT file system.
- **Further Timestamps:** The exFAT file system contains an access time value which is not found in the traditional FAT file system.

- **Timestamp Granularity:** All timestamps in exFAT operate at 10^{-1}s granularity. This provides a more accurate indication of the temporal ordering of events than was possible in FAT which only provided a two second granularity for time values.
- **Timezone Information:** The FAT file system recorded all time values in the local time of the computer which accessed the file system. Hence without access to the computer in question it was impossible to determine the timezone in which the operation occurred. The exFAT file system now records a timezone value which removes this difficulty.

Exercises

1 Table 6.2 provides the entry-type codes for allocated directory entries of various types. For each of these entry types what is the corresponding type value for a deleted entry?

2 The following questions require access to **ExFAT_V3.E01** which is available from the book's website. In each case you should solve the task using manual analysis and verify your results using automated forensic tools.
   a) Where does the data region commence?
   b) How many FAT structures are present on the device?
   c) What is the volume label?
   d) At what byte offset is the root directory located?
   e) The root directory contains a directory entry for an item called **Files**. Is this a directory or a regular file?
   f) The root directory contains a file called **cove.jpg**. What is the MD5 sum of this file?
   g) In relation to **cove.jpg** when was this file last modified?

Bibliography

ExFAT Filesystem (2024). ExFAT Filesystem [Internet]. elm-chan.org. [updated 2017; cited 2024 March 31]. http://elm-chan.org/docs/exfat_e.html (accessed 13 August 2024).

Hamm, J. (2009). Paradigm Solutions Extended FAT File System ExFAT. J Hamm [Internet]. 2009 January. https://paradigmsolutions.files.wordpress.com/2009/12/exfat-excerpt-1-4.pdf (accessed 13 August 2024).

Heeger, J., Yannikos, Y., and Steinebach, M. (2022). An introduction to the ExFAT file system and how to hide data within. *Journal of Cyber Security and Mobility* 11 (02): 239–264.

Munegowda, K., Raju, G.T., and Raju, V.M. (2014a). Directory compaction techniques for space optimizations in ExFAT and FAT file systems for embedded storage devices. *International Journal of Computer Science Issues (IJCSI)* 11 (1): 144.

Munegowda, K., Raju, G.T., and Maninkandanraju, V. (2014b). Design and implementation of log structured fat and ExFAT file systems. *International Journal of Engineering and Technology* 6 (4): 1708–1727.

Munegowda, K., Raju, G.T., and Maninkandanraju, V. (2014c). Adapting Endurance and Performance Optimization Strategies of ExFAT file system to FAT file system for embedded storage devices. *International Journal of Engineering and Technology* 6 (1): 204–211.

Nordvik, R. (2024). Interpretation of file system metadata in a criminal investigation context. PhD Dissertation. Norway: Norwegian University of Science and Technology.

Nordvik, R. and Axelsson, S. (2022). It is about time–do exFAT implementations handle timestamps correctly? *Forensic Science International Digital Investigation* 42-43: 301476–301476.

SANS (2024). Digital Forensics and Incident Response Blog –FAT and FAT Directory Entries –SANS Institute [Internet]. www.sans.org. [cited 2024 March 31]. https://www.sans.org/blog/fat-and-fat-directory-entries/ (accessed 13 August 2024).

Shullich, R. (2010). *Reverse Engineering the Microsoft ExFAT File System*. The SANS Institute.

Vandermeer, Y., Le-Khac, N.A., Carthy, J., and Kechadi, T. (2018). Forensic analysis of the ExFAT artefacts. arXiv preprint arXiv:1804.08653.

Windows App Development (2024). ExFAT file system specification - Win32 apps [Internet]. docs .microsoft.com. [cited 2024 May 23]. https://docs.microsoft.com/en-us/windows/win32/fileio/exfat-specification (accessed 13 August 2024).

7

The NTFS File System

The New Technology File System (NTFS) is traditionally one of the most 'interesting' file systems from a file system forensic perspective. The main reason for interest in NTFS is due to its use as the primary drive's (i.e. C:) file system in every Windows version since Windows NT. The file system was first introduced in Windows NT 3.1 in 1993 and to this day is still the default Windows file system.

The NTFS file system was a fork of HPFS (the High-Performance File System), a file system that Microsoft and IBM were designing in partnership. Hence it shares many features with HPFS including the MBR partition identifier (0x07).[1] Prior to the introduction of NTFS, the FAT family of file systems had been the default on Windows. As disks grew in size the FAT family provided an obvious limitation. Cluster addresses were only four bytes in size (actually less than this in reality). In NTFS cluster addresses could be up to eight bytes, allowing for many more clusters to be addressed, thereby supporting large disks. Additionally NTFS was designed to ensure that the basic operations (file read/write) were very efficient, again helping the file system to scale to larger systems.

In its day NTFS was a very modern file system. NTFS provided support for the following functionality (many of which are still encountered in new file systems to this day):

- **B-Tree-Based Directories:** Directory storage in NTFS, as in many modern file systems, is based on B-Trees. These structures maintain sorted data that are very quick to search, but also allowing for efficient insertions and deletions.
- **Alternate Data Streams:** Alternate data streams (ADS) are the name provided for forks in NTFS. Forks allow more than one single data stream to be associated with a filename. Generally ADS are not listed in Windows explorer when viewing the contents of a directory. Only the primary data stream is visible. Forensic tools will present the alternate data stream in addition to the primary stream.

  The ADS functionality was initially created for compatibility with Macintosh resource forks. The most commonly encountered use of these is for downloaded files. Internet Explorer began to create a *Zone.Identifier* ADS for every file downloaded from the web. This provided the URL from which the content was downloaded. It meant that other software was warned that the file was from the web and possibly untrustworthy. Other browsers have followed suit since. From an investigative perspective ADS can be used to hide information.

1 Now also shared with ExFAT.

File System Forensics, First Edition. Fergus Toolan.

- **Journaling:** NTFS is a journaling file system. The journal is available through the special system file ($LogFile). NTFS journals record metadata changes to the file system. The use of journaling made NTFS more fault tolerant than previous file systems.
- **Sparse Files:** A sparse file contains many clusters of empty space in the file. Most file systems will store these zero'd clusters as part of the file's contents. In NTFS, on the other hand, these empty regions are not actually stored on the disk. They are recorded in the metadata structures but the space can be used for other files.
- **Compression:** Compression in NTFS is implemented at the file system level. Folders (or files) can be marked as compressed. Any file that is moved to a compressed folder will automatically be compressed. Compression is achieved using algorithms that are based on the LZ77 compression algorithm.
- **Encryption:** Certain server versions of Windows allow for the encryption of files. Files are encrypted using a file encryption key which is used for symmetric encryption. This symmetric key is encrypted using asymmetric encryption with the public key held in an alternate data stream and the private key available from the logged in user details.
- **Access Control Lists:** NTFS uses security descriptors to define the owner. Each security descriptor contains two access control lists (ACLs). The discretionary access control list (DACL) defines the actions (read, write, etc.) that are allowed/forbidden for each user/group. The system access control list (SACL) defines the activities that should be logged.

The remainder of this chapter firstly examines the on-disk structure of NTFS (Section 7.1), before proceeding to introduce the basic analysis methods used for the NTFS file system (Section 7.2). This section will show the reader how digital forensic tools recover files from NTFS file systems. Finally the reader is introduced to some advanced concepts in the analysis of NTFS (Section 7.3) such as file deletion, fragmented files, alternate data streams and large MFT records.

7.1 On-Disk Structures

The NTFS file system consists of a number of system files which are summarised in Table 7.1. With one exception the location of these files is not defined. They may appear anywhere in the file system. Their location is determined from the Master File Table (MFT), which keeps a record of all metadata/content location information. The one exception is the $Boot file, which is always found in Sector 0.

7.1.1 $Boot

The $Boot metadata file is the only file on the NTFS file system for which the position is known. This file always occupies sector 0 on the device. The $Boot file serves an identical purpose to that of the volume boot record in FAT/ExFAT, and indeed the $Boot file is often referred to as the volume boot record or VBR for NTFS.

$Boot is 512_d bytes (one sector) in size. It contains bootstrap code and information about the volume structure. Table 7.2 provides the structure of $Boot. The $Boot file is the first step in the analysis of an NTFS file system. From a digital forensics perspective, the most important aspect of this structure is that it allows the location of $MFT to be determined. From $MFT all files on the file system can be recovered. $Boot also provides other information vital to further analysis such as the cluster size (a combination of sector size and sectors per cluster) and the $MFT record size. The remainder of the first sector in the file system is composed of the bootstrap code itself.

Table 7.1 Special files in NTFS.

MFT #	Name	Description
0	$MFT	This is the Master File Table (MFT) which contains an entry for every file in the NTFS file system. It is the most important structure in terms of NTFS forensic analysis.
1	$MFTMirr	The MFT Mirror mirrors the first cluster of the MFT itself.
2	$Logfile	Contains a journal which logs metadata changes. Information can be recovered from $Logfile in relation to previous states of the file system.
3	$Volume	Contains volume information such as the label, identifier and version.
4	$AttrDef	Contains information about the attributes used in the MFT such as names, identifiers and sizes.
5	.	Contains the file system's root directory.
6	$Bitmap	This structure contains the allocation status (used or unused) of every cluster in the file system.
7	$Boot	Contains the boot sector and boot code, often called the Volume Boot Record (VBR). This is the only file with a guaranteed position, always occurring in sector 0. $Boot is used to locate the first cluster of $MFT.
8	$BadClus	Contains a list of clusters that have bad sectors.
9	$Secure	Contains information about security and access control for files.
10	$Upcase	Contains the Uppercase version of every unicode character.
11	$Extend	A directory that contains file system extensions which have no reserved MFT record number.

7.1.2 Indexes

Indexes are used to store groups of attributes in a sorted order. One of the most commonly encountered index structures in NTFS is the directory. In this case a number of $FILENAME attributes (Section 7.1.6) are stored in the index. NTFS uses a B-Tree structure for storing indexes. A B-Tree is a self-balancing tree data structure which is often encountered in modern file systems. B-Trees are composed of nodes which are linked in a hierarchical manner. Each B-Tree has a top-level, head node, which has two or more children.[2] Internal nodes have a parent and two or more children, while leaf nodes have a parent and zero children.

Index structures (i.e. B-Trees) provide a large performance advantage over linear storage structures (such as FAT directory entries) as they are much quicker to search. B-Trees allow for searching, insertion and deletion in logarithmic time. Consider the sample B-Tree shown in Figure 7.1[3] and a search for the value 7_d.

The head node contains the value 6_d which is less than the desired value. This means that, if present in the tree, the value 7_d must be in the right child of the head node. Examining this node shows that value to be 8_d which is larger than the target. This results in the left child being searched. This node contains the desired value. Compare this to a linear data structure such as:

$$[6, 3, 8, 1, 4, 7, 10]$$

This would require six checks to locate the value 7_d as opposed to three checks in the B-Tree.

2 A B-Tree with two children for each node is called a binary tree.
3 This is a binary tree as each node has two children.

Table 7.2 NTFS $Boot structure.

Offset	Size	Name	Description
0x00	0x03	Jump	Jump instruction to access the boot strap code.
0x03	0x08	OEM Name	The original equipment manufacturer name. Always "NTFS".
0x0B	0x02	Sector Size	The sector size in bytes. This is generally 0x200 (512_d) bytes.
0x0D	0x01	Sectors/Cluster	The number of sectors per cluster. This is always a power of two.
0x0E	0x02	Reserved	Reserved Sectors. Must be zero.
0x10	0x03	Reserved	Zero'd.
0x13	0x02	Unused	Unused.
0x15	0x01	Media Descriptor	The type of media on which the file system is resident. This is generally 0xF8 for standard hard drives.
0x16	0x02	Reserved	Zero'd.
0x18	0x02	Sectors/Track	The number of sectors per physical track. This value is related to the old format CHS addressing in disks.
0x1A	0x02	# Heads	The number of heads on the disk. This value is related to the old format CHS addressing.
0x1C	0x04	Hidden Sectors	Meaning uncertain.
0x20	0x04	Unused	Unused.
0x24	0x04	Unused	Unused.
0x28	0x08	# Sectors	The total number of sectors on the device.
0x30	0x08	MFT Location	The logical cluster number for the first cluster of the $MFT file.
0x38	0x08	MFTMirr Location	The logical cluster number for the first cluster of the $MFTMirr file.
0x40	0x01	MFT Record Size	A two's complement number. A positive number represents the MFT record size in bytes. In the case of a negative number, x, the MFT record size is given by $2^{\|x\|}$ bytes.
0x41	0x03	Unused	Unused.
0x44	0x01	Clusters/Index	Num. clusters in the index buffer.
0x45	0x03	Unused	Unused.
0x48	0x08	Serial Number	The volume serial number.
0x50	0x04	Unused	Unused.

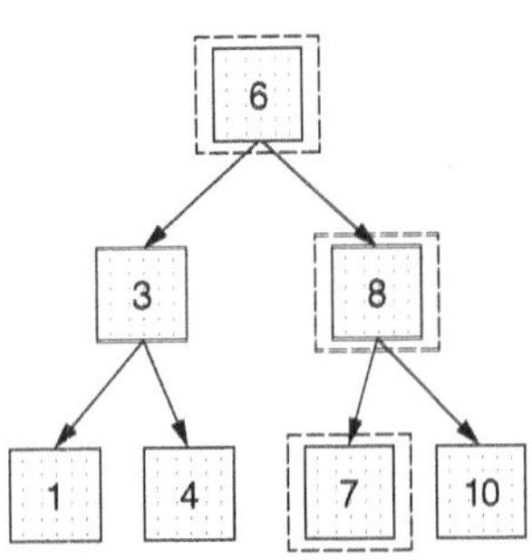

Figure 7.1 A sample B-Tree structure showing the three nodes that are examined in order to find the value 7_d.

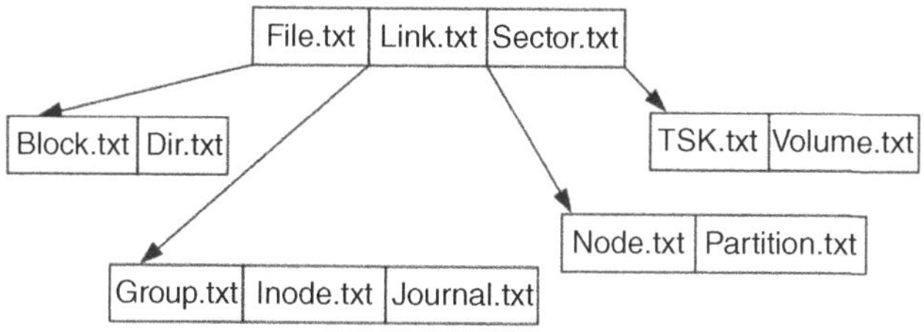

Figure 7.2 A sample B-Tree structure with filenames as values. Similar to that seen in many file systems.

In general B-Trees nodes can hold more than one single value in each node unlike the tree shown in Figure 7.1. Figure 7.2 provides a more accurate interpretation of a B-Tree that might be encountered in NTFS (or indeed in any modern file system). This B-Tree is being used to store file names, with each node being able to store a maximum of three values.

While searching is an extremely efficient operation insertion and deletion sometimes require the tree to be re-structured. This restructuring will sometimes overwrite old data (i.e. deleted file names for instance).

Indexes are stored in $INDEX_ROOT and $INDEX_ALLOCATION attributes (see Section 7.1.6). In the case of small indexes they will use the resident $INDEX_ROOT attribute, while large indexes use $INDEX_ALLOCATION, a non-resident attribute. Each index entry consists of a header and an attribute (e.g. $FILENAME for directories). The processing of these attributes (and all indexes) is shown later in this chapter (Section 7.2.3).

7.1.3 Fixup Arrays

NTFS uses a concept of fixup arrays (also called the Update Sequence Array) to increase reliability. The final two bytes in each sector of a metadata structure (such as an MFT record) are replaced with a signature. When the structure is accessed these signatures can be checked to ensure that all sectors are components of the same metadata structure. Figure 7.3 shows an NTFS metadata structure before and after applying fixup values.

In Figure 7.3, before the application of the fixup values, we see that the first sector's final two bytes are 0x1234 and the second sector's final two bytes are 0xCDEF. The fixup array portion of the structure is zero'd. In order to apply the fixup values, the following steps occur:

1. The signature value is increased (it becomes 0x0001)
2. The final two bytes of the first sector are stored in the first position in the fixup array
3. The signature is written to the final two bytes of the first sector (0x0001)
4. Steps 2 and 3 are repeated for each sector in the structure.

In order to interpret these fixup arrays it is necessary to first process the fixup array itself. Note an MFT record is used as an example in this case. The offset to the fixup array is given by two bytes at 0x04 in the $MFT header and the length of the fixup array is given in the subsequent two bytes. The Fixup Array begins with an update sequence number (the signature in Figure 7.3) and is followed by the actual fixup values themselves. Listing 7.1 shows an excerpt from an MFT Record (note some content has been removed for presentation purposes).

From Listing 7.1 we see that the Fixup Array is located at offset 0x30 and contains 0x03 elements. Each element is two bytes in size. The fixup array itself is also highlighted. The first element in the array is the signature (0x1D00), while the remaining elements are the original values that were replaced with the signature. At the end of each sector in the MFT Record, the last two bytes have

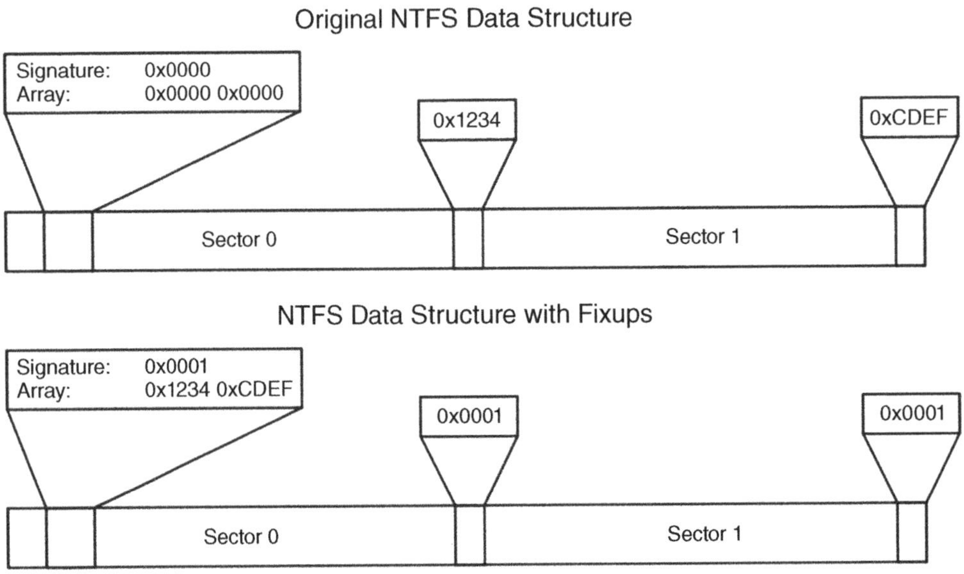

Figure 7.3 An original NTFS metadata structure (top) and the same metadata structure after the application of fixup values (bottom).

```
010400: 4649 4c45 3000 0300 0000 0000 0000 0000 FILE0...........
010410: 0200 0100 3800 0100 b801 0000 0004 0000 ....8...........
010420: 0000 0000 0000 0000 0400 0000 4100 0000 ............A...
010430: 1d00 0000 0000 0000 1000 0000 4800 0000 ............H...
...[snip]...
0105f0: 0000 0000 0000 0000 0000 0000 0000 1d00 ................
010600: 0000 0000 0000 0000 0000 0000 0000 0000 ................
...[snip]...
0107f0: 0000 0000 0000 0000 0000 0000 0000 1d00 ................
```

Listing 7.1 An MFT record demonstrating the use of the fixup array.

been replaced with the signature value. This signature values show that the two sectors in question are linked!

Forensic tools that support NTFS will include an ability to process these values, replacing the signature values with the original content during analysis. This concept is applicable in many metadata files in NTFS and as such is important to understand.

7.1.4 Time in NTFS

Most time values in NTFS are stored as 64-bit signed values, counting the number of 100 ns (10^{-7} s) intervals since 1 January 1601. All of these time values are stored in the UTC+0 timezone. When encountering these values there are a number of online converters that can be used to process the values. Listing 7.2 shows a means of getting the human-readable time for a particular Windows Filetime value: 0x1D7FED75319AEB1 (132854914796334769_d).

The Unix epoch time counts the number of seconds since 1 January 1970. In order to convert Windows filetime values to a human-readable format the **date** command can be used. The date

```
$ date -ud @$(( (0x1D7FED75319AEB1 / 10000000) - 11644473600))
Sat 01 Jan 2022 06:17:59 UTC
```

Listing 7.2 Using **date** to convert a Windows filetime (0x1D7FED75319AEB1) to a human-readable format.

command operates on Unix time stamps, so the Windows filetime value must first be converted to Unix time. This is a two-step process. Firstly the Windows time value must be converted from 100ns intervals to seconds. This requires division by $10,000,000_d$. The result of this calculation is the number of seconds since 1601. The second step is to remove the number of seconds between 1601 and 1970, in other words, to shift the epoch. This entails subtracting the value $11,644,473,600_d$ from the first result. The combination of these steps results in the Unix time-equivalent value. The process (including the **date** command) is shown in Listing 7.2.

7.1.5 Master File Table

The Master File Table ($MFT) is one of the most important structures in NTFS. $MFT contains information about all files and directories in the file system. It is the structure that is processed by forensic tools when they wish to list files in a file system, recover file metadata and also recover file content. Not only does $MFT contain information about user-created files, it always contains entries for all of the NTFS system files (including $MFT itself!)

$MFT is composed of a number of MFT records, at least one per file. The structure of each record is shown in Figure 7.4. Each record begins with a record header and is followed by a number of attributes. Attributes are composed of header and data components. The data for an attribute can be resident (stored inside the MFT Record itself) or non-resident (stored somewhere else in the file system). In the case of non-resident data the attribute will contain a pointer to the location of said non-resident data. Generally each MFT record is 1024_d bytes; however, this should be confirmed in $Boot.

From a forensic perspective, notice that there is often unused (slack) space at the end of an MFT Record. This provides the potential for partial recovery of old MFT entries. The attributes in NTFS include the following (note that the attribute-type identifier is provided in brackets):

- **$STANDARD_INFORMATION (0x10):** This attribute contains the metadata associated with a file. This includes MACB times, owner, security information, etc. This is of vital importance for recovering metadata for forensics.
- **$ATTRIBUTE_LIST (0x20):** Used in the case that a file needs multiple MFT Records. If present it points to other locations at which the remaining attributes will be found.
- **$FILE_NAME (0x30):** This contains the file name for the file/directory in question. Note that there can be multiple $FILE_NAME attributes, in the case of hard links or long file names. There are also timestamps present in this attribute.

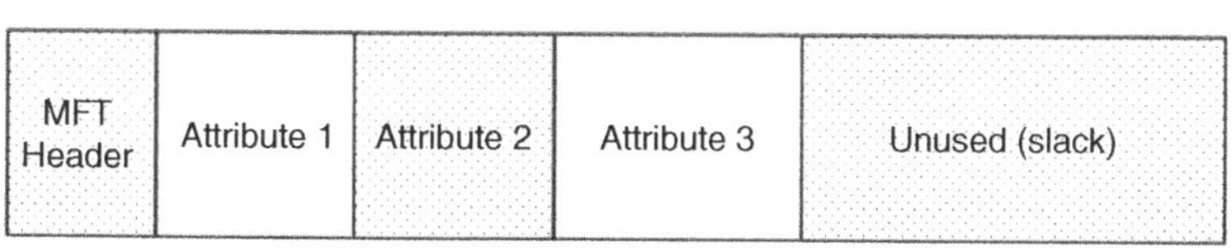

Figure 7.4 MFT record structure.

- **$OBJECT_ID (0x40):** This is a unique identifier for a file that allows tracking of a file even if the file name changes (or even if it is moved between systems). This is only available in later versions of NTFS.
- **$SECURITY_DESCRIPTOR (0x50):** Security properties/access control lists for the file.
- **$VOLUME_NAME (0x60):** This contains the volume name for a file system and is generally found only in MFT record 3 ($VOLUME).
- **$VOLUME_INFORMATION (0x70):** File system version information is found in this structure. This attribute is also found only in MFT record 3 ($VOLUME).
- **$DATA (0x80):** This is another vital attribute for digital forensics, as this attribute tells us how to find the file content! As stated previously this can be resident (for very small files) in which case the content is stored in the MFT record itself, or non-resident, in which case $DATA will provide us with the location of the content. Files in NTFS can have multiple $DATA attributes for a number of reasons. One of these is due to the possibility of Alternate Data Streams (ADS), a separate piece of data independent of the actual file content.
- **$INDEX_ROOT (0x90):** This is a B-Tree node used to locate other nodes in a B-Tree. These are used for storing files in directories.
- **$INDEX_ALLOCATION (0xA0):** In the case that there is insufficient space to store information in the $INDEX_ROOT structure, $INDEX_ALLOCATION is used to allocate extra clusters to the structure.
- **$BITMAP (0xB0):** A bitmap structure which informs on cluster allocation status.
- **$REPARSE_POINT (0xC0):** These are soft links, pointers to other files in the MFT.
- **$EA_INFORMATION (0xD0):** Used for implementing OS2[4] extended attributes for backwards compatibility.
- **$EA (0xE0):** Used for implementing OS2 extended attributes for backwards compatibility.
- **$LOGGED_UTILITY_STREAM (0x100):** Contains keys and information about encrypted attributes in recent versions of NTFS.

The above attributes will be covered in more detail later in this section.

7.1.6 MFT Record Structure

Figure 7.4 provided a graphical view of the MFT record structure. This consists of an MFT record header followed by a number of attributes. Attributes consist of header and data sections. The attribute can be resident, in which case the data is stored in the MFT record itself, or non-resident, in which case the data is stored at another location in the file system. Resident and non-resident attributes have independent headers.

7.1.6.1 MFT Record Header

The MFT record header structure is a 42_d byte structure found at the beginning of every MFT record. The structure of this record header is shown in Table 7.3.

Every attribute begins with a 16-byte header. This is followed by information on where the attribute data can be encountered. There are two possibilities: either the data is resident or non-resident. Resident data is located in the actual MFT record itself, whereas non-resident data is found in other locations in the file system. Table 7.4 provides the attribute header structure.

The attribute header is followed by a secondary header. The structure of this is dependent on whether the attribute is resident or non-resident. The structure of the resident attribute header is shown in Table 7.5 and the non-resident attribute header in Table 7.6.

4 OS/2 was an operating system created jointly by Microsoft and IBM until 1992 and solely by IBM until 2001.

Table 7.3 MFT record header structure.

Offset	Size	Name	Description
0x00	0x04	Signature	The MFT record signature value (FILE).
0x04	0x02	Fixup Array Offset	The offset to the fixup array.
0x06	0x02	Fixup Array Size	The number of entries in the fixup array.
0x08	0x08	LSN	$LOGFILE sequence number.
0x10	0x02	Sequence Value	The number of times this MFT record has been reused.
0x12	0x02	Link Count	The number of links to this file.
0x14	0x02	First Attribute Offset	The byte offset to the first attribute in the record.
0x16	0x02	Flags	Record Flags: 0x01 - Record in Use; 0x02 Directory.
0x18	0x04	Record Size (used)	The actual size of the MFT record in bytes.
0x1C	0x04	Record Size (alloc)	The allocated size of the MFT record in bytes. This is generally the same as that in the $Boot structure for MFT record size.
0x20	0x08	File Reference	File reference to base record.
0x28	0x02	Next Attribute ID	The ID for the next attribute in the record. This is one more than the current number of attributes in the record.

Table 7.4 Attribute header structure.

Offset	Size	Name	Description
0x00	0x04	Attribute Type	The attribute type identifier (see Section 7.1.5 for the list of attributes (with identifiers)).
0x04	0x04	Attribute Size	Attribute size in bytes.
0x08	0x01	Non-Resident Flag	This flag is 0x01 when an attribute is non-resident, and 0x00 for resident attributes.
0x09	0x01	Name Length	Length of the attribute name in bytes.
0x0A	0x02	Name Offset	Offset to the attribute name in bytes.
0x0C	0x02	Flags	Flags relating to the attribute. Some flags include: 0x0001 (compressed); 0x4000 (encrypted) and 0x8000 (sparse).
0x0E	0x02	Attribute ID	An ID number unique to this attribute in this MFT record.

Table 7.5 Resident attribute header structure.

Offset	Size	Name	Description
0x00	0x10	Common Header	The common attribute header (see Table 7.4)
0x10	0x04	Content Size	The size of the attribute content in bytes.
0x14	0x02	Content Offset	The offset to the start of the attribute data in bytes. This offset is relative to the start of the attribute.

Table 7.6 Non-resident attribute header structure.

Offset	Size	Name	Description
0x00	0x10	Common Header	The common attribute header (see Table 7.4).
0x10	0x08	Starting VCN	The starting virtual cluster number (VCN) of the runlist (in other words the position in the file content that this run list represents).
0x18	0x08	Ending VCN	The ending VCN of the runlist.
0x20	0x02	Runlist Offset	The location of the runlist relative to the start of the attribute.
0x22	0x02	Compression Unit	Compression algorithm used.
0x24	0x04	Unused	Unused.
0x28	0x08	Allocated Size	The allocated size of the attribute content.
0x30	0x08	Actual Size	The actual size of the attribute content.
0x38	0x08	Initialised Size	The initialised size of the attribute content.

Resident attribute headers allow the direct location of the resident attribute data to be determined by providing a byte offset to the beginning of the data and the size of the data in bytes. Non-resident attributes are slightly more complex when locating the actual data. The key component in data location in a non-resident attribute is the runlist. The non-resident attribute header structure provides the offset to the runlist, relative to the start of the attribute (see Table 7.6). The run list itself is a variable length (null terminated) structure. As the name suggests a run list is composed of one or more runs. Each run provides the starting cluster and number of clusters in which the data can be located.

Run lists are themselves composed of three parts. The first part (one single byte) describes the structure of the run list. The second part provides the number of clusters in the run and the third provides the starting cluster of the run list. The final two parts of the run list structure are variable length. The first byte informs the analyst of the length of each part. Consider the runlist 0x21112001 as shown in Figure 7.5.

The first byte describes the structure. The high-order nibble of this byte provides the number of bytes used in the starting cluster, while the low-order nibble provides the number of bytes used to store the number of contiguous clusters in the run. This is followed by the number of contiguous clusters in the run. The length of this value is identified by the low-order nibble in the first byte. This is 0x11 (17_d) in Figure 7.5. Finally the starting cluster is found. The length of this value is determined by the high-order nibble in the first byte. In Figure 7.5 the value of the starting cluster is 0x120 (288_d).

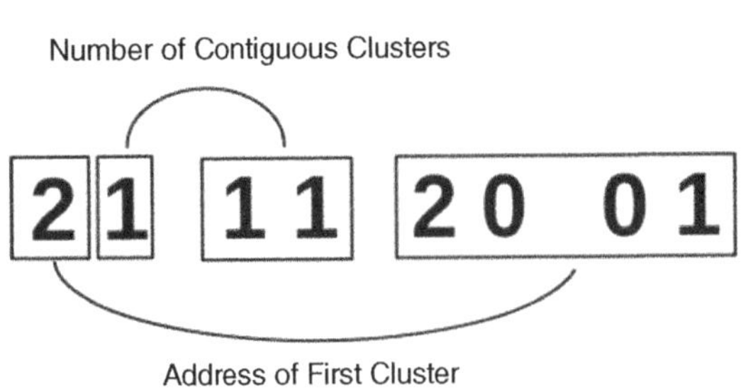

Figure 7.5 A sample run list. The first byte describes the structure which is followed by the number of clusters and the starting cluster.

7.1.6.2 Browsing Attributes

Generally when processing an MFT record it is necessary to process all of the attributes present. The method for doing this is as follows:

1. Process the MFT record header (Table 7.3) and locate the offset to the first attribute.
2. Process the common attribute header for attribute 1 and find the length of the attribute. Extract this content (this is attribute 1)
3. Repeat step 2 (using the attribute length to move to the start of the next attribute). This process is shown in Listing 7.3 for a sample MFT record.

In Listing 7.3 the offset to the first attribute is given as 0x38 bytes. At this offset begins the attribute header for the first attribute. The first four bytes of this header determine the attribute type. In this case the value is 0x10 (which is the $STANDARD_INFORMATION attribute – see Section 7.1.5). The next four bytes contain the length of this attribute (0x48 bytes). Moving forward 0x48 bytes will find the start of the next attribute. This process continues as described. The results of this process are shown in Table 7.7.

```
010800: 4649 4c45 3000 0300 0000 0000 0000 0000 FILE0...........
010810: 0100 0100 3800 0100 a801 0000 0004 0000 ....8...........
010820: 0000 0000 0000 0000 0400 0000 4200 0000 ............B...
010830: 8b00 0000 0000 0000 1000 0000 4800 0000 ............H...
010840: 0000 0000 0000 0000 3000 0000 1800 0000 ........0.......
010850: 8ee3 3a81 bc0b da01 8e90 3b81 bc0b da01 ..:.......;.....
010860: 8e90 3b81 bc0b da01 8ee3 3a81 bc0b da01 ..;.......:.....
010870: 2000 0000 0000 0000 0000 0000 0000 0000  ...............
010880: 3000 0000 7000 0000 0000 0000 0000 0300 0...p...........
010890: 5400 0000 1800 0100 4100 0000 0000 0100 T.......A.......
0108a0: 8ee3 3a81 bc0b da01 8ee3 3a81 bc0b da01 ..:.......:.....
0108b0: 8ee3 3a81 bc0b da01 8ee3 3a81 bc0b da01 ..:.......:.....
0108c0: 0040 0400 0000 0000 0000 0000 0000 0000 .@..............
0108d0: 2000 0000 0000 0000 0900 6800 6900 6c00  .........h.i.l.
0108e0: 6c00 7300 2e00 6a00 7000 6700 1800 0000 l.s...j.p.g.....
0108f0: 5000 0000 6800 0000 0000 0000 0000 0100 P...h...........
010900: 5000 0000 1800 0000 0100 0480 1400 0000 P...............
010910: 2400 0000 0000 0000 3400 0000 0102 0000 $.......4.......
010920: 0000 0005 2000 0000 2002 0000 0102 0000 .... ... .......
010930: 0000 0005 2000 0000 2002 0000 0200 1c00 .... ... .......
010940: 0100 0000 0003 1400 ff01 1f00 0101 0000 ................
010950: 0000 0001 0000 0000 8000 0000 4800 0000 ............H...
010960: 0100 4000 0000 0200 0000 0000 0000 0000 ..@.............
010970: 4300 0000 0000 0000 4000 0000 0000 0000 C.......@.......
010980: 0040 0400 0000 0000 3d31 0400 0000 0000 .@......=1......
010990: 3d31 0400 0000 0000 2144 0042 0000 0000 =1......!D.B....
0109a0: ffff ffff 0000 0000 ffff ffff 0000 0000 ................
```

Listing 7.3 An MFT record showing the offset to the first attribute (0x38) and the attribute types and lengths along with the end of record marker.

7.1.6.3 $STANDARD_INFORMATION (0x10)

Much of the metadata in NTFS is stored in the $STANDARD_INFORMATION attribute. The structure of this is shown in Table 7.8. This attribute is always resident. As such the common header (Table 7.4) will be followed by the resident header structure (Table 7.5).

Table 7.7 The attributes and their lengths from the MFT record in Listing 7.3.

Attribute Type	Attribute Name	Length
0x10	$STANDARD_INFORMATION	0x48
0x30	$FILENAME	0x70
0x50	$SECURITY_DESCRIPTOR	0x68
0x80	$DATA	0x48

Table 7.8 The $STANDARD_INFORMATION attribute structure.

Offset	Size	Name	Description
0x00	0x08	Creation Time	The time at which the file was created.
0x08	0x08	Modification Time	The time at which the file's contents were modified.
0x10	0x08	MFT Change Time	The time at which the file's metadata was last modified.
0x18	0x08	Access Time	The time at which the file was last accessed.
0x20	0x04	Flags	This provides information about the file referenced by this MFT record. The flag values are found in Table 7.9.
0x24	0x04	Max. # Versions	The maximum number of versions.
0x28	0x04	Version Number	The current version number.
0x2C	0x04	Class ID	The class ID.
0x30	0x04	Owner ID	The owner ID (Not always present).
0x34	0x04	Security ID	The security ID mapping to $SECURE (not to a Windows SID).
0x38	0x08	Quota Changed	Quota change.
0x40	0x08	USN	The Update Sequence Number (USN) (not always present).

$STANDARD_INFORMATION contains the file timestamps. NTFS records MACB timestamps, modification, access, change and birth (creation). These values are Windows 64 bit timestamps which can be converted as shown in Section 7.1.4.

7.1.6.4 $ATTRIBUTE_LIST (0x20)

In the case in which the attributes for the MFT record will not fit into a single MFT record, there exists the $ATTRIBUTE_LIST attribute which will provide the locations of other attributes. $ATTRIBUTE_LIST may be resident or non-resident. The contents of $ATTRIBUTE_LIST are a list of 32_d byte structures each of which follows the structure shown in Table 7.10. Section 7.3.5 provides an example of an MFT record that uses $ATTRIBUTE_LIST.

7.1.6.5 $FILENAME (0x30)

As the name suggests $FILENAME attributes store filenames for particular MFT records. Both files and directories have at least one $FILENAME attribute. In addition to the filename these attributes also store further MACB times. Similar to $STANDARD_INFORMATION these timestamps are

Table 7.9 Flag values for the $STANDARD_INFORMATION attribute.

Value	Description	Value	Description
0x0001	Read-Only	0x0200	Sparse File
0x0002	Hidden	0x0400	Reparse Point
0x0004	System	0x0800	Compressed
0x0020	Archive	0x1000	Offline
0x0040	Device	0x2000	Content not indexed
0x0080	Normal	0x4000	Encrypted
0x0100	Temporary		

Table 7.10 $ATTRIBUTE_LIST structure.

Offset	Size	Name	Description
0x00	0x04	Attribute Type	The attribute-type identifier for the specific attribute.
0x04	0x02	Entry Length	The size of this structure in bytes.
0x06	0x01	Name Length	The size of the name in bytes.
0x07	0x01	Name Offset	The offset to the attribute name.
0x08	0x08	Starting VCN	Used if the attribute requires multiple MFT entries to describe the content.
0x10	0x08	File Reference	File reference of where the attribute is located. The first four bytes represent the MFT record number.
0x18	0x01	Attribute ID	Attribute ID.

Windows filetime objects (100 ns intervals since 1 January 1601). The structure of $FILENAME is provided in Table 7.11.

An interesting item in relation to the $FILENAME attribute is that this is the attribute that is used to determine file size. In order to recover the complete file content this attribute must be consulted along with the $DATA attribute. $DATA provides the location of the file's data while $FILENAME provides the actual file size. Also, unlike other file systems, NTFS contains a second set of timestamps in relation to each file in the $FILENAME attribute. These timestamps are related to the filename itself and are generally updated when files are created, moved, renamed, etc., rather than when content is modified or accessed.

7.1.6.6 $OBJECT_ID (0x40)

The $OBJECT_ID (OID) attribute is used by the distributed link tracking service in Windows which is used to locate a file even after it has been moved or renamed. $OBJECT_ID contains an Universally Unique IDentifier (UUID) for each file created on the system. These are indexed in the system file **$Extend\$ObjID** which allows the files to be located even after renaming/moving.

The $OBJECT_ID attribute is always resident with a maximum size of 64_d bytes. The structure of $OBJECT_ID is shown in Table 7.12. Many modern implementations specify only the first field in this structure. In other words it is now common to encounter $OBJECT_ID attributes which consist of a 16_d byte Object ID and nothing else.

Table 7.11 $FILENAME attribute structure.

Offset	Size	Name	Description
0x00	0x08	Parent MFT	MFT file reference of the parent directory.
0x08	0x08	Creation Time	Time at which the MFT record was created.
0x10	0x08	Modification Time	Time at which the contents were modified.
0x18	0x08	Change Time	Time at which the MFT record was changed.
0x20	0x08	Access Time	Time at which the contents were last accessed.
0x28	0x08	Allocated Size	The space, in bytes, allocated on disk to store this file.
0x30	0x08	Actual Size	The actual file size in bytes.
0x38	0x04	Flags	Flags (same as those in $STANDARD_INFORMATION – see Table 7.9).
0x3C	0x04	Reparse Value	Reparse value.
0x40	0x01	Name Length (n)	The number of UTF-16 characters in the name ($n \times 2$ provides the number of bytes for the name).
0x41	0x01	Name Space	The namespace type. Valid values are: 0x00: POSIX – case sensitive unicode; 0x01: Win32 – Unicode case insensitive; 0x02: DOS – Case insensitive, no special characters, 8.3 format required; and 0x03: Win32/DOS – Original name fits DOS standard and two names are not required.
0x42	$n \times 2$	Name	The actual name (in UTF-16 encoding).

Table 7.12 $OBJECT_ID attribute structure. Note that often in recent Windows versions only the first 16_d bytes are used.

Offset	Size	Name	Description
0x00	0x10	OID UUID	The Object ID for the item in question. This value should be unique for each item on the file system. Note that this uniqueness property should hold for network file systems also, meaning that it might cover more than one device.
0x10	0x10	Birth VID	The UUID of the volume on which this item was originally created. This should not change during the object's lifetime, even if it is moved to a different system.
0x20	0x10	Birth OID	The original OID of the item. The OID might change if an item is moved to a different system but this birth OID should always remain constant.
0x30	0x10	Domain ID	The UUID for the domain on which the item was created. This is generally unused.

The $OBJECT_ID attribute is created as part of the Distributed Link Tracking Service in Windows. As such it will generally not be found when files are created/opened on other operating systems. The attribute is created only when a file is created or opened using Windows. The majority of operations (e.g. moving and renaming) will preserve the OID value but copying the file will alter it. This is due to the creation of a new item from the copy which cannot have the same OID as the original item.

OID values are generated following a specific pattern. Consider the OID shown in Listing 7.4. This is composed of three components. The first eight bytes represent the time at which the item was created. The next two bytes are a counter, while the final six bytes are the MAC address of the computer on which the item was created. This can be used to link a file to a specific computer; however, this information could be spoofed. If no MAC address is present a random value is used instead.

```
00e5a8: 47f8 44e4 3478 ec11 88c9 0800 2771 5e21
```

Listing 7.4 An OID discovered in an MFT record's $OBJECT_ID attribute.

The time that is used in the $OBJECT_ID is not the same as that used in the rest of NTFS. In this case time is a 60_d bit value which counts the number of 100_dns intervals since 1 January 1582. In order to convert the little-endian 64_d bit value in Listing 7.4 the first step is to convert to big-endian and drop the most significant nibble (i.e. the most significant 4_d bits). From Listing 7.4 this results in 0x1EC7834E444F847. The next step is to subtract the number of 100_dns intervals between 1582 and 1601 (the start of traditional NTFS time). This value is 0x146BF33E42C000 which results in 0x1D80C4196023847. This can be converted using the method shown previously. Converting this value to a human-readable format results in Tuesday, 18 January 2022 8:01:23 AM.

7.1.6.7 $SECURITY_DESCRIPTOR (0x50)

$SECURITY_DESCRIPTOR attributes are generally encountered only in the $SECURE file rather than in MFT records. The attribute may be resident or non-resident. Structurally the attribute's data is composed of a 0x14 byte header, followed by two ACLs: one, the SACL for auditing purposes and the other, DACL for permissions. Each ACL is composed of one or more Access Control Entries (ACE) and SID pairs. The attribute's data is finalised with two security identifiers (SID) representing the owner and the group. The $SECURITY_DESCRIPTOR attribute header structure is shown in Table 7.13.

All offsets provided in Table 7.13 are relative to the start of the attribute's data. The header contains information on the locations of the User and Group Security Descriptors (SID) and also the offset to the System and Discretionary ACLs.

The SID uniquely identifies a user (or group) in the Windows operating system and can be used by NTFS to show ownership of a file. The SID is a variable length structure which is shown in Table 7.14. Each SID comprised of a minimum of two components (the version

Table 7.13 $SECURITY_DESCRIPTOR attribute header structure.

Offset	Size	Name	Description
0x00	0x01	Revision	Revision Number.
0x01	0x01	Padding	Padding Byte (0x00).
0x02	0x02	Control Flags	Control Flags.
0x04	0x04	User SID Offset	Byte offset to the User SID.
0x08	0x04	Group SID Offset	Byte offset to the Group SID.
0x0C	0x04	SACL Offset	Byte offset to the SACL.
0x10	0x04	DACL Offset	Byte offset to the DACL.

Table 7.14 The Security ID (SID) structure.

Offset	Size	Name	Description
0x00	0x01	Version	The version is the first component of the SID (and is generally 1). S- is added before the version for presentation purposes.
0x01	0x01	Sub-Auth Count (n)	The number of subauthorities that are present in this SID.
0x02	0x06	Authority ID	The authority ID, i.e. the X is S-1-X.
0x08	0x04× 4	SubAuthority[]	Each four-byte element in this array is appended to the SID in the order in which they are found in these fields.

Table 7.15 Access control list (ACL) structure.

Offset	Size	Name	Description
0x00	0x01	ACL Revision	Revision number associated with the ACL.
0x01	0x01	Padding	Padding.
0x02	0x02	ACL Size	The size of the ACL in bytes.
0x04	0x02	ACE Count	The number of ACEs in the ACL.
0x06	0x02	Padding	Padding.

and authority ID) and any number of optional subauthority IDs. In Windows SIDs are written in a particular pattern, an example of this is S-1-5-32-544.[5] The letter S merely identifies the following value as an SID. Next is the revision level (1) which is followed by an identifier authority (5 - SECURITY_NT_AUTHORITY),[6] and two subauthority values (32 and 544).

Consider the SID shown in Listing 7.5. Alternate fields are underlined.

```
0000000: 0102 0000 0000 0005 2000 0000 2002 0000  ................
```

Listing 7.5 A sample SID.

The resulting SID would appear as S-1-5-32-544. This is version 1_d, consisting of two subauthorities. The main authority ID is 5_d, while the subauthorities are 32_d and 544_d. In the case of multiple subauthorities in an SID the final part is the relative ID (which should be unique in the domain in question) while the other subauthorities represent the domain. Each domain should have a unique subauthority value.

The next component of $SECURITY_DESCRIPTOR is that of the ACLs. The ACL structure is shown in Table 7.15. There can be two types of ACL, the SACL and the DACL. The DACL defines the users/groups and the actions that they are permitted to perform on the item. The SACL on the other hand defines the attempted actions that should be logged in the Windows event log.

Each ACL consists of a list of Access Control Entries (ACE). Each ACE specifies the access rights which should be permitted/disallowed (or logged in the case of an ACE in the SACL) for a particular

5 This is the SID of the Windows local administrators group.
6 Some common keys and authority meanings can be found at https://docs.microsoft.com/en-us/windows/win32/secauthz/well-known-sids.

Table 7.16 Access control entry (ACE) structure.

Offset	Size	Name	Description
0x00	0x01	Type	Describes the permission represented by the ACE. Valid values include 0x00 – Access Allowed; 0x01 – Access Denied; and 0x02 – System Audit.
0x01	0x01	Flags	ACE flags.
0x02	0x02	ACE Size	The size of the ACE in bytes.
0x04	0x04	Access Mask	The access mask defines the types of access that are permitted.
0x08	Variable	SID	The SID to which the ACE refers.

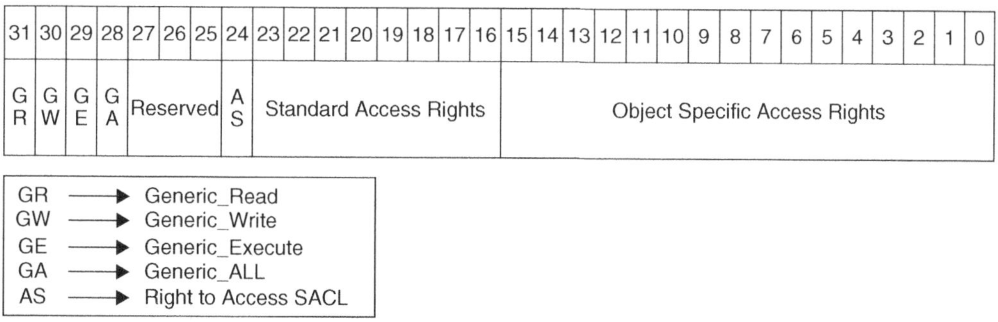

Figure 7.6 The Access Mask bit field structure.

user/group. Note that if there is no DACL present the system will grant full rights to all users but if a DACL is present which contains no ACEs the system will deny all rights to all users. The ACE structure is shown in Table 7.16.

The access mask in the ACE is used to define the exact types of access that are permitted. The access mask is a bit-field structure as shown in Figure 7.6. The meanings of the object specific access rights and the standard access rights are provided in Tables 7.17 and 7.18, respectively.

Table 7.17 Object specific access mask bits.

Bit	Meaning
0	FILE_READ_DATA/FILE_LIST_DIRECTORY
1	FILE_WRITE_DATA/FILE_ADD_FILE
2	FILE_APPEND_DATA/FILE_ADD_SUBDIRECTORY/FILE_CREATE_PIPE_INSTANCE
3	FILE_READ_EA/FILE_READ_PROPERTIES
4	FILE_WRITE_EA/FILE_WRITE_PROPERTIES
5	FILE_EXECUTE (File)/FILE_TRAVERSE (Directory)
6	FILE_DELETE_CHILD
7	FILE_READ_ATTRIBUTES
8	FILE_WRITE_ATTRIBUTES

Table 7.18 Standard access mask bits.

Bit	Meaning
16	DELETE
17	READ_CONTROL
18	WRITE_DAC
19	WRITE_OWNER
20	SYNCHRONIZE

The access mask bit field combined with the access type and the SID shows what actions certain users are allowed/disallowed from performing.

7.1.6.8 $VOLUME_NAME (0x60)

$VOLUME_NAME is found only in the MFT record for the $VOLUME file (MFT record: 3_d). This attribute contains the volume label which was assigned to the device at creation time. Listing 7.6 shows a $VOLUME_NAME attribute. The attribute header, resident header and data are highlighted.

```
000d68: 6000 0000 2800 0000 0000 1800 0000 0400  `...(...........
000d78: 0e00 0000 1800 0000 4e00 5400 4600 5300  ........N.T.F.S.
000d88: 2d00 4600 5300 0000                      -.F.S...
```

Listing 7.6 A sample $VOLUME_NAME attribute.

The structure of this attribute's data is very simple, it is merely the UTF-16 encoded volume label. The offset to the data and the size of the data is found in the resident attribute header ($VOLUME_NAME is always resident). In Listing 7.6 the offset to the data is 0x18 and the data is 0x0E bytes in size. The value of the volume label is "NTFS-FS".

7.1.6.9 $VOLUME_INFORMATION (0x70)

Similar to $VOLUME_NAME, $VOLUME_INFORMATION is another attribute that is found only in the $VOLUME file (MFT record: 3). Listing 7.7 shows the contents of a sample $VOLUME_INFORMATION attribute.

```
000d90: 7000 0000 2800 0000 0000 1800 0000 0500  p...(...........
000da0: 0c00 0000 1800 0000 0000 0000 0000 0000  ................
000db0: 0301 0000 0000 0000                      ........
```

Listing 7.7 Contents of a sample $VOLUME_INFORMATION attribute in the $Volume MFT record.

Again, this attribute is always resident and is 0x28 bytes in size. The resident header informs the analyst that the data begins at 0x18 and is 0x0C bytes in length. The data is interpreted using Table 7.19.

Table 7.19 The $VOLUME_INFORMATION attribute structure. The values are from Listing 7.7.

Offset	Size	Name	Description	Value
0x00	0x08	Unused	Unused – generally zero'd.	0x00
0x08	0x01	FS Major Version	The major version number of the file system.	0x03
0x09	0x01	FS Minor Version	The minor version number of the file system	0x01
0x0A	0x02	Flags	Volume flags (see Table 7.20)	0x00

Table 7.20 Flag values for the $VOLUME_INFORMATION attribute in NTFS.

Flag	Description
0x0001	Dirty
0x0002	Resize $Logfile
0x0004	Upgrade Volume next time
0x0008	Mounted in NT
0x0010	Deleting Change Journal
0x0020	Repair Object IDs
0x8000	Modified by **chkdsk**

The combination of major/minor version in $VOLUME_INFORMATION is used to give some indication of the file system's age. A version of 1.2 is generally created under Windows NT, 3.0 is created under Windows 2000, while 3.1 is anything created since the time of Windows XP. Most encountered NTFS file systems will have a version of 3.1.

7.1.6.10 $DATA (0x80)

The $DATA attribute is used to discover the location of file content. $DATA attributes can be resident or non-resident. They have no actual structure being fully dependent on the file's content. The attribute is merely used to locate the content. In the case of a resident primary $DATA attribute (for instance in the case of a very small file), the file's contents are found directly in the MFT record itself, and therefore do not occupy any clusters on disk. Non-resident $DATA is located through the data run found in the non-resident attribute header.

A single MFT record can contain multiple $DATA attributes. These are referred to as alternate data streams and are generally named attributes (for instance the Zone.Identifier ADS mentioned previously). Processing of these ADS is demonstrated in Section 7.3.4.

7.1.6.11 $INDEX_ROOT (0x90)

NTFS index structures are used to hold directory entries and are organised as B-Trees. There are two forms of index attribute, $INDEX_ROOT and $INDEX_ALLOCATION. In the case of small index structures (for instance directories with only a small number of files) all of the items are listed in the resident $INDEX_ROOT structure. In the case that the volume of data is too large for a resident structure, the non-resident $INDEX_ALLOCATION structure is used instead.

Listing 7.8 shows a sample $INDEX_ROOT attribute. The $INDEX_ROOT attribute is a named attribute, the name is always $I30. The attribute's data is composed of a 16_d byte $INDEX_ROOT header, followed by a node header, followed by a sequence of directory entries. These directory entries contain, among other things, a $FILENAME attribute which provides information about each file in the directory.

```
014550: 9000 0000 2001 0000 0004 1800 0000 0200 .... ...........
014560: 0001 0000 2000 0000 2400 4900 3300 3000 .... ...$.I.3.0.
014570: 3000 0000 0100 0000 0010 0000 0100 0000 0...............
014580: 1000 0000 f000 0000 f000 0000 0000 0000 ................
014590: 4400 0000 0000 0100 6800 5600 0000 0000 D.......h.V.....
0145a0: 4100 0000 0000 0100 5af1 3490 bc0b da01 A.......Z.4.....
0145b0: 9d03 3590 bc0b da01 9d03 3590 bc0b da01 ..5.......5.....
0145c0: 5af1 3490 bc0b da01 4800 0000 0000 0000 Z.4.....H.......
0145d0: 4200 0000 0000 0000 2000 0000 0000 0000 B....... .......
0145e0: 0a00 6400 6500 6c00 6500 7400 6500 2e00 ..d.e.l.e.t.e...
0145f0: 7400 7800 7400 0000 4200 0000 0000 4b00 t.x.t...B.....K.
014600: 6800 5400 0000 0000 4100 0000 0000 0100 h.T.....A.......
014610: 8ee3 3a81 bc0b da01 8e90 3b81 bc0b da01 ..:.......;.....
014620: 8e90 3b81 bc0b da01 8ee3 3a81 bc0b da01 ..;.......:.....
014630: 0040 0400 0000 0000 3d31 0400 0000 0000 .@......=1......
014640: 2000 0000 0000 0000 0900 6800 6900 6c00 ..........h.i.l.
014650: 6c00 7300 2e00 6a00 7000 6700 0000 0000 l.s...j.p.g.....
014660: 0000 0000 0000 0000 1000 0000 0200 0000 ................
```

Listing 7.8 The $INDEX_ROOT attribute from MFT record number 65_d in **NTFS_V1.E01**.

Table 7.21 presents the structure of the $INDEX_ROOT header. The values included in this table are taken from Listing 7.8. One of the most important pieces of information provided in the header is the attribute type used in the index. In Table 7.21 the attribute type is 0x30 which is a $FILENAME attribute. This is expected, as the $FILENAME attribute contains the file names allowing for directory contents to be listed.

The $INDEX_ROOT header is immediately followed by the node header. This structure allows the index entries to be located. The structure of the node header is provided in Table 7.22. The values shown in this table are taken from Listing 7.8.

The node header allows the first entry in the index to be located (0x10). The byte offset provided is relative to the start of the node header. The type value from the $INDEX_ROOT header determines

Table 7.21 $INDEX_ROOT header structure with values from Listing 7.8.

Offset	Size	Name	Description	Value
0x00	0x04	Type	The type of attribute in the index.	0x30 (48_d)
0x04	0x04	Collation	The collation sorting rule to use.	0x01 (1_d)
0x08	0x04	Record Size	The size of each index record in bytes.	0x1000 (4096_d)
0x0C	0x01	Record Size	The size of each index record in clusters.	0x01 (1_d)
0x0D	0x03	Unused		0x00 (0_d)

the type of entry that is present. In this case these are $FILENAME attributes. A quick glance at Listing 7.8 shows that two files are present, **delete.txt** and **hills.jpg**.

7.1.6.12 $INDEX_ALLOCATION (0xA0)

When the number of entries in an index is too large for the resident $INDEX_ROOT structure, a non-resident $INDEX_ALLOCATION structure is used instead. In this case the $INDEX_ROOT attribute will still be present, along with the $INDEX_ALLOCATION attribute and also a $BITMAP attribute which outlines the allocation status of the index records.

Each $INDEX_ALLOCATION attribute contains fixed-size index records, each of which contains a single tree node. The size of each index record is defined in the $INDEX_ROOT structure.

Each record is composed of an index record header, followed by a node header and then a list of entries. The node header follows the exact same structure as in the $INDEX_ROOT attribute (Table 7.22). The index record header structure is given in Table 7.23.

7.1.6.13 $BITMAP (0xB0)

A bitmap (or allocation status) describes the allocation status of an item in a computer system. In NTFS the $BITMAP attribute contains this information.[7] The $Bitmap attribute is always found in the MFT Record for $MFT itself. In this case the bitmap represents the allocation status of individual MFT records. Listing 7.9 shows an extract from an allocation bitmap.

Table 7.22 $INDEX_ROOT node header structure with values from Listing 7.8.

Offset	Size	Name	Description	Value
0x00	0x04	Index List Offset	The byte offset to the start of the Index Entry List (relative to the start of the node header)	0x10 (16_d)
0x04	0x04	Index End Offset	The byte offset to the end of the Index Entry list (relative to the start of the node header)	0xF0 (240_d)
0x08	0x04	Index Buffer Offset	Offset to the end of the allocated index entry list buffer (relative to the start of the node header)	0xF0 (240_d)
0x0C	0x04	Flags		0x00 (0_d)

Table 7.23 The index record header structure.

Offset	Size	Name	Description
0x00	0x04	Signature	The index record header signature (INDX).
0x04	0x02	Fixup Offset	The offset to the fixup array.
0x06	0x02	Fixup Size	The number of entries in the fixup array.
0x08	0x08	LSN	The Log File Sequence number.
0x10	0x10	VCN	The virtual cluster number of this record in the index stream.

7 Note that there is also a $Bitmap file, which contains the allocation status of clusters in the file system (MFT Record 6). It is important not to confuse the two.

In a bitmap structure each item is represented by one single bit. A bit value of one means the item is allocated while zero means that it is unallocated. The first byte represents items 0–7 (item zero is represented by the least significant bit, while item 7 is represented by the most significant). The second byte represents items 8–15, and so forth.

```
002000: ffff 0007 0000 0000 0706 0000 0000 0000 ................
```

Listing 7.9 An excerpt from a sample bitmap structure representing MFT record allocation status.

Consider the byte at offset 0x03 in Listing 7.9. This has the value 0x07 which, in binary, is 0b00000111. As it is the fourth byte in the bitmap it represents the allocation status of items 24_d–31_d. The three least significant bits are marked as being allocated which means that items 24_d, 25_d and 26_d are allocated while the remaining items represented by this byte are unallocated (all have zero values).

7.1.6.14 $REPARSE_POINT (0xC0)

A reparse point provides a means of extending the NTFS file system. Reparse points consist of a tag and data. The tag identifies the application/filter that should be applied to the data. Different reparse point tags can be defined by an application/vendor, but there are some standard tags in existence. These include symbolic links, directory junction points, volume mount points, etc. Table 7.24 provides the structure for a $REPARSE_POINT attribute.

The reparse type value is divided into three sub-parts. The least significant 16_d bits represent the type of reparse point that is represented by the $REPARSE_POINT attribute. The following 13_d bits are reserved for future use, while the three most significant bits have a special meaning. Bit 29_d, if set, informs the analyst that this $REPARSE_POINT is an alias for another system object. Bit 30_d, if set, informs the analyst that accessing the first byte of data will be slow (for instance if the data resides on an external tape drive). This is known as the high-latency bit. Finally, the most significant bit is commonly called the Microsoft bit. This is set when the tag is owned by Microsoft. User-defined tags must use 0 in this position.

Consider the reparse type value of 0xA0000003. The 16_d least significant bits represent the value 3_d, which provides the record type (junction/mount point in this case). The three most significant bits have the value 0b101, meaning that this is a Microsoft tag and an alias to another file system object.

The data is dependent on the $REPARSE_POINT attribute's type. In the case of a mount point/junction (type: 0xA0000003) the structure of the data is shown in Table 7.25.

Table 7.24 The structure of $REPARSE_POINT attribute.

Offset	Size	Name	Description
0x00	0x04	Reparse Type	The type of reparse point being used.
0x04	0x02	Length (n)	The length of the $REPARSE_POINT attribute's data (n).
0x06	0x02	Padding	Padding (zeros).
0x08	(n)	Data	The data for this $REPARSE_POINT. The structure of this is dependent on the type of $REPARSE_POINT that is encountered.

Table 7.25 The structure of $REPARSE_POINT attribute.

Offset	Size	Name	Description
0x00	0x02	Target Name Offset	The byte offset to the start of the target name relative to the end of this structure (0x08 into the data/0x10 into the $REPARSE_POINT attribute structure).
0x02	0x02	Target Name Length (n)	The length of the target name in bytes.
0x04	0x02	Print Name Offset	The byte offset to the start of the print name relative to the end of this structure (0x08 into the data/0x10 into the $REPARSE_POINT attribute structure).
0x06	0x02	Print Name Length (p)	The length of the print name in bytes.

Table 7.26 $EA_INFORMATION attribute structure.

Offset	Size	Name	Description
0x00	0x02	Packed Size	Size of the packed extended attribute.
0x02	0x02	Num. EA	The number of extended attributes that have the NEED_EA flag set.
0x04	0x04	Unpacked Size	The unpacked size of the attribute.

Table 7.27 $EA attribute structure.

Offset	Size	Name	Description
0x00	0x04	Next EA Offset	Offset to the next EA
0x04	0x01	Flags	Flags – 0x80: NEED_EA
0x05	0x01	Name Length (n)	The length of the extended attribute name.
0x06	0x02	Value Length (v)	The length of the extended attribute value.
0x08	(n)	Name	The name of the extended attribute.
0x08 + n	(v)	Value	The value of the extended attribute.

7.1.6.15 $EA_INFORMATION (0xD0) and $EA (0xE0)

The $EA_INFORMATION attribute along with the $EA attribute are used to implement Extended Attributes from OS/2's HPFS file system. These attributes are rarely encountered; hence, this section merely gives the structure of the attributes in Tables 7.26 and 7.27. Both attributes can be resident or non-resident.

While not generally used one of the most frequent instances in which extended attributes are encountered is as a means of hiding malware. On the few occasions that these attributes are encountered during an investigation, they may be of interest!

7.2 Analysis of NTFS

In this section the manual analysis of the NTFS file system is described. This section focuses on the basic analysis techniques used to perform simple forensic tasks such as gathering file system information, listing files and recovering file metadata and content. In the following section more advanced NTFS analysis topics will be introduced.

7.2.1 Creating NTFS File Systems

Before commencing analysis it is necessary to create some sample NTFS file systems for analysis. NTFS is generally encountered on system drives (on Windows systems); however, the complexity of an entire system drive can provide some challenges for understanding manual analysis. As with previous file systems a basic file system will be created for initial analysis. Changes will be made to this initial file system to demonstrate more advanced topics in NTFS.

Listing 7.10 shows the command used to create an NTFS file system on Linux. In this example only a volume label is specified.

```
$ sudo mkfs.ntfs -L "NTFS FS" /dev/sdb1
Cluster size has been automatically set to 4096 bytes.
Initializing device with zeroes: 100% - Done.
Creating NTFS volume structures.
mkntfs completed successfully. Have a nice day.
$
```

Listing 7.10 Creating an NTFS file system from the Linux terminal.

7.2.2 Supplied NTFS Image Files

Throughout this chapter a number of NTFS disk images are used for demonstration purposes. These images are available through the book's website. Table 7.28 summarises the available disk images.

7.2.3 NTFS Manual Analysis

There are a number of steps that must be performed in order to successfully analyse an NTFS file system. These steps are described in detail subsequently in this section. The necessary steps are:

1. **Process $Boot:** In order to locate other file system structures (especially $MFT) and to gather information about the file system as a whole it is necessary to process the $Boot structure.
2. **Recover $MFT:** The master file table ($MFT) is the single most important file used in the analysis of NTFS. It contains information about every single file in the file system. When it is considered that everything in NTFS is a file this means this structure contains information about all structures in the filesystem along with all user-created files and directories.

Table 7.28 NTFS disk images available from the book's website.

Image File	Description
NTFS_V1.E01	A basic NTFS file system which contains four files and one directory. One of the files contains an alternate data stream.
NTFS_V2.E01	**NTFS_V1.E01** with multiple hard links created to one file and two other files deleted.
NTFS_V3.E01	This image contains a fragmented file.

3. **Process Directories:** Files can be listed by processing directories. This allows for all content to be listed in the file system.
4. **Recover Metadata:** File metadata is stored in $MFT. The next step is to recover this metadata for each file in the file system.
5. **Recover Content:** File content recovery is the final step in the analysis of NTFS.

7.2.3.1 Process $Boot

As with all file system forensic analysis tasks, analysis of NTFS begins by recovering information about the file system as a whole. This will include the basic storage unit sizes (sectors/clusters) and also the location of vital file system structures such as $MFT (and also $MFTMirr in case of corruption of the primary $MFT). Sleuthkit provides the **fsstat** command to provide this information automatically. Listing 7.11 shows the output of **fsstat** when executed on the **NTFS_V1.E01** disk image.

```
FILE SYSTEM INFORMATION
--------------------------------------------
File System Type: NTFS
Volume Serial Number: 2BEFA0611D6F5839
OEM Name: NTFS
Volume Name: NTFS-FS
Version: Windows XP

METADATA INFORMATION
--------------------------------------------
First Cluster of MFT: 4
First Cluster of MFT Mirror: 16383
Size of MFT Entries: 1024 bytes
Size of Index Records: 4096 bytes
Range: 0 - 69
Root Directory: 5

CONTENT INFORMATION
--------------------------------------------
Sector Size: 512
Cluster Size: 4096
Total Cluster Range: 0 - 32766
Total Sector Range: 0 - 262142

$AttrDef Attribute Values:
$STANDARD_INFORMATION (16) Size: 48-72 Flags: Resident
$ATTRIBUTE_LIST (32) Size: No Limit Flags: Non-resident
$FILE_NAME (48) Size: 68-578 Flags: Resident,Index
...[snip]...
```

Listing 7.11 Partial output from **fsstat** on **NTFS_V1.E01**. The underlined information can be recovered directly from $Boot.

The output from **fsstat** is actually generated by processing two file system structures. The first three sections (File System Information, Metadata Information and Content Information) are generated from the $Boot file in NTFS which is examined in this section. The remaining section,

Table 7.29 Processed values from $Boot structure in **NTFS_V1.E01**.

Offset	Size	Name	Value
0x03	0x08	OEM Name	NTFS
0x0B	0x02	Sector Size	0x200 (512_d)
0x0D	0x01	Sectors/Cluster	0x08 ($512 \times 8 = 4096_d$)
0x28	0x08	# Sectors	0x3FFFF ($262,143_d$)
0x30	0x08	MFT Location	0x04 (4_d)
0x38	0x08	MFTMirr Loc.	0x3FFF ($16,383_d$)
0x40	0x01	MFT Record Size	0xF6 (-10_d) ($-10_d \rightarrow 2^{10} = 1024_d$)
0x48	0x08	Serial Number	0x2BEFA0611D6F5839

$AttrDef Attribute Values, is generated from the $AttrDef file. This file contains information about all possible attributes in the NTFS file system. Listing 7.12 shows the contents of $Boot from **NTFS_V1.E01** while table 7.29 shows some of the processed values from $Boot.

```
000000: eb52 904e 5446 5320 2020 2000 0208 0000 .R.NTFS .....
000010: 0000 0000 00f8 0000 3f00 ff00 0008 0000 ........?.......
000020: 0000 0000 8000 8000 ffff 0300 0000 0000 ................
000030: 0400 0000 0000 0000 ff3f 0000 0000 0000 .........?......
000040: f600 0000 0100 0000 3958 6f1d 61a0 ef2b ........9Xo.a..+
```

Listing 7.12 An excerpt from $Boot in **NTFS_V1.E01**.

Comparing the output of **fsstat** (Listing 7.11) with the contents of Table 7.29 shows that much of the information about the file system can be recovered from $Boot. For instance the OEM name is present in this structure along with the sector and cluster sizes. The ranges for sectors and clusters can be calculated from the information available. The total number of sectors is $262,143_d$; as numbering starts at 0_d for all structures in NTFS this means that the range of sectors is from 0_d to $262,142_d$ as **fsstat** shows.

There is no corresponding figure for the number of clusters; however, the number of sectors per cluster (8_d) is provided. The total number of clusters can then be calculated using:

$$numClusters = int\left(\frac{numSectors}{sectorsPerCluster}\right)$$

This provides $32,767_d$ in this case. Again, as all numbering begins at 0_d, this results in a cluster range of 0_d to $32,766_d$. Note also that in this example there are seven sectors at the end of the device which do not belong to any cluster!

$Boot also provides information about the master file table. The $MFT structure's first cluster is found in the $Boot structure. In Table 7.29 this value is 4_d; knowing the cluster size in this image it is now possible to state that the $MFT's first cluster will be found at byte offset $4 \times 4096 = 16,384_d$. However, this provides only the first cluster of the $MFT file. In order to recover the content of $MFT, the first $MFT record in this cluster should be processed. This will allow the entire $MFT file to be recovered.[8] $MFT is of such vital importance to the operation of an NTFS file system that a mirror of the first cluster of the $MFT file is maintained. The location of this can also be found in $Boot. According to Table 7.29 this can be found in cluster $16,383_d$.

The final piece of information required in order to proceed with analysis is that of MFT record size. While this is generally 1024_d bytes, it can be altered during file system creation. The value that is located in $Boot for this is 0xF6. This is a two's complement number (see Section 3.2.7) which has the value -10_d. As this is a negative number the MFT record size is 2, raised to the power of the absolute value of this number. In other words the MFT record size is $2^{10} = 1024_d$ bytes.

7.2.3.2 Recover $MFT

After processing $Boot the next step is to recover the master file table. The first cluster of this structure is obtained from $Boot along with the size of each MFT record. The very first MFT record is always that of $MFT itself.[9] From Table 7.29 the MFT record size is known to be 1024_d. Listing 7.13 shows the MFT record for $MFT from **NTFS_V1.E01** (note that some zero bytes at the end of the record have been removed). This record commences with the MFT Record Header, following this alternate attributes highlighted.

```
004000: 4649 4c45 3000 0300 0000 0000 0000 0000 FILE0...........
004010: 0100 0100 3800 0100 9801 0000 0004 0000 ....8...........
004020: 0000 0000 0000 0000 0400 0000 0000 0000 ................
004030: 0700 0000 0000 0000 1000 0000 6000 0000 ............`...
004040: 0000 1800 0000 0000 4800 0000 1800 0000 ........H.......
004050: 0000 0000 0000 0000 0000 0000 0000 0000 ................
004060: 0000 0000 0000 0000 0000 0000 0000 0000 ................
004070: 0600 0000 0000 0000 0000 0000 0000 0000 ................
004080: 0000 0000 0000 0000 0000 0000 0000 0000 ................
004090: 0000 0000 0000 0000 3000 0000 6800 0000 ........0...h...
0040a0: 0000 1800 0000 0200 4a00 0000 1800 0100 ........J.......
0040b0: 0500 0000 0000 0500 0069 b830 bc0b da01 .........i.0....
0040c0: 0069 b830 bc0b da01 0069 b830 bc0b da01 .i.0.....i.0....
0040d0: 0069 b830 bc0b da01 0070 0000 0000 0000 .i.0.....p......
0040e0: 006c 0000 0000 0000 0600 0000 0000 0000 .l..............
0040f0: 0403 2400 4d00 4600 5400 0000 0000 0000 ..$.M.F.T.......
004100: 8000 0000 4800 0000 0100 4000 0000 0100 ....H.....@.....
004110: 0000 0000 0000 0000 1200 0000 0000 0000 ................
004120: 4000 0000 0000 0000 0030 0100 0000 0000 @........0......
004130: 0014 0100 0000 0000 0014 0100 0000 0000 ................
004140: 1113 0400 0000 0000 b000 0000 4800 0000 ............H...
004150: 0100 4000 0000 0300 0000 0000 0000 0000 ..@.............
004160: 0000 0000 0000 0000 4000 0000 0000 0000 ........@.......
004170: 0010 0000 0000 0000 1000 0000 0000 0000 ................
004180: 1000 0000 0000 0000 1101 0200 0000 0000 ................
004190: ffff ffff 0000 0000 0000 0000 0000 0000 ................
```

Listing 7.13 The MFT record for $MFT in **NTFS_V1.E01**.

Table 7.30 summarises the attributes that are present in the MFT record for $MFT. As expected there is a $STANDARD_INFORMATION attribute present which will provide metadata about the

8 In all NTFS file systems the first MFT record (0_d) is the record for $MFT itself!
9 The second record is that of $MFTMirr in case of error with the $MFT file.

Table 7.30 The attributes discovered in the MFT record for $MFT in **NTFS_V1.E01**.

Type ID	Name	Size	Resident
0x10	$STANDARD_INFORMATION	0x60 (96_d)	Yes
0x30	$FILENAME	0x68 (104_d)	Yes
0x80	$DATA	0x48 (72_d)	No
0xB0	$BITMAP	0x48 (72_d)	No

$MFT file itself. This is followed by a $FILENAME attribute. Examining the ASCII values of the $FILENAME attribute in Listing 7.13 shows the name of this file to be, as expected, $MFT. The final two attributes are $DATA and $BITMAP. The $DATA attribute will provide the location of the file content and the $BITMAP attribute will tell which MFT records are in use/free.

In order to recover the entire contents of the MFT file itself the $DATA attribute must be analysed. From Table 7.30 this attribute is seen to be non-resident. The attribute itself is presented in Listing 7.14. The attribute begins with the common attribute header followed by the non-resident header (highlighted). The processed headers are shown in Table 7.31.

```
004100: 8000 0000 4800 0000 0100 4000 0000 0100  ....H.....@.....
004110: 0000 0000 0000 0000 1200 0000 0000 0000  ................
004120: 4000 0000 0000 0000 0030 0100 0000 0000  @........0......
004130: 0014 0100 0000 0000 0014 0100 0000 0000  ................
004140: 1113 0400 0000 0000                      ........
```

Listing 7.14 The $DATA attribute for MFT Record 0 ($MFT file) in **NTFS_V1.E01**. The attribute and non-resident headers are highlighted.

From Table 7.31 the following information is obtained.

- This $DATA attribute represents the first 19_d clusters of the file's content (the starting VCN is cluster 0 and the ending VCN is 18_d).
- The file has been allocated 19_d clusters in total (the allocated space is 0x13000, while the cluster size is 0x1000). Combining this with the previous point means that only one single $DATA attribute is required for this file.
- There is potentially some slack space at the end of the file. The allocated file is 0x13000 but the actual file size is 0x11400. This means there is a potential for 0x1C00 bytes of slack space at the end of the file.
- The runlist can be found at offset 0x40 from the start of the attribute. The runlist is 0x111304.

In order to recover the content it is next necessary to interpret the run list content. Referring to Figure 7.5 shows that in this case the number of bytes used for both the starting cluster and the number of contiguous clusters is 1_d. This means that the run list represents 0x13 contiguous clusters beginning at cluster 0x04. Listing 7.15 shows a **dd** command that can be used to extract this file. The sleuthkit is also shown with both results compared based on their MD5 values.

Once $MFT has been recovered all information about the file system is now available to the analyst. The process continues with the listing of all files/directories that are present in the file system.

Table 7.31 Partially processed non-resident attribute header structure in the $MFT's $DATA attribute.

Offset	Size	Name	Value
0x00	0x10	Common Header	Type: 0x80 ($DATA)
			Size: 0x48 (72_d)
			Resident: No
			Name Length: 0x00 (0_d)
			Name Offset: 0x40 (64_d)
			Flags: 0x00 (0_d)
			Attribute ID: 0x01 (1_d)
0x10	0x08	Starting VCN	0x00 (0_d)
0x18	0x08	Ending VCN	0x12 (18_d)
0x20	0x02	Runlist Offset	0x40 (64_d)
0x28	0x08	Allocated Size	0x13000 ($77,824_d$)
0x30	0x08	Actual Size	0x11400 ($70,656_d$)
0x38	0x08	Initialised Size	0x11400 ($70,656_d$)

```
$ dd if=mnt/ewf1 of=mft.dd.raw bs=1 skip=$((4*4096))
    count=$((0x11400))
70656+0 records in
70656+0 records out
70656 bytes (71 kB, 69 KiB) copied, 1.83432 s, 38.5 kB/s
$
$ md5sum mft.*
dc382d0e7992af4dfad9d35f708eace9 mft.dd.raw
dc382d0e7992af4dfad9d35f708eace9 mft.tsk.raw
```

Listing 7.15 Using **dd** to recover the contents of $MFT from **NTFS_V1.E01**.

7.2.3.3 Process Directories

File listing begins from the root directory of any file system. In NTFS the root directory (.) always has the MFT record number 5. In order to view the contents of this record five records must be skipped (remember there is a record number 0!). The MFT record for record 5 is shown in Listing 7.16. The record begins with the record header and is followed by the attributes (alternate attributes highlighted). The attributes present in this are shown in Table 7.32.

In order to list the files/directories in a directory it is necessary to process the $INDEX_ROOT and/or $INDEX_ALLOCATION attributes. The $INDEX_ROOT structure is found in all directories and is always a resident attribute. In the case of small directories the actual directory contents will be stored here. In larger directories where the $INDEX_ROOT structure is not sufficiently large to store information about the files $INDEX_ALLOCATION is used to store the relevant information. In the case that both $INDEX_ROOT and $INDEX_ALLOCATION are present processing starts with $INDEX_ALLOCATION as this will contain the relevant data. The $INDEX_ALLOCATION (Type: 0xA0) node from Listing 7.16 is shown again in Listing 7.17. The processed values from this are shown in Table 7.33.

```
$ xxd -s $((5*1024)) -l 1024 mft.dd.raw
005400: 4649 4c45 3000 0300 0000 0000 0000 0000 FILE0...........
005410: 0500 0100 3800 0300 0002 0000 0004 0000 ....8...........
005420: 0000 0000 0000 0000 0600 0000 0500 0000 ................
005430: 0800 0000 0000 0000 1000 0000 4800 0000 ............H...
005440: 0000 1800 0000 0000 3000 0000 1800 0000 ........0.......
005450: 0069 b830 bc0b da01 1f24 428c bc0b da01 .i.0.....$B.....
005460: 1f24 428c bc0b da01 4716 728f bc0b da01 .$B.....G.r.....
005470: 2600 0000 0000 0000 0000 0000 0000 0000 &...............
005480: 3000 0000 6000 0000 0000 1800 0000 0100 0...`...........
005490: 4400 0000 1800 0100 0500 0000 0000 0500 D...............
0054a0: 0069 b830 bc0b da01 0069 b830 bc0b da01 .i.0.....i.0....
0054b0: 0069 b830 bc0b da01 0069 b830 bc0b da01 .i.0.....i.0....
0054c0: 0000 0000 0000 0000 0000 0000 0000 0000 ................
0054d0: 0600 0010 0000 0000 0103 2e00 0000 0000 ................
0054e0: 5000 0000 4800 0000 0100 4000 0000 0200 P...H.....@.....
0054f0: 0000 0000 0000 0000 0100 0000 0000 0000 ................
005500: 4000 0000 0000 0000 0020 0000 0000 0000 @........ ......
005510: 2c10 0000 0000 0000 2c10 0000 0000 0000 ,.......,.......
005520: 2102 0310 0000 0000 9000 0000 5800 0000 !...........X...
005530: 0004 1800 0000 0300 3800 0000 2000 0000 ........8... ...
005540: 2400 4900 3300 3000 3000 0000 0100 0000 $.I.3.0.0.......
005550: 0010 0000 0100 0000 1000 0000 2800 0000 ............(...
005560: 2800 0000 0100 0000 0000 0000 0000 0000 (...............
005570: 1800 0000 0300 0000 0000 0000 0000 0000 ................
005580: a000 0000 5000 0000 0104 4000 0000 0500 ....P.....@.....
005590: 0000 0000 0000 0000 0000 0000 0000 0000 ................
0055a0: 4800 0000 0000 0000 0010 0000 0000 0000 H...............
0055b0: 0010 0000 0000 0000 0010 0000 0000 0000 ................
0055c0: 2400 4900 3300 3000 2101 0510 0000 0000 $.I.3.0.!.......
0055d0: b000 0000 2800 0000 0004 1800 0000 0400 ....(...........
0055e0: 0800 0000 2000 0000 2400 4900 3300 3000 .... ...$.I.3.0.
0055f0: 0100 0000 0000 0000 ffff ffff 0000 0800 ................
```

Listing 7.16 Contents of MFT record 5 (the root directory) in **NTFS_V1.E01**.

Table 7.32 The attributes discovered in the MFT record for the root directory in **NTFS_V1.E01**.

Type ID	Name	Length	Resident
0x10	$STANDARD_INFORMATION	0x48 (72_d)	Yes
0x30	$FILENAME	0x60 (96_d)	Yes
0x50	$SECURITY_DESCRIPTOR	0x48 (72_d)	No
0x90	$INDEX_ROOT	0x58 (88_d)	Yes
0xA0	$INDEX_ALLOCATION	0x50 (88_d)	No
0xB0	$BITMAP	0x28 (40_d)	Yes

```
005580: a000 0000 5000 0000 0104 4000 0000 0500 ....P.....@.....
005590: 0000 0000 0000 0000 0000 0000 0000 0000 ................
0055a0: 4800 0000 0000 0000 0010 0000 0000 0000 H...............
0055b0: 0010 0000 0000 0000 0010 0000 0000 0000 ................
0055c0: 2400 4900 3300 3000 2101 0510 0000 0000 $.I.3.0.!.......
```

Listing 7.17 The $INDEX_ALLOCATION attribute for the root directory in **NTFS_V1.E01**.

Table 7.33 Partially processed values for the $INDEX_ALLOCATION attribute in the root directory in **NTFS_V1.E01**.

Offset	Size	Name	Value
0x00	0x10	Common Header	Type: 0xA0 ($INDEX_ALLOCATION) Size: 0x50 (96_d) Resident: No Name Length: 0x04 (4_d) Name Offset: 0x40 (64_d) Flags: 0x00 (0_d) Attribute ID: 0x05 (5_d)
0x10	0x08	Starting VCN	0x00
0x18	0x08	Ending VCN	0x00
0x28	0x08	Allocated Size	0x1000 ($4,096_d$)
0x30	0x08	Actual Size	0x1000 ($4,096_d$)
0x38	0x08	Initialised Size	0x1000 ($4,096_d$)

The $INDEX_ALLOCATION attribute has a name associated with it. This name is found at offset 0x40 and is 0x04 characters in size. These are UTF-16-encoded characters and as such each character occupies two bytes. The values found at this location give the attribute name as $I30. The runlist for the data content is found at offset 0x48, the value of which is 0x2101051000. This translates to a run consisting of one cluster starting at cluster 0x1005 ($4,101_d$). Listing 7.18 shows the contents of this location.

The directory contents are an index entry in an NTFS B-Tree. In the case of small directories (as is seen in this example) the actual files will be present (examining the ASCII values in Listing 7.18 will show file names); however, in larger directories this index record will point to other tree nodes.

The data is composed of an index record header followed by a node header structure. The index record header is 0x18 bytes in size while the node header is 0x10 bytes. The headers are followed by an index list which is the actual list of $FILENAME attributes for each of the files/directories contained in the directory. Listing 7.18 shows the index record header and the node header. Four index list items are also included (alternate items are underlined). For presentation purposes much of the intervening information has been removed. There are many other files in this directory than those listed here! As an exercise the reader is asked to process the remaining files and list the entire contents of the directory.

```
01005000: 494e 4458 2800 0900 0000 0000 0000 0000 INDX(...........
01005010: 0000 0000 0000 0000 2800 0000 0006 0000 ........(.......
01005020: e80f 0000 0000 0000 5200 da01 0000 7300 ........R.....s.
01005030: 0000 0000 0000 0000 0000 0000 0000 0000 ................
01005040: 0400 0000 0000 0400 6800 5200 0000 0000  ........h.R.....
01005050: 0500 0000 0000 0500 0069 b830 bc0b da01 .........i.0....
01005060: 0069 b830 bc0b da01 0069 b830 bc0b da01 .i.0.....i.0....
01005070: 0069 b830 bc0b da01 0010 0000 0000 0000 .i.0............
01005080: 000a 0000 0000 0000 0600 0000 0000 0000  ................
01005090: 0803 2400 4100 7400 7400 7200 4400 6500 ..$.A.t.t.r.D.e.
010050a0: 6600 0000 0000 0100 0800 0000 0000 0800 f...............
...[snip]...
010054d0: 0103 2e00 0000 0000 4100 0000 0000 0100  ........A.......
010054e0: 6000 4c00 0000 0000 0500 0000 0000 0500 `.L.............
010054f0: 4351 eb62 bc0b da01 bbf1 3490 bc0b da01 CQ.b......4.....
01005500: bbf1 3490 bc0b da01 67af 9492 bc0b da01 ..4.....g.......
01005510: 0000 0000 0000 0000 0000 0000 0000 0000 ................
01005520: 2000 0010 0000 0000 0500 4600 6900 6c00 .........F.i.l.
01005530: 6500 7300 0000 0000 4000 0000 0000 0100 e.s.....@.......
01005540: 6800 5200 0000 0000 0500 0000 0000 0500 h.R.............
01005550: 1d6b fc37 bc0b da01 0089 fc37 bc0b da01 .k.7.......7....
01005560: 0089 fc37 bc0b da01 1d6b fc37 bc0b da01 ...7.....k.7....
01005570: a800 0000 0000 0000 a600 0000 0000 0000 ................
01005580: 2000 0000 0000 0000 0800 6900 6e00 6600 .........i.n.f.
01005590: 6f00 2e00 7400 7800 7400 0000 0000 0000 o...t.x.t.......
010055a0: 4300 0000 0000 0100 6800 5800 0000 0000 C.......h.X.....
010055b0: 0500 0000 0000 0500 ba23 428c bc0b da01  .........#B.....
010055c0: 03ae 428c bc0b da01 84ea 74e3 c40b da01  ..B.......t.....
010055d0: ba23 428c bc0b da01 0010 0400 0000 0000  .#B.............
010055e0: 6905 0400 0000 0000 2000 0000 0000 0000 i....... .......
010055f0: 0b00 6900 7300 6c00 6100 6e00 6400 5200  ..i.s.l.a.n.d.R.
01005600: 2e00 6a00 7000 6700 0000 0000 0000 0000 ..j.p.g.........
```

Listing 7.18 Excerpt from the content of root directory's $INDEX_ALLOCATION attribute in **NTFS_V1.E01**.

Processing of these entries is a three-part process. Firstly the index header is processed which is followed by the node header. Finally each individual entry is processed. The processing of the index header is shown in Table 7.34.

Every index record header begins with a signature value (INDX). The most interesting information available in the header is the reference to the fixup array. This is located at offset 0x28 and contains 0x09 elements. Each element in the fixup array is two bytes in size. The fixup array itself is shown in Listing 7.19.

The first element in the fixup array (0x5200) is the value which will be placed at the end of every sector in this structure. The replacement values for the eight sectors are listed in the subsequent byte pairs. Once the index record header has been processed the node header is next. This is shown in Table 7.35.

The node header structure informs the analyst of the location of the directory entry list itself. The index list offset is relative to the start of the node header. The value in Table 7.35 is 0x28, meaning that the offset to the first directory entry is 0x28 + 0x18 = 0x40.

Table 7.34 Processed index record header from Listing 7.18.

Offset	Size	Name	Value
0x00	0x04	Signature	INDX
0x04	0x02	Fixup Array Offset	0x28 (40_d)
0x06	0x02	Fixup Array Size	0x09 (9_d)
0x08	0x08	LSN	0x00 (0_d)
0x10	0x08	Current VCN	0x00 (0_d)

```
01005028: 5200 da01 0000 7300 0000 0000 0000 0000 R.....s.........
01005038: 0000                                    ..
```

Listing 7.19 The contents of the fixup array from the root directory index record in **NTFS_V1.E01**.

Table 7.35 Processed node header from Listing 7.18.

Offset	Size	Name	Value
0x00	0x04	Index List Offset	0x28 (40_d)
0x04	0x04	Index List End Offset	0x600 ($1,536_d$)
0x08	0x04	Index List Buffer Offset	0xFE8 ($4,072_d$)
0x0C	0x04	Flags	0x00 (0_d)

Table 7.36 shows the processed values for the four directory entries shown in Listing 7.18. As expected in each of the four $FILENAME attributes that are processed the parent directory is 0x05, in other words the root directory. Note that the parent directory value is provided as an MFT file reference. The most significant two bytes represent the sequence number (0x05) and the least significant six bytes represent the MFT record number (0x05). Examining the MFT File reference values for each individual file shows that the MFT record numbers for **$AttrDef** is 0x04 ($4_d$), **Files** is 0x41 ($65_d$), **info.txt** is 0x40 (64_d) and **islands.jpg** is 0x43 (67_d). This can be compared with the output of **fls** (other files have been removed from the output) as shown in Listing 7.20.

Examining the flag values in each $FILENAME attribute shows that **$AttrDef** is a hidden system file, **info.txt** and **islands.jpg** are files and **Files** is a directory. The MFT record number for Files is 0x40 (64_d). In order to continue listing files, it is necessary to extract this MFT record and process this in the same manner as that shown for the root directory. This process continues until there are no further files to be processed.

The listing of the remaining files in the root directory and the processing of the **Files** directory is left as an exercise for the reader.

7.2.3.4 Recover File Metadata

The primary structure for storing metadata in NTFS is $STANDARD_INFORMATION but many other attributes can be used to provide information relevant to an investigation. Listing 7.21 shows the output from the **istat** command for the small **info.txt** file in **NTFS_V1.E01**. This shows the complexity of information available in NTFS when compared to simpler file systems such as FAT and ExFAT.

Table 7.36 Processed directory entries from Listing 7.18. Note that some values have been truncated and others have been omitted for presentation purposes.

Offset	Size	Name	Record 1 Value	Record 2 Value
0x00	0x08	MFT File Ref.	0x0004...0004	0x0001...0041
0x08	0x02	Entry Size	0x68 (104_d)	0x60 (96_d)
0x0A	0x02	Filename Size	0x52 (82_d)	0x4C (60_d)
0x0C	0x04	Flags	0x00 (0_d)	0x00 (0_d)
0x10	(n)	$FILENAME	—	—
		$FILENAME attributes		
0x00	0x08	Parent Dir.	0x0005...0005	0x0005...0005
0x28	0x08	Alloc. Size	0x1000 (4096_d)	0x00 (0_d)
0x30	0x08	Actual Size	0x0A00 (2560_d)	0x00 (0_d)
0x38	0x04	Flags	0x06	0x10000020
0x3C	0x04	Reparse Value	0x00 (0_d)	0x00 (0_d)
0x40	0x01	Name Length	0x08 (8_d)	0x05 (5_d)
0x41	0x01	Name Space	0x03 (3_d)	0x00 (0_d)
0x42	($n \times 2$)	Name	$AttrDef	Files
Offset	**Size**	**Name**	**Record 3 Value**	**Record 4 Value**
0x00	0x08	MFT File Ref.	0x0001...0040	0x0001...0043
0x08	0x02	Entry Size	0x68 (104_d)	0x68 (104_d)
0x0A	0x02	Filename Size	0x52 (82_d)	0x58 (88_d)
0x0C	0x04	Flags	0x00 (0_d)	0x00 (0_d)
0x10	(n)	$FILENAME	—	—
		$FILENAME attributes		
0x00	0x08	Parent Dir.	0x0005...0005	0x0005...0005
0x28	0x08	Alloc. Size	0xA8 (168_d)	0x41000 ($266,240_d$)
0x30	0x08	Actual Size	0xA6 (166_d)	0x40569 ($263,529_d$)
0x38	0x04	Flags	0x20	0x20
0x3C	0x04	Reparse Value	0x00 (0_d)	0x00 (0_d)
0x40	0x01	Name Length	0x08(8_d)	0x0B (11_d)
0x41	0x01	Name Space	0x00 (0_d)	0x00 (0_d)
0x42	($n \times 2$)	Name	info.txt	islands.jpg

```
$ fls mnt/ewf1
r/r 4-128-1: $AttrDef
...[snip]...
d/d 65-144-2: Files
r/r 64-128-2: info.txt
r/r 67-128-2: islands.jpg
...[snip]...
```

Listing 7.20 An excerpt from **fls** on **NTFS_V1.E01** showing the four files that appear in Listing 7.18.

```
MFT Entry Header Values:
Entry: 64 Sequence: 1
$LogFile Sequence Number: 0
Allocated File
Links: 1

$STANDARD_INFORMATION Attribute Values:
Flags: Archive
Owner ID: 0
Security ID: 0 ()
Created: 2023-10-31 05:36:38.189750100 (GMT)
File Modified: 2023-10-31 05:36:38.190515200 (GMT)
MFT Modified: 2023-10-31 05:36:38.190515200 (GMT)
Accessed: 2023-10-31 05:36:38.189750100 (GMT)

$FILE_NAME Attribute Values:
Flags: Archive
Name: info.txt
Parent MFT Entry: 5 Sequence: 5
Allocated Size: 168 Actual Size: 0
Created: 2023-10-31 05:36:38.189750100 (GMT)
File Modified: 2023-10-31 05:36:38.189750100 (GMT)
MFT Modified: 2023-10-31 05:36:38.189750100 (GMT)
Accessed: 2023-10-31 05:36:38.189750100 (GMT)

Attributes:
Type: $STANDARD_INFORMATION (16-0) Name: N/A Resident size: 48
Type: $FILE_NAME (48-3) Name: N/A Resident size: 82
Type: $SECURITY_DESCRIPTOR (80-1) Name: N/A Resident size: 80
Type: $DATA (128-2) Name: N/A Resident size: 166
```

Listing 7.21 Metadata recovered from an NTFS file system when using **istat**.

The **istat** output shows the areas in which metadata can be found. The first pieces of information recovered are from the MFT record header. The command then proceeds to process the $STANDARD_INFORMATION and $FILENAME attributes. Finally **istat** lists all the attributes that are present in the record.

Listing 7.22 shows the contents of MFT record number 64_d (**info.txt**). Alternate attributes are highlighted. Tables 7.37–7.39 process this attribute showing the header, $STANDARD_INFORMATION, and $FILENAME, respectively.

```
010000: 4649 4c45 3000 0300 0000 0000 0000 0000 FILE0...........
010010: 0100 0100 3800 0100 2002 0000 0004 0000 ....8... .......
010020: 0000 0000 0000 0000 0400 0000 4000 0000 ............@...
010030: 0500 6c61 0000 0000 1000 0000 4800 0000  ..la........H...
010040: 0000 0000 0000 0000 3000 0000 1800 0000 ........0.......
010050: 1d6b fc37 bc0b da01 0089 fc37 bc0b da01 .k.7.......7....
010060: 0089 fc37 bc0b da01 1d6b fc37 bc0b da01 ...7.....k.7....
010070: 2000 0000 0000 0000 0000 0000 0000 0000  ................
010080: 3000 0000 7000 0000 0000 0000 0000 0300 0...p...........
010090: 5200 0000 1800 0100 0500 0000 0000 0500 R...............
0100a0: 1d6b fc37 bc0b da01 1d6b fc37 bc0b da01 .k.7.....k.7....
0100b0: 1d6b fc37 bc0b da01 1d6b fc37 bc0b da01 .k.7.....k.7....
0100c0: a800 0000 0000 0000 0000 0000 0000 0000 ................
0100d0: 2000 0000 0000 0000 0800 6900 6e00 6600 .........i.n.f.
0100e0: 6f00 2e00 7400 7800 7400 0000 1800 0000 o...t.x.t.......
0100f0: 5000 0000 6800 0000 0000 0000 0000 0100  P...h...........
010100: 5000 0000 1800 0000 0100 0480 1400 0000 P...............
010110: 2400 0000 0000 0000 3400 0000 0102 0000 $.......4.......
010120: 0000 0005 2000 0000 2002 0000 0102 0000 .... ... .......
010130: 0000 0005 2000 0000 2002 0000 0200 1c00 .... ... .......
010140: 0100 0000 0003 1400 ff01 1f00 0101 0000  ................
010150: 0000 0001 0000 0000 8000 0000 c000 0000 ................
010160: 0000 0000 0000 0200 a600 0000 1800 0000 ................
010170: 5468 6973 2069 7320 6120 7369 6d70 6c65 This is a simple
010180: 204e 5446 5369 6d61 6765 2063 6f6e 7461 NTFSimage conta
010190: 696e 696e 6720 6f6e 6520 6469 7265 6374 ining one direct
0101a0: 6f72 7920 616e 6420 666f 7572 2066 696c ory and four fil
0101b0: 6573 2e0a 5468 6520 7374 7275 6374 7572 es..The structur
0101c0: 6520 6f66 2074 6869 7320 6973 3a0a 0a2f e of this is:../
0101d0: 2d20 4669 6c65 730a 2020 202f 2d20 6465 - Files. /- de
0101e0: 6c65 7465 2e74 7874 0a20 2020 2f2d 2068 lete.txt. /- h
0101f0: 696c 6c73 2e6a 7067 0a2f 2d20 6973 0500 ills.jpg./- is..
010200: 6e64 732e 6a70 670a 2f2d 2069 6e66 6f2e nds.jpg./- info.
010210: 7478 740a 0a0a 0000 ffff ffff 0000 0000 txt.............
```

Listing 7.22 MFT record 64_d (**info.txt**) from $MFT in **NTFS_V1.E01**.

Processing the attribute header shows the location of the fixup array (offset 0x30, 0x03 elements). The value of the fixup array is 0x0500 0x6C61 0x0000. The actual size of the record is 0x220 which is greater than a single sector (sector size is 0x200). This means the fixup array is required. The fixup locations are not part of the actual space used by the metadata structure. The header also informs the analyst that there is one link to this file and also that the MFT record has 4_d attributes (the next attribute ID value!). Most importantly the header informs the analyst that the first attribute can be found at offset 0x38.

When recovering metadata, tools process $STANDARD_INFORMATION as a matter of priority. This contains the file creation, modification, change and access time values. Note that in this example the $STANDARD_INFORMATION is not as long as it might be. Some of the optional values are not present. Before processing any attribute it is important to check the attribute size in the common attribute header.

Table 7.37 The processed MFT record header for **info.txt** in **NTFS_V1.E01**.

Offset	Size	Name	Value
0x00	0x04	Signature	FILE
0x04	0x02	Fixup Array Offset	0x30 (48_d)
0x06	0x02	Fixup Array Size	0x03 (3_d)
0x08	0x08	LSN	0x00 (0_d)
0x10	0x02	Sequence Value	0x01 (1_d)
0x12	0x02	Link Count	0x01 (1_d)
0x14	0x02	First Attribute Offset	0x38 (56_d)
0x16	0x02	Flags	0x01 (1_d)
0x18	0x04	Record Size (used)	0x220 (544_d)
0x1C	0x04	Record Size (alloc)	0x400 (1024_d)
0x20	0x08	File Reference	0x00 (0_d)
0x28	0x02	Next Attribute ID	0x04 (4_d)

Table 7.38 The processed $STANDARD_INFORMATION attribute in **info.txt** in **NTFS_V1.E01**.

Offset	Size	Name	Value
0x00	0x08	Creation Time	0x01DA0BBC37FC6B1D 2023-10-31 05:36:38
0x08	0x08	Modification Time	0x01DA0BBC37FC8900 2023-10-31 05:36:38
0x10	0x08	MFT Change Time	0x01DA0BBC37FC8900 2023-10-31 05:36:38
0x18	0x08	Access Time	0x01DA0BBC37FC6B1D 2023-10-31 05:36:38
0x20	0x04	Flags	0x20 (Archive)
0x24	0x04	Max. # Versions	0x00 (0_d)
0x28	0x04	Version Number	0x00 (0_d)
0x2C	0x04	Class ID	0x00 (0_d)

Another attribute that contains much metadata is $FILENAME. This attribute contains timestamps related to the filename itself. This attribute also provides the allocated and actual size values for the attribute. Finally, as expected, $FILENAME also contains the file name itself.

The final part of the **istat** output merely lists all the attributes present in the MFT record and provides the attribute type, size and resident/non-resident status of each. This is achieved by processing the individual attribute headers.

Table 7.39 The processed $FILENAME attribute in **info.txt** in **NTFS_V1.E01**.

Offset	Size	Name	Value
0x00	0x08	Parent MFT	Seq No: 0x05 MFT Rec. No: 0x05
0x08	0x08	Creation Time	0x01DA0BBC37FC6B1D 2023-10-31 05:36:38
0x10	0x08	Modification Time	0x01DA0BBC37FC6B1D 2023-10-31 05:36:38
0x18	0x08	Change Time	0x01DA0BBC37FC6B1D 2023-10-31 05:36:38
0x20	0x08	Access Time	0x01DA0BBC37FC6B1D 2023-10-31 05:36:38
0x28	0x08	Allocated Size	0xA8 (168_d)
0x30	0x08	Actual Size	0x00 (0_d)
0x38	0x04	Flags	0x20 (Archive)
0x3C	0x04	Reparse Value	0x00 (0_d)
0x40	0x01	Name Length (n)	0x08 (8_d)
0x41	0x01	Name Space	0x00 (0_d)
0x42	$n \times 2$	Name	info.txt

7.2.3.5 Recover File Content

The final step in the manual analysis of an NTFS file system is to recover the file's content. The content is located through the $DATA attribute which can be resident or non-resident. In the case of resident data the actual file content is stored in the MFT record itself. This is the preferred method of storage for very small files. However, larger files will obviously not fit into a 1024_d byte structure and as such these need to be stored in another location. To achieve this a non-resident $DATA attribute can be used.

Listing 7.23 shows the $DATA attribute for the file **info.txt** in **NTFS_V1.E01**. From this listing it is obvious that the content is stored in a resident fashion. The ASCII values are displaying the actual file content. The question is, how are these values recovered by forensic tools?

Processing the common attribute header shows that this is a $DATA attribute (type 0x80). It also shows that the data is resident. As this is a resident attribute, the common header is immediately followed by the resident attribute header. This informs the analyst that there are 0xA6 (166_d) bytes of data commencing at 0x18 (24_d) relative to the start of the attribute. This data in Listing 7.23 is the actual file content itself.

This should provide sufficient information to recover the file's content. The actual data exists at offset 0x170 in the MFT record itself. The command **dd if=mft.dd.raw skip=$((64*1024 + 0x170)) bs=1 count=$((0xA6)) of=info.manual.txt** can be used to extract this directly from the recovered MFT file. Listing 7.24 shows the MD5 sums for this file and the same file recovered using the sleuthkit. Why do these MD5 values differ?

The reason for this discrepancy becomes clear when the entire MFT record is analysed. The data for this resident attribute crosses the sector boundary inside the MFT record. Hence the fixup array

```
010158: 8000 0000 c000 0000 0000 0000 0000 0200 ................
010168: a600 0000 1800 0000 5468 6973 2069 7320 ........This is
010178: 6120 7369 6d70 6c65 204e 5446 5369 6d61 a simple NTFSima
010188: 6765 2063 6f6e 7461 696e 696e 6720 6f6e ge containing on
010198: 6520 6469 7265 6374 6f72 7920 616e 6420 e directory and
0101a8: 666f 7572 2066 696c 6573 2e0a 5468 6520 four files..The
0101b8: 7374 7275 6374 7572 6520 6f66 2074 6869 structure of thi
0101c8: 7320 6973 3a0a 0a2f 2d20 4669 6c65 730a s is:../- Files.
0101d8: 2020 202f 2d20 6465 6c65 7465 2e74 7874 /- delete.txt
0101e8: 0a20 2020 2f2d 2068 696c 6c73 2e6a 7067 . /- hills.jpg
0101f8: 0a2f 2d20 6973 0500 6e64 732e 6a70 670a ./- is..nds.jpg.
010208: 2f2d 2069 6e66 6f2e 7478 740a 0a0a       /- info.txt.....
```

Listing 7.23 The $DATA attribute for the **info.txt** file in **NTFS_V1.E01** (Record 64_d in $MFT).

```
$ md5sum info.manual.txt info.tsk.txt
0736d6d8fe902aa9056ba83b7d068939 info.manual.txt
defed800a77b3b68fd7130bf8fef0f6f info.tsk.txt
```

Listing 7.24 Two versions of the recovered info.txt file from **NTFS_V1.E01** showing different MD5 values.

needs to be consulted. Listing 7.22 showed the entire MFT record for this file. Notice the fixup array contains the content shown in Listing 7.25. The value 0x0500 has replaced the two bytes at offset 0x1FE in the MFT record. The original value of these bytes was 0x6C61. Replacing the 0x0500 value with 0x6C61 will result in the same MD5 sum being obtained. Listing 7.26 shows the MD5 sums of the three files. The newly modified file is underlined.

```
00011030: 0500 6c61 0000 0000                    ..la....
```

Listing 7.25 The contents of the fixup array in MFT record 68_d.

```
0736d6d8fe902aa9056ba83b7d068939 info.manual.txt
defed800a77b3b68fd7130bf8fef0f6f info.manual.fixup.txt
defed800a77b3b68fd7130bf8fef0f6f info.tsk.txt
```

Listing 7.26 The MD5 sums of the manually recovered **info.txt** file after the fixup array elements have been replaced.

But what of the case where the $DATA attribute is non-resident? Listing 7.27 shows a non-resident $DATA attribute for the file called **hills.jpg** (MFT Record #: 66_d) in **NTFS_V1.E01**. Processing the common attribute header shows this to be a $DATA attribute (type 0x80) of size 0x48 bytes, but in this case the attribute is non-resident. The common header is therefore immediately followed by the non-resident header. This is processed in Table 7.40.

The runlist in this $DATA attribute represents clusters 0_d to 67_d (a total of 68_d clusters). From $Boot it is known that the cluster size is 0x1000 bytes, and this structure shows that 0x44000 bytes have been allocated for this file (in other words 68_d clusters). The actual size is slightly less than this, 0x4313D ($274,749_d$ bytes), meaning that there will be some slack space present.

```
014958: 8000 0000 4800 0000 0100 4000 0000 0200 ....H.....@.....
014968: 0000 0000 0000 0000 4300 0000 0000 0000 ........C.......
014978: 4000 0000 0000 0000 0040 0400 0000 0000 @........@......
014988: 3d31 0400 0000 0000 3d31 0400 0000 0000 =1......=1......
014998: 2144 0042 0000 0000                     !D.B....
```

Listing 7.27 The non-resident $DATA attribute in the file **hills.jpg** (MFT Record: 66_d) in **NTFS_V1.E01**.

Table 7.40 Non-resident attribute header structure.

Offset	Size	Name	Value
0x00	0x08	Starting VCN	0x00 (0_d)
0x08	0x08	Ending VCN	0x43 (67_d)
0x10	0x02	Runlist Offset	0x40 (64_d)
0x12	0x02	Compression Unit	0x00 (0_d)
0x14	0x04	Unused	0x00 (0_d)
0x18	0x08	Allocated Size	0x44000 ($278,528_d$)
0x20	0x08	Actual Size	0x4313D ($274,749_d$)
0x28	0x08	Initialised Size	0x4313D ($274,749_d$)

The key information in a non-resident attribute header is the location of the run list. In this case the offset to the run list is 0x40. Examining this provides the information: 0x21 44 0042. Interpreting this shows that 0x2 bytes are used for the starting cluster and a single byte is used for the number of contiguous clusters. The number of contiguous clusters is 0x44 and the starting cluster is 0x4200. Listing 7.28 shows the recovery of $274,749_d$ bytes from the start of cluster 0x4200 using **dd** and the recovery of the same file using **icat**. Comparing their MD5 values shows the content to be equivalent.

```
$ dd if=mnt/ewf1 of=hills.dd.jpg bs=1 skip=$((0x4200 * 0x1000))
     count=274749
274749+0 records in
274749+0 records out
274749 bytes (275 kB, 268 KiB) copied, 6.981 s, 39.4 kB/s
$
$ icat mnt/ewf1 66 > hills.tsk.jpg
$
$ md5sum hills.*
9fa50a1b41a8565131036ee098bdebfd hills.dd.jpg
9fa50a1b41a8565131036ee098bdebfd hills.tsk.jpg
```

Listing 7.28 Using **dd** to recover **hills.jpg** from **NTFS_V1.E01** and showing the equivalence of this result to the file recovery function in **icat**.

This section has shown the method for the recovery of both resident and non-fragmented non-resident files in the NTFS file system. Section 7.3.3 will examine the effect of file fragmentation on the recovery process.

7.3 NTFS Advanced Analysis

The previous section demonstrated the basic techniques used in file system forensic analysis of an NTFS system. In this section some of the more advanced analysis techniques are examined. These include how tools such as **fsstat** gather all of the file system information by processing more than just the $Boot file, how fragmented files are recovered, how deleted files are recovered and how alternate data streams affect the digital forensic process.

7.3.1 Further File System Information

Listing 7.11 provided the information that was available about an NTFS file system from the **fsstat** command. Most of this information was manually recovered from the $Boot file; however, not all information was found there. In particular the volume name, NTFS version and the attribute definition information were not found in $Boot.

The **fsstat** command actually looks beyond the $Boot structure. It also processes the $VOLUME_NAME and $VOLUME_INFORMATION attributes to get the volume name and NTFS version information. Listing 7.29 shows these two attributes found in MFT Record 3 in **NTFS_V1.E01**.

```
004d68: 6000 0000 2800 0000 0000 1800 0000 0400 `...(...........
004d78: 0e00 0000 1800 0000 4e00 5400 4600 5300 ........N.T.F.S.
004d88: 2d00 4600 5300 0000 7000 0000 2800 0000 -.F.S...p...(...
004d98: 0000 1800 0000 0500 0c00 0000 1800 0000 ................
004da8: 0000 0000 0000 0000 0301 0000 0000 0000 ................
```

Listing 7.29 The contents of the $VOLUME_NAME (underlined) and $VOLUME_INFORMATION attributes in the $Volume MFT Record (number 3) in **NTFS_V1.E01**.

Referring to Section 7.1.6 shows how these structures can be processed. The $VOLUME_NAME attribute contains the volume name as resident data encoded in UTF-16. From Listing 7.29 this value is **NTFS-FS**.

The $VOLUME_INFORMATION resident data can be processed using Table 7.19. This shows major and minor version information of 0x03 and 0x01, respectively. This equates to version 3.1 which is the version of NTFS associated with any file system created since Windows NT.

The final piece of information in Listing 7.11 that has not yet been found is the attribute definition information. While there is a standard association between attribute-type identifiers and names (e.g. $DATA is 0x80) it can be changed, or new attributes can be defined. NTFS maintains a file called $AttrDef (MFT record 4) which contains a 160_d byte entry for each attribute. Listing 7.30 shows the $AttrDef entry for the $FILENAME attribute in **NTFS_V1.E01**. Table 7.41 shows the structure of this and also the values from Listing 7.30.

Examining this data shows some expected results, for instance the type ID is 0x30 (48_d) – which is the default for the $FILENAME attribute. The attribute can be used in an index and is resident (the flags are 0x42). This means, as seen previously, that filenames can be used in index structures (as they are in directories) and also that the attribute is always resident. It is never necessary to interpret a data run to locate a $FILENAME's data, it will always be present in the MFT record itself. Listing 7.31 shows the **fsstat** output for this attribute showing the information discovered in $AttrDef.

```
000140: 2400 4600 4900 4c00 4500 5f00 4e00 4100 $.F.I.L.E._.N.A.
000150: 4d00 4500 0000 0000 0000 0000 0000 0000 M.E.............
000160: 0000 0000 0000 0000 0000 0000 0000 0000 ................
000170: 0000 0000 0000 0000 0000 0000 0000 0000 ................
000180: 0000 0000 0000 0000 0000 0000 0000 0000 ................
000190: 0000 0000 0000 0000 0000 0000 0000 0000 ................
0001a0: 0000 0000 0000 0000 0000 0000 0000 0000 ................
0001b0: 0000 0000 0000 0000 0000 0000 0000 0000 ................
0001c0: 3000 0000 0000 0000 0000 0000 4200 0000 0...........B...
0001d0: 4400 0000 0000 0000 4202 0000 0000 0000 D.......B.......
```

Listing 7.30 The $AttrDef entry for $FILENAME in **NTFS_V1.E01**

Table 7.41 Partially processed $AttrDef entry structure with values from Listing 7.30.

Offset	Size	Name	Description	Value
0x00	0x80	Name	The attribute's name (UTF-16 encoding).	$FILENAME
0x80	0x04	Type ID	The type ID used in the attribute header.	0x30
0x8C	0x04	Flags	Flag values. 0x02 attribute can be used in index; 0x40 attribute is always resident; 0x08 attribute can be resident.	0x42
0x90	0x08	Minimum Size	The minimum size of the attribute in bytes.	0x44 (68_d)
0x98	0x08	Maximum Size	The maximum size of the attribute in bytes.	0x242 (578_d)

```
$FILE_NAME (48) Size: 68-578 Flags: Resident,Index
```

Listing 7.31 Information about the $FILENAME attribute provided by **fsstat** when run on **NTFS_V1.E01**.

The attribute's minimum and maximum size are also specified in the $AttrDef entry. In the case of $FILENAME in this example these are 0x44 (68_d) bytes and 0x242 (578_d) bytes, respectively. In the case of attributes such as $DATA which have an unlimited size, these values will be 0x00 and 0xFFFFFFFFFFFFFFFF, respectively.

7.3.2 Deleted Files

The **Files** directory in **NTFS_V1.E01** contains two files. In **NTFS_V2.E01** these two files, **hills.jpg** and **delete.txt** (MFT record numbers 66_d and 68_d respectively), have been deleted. The **delete.txt** file consisted solely of resident data, while the **hills.jpg** file contains non-resident data. Listing 7.32 shows an excerpt from **istat** on both of these files *before* they were deleted (i.e. in **NTFS_V1.E01**).

Examining the resident file **delete.txt** (MFT Record Number 68_d) after deletion (**NTFS_V2.E01**) initially shows the following MFT Record. This is shown in Listing 7.33. It is obvious from this that the data is still present – the resident data attribute is still present and can be interpreted. Indeed almost all of the same information is present as was present before deletion. The MFT Record is marked as being unallocated in the $BITMAP attribute associated with the $MFT file (MFT Record 0).

```
delete.txt - MFT Record 68

Entry: 68 Sequence: 1
$LogFile Sequence Number: 0
Allocated File
Links: 1
...[snip]...
Attributes:
Type: $STANDARD_INFORMATION (16-0) Name: N/A Resident size: 48
Type: $FILE_NAME (48-3) Name: N/A Resident size: 86
Type: $SECURITY_DESCRIPTOR (80-1) Name: N/A Resident size: 80
Type: $DATA (128-2) Name: N/A Resident size: 66

hills.jpg - MFT Record 66

Entry: 66 Sequence: 1
$LogFile Sequence Number: 0
Allocated File
Links: 1
...[snip]...
Attributes:
Type: $STANDARD_INFORMATION (16-0) Name: N/A Resident size: 48
Type: $FILE_NAME (48-3) Name: N/A Resident size: 84
Type: $SECURITY_DESCRIPTOR (80-1) Name: N/A Resident size: 80
Type: $DATA (128-2) Name: N/A Non-Resident size: 274749
init_size: 274749
16896 16897 16898 16899 16900 16901 16902 16903
...[snip]...
```

Listing 7.32 **istat** output for **delete.txt** and **hills.jpg** prior to deletion.

But what about non-resident $DATA attributes? MFT record 66_d, **hills.jpg**, was a large file that used a non-resident data attribute. Originally this file occupied 68_d clusters beginning at $16,896_d$. Listing 7.34 shows an excerpt from cluster $16,896_d$ after the file has been deleted. This shows that the file content is still present in the file system.

Examining the MFT record for this file shows only one single change, the link count is reset to zero. As with the resident file the $BITMAP attribute in MFT record 0_d is also unset so as to indicate that this MFT record number can now be reused. Additionally in the case of a non-resident data attribute, the contents of the bitmap file are updated to show that the clusters are no longer in use. The entry for cluster $16,896_d$ is located in byte $2,112_d$ in the bitmap file (least significant bit). The contents of the file are found in the 68_d clusters beginning at cluster $16,896_d$. Hence 9_d bytes from this point will provide the bitmap information. Listing 7.35 shows these bytes both before and after deletion.

Examining the data from $Bitmap shows the 68_d clusters before their deallocation. An extract from this bitmap structure (the final two bytes - 0xFF0F) is shown in Figure 7.7. Examining Listing 7.35 shows that all of these are deallocated after deletion (all zero values).

7.3.3 Fragmented Files

Fragmented files are files for which the content is stored in a number of fragments rather than in a single block of data. On busy file systems this is a common means of storing a large file. It occurs

```
011000: 4649 4c45 3000 0300 0000 0000 0000 0000 FILE0...........
011010: 0200 0000 3800 0000 c001 0000 0004 0000 ....8...........
011020: 0000 0000 0000 0000 0400 0000 4400 0000 ............D...
011030: 0600 0000 0000 0000 1000 0000 4800 0000 ............H...
011040: 0000 0000 0000 0000 3000 0000 1800 0000 ........0.......
011050: 5af1 3490 bc0b da01 9d03 3590 bc0b da01 Z.4.......5.....
011060: 9d03 3590 bc0b da01 5af1 3490 bc0b da01 ..5.....Z.4.....
011070: 2000 0000 0000 0000 0000 0000 0000 0000 ...............
011080: 3000 0000 7000 0000 0000 0000 0000 0300 0...p...........
011090: 5600 0000 1800 0100 4100 0000 0000 0100 V.......A.......
0110a0: 5af1 3490 bc0b da01 5af1 3490 bc0b da01 Z.4.....Z.4.....
0110b0: 5af1 3490 bc0b da01 5af1 3490 bc0b da01 Z.4.....Z.4.....
0110c0: 4800 0000 0000 0000 0000 0000 0000 0000 H...............
0110d0: 2000 0000 0000 0000 0a00 6400 6500 6c00 .........d.e.l.
0110e0: 6500 7400 6500 2e00 7400 7800 7400 0000 e.t.e...t.x.t...
0110f0: 5000 0000 6800 0000 0000 0000 0000 0100 P...h...........
011100: 5000 0000 1800 0000 0100 0480 1400 0000 P...............
011110: 2400 0000 0000 0000 3400 0000 0102 0000 $.......4.......
011120: 0000 0005 2000 0000 2002 0000 0102 0000 .... ... .......
011130: 0000 0005 2000 0000 2002 0000 0200 1c00 .... ... .......
011140: 0100 0000 0003 1400 ff01 1f00 0101 0000 ................
011150: 0000 0001 0000 0000 8000 0000 6000 0000 ............`...
011160: 0000 0000 0000 0200 4200 0000 1800 0000 ........B.......
011170: 5468 6973 2066 696c 6520 7769 6c6c 2062 This file will b
011180: 6520 6465 6c65 7465 6420 696e 2061 206c e deleted in a l
011190: 6174 6572 2076 6572 7369 6f6e 206f 6620 ater version of
0111a0: 7468 6973 2066 696c 6520 7379 7374 656d this file system
0111b0: 2e0a 0000 0000 0000 ffff ffff 0000 0000 ................
```

Listing 7.33 The MFT Record entry for **delete.txt** in **NTFS_V2.E01**. This is after the file has been deleted. Notice that the link count (highlighted) has been decreased to 0.

```
04200000: ffd8 ffe0 0010 4a46 4946 0001 0100 0001 ......JFIF......
04200010: 0001 0000 ffdb 0043 0002 0202 0202 0102 .......C........
04200020: 0202 0203 0202 0303 0604 0303 0303 0705 ................
04200030: 0504 0608 0709 0808 0708 0809 0a0d 0b09 ................
...[snip]...
```

Listing 7.34 An excerpt from the first cluster of the 'deleted' **hills.jpg** file in **NTFS_V2.E01**.

```
[[Before deletion]]
00000840: ffff ffff ffff ffff 0f

[[After deletion]]
00000840: 0000 0000 0000 0000 00
```

Listing 7.35 The contents of $Bitmap file both before and after deletion of **hills.jpg**.

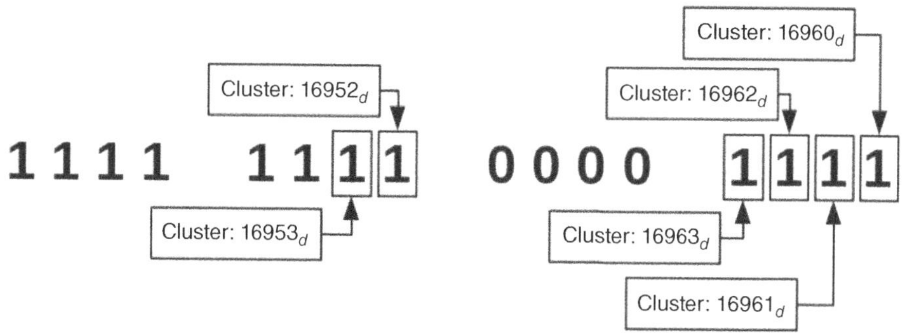

Figure 7.7 The relevant bitmap values for **hills.jpg** before file deletion.

when there is insufficient space in one single area of the disk for the file's contents. Instead, parts of the file are stored in different locations.

In NTFS these locations are referenced through data runs in the run list. To this point the encountered runlists have contained a single data run, in other words the files have been contiguous. More complex runlists contain multiple runs, as shown in Listing 7.36.

```
310B 002A 0121 02C7 FF21 0600 1000
```

Listing 7.36 Run list for a fragmented file.

Knowing that the runlist is composed of a number of data runs means that processing begins from the left most byte. This byte is 0x31. As with all runs the first nibble represents the number of bytes in the starting cluster, and the second nibble represents the number of bytes in the size of the data run. The total of these nibbles ($3 + 1 = 4_d$) is the number of bytes in total for the data run (excluding the first byte). This means that the first data run is 0x310B002A01. The next byte commences the second data run and is 0x21 meaning that the data run consists of a total of three bytes (after the first) giving 0x2102C7FF. This is followed by 0x21 giving a data run of 0x21060010. Finally the byte value 0x00 is encountered marking the end of the run list. Hence the runlist in Listing 7.36 is composed of three individual data runs.

The data runs can be processed as we saw in Section 7.1.6. For instance the first data run (0x310B002A01) consists of 0x0B clusters starting at cluster 0x12A00. Converting these values to decimal gives: 11_d clusters beginning at cluster $76,288_d$. This means that the clusters: $76,288_d$, $76,289_d$, $76,290_d$, $76,291_d$, $76,292_d$, $76,293_d$, $76,294_d$, $76,295_d$, $76,296_d$, $76,297_d$ and $76,298_d$ contain file content.

The second data run is: 0x2102C7FF. Processing this gives 0x02 clusters starting at 0xFFC7; however, the starting cluster is a signed number that is relative to the start of the previous data run. 0xFFC7 is -57_d, meaning that the second data run commences at $76,288 - 57 = 76,231_d$. Hence the clusters: $76,231_d$ and $76,232_d$ are the next two clusters encountered in the file.

The third data run is 0x21060010 meaning that it consists of 0x06 clusters beginning at cluster number 0x1000 (4096_d), which is relative to the start of the last run. The last run commenced at $76,231_d$ meaning that this third run commences at $76,231 + 4096 = 80,327_d$. This means that $80,327_d$, $80,328_d$, $80,329_d$, $80,330_d$, $80,331_d$ and $80,332_d$ are also part of the file's contents. The next byte is 0x00 signalling the end of the run list!

Hence the run list shown in Listing 7.36 represents the following clusters: $76,288_d$, $76,289_d$, $76,290_d$, $76,291_d$, $76,292_d$, $76,293_d$, $76,294_d$, $76,295_d$, $76,296_d$, $76,297d$, $76,298_d$, $76,231_d$,

$76,232_d$, $80,327_d$, $80,328_d$, $80,329_d$, $80,330_d$, $80,331_d$ and $80,332_d$. The key point to remember when processing subsequent data runs in NTFS is that the starting cluster of subsequent runs is relative to the start of the previous run.

7.3.4 Alternate Data Streams

Alternate data streams (ADS) are named secondary $DATA attributes which often provide information about a file. One of the most common uses is to identify the source on the Internet from which a file was downloaded. This ADS, called *Zone.Identifier*, shows applications that the file might not be fully trusted! ADS can also be used as an anti-forensic technique allowing data to be hidden in a named secondary $DATA stream. Listing 7.37 shows the MFT record for **islands.jpg** in **NTFS_V1.E01**. Processing the alternate data stream in Listing 7.37 is shown in Table 7.42.

```
014c00: 4649 4c45 3000 0300 0000 0000 0000 0000 FILE0...........
014c10: 0100 0100 3800 0100 f001 0000 0004 0000 ....8...........
014c20: 0000 0000 0000 0000 0500 0000 4300 0000 ............C...
014c30: 8700 0000 0000 0000 1000 0000 4800 0000 ............H...
014c40: 0000 0000 0000 0000 3000 0000 1800 0000 ........0.......
...[snip]...
014d40: 0100 0000 0003 1400 ff01 1f00 0101 0000 ................
014d50: 0000 0001 0000 0000 8000 0000 4800 0000 ............H...
014d60: 0100 4000 0000 0200 0000 0000 0000 0000 ..@.............
014d70: 4000 0000 0000 0000 4000 0000 0000 0000 @.......@.......
014d80: 0010 0400 0000 0000 6905 0400 0000 0000 ........i.......
014d90: 6905 0400 0000 0000 2141 0052 0000 0000 i.......!A.R....
014da0: 8000 0000 4800 0000 0009 1800 0000 0400 ....H...........
014db0: 1200 0000 3000 0000 4800 6900 6400 6400 ....0...H.i.d.d.
014dc0: 6500 6e00 4100 4400 5300 0000 0000 0000 e.n.A.D.S.......
014dd0: 4869 6464 656e 2049 6e66 6f72 6d61 7469 Hidden Informati
014de0: 6f6e 0000 0000 0000 ffff ffff 0000 0000 on..............
```

Listing 7.37 An MFT record containing two $DATA attributes. The primary $DATA attribute is underlined and is immediately followed by the ADS. Some content from the MFT record has been removed.

The Sleuthkit can also process ADS. Listing 7.38 shows an excerpt from the **fls** command when run on **NTFS_V1.E01**. This shows that there are two instances for **islands.jpg** with ID values 67-128-2 and 67-128-4. Previously with FAT and ExFAT, fls returned a single number to uniquely identify each file. In NTFS, due to alternate data streams this is not possible. Hence every ID number used by Sleuthkit for NTFS is a complex number in the form:

mftRecordNum-attributeType-attributeId

```
r/r 67-128-2: islands.jpg
r/r 67-128-4: islands.jpg:HiddenADS
```

Listing 7.38 The output from **fls** showing the file **islands.jpg** and its ADS **islands.jpg: HiddenADS**.

Table 7.42 Processing the alternate data stream in Listing 7.37. The offsets for the name/data are found in the common attribute header.

		Attribute Header	
Offset	**Size**	**Name**	**Value**
0x00	0x04	Attribute Type	0x80 ($DATA)
0x04	0x04	Attribute Size	0x48 (72_d)
0x08	0x01	Non-resident	0x00 (Resident)
0x09	0x01	Name Length	0x09 (9_d)
0x0A	0x02	Name Offset	0x18 (24_d)
0x0C	0x02	Flags	0x00 (0_d)
0x0E	0x02	Attribute ID	0x04 (4_d)
		Resident Header	
0x10	0x04	Content Size	0x12 (18_d)
0x14	0x02	Content Offset	0x30 (48_d)
		Data	
0x18	0x09	Name	HiddenADS
0x30	0x12	Data	Hidden Information

Consider the alternate data stream **islands.jpg:HiddenADS** in Listing 7.38. Sleuthkit's ID number for this is 67-128-4. This is the MFT record number (67_d), the attribute type ($DATA is 0x80 which is 128_d) and the attribute ID (which is 4_d – see Table 7.42). With the **icat** command the MFT record number can be used by itself (i.e. 67_d), in which case the primary $DATA attribute is recovered, or an alternate data stream can be recovered by giving the complete ID number. The recovery of the primary and alternate data streams is shown in Listing 7.39.

```
$ icat ntfs_V1.E01 67 > islands.jpg
$ icat ntfs_V1.E01 67-128-4
Hidden Information
```

Listing 7.39 Recovering the primary and alternate data streams using **icat**.

This generic structure of *mftRecordNumber-attributeType-attributeID* can be used to recover any attribute from an NTFS file system. Consider Listing 7.37. The second attribute in this is a filename attribute (type 0x30) with an attribute ID of 0x03. Listing 7.40 shows the recovery of this attribute's data using **icat**.

7.3.5 Large MFT Records

In the case in which the attributes for the MFT record will not fit into a single MFT record, there exists the $ATTRIBUTE_LIST attribute which will provide the locations to the other attributes.

```
$ icat mnt/ewf1 67-48-3 | xxd
000000: 0500 0000 0000 0500 ba23 428c bc0b da01 .........#B.....
000010: ba23 428c bc0b da01 ba23 428c bc0b da01 .#B......#B.....
000020: ba23 428c bc0b da01 0010 0400 0000 0000 .#B.............
000030: 0000 0000 0000 0000 2000 0000 0000 0000 ....... .......
000040: 0b00 6900 7300 6c00 6100 6e00 6400 7300 ..i.s.l.a.n.d.s.
000050: 2e00 6a00 7000 6700                     ..j.p.g.
```

Listing 7.40 Using **icat** to recover $FILENAME by specifying the MFT record number (67_d) along with the attribute type ($0x30 = 48_d$) and ID (3_d).

Listing 7.41 shows a MFT record in which many hard links were created to the file (MFT record 67_d in **NTFS_V2.E01**), thereby creating a $FILE_NAME attribute for each link. Once the storage space required for these exceeded the MFT Record Size (1024_d bytes) the $ATTRIBUTE_LIST attribute was created. This file is **islands.jpg** (MFT Record: 67_d) in **NTFS_V2.E01**.

```
014c00: 4649 4c45 3000 0300 0000 0000 0000 0000 FILE0...........
014c10: 0100 0700 3800 0100 f803 0000 0004 0000 ....8...........
014c20: 0000 0000 0000 0000 0a00 0000 4300 0000 ............C...
014c30: 8f00 0000 0000 0000 1000 0000 4800 0000 ............H...
014c40: 0000 0000 0000 0000 3000 0000 1800 0000 ........0.......
014c50: ba23 428c bc0b da01 03ae 428c bc0b da01 .#B.......B.....
014c60: 56fc a0bf 0a0c da01 ba23 428c bc0b da01 V........#B.....
014c70: 2000 0000 0000 0000 0000 0000 0000 0000 ...............
014c80: 2000 0000 4800 0000 0100 4000 0000 0900 ...H.....@.....
014c90: 0000 0000 0000 0000 0000 0000 0000 0000 ................
014ca0: 4000 0000 0000 0000 0010 0000 0000 0000 @...............
014cb0: 7001 0000 0000 0000 7001 0000 0000 0000 p.......p.......
014cc0: 2101 4152 000b da01 3000 0000 7000 0000 !.AR....0...p...
014cd0: 0000 0000 0000 0300 5800 0000 1800 0100 ........X.......
014ce0: 0500 0000 0000 0500 ba23 428c bc0b da01 .........#B.....
...[snip]...
```

Listing 7.41 MFT record 67_d from **NTFS_V2.E01** showing an $ATTRIBUTE_LIST attribute.

Processing the highlighted $ATTRIBUTE_LIST attribute shows the data to be non-resident with a data run composed of 0x21014152, meaning that the run consists of a single cluster beginning at cluster 0x5241 ($21,057_d$). Listing 7.42 shows an excerpt from this cluster.

```
...[snip]...
05241080: 3000 0000 2000 001a 0000 0000 0000 0000 0... ...........
05241090: 4300 0000 0000 0100 0600 0000 0000 0000 C...............
052410a0: 3000 0000 2000 001a 0000 0000 0000 0000 0... ...........
052410b0: 4300 0000 0000 0100 0800 0000 0000 0000 C...............
052410c0: 3000 0000 2000 001a 0000 0000 0000 0000 0... ...........
052410d0: 4600 0000 0000 0100 0000 0000 0000 0000 F...............
...[snip]...
```

Listing 7.42 An excerpt from cluster $21,057_d$ in **NTFS_V2.E01** showing attribute entries 5_d–7_d.

Table 7.43 Processed attribute entries from Listing 7.42.

Offset	Size	Name	Entry 1	Entry 2	Entry 3
0x00	0x04	Attribute Type	0x30	0x30	0x30
0x04	0x02	Entry Length	0x20 (32_d)	0x20 (32_d)	0x20 (32_d)
0x06	0x01	Name Length	0x00 (0_d)	0x00 (0_d)	0x00 (0_d)
0x07	0x01	Name Offset	0x1A (26_d)	0x1A (26_d)	0x1A (26_d)
0x08	0x08	Starting VCN	0x00 (0_d)	0x00 (0_d)	0x00 (0_d)
0x10	0x08	File Reference	Seq: 0x01 (1_d) MFT: 0x43 (67_d)	Seq: 0x01 (1_d) MFT: 0x43 (67_d)	Seq: 0x01 (1_d) MFT: 0x46 (70_d)
0x18	0x01	Attribute ID	0x06 (6_d)	0x08 (8_d)	0x00 (0_d)

Each 32_d byte entry in this cluster contains information about a single attribute and where those attributes can be found. Listing 7.42 shows three attribute entries. These are processed in Table 7.43.

The results from processing this data show that the three attributes reside in two different MFT records, the original record, 0x43 (67_d) and a secondary record 0x46 (70_d). During full analysis the remainder of the attribute entries would be processed and any other MFT records identified. In doing so the reader will discover two $FILENAME attributes in MFT Record 70_d, with the remaining attributes (including the $ATRRIBUTE_LIST attribute located in the original MFT Record (67_d)).

What happens when a forensic tool is run on these two MFT records? Running **istat** on Record 67_d will show the attribute header information and information on all of the attributes present in the MFT record. This includes $STANDARD_INFORMATION, eight $FILE_NAME attributes (two of which are actually in MFT Record 70_d) and the $ATTRIBUTE_LIST attribute. The **istat** output for the $ATTRIBUTE_LIST attribute is shown in Listing 7.43.

```
$ATTRIBUTE_LIST Attribute Values:
Type: 16-0 MFT Entry: 67 VCN: 0
Type: 48-3 MFT Entry: 67 VCN: 0
Type: 48-7 MFT Entry: 67 VCN: 0
Type: 48-5 MFT Entry: 67 VCN: 0
Type: 48-6 MFT Entry: 67 VCN: 0
Type: 48-8 MFT Entry: 67 VCN: 0
Type: 48-0  MFT Entry: 70 VCN: 0
Type: 48-1  MFT Entry: 70 VCN: 0
Type: 80-1 MFT Entry: 67 VCN: 0
Type: 128-2 MFT Entry: 67 VCN: 0
Type: 128-4 MFT Entry: 67 VCN: 0
```

Listing 7.43 $ATTRIBUTE_LIST contents as shown by **istat**. The attributes in the second MFT record are highlighted.

7.4 Summary

Knowledge of NTFS is of vital importance in traditional digital forensics. The NTFS file system is the standard file system for Windows machines and as such is very commonly encountered in file system forensic analysis.

For its day, NTFS is a modern file system. It was one of the first file systems that was based on B-Trees, a structure that has become standard in most modern file systems. It was also one of the first to use data runs to locate information. These structures are again commonly encountered in modern-day file systems (although generally by a different name!). Hence, while the popularity of NTFS may be waning, indeed the popularity of traditional computers/laptops is waning, knowledge of the NTFS file system is still of vital importance for any digital forensic analyst.

Exercises

1 In Section 7.2.3 the **NTFS_V1.E01** file system was partially analysed. As exercises please try the following:

a) During the listing of files the contents of the Root Directory were partially listed (Listing 7.18 and Table 7.36). Complete this process and compare the results to that of **fls**.

b) When listing files in the root directory another directory (Files) was discovered. Locate the MFT record for this directory and list the contents of this directory.

2 In relation to the $DATA attribute shown in Listing 7.44 answer the following questions.

```
000160: 8000 0000 5800 0000 0100 4000 0000 0200 ....X.....@.....
000170: 0000 0000 0000 0000 1400 0000 0000 0000 ................
000180: 4000 0000 0000 0000 0050 0100 0000 0000 @........P......
000190: 414e 0100 0000 0000 414e 0100 0000 0000 AN......AN......
0001a0: 3106 d04b 0131 0615 15ff 2106 f41c 3103 1..K.1....!...1.
0001b0: 58aa 0000 0000 0000                     X.......
```

Listing 7.44 Sample $DATA attribute.

a) What is the attribute size?

b) List the clusters in which the file content can be found.

3 In relation to the image provided in **NTFS_V3.E01** please answer the following questions.

a) What is the volume label?

b) How many clusters are in the file system?

c) What is the MD5 sum for the $MFT file?

4 There is a file in **NTFS_V3.E01** called **hills.jpg** (MFT Record #: 4840_d). In relation to this file answer the following:

a) Extract the MFT record for this file from the file and calculate its MD5 sum.

b) When was this file created?

c) What is the file size in bytes?

d) This file is fragmented. How many data runs are present?

e) Recover the file content.

Bibliography

Alazab, M., Venkatraman, S., and Watters, P. (2009). Effective digital forensic analysis of the NTFS disk image. *Ubiquitous Computing and Communication Journal* 4 (1): 551–558.

Alazab, M., Venkatraman, S., and Watters, P. (2009). Digital forensic techniques for static analysis of NTFS images. In: *Proceedings of ICIT2009, 4th International Conference on Information Technology*. IEEE Xplore 551–558.

Carrier, B. (2005). *File System Forensic Analysis*. Boston, MA; London: Addison-Wesley.

Cho, G.S. (2015). A new NTFS anti-forensic technique for NTFS index entry. *The Journal of Korea Institute of Information, Electronics, and Communication Technology* 8 (4): 327–337.

Chow, K.P., Law, F.Y., Kwan, M.Y., and Lai, P.K. (2007). The rules of time on NTFS file system. In: *2nd International Workshop on Systematic Approaches to Digital Forensic Engineering (SADFE'07)*, 71–85. IEEE.

Galhuber, M. and Luh, R. (2021). Time for truth: Forensic analysis of NTFS timestamps. In: *Proceedings of the 16th International Conference on Availability, Reliability and Security*, 1–10. ACM.

Huebner, E., Bem, D., and Wee, C.K. (2006). Data hiding in the NTFS file system. *Digital Investigation* 3 (4): 211–226.

Kai, Z., En, C., and Qinquan, G. (2010). Analysis and implementation of NTFS file system based on computer forensics. In: *2010 2nd International Workshop on Education Technology and Computer Science*, vol. 1, 325–328. IEEE.

Karresand, M., Axelsson, S., and Dyrkolbotn, G.O. (2019). Using NTFS cluster allocation behavior to find the location of user data. *Digital Investigation* 29: S51–S60.

Karresand, M., Dyrkolbotn, G.O., and Axelsson, S. (2020). An empirical study of the NTFS cluster allocation behavior over time. *Forensic Science International: Digital Investigation* 33: 301008.

Knutson, T. (2024). Filesystem Timestamps: What Makes Them Tick? –SANS Institute [Internet]. www.sans.org. [cited 2024 April 3]. https://www.sans.org/white-papers/36842/ (accessed 13 August 2024).

van der Meer, V., Jonker, H., and van den Bos, J. (2021). A contemporary investigation of NTFS file fragmentation. *Forensic Science International: Digital Investigation* 38: 301125.

Microsoft (2019). NTFS Overview [Internet]. Microsoft.com. [cited 2024 April 3]. https://docs.microsoft.com/en-us/windows-server/storage/file-server/ntfs-overview (accessed 13 August 2024).

Microsoft (2021). Distributed Link Tracking and Object Identifiers - Win32 apps [Internet]. learn.microsoft.com. [cited 2024 April 3]. https://docs.microsoft.com/en-us/windows/win32/fileio/distributed-link-tracking-and-object-identifiers (accessed 13 August 2024).

Microsoft (2024). Security identifiers (Windows 10) - Windows security [Internet]. docs.microsoft.com. [cited 2024 April 3]. https://docs.microsoft.com/en-us/windows/security/identity-protection/access-control/security-identifiers (accessed 13 August 2024).

Mohamed, A. and Khalid, C. (2021). Detection of suspicious timestamps in NTFS using volume shadow copies. *International Journal of Computer Network and Information Security* 13 (4): 62–69.

Nordvik, R., Toolan, F., and Axelsson, S. (2019). Using the object ID index as an investigative approach for NTFS file systems. *Digital Investigation* 28: S30–S39.

Oh, J., Lee, S., and Hwang, H. (2021). NTFS Data Tracker: tracking file data history based on $LogFile. *Forensic Science International: Digital Investigation* 39: 301309.

Palmbach, D. and Breitinger, F. (2020). Artifacts for detecting timestamp manipulation in NTFS on windows and their reliability. *Forensic Science International: Digital Investigation* 32: 300920.

Parsonage, H. (2008). The Meaning of Linkfiles In Forensic Examinations A look at the practical value to forensic examinations of dates and times, and object identifiers in Windows shortcut files [Internet] [cited 2024 April 3]. http://computerforensics.parsonage.co.uk/downloads/TheMeaningofLIFE.pdf (accessed 13 August 2024).

Updyke, D. and Jaconski, M. (2024). Using Alternate Data Streams in the Collection and Exfiltration of Data s]. SEI Blog [cited 2024 April 3]. https://insights.sei.cmu.edu/blog/using-alternate-data-streams-in-the-collection-and-exfiltration-of-data/ (accessed 13 August 2024).

Part III

Linux File Systems

8

The EXT2 File System

The most commonly encountered file systems in Linux systems are the ext family of file systems. Most modern distributions use ext4 as their default file system. Ext2 and ext3 are less frequently encountered, but are still used for removable media. Additionally some older installations still use ext3 as their main file system. The ext file system is also found on many Android phones, meaning that even if a true Linux system is never encountered, knowledge of ext is required in order to perform small-scale device forensics effectively.

This chapter initially provides some background on the ext family of file systems and then proceeds to describe the structures of the ext2 file system in detail. This allows an understanding of how the file system stores information and how digital forensic tools process the file system. The next chapter examines the advanced features introduced in ext3 and ext4.

The Extended File System (ext) family of file systems has long been the standard on the Linux OS. In 1992 the ext file system was released with the aim of developing it as the standard for Linux. Little under a year later version 2 (ext2) was released. This file system proved to be very successful and is still in use today. Usually ext2 is encountered on USB/Flash drives as it is not a journaled file system, and hence effective for removable media where the journaling overhead may cause performance issues.

Ext3 was released in 2001 and was the first Linux file system to provide support for journaling. Journaling allows for more robust and resilient file systems in which a catastrophic failure is less likely to corrupt and/or lose data. The journal is a temporary storage area to which changes to the file system are written prior to writing them to the actual file system. This means that if power is lost during the file system write operation the file system can be repaired by accessing the journal.

Ext4 began as additional functionality for ext3 but was forked early in its development. For this reason many people view ext4 as being an extension of ext3 rather than a new file system. The changes between ext3 and ext2 were sufficiently large to call it a new file system but this is not the case from ext3 to ext4. Ext4 improves the recovery abilities of the journal by adding checksums, ensuring that journal entries themselves are not corrupt prior to recovery and also provides for delayed file allocation. This means that space on disk is not allocated until the write is about to take place. In ext3 the space was allocated when the information was written to the journal.

One of the major benefits of the ext family (at least from 2 onwards) is the backwards compatibility. An ext2 file system can be upgraded to ext4 with no need to reformat! This is unlike the Microsoft family (although families might be better) of file systems: FAT, NTFS and ReFS which have no backwards compatibility.

Table 8.1 shows some information about the ext family of file systems in comparison to FAT32 and NTFS file systems.

File System Forensics, First Edition. Fergus Toolan.

Table 8.1 Comparison of ext file systems with traditional Windows file systems.

File System	Max. Filename Length[a)]	Max. File Size	Max. Volume Size	Timestamps[b)]
FAT32	255	4_d GiB	16_d TiB	MAB
NTFS	255	8_d PiB	8_d PiB	MACB
Ext2	255	2_d TiB	32_d TiB	MAC
Ext3	255	2_d TiB	32_d TiB	MAC
Ext4	255	16_d TiB	1_d EiB	MACB

a) This length is given in bytes. If unicode characters are used the number of characters will be less.
b) Timestamps are an important piece of information in forensics. The four traditional times are MACB: M – Content modification; A – File access; C – Metadata modification; B – Birth time (i.e. Creation).

8.1 On-Disk Structures

The ext file systems are divided into a number of mini file systems known as block groups. Each block group is capable of managing its own storage space and file metadata. Each block group also contains information about all other block groups in the file system. Figure 8.1 shows the general structure of the file system.

From Figure 8.1 the block group structure is clear. With the exception of the beginning of the volume the entire volume is composed of equal-sized block groups.[1] All ext volumes begin with 1024_d bytes of unallocated space. Block Group 0 begins immediately after this area.

Block groups, as mini file systems, have their own internal structure. Figure 8.2 shows the structure of block group 0 (BG0). Not all block groups will contain the superblock structure (although the structure is duplicated in a number of locations on the file system). However, BG0 will always contain a superblock structure.

The superblock itself is one of the most important structures in ext and the beginning of any analysis of the file system. The superblock is similar to the volume boot record of FAT and $Boot of NTFS. It contains information about the file system layout and describes the block group structure.

Each block group contains a block group descriptor table which provides a description of all block groups in the file system. This structure is identical in every block group. The block group descriptor allows every structure inside the block groups to be mapped.

The block group descriptor is followed by a reserved area to allow for the file system size to increase. Ext is one of the few file systems that allows for the file system's size to be increased during its life time. This reserved area provides space for growth of the block group descriptor table.

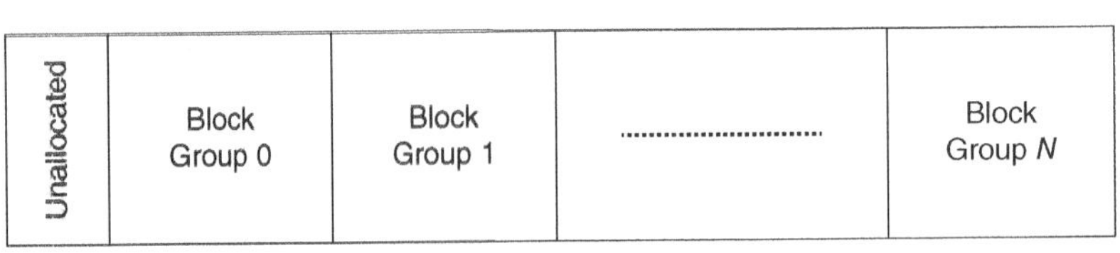

Figure 8.1 General layout of an ext volume.

1 Depending on the size of the device, the final block group may be smaller than the others.

Figure 8.2 Internal block group structure.

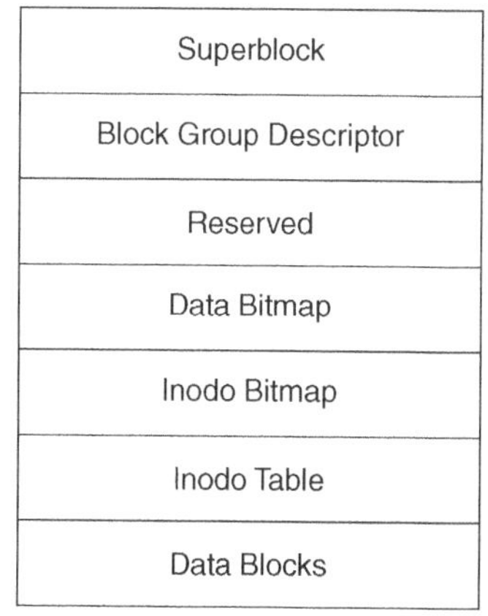

The bitmap structures are also found in the block group. These structures show the allocation status of the block group's data blocks and inodes. The inodes are the structures that contain the metadata information. The bitmaps are followed by the inode table, the area of the block group that contains all the inode information. Inodes in ext contain all the metadata about the file, except for the file name itself. The file name is instead stored in a directory entry. The inode also provides the location of the file's data blocks. The actual file contents are stored in these data blocks.

In ext metadata storage can be viewed as a combination of FAT and NTFS. In FAT all the metadata is stored in the directory entry, which provides the name and metadata for every file in a particular directory. In ext, directory entries are used to store the filename. In NTFS all metadata information (including the filename) is stored in the MFT, a structure similar to the inode table found in ext.

The remainder of this section examines these individual structures in more detail.

8.1.1 The Superblock

The superblock is one of the most important structures in the ext file system. It contains information about the file system itself. The information in the superblock provides the number and size of block groups in the file system. The number of blocks and inodes available in the file system are discovered in the superblock. In later versions of the superblock (all modern ones) the UUID and volume name (if present) are also found. Even the time at which the file system was last mounted and last written can be found here. Occasionally even the directory upon which the file system was last mounted can be found in the superblock.[2]

The structure of block group 0, in which a superblock is always found, was shown previously (Figure 8.2). Based on the fact that file systems have 1024_d bytes of unallocated space before the superblock and that the superblock is 1024_d bytes in size the **dd** command shown in Listing 8.1 can be used to extract the superblock.[3]

```
# dd if=/dev/sdb1 of=sb.dd bs=1024 skip=1 count=1
```

Listing 8.1 The **dd** command to extract the superblock from **/dev/sdb1**.

---

2 The path on which it was mounted is contained in the superblock; however, the superblock provides no information regarding the machine upon which it was mounted.

3 In this case the superblock is being extracted from a partition on a physical device (**/dev/sdb1**). This value can be replaced with a raw image filename in order to extract the superblock from an image file.

Table 8.2 Block groups in ext that contain superblock structures.

0	1	3	5	7
		9	25	49
		27	125	343
		81	625	2401
		...	...	...

Table 8.3 Superblock structure. Note that some values have been omitted.

Offset	Size	Name	Description
0x00	0x04	Total # Inodes	The total number of inodes in the file system.
0x04	0x04	Total # Blocks	The total number of blocks in the file system.
0x08	0x04	# Reserved Blocks	Ext can reserve a portion of blocks that only root can write to. This allows for rescue if the non-reserved space is fully occupied.
0x0C	0x04	Free Block Count	The number of blocks that are unused.
0x10	0x04	Free Inode Count	The number of unused inodes in the file system.
0x18	0x04	Log Block Size	The block size (in bytes) is given by the formula $2^{(10+log\_block\_size)}$.
0x20	0x04	Blocks/Group	The number of blocks in each block group. Using this and the total number of blocks the number of block groups can be calculated.
0x28	0x04	Inodes/Group	The number of inodes in each block group.
0x2C	0x04	Mount Time	The unix time at which the file system was last mounted.
0x30	0x04	Write Time	The unix time at which the file system was last written.
0x34	0x02	# mounts	The number of mounts since the last file system check (**fsck**).
0x36	0x02	max. # mounts	The maximum number of mounts before the file system's consistency is checked.
0x38	0x02	Magic	A magic number (0xEF53).
0x3A	0x02	File System State	The current state of the file system. Values: 0x01 – Clean; and 0x02 – Errors.
0x3C	0x02	File System Errors	What to do if errors are detected. Values: 1 – Continue; 2 – Remount read-only; and 3 – Panic.
0x3E	0x02	Minor Revision Version	Minor revision level of the file system.
0x40	0x04	Time Last Check	Unix time representing the last file system check.
0x48	0x04	Creator OS	Identifier of the OS that created the file system. Values: 0 – Linux; 1 – GNU Hurd; 2 – Masix; 3 – FreeBSD; and 4 – Lites.
0x50	0x02	UID Reserved Blocks	The UID that can use reserved blocks (default is 0, i.e. root).

Table 8.3 (Continued)

Offset	Size	Name	Description
0x52	0x02	GID Reserved Blocks	The GID that can use reserved blocks (default is 0).
0x54	0x04	First Inode	The first inode that is available for standard files. In older versions of ext this was 11. In more recent versions it may be different.
0x58	0x02	Inode Size	The inode size in bytes. In revision 0 this was always 128 bytes.
0x5A	0x02	Block Group Number	This is the block group number in which this superblock resides.
0x5C	0x04	Compatible Features	If the file system driver does not support these features the file system can still be mounted.
0x60	0x04	Incompatible Features	If the file system driver does not support these features then the file system should not be mounted.
0x64	0x04	RO-Compatible Features	If the file system driver does not support these features then the file system should be mounted as read-only.
0x68	0x10	UUID	A universally unique identifier for the file system.
0x78	0x10	Volume Name	The volume name.
0x88	0x40	Last Mounted Directory	The directory on which the file system was last mounted. Not normally used in most file system drivers.
0xD0	0x10	Journal UUID	The UUID for the journal file.
0xE0	0x04	Journal Inode	The inode for the journal file.
0xE4	0x04	Journal Device Number	A device identifier in the case where the journal is stored on a separate file system.

The superblock is regarded as one of the most important structures in the ext family of file systems. Therefore in early versions of the file system a copy of the superblock was found in every single block group. In later versions the default was to use the *sparse_superblock* feature when creating the file system in which a copy of the superblock was located only in certain block groups. These block groups were 0 and 1 and then all powers of 3, 5 and 7. Table 8.2 summarises the locations in which they can be found.

The superblock, like most ext structures, defaults to storing information in a little-endian format. The superblock is 1024_d bytes in size but much of this space is unused. Table 8.3 shows the structure of the superblock. Some values in this structure have been omitted.

The Sleuth Kit supports the ext family of file systems. The **fsstat** command generally reads the superblock structure and provides the information shown in Listing 8.2.

The superblock contains three features fields, for compatible, incompatible and read-only compatible features. In the case of compatible features these features are optional and generally provide performance improvements; however, if a file system driver does not support any of these features the file system can still be mounted. The incompatible features require that the file system driver must support that feature. If the driver does not support the features then the file system will not be mounted. Finally the read-only compatible features allow the file system to be mounted as a read-only file system in the case that the driver does not support one or more of these features. Table 8.4 shows the flag values for all of the features.

```
FILE SYSTEM INFORMATION
--------------------------------------------
File System Type: Ext2
Volume Name: ext2-FS
Volume ID: 8af32ee02bb3698ae24cdb848be4a795

Last Written at: 2023-11-03 05:36:06 (GMT)
Last Checked at: 2023-11-03 05:29:34 (GMT)

Last Mounted at: 2023-11-03 05:35:54 (GMT)
Unmounted properly
Last mounted on: /media/ext2

Source OS: Linux
Dynamic Structure
Compat Features: Ext Attributes, Resize Inode, Dir Index
InCompat Features: Filetype,
Read Only Compat Features: Sparse Super, Large File,

METADATA INFORMATION
--------------------------------------------
Inode Range: 1 - 65537
Root Directory: 2
Free Inodes: 65520

CONTENT INFORMATION
--------------------------------------------
Block Range: 0 - 65535
Block Size: 4096
Free Blocks: 63354

BLOCK GROUP INFORMATION
--------------------------------------------
Number of Block Groups: 2
Inodes per group: 32768
Blocks per group: 32768
```

Listing 8.2 Output from **fsstat** on **Ext2_V1.E01**.

8.1.2 The Block Group Descriptor Table

A copy of the block group descriptor table is found in every block group in the ext file system that also contains a superblock.[4] The table is composed of a number of block group descriptors, which describe a block group. Information contained in the block group descriptor includes the location of the inode bitmap, the inode table and the block bitmap. It also contains the number of free blocks and inodes in the particular block group. The location information in each block group descriptor is identical in all copies of the block group descriptor table found throughout the file system. This information is created at file system creation and rarely changes. The statistical

4 In the case of early ext2 file systems the superblock and the block group descriptor table were found in every block group.

Table 8.4 Compatible, incompatible and read-only compatible features.

Flag	Compatible	Incompatible	Read-Only
0x0001	Pre-allocate directories.	Compression.	Sparse superblocks/descriptor tables.
0x0002	AFS Server inodes exist.	Directory entries contain a type field.	File system uses a 64-bit file size.
0x0004	File system has a journal (ext3/4 only).	File system needs to replay the journal.	Directory contents stored as a tree.
0x0008	Inodes have extended attributes.	File system uses a journal device.	
0x0010	Inode resized.		
0x0020	Directories use hash index.		

information in the block group descriptor (free nodes, free inodes, etc.) is not guaranteed to be identical. Generally this information is only updated in block group 0.

Each block group descriptor is 32_d bytes in size. The block group descriptor table contains one descriptor for each of the block groups in the file system. The size of the block group descriptor table can be calculated from the superblock. In order to do this it is necessary to discover the block size, the number of blocks per group and the total number of blocks. From this the number of block groups that are present can be calculated. Each block group will comprise a single 32_d byte block group descriptor entry in the table. Using this information it is possible to determine how many blocks are needed for the block group descriptor table. Consider a file system in which the block size is 4096_d bytes, consisting of $166,986,752_d$ blocks, $32,768_d$ blocks in each block group. The total number of block groups[5] is given by:

$$\left\lceil \frac{166,986,752}{32,768} \right\rceil = 5097$$

Hence the number of block groups is 5097_d. The block group descriptor table must therefore contain 5097_d 32-byte entries. The bytes required to store the entire block group are given by:

$$5097 \times 32 = 163,104$$

This result means that $163,104_d$ bytes are required to store the entire block group structure which is:

$$\left\lceil \frac{163,104}{4096} \right\rceil = 40$$

blocks. Hence 40_d blocks are required to store the block group descriptor table.

The structure of a block group descriptor entry is given in Table 8.5. The block group descriptor table will allow the mapping of all block groups in the file system.

8.1.3 The Inode Table

Inodes are the key metadata structure in the ext family of file systems. Traditionally in ext2, inodes are 128_d bytes in size. The inode table is the area in which inodes are located. The inodes in the inode

5 Generally the final block group will be smaller than the other block groups. The final block group occupies the remaining block groups in the file system.

Table 8.5 Block group descriptor structure.

Offset	Size	Name	Description
0x00	0x04	Data Bitmap	Starting block of the data bitmap.
0x04	0x04	Inode Bitmap	Starting block of the inode bitmap.
0x08	0x04	Inode Table	Starting block of the inode table.
0x0C	0x02	Free Block Count	The number of free blocks.
0x0E	0x02	Free Inode Count	The number of free inodes.
0x10	0x02	Used Directory Count	The number of inodes that are allocated to directories.
0x12	0x02	Padding	2 bytes of padding.
0x14	0xC	Reserved	Reserved for future use.

Table 8.6 Ext2 inode structure.

Offset	Size	Name	Description
0x00	0x02	Mode	File type and file permissions (see Mode and Permissions).
0x02	0x02	UID	User ID of the file owner.
0x04	0x04	Size	File size in bytes.
0x08	0x04	Access Time	Unix time value representing the time the file was last accessed.
0x0C	0x04	Change Time	Unix time value representing the time the file's metadata was last modified.
0x10	0x04	Modified Time	Unix time value representing the time the file's content was last modified.
0x14	0x04	Deletion Time	Unix time value representing the time the file was deleted. If the file has not been deleted this value will be 0x00.
0x18	0x02	GID	The group ID of the owning group.
0x1A	0x02	Link Count	The number of references to this file.
0x1C	0x04	Blocks	Number of 512 byte blocks used for this inode's content.
0x20	0x04	Flags	Inode Flags (see Inode Flags).
0x24	0x04	OS Dependent 1	OS-dependent information.
0x28	0x3C	Content Location	15 × 0x04 byte block pointers. (see Block Pointers).
0x64	0x04	Generation	File version (used by NFS).
0x68	0x04	File XAttr	Block number containing the file's extended attributes (if present).
0x6C	0x04	Dir XAttr	Block number containing the directory's extended attributes (if present).
0x70	0x04	Fragment Address	Never used (marked obsolete in Ext 4).
0x74	0x0C	OS Dependent 2	Further bytes for OS-dependent information.

Table 8.7 Interpretation of the most significant nibble in the ext mode structure.

Value	Meaning
0x1	FIFO
0x2	Character device
0x4	Directory
0x6	Block device
0x8	Regular file
0xA	Symbolic link
0xC	Socket

table refer to files that are present in that block group. Hence each inode table (unlike superblocks and block group descriptor tables) is different.

Inodes record metadata such as MAC time, file permissions, file owner, file size and file location. However, unlike many other file systems the inode does not record the file name. This is to be found in the contents of a directory. The structure of an inode is given in Table 8.6.

8.1.3.1 Mode/Permissions

In Linux file systems the file permissions are stored inside the file system itself. In ext the inode's mode value stores this information in addition to the file type. The mode is a two-byte value at the very start of the inode entry. Consider the value 0x41C0. The most significant nibble, 0x4, represents the file type. In this case this value represents a directory. The possible values for this nibble are shown in Table 8.7.

The remaining three nibbles provide the permissions for the file in question. These nibbles are converted to binary and the nine least significant bits represent the rwxrwxrwx permissions. A permission is set if the corresponding bit is 1. In the sample value, 0x41C0, the three least significant nibbles are 0x1C0. Converting this to binary gives 0b000111000000. Of the nine least significant bits the first three represent the owner permissions, the next three represent the group permissions and the final three bits represent the permissions for all other users on the system. The corresponding Linux permission string would be rwx------.

The second most significant nibble (0x1 in this case) can also have special meanings. In addition to the least significant bit of this nibble representing the file owner's read permission, the other three bits can also have special meanings. The most significant bit represents a set UID file, the next most significant represents a set GID file and the second least significant bit represents the sticky bit. The set UID permission is found on executable files in Linux. If this bit is set then the executable will run with the permission of the owning user, not the user who executes the file. The set GID performs a similar task for the executable file's group. Listing 8.3 shows a common example of the setuid bit. The **/bin/passwd** command can be run by any user in order to change their Linux password; however, in order to change the password one must be root. Hence this command is a setuid command denoted by the **s** in the permission string.

The purpose of the sticky bit is to protect files from deletion by the wrong person. Deletion is generally controlled by the write permission. If a user can write to a file/directory then they can also delete said file. Generally this is acceptable. However there are certain shared areas of the file

```
$ ls -l /bin/passwd
-rwsr-xr-x 1 root root 68208 Jul 14 23:08 /bin/passwd
```

Listing 8.3 Permissions of **/bin/passwd** showing the setuid bit.

system in which only the owner should be able to delete a file. For instance consider the **/tmp** area of the file system. This area is used by processes to write temporary information to disk. However, so that all users can use this area it is universally writable, meaning that anyone can delete a file. If a process stores information in **/tmp** it should be the only process allowed to delete said information. If the sticky bit is set, then only the file owner can delete the file. Listing 8.4 shows the **/tmp** directory with the sticky bit set. This is represented by the **t** in the execute permission for all other users.

```
$ ls -l /
...
drwxrwxrwt 17 root root 12288 Oct 26 09:34 tmp
...
```

Listing 8.4 Permissions of **/tmp** showing the sticky bit.

8.1.3.2 Inode Flags

The four-byte flag value provides information that tells the ext family of file systems of any special characteristics of the file or requirements for accessing the file. Table 8.8 summarises the various flag values. Note that these flag values are from ext2, ext3 and ext4 file systems. Not all of them are found in each file system.

Be aware that the vast majority of the flags listed in Table 8.8 are dependent on the file system implementation. Not all file system drivers will implement all of these flags!

8.1.3.3 Block Pointers

In addition to metadata, the inode structure also contains the location of the file's content. This information is recorded using block pointers. There are 15_d four-byte values in the inode

Table 8.8 Selection of inode flag values in various ext file systems.

Value	Meaning
0x00000004	Compressed file.
0x00000010	Immutable file [File's location will not be changed on disk].
0x00000020	Append only [Writing can only append content to the file].
0x00000040	Do not dump file.
0x00000080	Do not update access time.
0x00001000	Hash indexed directory.
	Ext 3/4
0x00080000	Extent-based storage used.
0x10000000	Inline storage used.

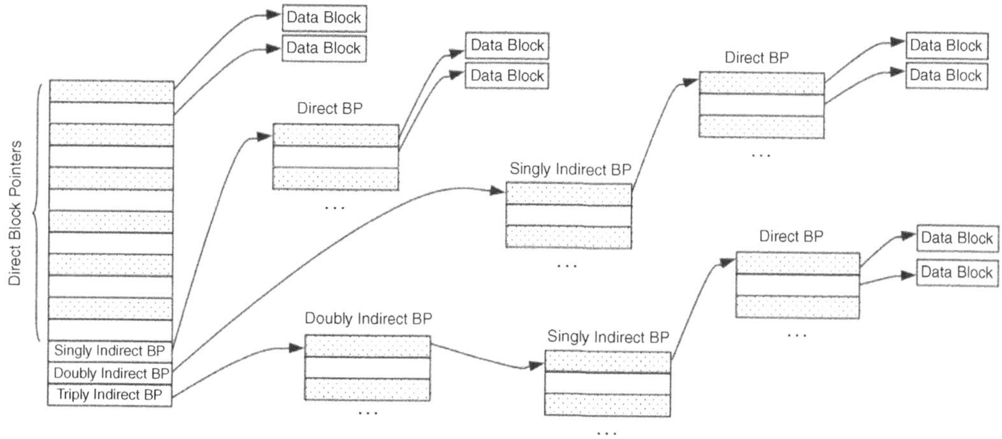

Figure 8.3 Block pointer structure.

that can be used for block pointers. The first 12_d of these are direct block pointers. The block addresses stored in these 12_d locations are the first 12_d blocks of the file's content. The remaining block pointers are indirect. There is one singly indirect block, which contains a block pointer to a block containing block pointers, one doubly indirect block pointer which contains a pointer to a block of singly indirect block pointers, and finally a single triply indirect block pointer which contains a pointer to a block consisting of doubly indirect block pointers. The overall block pointer structure is shown in Figure 8.3.

8.1.4 The Data and Inode Bitmaps

The bitmap structures are used to show used and unused items in the block group. The data bitmap shows the usage status of each block in the block group, while the inode bitmap performs the same task for the inodes in the block group. In both cases a single bit is used to represent each item, with a value of 1 signifying that the value is in use and a value of zero signifying that the value is not being used.

In the case of the data bitmap the least significant bit of byte 0 represents block 0 in the block group's data area. The most significant bit in byte 0 represents block 7 in the data area. In byte 1, the least significant bit represents block 8, and so on. The process is the same in the inode bitmap except that the first inode number is 1, rather than 0. Hence, the least significant bit in byte 0 of the inode bitmap represents the allocation status of inode 1. The most significant bit represents the allocation status of inode 8 and so on.

8.1.5 Locating an Inode

A necessary skill in order to process an ext file system is to locate an inode. Each block group contains a number of inodes. When locating a particular inode number it is necessary to first locate the block group in which it can be found. Using the inodes per block group (*iBG*) value from the superblock, Equation 8.1 provides the formula to locate the block group, *BG*, in which a given inode number, *n*, occurs.

$$BG = \left\lfloor \frac{n}{iBG} \right\rfloor \tag{8.1}$$

However, knowing which block group an inode occurs in is not by itself sufficient. It is also necessary to know where in the inode table the inode entry occurs. The starting block of the inode table, IT_{block}, is found in the block group descriptor. The byte offset, i_{offset}, to the start of the desired inode is then given in Equation 8.2 where B_{size} is the block size in bytes and I_{size} is the inode size in bytes.

$$i_{offset} = (IT_{block} \times B_{size}) + [(n \,\%\, iBG) - 1] \times i_{size}) \tag{8.2}$$

The final value in Equation 8.2 is the actual byte offset in the file system in which the inode is found. In ext2 the inode size is always 128_d bytes, meaning that extracting 128_d bytes from i_{offset} will provide the entire contents of the inode which can then be processed using Table 8.6.

8.2 Analysis of ext2

In this section the analysis of the ext2 file system is described in detail. While this file system is supported by many commercial and open source tools, it is, as argued throughout this book, necessary for the analyst to understand how these tools might function. This in turn allows for greater confidence in the results of file system forensic tools and even for dual tool verification purposes.

This section follows the same structure as the other file systems presented in this book. It commences with an introduction to the creation of ext2 file systems and continues to describe the sample file systems provided in this book, which are used throughout the remainder of this chapter to demonstrate the recovery methods generally employed in ext2. Finally, this section will describe the entire ext2 analysis process.

8.2.1 Creating ext2 File Systems

Before proceeding with analysis it is necessary to determine how ext2 file systems are created. While some are provided from this book's website for the reader to practice some of the described analysis techniques, the ability to create further file systems will aid the reader in perfecting said techniques.

Linux provides direct support for creating ext file systems. The command **mkfs.ext2** can be used to create a file system. An example of this is shown in Listing 8.5 in which a basic ext2 file system is created on **/dev/sdb1**. This file system label is set to ext2-FS.

```
# mkfs.ext2 -L "ext2-FS" /dev/sdb1
```

Listing 8.5 Command used to create an ext2 file system.

8.2.2 Supplied ext2 Image Files

There are a number of disk image files available from the book's website. These are summarised in Table 8.9. The file systems shown in Table 8.9 will be used in the remainder of this chapter to demonstrate the analysis method for ext2 file systems. Readers are advised to follow the examples while reading.

Table 8.9 Disk images available from the book's website.

File Name	Description
Ext2_V1.E01	A newly created ext2 file system with four files and 1 directory.
Ext2_V2.E01	**Ext2_V1.E01** with a hard and symbolic link added and two files deleted.
Ext2_V3.E01	An Ext2 file system for use in the exercises.

8.2.3 Ext2 Manual Analysis

In order to analyse an ext2 file system forensic tools follow a specific sequence of steps. These steps are:

1. **Process the Superblock:** As with most file system analysis tasks the first step is to process the superblock structure. This structure contains general information about the filesystem, such as size and volume label. This structure also allows the number of block groups and the size of each block group to be determined, allowing the entire file system to be mapped.
2. **Map the Block Groups:** Once an overview of the file system has been gathered, the second step provides deeper knowledge of the structures. In this step the exact layout of each individual block group in the file system is discovered. From this step the data area, inode table and data/inode bitmaps in every block group can be located. These first two steps are the tasks that the Sleuth Kit tool, **fsstat**, performs.
3. **Process the Root Directory Inode:** The next task is to list all the files that are present in the file system. To do this the root directory must be located by first locating the root directory's inode and then processing this structure in order to determine where directory contents are stored.
4. **Process the Root Directory:** Once the directory entries associated with the root directory are located, they must be processed to determine what files/directories are present in the root directory.
5. **Process Directories:** Each directory found in the root directory must also be processed in the same manner as that of the root directory itself. That is, the inode entry for that directory is located and processed to find the content. Finally the content is processed to discover what files are present in the directory. This process is repeated for all subsequent directories that are found. Once complete all files/directories on the device are listed.
6. **Process Files:** Finally the file metadata and content is recovered. Both these tasks involve processing the relevant inode values and, as will be seen, are very similar to previous tasks performed in order to list the files in the file system.

The following sections describe each of these steps in detail using the **Ext2_V1.E01** disk image for demonstration purposes.

8.2.3.1 Process the Superblock

From Section 8.1.1 it is known that the superblock structure contains information about the file system as a whole. While there are generally multiple copies of the superblock (Table 8.2) the primary superblock always appears at offset 1024_d bytes into the file system.

```
000400: 0000 0100 0000 0100 cc0c 0000 7af7 0000 ............z...
000410: f0ff 0000 0000 0000 0200 0000 0200 0000 ................
000420: 0080 0000 0080 0000 0080 0000 ba86 4465 ..............De
000430: c686 4465 0200 ffff 53ef 0100 0100 0000 ..De....S.......
000440: 3e85 4465 0000 0000 0000 0000 0100 0000 >.De............
000450: 0000 0000 0b00 0000 8000 0000 3800 0000 ............8...
000460: 0200 0000 0300 0000 95a7 e48b 84db 4ce2 ..............L.
000470: 8a69 b32b e02e f38a 6578 7432 2d46 5300 .i.+....ext2-FS.
000480: 0000 0000 0000 0000 2f6d 6564 6961 2f65 ......../media/e
000490: 7874 3200 0000 0000 0000 0000 0000 0000 xt2.............
0004a0: 0000 0000 0000 0000 0000 0000 0000 0000 ................
0004b0: 0000 0000 0000 0000 0000 0000 0000 0000 ................
```

Listing 8.6 Excerpt from the superblock structure found in **Ext2_V1.E01**.

Listing 8.6 shows the superblock in **Ext2_V1.E01** with processed values in Table 8.10. From this it is clear that much information is to be found in the superblock. For instance there are $65,536_d$ inodes in the file system along with $65,536_d$ blocks. The block size value must be calculated. To do this take the value for the log block size (l_{BS}), 0x02, and calculate, $2^{(10+l_{BS})} = 2^{12} = 4096_d$. The same calculation is performed to calculate the fragment size (although this feature is generally no longer used in modern versions of ext2).

One of the main things that must be determined is the number of block groups present in the file system and also the size of each block group. The size of the block group is given directly in the superblock. From Table 8.10 there are $32,768_d$ blocks in each block group. Knowing already that there are a total of $65,536_d$ blocks in total then there are

$$\left\lceil \frac{65,536}{32,768} \right\rceil = 2$$

block groups in total. These block groups will be numbered 0–1. Note that the same method can be used with the total number of inodes and the number of inodes per block group values in order to calculate the total number of block groups in the file system.

The ext superblock also records certain time values. These are the last mount time; the last write time; and the last check (**fsck**) time. These values are all stored in UTC as unix time values. Other important information available from the superblock includes the inode size (128_d bytes) and the first inode (11_d). This is the first inode number that will be used for non-system files.

The superblock also provides the volume label (**ext2-FS**) and, sometimes even the directory upon which the file system was last mounted. In the sample provided this directory is **/media/ext2**. This information may be of interest to an investigator.

The compatible, incompatible and RO-compatible features are also found in the superblock. These values are 0x38, 0x02 and 0x03, respectively. The compatible feature value can be rewritten as 0x38 = 0x08 + 0x10 + 0x20. Referring to Table 8.4 shows the file system supports extended inode attributes, that inodes are not standard sized and that directories can use hash trees. This process is repeated for the incompatible and RO-compatible feature values.

Listing 8.7 shows some of the output of the **fsstat** command when run on the **Ext2_V1.E01** disk image. In this all of the information manually gathered from the superblock is present. However, there is further information provided by the **fsstat** command in relation to every block group in the file system. This information is not discovered from the superblock itself, but instead is found in the block group descriptors. Hence the next step is to process these structures in order to determine the exact layout of the file system.

Table 8.10 Selected superblock values from **Ext2_V1.E01**.

Offset	Size	Name	Value
0x00	0x04	Total # Inodes	0x10000 $(65,536_d)$
0x04	0x04	Total # Blocks	0x10000 $(65,536_d)$
0x08	0x04	# Reserved Blocks	0xCCC (3276_d)
0x0C	0x04	Free Block Count	0xF77A $(63,354_d)$
0x10	0x04	Free Inode Count	0xFFF0 $(65,520_d)$
0x18	0x04	Log Block Size	0x02 $\rightarrow 2^{12}$ (4096_d)
0x20	0x04	Blocks/Group	0x8000 $(32,768_d)$
0x28	0x04	Inodes/Group	0x8000 $(32,768_d)$
0x2C	0x04	Mount Time	0x654486BA 2023-11-03 05:35:54 UTC
0x30	0x04	Write Time	0x654486C6 2023-11-03 05:36:06 UTC
0x34	0x02	# mounts	0x02 (2_d)
0x38	0x02	Magic	0xEF53
0x40	0x04	Time Last Check	0x6544853E 2023-11-03 05:29:34 UTC
0x44	0x04	Check Interval	0x00 (0_d)
0x54	0x04	First Inode	0x0B (11_d)
0x58	0x02	Inode Size	0x80 (128_d)
0x5C	0x04	Compatible Features	0x38
0x60	0x04	Incompatible Features	0x02
0x64	0x04	RO-Compatible Features	0x03
0x68	0x10	UUID	0x95A7...F38A
0x78	0x10	Volume Name	ext2-FS
0x88	0x40	Last Mounted Directory	/media/ext2

8.2.3.2 Map the Block Groups

In order to map the block groups the block group descriptor (BGD) table is processed. From Step 1 it is known that the file system present in **Ext2_V1.E01** contains 2_d block groups. Section 8.1.2 informs that each block group descriptor is 32_d bytes in size. This means that the entire table is $32 \times 2 = 64_d$ bytes in size.

The block group descriptor table begins in the block immediately after the superblock. The first superblock is located at byte offset 1024_d and is 1024_d bytes in size. This is fully contained in block 0 (which is 4096_d bytes in size). This means that the Block Group Descriptor table is located in block 1 (byte offset 4096_d). The 64_d bytes at this point are shown in Listing 8.8. The first block group descriptor (BG0) is underlined in Listing 8.8.

Table 8.5 describes the structure of the block group descriptor. Table 8.11 processes the first block group descriptor in Listing 8.8.

From Table 8.11 the start of the data bitmap (block 17_d), the inode bitmap (block 18_d) and the inode table (block 19_d) are provided but the size of the inode table is not present. Remember from

```
FILE SYSTEM INFORMATION
--------------------------------------------
File System Type: Ext2
Volume Name: ext2-FS
Volume ID: 8af32ee02bb3698ae24cdb848be4a795

Last Written at: 2023-11-03 05:36:06 (GMT)
Last Checked at: 2023-11-03 05:29:34 (GMT)

Last Mounted at: 2023-11-03 05:35:54 (GMT)
Unmounted properly
Last mounted on: /media/ext2

Source OS: Linux
Dynamic Structure
Compat Features: Ext Attributes, Resize Inode, Dir Index
InCompat Features: Filetype,
Read Only Compat Features: Sparse Super, Large File,

METADATA INFORMATION
--------------------------------------------
Inode Range: 1 - 65537
Root Directory: 2
Free Inodes: 65520

CONTENT INFORMATION
--------------------------------------------
Block Range: 0 - 65535
Block Size: 4096
Free Blocks: 63354

BLOCK GROUP INFORMATION
--------------------------------------------
Number of Block Groups: 2
Inodes per group: 32768
Blocks per group: 32768
```

Listing 8.7 Partial output from **fsstat** command when run on the **Ext2_V1.E01** disk image.

```
001000: 1100 0000 1200 0000 1300 0000 b07b f37f .............{..
001010: 0200 0400 0000 0000 0000 0000 0000 0000 ................
001020: 1180 0000 1280 0000 1380 0000 ca7b fd7f .............{..
001030: 0100 0400 0000 0000 0000 0000 0000 0000 ................
```

Listing 8.8 The block group descriptor table from **Ext2_V1.E01**. The block group descriptor for block group 0 is highlighted.

Table 8.11 Partially processed BG0 descriptor from Listing 8.8.

Offset	Size	Name	Value
0x00	0x04	Data Bitmap	0x11 (17_d)
0x04	0x04	Inode Bitmap	0x12 (18_d)
0x08	0x04	Inode Table	0x13 (19_d)
0x0C	0x02	Free Block Count	0x7BB0 ($31,664_d$)
0x0E	0x02	Free Inode Count	0x7FF3 ($32,755_d$)
0x10	0x02	Used Directory Count	0x02 (2_d)

the superblock (Table 8.10) it was discovered that the inode size is 128_d bytes, the inodes per block group is $32,768_d$ and that the block size is 4096_d bytes. Using this information the number of blocks that the inode table occupies can be calculated as:

$$\left\lceil \frac{32,768 \times 128}{4096} \right\rceil = 1024$$

This result means that there are 1024_d blocks in the inode table which implies that the first block of the inode table is block 19_d and the final block is 1042_d. This means that the data area will begin in block 1043_d. The structure of BG0 is shown in Figure 8.4. For comparison purposes Listing 8.9 shows the output from **fsstat** showing the structure of BG0.

The process shown in this section can be continued for the remaining block group descriptors in the block group descriptor table (Listing 8.8). Once complete the output can be compared to that of **fsstat**.

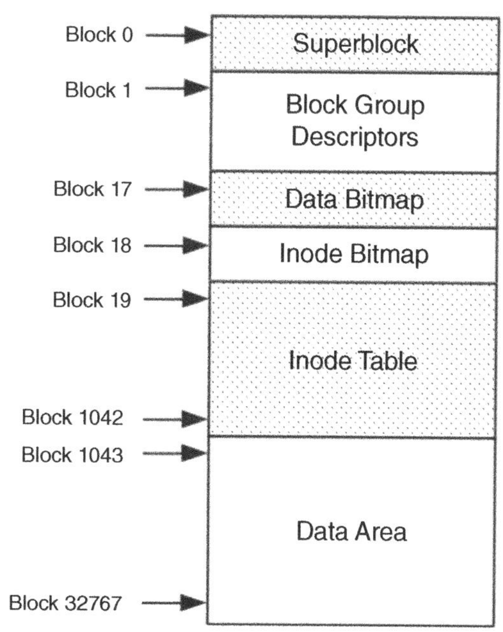

Figure 8.4 BG0 structure in **Ext2_V1.E01**.

```
Group: 0:
  Inode Range: 1 - 32768
  Block Range: 0 - 32767
  Layout:
    Super Block: 0 - 0
    Group Descriptor Table: 1 - 1
    Data bitmap: 17 - 17
    Inode bitmap: 18 - 18
    Inode Table: 19 - 1042
    Data Blocks: 1043 - 32767
  Free Inodes: 32755 (99%)
  Free Blocks: 31664 (96%)
  Total Directories: 2
```

Listing 8.9 Partial output from **fsstat** showing the information for BG0 in **Ext2_V1.E01**.

8.2.3.3 Process Root Directory Inode

Once the entire file system structure is mapped it is then possible to begin listing the files present in the file system. The first step in this task is to locate the root directory inode and process this structure.

In the ext2 file system the inode of the root directory is always 2. Hence this inode must be located. Using Equations 8.1 and 8.2 the block group in which the inode will be found is firstly calculated using:

$$\left\lfloor \frac{2}{32,768} \right\rfloor = 0$$

Equation 8.2 is then used to calculate inode 2's position in BG0. This is given as:

$$(19 * 4096) + (((2 \% 32,768) - 1) \times 128) = 77,824 + (1 * 128) = 77,952$$

Hence the root directory inode can be found at byte offset $77,952_d$. Every inode in this file system is 128_d bytes in size. Listing 8.10 shows the contents of the root directory inode. The processed values are shown in Table 8.12.

```
013080: ed41 0000 0010 0000 1386 4465 c186 4465 .A........De..De
013090: c186 4465 0000 0000 0000 0400 0800 0000 ..De............
0130a0: 0000 0000 0300 0000 1304 0000 0000 0000 ................
0130b0: 0000 0000 0000 0000 0000 0000 0000 0000 ................
0130c0: 0000 0000 0000 0000 0000 0000 0000 0000 ................
0130d0: 0000 0000 0000 0000 0000 0000 0000 0000 ................
0130e0: 0000 0000 0000 0000 0000 0000 0000 0000 ................
0130f0: 0000 0000 0000 0000 0000 0000 0000 0000 ................
```

Listing 8.10 Contents of the root directory inode.

In order to proceed the contents of the root directory itself are located. This is found using the block pointers. As discussed in Section 8.1.3.3 the inode contains 12 direct block pointers and 3 indirect block pointers. In the case of the root directory inode only a single block pointer is allocated.

Table 8.12 Partially processed root directory inode in **Ext2_V1.E01**.

Offset	Size	Name	Value
0x00	0x02	Mode	0x41ED Directory rwxr-xr-x
0x02	0x02	UID	0x00 (0_d)
0x04	0x04	Size	0x1000 (4096_d)
0x08	0x04	Access Time	0x65448613 2023-11-03 05:33:07 UTC
0x0C	0x04	Change Time	0x654486C1 2023-11-03 05:36:01 UTC
0x10	0x04	Modified Time	0x654486C1 2023-11-03 05:36:01 UTC
0x14	0x04	Deletion Time	0x00 (0_d)
0x28	0x3C	Content Location	0x413 (1043_d)

The value of that is 0x413 (1043_d), meaning that the content of the root directory can be found in block number 1043_d. The next step is to process this content.

8.2.3.4 Process the Root Directory

Listing 8.11 shows the contents of the root directory in **Ext2_V1.E01**. From this output filenames are seen in the ASCII values. These can be compared to the output of the **fls** command (Listing 8.12) showing similar content. The next step is to process this information to determine the actual filenames present in the directory.

```
413000: 0200 0000 0c00 0102 2e00 0000 0200 0000 ................
413010: 0c00 0202 2e2e 0000 0b00 0000 1400 0a02 ................
413020: 6c6f 7374 2b66 6f75 6e64 0000 0180 0000 lost+found......
413030: 1000 0502 4669 6c65 7300 0000 0c00 0000 ....Files.......
413040: 1000 0801 6c61 6b65 2e6a 7067 0d00 0000 ....lake.jpg....
413050: b40f 0801 696e 666f 2e74 7874 0000 0000 ....info.txt....
```

Listing 8.11 The contents of the root directory in **Ext2_V1.E01**.

```
$ fls mnt/ewf1
d/d 11: lost+found
d/d 32769: Files
r/r 12: lake.jpg
r/r 13: info.txt
V/V 65537: $OrphanFiles
```

Listing 8.12 The output from the **fls** command on **Ext2_V1.E01**.

In ext root directory entries are not of a fixed length. This is due to the variable length filename field that is held with an entry. The structure of a root directory entry is given in Table 8.13. The root directory entries in Listing 8.11 are processed in Table 8.14.

Table 8.14 shows the same information that Sleuth Kit's **fls** command provided (Listing 8.12). There are a number of items of note about the directory entry structures. These include:

- **Directory Entry Slack Space:** It is possible for directory entries to have slack space. This can occur when a directory name is changed to a shorter name. The directory record length will remain the same as the original (so that it is possible to correctly skip to the next record) but the name length will be reduced. Information that exists between the end of the name and the end of the directory entry is slack space.
- **Final Directory Entry Length:** The record length for the final directory entry in a directory always runs to the end of the block. Hence the final record entry has a length of 0xFB4 bytes – much longer than actually needed.
- **./.. Directories:** Every directory in ext contains a . and .. directory. These are the current and parent directories, respectively. In the case of the root directory, the current directory is the root directory which is inode 2; however, there is no parent, so the .. directory is also inode 2 in this

Table 8.13 Root directory entry structure.

Offset	Size	Name	Description
0x00	0x04	Inode	The inode number of the file/directory.
0x04	0x02	Record Length	The size of the directory entry in bytes.
0x06	0x01	Name Length (n)	The size of the filename in bytes.
0x07	0x01	File Type	See Table 8.15.
0x08	n	Filename	The name of the file.

Table 8.14 Processed root directory entries.

	Record 1	Record 2	Record 3
Inode	0x02 (2_d)	0x02 (2_d)	0x0B (11_d)
Record Length	0x0C (12_d)	0x0C (12_d)	0x14 (20_d)
Name Length	0x01 (1_d)	0x02 (2_d)	0x0A (10_d)
Type	0x02 – Dir.	0x02 – Dir.	0x02 – Dir.
Filename	.	..	lost+found
	Record 4	**Record 5**	**Record 6**
Inode	0x8001 ($32{,}769_d$)	0x0C (12_d)	0x0D (13_d)
Record Length	0x10 (16_d)	0x10 (16_d)	0xFB4 ($4{,}020_d$)
Name Length	0x05 (5_d)	0x08 (8_d)	0x08 (8_d)
Type	0x02 – Dir	0x01 – File	0x01 – File
Filename	Files	lake.jpg	info.txt

Table 8.15 Possible file type field values in a root directory entry.

Value	Meaning
0x00	Unknown file type
0x01	Regular file
0x02	Directory
0x03	Character device
0x04	Block device
0x05	Buffer file
0x06	Socket file
0x07	Symbolic link

case. You can see this for yourself on a Linux system, by running the command **cd /** to change to the root directory and then running **cd ..**. The second command will 'change' to the parent directory, which is still /.

- **lost+found:** This directory is found on all Linux/Unix/MacOS file systems. It is used in the case of file system checking tools such as **fsck** discovering errors. It stores corrupted files that were discovered by these tools.

8.2.3.5 Process Directories

Using the method presented in Step 4, the same actions are performed for all discovered directories. Table 8.14 shows that there are two other directories present, **lost+found** (Inode 0x0B) and **Files** (Inode 0x8001). It is left as an exercise for the reader to process these directories and rebuild the entire file system content.

8.2.3.6 Process Files

The final step in the analysis of an ext2 file system is to recover file metadata and content. The recovery of file metadata involves the processing of the inode values as shown in Step 3. Listing 8.13 shows the output of the **istat** command when run on inode 13_d (**info.txt**).

From this output it is clear that the inode structure is being processed in order to gather this information. The UID/GID values, the mode and file permissions,[6] the file size, the number of links, the timestamps, etc. are all found in the inode structure. Hence the metadata information of any file can be accessed, by first locating the inode in the file system and then processing this value.

The final step in analysis is to extract the file's content. It has already been shown how the root directory content can be extracted. However, in the case of a directory, the content always occupies entire blocks (the file size in that case was 4096_d bytes). Listing 8.13 shows that the file size is only 176_d bytes in size. In order to extract this the inode is processed to discover the block(s) occupied by the file in question. The output from **istat** shows that inode 13_d contains only a single direct block pointer ($1,536_d$). The command shown in Listing 8.14 will extract the content of this file.

The **info.txt** file is a small file that only occupied a single block in the file system. Now consider a larger file, in this case inode 12_d. Listing 8.15 shows the actual content of the inode itself along with the command used to extract it. The file size and block pointers are highlighted.

6 Sleuth Kit presents the file type as an extra permission bit. The first r in the permission string refers to a regular file.

```
inode: 13
Allocated
Group: 0
Generation Id: 3762329016
uid / gid: 0 / 0
mode: rrwxr-x---
size: 176
num of links: 1

Inode Times:
Accessed:       2023-11-03 05:36:01 (GMT)
File Modified:  2023-11-03 05:36:01 (GMT)
Inode Modified: 2023-11-03 05:36:01 (GMT)

Direct Blocks:
1536
```

Listing 8.13 Output from the **istat** command when run on inode 13_d on **Ext2_V1.E01**.

```
$ dd if=mnt/ewf1 of=info.txt bs=1 count=176 skip=$((4096*1536))
176+0 records in
176+0 records out
176 bytes copied, 0.00641918 s, 27.4 kB/s
$
$ more info.txt
This is an ext2 file system with four files and one user created
directory.
The structure of this device is:

/- Files
   /- delete.txt
   /- beach.jpg
/- lake.jpg
/- info.txt
```

Listing 8.14 Extracting and viewing the **info.txt** file in Ext2_V1.E01.

```
$ xxd -s $(( (4096 * 19) + (11 * 128) )) -l 128 mnt/ewf1
013580: e881 0000 48e3 0000 0786 4465 0786 4465  ....H.....De..De
013590: 0786 4465 0000 0000 0000 0100 8000 0000  ..De............
0135a0: 0000 0000 0100 0000 0186 0000 0286 0000  ................
0135b0: 0386 0000 0486 0000 0586 0000 0686 0000  ................
0135c0: 0786 0000 0886 0000 0986 0000 0a86 0000  ................
0135d0: 0b86 0000 0c86 0000 1484 0000 0000 0000  ................
0135e0: 0000 0000 7b87 1f3f 0000 0000 0000 0000  ....{..?........
0135f0: 0000 0000 0000 0000 0000 0000 0000 0000  ................
```

Listing 8.15 Contents of inode 12 in **Ext2_V1.E01**.

Analysing this shows the file size to be 0xE348 ($58,184_d$) bytes, much larger than the 4096_d byte block size. Hence this file will require multiple blocks in order to store its content. Processing the 12_d direct blocks gives values of 0x8601–0x860C ($34,305_d$–$34,316_d$). In this example the singly indirect block pointer value is also used. The value of this is 0x8414 ($33,812_d$). The contents of this are shown in Listing 8.16. This clearly shows that three further blocks are occupied by this file. These blocks are 0x860D ($34,317_d$)–0x860F ($34,319_d$).

```
$ xxd -s $((0x8414 * 4096)) mnt/ewf1 | more
08414000: 0d86 0000 0e86 0000 0f86 0000 0000 0000
08414010: 0000 0000 0000 0000 0000 0000 0000 0000
```

Listing 8.16 Contents of singly indirect block pointer for inode 12_d in **Ext2_V1.E01**.

The file size is 0xE348 ($58,184_d$) bytes; hence, the file will occupy 14_d blocks in their entirety. Fourteen blocks allow for $14 \times 4096 = 57,344_d$ bytes, meaning that block 15_d contains $58,184 - 57,344 = 840_d$ bytes. The remaining $4096 - 840 = 3256_d$ bytes are slack space. Fourteen blocks could be extracted followed by the 840_d bytes from block 15_d and combine these to get the file or, as all blocks are contiguous, $58,184_d$ bytes could be extracted from the start of the first block (if the file were fragmented this is not possible). Listing 8.17 shows this approach being used to extract the file's contents. The resulting file is shown in Figure 8.5.

```
$ dd if=mnt/ewf1 of=lake.jpg bs=1 skip=$((0x8601 * 4096))
     count=58184
58184+0 records in
58184+0 records out
58184 bytes (58 kB, 57 KiB) copied, 1.41899 s, 41.0 kB/s
```

Listing 8.17 Extracting the content of **lake.jpg** from **Ext2_V1.E01**.

The method that has been presented in this section is the basic method used by all file system forensic tools when processing an ext2 file system. The remainder of this chapter will focus on some of the more advanced topics in the ext2 file system, such as handling fragmented files, deleted files and both hard and soft links.

Figure 8.5 The extracted **lake.jpg** file.

8.3 Ext2 Advanced Analysis

The basic tasks presented to this point allow for the analysis of most ext2 file systems. However, there are some commonly encountered items in the ext2 file system which require a little more care during analysis. In this section we will examine some of these topics, including fragmented files (Section 8.3.1), links (Section 8.3.2) and deleted files (Section 8.3.3).

8.3.1 Fragmented Files

The files recovered to this point have been contiguous on disk. There is no requirement for files to be contiguous; hence, it may be required to handle fragmented files during analysis. The **Ext2_V1.E01** disk image contains one fragmented file, **Files/beach.jpg** - inode $32,771_d$. Listing 8.18 shows the output of the **istat** command on this file.

```
...[snip]...
size: 284611
...[snip]...

Direct Blocks:
34320 34321 34322 34323 34324 34325 34326 34327
34328 34329 34330 34331 34332 34333 34334 34335
1072 1073 1074 1075 1076 1077 1078 1079
1080 1081 1082 1083 1084 1085 1086 1087
...[snip]...
1112 1113 1114 1115 1116 1117 1118 1119
1152 1153 1154 1155 1156 1157

Indirect Blocks:
33813
```

Listing 8.18 Excerpt from the **istat** command's output for inode $32{,}771_d$ in **Ext2_V1.E01**.

Listing 8.18 clearly shows the fragmented nature of the file's content. The first 16 blocks of content are contiguous, from block $34,320_d$–$34,335_d$, the next block is found in block 1072_d.

But how are the block pointers actually stored? Listing 8.19 shows the inode for this file. The block group containing inode $32,771_d$ is found using:

$$\left\lfloor \frac{32,771}{32,768} \right\rfloor = 1$$

Its position in the inode table in block group 1 is given by:

$$(32,771\%32,768) - 1 \times 128 = 256$$

The inode table in block group 1 begins at block number $32,787_d$ (found by processing the relevant block group descriptor). This means that the byte offset to the inode is $32,787 \times 4096 + 256 = 134,295,808_d$. Listing 8.19 provides the contents of this inode with the file size and block pointers underlined.

The 12 direct block pointers contain the values 0x8610–0x861B ($34,320_d$–$34,331_d$). The next block pointer is a singly indirect block pointer. The value of this is 0x8415 ($33,813_d$). An excerpt from the contents of this block is shown in Listing 8.20.

```
08013100: e881 0000 c357 0400 1c86 4465 1c86 4465 .....W....De..De
08013110: 1c86 4465 0000 0000 0000 0100 3802 0000 ..De........8...
08013120: 0000 0000 0100 0000 1086 0000 1186 0000 ................
08013130: 1286 0000 1386 0000 1486 0000 1586 0000 ................
08013140: 1686 0000 1786 0000 1886 0000 1986 0000 ................
08013150: 1a86 0000 1b86 0000 1584 0000 0000 0000 ................
08013160: 0000 0000 5a0b 4f07 0000 0000 0000 0000 ....Z.O.........
08013170: 0000 0000 0000 0000 0000 0000 0000 0000 ................
```

Listing 8.19 Contents of inode 32,771$_d$ in **Ext2_V1.E01**.

```
08415000: 1c86 0000 1d86 0000 1e86 0000 1f86 0000 ................
08415010: 3004 0000 3104 0000 3204 0000 3304 0000 0...1...2...3...
08415020: 3404 0000 3504 0000 3604 0000 3704 0000 4...5...6...7...
08415030: 3804 0000 3904 0000 3a04 0000 3b04 0000 8...9...:...;...
08415040: 3c04 0000 3d04 0000 3e04 0000 3f04 0000 <...=...>...?...
08415050: 4004 0000 4104 0000 4204 0000 4304 0000 @...A...B...C...
...[snip]...
```

Listing 8.20 Contents of the indirect block pointer in block 33,813$_d$ in **Ext2_V1.E01**.

This block contains a list of four byte block pointers. The list continues until the first zero value block pointer is encountered. In block 33,813$_d$ there are 58$_d$ further block pointers found. The first four of these are contiguous with the initial 12 direct block pointers seen in Listing 8.19 with values 0x861C–0x861F (34,332$_d$–34,335$_d$). The next block pointer points to 0x430 (1072$_d$). Each of the remaining block pointers is processed in order to rebuild the entire file content.

8.3.2 Links

Links are a means provided by Linux (and other Unix-like operating systems) to allow for multiple references to a file to exist in the file system. The inode structure (Table 8.6) contains the number of links to a file. Listing 8.21 shows the creation of both soft (also called symbolic) and hard links. In both cases links are created to the file **lake.jpg**. The resulting disk image is available as **Ext2_V2.E01**.

```
$ ln -s lake.jpg softlink.jpg
$ ln lake.jpg hardlink.jpg
$
$ ls -iR
32769 Files          13 info.txt    11 lost+found
   12 hardlink.jpg   12 lake.jpg    14 softlink.jpg
```

Listing 8.21 Commands to create soft and hard links.

Take note of the inodes in Listing 8.21. The softlink file has a different inode number than its source. The source file (**lake.jpg**) has inode 12$_d$ while the file **softlink.jpg** has inode 14$_d$. In contrast to this the hard link has the exact same inode number as that of the source file (12$_d$). Listings 8.22 and 8.23 show the output of the **istat** command on inodes 12$_d$ and 14$_d$, respectively.

```
inode: 12
Allocated
Group: 0
Generation Id: 1059030907
uid / gid: 0 / 0
mode: rrwxr-x---
size: 58184
num of links: 2

Inode Times:
Accessed:       2023-11-03 05:32:55 (GMT)
File Modified:  2023-11-03 05:32:55 (GMT)
Inode Modified: 2023-11-03 13:24:32 (GMT)

Direct Blocks:
34305 34306 34307 34308 34309 34310 34311 34312
...[snip]...
```

Listing 8.22 Output of **istat** on inode 12_d in **Ext2_V2.E01**.

```
inode: 14
Allocated
Group: 0
Generation Id: 365031907
symbolic link to: lake.jpg
uid / gid: 0 / 0
mode: lrwxrwxrwx
size: 8
num of links: 1

Inode Times:
Accessed:       2023-11-03 13:24:26 (GMT)
File Modified:  2023-11-03 13:24:26 (GMT)
Inode Modified: 2023-11-03 13:24:26 (GMT)

Direct Blocks:
0
```

Listing 8.23 Output of the **istat** command on the soft link file, inode 14.

In the case of the hard link the number of links to the file is increased – there are now two links to the file. The content is identical in both cases. If the original file is deleted the content will still exist through the hard link. In the case of the softlink there is no direct block address present. The file type is now marked as l, compared to r (regular file) for the hard link. Listing 8.24 shows the actual content of the inode. The most significant nibble of the mode value is 0xA signifying this to be a symbolic (soft) link file.

In the softlink case, instead of containing block pointers, the inode contains the actual path to the source file. The number of links to the source file would still be 1. Hence if the source file is deleted, the symbolic link will no longer point to a valid file, rendering the link invalid also.

```
013680: ffa1 0000 0800 0000 8af4 4465 8af4 4465 ..........De..De
013690: 8af4 4465 0000 0000 0000 0100 0000 0000 ..De............
0136a0: 0000 0000 0100 0000 6c61 6b65 2e6a 7067 ........lake.jpg
0136b0: 0000 0000 0000 0000 0000 0000 0000 0000 ................
0136c0: 0000 0000 0000 0000 0000 0000 0000 0000 ................
0136d0: 0000 0000 0000 0000 0000 0000 0000 0000 ................
0136e0: 0000 0000 e3f1 c115 0000 0000 0000 0000 ................
0136f0: 0000 0000 0000 0000 0000 0000 0000 0000 ................
```

Listing 8.24 Contents of inode 14_d in **Ext_V2.E01** showing a symbolic link.

8.3.3 Deleted Files

The next topic that must be discussed is that of deleted files. From other file systems such as FAT it is known that a file is often merely marked as deleted in the metadata structure. All the content and metadata is still intact. But what occurs in ext2? For this topic the **Ext2_V2.E01** is used in which the files **Files/delete.txt** and **beach.jpg** have been deleted. Previous analysis of the file system showed that before the **beach.jpg** file was deleted the first block of file content was found to be 0x8610. Listing 8.25 shows the beginning of this block after deletion. It is clear that the file's contents are still present on the disk. Indeed re-running the command in Listing 8.17 allows for the file to be recovered in its entirety.

```
08610000: ffd8 ffdb 0043 0002 0202 0202 0102 0202 .....C..........
08610010: 0203 0202 0303 0604 0303 0303 0705 0504 ................
08610020: 0608 0709 0808 0708 0809 0a0d 0b09 0a0c ................
08610030: 0a08 080b 0f0b 0c0d 0e0e 0f0e 090b 1011 ................
...[snip]...
```

Listing 8.25 The contents of block 0x8610 on **Ext2_V2.E01** after the deletion of **beach.jpg**.

Next the inode itself is examined. Listing 8.26 shows the contents of inode $32,771_d$. Deletion has caused a number of changes to the file system. Firstly the file size has become zero, secondly the deletion time has been set and finally the block pointers have been zero'd.

```
08013100: e881 0000 0000 0000 1c86 4465 9ff4 4465 ..........De..De
08013110: 9ff4 4465 9ff4 4465 0000 0000 0000 0000 ..De..De........
08013120: 0000 0000 0100 0000 0000 0000 0000 0000 ................
08013130: 0000 0000 0000 0000 0000 0000 0000 0000 ................
08013140: 0000 0000 0000 0000 0000 0000 0000 0000 ................
08013150: 0000 0000 0000 0000 0000 0000 0000 0000 ................
08013160: 0000 0000 5a0b 4f07 0000 0000 0000 0000 ....Z.O.........
08013170: 0000 0000 0000 0000 0000 0000 0000 0000 ................
```

Listing 8.26 The contents of inode $32,771_d$ on **Ext2_V2.E01** after the deletion of **beach.jpg**.

This information is confirmed by the **istat** command as shown in Listing 8.27. From this the conclusion can be drawn that while some metadata will still exist for a deleted file and that the contents of the file will still exist, it is impossible to link the metadata to the file content.

Finally checking the root directory will show that the file name/inode number has not been overwritten in this case.

```
inode: 32771
Not Allocated
Group: 1
Generation Id: 122620762
uid / gid: 0 / 0
mode: rrwxr-x---
size: 0
num of links: 0

Inode Times:
Accessed:        2023-11-03 05:33:16 (GMT)
File Modified:   2023-11-03 13:24:47 (GMT)
Inode Modified:  2023-11-03 13:24:47 (GMT)
Deleted:         2023-11-03 13:24:47 (GMT)

Direct Blocks:
```

Listing 8.27 The output from **istat** on inode $32,771_d$ in **Ext2_V2.E01** showing the changes to the stored metadata information.

8.4 Summary

In this chapter the ext2 file system was introduced. The main structures of this file system were introduced and a method of recovering file content and metadata was proposed. Additionally some of the more advanced topics in ext2, such as fragmentation, deletion and links, were introduced to the reader. In the next chapter the examination of the ext family of file systems continues. While all later versions (ext3 and ext4) are very similar to ext2 in overall structure there are some differences that make their analysis slightly different. Hence the next chapter can be viewed as discussing these differences!

Exercises

In relation to the ext2 file system supplied in **Ext2_V3.E01** answer the following questions. You should attempt to answer these questions manually and verify your results using a forensic tool.

1 What is the volume name?

2 What block size is used in this file system?

3 What is the inode size?

4 How many block groups are present in this file system?

5 Map the structure of BG0.

6 In relation to inode 12_d answer the following questions.
   a) In which block group is this inode found?
   b) What is the byte offset to this inode?
   c) What are the file permissions?

d) In which block(s) are the file contents stored?
e) What is the file size in bytes?
f) What is the MD5 sum of this file?

7 When the file system contents are listed using **fls** it would appear that two files have the same inode number (12_d). How is this possible?

8 List the contents of the root directory in this file system.

Bibliography

Barik, M.S., Gupta, G., Sinha, S. et al. (2007). An efficient technique for enhancing forensic capabilities of Ext2 file system. *Digital Investigation* 4: 55–61.

Card, R., Ts'o, T., and Tweedie, S. (2001). Design and Implementation of the Second Extended Filesystem [Internet]. e2fsprogs.sourceforge.net. https://e2fsprogs.sourceforge.net/ext2intro.html (accessed 13 August 2024).

Carrier, B. (2005). *File System Forensic Analysis*. Boston, MA; London: Addison-Wesley.

Dilger, A.E. (2002). Online ext2 and ext3 Filesystem Resizing. Ottawa Linux Symposium 2002 (26 Jun 2002), p. 117.

Ext2 (2024). OSDev Wiki [Internet]. wiki.osdev.org. https://wiki.osdev.org/Ext2 (accessed 13 August 2024).

Heintzkill, R. (2021). Linux Hard Links versus Soft Links Explained [Internet]. CBT Nuggets Blog. https://www.cbtnuggets.com/blog/certifications/open-source/linux-hard-links-versus-soft-links-explained (accessed 13 August 2024).

Phillips, D. (2001). A directory index for EXT2. 5th Annual Linux Showcase & Conference (ALS 01).

Piper, S., Davis, M., Manes, G., and Shenoi, S. (2005). Detecting hidden data in Ext2/Ext3 file systems. *Advances in Digital Forensics: IFIP International Conference on Digital Forensics*, National Center for Forensic Science, Orlando, Florida (13–16 February 2005), 245–256. Springer US.

Poirier, D. (2001). The Second Extended File System [Internet]. www.nongnu.org. https://www.nongnu.org/ext2-doc/ext2.html (accessed 13 August 2024).

Polstra, P. (2015). *Linux Forensics: With Python and Shell Scripting*. Createspace Independent Publishing Platform.

9

The EXT3/EXT4 File Systems

By the late 1990s ext2 was beginning to show its age. At the time, newer file systems containing modern features such as journaling were becoming increasingly common. As ext2 did not contain any of these features the need for a third extended file system was realised. Development of ext3 was first proposed in 1998 and fully integrated into the Linux kernel in November 2001.

However, as time passed it was again realised that ext3 was no longer fit for purpose. This was mainly due to the addressing issues that it faced. For modern devices the ability to create larger files (and volumes) was essential. Ext4 is more an extension of ext3 than a new file system. It was initially created as a set of extensions for ext3 but the project was forked during development to become ext4. Development of ext4 concluded in October 2008 with its inclusion in the Linux kernel.

This chapter will examine the developments in terms of the ext file system family. Chapter 8 described the ext2 file system structures and showed how these can be processed to recover file and metadata content. This chapter will proceed to show how ext3 and ext4 differ from ext2. Unless otherwise stated the information used to process an ext2 file system is also used to process these file systems. Before commencing, the disk images used for this chapter are introduced.

9.1 Supplied Image Files

Four distinct image files are used throughout this chapter, an ext3 file system with journaling, an ext3 file system with HTree directories, an ext4 file system using multiple storage mechanisms and an ext4 file system with extended attributes and deleted files. Table 9.1 summarises these image files.

9.2 The ext3 File System

The ext3 file system is an extension of ext2 which provides a number of added features. One of the overriding design goals of ext3 was to ensure its backwards compatibility with ext2. This meant that ext2 file systems could be upgraded in place (without the need of back-up/restore).

Ext3 added a number of new features to ext2. The most important of these, from a file system forensic perspective, was the journal. The journal (Section 9.2.1) records changes to the file system that have yet to be committed to the file system. The use of a journal reduces the time required to restore a crashed file system and also reduces the likelihood of file system corruption.

File System Forensics, First Edition. Fergus Toolan.

Table 9.1 Ext3/4 disk images available from the book's website.

Image File	Description
Ext3_V1.E01	An ext3 file system with journaling.
Ext3_V2.E01	An ext3 file system with HTree directories enabled.
Ext4_V1.E01	An ext4 file system with extents, inline storage and symbolic links.
Ext4_V2.E01	An ext4 file system with extended attributes and deleted files.

In addition to the journal ext3 introduced two other features, online resizing of the file system and the use of HTree directory indexing. Online resizing allows the file system to grow while mounted. Consider the scenario in which a deployment server is running out of disk space. Generally this file system would need to be taken offline (unmounted) and its data relocated to a larger file system. With ext3 this is not necessary as the file system itself can be resized when mounted. This means that there is no need to take a file system offline in order to allocate more space. While highly beneficial for system administrators this feature has little relevance to digital forensics.

HTree directory indexing was introduced to improve the efficiency of the ext file system. Ext2 used a linear structure for directory indexing. Directory entries appeared one after the other in a directory (Section 8.2.3). These entries were not even of fixed size (as they contain the variable length file name) and as such could not be quickly searched. The modern file system approach is to use a B-Tree structure (e.g. NTFS) for directory indexing. However, this can lead to trees with many levels and potential data loss if high-level nodes become corrupt. The B-Tree structure is also very complex to implement and was considered to be opposed to ext's design philosophy. Hence a compromise was reached which involved the use of HTrees. These trees have much higher fan-out (number of children per node) than B-Trees, meaning that more files can be represented using a smaller tree height.

Other than the features mentioned above, the structures in ext3 are identical to those found in ext2. The remainder of this section will examine the forensic implications of the ext journal and also of HTree directory indexing.

9.2.1 The Ext Journal

A file system journal records changes that have been made to the file system before they are committed to disk. In this way the journal serves as a protection against crashes that might destroy file system consistency. Of course the journal also has wonderful applications for digital forensic analysts, as they look into the past as it were, potentially viewing deleted files and older versions of current files.

The journal in ext (and in most file systems) is a fixed-size file that is updated in a circular manner. This implies that when the journal is full it will begin to overwrite the start of the file. The basic journal storage unit is the block, so if a single inode is updated, the contents of the entire block that contains the inode in question will be copied to the journal.

There are three journaling levels available in ext3 (and also ext4):

- **Journal:** Records all modified metadata blocks and data blocks in the journal. This is very slow as data is written twice to disk, once to the journal and once to the main part of the disk. From a forensic perspective it is also the most informative as it contains both content and metadata.

- **Ordered:** This is the default type in ext3 – the metadata is recorded in the journal, but data is flushed before metadata is updated. This ensures that consistency is maintained but only metadata is available to the analyst.
- **Write-back:** This is the fastest journal type in which the metadata is recorded in the journal and the data is flushed by the file system. This means that there may be a delay in flushing the data. Both ordered and write-back journaling record only metadata in the journal (the difference is in the timing of the journal metadata and content write operations), and hence from a forensic perspective both are of similar value.

In general the journal file is located at inode 8 in the file system. This can be checked in the superblock. Using the supplied file, **Ext3_V1.E01**, the contents of this file system are shown in Listing 9.1.

```
$ fls -r Ext3_V1.E01
d/d 11: lost+found
r/r 12: testFile.txt
r/r * 13: deleteMe.txt
V/V 4097: $OrphanFiles
```

Listing 9.1 The contents of **Ext3_V1.E01** showing the deleted file **deleteMe.txt**.

Running **fsstat** on the supplied disk image shows that, as expected, the journal is located at inode 8 (Listing 9.2).

```
$ fsstat Ext3_V1.E01
...[snip]...
File System Type: Ext3
...[snip]...
Journal ID: 00
Journal Inode: 8
```

Listing 9.2 Using **fsstat** to locate the journal inode in **Ext3_V1.E01**. Note that the output has been truncated for presentation purposes.

Examining the output from the **istat** command for inode 13_d shows that the information about the direct blocks is no longer present (Listing 9.3). This is confirmed by analysing the inode's underlying data itself (Listing 9.4) which shows that all direct block pointers have been overwritten. Hence, while the metadata for the file is still present, there is no indication of where the file content is located. Instead it is necessary to examine the journal to determine the actual location of the file's content (if it is still present on disk).

The ext journal structure is shown in Figure 9.1. The journal begins with a Journal Superblock (JSB) which describes the structure of the journal as a whole. It is a much simpler structure than the file system superblock. Transactions are recorded sequentially after this, with each receiving a new sequence number. As stated previously, once the end of the journal is encountered it loops back to the beginning, overwriting the data previously found at that location. Each transaction is composed of a descriptor block which describes the structure of the transaction. This is then followed by one or more metadata blocks (and data blocks if full journaling is used). These are the actual blocks that

```
$ istat Ext3_V1.E01 13
inode: 13
Not Allocated
Group: 0
Generation Id: 2297719927
uid / gid: 0 / 0
mode: rrw-r--r--
size: 0
num of links: 0

Inode Times:
Accessed: 2018-03-05 07:15:36 (GMT)
File Modified: 2018-03-05 07:18:24 (GMT)
Inode Modified: 2018-03-05 07:18:24 (GMT)
Deleted: 2018-03-05 07:18:24 (GMT)

Direct Blocks:
$
```

Listing 9.3 Using **istat** to read metadata for the deleted file (inode 13_d) clearly showing that the content location can no longer be determined.

```
$ xxd -s $(( (1024*68) + (128*12))) -l 128 mnt/ewf1
011600: a481 0000 0000 0000 98ee 9c5a 40ef 9c5a ...........Z@..Z
011610: 40ef 9c5a 40ef 9c5a 0000 0000 0000 0000 @..Z@..Z........
011620: 0000 0000 0100 0000 0000 0000 0000 0000 ................
011630: 0000 0000 0000 0000 0000 0000 0000 0000 ................
011640: 0000 0000 0000 0000 0000 0000 0000 0000 ................
011650: 0000 0000 0000 0000 0000 0000 0000 0000 ................
011660: 0000 0000 776c f488 0000 0000 0000 0000 ....wl..........
011670: 0000 0000 0000 0000 0000 0000 0000 0000 ................
```

Listing 9.4 Raw data for inode 13_d showing the first block pointer value has been overwritten.

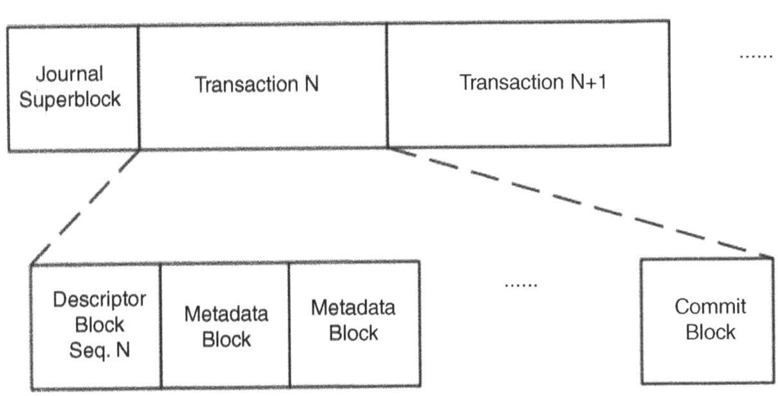

Figure 9.1 Ext journal structure.

were updated. The transaction ends with a commit block, in the case of successful transactions and a revoke block otherwise.

The Sleuth Kit provides a set of commands which can access the ext journal. The **jls** command will list information about the blocks contained in the journal, while **jcat** will allow for particular blocks to be extracted from the journal. The output from **jls** is shown in Listing 9.5.

```
$ jls Ext3_V1.E01
JBlk Description
0: Superblock (seq: 0)
sb version: 4
sb version: 4
sb feature_compat flags 0x00000000
sb feature_incompat flags 0x00000000
sb feature_ro_incompat flags 0x00000000
1: Unallocated Descriptor Block (seq: 8)
2: Unallocated FS Block 68
3: Unallocated FS Block 324
4: Unallocated FS Block 1
5: Unallocated FS Block 69
6: Unallocated FS Block 66
7: Unallocated FS Block 2
8: Unallocated FS Block 67
9: Unallocated Commit Block (seq: 8, sec: 1520234305.3395741952)
10: Unallocated Descriptor Block (seq: 5)
...
$
```

Listing 9.5 Using **jls** to list details of each individual journal block.

Listing 9.5 shows the journal superblock (JSB – Block 0) and some information from that structure. Block 1 contains a descriptor for sequence 8 followed by 7 metadata blocks (2–8) and a commit block in block 9. Recall that the deleted file was located in inode 13_d (Listing 9.1). The output from **istat** (Listing 9.3) showed that the data blocks for this inode are no longer present; however, it may be possible to recover the file content using the journal!

Firstly it is necessary to calculate which block on the file system contains inode 13_d. It is known from **fsstat** (or the superblock) that there are 2048_d inodes in each block group, and therefore inode 13_d must be in block group 0_d. Again from **fsstat** it is determined that the inode table begins in block 68_d. If each inode is 128_d bytes in size and blocks are 1024_d bytes, then inode 13_d must occur in the second block of the inode table, i.e. block 69_d. Next it is necessary to search the output of **jls** to find any mention of block 69_d. We see that journal blocks 5_d, 13_d and 20_d contain changes to block 69_d (remember there are 8_d inodes in a block so not all of these changes will refer to inode 13_d, but an old copy of the inode may be found). These blocks can be extracted using the **jcat** command as shown in Listing 9.6.

Inode 13_d will be the fifth inode present in the inode table block meaning that it is necessary to skip 512_d bytes in each block. The data in **J5.dd** and **J13.dd** are shown in Listing 9.7.

As each block on this file system is 1024_d bytes in size, and inode 13_d's file size is 32_d bytes, the contents of block 0x202 (514_d) can be found using the command shown in Listing 9.8.

```
$ jcat Ext3_V1.E01 8 5 > J5.dd
$ jcat Ext3_V1.E01 8 13 > J13.dd
$ jcat Ext3_V1.E01 8 20 > J20.dd
$
```

Listing 9.6 Using **jcat** to recover the relevant journal blocks.

```
$ xxd -s 512 -l 128 J5.dd
000200: a481 0000 0000 0000 98ee 9c5a 40ef 9c5a ...........Z@..Z
000210: 40ef 9c5a 40ef 9c5a 0000 0000 0000 0000 @..Z@..Z........
000220: 0000 0000 0100 0000 0000 0000 0000 0000 ................
000230: 0000 0000 0000 0000 0000 0000 0000 0000 ................
000240: 0000 0000 0000 0000 0000 0000 0000 0000 ................
000250: 0000 0000 0000 0000 0000 0000 0000 0000 ................
000260: 0000 0000 776c f488 0000 0000 0000 0000 ....wl..........
000270: 0000 0000 0000 0000 0000 0000 0000 0000 ................
$ xxd -s 512 -l 128 J13.dd
000200: a481 0000 2000 0000 98ee 9c5a 98ee 9c5a .... ......Z...Z
000210: 98ee 9c5a 0000 0000 0000 0100 0200 0000 ...Z............
000220: 0000 0000 0100 0000 0202 0000 0000 0000 ................
000230: 0000 0000 0000 0000 0000 0000 0000 0000 ................
000240: 0000 0000 0000 0000 0000 0000 0000 0000 ................
000250: 0000 0000 0000 0000 0000 0000 0000 0000 ................
000260: 0000 0000 776c f488 0000 0000 0000 0000 ....wl..........
000270: 0000 0000 0000 0000 0000 0000 0000 0000 ................
$
```

Listing 9.7 The contents of inode 13_d in Journal Blocks 5_d and 13_d. The highlighted values show the uninitialised deletion time and the direct block pointer in **J13.dd** prior to file deletion.

```
$ xxd -s $((1024*514)) -l 32 mnt/ewf1
080800: 5468 6973 2077 696c 6c20 6265 2064 656c This will be del
080810: 6574 6564 2065 7665 6e74 7561 6c6c 790a eted eventually.
$
```

Listing 9.8 The contents of block 514_d in **Ext3_V1.E01** recovered through use of the journal.

Note that examining **J20.dd** will show a different block for content (515_d). Examining the content of this block will also locate the file's content. This block stored another version of this file. Analysts can study the timestamp values that are present in each of these metadata blocks to determine the order of events that are logged in the journal.

At this stage Sleuth Kit tools can be used to recover information from the journal. The next question to ask is how do these tools perform that recovery task. The overall structure of the journal has already been described. It commences with a journal superblock, which is followed by a list of transactions. Each transaction contains a journal descriptor block, followed by a list of data blocks, terminated by a commit or revocation block. The next step is to determine the underlying structure of these various items.

Table 9.2 Ext3 journal block header structure.

Offset	Size	Name	Description
0x00	0x04	Magic	All journal blocks begin with the JBD2 magic header (0xC03B3998).
0x04	0x04	Block Type	Field describing the block type of the current block: - 1: Descriptor block - 2: Commit block - 3: Superblock (V1) - 4: Superblock (V2) - 5: Revocation block
0x08	0x04	Seq. Num.	The transaction ID containing this block.

The first thing to note is that the journaling structures used in ext3 (and 4) are ***big-endian*** by default. This is quite unusual in ext (and in file systems in general!). Every superblock, commit, revoke and descriptor block begins with the same 12_d byte journal header. The structure of this header is shown in Table 9.2.

Recall the output from the **jls** command when run on **Ext3_V1.E01** (Listing 9.5). Using Table 9.2 it should be possible to rebuild that structure. The journal file (**journal.dd**) was first recovered using **icat**. Each block begins with the hex values (0xC03B3998) which can be used to search for journal blocks as shown in Listing 9.9. The offsets provided here are offsets to the start of the block. Each block is 1024_d bytes in size, so dividing each offset by this gives a list of blocks as: 0, 1, 9, 10, 17, 18 and 23. Comparing this to the output of **jls** confirms that these blocks are the version 2 Superblock (Block 0), descriptor blocks (blocks 1, 10 and 18) and commit blocks (blocks 9, 17 and 23).

```
000000: c03b 3998 0000 0004 0000 0000 0000 0400.;9.............
000400: c03b 3998 0000 0001 0000 0008 0000 0044.;9............D
002400: c03b 3998 0000 0002 0000 0008 0000 0000.;9.............
002800: c03b 3998 0000 0001 0000 0005 0000 0043.;9............C
004400: c03b 3998 0000 0002 0000 0005 0000 0000.;9.............
004800: c03b 3998 0000 0001 0000 0006 0000 0001.;9.............
005c00: c03b 3998 0000 0002 0000 0006 0000 0000.;9.............
```

Listing 9.9 Journal block headers found in the journal file in **Ext3_V1.E01**. The journal signature values are highlighted.

Each of these block types then needs to be processed individually. Analysis of the journal begins with the journal superblock. The version 1 superblock structure is shown in Table 9.3 with the version 2 superblock additions shown in Table 9.4.

The superblock must be consulted in order to process the descriptor blocks. Specifically it is needed to determine if the version 3 checksum and 64-bit block flags are set. If not then the descriptor blocks can be processed using the structure in Table 9.5. If they are set then the structure in Table 9.6 is necessary. The descriptor block will describe all of the blocks that are in the transaction record.

Table 9.3 Ext3 journal superblock version 1 structure.

Offset	Size	Name	Description
0x00	0x0C	Header	Block header structure (Table 9.2).
0x0C	0x04	Block Size	Size of each journal block in bytes.
0x10	0x04	Num. Blocks	Total number of blocks in the journal.
0x14	0x04	First Block	The first block of journal information.
0x18	0x04	First Commit	The first commit ID expected.
0x1C	0x04	Start Block	Block number of the starting block of the log.
0x20	0x04	Error	Error number.

Table 9.4 Ext3 journal superblock version 2 structure. The first 0x24 bytes are common with the version 1 structure (Table 9.3).

Offset	Size	Name	Description
0x24	0x04	Compat. Features	Only one possible value 0x01 meaning that checksums are enabled.
0x28	0x04	Incompat. Features	Possible Values: - 0x01: Journal has revocation blocks; - 0x02: 64-bit block numbers; - 0x04: Asynchronous commit; - 0x08: Version 2 checksum; - 0x10: Version 3 checksum.
0x2C	0x04	RO Compat. Features	Not implemented.
0x30	0x10	UUID	UUID for the journal.

Table 9.5 Default journal descriptor block structure.

Offset	Size	Name	Description
0x00	0x04	Block Num.	The block number represented by this entry.
0x04	0x02	Checksum	A checksum value.
0x06	0x02	Flags	Possible values: 0x01: On disk block escaped; 0x02: Same UUID as previous; 0x04: Data block deleted by transaction; 0x08: Last tag in block.
0x08	0x10	UUID	Not present if same UUID as previous flag is set.

Table 9.6 Version 3 journal descriptor block structure.

Offset	Size	Name	Description
0x00	0x04	Block Num. (Lo)	Least significant 32_d-bits of the block number.
0x04	0x04	Flags	Possible values: 0x01: On disk block escaped; 0x02: Same UUID as previous; 0x04: Data block deleted by transaction; 0x08: Last tag in block.
0x08	0x04	Block Num. (Hi)	Most significant 32_d-bits of the block number.
0x0C	0x04	Checksum	A checksum value.
0x10	0x10	UUID	Not present if same UUID as previous flag is set.

Listing 9.10 shows the contents of block 1_d in the journal file found in **Ext_V1.E01**. The journal header shows that this is a descriptor block for sequence number 8_d. Alternate descriptors are highlighted in Listing 9.10. In the first descriptor the 'Same UUID as Previous' flag is not set. This means that the entry is 24_d bytes in size. Subsequent entries in this descriptor block have this flag set, meaning that they do not contain a UUID field and hence consist only of 8_d bytes. The processed values are shown in Table 9.7. This output can be compared to that of **jls** in which the block numbers are shown (Listing 9.5).

```
000400: c03b 3998 0000 0001 0000 0008 0000 0044 .;9............D
000410: 0000 0000 0000 0000 0000 0000 0000 0000 ................
000420: 0000 0000 0000 0144 0000 0002 0000 0001 .......D........
000430: 0000 0002 0000 0045 0000 0002 0000 0042 .......E.......B
000440: 0000 0002 0000 0002 0000 0002 0000 0043 ...............C
000450: 0000 000a 0000 0000 0000 0000 0000 0000 ................
```

Listing 9.10 An excerpt from block 1_d in the journal file from **Ext3_V1.E01**. The block begins with a header and is followed by the entries.

Further information about processing of the ext journal structures can be found in the Kernel wiki.[1]

9.2.2 HTree Directory Indexing

The traditional ext2 file system used a linear array for directory entries. This structure contained no internal organisation. In order to locate a particular file in a directory, potentially all files need to be searched. Additionally, directory entries are of variable length meaning that it was impossible to jump to a specific entry, rather $x - 1$ entries had to be processed in order to locate the xth entry in the directory. This inherent inefficiency led to the development of HTree (Hash Tree)-based directory indexing.

1 https://ext4.wiki.kernel.org/index.php/Ext4_Disk_Layout#Descriptor_Block.

Table 9.7 Processed entries from the **Ext3_V1.E01** descriptor block (block number 1_d).

	Entry 1	**Entry 2**	**Entry 3**	**Entry 4**
Block	0x44	0x144	0x01	0x45
C-sum	0x00	0x00	0x00	0x00
Flags	0x00	0x02	0x02	0x02
UUID	0x00	—	—	—
	Entry 5	**Entry 6**	**Entry 7**	
Block	0x42	0x02	0x43	
C-Sum	0x00	0x00	0x00	
Flags	0x02	0x02	0x0A	
UUID	—	—	—	

HTrees are similar to B-Trees as seen in NTFS (Chapter 7). They differ in the overall structure in which a HTree has a maximum depth of only two layers and therefore much fanout (there exist many children for each node). HTrees are indexed based on a hash of the filename and not on the filename itself. The use of HTrees increased the practical limits for the number of files per directory in Linux systems from multiple thousands of files for linear array directories, to tens of millions of files for HTree-based directories.

Although HTrees are supported in ext3 and ext4[2] smaller directories in these file systems still use a linear directory structure. In the case of larger directories with many files, the HTree directory structure is utilised. To determine if linear or HTree directory entries are in use the inode flags are consulted. Listing 9.11 shows the contents of the root directory's inode in **Ext3_V2.E01** with the inode flags highlighted. Referring to Table 8.8 shows that the bit which is set (0x1000) refers to the use of tree-based directory indexing. Hence this directory uses a HTree structure for directory entry storage.

```
$ xxd -s $((19*4096 + 128)) mnt/ewf1
013080: ed41 0000 0040 1a00 9570 5562 9270 5562 .A...@...pUb.pUb
013090: 9270 5562 0000 0000 0000 0300 280d 0000 .pUb........(...
0130a0: 0010 0000 50c3 0000 1304 0000 1e14 0000 ....P...........
0130b0: 1f14 0000 2014 0000 2114 0000 2214 0000 .... ...!..."...
0130c0: 2314 0000 2414 0000 2514 0000 2614 0000 ....$...%...&...
0130d0: 2714 0000 2814 0000 2914 0000 0000 0000 '...(...).......
0130e0: 0000 0000 0000 0000 0000 0000 0000 0000 ................
0130f0: 0000 0000 0000 0000 0000 0000 0000 0000 ................
```

Listing 9.11 The root directory inode content in **Ext3_V2.E01**.

Listing 9.11 also shows the content location for the directory itself. Notice that all 12_d direct block pointers are in use along with one singly indirect block pointer. The twelve direct block pointers are: 0x413, 0x141E, 0x141F, 0x1420, 0x1421, 0x1422, 0x1423, 0x1424, 0x1425, 0x1426, 0x1427

2 HTrees were originally developed for ext2 but were never officially included in the file system release.

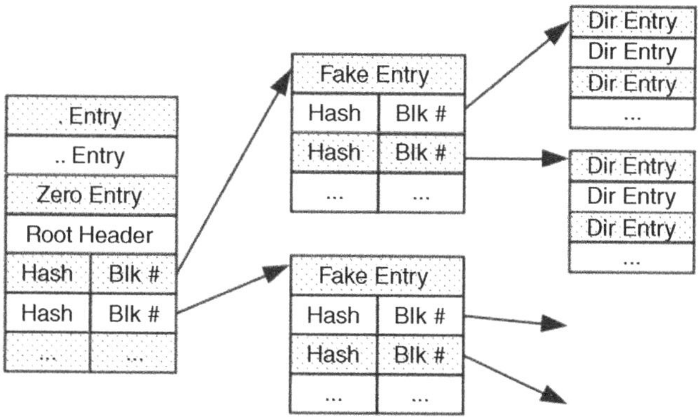

Figure 9.2 HTree structure.

and 0x1428. The indirect block pointer is 0x1429. For ease of further analysis **icat** can be used to recover this 'file'. This is achieved through **icat Ext3_V2.E01 2 > root.dd**. Further analysis will be performed on the **root.dd** file.

The ext HTree contains three types of node. A single root node is found at the start of the root directory file. This then links to internal or leaf nodes. Leaf nodes in the HTree structure are merely a linear array of directory entries which can be processed as with the traditional ext2 processing algorithms. The leaf nodes are sometimes referred to as directory entry blocks as they merely contain traditional directory entries. The root node contains a set of hash values and the block number that files hashing to that value can be found in. In the case of sufficient collisions to require more than a single block, the major hash value will point to an intermediate node (also called the directory index block) which uses minor hashes to map to subsequent leaf nodes. The overall structure of the HTree is shown in Figure 9.2.

As stated previously the root node is found in the first block of the recovered directory. Figure 9.2 provides an idea of the root node's structure. For backwards compatibility the root node begins with two traditional directory entries for the . and .. directories, respectively. This is followed by four zero bytes. These zeros fool ext2 file systems, which are unable to process HTrees, into believing that the directory entries are finished. This is due to the special meaning of inode zero which is that no further processing should take place. The zero value is followed by a 12_d byte HTree Root Header structure. Listing 9.12 shows the contents of the root node in **Ext3_V2.E01** while Table 9.8 shows the structure of this root node and the interpreted values.

```
000000: 0200 0000 0c00 0102 2e00 0000 0200 0000 ................
000010: f40f 0202 2e2e 0000 0000 0000 0108 0000 ................
000020: fc01 a301 0100 0000 9a49 7400 9b01 0000 .........It.....
000030: 4cd9 e400 e100 0000 22ff b801 6d00 0000 L......."...m...
...[snip]...
```

Listing 9.12 The contents of the HTree root node in **Ext3_V2.E01**. The zero entry is highlighted and followed by the node header. Alternate entries are highlighted.

The entries follow the header and consist of a four-byte hash value followed by a four-byte block number. This block number is relative to the beginning of the directory file. The first entry

Table 9.8 HTree root node structure with interpreted values from Listing 9.12. Offset 0x00 represents the beginning of the unhighlighted area of raw data, after the zero inode (highlighted).

Offset	Size	Name	Description	Value
0x00	0x01	Hash Version	Hash algorithm used. The algorithm is one of: 0x0 – Legacy; 0x1 – Half MD4; 0x2 – Tea; 0x3 – Legacy (unsigned); 0x04 – Half MD4 (unsigned); 0x5 – Tea (unsigned).	0x01 (1_d)
0x01	0x01	Header Length	Length of the record header structure. Note that this does not include the zero hash block number (4_d bytes).	0x08 (8_d)
0x02	0x01	Levels	The number of levels in the tree. This value can't exceed 3_d.	0x00 (0_d)
0x03	0x01	Unused	Unused.	0x00 (0_d)
0x04	0x02	Limit	Maximum number of index entries (plus 1 for the header) that can follow this header.	0x1FC (508_d)
0x06	0x02	Count	The actual number of index entries that follow the header (plus 1 for the header).	0x1A3 (419_d)
0x08	0x04	Block	The block number (within the directory file) associated with a zero hash value.	0x01 (1_d)
0x0C	0x08	Entries	Each structure contains a four-byte hash and a four-byte block number (relative to the directory file). The count value (offset 0x06) informs the analyst of the number of entries present in this structure.	

(underlined) in Listing 9.12 has a hash value of 0x0074499A with a corresponding block number of 0x19B. The contents of this block are shown in Listing 9.13 which clearly shows traditional directory entries.

```
19b000: 7668 0000 1800 0d01 6669 6c65 3236 3733 vh......file2673
19b010: 312e 7478 7434 3536 2885 0000 1800 0d01 1.txt456(.......
19b020: 6669 6c65 3334 3037 372e 7478 7400 0d01 file34077.txt...
19b030: ec7a 0000 1800 0d01 6669 6c65 3331 3435 .z......file3145
...[snip]...
```

Listing 9.13 Contents of block 0x19B in the root directory of **Ext3_V2.E01**.

Interior nodes begin with a *fake record*, which is merely four 0x00 bytes. This is followed by a two-byte record length field which will hide the subsequent header information. The use of zero inode values allows for the entire directory content to be read by ext2 file system drivers which do not provide support for the HTree structure as these drivers will cease processing the block on encountering a zero inode.

9.3 The Ext4 File System

Since 2008 the fourth extended file system (ext4) has become standard on most Linux distributions. This file system is backward compatible with previous versions but adds modern storage methods to the ext file system. Ext4 added a raft of new features which distinguish it from previous versions. From a file system forensic perspective this section will cover the most important features of ext4.

Firstly the new inode structure is described. While compatible with the previous inode structure the default size is now 256_d bytes allowing more space for extra metadata information. The data storage mechanisms are dramatically changed in ext4, with extents being used as the default storage mechanism rather than block pointers. This allows for more efficient storage of large files and follows the storage mechanism used in most modern file systems. In addition to this, ext4 also allows for inline storage (analogous to resident $DATA attributes in NTFS) which allow for small file content to be stored in the metadata (i.e. inode) structure itself. Ext4 also includes a creation time and improves the granularity of all timestamps in the file system (nanosecond as opposed to second granularity). The remainder of this section will examine these new structures in detail.

9.3.1 Large Inodes

Ext4 defaults to an inode size of 256_d bytes, twice that of previous versions of the ext file system. The first 128_d bytes of the ext4 inode are identical to those of previous ext versions (Table 8.6). Table 9.9 shows the meaning of the extra bytes in the ext4 inode.

The size of the ext4 inode is generally 256_d bytes allocated on disk but not all of this is used. In the extended inode structure the first value (2 bytes at 0x80) provides the size of the inode above that of the ext2 inode size (128_d bytes). The remaining bytes in the inode can then be used for extended attributes. However, from a file system forensic perspective the most interesting information in the extended inode is that of time stamps which are covered in the next section.

9.3.1.1 Timestamps

Listing 9.14 shows the output from two **istat** commands. The first of these is run on an ext2 file system while the second is run on ext4. From this output it is clear that the ext4 file system provides an extra timestamp value (that of creation time) and also provides nanosecond granularity.

Table 9.9 Ext4 inode structure.

Offset	Size	Name	Description
0x00	0x80	Ext2 Inode	Structure as shown in Table 8.6.
0x80	0x02	Extra Size	The extra bytes (above 128_d) occupied by this inode.
0x82	0x02	Checksum (Hi)	Upper 16_d bits of the inode checksum.
0x84	0x04	ctime (extra)	Extra metadata change time value providing nanosecond granularity.
0x88	0x04	mtime (extra)	Extra content modification time value providing nanosecond granularity.
0x8C	0x04	atime (extra)	Extra access time value providing nanosecond granularity.
0x90	0x04	Creation Time	Unix time value representing the file creation time.
0x94	0x04	crtime (extra)	Extra creation time value providing nanosecond granularity.
0x98	0x04	Version (Hi)	Upper 32_d bits for version number.
0x9C	0x04	Project ID	Project ID value.

```
[ext2]
...
Inode Times:
Accessed: 2018-03-05 07:15:20 (GMT)
File Modified: 2018-03-05 07:15:20 (GMT)
Inode Modified: 2018-03-05 07:15:20 (GMT)
...
[ext4]
...
Inode Times:
Accessed: 2018-03-13 05:53:38.984979508 (GMT)
File Modified: 2018-03-13 05:53:38.984979508 (GMT)
Inode Modified: 2018-03-13 05:53:38.984979508 (GMT)
File Created: 2018-03-13 05:53:38.984979508 (GMT)
...
```

Listing 9.14 Comparison of the timestamps found in ext2 (top) and ext4 (bottom) file systems as recovered by **istat**.

The extra detail is achieved through the addition of a creation time value and the use of four extra bytes for each timestamp which store the nanosecond component (and a little more, as will be seen in a moment). These extra fields are found in the extended ext4 inode structure (Table 9.9). The extra timestamps and improved granularity allow for the generation of more precise and detailed timelines for ext4 than for previous versions of the extended file system.

Consider the output of the **stat**[3] command on the file **reflect.jpg** in **Ext4_V1.E01** (Listing 9.15). The file's access time was altered using **touch -a -t 212201011200**.

```
  Size: 273177 Blocks: 536 IO Block: 4096 regular file
Device: 700h/1792d Inode: 13 Links: 1
Access: (0750/-rwxr-x---) Uid: ( 0/ root) Gid: ( 0/ root)
Access: 2122-01-01 12:00:00.000000000 +0000
Modify: 2023-12-06 07:54:04.657865029 +0000
Change: 2023-12-06 08:00:24.665854951 +0000
 Birth: -
```

Listing 9.15 Output from the **stat** command showing the access timestamp. This time value is past the end of Unix time (Y2038)!

Listing 9.16 shows the output of Sleuth Kit's **istat** command on this particular inode in the filesystem.[4] Notice the access time value is from the year 1985, rather than 2122 as seen in the output from **stat**. What has happened? Which of these values is correct?

From knowledge of previous versions of the ext file system it is known that Unix time expires in 2038. This is due to the fact that Unix time traditionally was a 32_d bit signed integer value measuring the number of seconds since 1 January 1970. This allows for a maximum value of 2^{31} seconds which provides a final time of 19 January 2038 at 3:14:07 AM. This was a potential issue in the ext file system going forward. Therefore ext4 made two significant changes to the timestamp format.

3 The **stat** command is used only for gathering metadata information about live files on the currently running file system. It is not a digital forensic tool and should not be used as a substitute for one.
4 Sleuth Kit version 4.12 was used for this example.

```
Inode Times:
Accessed: 1985-11-25 05:31:44.000000000 (GMT)
File Modified: 2023-12-06 07:54:04.657865029 (GMT)
Inode Modified: 2023-12-06 08:00:24.665854951 (GMT)
File Created: 2023-12-06 07:54:04.657865029 (GMT)
```

Listing 9.16 Excerpt from running **istat** on the timestamp file showing the timestamp values, clearly showing the error in timestamp interpretation in Sleuth kit (Version 4.12).

The first of these changes was to store the original access, modified and changed time fields as unsigned values. This allows for 2^{32} possible values which means that Unix time would now expire on 7 February 2106 at 6:28:15 AM. However, even this value is unable to explain the time value shown in the **stat** output (Listing 9.15). The year 2122 exceeds the maximum year possible in a 32-bit system.

This leads to the second change. From Table 9.9 the extra fields in the inode structure are shown. Each of the access, modification and change times have an extra field associated with them. This is often interpreted as being nanoseconds; however, it is actually more than mere nanoseconds. The two least significant bits represent the high value bits of the basic time. This means that 2^{34} seconds can now be represented (the 32_d bits from the original inode timestamp value along with the 2_d extra bits from the file system). The use of 34_d bits results in a maximum time value in the ext4 filesystem of 30 May 2514 at 1:53:03 AM.

Consider the raw content of the **reflect.jpg** file's inode as seen in Listing 9.17. The access time and the access time (extra) fields are highlighted and have the values 0x1DE80440 and 0x00000001. A naive approach to time stamp interpretation would interpret 0x1DE80440 as 25 November 1985 05:31:44 UTC just as seen in the **istat** output.

```
049c00: e881 0000 192b 0400 4004 e81d 182a 7065 .....+..@....*pe
049c10: 9c28 7065 0000 0000 0000 0100 1802 0000 .(pe............
049c20: 0000 0800 0100 0000 0af3 0100 0400 0000 ................
049c30: 0000 0000 0000 0000 4300 0000 4180 0000 ........C...A...
049c40: 0000 0000 0000 0000 0000 0000 0000 0000 ................
049c50: 0000 0000 0000 0000 0000 0000 0000 0000 ................
049c60: 0000 0000 4948 2863 0000 0000 0000 0000 ....IH(c........
049c70: 0000 0000 0000 0000 0000 0000 0d42 0000 .............B..
049c80: 2000 1049 9c8f c09e 14e5 d89c 0100 0000 ..I............
049c90: 9c28 7065 14e5 d89c 0000 0000 0000 0000 .(pe............
049ca0: 0000 0000 0000 0000 0000 0000 0000 0000 ................
049cb0: 0000 0000 0000 0000 0000 0000 0000 0000 ................
049cc0: 0000 0000 0000 0000 0000 0000 0000 0000 ................
049cd0: 0000 0000 0000 0000 0000 0000 0000 0000 ................
049ce0: 0000 0000 0000 0000 0000 0000 0000 0000 ................
049cf0: 0000 0000 0000 0000 0000 0000 0000 0000 ................
```

Listing 9.17 Sample ext4 inode showing access time and access time (extra) fields.

The correct approach to this conversion is to consider the two least significant bits of the access time's extra field. These have the value 01_b. This means that the actual time value is 0x11DE80440 which is 1 January 2122 12:00:00 UTC, exactly what was seen in the output from the **stat** command.

9.3.2 Ext4 Data Storage

Ext4 provides a number of new means to locate the file content from the inode. Traditionally all files in ext were located using block pointers (both direct and indirect) but modern file systems use other methods of content location. To this end, ext4 introduces a number of new storage mechanisms which include extent-based storage, inline storage and symbolic links. These topics are shown in the remainder of this section.

9.3.2.1 Extent-Based Storage

Extents are used in many modern file systems as an efficient means of locating a large number of contiguous blocks (or clusters).[5] Consider a file which consists of 1000_d contiguous blocks. In ext2 and ext3, block pointers are used to locate each individual block of the file's data. There is a one-to-one correspondence between the file size and the number of block pointers that are required for storage. Extent-based storage records the starting block number and the number of blocks in the particular extent, allowing one extent structure to store all information about the file's location in the case of unfragmented files.

Extents are formed in a tree-like structure. Each extent block begins with an extent header. It is then followed by leaf nodes (depth = 0) which contain extents pointing to the data blocks for the file. In the case of depth greater than 0, the header is followed by an index block which points to blocks that contain further nodes in the tree. In the case of small extent trees (i.e. files with little or no fragmentation) the entire extent tree can be stored in the inode structure (using the block pointer area in the basic inode). The extent header itself is 12_d bytes in size and its structure is shown in Table 9.10.

Extent leaf nodes contain the actual extents themselves. These are also 12_d-byte structures. The leaf node structure is shown in Table 9.11.

Index nodes follow the same structure as shown in Table 9.10. The only difference is that in an index node the depth will be greater than one. This means that extents point to other extent-tree nodes rather than directly to data blocks.

Listing 9.18 shows inode 15_d from **Ext4_V1.E01**. In this the extent header is highlighted. The 12_d-byte extent appears immediately following the header. The processed values of these two structures are shown in Table 9.12.

Table 9.10 The extent header structure in ext4.

Offset	Size	Name	Description
0x00	0x02	Magic	A magic value identifying an extent header structure (0xF30A).
0x02	0x02	Num. Entries	The number of entries following the extent header.
0x04	0x02	Max. Entries	The maximum number of entries that might follow the extent header.
0x06	0x02	Depth	Tree depth. If this value is 0 the extents point to data blocks. Any value greater than zero means that the extents are pointing to other extent-tree blocks.
0x08	0x04	Generation	Tree generation.

5 NTFS uses extents but refers to them as data runs.

Table 9.11 The extent leaf node structure in ext4.

Offset	Size	Name	Description
0x00	0x04	First Block	The file's logical block of the first block covered by this extent. In the case of zero this extent represents the start of the file content.
0x04	0x02	Num. Blocks	The number of blocks in the extent. Assuming value in this field is x, if $x <= 0x8000$ then the extent is initialised and contains x blocks. If $x > 0x8000$ then the extent is uninitialised and contains $x - 32,768$ blocks. Due to this the maximum length of an initialised extent is $32{,}678_d$ blocks.
0x06	0x02	Start (Hi)	Upper 16_d bits of the starting block number.
0x08	0x04	Start (Lo)	Lower 32_d bits of the starting block number.

```
049e00: e881 0000 5630 0b00 ba28 7065 ba28 7065 ....V0...(pe.(pe
049e10: ba28 7065 0000 0000 0000 0100 a005 0000 .(pe............
049e20: 0000 0800 0100 0000 0af3 0100 0400 0000 ................
049e30: 0000 0000 0000 0000 b400 0000 8480 0000 ................
049e40: 0000 0000 0000 0000 0000 0000 0000 0000 ................
049e50: 0000 0000 0000 0000 0000 0000 0000 0000 ................
049e60: 0000 0000 ac9f d98c 0000 0000 0000 0000 ................
049e70: 0000 0000 0000 0000 0000 0000 6e5b 0000 ............n[..
049e80: 2000 8970 d888 382e d888 382e d864 442d ..p..8...8..dD-
049e90: ba28 7065 d864 442d 0000 0000 0000 0000 .(pe.dD-........
```

Listing 9.18 Extract from inode 15_d in **Ext4_V1.E01**. The extent header and single 12_d byte extent are highlighted.

Table 9.12 Processed extent tree from Listing 9.18.

Offset	Size	Name	Value
		Extent Header	
0x00	0x02	Magic	0xF30A
0x02	0x02	Num. Entries	0x01 (1_d)
0x04	0x02	Max. Entries	0x04 (4_d)
0x06	0x02	Depth	0x00 (0_d)
0x08	0x04	Generation	0x00 (0_d)
		Extent 1	
0x00	0x04	First Block	0x00 (0_d)
0x04	0x02	Num. Blocks	0xB4 (180_d)
0x06	0x02	Start (Hi)	0x00 (0_d)
0x08	0x04	Start (Lo)	0x8084 ($32,900_d$)

Table 9.12 shows the processed header showing that this tree contains a single entry (of a maximum of four) that will fit in the 60_d bytes available in the inode (12_d bytes are reserved for the header, leaving 48_d bytes available for actual extents). The header informs the analyst that the depth is zero meaning that each of the extents in this tree node point to data blocks and not to other extent trees. Processing the single extent provides a starting block of 0x8084 ($32,900_d$) and a length of 0xB4 (180_d) blocks. This can be confirmed using **istat** as shown in Listing 9.19.

```
inode: 15
Allocated
Group: 0
Generation Id: 2363072428
uid / gid: 0 / 0
mode: rrwxr-x---
Flags: Extents,
size: 733270
num of links: 1

Inode Times:
Accessed: 2023-12-06 07:54:34.189864246 (GMT)
File Modified: 2023-12-06 07:54:34.193864246 (GMT)
Inode Modified: 2023-12-06 07:54:34.193864246 (GMT)
File Created: 2023-12-06 07:54:34.189864246 (GMT)

Direct Blocks:
32900 32901 32902 32903 32904 32905 32906 32907
...[snip]...
33076 33077 33078 33079
```

Listing 9.19 The output from **istat** for inode 15_d in **Ext4_V1.E01** showing the direct blocks after interpretation of the extent structure.

In the case of file fragmentation multiple extents will be found in the inode. In the case of a file with more than four fragments the inode structure is not sufficiently large to store this information. In this case an extent-tree structure is used instead. Due to the nature of extents, each individual extent is limited to 128MiB in size (assuming the default 4096_d block size). Each extent uses 15_d bits to represent the number of blocks in the extent. This leads to a maximum of $32,767_d$ blocks that can be found in one single extent. Hence any file larger than this will use multiple extents in storage.

Listing 9.20 shows an inode from a large (c. 390 MB) file that was created on an ext4 file system. Examining the inode structure itself shows an extent header as expected. This header shows that there is one single extent following this (from a maximum of four possible extents) and that the depth of this node is 0x01.

The extent that was shown in Listing 9.18 had a depth value of zero. This meant that it was a leaf node, meaning that it contained extent structures. In the case of Listing 9.20 the node depth is one. This signifies that this is an index (also called internal or interior) node. This node does not contain extents; instead, it contains pointers to other nodes in the tree. Each index node of an extent tree contains a number of 12_d-byte extent index structures (Table 9.13).

```
30037bc00: b481 e803 0000 6a18 49ea c362 7809 c462 ......j.I..bx..b
30037bc10: eb08 c462 0000 0000 e803 0100 0835 0c00 ...b.........5..
30037bc20: 0000 0800 0100 0000 0af3 0100 0400 0100 ................
30037bc30: 0000 0000 0000 0000 ed88 3000 0000 1500 ..........0.....
30037bc40: 0028 0000 0080 0000 0060 1500 00a8 0000 .(.......`......
30037bc50: 0008 0000 00e0 1500 00b0 0000 0018 0000 ................
30037bc60: 00f8 1500 45ad 1d98 0000 0000 0000 0000 ....E...........
30037bc70: 0000 0000 0000 0000 0000 0000 2b0e 0000 ............+...
30037bc80: 2000 1957 c88b 213d b8ec a299 9047 6abf ..W..!=.....Gj.
30037bc90: 7809 c462 accf ad08 0000 0000 0000 0000 x..b............
30037bca0: 0000 0000 0000 0000 0000 0000 0000 0000 ................
```

Listing 9.20 An ext4 inode utilising an extent-tree structure. The extent header and extent index are highlighted.

Table 9.13 The ext4 extent index structure.

Offset	Size	Name	Description
0x00	0x04	Logical Block	This extent index covers blocks from this point onwards. A value of zero signifies the start of the file.
0x04	0x04	Block Number (lo)	Lower 32_d bits of the block number of the extent node.
0x08	0x02	Block Number (hi)	Upper 16_d bits of the previous field.
0x0A	0x02	Unused	Unused.

Examining the extent index in Listing 9.20 shows that this extent index refers to the start of the file's content (logical block number is zero). The physical block number at which the next node is found is 0x3088ED. Listing 9.21 shows the content of this block.

```
3088ed000: 0af3 0800 5401 0000 0000 0000 0000 0000 ....T...........
3088ed010: 0028 0000 0028 1500 0028 0000 0080 0000 .(...(...(......
3088ed020: 0060 1500 00a8 0000 0008 0000 00e0 1500 .`..............
3088ed030: 00b0 0000 0018 0000 00f8 1500 00c8 0000 ................
3088ed040: 0080 0000 0078 1700 0048 0100 0008 0000 .....x...H......
3088ed050: 00f8 1700 0050 0100 0030 0000 00a8 1800 .....P...0......
3088ed060: 0080 0100 a006 0000 0000 1900 0000 0000 ................
```

Listing 9.21 The contents of the extent block showing the header and individual extents. Alternate extents are highlighted.

The extent header is discovered first (magic value 0xF30A as expected). This informs the analyst that this node contains 8_d entries from a maximum of 0x154 (340_d). The depth of this node is zero, meaning this node contains extents. Table 9.14 contains the processed extents.

The processed extents can then be used to recover the file content in its entirety. From Table 9.14 the total number of blocks occupied by the file is 0x186A0 ($100,000_d$) which is the correct number of blocks for this file. Using the extent information each individual extent can be recovered and the file can then be recreated using the extents.

Table 9.14 Processed extents from Listing 9.21.

Extent	1	2	3	4
Logical Blk	0x00	0x2800	0xA800	0xB000
Num. Blks	0x2800	0x8000	0x8000	0x1800
Start (Hi)	0x00	0x00	0x00	0x00
Start (Lo)	0x152800	0x156000	0x15E000	0x15F800
Extent	**5**	**6**	**7**	**8**
Logical Blk	0xC800	0x14800	0x15000	0x18000
Num. Blks	0x8000	0x0800	0x3000	0x6A0
Start (Hi)	0x00	0x00	0x00	0x00
Start (Lo)	0x177800	0x17F800	0x18A800	0x190000

As files are being created extents are firstly created in the inode as needed. Initially the first four extents would have been located in the inode structure. Once a fifth extent is required, the first extent entry is overwritten in the inode with an extent index and all four existing extents are copied to the extent index block. However, it would appear from Listing 9.20 that extents 2–4 are not overwritten. Examining the inode in Listing 9.20 shows that these three extents are still present; hence, even in the case in which the extent index block is no longer available it is still be possible to recover some of the file content.

9.3.2.2 Inline Storage

Another form of storage introduced in ext4 is that of inline storage. In this storage mechanism small files are stored in the inode itself. This method of storage is similar to resident $DATA attributes in NTFS. Up to 60_d bytes can be stored using this method (although the use of extended attributes can increase this value). Note also that the inline storage is not normally enabled by default in most ext4 file systems. When creating the file system the option **-O inline_data** must be provided to the **mkfs** command. If this option is not provided only extent-based storage will be utilised.

Inode 14_d in **Ext4_V1.E01** contains a small text file which is stored inline. The inline data flag is set in the inode meaning that the data can be read directly from the inode structure itself. Listing 9.22 shows the output of **istat** when run on inode 14_d in **Ext4_V1.E01**. This shows the flag value and also that there are no direct blocks listed.

Listing 9.23 shows the content of the inode itself. The file size is 0x2E (46_d) bytes. The flags show that the data is inline and the actual data itself reads 'This file will be deleted in a later version. \n'.

9.3.2.3 Symbolic Links

Symbolic links are implemented using a feature that is similar to inline storage (even if inline storage is not enabled on a particular file system). A symbolic link is a special type of file that points to another file. Listing 9.24 shows the **istat** output for a symbolic link while Listing 9.25 shows the actual inode content (inode 16_d in **Ext4_V1.E01**).

From Listing 9.25 the file size is found to be 0x0B (11_d) bytes. For a symbolic link this is interpreted not as file size, but as the size of the link name (i.e. the filename of the file being linked to).

```
inode: 14
Allocated
Group: 0
Generation Id: 667396484
uid / gid: 0 / 0
mode: rrwxr-x---
Flags: Inline Data,
size: 46
num of links: 1

Inode Times:
Accessed: 2023-12-06 07:54:26.613864447 (GMT)
File Modified: 2023-12-06 07:54:26.613864447 (GMT)
Inode Modified: 2023-12-06 07:54:26.613864447 (GMT)
File Created: 2023-12-06 07:54:26.613864447 (GMT)
```

Listing 9.22 The output from the **istat** command when run on inode 14_d showing the inline data flag. Note that no direct blocks are listed.

```
049d00: e881 0000 2e00 0000 b228 7065 b228 7065 .........(pe.(pe
049d10: b228 7065 0000 0000 0000 0100 0000 0000 .(pe............
049d20: 0000 0010 0100 0000 5468 6973 2066 696c ........This fil
049d30: 6520 7769 6c6c 2062 6520 6465 6c65 7465 e will be delete
049d40: 6420 696e 2061 206c 6174 6572 2076 6572 d in a later ver
049d50: 7369 6f6e 2e0a 0000 0000 0000 0000 0000 sion............
049d60: 0000 0000 84a9 c727 0000 0000 0000 0000 .......'........
049d70: 0000 0000 0000 0000 0000 0000 67bf 0000 ............g...
049d80: 2000 2fd3 fc4f 5b92 fc4f 5b92 fc4f 5b92 ./..O[..O[..O[.
049d90: b228 7065 fc4f 5b92 0000 0000 0000 0000 .(pe.O[.........
049da0: 0000 02ea 0407 0000 0000 0000 0000 0000 ................
049db0: 0000 0000 6461 7461 0000 0000 0000 0000 ....data........
049dc0: 0000 0000 0000 0000 0000 0000 0000 0000 ................
```

Listing 9.23 Raw inode data for an inline file. The flags show that the data is stored inline. Data is found at offset 0x28 (the block pointer location). In this example the data is 0x2E bytes in size. The resulting data is 'This file will be deleted in a later version.\n'

The mode value is 0xA1FF. The most significant nibble provides the file type. 0xA000 refers to a symbolic link. The block pointers (60_d bytes at offset 0x28) are then used to store the data, in this case the file name, which is found to be **reflect.jpg**. Hence this inode represents a symbolic link to a file in the same directory called **reflect.jpg**.

9.3.3 File Deletion in Ext4

In traditional ext file systems the act of deletion involves setting the deleted timestamp and overwriting the block pointer structures. Ext4 provides a number of means of storing files. This section examines each of these methods of file storage and the forensic implications of deletion with each method.

We commence with an analysis of inline storage. Listing 9.23 shows an inode for a file that is utilising inline storage. Listing 9.26 shows the same inode after deletion.

```
inode: 16
Allocated
Group: 0
Generation Id: 4236569570
symbolic link to: reflect.jpg
uid / gid: 0 / 0
mode: lrwxrwxrwx
size: 11
num of links: 1

Inode Times:
Accessed: 2023-12-06 08:32:12.689804347 (GMT)
File Modified: 2023-12-06 08:32:07.597804482 (GMT)
Inode Modified: 2023-12-06 08:32:07.597804482 (GMT)
File Created: 2023-12-06 08:32:07.597804482 (GMT)

Direct Blocks:
0
```

Listing 9.24 The output of **istat** when run on a symbolic link (inode 16_d in **Ext4_V1.E01**).

```
049f00: ffa1 0000 0b00 0000 8c31 7065 8731 7065 .........1pe.1pe
049f10: 8731 7065 0000 0000 0000 0100 0000 0000 .1pe............
049f20: 0000 0000 0100 0000 7265 666c 6563 742e ........reflect.
049f30: 6a70 6700 0000 0000 0000 0000 0000 0000 jpg.............
049f40: 0000 0000 0000 0000 0000 0000 0000 0000 ................
049f50: 0000 0000 0000 0000 0000 0000 0000 0000 ................
049f60: 0000 0000 e2eb 84fc 0000 0000 0000 0000 ................
049f70: 0000 0000 0000 0000 0000 0000 af6c 0000 .............l..
049f80: 2000 86b1 0817 878e 0817 878e ec50 76a4 ............Pv.
049f90: 8731 7065 0817 878e 0000 0000 0000 0000 .1pe............
049fa0: 0000 0000 0000 0000 0000 0000 0000 0000 ................
```

Listing 9.25 An inode for a symbolic link showing the mode which informs the analyst that this is a symbolic link (0xA000) and the actual link content itself.

```
049d00: e881 0000 2e00 0000 b228 7065 8336 7065 .........(pe.6pe
049d10: b228 7065 8336 7065 0000 0000 0000 0000 .(pe.6pe........
049d20: 0000 0010 0100 0000 5468 6973 2066 696c ........This fil
049d30: 6520 7769 6c6c 2062 6520 6465 6c65 7465 e will be delete
049d40: 6420 696e 2061 206c 6174 6572 2076 6572 d in a later ver
049d50: 7369 6f6e 2e0a 0000 0000 0000 0000 0000 sion............
049d60: 0000 0000 84a9 c727 0000 0000 0000 0000 .......'........
049d70: 0000 0000 0000 0000 0000 0000 80e1 0000 ................
049d80: 2000 97ba 30f2 e5af fc4f 5b92 fc4f 5b92 ...0....O[..O[.
049d90: b228 7065 fc4f 5b92 0000 0000 0000 0000 .(pe.O[.........
049da0: 0000 02ea 0407 0000 0000 0000 0000 0000 ................
049db0: 0000 0000 6461 7461 0000 0000 0000 0000 ....data........
```

Listing 9.26 Inode 14_d in **Ext4_V2.E01** using inline storage after file deletion. While the deletion time has been set the content is still present.

As with all versions of the ext file system the deletion time value has been set. However, unlike traditional block pointers the actual data content has not been overwritten.

Examining symbolic links after deletion shows different behaviour. The symbolic link in Listing 9.25 is shown again in Listing 9.27 after deletion. The deletion time is set but in this case the data (the filename) has been zero'd. This means that this data is unrecoverable.

```
049f00: ffa1 0000 0b00 0000 8c31 7065 8b36 7065 .........1pe.6pe
049f10: 8731 7065 8b36 7065 0000 0000 0000 0000 .1pe.6pe........
049f20: 0000 0000 0100 0000 0000 0000 0000 0000 ................
049f30: 0000 0000 0000 0000 0000 0000 0000 0000 ................
049f40: 0000 0000 0000 0000 0000 0000 0000 0000 ................
049f50: 0000 0000 0000 0000 0000 0000 0000 0000 ................
049f60: 0000 0000 e2eb 84fc 0000 0000 0000 0000 ................
049f70: 0000 0000 0000 0000 0000 0000 bf9b 0000 ................
049f80: 2000 2a1a f476 0784 0817 878e ec50 76a4 .*..v.......Pv.
049f90: 8731 7065 0817 878e 0000 0000 0000 0000 .1pe............
049fa0: 0000 0000 0000 0000 0000 0000 0000 0000 ................
```

Listing 9.27 Inode 16_d in **Ext4_V2.E01** containing a symbolic link after deletion. In this case the content is overwritten.

The final type of storage to examine is that of extent-based storage (including extent trees). Listing 9.18 showed a file using a single extent. Listing 9.28 shows this same file after deletion.

```
049e00: e881 0000 0000 0000 ba28 7065 8736 7065 .........(pe.6pe
049e10: 8736 7065 8736 7065 0000 0000 0000 0000 .6pe.6pe........
049e20: 0000 0800 0100 0000 0af3 0000 0400 0000 ................
049e30: 0000 0000 0000 0000 0000 0000 0000 0000 ................
049e40: 0000 0000 0000 0000 0000 0000 0000 0000 ................
049e50: 0000 0000 0000 0000 0000 0000 0000 0000 ................
049e60: 0000 0000 ac9f d98c 0000 0000 0000 0000 ................
049e70: 0000 0000 0000 0000 0000 0000 8d7d 0000 .............}..
049e80: 2000 935e b0b8 4056 b0b8 4056 d864 442d ..^..@V..@V.dD-
049e90: ba28 7065 d864 442d 0000 0000 0000 0000 .(pe.dD-........
```

Listing 9.28 Inode 15_d in **Ext4_V2.E01** using extent-based storage inode after deletion.

Again the deletion time has been initialised marking the file as deleted. The extent-header structure is still present (at least the identifying value 0xF30A is present), but it would appear that the extent itself has been overwritten. Hence it is impossible to recover this file using file system forensic techniques as there is no content location information available after deletion. The content is still present on the device by default and might be recoverable using data carving techniques.

What happens in the case of an extent-tree storage mechanism? Listings 9.20 and 9.21 showed the contents of an inode that required an extent tree for storage and the content of the extent block itself. Listing 9.29 shows the same inode after file deletion.

Examining the extent header shows that the number of extents in the structure has been zero'd. However, it appears that the data is still present. Interpreting the extent index node (immediately after the header) shows that the extent block is 0x3088ED (3, 180, 781_d). The contents of this block, after deletion, are shown in Listing 9.30.

```
000000: b481 e803 0000 0000 49ea c362 9b12 c462 ........I..b...b
000010: 9b12 c462 9b12 c462 e803 0000 0000 0000 ...b...b........
000020: 0000 0800 0100 0000 0af3 0000 0400 0000 ................
000030: 0000 0000 0000 0000 ed88 3000 0000 1500 ..........0.....
000040: 0028 0000 0080 0000 0060 1500 00a8 0000 .(.......`......
000050: 0008 0000 00e0 1500 00b0 0000 0018 0000 ................
000060: 00f8 1500 45ad 1d98 0000 0000 0000 0000 ....E...........
000070: 0000 0000 0000 0000 0000 0000 e3ad 0000 ................
000080: 2000 b229 fc9a e104 fc9a e104 9047 6abf ..)........Gj.
000090: 7809 c462 accf ad08 0000 0000 0000 0000 x..b............
```

Listing 9.29 The contents of an inode using extent trees after deletion.

```
000000: 0af3 0000 5401 0000 0000 0000 0000 0000 ....T...........
000010: 0000 0000 0000 0000 0028 0000 0000 0000 .........(......
000020: 0000 0000 00a8 0000 0000 0000 0000 0000 ................
000030: 00b0 0000 0000 0000 0000 0000 00c8 0000 ................
000040: 0000 0000 0000 0000 0048 0100 0000 000  .........H......
000050: 0000 0000 0050 0100 0000 0000 0000 0000 .....P..........
000060: 0080 0100 0000 0000 0000 0000 0000 0000 ................
```

Listing 9.30 Contents of the extent block after file deletion.

The extent header is almost fully intact. The only change is that number of entries has been zero'd. The first extent has also been completely erased but subsequent extents have some information available. However, the information remaining is only the logical addresses of file content. Information about the physical blocks (starting block and number of blocks) has been overwritten. This means that it is not possible to recover information from the extent block. However, remember that some information is still contained in the inode itself. From Listing 9.29 three of the extents (from a total of 8) are recoverable. This means that when extent trees are used some of the content is recoverable.

9.3.4 Extended Attributes

Extended attributes (xattr) are extra pieces of data that can be stored in the metadata structures. They are similar to alternate data streams in NTFS. These name value pairs can be stored after the inode (space permitting) or in a separate block on disk. Listing 9.31 shows an inode with an extended attribute (Inode 13_d in **Ext4_V2.E01**).

When xattr values are stored in the inode itself, the xattr magic value (0xEA200000) is encountered at offset 0xA0. This is highlighted in Listing 9.31. Immediately following this is found the first xattr. This can be processed using Table 9.15.

Using Table 9.15 it is determined that the attribute name is *user.Hidden* (the index value 0x01, implies this is a user attribute with a name Hidden). This means that the complete name is *user.Hidden*. The content is located at offset 0x50 relative to the start of the first extended attribute. This means that the content occupies 0x0C (12_d) bytes beginning at offset 0xF4 in the inode in Listing 9.31. The value of this is **Hidden Value**.

```
049c00: e881 0000 192b 0400 4004 e81d b932 7065 .....+..@....2pe
049c10: 9c28 7065 0000 0000 0000 0100 1802 0000 .(pe............
049c20: 0000 0800 0100 0000 0af3 0100 0400 0000 ................
049c30: 0000 0000 0000 0000 4300 0000 4180 0000 ........C...A...
049c40: 0000 0000 0000 0000 0000 0000 0000 0000 ................
049c50: 0000 0000 0000 0000 0000 0000 0000 0000 ................
049c60: 0000 0000 4948 2863 0000 0000 0000 0000 ....IH(c........
049c70: 0000 0000 0000 0000 0000 0000 5698 0000 ............V...
049c80: 2000 cd3c 10d0 2be8 14e5 d89c 0100 0000 ..<..+.........
049c90: 9c28 7065 14e5 d89c 0000 0000 0000 0000 .(pe............
049ca0: 0000 02ea 0601 5000 0000 0000 0c00 0000 ......P.........
049cb0: 0000 0000 4869 6464 656e 0000 0000 0000 ....Hidden......
049cc0: 0000 0000 0000 0000 0000 0000 0000 0000 ................
049cd0: 0000 0000 0000 0000 0000 0000 0000 0000 ................
049ce0: 0000 0000 0000 0000 0000 0000 0000 0000 ................
049cf0: 0000 0000 4869 6464 656e 2056 616c 7565 ....Hidden Value
```

Listing 9.31 Inode 13_d in **Ext4_V2.E01** showing an extended attribute. The 'magic' value and extended attribute are highlighted.

Table 9.15 Extended attribute structure. The values are from Listing 9.31.

Offset	Size	Name	Description	Value
0x00	0x01	Name Len. (X)	The length of the attribute name.	0x06 (6_d)
0x01	0x01	Name Index	The attribute name index. Possible values include: 0x00: No prefix 0x01: user. 0x02: system.posix_acl_access. 0x03: system.posix_acl_default. 0x04: trusted. 0x06: security. 0x07: system. 0x08: system.richael	0x01 (1_d)
0x02	0x02	Value Offset	Location of attribute value relative to the start of the extended attribute structure.	0x50 (80_d)
0x04	0x04	Value Inum	The inode in which this value is stored. Zero means it is stored in the same block as this entry.	0x00 (0_d)
0x08	0x04	Value Size	The size of the value in bytes.	0x0C (12_d)
0x0C	0x04	Hash	Hash of attribute name and value.	0x00 (0_d)
0x10	X	Name	Attribute name. The length is in the name length field.	Hidden

Multiple xattrs can be stored in a single inode. This is shown in Listing 9.32. The magic value and second attribute along with its corresponding value are highlighted. Once the space between attributes and values can no longer fit extra attributes the attributes are stored in a separate block. This is shown in Listing 9.33.

```
04a1a0: 0000 02ea 0601 5000 0000 0000 0b00 0000 ......P.........
04a1b0: 0000 0000 4869 6464 656e 0000 0201 4800 ....Hidden....H.
04a1c0: 0000 0000 0700 0000 0000 0000 5832 0000 ............X2..
04a1d0: 0000 0000 0000 0000 0000 0000 0000 0000 ................
04a1e0: 0000 0000 0000 0000 0000 0000 5661 6c75 ............Valu
04a1f0: 6520 3200 4869 6464 656e 2044 6174 6100 e 2.Hidden Data.
```

Listing 9.32 An inode containing two xattrs (Inode 18_d in **Ext4_V2.E01**).

```
04a200: e881 0000 192b 0400 8335 7065 9c35 7065 .....+...5pe.5pe
04a210: 8335 7065 0000 0000 0000 0100 2002 0000 .5pe........ ...
04a220: 0000 0800 0100 0000 0af3 0100 0400 0000 ................
04a230: 0000 0000 0000 0000 4300 0000 7b81 0000 ........C...{...
04a240: 0000 0000 0000 0000 0000 0000 0000 0000 ................
04a250: 0000 0000 0000 0000 0000 0000 0000 0000 ................
04a260: 0000 0000 d286 4fea 4e08 0000 0000 0000 ......O.N.......
04a270: 0000 0000 0000 0000 0000 0000 68a3 0000 ............h...
04a280: 2000 bab4 e445 edc3 5448 3e94 5448 3e94 ....E..TH>.TH>.
04a290: 8335 7065 5448 3e94 0000 0000 0000 0000 .5peTH>.........
04a2a0: 0000 02ea 0601 5000 0000 0000 0b00 0000 ......P.........
04a2b0: 0000 0000 4869 6464 656e 0000 0201 4800 ....Hidden....H.
04a2c0: 0000 0000 0700 0000 0000 0000 5832 0000 ............X2..
04a2d0: 0000 0000 0000 0000 0000 0000 0000 0000 ................
04a2e0: 0000 0000 0000 0000 0000 0000 5661 6c75 ............Valu
04a2f0: 6520 3200 4869 6464 656e 2044 6174 6100 e 2.Hidden Data.
```

Listing 9.33 An inode (19_d in **Ext4_V2.E01**) containing two attributes in the inode. The file acl field (highlighted) contains the value 0x84E. This is the block which contains further attributes.

The File ACL (four bytes at offset 0x68) provides the location of the block used for further storage of attributes which will no longer fit in the inode's free space. In Listing 9.33 this block number is 0x84E. Listing 9.34 shows the content of this block.

```
84e000: 0000 02ea 0100 0000 0100 0000 583f 583f ............X?X?
84e010: db69 0095 0000 0000 0000 0000 0000 0000 .i..............
84e020: 0201 f80f 0000 0000 0700 0000 3a5e 6561 ............:^ea
84e030: 5833 0000 0201 f00f 0000 0000 0700 0000 X3..............
84e040: 3d5e 6261 5834 0000 0000 0000 0000 0000 =^baX4..........
84e050: 0000 0000 0000 0000 0000 0000 0000 0000 ................
...[snip]...
84efe0: 0000 0000 0000 0000 0000 0000 0000 0000 ................
84eff0: 5661 6c75 6520 3400 5661 6c75 6520 3300 Value 4.Value 3.
```

Listing 9.34 Contents of an extended attribute block. The extended attribute block header is highlighted along with alternate attributes and their corresponding values.

The extended attribute block begins with an extended attribute block header. The structure of this, along with the values from Listing 9.34, is shown in Table 9.16. The remaining attributes are found after this.

Table 9.16 Extended attribute header block structure. The values are from Listing 9.34.

Offset	Size	Name	Description	Value
0x00	0x04	Magic	Magic value.	0xEA200000
0x04	0x04	Ref. Count	Reference count.	0x01 (1_d)
0x08	0x04	Num. Blocks	The number of blocks used.	0x01 (1_d)
0x0C	0x04	Hash	Hash value of all attributes.	0x3F583F58
0x10	0x04	Checksum	Checksum of the extended attribute block.	0x950069DB
0x14	0x0C	Reserved	Reserved.	

9.3.5 Ext4 Block Group Descriptors

All versions of the ext file system contain block group descriptor structures. These provide information on the structure of each block group. The block group descriptor structure is found in all block groups directly after the superblock (in blocks which contain a superblock) or at the beginning of the block group. Traditional block group descriptors (ext2 and ext3) contain a single 32_d-byte entry for each block group in the file system. Ext4 requires more information. In particular ext4 requires 64_d-bit addressing, meaning that ext4 block group descriptor entries require 64_d bytes of storage. Table 9.17 shows the structure of the ext block group descriptor structure.

The first 0x12 bytes in the ext4 block group descriptor structure are identical to those in earlier versions of ext. The extra information is added after this point. This includes some extra count information, checksums and the location of the snapshot exclusion block (which will exclude certain files/directories from backups/snapshots in ext4). The main change in the block group descriptor structure is that addresses are now 8_d bytes in size. This is achieved through a combination of the original four bytes (which become the least significant bytes) and the extra four bytes (which become the most significant bytes). The combination of these values provides the block address in question. The same process is used for counts and checksums in the block group descriptor entry.

9.3.6 Flexible Block Groups

The traditional block group structure in the ext file system leads to fragmentation, especially in the case of large files. Large files will occupy multiple block groups, meaning that both data and metadata are separated. Multiple non-contiguous reads are often required to access the contents of large files. This means that reading a large file can be a slow process and writing one even slower. Ext4 introduced flexible block groups in order to address this problem. In this, multiple block groups are chained together as one logical block group. In order to do this, the bitmaps (data and inode) and inode tables are gathered together in the first block group. The remaining block groups are used for data only. Consider a scenario in which flexible block groups are composed of two traditional block groups. The effect of this can be seen in Figure 9.3 in which Flexible Block Group (FBG) 0, contains Block Group (BG) 0 and 1's metadata structures.

This can be seen from the output of Sleuth Kit's **fsstat** command as seen in Listing 9.35. On the left is the output from an ext2 file system. This does not support flexible block groups. On the right the first two block groups in an ext4 file system using flexible block groups are shown. It is clear that in the ext4 file system the data bitmap, inode bitmap and inode table for group 1 are actually located in BG0.

Table 9.17 Ext4 block group descriptor entry structure.

Offset	Size	Name	Description
0x00	0x04	Block Bitmap (Lo)	Block bitmap address – least significant 32-bits.
0x04	0x04	Inode Bitmap (Lo)	Inode bitmap address – least sig. 32-bits.
0x08	0x04	Inode Table (Lo)	Inode table address – least sig. 32-bits.
0x0C	0x02	Free Blocks (Lo)	Free blocks – least sig. 16-bits.
0x0E	0x02	Free Inodes (Lo)	Free inodes – least significant 16-bits.
0x10	0x02	Used Directories (Lo)	Used directories – least sig. 16-bits.
0x12	0x02	Flags	See description.
0x14	0x04	Exclusion Bitmap (Lo)	Exclusion bitmap – least sig. 32-bits.
0x18	0x02	Block BM CSum (Lo)	Block bitmap checksum – least significant 16-bits.
0x1A	0x02	Inode BM CSum (Lo)	Inode bitmap checksum – least sig. 16-bits.
0x1C	0x02	Unused Inodes (Lo)	Unused inodes – least significant 16-bits.
0x1E	0x02	Checksum	Checksum value for the group descriptor
0x20	0x04	Block Bitmap (Hi)	Block bitmap address – most sig. 32-bits.
0x24	0x04	Inode Bitmap (Hi)	Inode bitmap address – most sig. 32-bits.
0x28	0x04	Inode Table (Hi)	Inode table address – most sig. 32-bits.
0x2C	0x02	Free Block Count (Hi)	Free blocks – most sig. 16-bits.
0x2E	0x02	Free Inode Count (Hi)	Free inodes – most sig. 16-bits.
0x30	0x02	Used Directories (Hi)	Used directories – most sig. 16-bits.
0x32	0x02	Unused Inode (Hi)	Unused inodes – most sig. 16-bits.
0x34	0x04	Exclusion Bitmap (Hi)	Exclusion bitmap – most sig. 32-bits.
0x38	0x02	Blk BM CSUM (Hi)	Block bitmap checksum – most sig. 16-bits.
0x3A	0x02	Inode BM CSUM (Hi)	Inode bitmap checksum – most sig. 16-bits.
0x3C	0x04	Reserved	Padding.

From a raw filesystem it is possible to determine if a device supports flexible block groups. The use of flexible block groups is determined in the incompatible features value in the superblock. For instance, consider the superblock in Listing 9.36. The ext4 superblock contains two highlighted areas. The first represents the incompatible features and has a value of: 0x82C2. Incompatible features are specified as a bitfield and as such converting to binary is the easiest way to show what features are included. This is shown in Figure 9.4 where the meaning of each set bit is defined. Bit 9 represents the flexible block group.

Once it is determined that flexible block groups are being used it is then necessary to determine the size. Examining the single highlighted byte at offset 0x174 shows a value of 0x04. Raising 2 to the power of this value provides the number of block groups in each flexible block group. In this case $2^4 = 16$. So there are 16_d block groups in each flexible block group. This can be confirmed using **fsstat**. Processing the block group descriptors can proceed as normal. The relevant structures for later block groups in the flexible block group will appear in the first block group found in the flexible block group.

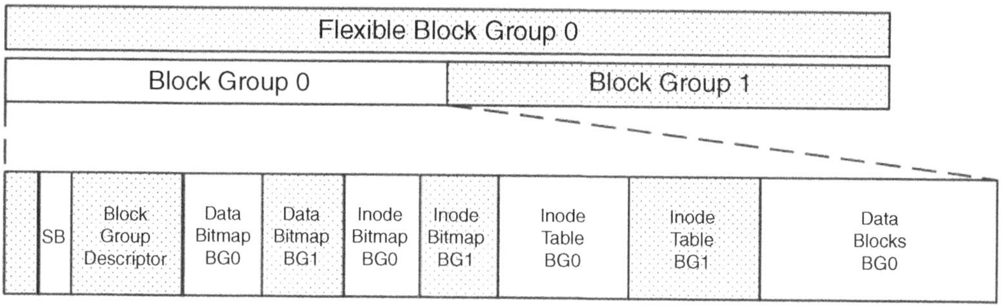

Figure 9.3 Flexible block group structure.

```
Group: 0:
  Inode Range: 1 - 32768
  Block Range: 0 - 32767
  Layout:
    Super Block: 0 - 0
    Group Descriptor Table: 1 - 1
    Data bitmap: 17 - 17
    Inode bitmap: 18 - 18
    Inode Table: 19 - 1042
    Data Blocks: 1043 - 32767
  Free Inodes: 32755 (99%)
  Free Blocks: 31664 (96%)
  Total Directories: 2

Group: 1:
  Inode Range: 32769 - 65536
  Block Range: 32768 - 65535
  Layout:
    Super Block: 32768 - 32768
    Group Descriptor Table: 32769...
    Data bitmap: 32785 - 32785
    Inode bitmap: 32786 - 32786
    Inode Table: 32787 - 33810
    Data Blocks: 33811 - 65535
  Free Inodes: 32765 (99%)
  Free Blocks: 31690 (96%)
  Total Directories: 1
```

```
Group: 0:
  Block Group Flags: [INODE_ZEROED]
  Inode Range: 1 - 8192
  Block Range: 0 - 32767
  Layout:
    Super Block: 0 - 0
    Group Descriptor Table: 1 - 1
    Group Descriptor Growth: 2 - 64
    Data bitmap: 65 - 65
    Inode bitmap: 69 - 69
    Inode Table: 73 - 584
    Uninit Data Bitmaps: 69 - 80
    Uninit Inode Bitmaps: 73 - 84
    Uninit Inode Table: 2121 - 8264
    Data Blocks: 8289 - 32767
  Free Inodes: 8176 (99%)
  Free Blocks: 30642 (93%)
  Total Directories: 3
  Stored Checksum: 0x3044

Group: 1:
  Block Group Flags: [INODE_UNINIT..
  Inode Range: 8193 - 16384
  Block Range: 32768 - 65535
  Layout:
    Super Block: 32768 - 32768
    Group Descriptor Table: 32769...
    Group Descriptor Growth: 32770..
    Data bitmap: 66 - 66
    Inode bitmap: 70 - 70
    Inode Table: 585 - 1096
    Data Blocks: 32833 - 65535
  Free Inodes: 8192 (100%)
  Free Blocks: 32456 (99%)
  Total Directories: 0
  Stored Checksum: 0xA5E8
```

Listing 9.35 Comparison of traditional block groups in ext2 (left) and flexible block groups in ext4. Note in ext4 that the data bitmap, inode bitmap and inode table for BG1 are actually located in BG0.

```
000400: 0080 0000 0000 0200 9919 0000 39e6 0100 ............9...
000410: f07f 0000 0000 0000 0200 0000 0200 0000 ................
000420: 0080 0000 0080 0000 0020 0000 4a29 7065 ..........J)pe
000430: dd31 7065 0300 ffff 53ef 0100 0100 0000 .1pe....S.......
000440: 7b27 7065 0000 0000 0000 0000 0100 0000 {'pe............
000450: 0000 0000 0b00 0000 0001 0000 3c00 0000 ............<...
000460: c282 0000 6b04 0000 9709 4d23 16ea 477d ....k.....M#..G}
000470: 8df6 0838 abc1 3622 4578 7434 2d46 5300 ...8..6"Ext4-FS.
000480: 0000 0000 0000 0000 2f6d 6564 6961 2f73 ......../media/s
...[snip]...
000560: 0100 0000 0000 0000 0000 0000 0000 0000 ................
000570: 0000 0000 0401 0000 2126 0000 0000 0000 ........!&......
000580: 0000 0000 0000 0000 0000 0000 0000 0000 ................
```

Listing 9.36 Excerpt from an ext4 superblock showing the incompatible features which indicates that flexible block groups are being used.

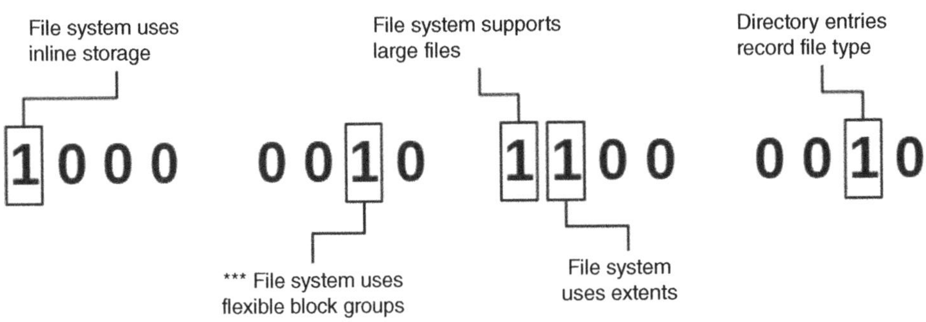

Figure 9.4 Incompatible features value 0x82C2 from Listing 9.36 showing the meaning of each individual bit field value.

9.4 Summary

While the ext2 file system was an excellent file system in its day, by the late 1990s it had begun to show its age. The development of ext3 led to many performance improvements some of which affected the digital forensic process. The traditional ext2 directory indexing structure, which merely used a linear array of directory entries, was unable to scale to large numbers of files. Hence, ext3 included HTree-based directory indexing which resulted in much faster access to files and consequently the ability to efficiently store large numbers of files in a single directory. The forensic implications of this were that the HTree structure is processed in a different manner to that of the linear array.

When compared to other file systems of the time, such as NTFS, ext2 suffered a lack of resilience. This was partially due to the absence of a journal structure to record changes to the file system prior to write operations. The journal structure was implemented in ext3, resulting in a circular journal system which (by default) provides historic metadata. Due to the nature of deletion in ext filesystems, whereby the block pointers are overwritten on deletion, the ability to locate older versions of inode structures allows for the potential recovery of deleted files.

Even with the developments introduced in ext3 this file system was still not sufficient for modern usage. Hence the file system was further developed to allow for modern forms of storage. This included inline data for small files (and symbolic links which are a minor alteration of this concept) and also the use of extents. This improved file system efficiency in terms of storage of both small and large files. This change means that forensic analysts require more knowledge of file storage and also file recovery techniques based on the four possible storage mechanisms (block pointers, inline data, extents and symbolic links) encountered in the ext file system family.

The use of block groups in the ext file system resulted in a number of mini file systems. This meant that some files could be recovered even in the event of the inode table being destroyed (it was generally only a single part (i.e. one block group) that was actually damaged). However, for larger files it led to more fragmentation. Ext4 addressed this through the use of flexible block groups. In this scenario the metadata information for multiple block groups is found in one single block group in the flexible block group.

One of the long-known limitations of the ext family of file systems was the Y2038 problem, in which signed 32_d-bit Unix time would expire in the year 2038. This has been improved in ext4 in which the basic 32_d timestamp value is now an unsigned value, and two extra bits from the extra time fields are used to create an unsigned 34_d bit timestamp value. This will not expire until the year 2514! While fixed for ext users, there is a potential problem in the forensic community in general, which is what the tools are actually interpreting! The version of Sleuth Kit used in Listing 9.16 was released in January 2022, more than ten years since the release of ext4 and still shows an incorrect timestamp. This shows how vital it is that tools are tested and that their limits are evaluated and understood.

While ext is not considered a 'standard' file system for the desktop computing world (as Linux is not the most popular of operating systems) it is commonly encountered in the server-level infrastructure. Many servers in the world use some form of Linux (and therefor ext) by default. Also when including the area of mobile phone forensics, it is conceivable that ext is one of the most common file systems in existence as it is now standard on Android devices! Hence knowledge of the functioning of the ext file system is of vital importance to all digital forensic analysts.

Exercises

1 Create an ext4 file system (which supports inline-data) and add some content to this file system. The content should include a directory containing many files (so that HTree indexing will be used), a large file (to demonstrate extents), a small file (to demonstrate inline storage) and a symbolic link. Create an image of this device, then delete all files (and the directory) and create a new image. Using these two images verify the following claims:
   a) The content of files that use inline storage can be recovered after file deletion.
   b) Symbolic link targets (i.e. the filename) are overwritten during deletion.
   c) Extent-tree blocks can be recovered, but the extents in these blocks contain insufficient information to recover the file's content.
   d) HTree directory structures are recoverable.

2 Listing 9.37 shows an ext4 inode. In relation to this inode answer the following questions:
   a) What is the creation time of this inode? Your answer should include the nanosecond component.
   b) How is this inode stored (extents or inline)?
   c) What is the content of this file?

```
00: a481 0000 0d00 0000 7eba c262 7eba c262
10: 7eba c262 0000 0000 0000 0100 0000 0000
20: 0000 0010 0100 0000 496e 6c69 6e65 2044
30: 6174 6121 0a00 0000 0000 0000 0000 0000
40: 0000 0000 0000 0000 0000 0000 0000 0000
50: 0000 0000 0000 0000 0000 0000 0000 0000
60: 0000 0000 4763 700f 0000 0000 0000 0000
70: 0000 0000 0000 0000 0000 0000 3963 0000
80: 2000 49ab 6456 5665 6456 5665 6456 5665
90: 7eba c262 6456 5665 0000 0000 0000 0000
a0: 0000 02ea 0407 0000 0000 0000 0000 0000
b0: 0000 0000 6461 7461 0000 0000 0000 0000
```

Listing 9.37 Ext4 inode.

3 Listing 9.38 shows an inode from an ext4 file system which uses extent-based storage. Process this inode and answer the following questions:

```
00: f881 e803 0070 3b00 cea5 c262 cea5 c262
10: cea5 c262 0000 0000 e803 0100 b81d 0000
20: 0000 0800 0100 0000 0af3 0100 0400 0000
30: 0000 0000 0000 0000 b703 0000 7722 3900
40: 0000 0000 0000 0000 0000 0000 0000 0000
50: 0000 0000 0000 0000 0000 0000 0000 0000
60: 0000 0000 9938 92d1 0000 0000 0000 0000
70: 0000 0000 0000 0000 0000 0000 38cf 0000
80: 2000 c937 fc3c 55de fc3c 55de 7ca9 9bd8
90: cea5 c262 7ca9 9bd8 0000 0000 0000 0000
```

Listing 9.38 Ext4 inode using extent-based storage.

a) Process the mode and determine the file type and file permissions.
b) How is it determined that this file uses extent-based storage?
c) What is the file size in bytes?
d) How many extents are present in this inode?
e) Determine the starting block and number of blocks in the first extent in this inode.

Bibliography

Carrier, B. (2005). *File System Forensic Analysis*. Boston, MA; London: Addison-Wesley.

Fairbanks, K.D. (2012). An analysis of Ext4 for digital forensics. *Digital Investigation* 1 (9): S118–S130.

Göbel, T. and Baier, H. (2018). Anti-forensics in Ext4: on secrecy and usability of timestamp-based data hiding. *Digital Investigation* 24: S111–S120.

Hrishikesh, C.Z. (2017). Addition of Ext4 Extent and Ext3 HTree DIR Read-Only Support in NetBSD [Internet]. [cited 2024 March 26]. https://www.netbsd.org/gallery/presentations/hrishikesh/2017_AsiaBSDCon/abc2017ext4_final_paper.pdf (accessed 14 August 2024).

Mathur, A., Cao, M., Bhattacharya, S. et al. (2007). The new Ext4 filesystem: current status and future plans. Proceedings of the Linux Symposium (27 Jun 2007), Volume 2, pp. 21–33.

Mingming, C. (2005). Features found in Linux 2.6 [Internet]. [cited 2024 March 26]. http://ext2.sourceforge.net/2005-ols/paper-html/node2.html (accessed 14 August 2024).

Nordvik, R. (2022). Ext4. In: *Mobile Forensics — The File Format Handbook: Common File Formats and File Systems Used in Mobile Devices*, 41–68. Cham: Springer International Publishing.

Polstra, P. (2015). *Linux Forensics: With Python and Shell Scripting*. Createspace Independent Publishing Platform.

Pomeranz, H. (2024). Understanding Ext4 (Parts 1 - 6) [Internet]. [cited 2024 March 26]. https://www.sans.org/blog/understanding-ext4-part-1-extents/ (accessed 14 August 2024).

SANS Digital Forensics and Incident Response (2017). EXT File System Recovery - SANS Digital Forensics and Incident Response Summit 2017 [Internet]. YouTube [cited 2024 March 26]. https://www.youtube.com/watch?v=6pzm6909IvY (accessed 14 August 2024).

The Linux Kernel (2013). ext4 Data Structures and Algorithms — The Linux Kernel documentation [Internet]. www.kernel.org. https://www.kernel.org/doc/html/latest/filesystems/ext4/index.html (accessed 14 August 2024).

Tweedie, S.C. (1998). Journaling the Linux Ext2Fs filesystem. In The Fourth Annual Linux Expo 1998 May 28.

Wong, D.J. (2013). Disk Layout - Ext4 [Internet]. https://djwong.org/docs/ext4_disk_layout.pdf (accessed 18 December 2024).

10

The XFS File System

The XFS file system was created by Silicon Graphics in the mid-1990s for their IRIX OS. In 2001 it was ported to Linux and became available on most Linux distributions soon after this. XFS is a 64-bit journaling file system.[1] Red Hat Enterprise Linux (RHEL) uses XFS as its default file system since version 7 (approximately 2014).

As with many modern file systems, XFS is based on B+Tree structures. It uses extents to determine where file content is stored. The combination of these allows for efficient processing of files, especially larger files. It can support file systems up to 8 EiB in size and can support files up to the same size. Theoretically an XFS file system can have up to 2^{64} files. XFS is a journaling file system in which metadata is routinely journaled. XFS also uses delayed writing to help ensure consistency of information on-disk.

XFS uses the concept of allocation groups (AG). These are similar to block groups in ext, but generally larger in size. Each allocation group acts as its own file system, managing its own inodes and data blocks. However, files can span multiple allocation groups. This use of allocation groups allows for greater parallelism in XFS when compared to other file systems, thereby exploiting modern multi-core/processor systems. The use of allocation groups also allows for striped allocation, creating a form of file system RAID.

Similar to NTFS, XFS allows for 'alternate data streams' allowing name/value pairs to be stored in addition to the file content. In XFS these structures are called extended attributes.

Unlike the other file systems discussed in this book, and indeed most file systems in common usage, XFS stores data in a big-endian fashion. This generally means that the interpretation of raw data in the XFS file system is a little easier than it is in other file systems as there is no need to convert from little to big-endian during analysis.

Like many modern file systems journaling is enabled by default in XFS. XFS provides journaling of metadata structures. Write operations are first written to the journal structure before being written to the actual disk itself. This reduces the risk of catastrophic failure in cases where power is lost during a critical update.

The XFS journal is a circular buffer of disk blocks. The location and size of the journal is determined from the superblock structure. By default the XFS journal is stored in the data section of the file system, although it can be implemented on a separate device. In the case of implementation on a separate device, the redundancy level is higher. XFS will automatically rebuild the file system from the journal in the event of a crash.

XFS uses extent-based data allocation. File contents are referenced by extent structures which provide a concise method of referencing large chunks of data. A single extent describes one or more

1 The current version of XFS is often referred to as Version 5. This is the version that is analysed in this chapter.

File System Forensics, First Edition. Fergus Toolan.

contiguous blocks of data. In comparison to ext's block pointer method, the extent-based allocation requires much less space to describe the location of large files on disk.

The free space B+Trees are used to manage space allocation on the XFS file system. They allow space to be located for the allocation of new files. One of the free space B+Trees is indexed based on the length of the contiguous blocks that are free, while the other is indexed based on the starting block of the free space. This method allows fragments of fragmented files to be stored in close proximity to other extents. Additionally, it also allows the file system to store a file in an area which has enough contiguous free blocks to minimise the amount of fragmentation that is required.

In a manner similar to that of NTFS, XFS allows the use of extended attributes. In this, the user (or the system) can define name/value pairs associated with an inode. Names are printable character strings of up to 256_d bytes in length. These names are null-terminated. The values can contain up to 64 kB of binary data. Caution must be taken when examining a file system that contains extended attributes as it may not be possible to store these extended attributes when a file is recovered. For instance, these extended attributes cannot be stored on the ext2 file system. Extended attributes mean that the investigator must be cautious to ensure that all data in the file system is correctly recovered.

10.1 On-Disk Structures

There are a number of concepts and on-disk structures which are of vital importance if wishing to conduct forensic analysis of XFS file systems. This section describes some of the key on-disk structures/concepts including:

- **Allocation Groups:** In a manner similar to ext, XFS uses mini-file systems known as allocation groups, each of which manages its own storage (both data storage and inodes).
- **B+Trees:** Like most modern file systems the main metadata storage structure is based on B+Trees.
- **Superblock:** Similar to the superblock structure in ext (and the volume boot record structures in most Windows-based file systems) this structure contains information about the file system as a whole.
- **Signatures:** Each XFS structure has a unique signature making them easy both to locate and to identify. Corrupt file systems can still be analysed by searching for these signature values in order to locate particular structures in the XFS file system.
- **Time:** The time structure used in XFS is that of Unix Time with a four-byte nanosecond component.
- **Addressing:** XFS provides two different addressing schemes (absolute and relative). Knowledge of these is required when wishing to access particular structures in the file system.

10.1.1 Allocation Groups

The key to the XFS file system is the use of allocation groups (AG). These can be thought of as mini-file systems that can be up to 1 TiB in size (regardless of underlying disk dimensions). Each AG maintains a copy of the superblock and is responsible for managing its own inodes and free space. Each AG is truly independent of others (unless a file spans multiple AGs) and as such each AG is able to operate in parallel, thereby greatly increasing access efficiency in modern computing systems. Figure 10.1 shows the AG structure.

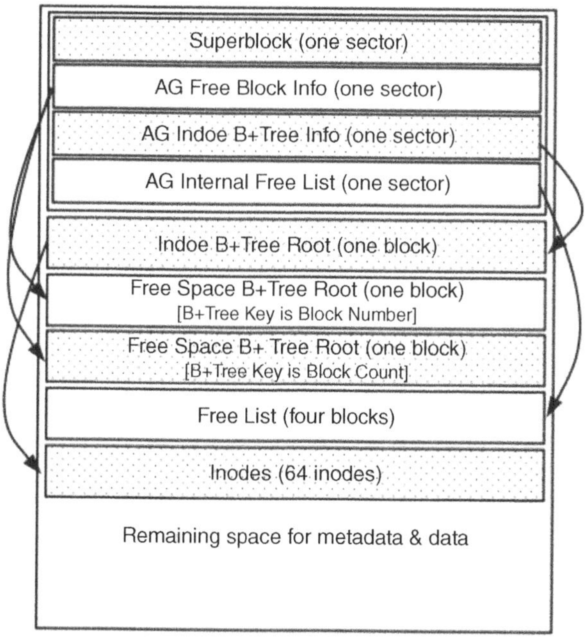

Figure 10.1 Allocation group structure.

The structures in the AG include:

- **Superblock:** The superblock contains information about the file system itself. The purpose of this structure in XFS is identical to that of the superblock in ext (and also the volume boot records in NTFS/FAT). For instance the XFS superblock will provide the size of allocation groups, inodes, blocks, sectors, etc. It can also contain information about the file system UUID and name. Like all file systems, the superblock is generally the first structure analysed when performing file system forensics on XFS. The superblock structure is shown in Section 10.1.4.
- **Free Block Info:** This provides information about the free space B+Trees. These trees are indexed either by block number (in order to find free space near to a particular point) or by block count (in order to find a particular amount of contiguous free blocks to minimise fragmentation). This structure also provides information about the overall free space in the AG. The structure of this sector is shown in Section 10.3.1.
- **Inode B+Tree Info:** Information about the inode B+Tree location and statistics.
- **Internal Free List:** Information about the free list blocks – these blocks are maintained for growth of the various AG B+Trees if required.
- **Inode B+Tree:** B+Trees that contain the inode allocation in the AG.
- **Free Space B+Tree:** Two B+Trees which maintain a list of free blocks in the AG. One is indexed by the block number at the start of the free space, and the other is indexed by the length of the free space.
- **Free List:** These blocks are kept free for growth of the Inode B+Tree.
- **Inodes:** Inodes are metadata structures which provide information about the file and also the location of the file's content.
- **Directory Entries:** As in ext, directory entries are found in directories and provide the link between the filename and inode number.

10.1.2 Addressing

As stated previously XFS is a 64-bit file system, and as such, generally uses 64-bit addressing. However, XFS has two forms of addressing: absolute and relative. As expected an absolute address is 64_d bits in length and addresses the exact block on disk. A relative address on the other hand is 32_d bits in size and provides an address of a block relative to the current AG.

The actual size of addresses depends on file system size. Absolute addresses are divided into two parts: (1) The allocation group; and (2) the block address inside that AG. As an example assume the journal address is 0x0000000000008005. This is an absolute address (eight bytes) which contains two parts, the AG part and the block address part. The sizes of these parts are dependent on file system size. In order to discover these it is necessary to find the $log_2(agSize)$ value in the superblock, which is located in a single byte at offset 0x7C. This is the number of bits that form the block address. In the case of a value 0x0E or 14_d for $log_2(agSize)$, the 14_d least significant bits provide the block address while the remaining bits form the AG address as seen in Figure 10.2.

In this case the hex address value, 0x8005 or $1000\ 0000\ 0000\ 0101_b$. The 14 least significant bits are: $00\ 0000\ 0000\ 0101_b$ which is 5_d. The remaining most significant bits are: 10_b which is 2_d. Hence the journal is located in AG 2 at block 5. But where is this in the file system? In order to calculate this the number of blocks in each AG and the size of each block is required. These values are also located in the superblock. Assuming these values are 0x4000 and 0x1000, respectively, the absolute byte offset to the Journal is given by $(0x4000 \times 2 + 5) \times 0x1000$.

10.1.2.1 Inode Addressing

Inode addressing is slightly more complex than block addressing as there are generally multiple inodes in each block. As with block addresses there are two types of inode address: absolute and relative. Absolute addresses are eight bytes in length and provide the AG and the position inside the AG. Relative addresses are four bytes and provide the position relative to the start of the current AG.

To determine the location of an inode from its XFS inode address the values of $log_2(agSize)$ and $log_2(inodesPerBlock)$ are required from the Superblock. Consider the inode address 0x00000060. Based on the length of this address it is a relative address. Assuming that block size is 0x1000 (4096_d), $log_2(agSize)$ is 0x10 (16_d) and that $log_2(inodesPerBlock)$ is 0x03 (3_d), the 0x03 least significant bits represent the inode offset in the block, the next 0x10 (16_d) bits represent the block location in the AG and the remaining most significant bits represent the AG itself. This structure is shown in Figure 10.3.

In the case of inode 0x80021 (Figure 10.3) it is found to be in AG 1, block 4, offset one. The three least significant bits provide the inode offset in the block (1_d), while the next 16_d bits provide the block's offset ($0b100 = 4_d$). The remaining most significant bits show that the inode is found in AG 1. The actual byte offset to this is shown in Equation 10.1.

$$((AG_{\#} \times AG_{Size} + block_{Offset}) \times block_{Size}) + (Inode_{Offset} \times Inode_{Size}) \tag{10.1}$$

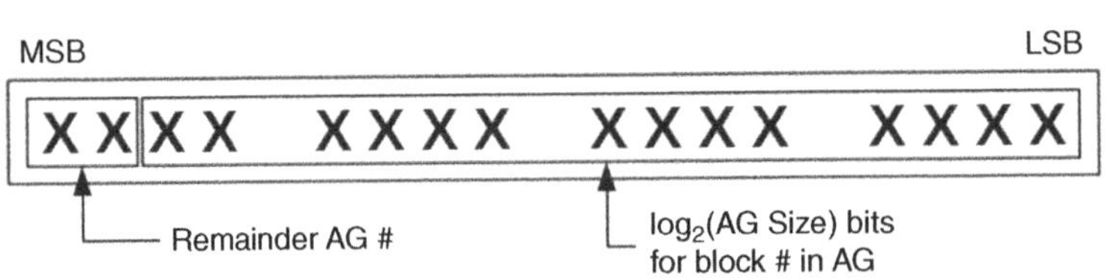

Figure 10.2 Absolute address structure in XFS where $log2(agSize)$ is 14_d.

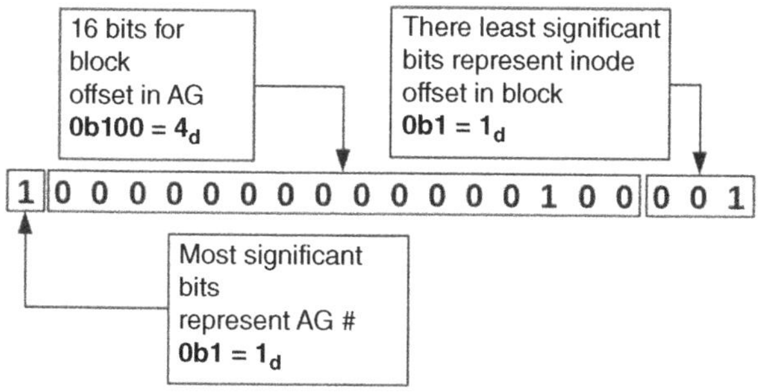

Figure 10.3 Absolute inode address structure in XFS where $log_2(AGSize)$ is 16_d and $log_2(inodes/block)$ is 3_d.

Given values of 512_d bytes for inode size, and $4,096_d$ bytes for block size, the above calculation results in a byte offset of $268,452,352_d$. Extracting 512_d bytes at offset $268,452,352_d$ in the file system should result in the inode content itself.

10.1.3 XFS B+ Trees

XFS, like many modern file systems, uses B+Trees for fast, efficient access. Due to the different forms of addressing (absolute and relative) there are two forms of B+Tree in XFS. The first is the short form B+Tree which is used inside a specific group in which addresses are four bytes in length. The second is the long form B+Tree in which addresses are eight bytes in length and cover absolute addressing.

Each block in a B+Tree (regardless of whether it is a short- or long-form tree) is either a leaf node or an internal node. Leaf nodes contain actual records, while internal nodes contain keys and pointers to other blocks in the B+Tree. Both of these types have the same abstract format of a header followed by an array of records.

The short form B+Tree references information contained in the current AG. Its header structure is defined in Table 10.1. The header for long form B+Tree nodes is very similar to that found in short

Table 10.1 Structure of the XFS short form B+Tree.

Offset	Size	Name	Description
0x00	0x04	Signature	Signature values identifying this particular tree.
0x04	0x02	Level	Level of this block in the tree. 0x00 represents a leaf node which contains records. Other values represent internal nodes containing pointers to other nodes.
0x06	0x02	# Records	The number of records in this node.
0x08	0x04	Left Sibling	AG (relative) block number of the left sibling node.
0x0C	0x04	Right Sibling	AG (relative) block number of the right sibling node.
			Version 5
0x10	0x08	Block #	The absolute block number of the block containing this node.
0x18	0x08	LSN	The log sequence number of the last write to this block.
0x20	0x10	UUID	UUID of this file system (should match superblock).
0x30	0x04	Owner	The AG number of the AG containing this tree block.
0x34	0x04	CRC	Block Checksum.

Table 10.2 Structure of the XFS long form B+Tree.

Offset	Size	Name	Description
0x00	0x04	Signature	Signature values identifying this particular tree.
0x04	0x02	Level	Level of this block in the tree. 0x00 represents a leaf node which contains records. Other values represent internal nodes containing pointers to other nodes.
0x06	0x02	# Records	The number of records in this node.
0x08	0x08	Left Sibling	AG (absolute) block number of the left sibling node.
0x10	0x08	Right Sibling	AG (absolute) block number of the right sibling node.
			Version 5
0x18	0x08	Block #	The absolute block number of the block containing this node.
0x20	0x08	LSN	The log sequence number of the last write to this block.
0x28	0x10	UUID	UUID of this file system (should match superblock).
0x38	0x04	Owner	The AG number of the AG containing this tree block.
0x3C	0x04	CRC	Block Checksum.
0x40	0x04	Padding	Padding.

form nodes. The key difference is that addressing is 64_d bits rather than 32_d bits as these represent absolute addressing. The structure is given in Table 10.2.

10.1.4 The Superblock

As with many other file systems XFS contains a superblock which describes the overall structure of the file system. In XFS, every AG contains a superblock. Generally, only the primary superblock is used (unless a file system is corrupt and needs to be rebuilt). The primary superblock is found in the first sector in AG0. Currently the superblock is 272_d bytes in size. Table 10.3 provides the basic structure of the XFS superblock while Table 10.4 provides extra structure information specific to version 5 file systems.

10.1.4.1 Locating Superblocks

As stated earlier the first superblock will appear at sector 0 – it is the first sector in the first allocation group. Each allocation group maintains a copy of the superblock (which occurs in the first sector in each allocation group). The number of allocation groups and the number of blocks in each allocation group can be determined from Table 10.3. Consider an XFS file system in which there are four allocation groups, each with $32,768_d$ blocks per group, and a block size of 4096_d bytes. In this scenario four superblocks would be expected, one at the start of each allocation group.This means that every $32,768 \times 4096 = 134,217,728_d$ bytes a superblock is found. Table 10.5 shows the expected locations of superblock copies in this file system.

This method relies on the primary superblock (sector 0) being present and uncorrupted. But what if this is not the case? All XFS structures contain signatures, and the superblock is no exception.

Table 10.3 XFS superblock structure.

Offset	Size	Name	Description
0x00	0x04	Signature	The magic signature for an XFS superblock (ASCII: XFSB).
0x04	0x04	Block Size	The size of each block in bytes.
0x08	0x08	# Blocks	The total number of blocks in the file system.
0x10	0x08	# Blocks in RT Dev.	The total number of blocks in the real-time device.
0x18	0x08	# Extents in RT Dev.	The number of extents in the real-time device.
0x20	0x10	UUID	The UUID for this file system.
0x30	0x08	Journal Block	The first block of the XFS journal.
0x38	0x08	Root Dir Inode	The inode # for the root directory.
0x40	0x08	RT Extents Bitmap Inode	The inode number for the real-time extents bitmap.
0x48	0x08	RT Bitmap Summary	The inode number for the real-time summary.
0x50	0x04	RT Extent Size	The size of the real-time extent structure in blocks.
0x54	0x04	AG Size	The size of each AG in blocks.
0x58	0x04	# AGs	The number of AGs in the file system.
0x5C	0x04	# RT Bitmap Blocks	The number of blocks in the real-time bitmap.
0x60	0x04	# Journal Blocks	The number of blocks in the journal.
0x64	0x02	FS Version/Flags	The file system version is contained in the low nibble (and is generally 5 in modern systems). The remainder contains the file system flags.
0x66	0x02	Sector Size	The sector size in bytes.
0x68	0x02	Inode Size	The size of each inode record in bytes.
0x6A	0x02	Inodes/Block	The number of inodes per block.
0x6C	0x0C	FS Name	The file system name.
0x78	0x01	$log_2(blockSize)$	Log to base 2 of the block size.
0x79	0x01	$log_2(sectorSize)$	Log to base 2 of the sector size.
0x7A	0x01	$log_2(inodeSize)$	Log to base 2 of the inode size.
0x7B	0x01	$log_2(inodeBlk)$	Log to base 2 of the inodes per block value.
0x7C	0x01	$log_2(agSize)$	Log to base 2 of the AG size – rounded up if necessary.
0x7D	0x01	$log_2(rtExtents)$	Log to base 2 of the RT extent size.
0x7E	0x01	Being Created	Set if the file system is currently being created.
0x7F	0x01	Max. Inode %	The maximum percentage of the file system that can be used for inodes.
0x80	0x08	# Allocated Inodes	The number of allocated inodes.
0x88	0x08	# Free Inodes	The number of free inodes.
0x90	0x08	# Free Blocks	The number of free blocks.
0x98	0x08	# Free RT Extents	The number of free RT extents.
0xA0	0x08	User Quota Inode	User quota information is referenced by this inode.
0xA8	0x08	Group Quota Inode	Group quota information is referenced by this inode.
0xB0	0x02	Quota Flags	Flags related to user/group quotas.
0xB2	0x01	Misc. Flags	Miscellaneous Flags.
0xB3	0x01	Reserved	Zero.

Table 10.3 (Continued)

Offset	Size	Name	Description
0xB4	0x04	Inode Alignment	The inode chunk alignment in blocks.
0xB8	0x04	RAID Unit	The block size of the underlying RAID unit.
0xBC	0x04	RAID Stripes	The block size of the underlying RAID stripes.
0xC0	0x01	$log_2(dirBlkAlloc)$	Log to base 2 of the directory block allocation.
0xC1	0x01	$log_2(jrnlSecSize)$	Log to base 2 of the sector size for the journaling device.
0xC2	0x02	Sect. Size Ext Journal	The sector size of the external journaling device.
0xC4	0x04	Stripe Size Ext Journal	The stripe size of the external journaling device.
0xC8	0x04	Additional Flags	Extra file system features.
0xCC	0x04	Repeated Flags	Repeated flags for alignment.

Table 10.4 XFS extended superblock structure (version 5).

Offset	Size	Name	Description
0xD0	0x04	RW Features	Read-write flags.
0xD4	0x04	RO Features	Read-only flags.
0xD8	0x04	RW Incompat	Read-write incompatibility flags.
0xDC	0x04	RW Incompat Log	Read-write incompatibility flags for log.
0xE0	0x04	Checksum	CRC32 checksum for the superblock.
0xE4	0x04	Sparse Inode Align	Sparse inode alignment.
0xE8	0x08	Project Quota Inode	Project quota inode.
0xF0	0x08	LSN	Log sequence number of last superblock update.
0xF8	0x10	UUID	UUID if incompat_meta_uuid is set.
0x108	0x08	RM B-Tree Inode	Root for the Real-Time Reverse Mapping B-Tree.

Table 10.5 Expected superblock locations in an XFS file system with a block size of 4096_d bytes, 4_d allocation groups and $32,768_d$ blocks per allocation group.

Allocation Group	Expected SB Offset (bytes)
0	0_d
1	$134,217,728_d$
2	$268,435,456_d$
3	$402,653,184_d$

The superblock signature is XFSB. Listing 10.1 shows an XFS image being searched for this signature using the **strings/grep** commands. The **-td** option to strings provides the byte offset in the file at which the match is found.

This method may on occasion provide some false positives. For instance if there was a document in the file system describing XFS signatures, it might contain the text XFSB. However, these can easily be eliminated as they will not fit the pattern of the other elements. For instance in Listing 10.1 the value repeats every $134,217,728_d$ bytes. Any hit that does not follow this pattern is most likely a false positive.

```
$ strings -td mnt/ewf1 | grep XFSB
        0 XFSB
134217728 XFSB
268435456 XFSB
268466264 XFSB
268475480 XFSB
402653184 XFSB
```

Listing 10.1 Using **strings** to search for XFS superblock signatures.

10.1.5 XFS Signatures

The majority of structures in XFS begin with a 'magic number' generally an ASCII string which quickly tells us the structure type. As these signatures are provided in ASCII (generally) they provide an easy way to quickly locate particular structures using **strings -td** as seen when locating superblocks in the previous section. Some of the relevant signatures are provided in Table 10.6.[2]

10.1.6 XFS Inodes

As in ext the inode is the structure that contains all the file metadata and also contains the location of the data content. Figure 10.4 shows the generic inode structure. There are three main parts to the inode. The inode core contains the main metadata information. This structure is 176_d bytes in size and is found at the very beginning of the inode. It is followed by the data fork, which provides the location of the data and finally contains an optional attribute fork. Table 10.7 provides the structure of the inode core.

There are three versions of the XFS inode structure. Generally in modern XFS file systems (i.e. version 5) only version 3 inodes are encountered. Versions 1 and 2 are now considered obsolete.

Table 10.6 A selection of signature values used in the XFS file system.

Structure	Magic Number	ASCII
Superblock	0x5846 5342	XFSB
AG Free Block Info	0x5841 4746	XAGF
Inode B+Tree Info	0x5841 4749	XAGI
AG Internal Free List	0x5841 464C	XAFL
Log Records (Journal)	0xFEED BABE	
Inodes	0x494E	IN
Symbolic Links	0x5853 4C4D	XSLM
Free Space By Block Tree	0x4142 5442	ABTB
Free Space By Block Tree (v5)	0x4142 3342	AB3B

2 For a complete list of signatures the reader is advised to consult XFS Algorithms and Data Structures (Chapter 7).

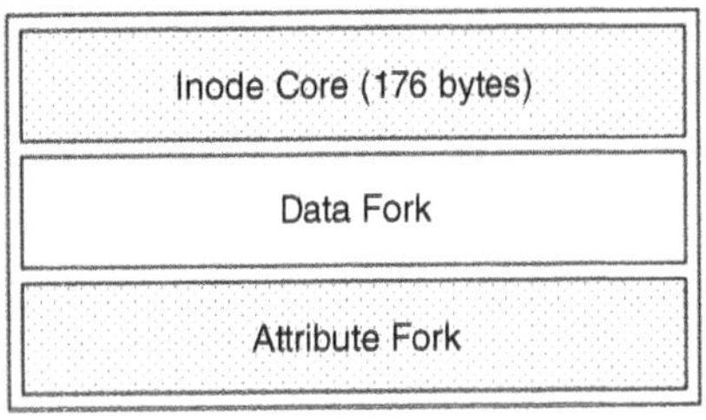

Figure 10.4 XFS inode structure.

Table 10.7 XFS inode core structure.

Offset	Size	Name	Description
0x00	0x02	Signature	XFS inode signature (ASCII: IN).
0x02	0x02	Mode	File type and permissions. Similar to ext, the most significant nibble provides the type while the remainder provides the permissions.
0x04	0x01	Version	Inode version (1, 2 or 3). XFS version 5 file systems will always have version 3 inodes.
0x05	0x01	Format	Identifies how information is stored in the data fork. Known values include: 1 – Resident data (i.e. the content is present in the inode); 2 – Extent array; There are other values but their meaning is unclear.
0x06	0x02	# Links (old)	Unused in version 3 inodes.
0x08	0x04	UID	User ID of the inode owner.
0x0C	0x04	GID	Group ID of the inode group.
0x10	0x04	# Links	Number of links to this file.
0x14	0x04	Project ID	Files may be grouped by project ID in XFS allowing quotas to be set for a particular project.
0x18	0x06	Padding	Padding bytes.
0x1E	0x02	Flushiter	Flush counter.
0x20	0x04	atime	Last access time.
0x24	0x04	atime (ns)	Nanosecond component of atime.
0x28	0x04	mtime	Last content modification time.
0x2C	0x04	mtime (ns)	Nanosecond component of mtime.
0x30	0x04	ctime	Last metadata change time.
0x34	0x04	ctime (ns)	Nanosecond component of ctime.
0x38	0x08	File Size	For regular files this is the file size, for directories it is the size of the directory entries, and for symbolic links it is the length of the link.
0x40	0x08	# Blocks	The number of blocks used to store the inode's data excluding extended attributes.
0x48	0x04	Extent Size	Extent size hint.
0x4C	0x04	# Extents	The number of extents associated with this file.
0x50	0x02	# ExtAttr Extents	The number of extents associated with the extended attributes.

Table 10.7 (Continued)

Offset	Size	Name	Description
0x52	0x01	Fork Offset	Offset in the inode at which the extended attribute fork begins. This number must be multiplied by 8_d to get the actual byte offset.
0x53	0x01	Attr. Format	Storage format of the attribute fork. This uses the same values as the data fork format.
0x54	0x04	DMAPI Event Mask	Related to the Data Management API.
0x58	0x02	DMAPI State	Related to the Data Management API.
0x5A	0x02	Flags	Flags.
0x5C	0x04	Generation	Generation ID.
0x60	0x04	Next Unlinked	Tracking of deleted attributes that are still in use by a program.
0x64	0x04	CRC	Inode checksum.
0x68	0x08	Change Count	Number of changes to the attributes in this inode.
0x70	0x08	LSN	Log sequence number of the last write to this file.
0x78	0x08	Flags2	Further inode flags.
0x80	0x04	COW Extent Size	Copy-on-Write extent size.
0x84	0x0C	Padding	Padding.
0x90	0x04	btime	Birth (Creation) time.
0x94	0x04	btime (ns)	Nanosecond component of btime.
0x98	0x08	Inode #	Absolute inode number for this inode.
0xA0	0x10	UUID	File system UUID.

10.1.7 Directories

Directories in XFS are composed of a directory header followed by a series of directory entries. The directory header is either 6_d or 10_d bytes in size. This size discrepancy is dependent on the addressing scheme being used. If 8_d byte (absolute) addressing is used in any of the directory entries then the structure will be 10_d bytes in size; otherwise, the header will be 6_d bytes in size. The header itself contains the number of entries that require 8 byte addresses. If any entry requires an 8-byte address then the header will be 10_d bytes. Table 10.8 shows the directory header structure.

Table 10.8 Directory header structure.

Offset	Size	Name	Description
0x00	0x01	# Dir. Entries	The number of directory entries in this directory.
0x01	0x01	# 8_d Byte Dir. Entries	The number of directory entries in this directory that require 8-byte addressing.
0x02	0x04/0x08	Parent Dir. Inode	The inode of the directory's parent directory. This is 0x04 bytes if the previous field's value is 0x00, and is 0x08 bytes otherwise.

Table 10.9 XFS directory entry structure.

Offset	Size	Name	Description
0x00	0x01	Name Length (n)	The size of the file name in bytes.
0x01	0x02	Offset	An offset value used for directory iteration. This value will affect the order in which files/directories are displayed.
0x03	(n)	Filename	The filename.
0x03 + n	0x01	Inode Type	The type of the inode (0x01 – regular file; 0x02 – directory).
0x03 + n + 1	0x04/0x08	Inode #	The inode address. In the case of 8_d byte addresses this is absolute. Four byte addresses are relative to the current AG.

The structure of the directory entries is shown in Table 10.9. In a manner similar to that used in ext, the XFS directory entry is used to map the filename to the inode number. Also the directory entry is the only place in which a file name is found. The inode itself contains no information about the file's name.

10.1.8 Extents

Data in XFS can be stored in a number of different ways. Inline (or resident) data is found directly in the inode's data fork (see Figure 10.4). Generally inline data storage is used only for small directories. All files, even ones with very small content, use an extent-based storage system.

Extents are similar to run-lists in NTFS (and to extents in ext4). Each extent records the number of blocks in the extent, the absolute block address of the starting block in the extent, the logical file block offset represented by the extent, and a flag which specifies if the extent has been pre-allocated. The XFS extent structure is 128_d bits (16_d bytes) in size. Figure 10.5 shows the extent structure.

The 21_d least significant bits represent the number of blocks in the current extent. Following this the subsequent 52_d bits represent the starting block in the extent. Combining these two pieces of information will allow for the entire extent to be extracted. In the case of contiguous files this information will be sufficient to extract the entire file content. However, in the case of fragmentation there will be multiple extents. In this case, the subsequent 54_d bits are used to provide the logical block address inside the file. The first extent will always have a logical block address of 0x00. The single most significant bit is used as a flag. If set (1), this informs that the extent has been pre-allocated (i.e. not written to yet).

A single extent can represent 2^{21} blocks of data. Given that the standard block size is 4096_d bytes, this implies that a single extent can represent a file of up to 8_d GiB in size. Anything larger than that requires multiple extents to represent it. Generally extents are stored in extent list format. This means that a list of extents is stored in the inode's data fork. In the case where there are too many extents for this storage method, extents are instead stored in a long format B+Tree structure. Generally in Version 5 XFS this requires more than 21 extents before a B+Tree is required.

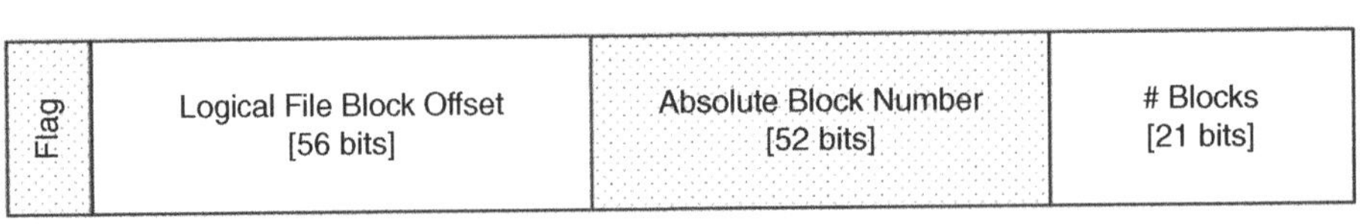

Figure 10.5 XFS extent structure.

10.1.9 Time in XFS

XFS version 5 records four timestamps in relation to every file/directory. These are:

- **mtime:** The time at which the file's contents were last modified.
- **atime:** The time at which the file's contents were last accessed.
- **ctime:** The time at which the file's metadata was last changed.
- **btime:** The time at which the file was created (birth time).

Prior to version 5, XFS recorded only MAC times (no creation time was recorded). In all versions of XFS time is stored as a four-byte unix time value, with a four-byte nanosecond component.

10.2 Analysis of XFS

This section examines the means of analysing the XFS file system. Support for this file system amongst digital forensic tools is limited. As such the manual analysis (Section 10.2.3) becomes even more important. Again the analysis is divided into two sections. Initially basic tasks such as listing files and recovering file metadata and content are examined. Following this more advanced topics in file system analysis such as fragmentation, deletion and journaling are introduced.

10.2.1 Creating XFS File Systems

Generally support for XFS is included in all Linux distributions. If not present it can be installed by installing **xfsprogs**. Once installed a file system is easily created as shown in Listing 10.2. Note the output from **mkfs.xfs** provides much information about the file system in question.

```
$ sudo mkfs.xfs -L "XFS-FS" /dev/sdb1
meta-data=/dev/sdb1      isize=512     agcount=4, agsize=32768 blks
         =               sectsz=512    attr=2, projid32bit=1
         =               crc=1         finobt=1, sparse=1, rmapbt=0
         =               reflink=1
data     =               bsize=4096    blocks=131072, imaxpct=25
         =               sunit=0       swidth=0 blks
naming   =version 2      bsize=4096    ascii-ci=0, ftype=1
log      =internal log   bsize=4096    blocks=1368, version=2
         =               sectsz=512    sunit=0 blks, lazy-count=1
realtime =none           extsz=4096    blocks=0, rtextents=0
```

Listing 10.2 Output from **mkfs.xfs** when creating an XFS file system.

Further details of **mkfs.xfs** can be found on the **man** page!

10.2.2 Supplied XFS Image Files

The files used in the remainder of this chapter are available from the book's website. Table 10.10 summarises these files.

The basic XFS image (**XFS_V1.E01**) contains four files and one directory. Two of the files, along with the directory are found in the root directory, while the remaining two files are found in the subdirectory. The **XFS_V2.E01** image file is created from the first image by deleting the two files in

Table 10.10 XFS image files used in this chapter.

Filename	Description
XFS_V1.E01	Basic XFS file system with four files and one directory.
XFS_V2.E01	**XFS_V1.E01** with two files deleted and an extended attribute added to a file in the root directory. Hard and soft links have also been added to this file system.
XFS_V3.E01	**XFS_V2.E01** with extra files added which overwrote the inode information for the deleted files.
XFS_V4.E01	This file system is used for the chapter exercises.

the subdirectory. In addition to that an extended attribute is added to a file in the root directory and hard and soft links created. The **XFS_V3.E01** image file is created from **XFS_V2.E01** and contains a number of new files which overwrite the inode information about the previously deleted files. The final image (**XFS_V4.E01**) is used in the chapter exercises.

10.2.3 XFS Manual Analysis

In order to manually analyse an XFS file system there are a number of steps that must be performed. In this section these steps are described through example. Throughout this section the file **XFS_V1.E01** is the file system being analysed. This was created using the **mkfs.xfs** program on a Linux system.

The process of analysing an XFS file system can be subdivided into six individual steps. These are:

1. **Process the Superblock:** As with most file systems the first step is to process the superblock in order to locate all the relevant file system structures. In the case of XFS it is necessary to locate the allocation groups and the structures inside these groups.
2. **Locate the Root Directory:** Analysis then proceeds to locate the root directory. The address of this structure is found in the superblock which is then mapped to a physical on-disk address.
3. **Process the Root Directory:** The root directory is processed to reveal the files/directories in the file system's root.
4. **Process the Subdirectories:** All subdirectories identified in step 3 (and in this step) are processed. Once all the subdirectories have been processed every file/directory has been listed.
5. **Recover File Metadata:** The next step is to recover the metadata about each file from the XFS inode structure.
6. **Recover File Content:** The final step in analysis is to recover the file's content.

10.2.3.1 Process the Superblock

As stated in Section 10.1.4 XFS has multiple copies of the superblock with one located in the first sector of each allocation group. In version 5 XFS file systems the superblock is 272_d bytes in size. Section 10.1.4 shows how to locate a superblock based on its signature. In the case of an intact file system it is easier to merely analyse the primary superblock located in AG 0, which begins in sector 0 on the volume. Listing 10.3 shows the contents of the superblock in **XFS_V1.E01**.

In order to proceed with analysis certain information needs to be recovered from the XFS superblock. This includes:

```
000000: 5846 5342 0000 1000 0000 0000 0002 0000 XFSB............
000010: 0000 0000 0000 0000 0000 0000 0000 0000 ................
000020: f7a7 81bd 6d02 4c30 b214 c797 936b bbfe ....m.L0.....k..
000030: 0000 0000 0001 0006 0000 0000 0000 0080 ................
000040: 0000 0000 0000 0081 0000 0000 0000 0082 ................
000050: 0000 0001 0000 8000 0000 0004 0000 0000 ................
000060: 0000 0558 b4a5 0200 0200 0008 5846 532d ...X........XFS-
000070: 4653 0000 0000 0000 0c09 0903 0f00 0019 FS..............
000080: 0000 0000 0000 0040 0000 0000 0000 0038 .......@.......8
000090: 0000 0000 0001 f90b 0000 0000 0000 0000 ................
0000a0: ffff ffff ffff ffff ffff ffff ffff ffff ................
0000b0: 0000 0000 0000 0008 0000 0000 0000 0000 ................
0000c0: 0000 0000 0000 0001 0000 018a 0000 018a ................
0000d0: 0000 0000 0000 0005 0000 0003 0000 0000 ................
0000e0: 06a7 47ba 0000 0004 ffff ffff ffff ffff..G............
0000f0: 0000 0001 0000 001d 0000 0000 0000 0000 ................
000100: 0000 0000 0000 0000 0000 0000 0000 0000 ................
```

Listing 10.3 The superblock structure from sector 0 of **XFS_V1.E01**.

- **Block Size:** The block is the basic storage structure and as such it is necessary to know how large this is. This value is given in bytes.
- **Root Directory Inode:** Step 2 involves processing the root directory. In order to do this the root directory structure must be located. The first step in this task is to discover the inode for the root directory.
- **AG Size:** Allocation groups are mini file systems inside XFS. These have their own internal structures. To locate information inside an allocation group it is necessary to know where the AG starts. Knowing the size of the AGs will allow the exact starting point of each AG to be determined.
- **Sector Size:** The sector size is necessary in order to locate other structures.
- **Inode Size:** Inodes are the basic metadata storage system in XFS. In order to successfully process these structures it is necessary to know their size.
- **Inodes/Block:** The number of inodes in each block will allow the position of a particular inode in the inode table to be determined.
- **$\log_2$(agSize):** The log of the AG Size is used in determining the absolute address of both blocks and inodes (Figures 10.2 and 10.3).
- **$\log_2$(inodesPerBlock):** The log of the inodes per block value is used to determine the absolute inode address in the file system.
- **UUID:** The UUID is necessary to ensure that all subsequent structures belong to the same file system.

Table 10.11 shows the extracted values from **XFS_V1.E01**. It is left as an exercise for the reader to complete the remainder of the analysis of the superblock (Tables 10.3 and 10.4).

10.2.3.2 Locate the Root Directory

After gathering information about the file system as a whole, analysis proceeds with the listing of files. This process commences by listing the contents of the root directory. However, in order to process the root directory the root directory structure must first be located. From step 1 the required information has already been obtained (see Table 10.11) which includes:

Table 10.11 Extracted values from the superblock in **XFS_V1.E01**.

Offset	Size	Name	Value
0x04	0x04	Block Size	0x1000 $(4,096_d)$
0x20	0x10	UUID	0xF7A7 … BBFE
0x38	0x08	Root Dir. Inode	0x80 (128_d)
0x54	0x04	AG Size	0x8000 $(32,768_d)$
0x58	0x04	# AGs	0x04 (4_d)
0x66	0x02	Sector Size	0x200 (512_d)
0x68	0x02	Inode Size	0x200 (512_d)
0x6A	0x02	Inodes/Block	0x08 (8_d)
0x7B	0x01	$log_2(inodesPerBlock)$	0x03 (3_d)
0x7C	0x01	$log_2(AG_{size})$	0x0F (15_d)

- **Inode Address:** 0x0000 0000 0000 0080
- **$\mathbf{log_2(AG_{size})}$:** 0x0F (15_d)
- **$\mathbf{log_2(inodesPerBlock)}$:** 0x03 (3_d)
- **Block Size:** 0x1000 (4096_d)
- **AG Size:** 0x8000 $(32,768_d)$
- **Inode Size:** 0x200 (512_d)

The root directory inode address is an 8_d-byte value. This implies that this is an absolute inode address. In order to process this value, it is necessary to also have the $log_2(agSize)$ and $log_2(inodesPerBlock)$ values also. These are 15_d and 3_d, respectively. The method of processing these values is provided in Section 10.1.2. The $log_2(inodesPerBlock)$ least significant bits represent the inode offset inside the block. The next $log_2(agSize)$ bits represent the block offset inside the allocation group, and the remaining bits represent the allocation group itself. The processing of the root directory's inode address is shown in Listing 10.4.

```
... 0000 0000 0000 0000 1000 0000
```

Listing 10.4 The processed root directory inode address (only the three least significant bytes are shown).

The result of this step shows that the root directory is located at inode offset 0_b in block offset $10000_b = 16_d$ in allocation group 0_b. Calculating the actual byte offset to this location is done using:

$$(((AG_{\#} \times AG_{size}) + blk_{off}) \times blk_{size}) + (inode_{off} \times inode_{size})$$

$$(((0 \times 32,768) + 16) \times 4096) + (0 \times 512) = 65,536_d$$

giving a byte offset of $65,536_d$ bytes. In the next step the root directory inode is extracted and processed.

10.2.3.3 Process the Root Directory

The contents of the root directory inode are shown in Listing 10.5. The inode is 512_d bytes in size; however, the output in Listing 10.5 has been truncated as not all of the content is in use. From Section 10.1.6 the structure of the inode is known. Each inode consists of up to three parts, a required inode core and optional data and attribute forks. The inode core is 176_d bytes in size and is highlighted in Listing 10.5.

```
010000: 494e 41ed 0301 0000 0000 0000 0000 0000 INA.............
010010: 0000 0003 0000 0000 0000 0000 0000 0000 ................
010020: 6548 bd3f 312c 8b8f 6548 bd32 3220 b0e7 eH.?1,..eH.22..
010030: 6548 bd32 3220 b0e7 0000 0000 0000 0036 eH.22 .........6
010040: 0000 0000 0000 0000 0000 0000 0000 0000 ................
010050: 0000 0002 0000 0000 0000 0000 0000 0000 ................
010060: ffff ffff bebe 31a7 0000 0000 0000 0006 ......1.........
010070: 0000 0001 0000 0014 0000 0000 0000 0000 ................
010080: 0000 0000 0000 0000 0000 0000 0000 0000 ................
010090: 6548 b9d3 1fd3 b868 0000 0000 0000 0080 eH.....h........
0100a0: f7a7 81bd 6d02 4c30 b214 c797 936b bbfe ....m.L0.....k..
0100b0: 0300 0000 0080 0500 6046 696c 6573 0200 ........'Files..
0100c0: 0000 8308 0078 696e 666f 2e74 7874 0100 .....xinfo.txt..
0100d0: 0000 850b 0090 7375 6e72 6973 652e 6a70 ......sunrise.jp
0100e0: 6701 0000 0086 0000 0000 0000 0000 0000 g...............
0100f0: 0000 0000 0000 0000 0000 0000 0000 0000
```

Listing 10.5 Contents of the root directory inode in **XFS_V1.E01**.

Table 10.12 shows the partially processed inode core structure in Listing 10.5. Only those values that are necessary for further analysis or of possible interest in investigation are shown. It is left as an exercise for the reader to process the remainder of the inode core Structure using Table 10.7.

Processing the root directory inode shows that this inode represents a directory (as expected) with permissions **rwxr-xr-x**. The data fork in this directory is resident meaning that the actual data is stored in the inode structure itself. Examining Listing 10.5 shows what appear to be file names in the data fork (immediately after the inode core) so this is also an unsurprising result. The time values are converted as normal unix time values. The file size is given as 0x36 bytes. As the data fork is resident these 0x36 bytes will appear immediately after the inode core structure. This data is shown in Listing 10.6. Alternate directory entries are highlighted.

```
0100b0: 0300 0000 0080 0500 6046 696c 6573 0200 ........'Files..
0100c0: 0000 8308 0078 696e 666f 2e74 7874 0100 .....xinfo.txt..
0100d0: 0000 850b 0090 7375 6e72 6973 652e 6a70 ......sunrise.jp
0100e0: 6701 0000 0086 0000 0000 0000 0000 0000 g...............
```

Listing 10.6 Directory entries from the root directory in **XFS_V1.E01**. The directory begins with the header followed by the directory entries.

Processing the directory header in Listing 10.6 shows that there are three directory entries present, none of which require 8-byte addressing. This results in the header structure being a

Table 10.12 Partially processed root directory inode in **XFS_V1.E01.**

Offset	Size	Name	Value
0x00	0x02	Signature	IN
0x02	0x02	Mode	0x41ED Directory rwxr-xr-x
0x05	0x01	Format	0x01 – resident
0x10	0x04	# Links	0x03 (3_d)
0x20	0x04	atime	0x6548BD3F 2023-11-06 10:17:35 UTC
0x24	0x04	atime (ns)	0x312C8B8F ($825,002,895_d$)
0x28	0x04	mtime	0x6548BD32 2023-11-06 10:17:22 UTC
0x2C	0x04	mtime (ns)	0x3220B0E7 ($841,003,239_d$)
0x30	0x04	ctime	0x6548BD32 2023-11-06 10:17:22 UTC
0x34	0x04	ctime (ns)	0x3220B0E7 ($841,003,239_d$)
0x38	0x08	File Size	0x36 (54_d)
0x90	0x04	btime	0x6548B9D3 2023-11-06 10:02:59 UTC
0x94	0x04	btime (ns)	0x1FD3B868 ($533,969,000_d$)
0x98	0x08	Inode #	0x80 (128_d)
0xA0	0x10	UUID	0xF7A7 … BBFE

mere 6_d bytes in size. The parent directory inode is given as 0x00000080 – in other words the root directory itself! Directory entries are processed based on Table 10.9. The results of this are shown in Table 10.13.

Processing the root directory results in two files (**info.txt** and **sunrise.jpg**) and one directory (**Files**). The file inode values are 0x85 and 0x86, respectively, while the directory's inode is 0x83.

Table 10.13 Processed directory entries in the root directory.

Name	Entry 1	Entry 2	Entry 3
Name Length (n)	0x05 (5_d)	0x08 (8_d)	0x0B (11_d)
Offset	0x60 (96_d)	0x78 (120_d)	0x90 (144_d)
Filename	Files	info.txt	sunrise.jpg
Inode Type	0x02 Directory	0x01 File	0x01 File
Inode #	0x83 (131_d)	0x85 (133_d)	0x86 (134_d)

10.2.3.4 Process the Subdirectories

Processing of subdirectories is identical to the method of processing the root directory. The inode structure is located (0x83 for the **Files** directory) and processed using the same method as in the previous step. This allows the listing of all files/directories in the subdirectory. Once all directories in the file system have been processed the analyst can be confident that all live files have been listed. The processing of the **Files** subdirectory in **XFS_V1.E01** is left as an exercise for the reader.

10.2.3.5 Recover File Content/Metadata

The final step in analysing an XFS file system is to recover file metadata and content. Metadata is recovered from the inode core, in exactly the same manner that was used when analysing the root directory. One scenario in file recovery has already been demonstrated, that of resident data recovery. In this scenario the data fork contains the actual file content. The file size can be read from the inode core, and the data extracted. However, resident data cannot be used if the file content would exceed the size of the inode. Consider the file **sunrise.jpg** (Inode 0x86) on the **XFS_V1.E01** disk image. This is a large file, too large to be stored as resident data. Hence another method must be used. Large files in XFS are generally stored using extents.

Listing 10.7 shows the contents of the inode core for Inode 0x86. The data fork format is given as 0x02 meaning that extent-based storage is being used. The file size is 0x83EF8 ($540,408_d$) bytes. The file content is stored in one single extent.

```
010c00: 494e 81e8 0302 0000 0000 0000 0000 0000 IN..............
010c10: 0000 0001 0000 0000 0000 0000 0000 0000 ................
010c20: 6548 bd32 3220 b0e7 6548 bd32 325d b9e7 eH.22..eH.22]..
010c30: 6548 bd32 325d b9e7 0000 0000 0008 3ef8 eH.22]........>.
010c40: 0000 0000 0000 0084 0000 0000 0000 0001 ................
010c50: 0000 0002 0000 0000 0000 0000 a818 785a ..............xZ
010c60: ffff ffff f740 8346 0000 0000 0000 0006 .....@.F........
010c70: 0000 0001 0000 0014 0000 0000 0000 0000 ................
010c80: 0000 0000 0000 0000 0000 0000 0000 0000 ................
010c90: 6548 bd32 3220 b0e7 0000 0000 0000 0086 eH.22 ..........
010ca0: f7a7 81bd 6d02 4c30 b214 c797 936b bbfe ....m.L0.....k..
010cb0: 0000 0000 0000 0000 0000 0000 0300 0084 ................
```

Listing 10.7 The contents of the inode core for inode 0x86.

Extents in XFS are 16_d-byte structures. Extents are found in the data fork, meaning that they are found immediately after the inode core. In the case of inode 0x86 there is only one single extent. This extent is shown in Listing 10.8.

```
010cb0: 0000 0000 0000 0000 0000 0000 0300 0084 ................
```

Listing 10.8 The extent structure found in inode 0x86.

Processing this allows the discovery that no flag value is set, the logical position in the file is 0_d, meaning that this is the first extent of the file's content – which is always the case when there is only a single extent. The absolute block number at which the extent starts is 24_d and the number

Figure 10.6 Contents of the recovered file **sunrise.jpg**.

of blocks in the extent is 132_d. This file can then be extracted using the command shown in Listing 10.9. Figure 10.6 shows the recovered picture.

```
$ dd if=mnt/ewf1 of=sunrise.jpg bs=1 skip=$((24*4096))
     count=$((0x83EF8))
540408+0 records in
540408+0 records out
540408 bytes (540 kB, 528 KiB) copied, 13.8077 s, 39.1 kB/s
$
$ file sunrise.jpg
sunrise.jpg: JPEG image data, JFIF standard 1.01, aspect ...
$
$ md5sum sunrise.jpg
2394c86c7a79019c63da8e394e8c7b35 sunrise.jpg
```

Listing 10.9 The **dd** command used to extract inode 0x86 (**sunrise.jpg**) from **XFS_V1.E01**.

This section has shown how to perform basic manual analysis of an XFS file system. However, XFS is a modern file system providing many features that have not been covered to this point. In the next section some of these advanced features are examined.

10.3 XFS Advanced Analysis

To this point the basic structures in XFS have been described and basic manual analysis has been performed. Manual analysis is more important in XFS than in many other file systems as forensic tools do not often provide support for this file system. At this stage the reader should be able to describe the layout of an XFS file system using the superblock; process the root directory and subsequent directories to list the files in the file system; and process inodes to recover file metadata and content.

In this section the focus turns toward more advanced topics in the XFS file system. This begins with block and inode management and then turns to file deletion and extended attributes. Finally this section concludes by examining the XFS journaling structure.

10.3.1 AG Free Space Management

Directly after the superblock sector the free block information area is found (i.e. byte offset 512_d). This provides information about the free space B+Trees and general information about the free space in the particular allocation group. The free space system is relevant to the particular AG in which it is found. There are two versions of the free space tree, one of which is indexed based on the block number and the other is indexed based on the count of empty blocks. The first method allows free space near a particular point to be located, while the second allows an area large enough for a particular file to be located in order to minimise fragmentation. Listing 10.10 shows the free block information area from **XFS_V1.E01**. Table 10.14 shows the processed values from Listing 10.10.

```
000200: 5841 4746 0000 0001 0000 0000 0000 8000 XAGF............
000210: 0000 0001 0000 0002 0000 0000 0000 0001 ................
000220: 0000 0001 0000 0000 0000 0001 0000 0004 ................
000230: 0000 0004 0000 7e71 0000 7e6d 0000 0000 ......~q..~m....
000240: f7a7 81bd 6d02 4c30 b214 c797 936b bbfe ....m.L0.....k..
000250: 0000 0000 0000 0001 0000 0005 0000 0001 ................
000260: 0000 0000 0000 0000 0000 0000 0000 0000 ................
000270: 0000 0000 0000 0000 0000 0000 0000 0000 ................
000280: 0000 0000 0000 0000 0000 0000 0000 0000 ................
000290: 0000 0000 0000 0000 0000 0000 0000 0000 ................
0002a0: 0000 0000 0000 0000 0000 0000 0000 0000 ................
0002b0: 0000 0000 0000 0000 0000 0000 0000 0000 ................
0002c0: 0000 0000 0000 0000 0000 0000 0000 0000 ................
0002d0: 0000 0001 0000 001a dd18 02b4 0000 0000 ................
0002e0: 0000 0000 0000 0000 0000 0000 0000 0000 ................
```

Listing 10.10 AG free block information area in AG 0 of **XFS_V1.E01**.

There are two B+Trees related to free space. Each of these trees addresses items inside the individual AG and as such they use the short form header. The records for these trees are a combination of offset/count pairs. The offset is to a relative block address and the count measures the number of blocks that are free from that point.

Both of the trees contain the exact same information but are sorted on different items. The first B+Tree is sorted based on the starting block number, while the second is sorted on the count of the number of blocks that are free. The roots of these trees are discovered from the AG free list information sector above. In this case, the free space by block number tree is located at block 0x01 and the free space by count tree is located at block 0x02. Listing 10.11 shows the free space by block number tree.

This structure is processed using the short form B+Tree header in Table 10.1. The results of this are shown in Table 10.15. Following the header there are two entries in this B+Tree. Each entry consists of an offset (4 byte block number) and a count of free blocks (four bytes). The two records are highlighted in Listing 10.11. The result of processing these is shown in Table 10.16.

Table 10.14 Partially processed AG free block information structure. The values are from Listing 10.10.

Offset	Size	Name	Description	Value
0x00	0x04	Signature	Magic number for XFS free block information area.	XAGF
0x04	0x04	Version #	The version number (currently 1).	0x01 (1_d)
0x08	0x04	AG #	The AG number to which this AGF belongs.	0x00 (0_d)
0x0C	0x04	AG Size (Blocks)	The size of the AG in blocks – generally identical to that found in the superblock. May differ for the final AG.	0x8000 ($32,768_d$)
0x10	3*4 bytes	Roots	Three relative block numbers, two for the free space B+Tree locations and one for the reverse mapping B+Tree if enabled.	0x01 (1_d); 0x02 (2_d); 0x00 (0_d)
0x1C	3*4 bytes	Levels	Specifies the depth of the above trees (two for free space trees and one for reverse mapping B+Tree).	0x01 (1_d); 0x01 (1_d); 0x00 (0_d)
0x28	0x04	First Free List Blk	Index of the first free list block.	0x01 (1_d)
0x2C	0x04	Last Free List Blk	Index of the last free list block.	0x04 (4_d)
0x30	0x04	# Blks in Free List	Number of blocks in the free list.	0x04 (4_d)
0x34	0x04	# Free Blks in AG	Number of free blocks in the AG.	0x7E71 ($32,369_d$)
0x38	0x04	# Blks Long Free	Number of blocks in the longest contiguous segment of free blocks.	0x7E6D ($32,365_d$)
0x3C	0x04	# Blks FSBT	Number of blocks used for free space B+Trees. Only used if certain features are enabled.	0x00 (0_d)
0x40	0x10	UUID	This UUID should be the same as that found in the superblock.	0xF7A7 … BBFE
0x68	0x08	LSN	Last write log sequence number.	0x00 (0_d)

```
001000: 4142 3342 0000 0002 ffff ffff ffff ffff AB3B............
001010: 0000 0000 0000 0008 0000 0001 0000 001a ................
001020: f7a7 81bd 6d02 4c30 b214 c797 936b bbfe ....m.L0.....k..
001030: 0000 0000 5a9a 764a 0000 000c 0000 0004 ....Z.vJ........
001040: 0000 0193 0000 7e6d 0000 0000 0000 0000 ......~m........
```

Listing 10.11 Free space by block number tree in AG 0 in **XFS_V1.E01**.

The first entry in Table 10.16 can be interpreted as four free blocks beginning at block 0x0C (12_d), meaning that blocks 12_d, 13_d, 14_d and 15_d are free. The second B+Tree (free space by length) will have the same records, but they will be sorted based on the count of the blocks rather than the starting block number. These structures are used to determine what free blocks are available for new files in the file system.

Table 10.15 Processed short form tree header from the free space block number B+Tree in AG0 of **XFS_V1.E01** (Listing 10.11).

Offset	Size	Name	Value
0x00	0x04	Signature	AB3B
0x04	0x02	Level	0x00 (0_d)
0x06	0x02	# Records	0x02 (2_d)
0x08	0x04	Left Sibling	0xFFFFFFFF
0x0C	0x04	Right Sibling	0xFFFFFFFF
		Version 5	
0x10	0x08	Block #	0x08 (8_d)
0x18	0x08	LSN	0x010000001A
0x20	0x10	UUID	0xF7A7...BBFE
0x30	0x04	Owner	0x00 (0_d)
0x34	0x04	CRC	0x5A9A764A

Table 10.16 Processed entries in Listing 10.11.

	Record 1	Record 2
Offset	0x0C (12_d)	0x193 (403_d)
Count	0x04 (4_d)	0x7E6D ($32,365_d$)

10.3.1.1 AG Free List

The allocation group free list is found in sector 3 in the allocation group. The signature for this is 0x5841464C (ASCII: XAFL). This structure contains a header, which is followed by an array of relative block addresses (four bytes each). These blocks are reserved for further free space B+Tree growth. The AG free list from AG 0 in **XFS_V1.E01** is shown in Listing 10.12. The header is 36_d bytes in size and is highlighted in Listing 10.12. Table 10.17 provides the structure of the AFL header along with the values from Listing 10.12.

```
000600: 5841 464c 0000 0000 f7a7 81bd 6d02 4c30 XAFL........m.L0
000610: b214 c797 936b bbfe 0000 0000 0000 0000 .....k..........
000620: 1ce4 1527 ffff ffff 0000 0006 0000 0007 ...'............
000630: 0000 0008 0000 0009 ffff ffff ffff ffff ................
```

Listing 10.12 AG free list from AG 0 in **XFS_V1.E01**.

The remainder of the free list structure is composed of four byte block numbers (0xFFFFFFFF (-1_d) is a NULL value); however, not all of these entries are active. To determine this refer back to the AG free block information area (Table 10.14) which refers to the first and last free list blocks (0x01 and 0x04, respectively). These are array index positions in the free list (note that the indexing begins at 0x00). The first free list block is index 0x01 (the second element in the list). The final free list index is 0x04. This means that the elements in positions 1_d–4_d are being used. The values

Table 10.17 AG Free list header structure with values from Listing 10.12.

Offset	Size	Name	Description	Value
0x00	0x04	Signature	Magic number for the AG Free List.	XAFL
0x04	0x04	AG #	Specifies the AG # containing this list.	0x00 (0_d)
0x08	0x10	UUID	File System UUID	0xF7A7...BBFE
0x18	0x08	LSN	Log Sequence Number for the last write to this block	0x00 (0_d)
0x20	0x04	CRC	Checksum for this sector	0x1CE41527

of these are 0x06, 0x07, 0x08 and 0x09, respectively. Hence these are the four blocks in AG0 of **XFS_V1.E01** that are being reserved for further growth of the free space trees.

10.3.2 AG Inode Management

Allocation group inodes are managed in a similar fashion to blocks. There is an AG inode information structure located in sector 2 of the allocation group (Signature XAGI). This structure provides information on the location of the inode B+Tree(s). Records in the inode B+Tree provide information relating to the allocation status of each inode in the file system. Note that inodes are allocated in XFS only when they are needed; hence, newer file systems (or file systems that very rarely change) will have only a limited number of inodes. Traditionally only a single inode tree is used which tracks the used inodes. However, certain systems allow for a second inode tree which tracks free inodes. This speeds file system performance when creating new inodes. Listing 10.13 shows the contents

```
000400: 5841 4749 0000 0001 0000 0000 0000 8000 XAGI............
000410: 0000 0040 0000 0003 0000 0001 0000 0038 ...@...........8
000420: 0000 0080 ffff ffff ffff ffff ffff ffff ................
000430: ffff ffff ffff ffff ffff ffff ffff ffff ................
000440: ffff ffff ffff ffff ffff ffff ffff ffff ................
000450: ffff ffff ffff ffff ffff ffff ffff ffff ................
000460: ffff ffff ffff ffff ffff ffff ffff ffff ................
000470: ffff ffff ffff ffff ffff ffff ffff ffff ................
000480: ffff ffff ffff ffff ffff ffff ffff ffff ................
000490: ffff ffff ffff ffff ffff ffff ffff ffff ................
0004a0: ffff ffff ffff ffff ffff ffff ffff ffff ................
0004b0: ffff ffff ffff ffff ffff ffff ffff ffff ................
0004c0: ffff ffff ffff ffff ffff ffff ffff ffff ................
0004d0: ffff ffff ffff ffff ffff ffff ffff ffff ................
0004e0: ffff ffff ffff ffff ffff ffff ffff ffff ................
0004f0: ffff ffff ffff ffff ffff ffff ffff ffff ................
000500: ffff ffff ffff ffff ffff ffff ffff ffff ................
000510: ffff ffff ffff ffff ffff ffff ffff ffff ................
000520: ffff ffff ffff ffff f7a7 81bd 6d02 4c30 ............m.L0
000530: b214 c797 936b bbfe 0310 01ee 0000 0000 .....k..........
000540: 0000 0001 0000 0014 0000 0004 0000 0001 ................
000550: 0000 0000 0000 0000 0000 0000 0000 0000 ................
```

Listing 10.13 The inode information area in AG0 of **XFS_V1.E01**.

Table 10.18 The inode information area. Values are from Listing 10.13.

Offset	Size	Name	Description	Value
0x00	0x04	Signature	Magic number identifying the structure.	XAGI
0x04	0x04	Version	Currently set to 1.	0x01 (1_d)
0x08	0x04	AG #	AG number containing this structure.	0x00 (0_d)
0x0C	0x04	AG Size	Size of the AG in blocks.	0x8000 ($32,768_d$)
0x10	0x04	Inode Count	Number of allocated inodes in this block.	0x40 (64_d)
0x14	0x04	IBT Root	The block number of the inode B+Tree root node.	0x03 (3_d)
0x18	0x04	IBT Level	The number of levels in the inode B+Tree.	0x01 (1_d)
0x1C	0x04	Free Inodes	The number of free inodes in this AG.	0x38 (56_d)
0x20	0x04	New Inode	Relative inode number of the most recently allocated chunk of inodes.	0x80 (128_d)
0x24	0x04	Dir Inode	Always 0xFFFFFFFF.	0xFFFFFFFF
0x28	0x04 x 64_d	Unlinked Inodes	A list of relative inode addresses representing inodes that have been deleted but are still referenced.	All NULL
			Version 5	
0x128	0x10	UUID	File system UUID.	0xF7A7 ... BBFE
0x138	0x04	CRC	Sector checksum.	0x031001EE
0x13C	0x04	Padding	Padding.	0x00 (0_d)
0x140	0x08	LSN	Log sequence number of last write to this sector.	0x0100000014
0x148	0x04	FIBT Root	Block number of the free inode B+Tree.	0x04 (4_d)
0x14C	0x04	FIBT Level	Number of levels in the free inode B+Tree.	0x01 (1_d)

of the inode information structure in AG0 of **XFS_V1.E01**. The inode information structure along with the processed values in Listing 10.13 are shown in Table 10.18.

From Table 10.18 it is clear that there are two inode trees in this file system. The root node of the inode B+Tree is located in Block 3, while the root node of the free inode B+Tree is located in Block 4. Listing 10.14 shows the contents of the inode B+Tree (Block 3) in **XFS_V1.E01**. This tree uses the short form header which is processed in Table 10.19.

```
003000: 4941 4233 0000 0001 ffff ffff ffff ffff IAB3............
003010: 0000 0000 0000 0018 0000 0001 0000 0014 ................
003020: f7a7 81bd 6d02 4c30 b214 c797 936b bbfe ....m.L0.....k..
003030: 0000 0000 e3f6 856b 0000 0080 0000 4038 .......k......@8
003040: ffff ffff ffff ff00 0000 0000 0000 0000 ................
```

Listing 10.14 The inode B+Tree in AG 0 from **XFS_V1.E01**.

Table 10.19 shows that this tree contains a single record. In the case of inode trees each record is 16_d bytes in size. In the simplest case these records consist of three fields. The first four bytes

Table 10.19 Processed inode B+Tree. from AG0 in **XFS_V1.E01**. Values are from Listing 10.14.

Offset	Size	Name	Value
0x00	0x04	Signature	IAB3
0x04	0x02	Level	0x00 (0_d)
0x06	0x02	# Records	0x01 (1_d)
0x08	0x04	Left Sibling	-1_d
0x0C	0x04	Right Sibling	-1_d
		Version 5	
0x10	0x08	Block #	0x18 (24_d)
0x18	0x08	LSN	0x100000014
0x20	0x10	UUID	0xF7A7...BBFE
0x30	0x04	AG #	0x00 (0_d)
0x34	0x04	Checksum	0xE3F6856B

represent the starting inode in the allocation chunk, the next four bytes represent the number of inodes in the allocation chunk and the final 8_d bytes represent the allocation bitmap itself. However, in file systems in which the sparse inodes flag is set the number of inodes in the chunk is removed and replaced with a more complex structure. This structure is shown in Table 10.20. The values are taken from the record in Listing 10.14.

From Table 10.20 there is only a single chunk of allocated inodes. This chunk begins at inode 0x80 (128_d) and contains 0x40 (64_d) inodes, 0x38 (56_d) of which are free. The remaining 8_d bytes contain the allocation bitmap for these 64_d inodes. To interpret the bitmap, it is first converted to binary (only the least significant bytes 0xFF00 are converted below) giving:

$$1111\ 1111\ 0000\ 0000_b$$

The least significant bit represents the first inode in the allocation chunk, while the most significant bit represents the final inode in the chunk. A value of 0 means that the inode is in use, while a value of 1 means that the inode is free. Hence in the supplied **XFS_V1.E01** file system's AG 0 the 8_d inodes, beginning at inode 0x80 (128_d) are occupied and the remainder are free.

Table 10.20 Inode B+Tree record structure. Processed values are from the record in Listing 10.14.

Offset	Size	Name	Description	Value
0x00	0x04	First Inode	The first inode in the allocation chunk.	0x80 (128_d)
0x04	0x02	Hole Bitmask	A 16-bit element showing which parts of the chunk are not allocated to inodes. Each bit represents four inodes.	0x0000
0x06	0x01	Num. Inodes	The number of inodes in the allocation chunk.	0x40 (64_d)
0x07	0x01	Num. Free Inodes	The number of free inodes in the allocation chunk.	0x38 (56_d)
0x08	0x08	Bitmap	A bitmap structure of allocated inodes.	0xFFFF...FF00

10.3.3 Deleted Files

The file system **XFS_V2.E01** was created from **XFS_V1.E01** by deleting two files from the original file system. These files were **delete.txt** (Inode: 0x84) and **tree.jpg** (Inode: 0x87), both in the **Files** directory. The **delete.txt** file's extent contained a single block at block 10_d, while **tree.jpg** contained 247_d blocks at block number 156_d. Listing 10.15 shows the content in both locations is still present. However, the question that must now be answered is whether these files can be recovered using file system structures, or is it only through carving that file recovery can be achieved?

```
$ xxd -s $((10*4096)) -l $((0x30)) mnt/ewf1
00a000: 5468 6973 2066 696c 6520 7769 6c6c 2062 This file will b
00a010: 6520 6465 6c65 7465 6420 696e 2061 206c e deleted in a l
00a020: 6174 6572 2076 6572 7369 6f6e 210a 0000 ater version!...
$
$ xxd -s $((156*4096)) -l $((0x30)) mnt/ewf1
09c000: ffd8 ffe0 0010 4a46 4946 0001 0100 0001 ......JFIF......
09c010: 0001 0000 ffdb 0043 0001 0101 0101 0101 .......C........
09c020: 0101 0101 0101 0101 0201 0101 0101 0201 ................
```

Listing 10.15 Content of deleted files is still to be found in the file system.

When manual analysis is performed, it is discovered that the directory entries still exist in this case. Listing 10.16 shows the contents of the directory entries for the **Files** directory. The number of entries is now zero because all files in the directory were removed but the old directory entries still exist in slack space.

```
0106b0: 0000 0000 0080 0a00 6064 656c 6574 652e ........`delete.
0106c0: 7478 7401 0000 0084 0800 7874 7265 652e txt.......xtree.
0106d0: 6a70 6701 0000 0087 0000 0000 0000 0000 jpg.............
```

Listing 10.16 The data fork in the **Files** directory inode. Both **delete.txt** and **tree.jpg** were deleted.

The final step is to check the status of the inodes for these files. Inodes 0x84 and 0x87 represent the deleted files. These inodes are located at byte offsets $67,584_d$ and $69,120_d$, respectively. Listing 10.17 shows the content of inode 0x87 after deletion, clearly showing that the file extent is still intact.

This section shows that not only does the file content remain, the metadata (i.e. inode content) also remains. However, if only **delete.jpg** had been deleted from the **Files** directory, the directory entries would have been restructured. This means the entry for **tree.jpg** would have been moved to the start of the directory, thereby overwriting the entry for **delete.txt**. Hence, it is only entries that remain in the directory's slack space that can be recovered using this method. The fact that the inode as well as the data are intact means that metadata carving techniques from the very simple such as searching for IN, the Inode signature, to the more complex such as Nordvik et al.'s generic metadata time carving, can be used in addition to traditional content-based carving approaches. The reader should however be aware that the inodes and/or blocks occupied by the deleted files are now marked as unallocated and may be overwritten at any stage. The recovery of **delete.txt** through the examination of Inode 0x84 is left as an exercise for the reader.

```
010e00: 494e 0000 0302 0000 0000 0000 0000 0000 IN..............
010e10: 0000 0000 0000 0000 0000 0000 0000 0000 ................
010e20: 6548 bd44 16b5 a416 6548 bd44 16b5 a416 eH.D....eH.D....
010e30: 6548 de0d 000b e79b 0000 0000 0000 0000 eH..............
010e40: 0000 0000 0000 0000 0000 0000 0000 0000 ................
010e50: 0000 0002 0000 0000 0000 0000 e6b6 cda8 ................
010e60: ffff ffff 2b70 cba3 0000 0000 0000 000c ....+p..........
010e70: 0000 0001 0000 002c 0000 0000 0000 0000 .......,........
010e80: 0000 0000 0000 0000 0000 0000 0000 0000 ................
010e90: 6548 bd44 16b5 a416 0000 0000 0000 0087 eH.D............
010ea0: f7a7 81bd 6d02 4c30 b214 c797 936b bbfe ....m.L0.....k..
010eb0: 0000 0000 0000 0000 0000 0000 1380 00f7 ................
```

Listing 10.17 The contents of inode 0x87 (**tree.jpg**) after deletion. The data fork is highlighted.

10.3.4 Extended Attributes

The XFS file system allows for extended attributes, similar to alternate data streams in NTFS. These extended attributes consist of name value pairs. Names are generally ASCII (or other printable) characters while the value can consist of up to 64Kb binary data. The **XFS_V2.E01** file system contains a file called **sunrise.jpg** (Inode: 0x86) to which an extended attribute was added. The **attr** command is used to manage extended attributes on the XFS file system. In this case the attribute was added using the command **attr -s "Hidden" -V "Hidden Information" sunrise.jpg**, to create an attribute called *Hidden* with the value "Hidden Information".

Extended attributes are stored in the attribute fork area of the inode (Figure 10.4). The location of this structure is different in each inode and is pointed to from the inode core. At offset 0x52 the location of the start of the attribute fork is found. This value is multiplied by 8 to get the byte offset to the start of the attribute fork relative to the end of the inode core (176_d bytes). The following byte, offset 0x53, provides the storage format for the attribute fork, which uses the same values as the data format byte. Listing 10.18 shows the inode for **sunrise.jpg** (Inode: 0x86) in **XFS_V2.dd**. In this case the offset is 0x25, and the storage format is 0x01, meaning that the data is resident. The byte offset to this attribute is given as $176 + (0x25 \times 8) = 472_d$

The attribute area contains a small header which provides in the first two bytes (0x1F) the length of the extended attribute fork, the number of attributes in the next byte (0x01) and is finalised with a single alignment byte (always 0x00). The extended attributes follow this header structure. Table 10.21 provides the extended attribute structure and values from the attribute shown in Listing 10.18.

Table 10.21 Extended attribute structures. Values are from Listing 10.18.

Offset	Size	Name	Description	Value
0x00	0x01	Name Length (n)	Length of the attribute name	0x06 (6_d)
0x01	0x01	Value Length (m)	Length of the attribute value	0x12 (18_d)
0x02	0x01	Flags	Flags	0x00 (0_d)
0x03	n	Name	Attribute name	Hidden
0x03 + n	m	Value	Attribute value	Hidden Information

```
010c00: 494e 81e8 0302 0000 0000 0000 0000 0000 IN..............
010c10: 0000 0002 0000 0000 0000 0000 0000 0000 ................
010c20: 6548 bd32 3220 b0e7 6548 bd32 325d b9e7 eH.22..eH.22]..
010c30: 6548 ddf3 2762 b73b 0000 0000 0008 3ef8 eH..'b.;......>.
010c40: 0000 0000 0000 0084 0000 0000 0000 0001 ................
010c50: 0000 2501 0000 0000 0000 0000 a818 785a..%...........xZ
010c60: ffff ffff c4f4 7338 0000 0000 0000 0009 ......s8........
010c70: 0000 0001 0000 0025 0000 0000 0000 0000 .......%........
010c80: 0000 0000 0000 0000 0000 0000 0000 0000 ................
010c90: 6548 bd32 3220 b0e7 0000 0000 0000 0086 eH.22 ..........
010ca0: f7a7 81bd 6d02 4c30 b214 c797 936b bbfe ....m.L0.....k..
010cb0: 0000 0000 0000 0000 0000 0000 0300 0084 ................
010cc0: 0000 0000 0000 0000 0000 0000 0000 0000 ................
...[snip]...
010dc0: 0000 0000 0000 0000 0000 0000 0000 0000 ................
010dd0: 0000 0000 0000 0000 001f 0100 0612 0048 ...............H
010de0: 6964 6465 6e48 6964 6465 6e20 496e 666f iddenHidden Info
010df0: 726d 6174 696f 6e00 0000 0000 0000 0000 rmation.........
```

Listing 10.18 The **sunrise.jpg** inode (0x86) in **XFS_V2.E01**. The header is highlighted and is followed by the extended attribute.

10.3.5 Links

As with many file systems XFS supports the creation of links. Both hard and soft links can be created. In **XFS_V2.E01** both a hard and soft link were created in the root directory to the **sunrise.jpg** file. Listing 10.19 shows the contents of the root directory's data fork after the creation of these links. Notice that in the case of the **hardlink.jpg** file, the inode number for this is 0x86, identical to that of the target file, **sunrise.jpg**.

```
0100b0: 0500 0000 0080 0500 6046 696c 6573 0200 ........'Files..
0100c0: 0000 8308 0078 696e 666f 2e74 7874 0100 .....xinfo.txt..
0100d0: 0000 850b 0090 7375 6e72 6973 652e 6a70 ......sunrise.jp
0100e0: 6701 0000 0086 0c00 a868 6172 646c 696e g........hardlin
0100f0: 6b2e 6a70 6701 0000 0086 0c00 c073 6f66 k.jpg........sof
010100: 746c 696e 6b2e 6a70 6707 0000 0088 0000 tlink.jpg.......
```

Listing 10.19 The root directory data fork after creation of hard and soft links.

The content of inode (0x86) is shown in Listing 10.20. In this, the number of links has been increased, showing that a hardlink has been created to this file. This inode is now associated with two separate directory entries. The inode will not be deleted until both of these are removed. Deleting either the **hardlink.jpg** or **sunrise.jpg** will result in the link count being decreased. The inode will not be deallocated until the link count reaches 0_d.

What about a symbolic, or soft link? Inode 0x88 in Listing 10.19 is an example of a softlink. The contents of this inode are provided in Listing 10.21. Firstly it is possible to tell that this is a softlink through the mode/permissions value. This is 0xA1FF, in which the most significant nibble, 0xA, represents a symbolic link structure.

The link itself is discovered by firstly determining the storage mechanism, which in this case is 0x01, meaning that the data is resident in this inode. The data is 0x0B bytes in size. Consulting

```
010c00: 494e 81e8 0302 0000 0000 0000 0000 0000 IN..............
010c10: 0000 0002 0000 0000 0000 0000 0000 0000 ................
010c20: 6548 bd32 3220 b0e7 6548 bd32 325d b9e7 eH.22..eH.22]..
010c30: 6548 ddf3 2762 b73b 0000 0000 0008 3ef8 eH..'b.;......>.
010c40: 0000 0000 0000 0084 0000 0000 0000 0001 ................
010c50: 0000 2501 0000 0000 0000 0000 a818 785a..%...........xZ
010c60: ffff ffff c4f4 7338 0000 0000 0000 0009 ......s8........
010c70: 0000 0001 0000 0025 0000 0000 0000 0000 .......%........
010c80: 0000 0000 0000 0000 0000 0000 0000 0000 ................
010c90: 6548 bd32 3220 b0e7 0000 0000 0000 0086 eH.22 ..........
010ca0: f7a7 81bd 6d02 4c30 b214 c797 936b bbfe ....m.L0.....k..
010cb0: 0000 0000 0000 0000 0000 0000 0300 0084 ................
```

Listing 10.20 The contents of inode 0x86 in **XFS_V2.E01** showing the increased link count field.

```
011000: 494e a1ff 0301 0000 0000 0000 0000 0000 IN..............
011010: 0000 0001 0000 0000 0000 0000 0000 0000 ................
011020: 6548 ddfd 229e 0234 6548 ddfd 229e 0234 eH.."..4eH.."..4
011030: 6548 ddfd 229e 0234 0000 0000 0000 000b eH.."..4........
011040: 0000 0000 0000 0000 0000 0000 0000 0000 ................
011050: 0000 0002 0000 0000 0000 0000 2a7d 7997 ............*}y.
011060: ffff ffff 0ec7 8f9c 0000 0000 0000 0002 ................
011070: 0000 0001 0000 0025 0000 0000 0000 0000 .......%........
011080: 0000 0000 0000 0000 0000 0000 0000 0000 ................
011090: 6548 ddfd 229e 0234 0000 0000 0000 0088 eH.."..4........
0110a0: f7a7 81bd 6d02 4c30 b214 c797 936b bbfe ....m.L0.....k..
0110b0: 7375 6e72 6973 652e 6a70 6700 0000 0000 sunrise.jpg.....
```

Listing 10.21 Inode 0x88 in **XFS_V2.E01** showing a softlink.

the data area shows that the symbolic link is **sunrise.jpg**. In the case that the symbolic link text is greater than the available data area, symbolic links can be stored using extents. In this case, the link text will be located elsewhere in the file system and the inode's data fork will contain an extent which points to this location.

10.3.6 The XFS Journal

XFS provides a journaling system for use with the file system. The journal structure is a set of contiguous blocks, the location of which is discovered in the XFS superblock. The XFS journal can exist on the same device as the file system or, for added redundancy and efficiency, it can also exist on a separate device. Listing 10.22 shows the contents of the superblock in **XFS_V3.E01** with the journal start block and the number of blocks in the journal highlighted. This information allows the journal to be extracted from the file system. For instance in Listing 10.22 the journal start block is 0x10006 and there are 0x558 blocks in the journal. As the block size is 0x1000 bytes the following command is used to extract the journal:

dd if=mnt/ewf1 of=journal.raw bs=$((0x1000)) skip=$((0x10006)) count=$((0x558)).

The journal consists of a series of log records which contain a transaction, or part of a transaction. Transactions comprised log operation headers and raw data. The start operation in a transaction describes the transaction ID while the final operation is a commit record. The XFS journal records

```
000000: 5846 5342 0000 1000 0000 0000 0002 0000 XFSB............
000010: 0000 0000 0000 0000 0000 0000 0000 0000 ................
000020: f7a7 81bd 6d02 4c30 b214 c797 936b bbfe ....m.L0.....k..
000030: 0000 0000 0001 0006 0000 0000 0000 0080 ................
000040: 0000 0000 0000 0081 0000 0000 0000 0082 ................
000050: 0000 0001 0000 8000 0000 0004 0000 0000 ................
000060: 0000 0558 b4b5 0200 0200 0008 5846 532d ...X........XFS-
000070: 4653 0000 0000 0000 0c09 0903 0f00 0019 FS..............
```

Listing 10.22 An excerpt from the superblock in **XFS_V3.E01** showing the journal's starting block and number of blocks.

changes to metadata structures made by the transaction. These changes are found between the start and commit operations.

Previously inode 0x87 (**tree.jpg**) was deleted. In this version of the file system, new files have been created which have overwritten inode 0x87. This section attempts to use the journal to recover the original metadata structure for inode 0x87 and from that to recover the contents of the deleted file. Linux provides some tools to work directly with XFS logs. Listing 10.23 shows an excerpt from the output of **xfs_logprint** for **XFS_V3.E01**.[3]

```
cycle: 1 version: 2 lsn: 1,26 tail_lsn: 1,20
length of Log Record: 1024 prev offset: 20 num ops: 12
uuid: f7a781bd-6d02-4c30-b214-c797936bbbfe
format: little endian linux
h_size: 32768
-------------------------------------------------------------------
Oper (0): tid: c3ba9e3 len: 0 clientid: TRANS flags: START
...[snip]...
Oper (8): tid: c3ba9e3 len: 56 clientid: TRANS flags: none
INODE: #regs: 3 ino: 0x87 flags: 0x5 dsize: 16
      blkno: 128 len: 32 boff: 3584
Oper (9): tid: c3ba9e3 len: 176 clientid: TRANS flags: none
INODE CORE
magic 0x494e mode 0100750 version 3 format 2
nlink 1 uid 0 gid 0
atime 0x6548bd44 mtime 0x6548bd44 ctime 0x6548bd44
size 0xf6f0e nblocks 0xf7 extsize 0x0 nextents 0x1
naextents 0x0 forkoff 0 dmevmask 0x0 dmstate 0x0
flags 0x0 gen 0xe6b6cda7
flags2 0x0 cowextsize 0x0
Oper (10): tid: c3ba9e3 len: 16 clientid: TRANS flags: none
EXTENTS inode data
```

Listing 10.23 Excerpt from **xfs_logprint** when used on **XFS_V3.E01**.

The log sequence number (LSN) provides the cycle number (1_d) and the sector in the journal in which this transaction is found (26_d). The first operation shown here is a transaction start operation. Three further operations are shown. Operation 8_d shows that inode 0x87 is being updated. The

3 The **xfs_logprint** command will not work on E01 files or files resulting from the **ewfmount** command. The raw image must be exported using the command **ewfexport XFS_V3.E01**.

following two operations show information about the inode core structure (operation 9_d) and the inode's data fork being updated (operation 10_d). It is in these operations that it may be possible to determine the old values for inode 0x87.

Each transaction begins with a journal log record header structure, an excerpt from which is shown in Listing 10.24 with the structure and interpreted values provided in Table 10.22. This log record header is found at sector 26_d in the recovered journal file and represents the transaction shown in Listing 10.23. The journal log record header occupies an entire sector (512_d bytes).

```
003400: feed babe 0000 0001 0000 0002 0000 0400 ................
003410: 0000 0001 0000 001a 0000 0001 0000 0014 ................
003420: 2c1f a8db 0000 0014 0000 000c 0c3b a9e3,............;..
003430: 0000 0000 0000 0000 0000 0000 0000 0000 ................
...[snip]...
003510: 0000 0000 0000 0000 0000 0000 0000 0000 ................
003520: 0000 0000 0000 0000 0000 0000 0000 0001 ................
003530: f7a7 81bd 6d02 4c30 b214 c797 936b bbfe ....m.L0.....k..
003540: 0000 8000 0000 0000 0000 0000 0000 0000 ................
```

Listing 10.24 The journal header from **XFS_V3.E01**.

Log record header structures can be located simply by searching for their magic signature 0xfeedbabe. This is shown in Listing 10.25 for **XFS_V3.E01**. Each of the $4,099_d$ hits discovered in this file represents a transaction.

Table 10.22 Processed values from the log record header in Listing 10.24.

Offset	Size	Name	Description	Value
0x00	0x04	Signature	Journal signature 0xFEEDBABE.	0xFEEDBABE
0x04	0x04	Cycle	Cycle number of the log record.	0x01 (1_d)
0x08	0x04	Version	Log record version (currently 2).	0x02 (2_d)
0x0C	0x04	Length	Log record length in bytes.	0x400 ($1,024_d$)
0x10	0x08	LSN	Log sequence number of this record.	0x10000001A
0x18	0x08	Tail LSN	Log sequence number of the first record with uncommitted buffers.	0x100000014
0x20	0x04	CRC	Checksum.	0x2C1FA8DB
0x24	0x04	Prev. Block	Block number of the previous log record.	0x14 (20_d)
0x28	0x04	# Log Ops.	The number of log operations in this record.	0x0C (12_d)
0x2C	0x04	Cycle Data	This array consists of 64_d four byte entries which represent a particular transaction number.	0x0C3BA9E3
0x12C	0x04	Format	Format of the log record. This is one of: 0x00: Unknown; 0x01: Linux LE; 0x02: Linux BE; 0x03 Irix BE.	0x01 (1_d)
0x130	0x10	UUID	File system UUID.	0xF7A7...BBFE
0x140	0x04	Size	Log record size.	0x8000 ($32,768_d$)

```
$ xxd journal.raw | grep "feed babe"
000000: feed babe 0000 0001 0000 0002 0000 0200  ................
000400: feed babe 0000 0001 0000 0002 0000 0200  ................
000800: feed babe 0000 0001 0000 0002 0000 0600  ................
001000: feed babe 0000 0001 0000 0002 0000 0400  ................
...[snip]...
```

Listing 10.25 Searching **XFS_V3.E01** for journal log record header structures.

Immediately after the journal log record header a series of log operations are located. These consist of a header and, in some cases, data associated with the particular operation. These describe the individual operations that are occurring. Operations such as transaction start and commit have only a header as there is no data associated with them. Table 10.23 provides the structure for a log operation header.

Listing 10.26 shows the first three log operation headers in sector 27_d of the recovered journal file from **XFS_V3.E01**. Alternate operation headers are highlighted. Unhighlighted information represents the data associated with the previous log operation header. From this the first operation contains no data, while operations 1_d and 2_d contain some data. Table 10.24 processes the three operation headers.

Operation 0_d marks the start of the transaction with ID 0x0C3BA9E3. The transaction ID (TID) value in this operation header is 0x01. This is not the TID itself, but a pointer to the position in the cycle array in the log record header (Listing 10.24). The flag value informs the analyst that this is a START operation. As this is a start operation it contains no data.

Operation 1_d consists of 0x10 bytes of data. From processing the log record header, it is determined that the journal data is stored in a little-endian format. The first four bytes represent

Table 10.23 Journal log operation header structure.

Offset	Size	Name	Description
0x00	0x04	TID	The transaction ID for this transaction. Note that this may be the actual TID or a pointer to the index position in the cycle array in the log record header.
0x04	0x04	Length	Length of the data region following this operation header.
0x08	0x01	Client ID	The instigator of this transaction. Possible values include: 0x69: XFS_TRANSACTION; 0x02: XFS_VOLUME; 0xAA: XFS_LOG.
0x09	0x01	Flags	Transaction-specific flags. Possible values include: 0x01: Transaction start; 0x02: Transaction commit; 0x04: Continue to new record; 0x08: Started in prev. record; 0x10: End of continued transaction; 0x20: Unmount transaction.
0x0A	0x02	Padding	0x0000

```
003600: 0000 0001 0000 0000 6901 0000 0c3b a9e3  ........i....;..
003610: 0000 0010 6900 0000 4e41 5254 2800 0000  ....i...NART(...
003620: e3a9 3b0c 0900 0000 0c3b a9e3 0000 0018 ..;......;......
003630: 6900 0000 3c12 0200 0028 0100 0100 0000 i...<....(......
003640: 0000 0000 0100 0000 0100 0000            ............
```

Listing 10.26 Operations 0, 1 and 2, in sector 27_d of the **XFS_V3.E01** journal.

Table 10.24 Processed operation headers from Listing 10.26.

Off.	Len.	Name	Op 0	Op 1	Op 2
0x00	0x04	TID	0x01 0x0C3BA9E3	0x0C3BA9E3	0x0C3BA9E3
0x04	0x04	Length	0x00 (0_d)	0x10 (16_d)	0x18 (24_d)
0x08	0x01	CID	0x69 (105_d)	0x69 (105_d)	0x69 (105_d)
0x09	0x01	Flags	0x01 (1_d) START	0x00 (0_d)	0x00 (0_d)
0x0A	0x02	Padding	0x00	0x00	0x00

Table 10.25 Processed transaction header from Listing 10.26.

Offset	Size	Name	Description	Value
0x00	0x04	Magic	Signature value.	TRAN
0x04	0x04	Transaction Type	See Table 10.26.	0x28 (40_d) Swap data fork
0x08	0x04	TID	The transaction ID	0x0C3BA9E3
0x0C	0x04	# Items	Number of operations after this, not including the commit operation.	0x09 (9_d)

the magic value TRAN. Generally it is necessary to process the first part of the data to determine the type of operation that is represented. Data items that begin with the TRAN signature are called transaction headers. The structure of these, with values from Listing 10.26, is given in Table 10.25. Remember that all data is stored in a little-endian format!

Operation 2_d contains 0x18 bytes of data. The first two bytes of this are 0x123C. This is a type of log item. To determine the exact type the value must be looked up in Table 10.27 which shows this to be a buffer write operation. The structure of a buffer write operation, with values from Listing 10.24, is shown in Table 10.28.

The next task is to continue processing the remaining operations in the transaction. The operations that are of particular interest for file recovery are operations 8_d, 9_d and 10_d which were seen in Listing 10.23. These operations appear to be those that altered the content of inode 0x87. The operations appear in Listing 10.27. For each operation the headers are highlighted. The processed values of these headers appear in Table 10.29.

Table 10.26 Transaction types as found in the transaction header structure.

Type	Name	Type	Name	Type	Name
1	Set inode attribute (not size)	15	Start write	29	Disable quotas
2	Set inode size	16	Block allocation	30	Allocate disk quota
3	Inactive inode	17	Unused	31	Adjust quota limits
4	File creation	18	Update inode's preallocation flag	32	Unknown
5	Create truncated	19	Add attribute fork	33	Create quota inode
6	Truncate quota file	20	Erase attribute fork	34	Finish disabling quotas
7	Remove a file	21	Unknown	35	Update SB unit
8	Link inode to directory	22	Set extended attribute	36	Update inode timestamps
9	Rename path	23	Remove extended attribute	37	Grow real-time bitmap
10	Crete directory	24	Unknown	38	Zero real-time bitmap
11	Remove directory	25	Clear bad inode point in AGI	39	Free space in real-time bitmap
12	Create symlink	26	Change superblock	40	Swap data forks
13	Set DMAPI attributes	27	Dummy 1	41	Update superblock inode/block counts
14	Expand file system	28	Dummy 2	42	Checkpoint create

Table 10.27 Log item magic values.

Signature	Meaning	Signature	Meaning
0x1236	Extent freeing intent	0x123F	Inode creation
0x1237	Extent freeing done	0x1240	Reverse mapping update intent
0x1238	Unknown	0x1241	Reverse mapping update done
0x123B	Inode updates	0x1242	Reference count update intent
0x123C	Buffer writes	0x1243	Reference count update done
0x123D	Quota update	0x1244	File block mapping update intent
0x123E	Quota off	0x1245	File block mapping update done

Examining the data of operation 8_d shows the magic value to be 0x123B (Table 10.30). Referring to Table 10.27 shows this to be an inode update. The structure of the inode update log operation along with the values from operation 8_d is provided in Table 10.30.

Examining the inode update operation provides much useful information. Firstly, and most importantly, the inode number to which this operation refers to is identified. This is 0x87 in this case. Next the block to be updated is discovered. This is block 0x80 (which was where the root directory was found) and the byte offset in this block is 0xE00. Remember that each inode occupies 0x200 bytes so this is the end of the seventh inode in the block (as would be expected!). There are a total of three operations in this update, meaning the next two operations (9_d and 10_d) are also part

Table 10.28 Buffer write operation structure. Values are taken from Listing 10.26.

Offset	Size	Name	Description	Value
0x00	0x02	Magic	Signature value.	0x123C
0x02	0x02	Size	Number of buffer data items following this one.	0x02 (2_d)
0x04	0x02	Flags	Flags associated with this buffer item.	0x2800
0x06	0x02	Length	Number of sectors changed.	0x01 (1_d)
0x08	0x08	Blk #	Sector number to be written.	0x01 (1_d)
0x10	0x04	Map size	The size of the data map in four-byte entries.	0x01 (1_d)
0x14	Var	Data Map		0x01 (1_d)

```
OPERATION 8
003838: 0c3b a9e3 0000 0038 6900 0000 3b12 0300.;.....8i...;...
003848: 0500 0000 0000 1000 0000 0000 8700 0000 ................
003858: 0000 0000 0000 0000 0000 0000 0000 0000 ................
003868: 0000 0000 8000 0000 0000 0000 2000 0000 ............ ...
003878: 000e 0000                               ....
---
OPERATION 9
00387c: 0c3b a9e3 0000 00b0 6900 0000 4e49 e881.;......i...NI..
00388c: 0302 0000 0000 0000 0000 0000 0100 0000 ................
00389c: 0000 0000 0000 0000 0000 0000 44bd 4865 ............D.He
0038ac: 16a4 b516 44bd 4865 16a4 b516 44bd 4865 ....D.He....D.He
0038bc: 16a4 b516 0e6f 0f00 0000 0000 f700 0000 .....o..........
0038cc: 0000 0000 0000 0000 0100 0000 0000 0002 ................
0038dc: 0000 0000 0000 0000 a7cd b6e6 ffff ffff ................
0038ec: 0000 0000 0600 0000 0000 0000 1400 0000 ................
0038fc: 0100 0000 0000 0000 0000 0000 0000 0000 ................
00390c: 0000 0000 0000 0000 0000 0000 44bd 4865 ............D.He
00391c: 16a4 b516 8700 0000 0000 0000 f7a7 81bd ................
00392c: 6d02 4c30 b214 c797 936b bbfe           m.L0.....k..
---
OPERATION 10
003938: 0c3b a9e3 0000 0010 6900 0000 0000 0000.;......i.......
003948: 0000 0000 0000 0000 1380 00f7           ............
```

Listing 10.27 Operations 8_d, 9_d and 10_d in block 27_d of the journal file.

of the update. Finally, it is necessary to determine which parts of the inode are to be updated. The fields value shows which should be updated. This value is 0x05 which is 0x01 + 0x04. Consulting Table 10.31 shows this to mean that the inode core (0x01) and the data fork's extent structure will be updated (0x04). The next two log operations should relate to these updates.

Processing continues with operation 9_d. Based on the content of the previous operation this should be the actual content of the inode core structure. Examining the data shows the first two bytes are NI, which is the little-endian version of the inode code IN. The most important piece of

Table 10.29 Processed operation headers from Listing 10.27.

Offset	Size	Name	Op 8	Op 9	Op 10
0x00	0x04	TID	0x0C3BA9E3	0x0C3BA9E3	0x0C3BA9E3
0x04	0x04	Length	0x38 (56_d)	0xB0 (176_d)	0x10 (16_d)
0x08	0x01	CID	0x69 (105_d)	0x69 (105_d)	0x69 (105_d)
0x09	0x01	Flags	0x00 (0_d)	0x00 (0_d)	0x00 (0_d)
0x0A	0x02	Padding	0x00 (0_d)	0x00 (0_d)	0x00 (0_d)

Table 10.30 Processed inode update for operation 8_d.

Offset	Size	Name	Description	Value
0x00	0x02	Type	Signature of inode update.	0x123B
0x02	0x02	Size	Number of operations involved including this operation.	0x03 (3_d)
0x04	0x04	Fields	The parts of the inode being updated (see Table 10.31).	0x05 (5_d)
0x08	0x02	Attr. Fork Size	Size of the attribute fork (bytes).	0x00 (0_d)
0x0A	0x02	Data Fork Size	Size of the data fork (bytes).	0x10 (16_d)
0x0C	0x04	Padding	Padding.	0x00 (0_d)
0x10	0x08	Inode	The inode number.	0x87 (135_d)
0x18	0x10	UUID	Device UUID.	0x00 (0_d)
0x28	0x08	Block #	Sector number of the inode buffer.	0x80 (128_d)
0x30	0x04	Length	Length of the inode buffer (in sectors).	0x20 (32_d)
0x34	0x04	Buffer offset	Byte offset of the inode in the buffer.	0xE00 (3584_d)

Table 10.31 Possible values for fields in the inode update operation.

Value	Description	Value	Description
0x0001	Inode core	0x0040	Attr fork (local)
0x0002	Data fork (local)	0x0080	Attr fork (extent)
0x0004	Data fork (extent)	0x0100	Attr fork (B-Tree)
0x0008	Data fork (B-Tree)	0x0200	Data fork (owner)
0x0010	Device number	0x0400	Attr fork (owner)
0x0020	UUID		

information to gather from this point in order to aid file recovery is the file size. This is located at offset 0x38 and contains the value 0xF6F0E. Hence the file in question is 0xF6F0E bytes in size.

Finally, the extent structure is located in operation 10_d. The extent value is 0x138000F7. When processed this results in an extent starting at block 156_d which is 247_d blocks in length. The combination of this information along with the file size allows for the file to be extracted. The command to do this is shown in Listing 10.28 along with the resulting picture (Figure 10.7).

```
$ dd if=mnt/ewf1 of=tree.jpg bs=1 skip=$((156*4096))
     count=$((0xF6F0E))
1011470+0 records in
1011470+0 records out
1011470 bytes (1.0 MB, 988 KiB) copied, 23.304 s, 43.4 kB/s
$
$ file tree.jpg
tree.jpg: JPEG image data, ...[snip]...
$
$ md5sum tree.jpg
6c0b1e5315fef70a2d2db760e4b557ca tree.jpg
```

Listing 10.28 Command to recover the deleted **tree.jpg** file.

Figure 10.7 The recovered **tree.jpg** file.

10.4 Summary

The XFS file system is encountered in certain Linux distributions as the standard file system in use. Although an older file system, it is generally regarded as being more effective than ext for large-scale data storage but it still has a number of issues that have meant it has not seen more widespread use. Particularly the resilience is not as good as that found in modern file systems.

From a file system forensic perspective, XFS presents a number of specific challenges that have not been encountered before. One of the main challenges is that forensic tools do not support this file system. This is the first file system examined in this book that is not supported by default by any of the file system forensic tools that are in common usage.[4] This means that the results obtained in this chapter are impossible to validate using other tools. Manual analysis is the only way forward. However, in Section 10.3.6, some of the file system tools were utilised to provide an overview of the journal structure (**xfs_logprint**). While this is not a forensic tool it provided a possible means of

4 There are some extensions written for Sleuth Kit that allow basic processing of XFS but they are not part of the official release.

verifying some of the results. However, while this tool allowed the file size to be obtained directly (see the output for operation 9_d in Listing 10.23) it would not allow for the actual extent itself to be recovered as operation 10_d was only described as being *EXTENTS Inode Data* with no interpretation of the extent values.

In the case that forensic tools are unable to support a particular file system it is always worth investigating the file system management tools that are available to see if they may aid the analysis task. However, the analyst must ensure that these tools do not change any of the data that will be relied upon later in the investigation, as these tools are not designed with the forensic process in mind.

Exercises

All questions in this section refer to the file system contained in **XFS_V4.E01**.

1 What is the volume label?

2 How many allocation groups exist in the filesystem?

3 What is the block size?

4 In which block is the root directory inode found?

5 Process the root directory and list the files/folders contained within.

6 The root directory contains a file called **info.txt**. What is the inode of this file?

7 In relation to **info.txt** answer the following questions:
   a) What is the file size?
   b) When was the file created?
   c) In which block(s) are the file content found?
   d) What is the MD5 of the file content?

8 Two directories were found in the root directory. List the contents of these directories.

9 Process the files **Links/hardlink.jpg** and **Links/softlink.jpg**. To which files are they linking?

10 A file called **sunrise.jpg** was deleted from the Pictures directory. Using any means at your disposal, recover the contents of this file.

Bibliography

Hellwig, C. (2009). XFS: the big storage file system for Linux.;login:: the magazine of USENIX. 34 (5): 10–18.

Kernel.org (2024). xfs/xfs-linux.git - XFS kernel development tree [Internet]. git.kernel.org. [cited 2024 May 28]. https://git.kernel.org/pub/scm/fs/xfs/xfs-linux.git/ (accessed 14 August 2024).

Kim, H., Kim, S., Shin, Y. et al. (2021). Ext4 and XFS file system forensic framework based on TSK. *Electronics* 10 (18): 2310.

Nikkel, B. (2021). *Practical Linux Foresnsics: A Guide for Digital Investigators*. San Francisco: No Starch Press.

Oracle (2024). Oracle Linux 6: Administrator's Solutions Guide [Internet]. docs.oracle.com. [cited 2024 March 26]. https://docs.oracle.com/en/operating-systems/oracle-linux/6/adminsg/index.html (accessed 14 August 2024).

Oracle Help Center (2024). Managing the XFS File System [Internet]. Oracle Help Center. [cited 2024 March 26]. https://docs.oracle.com/en/operating-systems/oracle-linux/8/fsadmin/fsadmin-ManagingtheXFSFileSystem.htmlxfs-main (accessed 14 August 2024).

Park, Y., Chang, H., and Shon, T. (2015). Data investigation based on XFS file system metadata. *Multimedia Tools and Applications* 75 (22): 14721–14743.

Pomeranz, H. (2018). XFS (Parts 1 –5) [internet]. righteousit.com. [cited 2024 June 19]. https://righteousit.com/2018/05/21/xfs-part-1-superblock/ (accessed 14 August 2024).

Red Hat Documentation (2024). Chapter 3. The XFS File System Red Hat Enterprise Linux 7 –Red Hat Customer Portal [Internet]. access.redhat.com. https://access.redhat.com/documentation/en-us/red_hatenterprise_linux/7/html/storage_administration_guide/ch-xfs (accessed 14 August 2024).

Tamma, K. and Venugopalan, S. (2024). Failure Analysis of SGI XFS File System [Internet]. [cited 2024 Mar 26]. https://pages.cs.wisc.edu/vshree/xfs.pdf (accessed 14 August 2024).

The Linux Kernel (n.d.). The SGI XFS Filesystem –The Linux Kernel documentation [Internet]. docs.kernel.org. [cited 2024 Mar 26]. https://docs.kernel.org/admin-guide/xfs.html (accessed 14 August 2024).

Vujičić, D., Marković, D., Đorđević, B., and Randić, S. (2016). Benchmarking performance of ext4, xfs, and btrfs as guest file systems under Linux environment. Proceedings of 3rd International Conference on Electrical, Electronic and Computing Engineering IcETRAN, pp. 13–16.

Wang, R.Y. and Anderson, T.E. (1993). xFS: A wide area mass storage file system. Proceedings of IEEE 4th Workshop on Workstation Operating Systems. WWOS-III (14 October 1993), pp. 71–78. IEEE.

Wiki (2024). XFS Linux [Wiki] [Internet]. xfs.wiki.kernel.org. [cited 2024 March 26 3]. https://xfs.wiki.kernel.org/ (accessed 14 August 2024).

XFS Algorithms & Data Structures 3rd Edition (2024). [cited 2024 March 26]. https://mirror.math.princeton.edu/pub/kernel/linux/utils/fs/xfs/docs/xfs_filesystem_structure.pdf (accessed 14 August 2024).

11

The Btrfs File System

Btrfs is a modern file system that uses B-Trees as its main storage mechanism. The name is an abbreviation of B-Tree file system and is pronounced in many ways such as 'butter fuss', 'b-tree FS', 'better FS' or most commonly by spelling it out! Development of Btrfs began in 2007 when Chris Mason joined Oracle. The first version of Btrfs was adopted into the mainline kernel in 2009. Currently (as of version 5) Oracle, Western Digital, Facebook and SUSE are actively involved in the Btrfs development process. A number of versions of SUSE Linux have used Btrfs as a replacement for ext as the primary file system. In August 2020, Fedora announced that Fedora 33 would use Btrfs as the default file system.

As a file system introduced to overcome space limitations of previous file systems Btrfs is able to store lots of large files! Table 11.1 shows some of the theoretical limits of the file system. They are theoretical as not all can be addressed in the current Linux kernel. While Btrfs can achieve these figures, the kernel cannot access them so some of the limits are never reached.

Btrfs is considered a modern file system, much more so than ext4 which was only ever considered a stop-gap until a better file system arrived. Therefore, Btrfs provides support for a multitude of modern file system principles such as:

- **B-Tree-Based File System:** Btrfs uses B-Trees to store all metadata information in the file system (except for the superblock). B-Trees consist of key-item pairs. There are a number of B-Trees used in all Btrfs file systems. These are discussed later.
- **Copy-on-Write (CoW):** Copy-on-write is a mechanism by which data is written to a disk only when changes are made to that data. Consider the action of copying a file on a single volume on a traditional file system. Copying exactly duplicates the underlying data, but makes no changes to that data. Btrfs (and other file systems that employ copy-on-write) will not duplicate the data when a copy occurs. Btrfs will increase the link count for the copy and will create another copy of the underlying data only when one of the links changes. Even in the case where data is modified on-disk, CoW generally means that the block is copied to a free location, changes are made to the block and the metadata is then updated. This means that Btrfs provides the possibility of finding older versions of files still in existence. The same principle applies to metadata blocks, meaning that older versions of metadata can also be found.
- **Multiple Device Support:** Btrfs provides for logical file systems that span multiple devices. This can take the form of JBOD (Just a Bunch of Disks) in which multiple physical devices are used to create one single (large) logical device, or it can be used to implement RAID at the file system level. Internally, in a logical Btrfs file system there are conceptually three areas on the device, the system, metadata and data areas. The system area stores information about the logical address mapping, the metadata area stores file system metadata and the data area stores file contents. By

File System Forensics, First Edition. Fergus Toolan.

Table 11.1 Btrfs file system limitations.

Metric	Value
Max. Volume Size	2^{64} bytes (16 EiB)
Max. File Size	2^{64} bytes (16 EiB)
Max. Number of Files	2^{64} bytes (16 EiB)
Max. Filename Length	255 bytes. This equates to 255 characters in ASCII encoding but less in other text encodings.

default, the system and metadata chunks are duplicated, allowing for a simple form of metadata RAID in almost all Btrfs filesystems.[1]

- **Extent-Based File Storage:** Extents provide a more flexible and scalable means of storing file content than ext's traditional block pointer system.[2] Extents are used in most modern file systems. Extents generally contain a starting location and a size, meaning that two numbers can define a run of data blocks. Files can have multiple extents.
- **Integrated Checksums:** Btrfs uses a block-level checksum feature, so that the integrity of each metadata block can be verified. Each node in a tree has its own internal checksum as part of that node. Btrfs also provides the CSUM_TREE which contains checksums of all extent data (file content) in the file system.
- **Subvolumes:** Subvolumes are smaller volumes inside the main Btrfs file system. All instances of Btrfs contain one subvolume, the top-level subvolume, which contains everything else in the file system. When a Btrfs device is mounted, it is actually a subvolume that is being mounted. By default the top-level subvolume is mounted; however, it is possible to specify a different subvolume to be mounted.
- **Snapshots:** Btrfs provides the ability to create snapshots, system states at particular points in time. Generally this is done through logical means. CoW means that no changes are made to data until the underlying structure is altered. Unlike a back-up, not everything is copied immediately in a snapshot, so a snapshot needs much less space than the backup. Snapshots are created in Btrfs by creating a subvolume which is a copy-on-write copy of another subvolume.
- **Compression:** At file system creation time Btrfs can be instructed to compress all data that is stored in the file system. Note as of Version 5.9, internal encryption has not been implemented, but it is expected as a feature in later versions.

Btrfs is a modern file system and is still under development. The current version is 5.17 (as of 2023).

11.1 On-Disk Structures

In order to analyse a Btrfs filesystem it is necessary to understand the types of structures that are present and where they will be encountered on the file system. In this section some of the common structures of interest to the analysis of Btrfs are described. It begins by describing the various

1 The exception is when Btrfs is installed on solid-state drives. In this case, the default behaviour is to have no duplication of any chunk area.
2 Extent-based storage is used in the ext4 file system.

B-Trees that are used for metadata storage in the file system. The internal structure of tree nodes is then described. All Btrfs trees are structured in the same manner so understanding these structures allows all metadata information in the file system to be located.

Btrfs trees store key-item pairs, the key provides information on the type of item and where it is located. There are a number of items in the Btrfs file system. In order to analyse the file system it is necessary to understand the various item types that are present in the file system. Of course it is also necessary to be able to locate the trees and items on the file system. Btrfs uses a single logical address space which is mapped to a physical address space using the chunk and device trees. These concepts are explained later in this section. Finally this section describes how time is stored in Btrfs. Please note that, unless otherwise stated, all structures in Btrfs are stored in a little-endian format.

An understanding of these structures will allow the manual processing of Btrfs file systems later in this chapter. As with XFS, this is important as, generally, forensic tools do not provide support for Btrfs.

11.1.1 The Superblock

Like many file systems Btrfs contains a superblock which provides information about the file system as a whole. The superblock serves the same purpose in Btrfs as it does in ext and as the volume boot record does in FAT and NTFS. From the superblock information relating to the data allocation units on the devices (sectors, nodes and leaves in the case of Btrfs), the logical addresses of certain trees that are required to rebuild all data and metadata in the file system, etc. are determined. The superblock is the initial starting point in the analysis of Btrfs.

There are multiple copies of the superblock structure in the file system. In Btrfs these superblocks are stored at specific absolute addresses. The primary copy of the superblock is stored at byte offset 0x10000 (64 KiB). Backup copies are stored at byte offsets 0x4000000 (64 MiB) and 0x4000000000 (256 GiB) if these locations are valid. In the case of Btrfs file systems with multiple devices, each device contains copies of the superblock at each of these offsets. All superblock copies are updated simultaneously.

The superblock can also be used to recognise a Btrfs file system. Listing 11.1 shows an excerpt from a Btrfs superblock structure. At offset 0x40 in the superblock structure the Btrfs signature is found. This value is **_BHRfS_M**.

```
010000: 3bdd f493 0000 0000 0000 0000 0000 0000 ;...............
010010: 0000 0000 0000 0000 0000 0000 0000 0000 ................
010020: 2f72 2027 c81b 4b8b bf6c b068 014b 7816 /r '..K..l.h.Kx.
010030: 0000 0100 0000 0000 0100 0000 0000 0000 ................
010040: 5f42 4852 6653 5f4d 0a00 0000 0000 0000 _BHRfS_M........
010050: 0080 d501 0000 0000 0040 5001 0000 0000 .........@P.....
```

Listing 11.1 Excerpt from the Btrfs superblock in **BtrFS_V1.E01** showing the magic identifier _BHRfs_M.

The structure of the superblock is provided in Table 11.2.

11.1.2 Btrfs Trees

The B-Tree in Btrfs is, as in many modern file systems, the basic structure for metadata storage. There are a number of system B-Trees that are located in Btrfs file systems. In this section these

Table 11.2 Btrfs superblock structure.

Offset	Size	Name	Description
0x00	0x20	Checksum	Checksum of all data in the superblock from the end of the checksum field to the end of the node.
0x20	0x10	UUID	The unique universal identifier for this file system.
0x30	0x08	Node Address	Logical address of this node.
0x38	0x07	Flags	File system flags.
0x3F	0x01	Backref Version	Always 1 in new file systems. A value of zero indicates an older file system.
0x40	0x08	Signature	Btrfs signature **_BHRfS_M**.
0x48	0x08	Generation	A counter used to ensure file system integrity.
0x50	0x08	ROOT_TREE Addr.	Logical address of the ROOT_TREE root.
0x58	0x08	CHUNK_TREE Addr.	Logical address of the CHUNK_TREE root.
0x60	0x08	LOG_TREE Addr.	Logical address of the LOG_TREE root.
0x68	0x08	Log Root Transid	Transaction ID tree address.
0x70	0x08	# Bytes	Total number of bytes in the file system.
0x78	0x08	# Bytes Used	Total number of bytes used in the file system.
0x80	0x08	Root Dir. OID	The object ID (OID) for the root directory (usually 0x06).
0x88	0x08	# Devices	The number of devices in the file system.
0x90	0x04	Sector Size	The sector size of the file system.
0x94	0x04	Node Size	The size of each tree node in the file system.
0x98	0x04	Leaf Size	The leaf node size of the file system.
0x9C	0x04	Stripe Size	The stripe size of the file system.
0xA0	0x04	CHUNK_ARRAY Size	The size of the CHUNK_ARRAY in bytes.
0xA4	0x08	Chunk Root Gen.	The chunk root generation.
0xAC	0x08	Compat Flags	Compatibility flags for mounting this file system.
0xB4	0x08	Compat RO Flags	Read-only compatibility flags. If a driver does not support any of these flags then the file system should be mounted as read-only.
0xBC	0x08	Incompat Flags	Drivers that do not support any of these flags may not use the file system.
0xC4	0x02	Checksum Type	Currently CRC32c.
0xC6	0x01	Root Level	The level of the ROOT_TREE.
0xC7	0x01	Chunk Root Level	The level of the CHUNK_TREE.
0xC8	0x01	Log Root Level	The level of the LOG_ROOT_TREE.
0xC9	0x62	DEV_ITEM	The DEV_ITEM for the device on which this superblock is found.
0x12B	0x100	File System Label	An 0x100 byte character array which contains the file system label.
0x32B	0x800	CHUNK_ARRAY	An excerpt from the CHUNK_TREE used to bootstrap logical/physical address mapping.

common trees are listed and the purpose of each is described. In each case the name of the tree is provided along with its object ID (OID).[3] The reserved trees include:

- **ROOT_TREE (OID: 0x01):** The ROOT_TREE (sometimes referred to as the tree of trees) is the primary structure required for rebuilding the file system and all other metadata structures. The ROOT_TREE contains information about the location of all other trees in the system. The logical address of the ROOT_TREE itself is located in the superblock.
- **EXTENT_TREE (OID: 0x02):** The EXTENT_TREE contains information about the data and metadata allocation in the file system. It provides information on the locations at which various types of data both can be and are currently stored in the file system.
- **CHUNK_TREE (OID: 0x03):** The CHUNK_TREE contains information about all devices that are present in the file system. The CHUNK_TREE is the structure used to map logical to physical addresses. The logical file system is divided into a number of chunks, entries for which appear in the CHUNK_TREE. These entries provide the physical stripes associated with the logical address, thereby allowing the logical addresses to be converted to physical addresses. The CHUNK_TREE is a vital structure required to locate other structures and file locations.
- **DEV_TREE (OID: 0x04):** The DEV_TREE is used in situations where it is necessary to map a logical to a physical address. This structure is generally used when device configuration is changed in a file system, which is not something that digital forensics aims to do. Hence, this tree is generally of little interest to the digital forensic process.
- **FS_TREE (OID: 0x05):** The FS_TREE (or file system tree) allows the contents of the entire file system to be rebuilt. This structure contains inode information about every file and directory. Processing this structure allows all files in the file system to be listed and recovered and also to recover associated metadata. This structure is one of the most vital in the digital forensic process.
- **The Root Directory Tree (generally OID: 0x06):** This provides a representation of the root directory (it actually points to the FS_TREE). To date all root directory trees have the OID 0x06. This is specified in the superblock and may change at a later date.
- **CSUM_TREE (OID: 0x07):** The CSUM_TREE is used to validate data. It contains checksums for each data extent in the file system.

11.1.3 Btrfs Tree Structure

B-trees are composed of one or more nodes. From the superblock the size of nodes in a particular file system is discovered. Btrfs provides two different types of node, internal and leaf nodes. Internal nodes contain pointers to other nodes, while leaf nodes contain the actual data in the form of key/item pairs. Every node, regardless of whether it is an internal or leaf node, begins with a node header. The remainder of this section describes the node structures in further details.

11.1.3.1 Node Header Structure

Every node in every B-Tree begins with a node header of 0x65 bytes in length. This header provides information about the node and the tree that contains it. It also provides the number of items that are present in the node and the node level. The structure of the node header is given in Table 11.3.

Subsequent data depends on the type of node in question, internal or leaf. Both internal and leaf node structures follow.

---

3 Every object (trees, files, etc.) in Btrfs has a unique object ID number. System objects have numbers between 0x01 and 0x100. OIDs greater than 0x100 are used by user-created files. There are also certain trees which have negative OIDs.

Table 11.3 Btrfs B-Tree node header structure.

Offset	Size	Name	Description
0x00	0x20	Checksum	Checksum of all data in the block from the end of the checksum field to the end of the node.
0x20	0x10	UUID	The unique universal identifier for this file system.
0x30	0x08	Node Addr.	Logical address of this node.
0x38	0x07	Flags	File system flags.
0x3F	0x01	Backref Revision	Always 1 in new file systems. A value of zero indicates an older file system.
0x40	0x10	UUID	CHUNK_TREE UUID.
0x50	0x08	Generation	As found in the superblock.
0x58	0x08	Tree OID Int	The OID of the tree that contains this node.
0x60	0x04	# Items	Number of items in this node.
0x64	0x01	Node Level	Leaf nodes are level 0. Any other numbers represent internal nodes. The number represents how many layers of internal nodes need to be traversed in order to reach a leaf node.

In a leaf node the header is immediately followed by a number of items. Item data is stored at the end of the node. A key to the item data location is stored immediately after the node header. This structure is shown in Figure 11.1.

Figure 11.1 shows a leaf node with three items. The key pointers commence immediately after the node header (node offset: 0x65). Key pointers are 0x19 (25_d) bytes in size and are composed of a 0x11 byte item key structure (see Section 11.1.4) followed by a four-byte value representing the offset to the start of the data item. This offset is relative to the end of the node header. The final four bytes in the key pointer contain the size of the data item (in bytes). Table 11.4 summarises this structure.

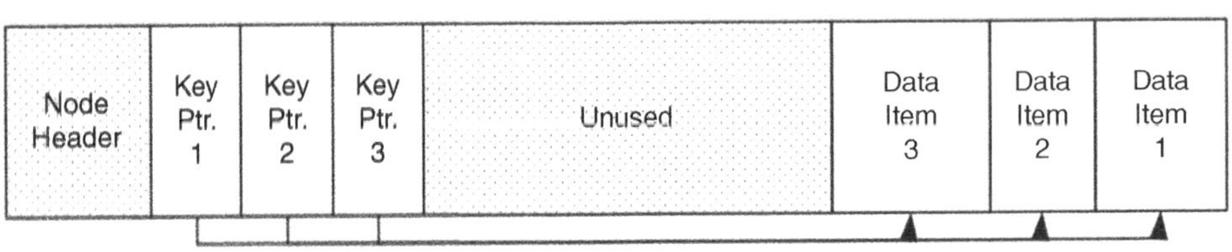

Figure 11.1 Btrfs B-Tree leaf node structure.

Table 11.4 Leaf node key pointer structure.

Offset	Size	Name	Description
0x00	0x11	Key	The item key (see Section 11.1.4).
0x11	0x04	Offset	Byte offset to the start of the data item relative to the end of the node header (0x65).
0x15	0x04	Size	Data item size in bytes.

Figure 11.2 Btrfs B-Tree internal node structure.

Table 11.5 Internal node key pointer structure.

Offset	Size	Name	Description
0x00	0x11	Key	The item key (see Section 11.1.4).
0x11	0x08	Node Addr.	Logical address of the next node in the tree.
0x19	0x08	Generation	Generation.

The data item structures are dependent on the type of item that is referenced. Section 11.1.5 describes each of the item types available in Btrfs in more detail.

11.1.3.2 Internal Node Structure

Internal nodes are used when trees become too large for a single node. Instead of containing pointers to data items inside the node itself, they contain pointers to other nodes in the tree. These other nodes may be leaf or internal nodes. In the latter case, they will contain pointers to yet more nodes.

Figure 11.2 shows the structure of an internal node in a Btrfs B-tree. The key pointer structure is provided in Table 11.5.

11.1.4 Btrfs Keys

When examining the structure of pointers in both the internal and leaf nodes the concept of the item key was encountered. These keys act as a form of identifier for item types. The key structure is 0x11 bytes in size and is shown in Table 11.6.

The key is used to sort items in a tree node. Note that when describing the various trees used in Btrfs some use negative OID values (Section 11.1.2); however, the OID field is an unsigned integer. This means that an OID of −1 (0xFFFFFFFFFFFFFFFF) will appear at the very end of the list and not before the positive OIDs as would be expected.

Table 11.6 Btrfs key structure.

Offset	Size	Name	Description
0x00	0x08	OID	The object ID to which this key refers.
0x08	0x01	Item Type	The type of item represented by this key (see Section 11.1.5).
0x09	0x08	Offset	The meaning of this value is dependent on the item type in question.

11.1.5 Btrfs Items

The item type field in the key describes the type of item that is present. There are a number of item types in Btrfs some of which are listed below. The reader should be aware that it is not generally necessary to fully understand all the item types as the majority have little use in the forensic process. Below are found the more commonly required items for forensic analysis of Btrfs. The reader is encouraged to discover more information at the Btrfs kernel wiki if required.[4]

- **INODE_ITEM (Type: 0x01):** The INODE_ITEM provides all metadata in relation to a file or directory. This is the structure that is read by the Linux **stat** command when it seeks information about a file. In Btrfs INODE_ITEMs are mainly located in file trees (e.g. FS_TREE) but can also be found in the ROOT_TREE. The key offset for an INODE_ITEM has no meaning and as such is always set to zero. Table 11.7 shows the structure of an INODE_ITEM.
  Again parallels exist with the ext inode structure. The reason for this is that these are all Linux file systems and must function with the **stat** command. From the INODE_ITEM we can also see that Btrfs stores four timestamps. The traditional ext times of modified, accessed and changed and also the time of inode creation. The Btrfs kernel wiki provides more information on the flags used in the INODE_ITEM.

Table 11.7 INODE_ITEM structure.

Offset	Size	Name	Description
0x00	0x08	Generation	Generation.
0x08	0x08	Transid	Transaction ID.
0x10	0x08	File Size (actual)	Size of the file in bytes.
0x18	0x08	File Size (alloc)	Size of the file in allocated bytes (complete blocks).
0x20	0x08	Block group	Generally unused related to free space management.
0x28	0x04	# Links	Number of links to the file. This is actually a count of the number of INODE_REF items pointing to this OID in Btrfs.
0x2C	0x04	UID	User ID (UID).
0x30	0x04	GID	Group ID (GID).
0x34	0x04	Mode	As in ext containing file type and permissions.
0x38	0x08	RDev	Generally unused in modern systems.
0x40	0x08	Flags	Inode Flags.
0x48	0x08	Sequence Num.	Used for NFS compatibility. This value is incremented every time the modification time changes.
0x50	0x20	Reserved	Reserved for future use.
0x70	0x0C	Access Time	Access time structure (see Section 11.1.6).
0x7C	0x0C	Change Time	Metadata change time structure (see Section 11.1.6).
0x88	0x0C	Modification Time	Modification time structure (see Section 11.1.6).
0x94	0x0C	Creation Structure	Inode creation time structure (see Section 11.1.6).

4 https://btrfs.readthedocs.io/en/latest/.

Table 11.8 INODE_REF structure.

Offset	Size	Name	Description
0x00	0x08	Directory Index	Used for ordering items in the directory.
0x08	0x02	Name Length (n)	The length of the name in bytes.
0x0A	(n)	File Name	The file name. The length is discovered in the previous field.

- **INODE_REF (Type: 0x0C):**
  The INODE_REF stores information about the filename. Specifically it maps an inode (Object ID) to a name in a directory similar to a directory entry in ext. The INODE_REF item is generally found in file trees but can also be found in the ROOT_TREE. The structure of an INODE_REF is given in Table 11.8.
  When dealing with an INODE_REF item, the key offset is the OID of the parent directory. Consider the key for an INODE_REF item shown in Listing 11.2.

```
10000: 1A01 0000 0000 0000 0C07 0100 0000 0000  ................
10010: 00                                       .
```

Listing 11.2 Item key for an INODE_REF item.

  In this we see that the OID of the Object being referred to is 0x1A1. The key offset is 0x107. This means that inode 0x107 is the parent of inode 0x11A.
- **DIR_ITEM (Type: 0x54):** The DIR_ITEM is found in directories and contains directory entries. The key offset for the DIR_ITEM contains the hashed value of the file name in the DIR_ITEM. This allows for faster searching for particular DIR_ITEM values. DIR_ITEMs can contain information about multiple files if those filenames' hash to the same value. Table 11.9 provides the DIR_ITEM structure.
  DIR_ITEMs are examined when attempting to rebuild the list of files/directories present in a file system.
- **DIR_INDEX (Type: 0x60):** The contents of the DIR_INDEX are identical to those of the DIR_ITEM but the key offset is different. The key offset provides an index to the position of the item in the directory. The first index position is 2, presumably to allow for the . and .. directories.
- **EXTENT_DATA (Type: 0x6C):** The EXTENT_DATA item provides information on where the file contents are stored. In Btrfs file content can be stored inline or using extents. In both cases the required information is available in the EXTENT_DATA item. The key offset for an EXTENT_DATA item provides the offset within the file that the particular extent represents. This value is 0x00 for files which have only a single extent or for the first extent in a file. EXTENT_ITEMs are found in file trees.
  The EXTENT_DATA item contains a 0x15 byte header. The structure of this is described in Table 11.10. In the case of inline storage, the file content is found immediately after the header. In the case of regular extent-based storage the structure in Table 11.11 is found.
  The size of the extent at 0x1D may differ from the size at 0x08. This is due to data encoding. Once the bytes located in the extent are decoded there should then be (n) bytes of data resulting.
- **EXTENT_CSUM (Type: 0x80):** EXTENT_CSUMs are found in the CSUM_TREE and contain checksums for particular data areas on the device.

Table 11.9 DIR_ITEM structure.

Offset	Size	Name	Description
0x00	0x11	Key	Key of the INODE_ITEM associated with this entry.
0x11	0x08	Transid	Transaction ID.
0x19	0x02	Xattr Length	Length of the extended attribute. 0 for standard dirs.
0x1B	0x02	Dir Name Length	Length of the directory name in bytes. The name follows immediately after this structure.
0x1D	0x01	Type	Valid values include: 0x00: Unknown 0x01: Regular File 0x02: Directory 0x03: Character Device 0x04: Block Device 0x05: FIFO Device 0x06: Socket Device 0x07: Symbolic Link 0x08: XATTR_ITEM

Table 11.10 EXTENT_DATA header structure.

Offset	Size	Name	Description
0x00	0x08	Generation	Generation.
0x08	0x08	Decoded Ext. Size (n)	The size of the decoded extent in bytes.
0x10	0x01	Compression	The compression algorithm used (0: none; 1: zlib; 2: LZO).
0x11	0x01	Encryption	The encryption algorithm used (0: none).
0x12	0x02	Other encoding	Any other encodings that might be used (0: none).
0x14	0x01	Extent Type	The storage mechanism used in this EXTENT_DATA item (0: Inline; 1: Regular; 2: Preallocated).

Table 11.11 Subsequent data in EXTENT_DATA structure for a regular file.

Offset	Size	Name	Description
0x15	0x08	Logical Address	Starting logical address of the extent. Zero means the entire extent consists of zero values.
0x1D	0x08	Size	Size of the extent.
0x25	0x08	Offset	Offset within the extent.
0x2D	0x08	# Bytes	Logical number of bytes in file (note this is not the file size, it is the allocated bytes). Consult the INODE_ITEM in order to determine the file size.

Table 11.12 ROOT_ITEM structure.

Offset	Size	Name	Description
0x00	0xA0	INODE_ITEM	An INODE_ITEM representing certain information about the tree root. Not all of the INODE_ITEM information is initialised.
0xA0	0x08	Transid	Transaction ID.
0xA8	0x08	Root Dir. ID	The root directory ID – always 0x100 for file trees, 0 otherwise.
0xB0	0x08	Root Node Addr.	The logical address of the root node of this tree.
0xB8	0x08	Unused	Unused.
0xC0	0x08	Unused	Unused.
0xC8	0x08	Transid (Snap)	The transid of the transaction that created the last snapshot of this root.
0xD0	0x08	Flags	Flags from INODE_ITEM apply.
0xD8	0x04	Ref. Count	Originally indicated a reference count. Now it is only 0 or 1.
0xDC	0x11	Key	Contains the key of the last item dropped during subvolume relocation. Zero otherwise.
0xED	0x01	Level	The tree level of the node described in the previous field.
0xEE	0x01	Height	The height of tree to which this ROOT_ITEM refers.

- **ROOT_ITEM (Type: 0x84):** ROOT_ITEMs are located only in the ROOT_TREE. The key offset for a ROOT_ITEM is 0x00 in the case of a normal subvolume. For a snapshot this key offset contains the transaction ID (TID) that created the snapshot. The ROOT_ITEM structure allows the root of a B-tree to be located. The structure of the ROOT_ITEM is given in Table 11.12.
  While the ROOT_ITEM structure contains more information than that listed in Table 11.12, most of it is relevant only if subvolumes are in use. The key field in the ROOT_ITEM is the logical address of the root node for the tree.
- **ROOT_BACKREF (Type: 0x90):** Contains the same content as the ROOT_REF (0x9C). The key for the ROOT_BACKREF item contains the subtreeID, the type (0x90) and the parent tree id.
- **ROOT_REF (Type: 0x9C):** ROOT_REF contains information about subvolumes such as the volume's name. This and the ROOT_BACKREF items are found only in the ROOT_TREE.
- **DEV_ITEM (Type: 0xD8):** The DEV_ITEM provides information about the Device. DEV_ITEMS are found in the CHUNK_TREE, which contains a DEV_ITEM for each individual device in the file system. The key offset for the DEV_ITEM is the device ID. Table 11.13 provides the structure of the DEV_ITEM.
- **CHUNK_ITEM (Type: 0xE4):** The Btrfs logical address space is broken into a number of non-overlapping chunks. The CHUNK_ITEM associates these logical address spaces with one or more physical addresses. There are three different types of chunk used depending on the type of data that is stored in them. These are data, metadata and system chunks. The data chunks are used to store data blocks only, while all file metadata is stored in the metadata chunk. Inline data is also stored in the metadata chunk. The system chunk is used to store B-Trees related to the address mapping process.
  The key offset for a CHUNK_ITEM contains the logical address at which the chunk starts. Table 11.14 describes the structure of the CHUNK_ITEM. CHUNK_ITEMs contain one or

Table 11.13 DEV_ITEM structure.

Offset	Size	Name	Description
0x00	0x08	Device ID	Device ID.
0x08	0x08	# Bytes	Total number of bytes on the device.
0x10	0x08	# Bytes Used	Number of used bytes on the device.
0x18	0x04	Opt. I/O Align.	Optimal I/O alignment.
0x1C	0x04	Opt. I/O Width	Optimal I/O width.
0x20	0x04	Sector Size	Sector size.
0x24	0x08	Type	Type.
0x2C	0x08	Generation	Generation.
0x34	0x08	Start Offset	Start Offset.
0x3C	0x04	Device Group	Device group.
0x40	0x01	Seek Speed	Seek speed.
0x41	0x01	Bandwidth	Bandwidth.
0x42	0x10	Device UUID	A UUID for the device represented by this DEV_ITEM.
0x52	0x10	FS UUID	A UUID for the file system present on this device.

more stripes which describe physical areas on the device. The number of stripes is found in the CHUNK_ITEM. The stripe structure is also found in Table 11.14.

Chunks which contain multiple stripes are actually duplicating data. If a chunk contains two stripes then there will exist two copies of any data stored in that chunk! The CHUNK_ITEM is the structure that allows this duplication (i.e. simple RAID) to occur.

Table 11.14 CHUNK_ITEM structure.

Offset	Size	Name	Description
0x00	0x08	Chunk Size	The size of this chunk in bytes.
0x08	0x08	OID	Root referencing this chunk.
0x10	0x08	Stripe Length	The length of each stripe in bytes.
0x18	0x04	Type	Purpose unknown.
0x1C	0x04	Opt. I/O Align	Optimal I/O alignment.
0x20	0x04	Opt. I/O Width	Optimal I/O width.
0x24	0x08	Sector Size	The sector size in bytes.
0x2C	0x08	# Stripes	The number of stripes.
0x34	0x08	# Sub-Stripes	The number of sub-stripes.
		Stripes (for each stripe defined above)	
0x00	0x08	Device ID	The device ID in the current file system.
0x08	0x08	Offset	The starting byte offset of the physical addresses associated with this stripe.
0x10	0x10	UUID	The UUID for the device.

- **STRING_ITEM (Type: 0xFD):** A STRING_ITEM merely contains a string in the data field. It is used exclusively for developmental testing and is never encountered in a deployed file system.

Other types of item in Btrfs include INODE_EXTREF (Type: 0x0D); XATTR_ITEM (Type: 0x18); ORPHAN_ITEM (Type: 0x30); DIR_LOG_ITEM (Type: 0x3C); DIR_LOG_INDEX (Type: 0x48); EXTENT_ITEM (Type: 0xA8); METADATA_ITEM (Type: 0xA9); TREE_BLOCK_REF (Type: 0xB0); EXTENT_DATA_REF (Type: 0xB2); EXTENT_REF_V0 (Type: 0xB4); SHARED_BLOCK_REF (Type: 0xB6); SHARED_DATA_REF (Type: 0xC0); BLOCK_GROUP_ITEM (Type: 0xC0); and DEV_EXTENT (Type: 0xCC). Further information on these items, if required, can be found in the Btrfs kernel wiki.

11.1.6 Time in Btrfs

As always in digital forensics the time storage mechanisms that are employed in any artefact are of interest. Btrfs uses a 64-bit Unix time with nano-second resolution. The time in Btrfs is stored as UTC. The resultant structure is a 12-byte structure shown in Table 11.15.

Consider the scenario in which a unix time value of $1,249,567,890_d$ and a nanosecond component of 1234_d are recovered. Listing 11.3 shows how this can be converted to a human-readable form.

```
$ date +"%Y-%m-%d %H:%M:%S.%N" -ud "@1249567890.1234"
2009-08-06 14:11:30.123400000
```

Listing 11.3 Converting a Btrfs unix time/nanosecond value to human-readable format.

Remember, with the Linux **date** command the exact output format can be specified. The above format will allow all times to be easily sorted using any standard sorting algorithm!

11.1.7 Logical and Physical Addressing

All addresses in Btrfs are provided as logical addresses. When a logical address is discovered, the first task is to map it to the corresponding physical address(es).[5] To do this, the CHUNK_TREE is used. However, the CHUNK_TREE address provided in the superblock is itself a logical address. Hence, an excerpt from the CHUNK_TREE is provided at offset 0x32B in the superblock. Generally this will just contain the system chunk in which the CHUNK_TREE will be stored. This area of the superblock is called the CHUNK_ARRAY and it consists of an array of (key, CHUNK_ITEM) pairs.

Table 11.15 Btrfs time structure.

Offset	Size	Name	Description
0x00	0x08	Unix Time	Seconds since the epoch (01-01-1970). This value is unsigned.
0x08	0x04	Nanoseconds	The nanosecond component of the time value.

5 Due to the implementation of file system-level RAID in Btrfs, it is possible for a single logical address to map to multiple physical addresses. Each of these addresses will contain identical content.

Table 11.16 Sample partial CHUNK_TREE for a single device file system.

Description	CHUNK 1	CHUNK 2	CHUNK 3
Key Offset	0xC00000	0x1400000	0x1C00000
	$(12,582,912_d)$	$(20,971,520_d)$	$(29,360,128_d)$
Chunk Size (bytes)	0x800000	0x800000	0x33300000
	$(8,388,608_d)$	$(8,388,608_d)$	$(858,783,744_d)$
Type	0x01 (1_d)	0x22 (34_d)	0x24 (36_d)
Num. Stripes	0x01 (1_d)	0x02 (2_d)	0x02 (2_d)
Sub-Stripes	0x00 (0_d)	0x00 (0_d)	0x00 (0_d)
	Stripe 1		
Device ID	0x01 (1_d)	0x01 (1_d)	0x01 (1_d)
Offset	0xC00000	0x1400000	0x2400000
	$(12,582,912_d)$	$(20,971,520_d)$	$(37,748,736_d)$
	Stripe 2		
Device ID	N/A	0x01 (1_d)	0x01 (1_d)
Offset	N/A	0x1C00000	0x5730000
		$(29,360,128_d)$	$(91,422,720_d)$

In order to map a logical address to a physical address, the entire CHUNK_TREE is required. Table 11.16 shows a CHUNK_TREE structure, with the key offsets provided. This CHUNK_TREE is from a single device file system created using the **mkfs.btrfs** default values.

Certain information about the file system can be discovered merely by examining the CHUNK_TREE. For instance both CHUNK_ITEMs 2 and 3 contain two stripes. This means that any information in either of these chunks is duplicated, whereas CHUNK_ITEM 1 contains only a single stripe meaning that there will be only one copy of this information.

In order to convert a target logical address (t_{log}) to a physical address (t_{phy}) the chunk in which t_{log} appears must be located. To do this the chunk logical address (c_{log}) which contains t_{log}, in other words, the value of c_{log} which is nearest to, but not greater than t_{log} must be located. The c_{log} value is the key offset in Table 11.16. The difference between t_{log} and c_{log} is calculated and added to one (or more) of the c_{phy} addresses. The result of this is the t_{phy} address.

Consider the logical address $t_{log} = 0x1D20000$ and the interpreted CHUNK_TREE provided in Table 11.16. The nearest c_{log} is in CHUNK_ITEM 3 ($c_{log} = 0x1C00000$). The target physical address is then given by:

$$
\begin{aligned}
t_{phy} &= (t_{log} - c_{log}) + c_{phy} \\
& \quad \{\textit{Substitute Values}\} \\
t_{phy} &= (0x1D20000 - 0x1C00000) + 0x2400000 \\
& \quad \{\textit{Calculate}\} \\
t_{phy} &= 0x2520000
\end{aligned}
$$

From the logical address of 0x1D20000 one of the corresponding physical addresses is 0x2520000, when using the stripe offset 0x2400000. As CHUNK_ITEM 3 contains 2_d stripes either of the stripe offsets could be used. The other corresponding physical address in the second stripe would be given as 0x5742000.

11.2 Analysis of Btrfs

At the time of writing, Btrfs is not supported by any of the forensic tools. None of the commercial tools mention Btrfs, and there is no official Sleuth Kit support. There are some additional packages available from other developers that integrate with the Sleuth Kit, but none of these have been tested by the author. With no tool support for Btrfs all analysis must be done manually. Image files are available from the book's website. The contents of these images are described in Section 11.2.2.

11.2.1 Creating Btrfs File Systems

Btrfs file systems are created using the **mkfs.btrfs** command which, if not already installed by default, is available in a package called **btrfs-tools** for most Debian-based systems. The output of the **mkfs.btrfs** command is shown in Listing 11.4.

```
Label:                 BtrFS-FS
UUID:                  2f722027-c81b-4b8b-bf6c-b068014b7816
Node size:             16384
Sector size:           4096
Filesystem size:       512.00MiB
Block group profiles:
  Data:               single          8.00MiB
  Metadata:           DUP             32.00MiB
  System:             DUP             8.00MiB
SSD detected:          no
Incompat features:     extref, skinny-metadata
Checksum:              crc32c
Number of devices:     1
Devices:
   ID                SIZE            PATH
    1           512.00MiB            /dev/sdb1
```

Listing 11.4 Output from the **mkfs.btrfs** command when creating a 512 Mb file system.

The output from this command immediately provides some of the information that can be located in the file system itself. For instance, this file system was created with the label 'BtrFS-FS' and the B-tree node size is $16,384_d$ bytes with a sector size of 4096_d bytes.

One of the more interesting aspects of this output is the Block Group Profiles. As mentioned previously, there are three types of block group (or chunk) in the Btrfs file system: data, metadata and system. The data and system block groups have 8.00 MiB used, while metadata has 32.00 MiB used. The schemes given are single for data and DUP (meaning duplicate) for the other block groups. This means that metadata and system chunks are duplicated; in other words, a second copy of each of these exists on the file system, allowing for some form of redundancy.

Once the file system was created multiple files/directories were created on the device. The structure of the device after these creation operations is shown in Listing 11.5. Note the inode numbers are included in the long listing.

```
$ ls -lihR
.:
total 292K
257 drwxr-xr-x 1 root root   38 Nov 16 11:31 Files
258 -rwxr-x--- 1 root root  166 Nov 16 11:30 info.txt
261 -rwxr-x--- 1 root root 288K Nov 16 11:31 sea.jpg

./Files:
total 196K
260 -rwxr-x--- 1 root root   44 Nov 16 11:31 delete.txt
259 -rwxr-x--- 1 root root 191K Nov 16 11:31 river.jpg
```

Listing 11.5 Files/directories created on the Btrfs file system.

An image, **Btrfs_V1.E01**, was then created of this device. A secondary image file was created after **Files/delete.txt** and **Files/river.jpg** were deleted from the original image. The resulting image file is called **Btrfs_V2.E01**. The structure of this is shown in Listing 11.6. Initially this section will manually analyse the **Btrfs_V1.E01** file.

```
$ ls -lihR
.:
total 292K
257 drwxr-xr-x 1 root root   38 Nov 16 11:31 Files
258 -rwxr-x--- 1 root root  166 Nov 16 11:30 info.txt
261 -rwxr-x--- 1 root root 288K Nov 16 11:31 sea.jpg

./Files:
total 0
```

Listing 11.6 Files/directories on the Btrfs file system after deletion.

11.2.2 Supplied Btrfs Image Files

There is a supporting file available from the book's website which provides an archive containing six image files of Btrfs file systems in various configurations. These files are summarised in Table 11.17. Note that the **BtrFS_Raid1*** files are both part of the same RAID 1 file system and will need to be analysed in parallel.

11.2.3 Btrfs Analysis Methodology

This section presents a method of analysing Btrfs file systems. Firstly the analysis process begins by trying to rebuild the current file system, listing all files/directories, recovering file contents and metadata. It then examines methods to perform more advanced forms of analysis on the Btrfs file system.

In order to recover the basic information about all files/directories present on the Btrfs file system, the following process is followed.

1) **Process the Superblock:** Like most file systems the superblock contains information about the file system as a whole. In particular it is used to discover the logical address for the

Table 11.17 Summary of provided Btrfs image files.

Filename	Description
BtrFS_V1.E01	New filesystem with four files and one directory.
BtrFS_V2.E01	**BtrFS_V1.E01** with two files deleted.
BtrFS_V3.E01	This file system contains a directory with a large number of files. This ensures that internal nodes are required in the file system tree.
BtrFS_V4.E01	A Btrfs file system containing a subvolume and snapshot.
BtrFS_Raid1_D1.E01	Device 1 from Btrfs RAID 1 array.
BtrFS_Raid1_D2.E01	Device 2 from Btrfs RAID 1 array.

CHUNK_TREE and the ROOT_TREE. It also contains interesting information such as the File System UUID and the number of devices in the file system.

2) **Process the CHUNK_ARRAY:** The CHUNK_TREE allows the mapping of logical addresses to their physical counterparts. However, after processing the superblock only a logical address for the CHUNK_TREE is found. In order to perform this mapping, part of the CHUNK_TREE is stored in the superblock. This is called the CHUNK_ARRAY. This structure is processed next to allow bootstrapping of the CHUNK_TREE.
3) **Locate the CHUNK_TREE:** The next step is to locate the physical address of the CHUNK_TREE. This is done using the logical address of the CHUNK_TREE located in Step 1, and the CHUNK_ARRAY discovered in Step 2.
4) **Process the CHUNK_TREE:** Following this the entire CHUNK_TREE is processed. Once this structure is rebuilt it allows all logical addresses to be converted to their physical counterparts.
5) **Locate the ROOT_TREE:** From the logical ROOT_TREE address discovered in Step 1, combined with the CHUNK_TREE in Step 4, the physical address of the ROOT_TREE is located.
6) **Locate the FS_TREE:** The ROOT_TREE is the 'tree-of-trees' containing information relating to all trees in the file system. In order to rebuild the file/directory structure the FS_TREE must be processed. In this step the FS_TREE is located by processing the ROOT_ITEM for the FS_TREE in the ROOT_TREE. The FS_TREE's OID is 0x05. The ROOT_ITEM will provide the logical address of the FS_TREE for which the CHUNK_TREE is then required in order to convert this to the physical address.
7) **Process the FS_TREE:** The FS_TREE provides information on all the files and directories in the file system. It allows the analyst to determine which objects are files and which are directories.
8) **Process Directories:** In order to rebuild the file system each individual directory in the file system must be processed. This allows the contents of the entire file system to be listed.
9) **Recover File Metadata:** It is then necessary to recover file (and directory) metadata. This is achieved by processing the INODE_ITEMs for each individual file/directory.
10) **Recover File Content:** The final step in the analysis is to recover the file's contents. Content locations are provided by the EXTENT_DATA structures.

There are some scenarios with Btrfs in which the analysis methodology may change slightly. For instance in the case of a Btrfs file system with snapshots or subvolumes there will be multiple file trees (similar to FS_TREE) which must be located and analysed. There is also a backup roots section of the superblock which can be analysed after the above process has been completed in order to see what older tree structures (and possibly data) are still present on the file system. Furthermore in the case of Btrfs file systems with multiple devices it might be necessary to rebuild the DEV_TREE in addition to the CHUNK_TREE. These special cases are considered later in the chapter; for now the next section analyses a simple Btrfs file system using the above steps.

11.2.4 Manual Analysis of a Single Device File System

For the remainder of this section the **BtrFS_V1.E01** file will be examined in detail. The aim of this task is to provide the reader with the skills necessary to list files in a Btrfs file system and to recover these files along with the associated metadata.

11.2.4.1 Process the Superblock

The first step in the forensic analysis of Btrfs is to analyse the superblock. The superblock provides information about the file system as a whole and also provides access to the chunk tree which is used to map the logical and physical addresses. The primary superblock is located at 0x10000. An excerpt from the superblock in **BtrFS_V1.E01** is shown in Listing 11.7.

```
010000: 3bdd f493 0000 0000 0000 0000 0000 0000 ;...............
010010: 0000 0000 0000 0000 0000 0000 0000 0000 ................
010020: 2f72 2027 c81b 4b8b bf6c b068 014b 7816 /r '..K..l.h.Kx.
010030: 0000 0100 0000 0000 0100 0000 0000 0000 ................
010040: 5f42 4852 6653 5f4d 0a00 0000 0000 0000 _BHRfS_M........
010050: 0080 d501 0000 0000 0040 5001 0000 0000 .........@P.....
010060: 0000 0000 0000 0000 0000 0000 0000 0000 ................
010070: 0000 0020 0000 0000 0080 0900 0000 0000 ... ............
010080: 0600 0000 0000 0000 0100 0000 0000 0000 ................
010090: 0010 0000 0040 0000 0040 0000 0010 0000 .....@...@......
0100a0: 8100 0000 0500 0000 0000 0000 0000 0000 ................
0100b0: 0000 0000 0000 0000 0000 0000 4101 0000 ............A...
0100c0: 0000 0000 0000 0000 0001 0000 0000 0000 ................
0100d0: 0000 0000 2000 0000 0000 0080 0500 0000 .... ...........
0100e0: 0000 1000 0000 1000 0000 1000 0000 0000 ................
0100f0: 0000 0000 0000 0000 0000 0000 0000 0000 ................
010100: 0000 0000 0000 0000 0000 0036 44fd 1489 ...........6D...
010110: 1844 9ea0 c9ed 54d7 911e ea2f 7220 27c8 .D....T..../r '.
010120: 1b4b 8bbf 6cb0 6801 4b78 1642 7472 4653 .K..l.h.Kx.BtrFS
010130: 2d46 5300 0000 0000 0000 0000 0000 0000 -FS.............
010140: 0000 0000 0000 0000 0000 0000 0000 0000 ................
```

Listing 11.7 Excerpt from the **BtrFS_V1.E01** superblock structure.

Listing 11.7 confirms this is a Btrfs superblock. The Btrfs signature value and file system UUID are highlighted. As analysis proceeds this value should be confirmed in all tree nodes to ensure they belong to this file system. Note that it may be possible to discover old file systems if validly formatted tree nodes which contain other UUID values are discovered. The interpretation of this superblock is provided in Table 11.18.

Table 11.18 Partially processed superblock values for **BtrFS_V1.E01**.

Offset	Size	Name	Value
0x00	0x20	Checksum	0x93F4DD3B
0x20	0x10	FS UUID	0x2F72...7816
0x30	0x08	Address	0x10000 ($65,536_d$)
0x38	0x08	Flags	0x01 (1_d)
0x40	0x08	Signature	_BHRfS_M
0x48	0x08	FS Generation	0x0A (10_d)
0x50	0x08	ROOT_TREE Addr.	0x1D58000 ($30,769,152_d$)
0x58	0x08	CHUNK_TREE Addr.	0x1504000 ($22,036,480_d$)
0x70	0x08	# Bytes	0x20000000 ($536,870,912_d$)
0x78	0x08	# Bytes Used	0x98000 ($622,592_d$)
0x80	0x08	Root Dir. OID	0x06 (6_d)
0x88	0x08	# Devices	0x01 (1_d)
0x90	0x04	Sector Size	0x1000 (4096_d)
0x94	0x04	Node Size	0x4000 ($16,384_d$)
0xA0	0x04	CHUNK_ARRAY Size	0x81 (129_d)
0xA4	0x08	Chunk Root Generation	0x05 (5_d)
0xC6	0x01	Root Level	0x00 (0_d)
0xC7	0x01	Chunk Root Level	0x00 (0_d)
0xC9	0x62	DEV_ITEM	See Section 11.1.5.
0x12B	0x100	Label	BtrFS-FS

From Table 11.18 some of the expected information based on the output of the **mkfs.btrfs** command is found. For instance the node size is 0x4000 ($16,384_d$) bytes and the sector size is 0x1000 (4096_d) bytes. Notice the file system generation value (0x0A). In Btrfs file systems, due to the copy-on-write principles, older versions of structures exist on the file system. The generation number identifies the stage at which this structure was created/modified. Finally the logical addresses for both the ROOT_TREE and the CHUNK_TREE, two structures that are needed in order to rebuild the file system, are also found.

11.2.4.2 Process the CHUNK_ARRAY

After processing the superblock the logical address for the ROOT_TREE has been determined but there is no means of mapping that logical address to a physical one. In order to do this the CHUNK_TREE must be rebuilt. However, only the logical address for the CHUNK_TREE is available. Btrfs provides a small part of the CHUNK_TREE in the superblock in a structure called the CHUNK_ARRAY. The CHUNK_ARRAY is always located at offset 0x32B in the superblock. The size of the array is given at offset 0xA0 in the Superblock and is 0x81 bytes (Table 11.18). The contents of the CHUNK_ARRAY are provided in Listing 11.8.

The CHUNK_ARRAY consists of (key, CHUNK_ITEM) pairs. Listing 11.8 begins with the 0x11 byte key which is followed by the CHUNK_ITEM. Alternate fields in the CHUNK_ITEM are highlighted. The processed key is shown in Table 11.19.

```
01032b: 0001 0000 0000 0000 e400 0050 0100 0000 ...........P....
01033b: 0000 0080 0000 0000 0002 0000 0000 0000 ................
01034b: 0000 0001 0000 0000 0022 0000 0000 0000 ........."......
01035b: 0000 0001 0000 0001 0000 1000 0002 0001 ................
01036b: 0001 0000 0000 0000 0000 0050 0100 0000 ...........P....
01037b: 0036 44fd 1489 1844 9ea0 c9ed 54d7 911e .6D....D....T...
01038b: ea01 0000 0000 0000 0000 00d0 0100 0000 ................
01039b: 0036 44fd 1489 1844 9ea0 c9ed 54d7 911e .6D....D....T...
0103ab: ea                                      .
```

Listing 11.8 The CHUNK_ARRAY from **BtrFS_V1.E01**.

Table 11.19 Processed key from first CHUNK_ARRAY item.

Offset	Size	Description	Value
0x00	0x08	Object ID	0x100 (256_d)
0x08	0x01	Type	0xE4 (CHUNK_ITEM)
0x09	0x08	Key Offset	0x1500000 ($22,020,096_d$)

Table 11.20 Processed CHUNK_ITEM found in the CHUNK_ARRAY.

Offset	Size	Name	Value
0x00	0x08	Size of Chunk (Bytes)	0x800000 ($8,388,608_d$)
0x08	0x08	Root Ref. Chunk	0x02 (2_d)
0x10	0x08	Stripe Length	0x10000 ($65,536_d$)
0x18	0x08	Type	0x22 (34_d)
0x20	0x04	Optimal I/O Align	0x10000 ($65,536_d$)
0x24	0x04	Optimal I/O Width	0x10000 ($65,536_d$)
0x28	0x04	Sector Size	0x1000 (4096_d)
0x2C	0x02	Number of Stripes	0x02 (2_d)
0x2E	0x02	Sub Stripes	0x01 (1_d)

The key offset for a CHUNK_ITEM is the logical address at which the address space begins, 0x1500000 in this case. Analysis proceeds to process the CHUNK_ITEM which is shown in Table 11.20. From this it is clear that there are two stripes in the CHUNK_ITEM. This means that any logical address that maps to this chunk will be duplicated. There will be two physical addresses corresponding to one logical address. Table 11.21 shows the processed stripes.

The CHUNK_ARRAY's CHUNK_ITEMs should contain the information needed to bootstrap the logical to physical address mapping process, by allowing the CHUNK_TREE to be located.

11.2.4.3 Locate the CHUNK_TREE

Next the CHUNK_ITEM located in the CHUNK_ARRAY is used to discover the location of the CHUNK_TREE. From the superblock the logical address of the CHUNK_TREE is 0x1504000. The

Table 11.21 Processed stripes from the CHUNK_ARRAY's CHUNK_ITEM.

Offset	Size	Description	Stripe 1	Stripe 2
0x00	0x08	Device ID	0x01 (1_d)	0x01 (1_d)
0x08	0x08	Offset	0x1500000 ($22,020,096_d$)	0x1D00000 ($30,408,704_d$)
0x10	0x10	Device UUID	0x3644...1EEA	0x3644...1EEA

CHUNK_ITEM recovered from the CHUNK_ARRAY has a key offset of 0x1500000. This is less than or equal to the desired logical address and as such the logical address must be part of this chunk. The calculation outlined in Section 11.1.7 is performed for the case of one single device in the file system.

$$
\begin{aligned}
t_{phy} &= (t_{log} - c_{log}) + c_{phy} \\
&\quad \{\mathit{Substitute\ Values}\} \\
t_{phy} &= (0x1504000 - 0x1500000) + 0x1500000 \\
&\quad \{\mathit{Calculate}\} \\
t_{phy} &= 0x1504000
\end{aligned}
$$

Therefore a copy of the CHUNK_TREE root node should be found at offset 0x1504000 and also, if the second stripe was used, at offset 0x1D04000. Listing 11.9 shows the first 64_d bytes at each location. Clearly the checksum, FS UUID and logical addresses are all identical. Hence two copies of the CHUNK_TREE root node have been discovered. The next step is to rebuild the entire CHUNK_TREE.

```
$ xxd -s $((0x1504000)) -l 64 mnt/ewf1
1504000: 2f66 96f7 0000 0000 0000 0000 0000 0000 /f..............
1504010: 0000 0000 0000 0000 0000 0000 0000 0000 ................
1504020: 2f72 2027 c81b 4b8b bf6c b068 014b 7816 /r '..K..l.h.Kx.
1504030: 0040 5001 0000 0000 0100 0000 0000 0001 .@P.............

$
$ xxd -s $((0x1D04000)) -l 64 mnt/ewf1
1d04000: 2f66 96f7 0000 0000 0000 0000 0000 0000 /f..............
1d04010: 0000 0000 0000 0000 0000 0000 0000 0000 ................
1d04020: 2f72 2027 c81b 4b8b bf6c b068 014b 7816 /r '..K..l.h.Kx.
1d04030: 0040 5001 0000 0000 0100 0000 0000 0001 .@P.............
```

Listing 11.9 First 64-bytes of both CHUNK_TREE root node locations.

11.2.4.4 Process the CHUNK_TREE

In processing the CHUNK_TREE, either of the physical locations discovered in the previous step can be used. Listing 11.10 shows an excerpt from the CHUNK_TREE root node at offset 0x1D04000.

```
1d04000: 2f66 96f7 0000 0000 0000 0000 0000 0000 /f..............
1d04010: 0000 0000 0000 0000 0000 0000 0000 0000 ................
1d04020: 2f72 2027 c81b 4b8b bf6c b068 014b 7816 /r '..K..l.h.Kx.
1d04030: 0040 5001 0000 0000 0100 0000 0000 0001 .@P.............
1d04040: be4e 1e7a bae9 4f90 b7ea 8e3c 359f f328 .N.z..O...<5..(
1d04050: 0500 0000 0000 0000 0300 0000 0000 0000 ................
1d04060: 0400 0000 0001 0000 0000 0000 00d8 0100 ................
1d04070: 0000 0000 0000 393f 0000 6200 0000 0001 ......9?..b.....
1d04080: 0000 0000 0000 e400 00d0 0000 0000 00e9 ................
1d04090: 3e00 0050 0000 0000 0100 0000 0000 00e4 >..P............
1d040a0: 0000 5001 0000 0000 793e 0000 7000 0000 ..P.....y>..p...
1d040b0: 0001 0000 0000 0000 e400 00d0 0100 0000 ................
1d040c0: 0009 3e00 0070 0000 0000 0100 0000 0000 ..>..p..........
1d040d0: 00e4 0000 d001 0000 0000 093e 0000 7000 ...........>..p.
1d040e0: 0000 0001 0000 0000 0000 e400 00d0 0100 ................
1d040f0: 0000 00b9 3d00 0070 0000 0000 0000 0000 ....=..p........
```

Listing 11.10 Excerpt from the CHUNK_TREE root node.

All tree nodes begin with a node header. Generally what follows the header is of more interest than the header itself. The number of items in the node shown in Listing 11.10 is 0x04 while the node is at level 0x00. A level 0 node is a leaf node and hence contains item pointers immediately after the node header, with the item data appearing at the very end of the node. Alternate item pointers are underlined. Also it appears that there are other item pointers after the four highlighted ones. Knowing that this device was zero'd before file system creation, it is possible that these are items that are no longer in use from this node. Table 11.22 shows the live item pointer values.

From the CHUNK_TREE item pointers (Table 11.22) it is seen that there is one DEV_ITEM (Type: 0xD8) and three CHUNK_ITEMs (Type: 0xE4). This is to be expected, as there should be one DEV_ITEM per device in the file system, and there is only a single device in this file system. Also there should be (at least) a CHUNK_ITEM for the data, metadata and system block groups, so three is the minimum expected. Based on the data size values for the CHUNK_ITEMs item 2 contains one stripe and items 3 and 4 contain two stripes each. Based on the key offset, item 3 is most likely the CHUNK_ITEM that was contained in the CHUNK_ARRAY.

Each of these items can now be processed. In order to extract the contents of each item four pieces of information are required: the physical offset to the start of the node, the length of the node header, the offset to the item data and the data size. For all of the items above, the physical offset to the node start is 0x1D04000 (or 0x1504000 depending on the stripe used) and the node header is always 0x65 bytes in size. Each individual item pointer is then examined to determine the offset to the item's data (relative to the end of the node header) and the size of that data. For instance the physical offset of the start of item 1's data is:

$$
\begin{aligned}
& \mathit{node\_offset} + \mathit{node\_header\_size} + \mathit{item\_offset} \\
= & \qquad \{\mathit{Substitution}\} \\
& \mathrm{0x1D04000} + \mathrm{0x65} + \mathrm{0x3F39}
\end{aligned}
$$

The size of this item is 0x62 bytes. The resulting DEV_ITEM is shown in Listing 11.11.

From Listing 11.11 it is clearly the correct file system as the FS UUID matches that found in the superblock. The partial processing of this DEV_ITEM is shown in Table 11.23.

Table 11.22 Processing of the four item pointers found in the CHUNK_TREE root node.

Offset	Size	Desc.	Item 1	Item 2
0x00	0x08	Object ID	0x01 (1_d)	0x100 (256_d)
0x08	0x01	Type	0xD8 (DEV_ITEM)	0xE4 (CHUNK_ITEM)
0x09	0x08	Key Offset	0x01 (1_d)	0xD00000 ($13,631,488_d$)
0x11	0x04	Data Offset	0x3F39 ($16,185_d$)	0x3EE9 ($16,105_d$)
0x15	0x04	Data Size	0x62 (98_d)	0x50 (80_d)
Offset	**Size**	**Desc.**	**Item 3**	**Item 4**
0x00	0x08	Object ID	0x100 (256_d)	0x100 (256_d)
0x08	0x01	Type	0xE4 (CHUNK_ITEM)	0xE4 (CHUNK_ITEM)
0x09	0x08	Key Offset	0x1500000 ($22,020,096_d$)	0x1D00000 ($30,408,704_d$)
0x11	0x04	Data Offset	0x3E79 ($15,993_d$)	0x3E09 ($15,881_d$)
0x15	0x04	Data Size	0x70 (112_d)	0x70 (112_d)

Table 11.23 Partially processed DEV_ITEM from the CHUNK_TREE.

Offset	Size	Description	Value
0x00	0x08	Device ID	0x01 (1_d)
0x08	0x08	# bytes on device	0x20000000 ($536,870,912_d$)
0x10	0x08	# bytes used	0x5800000 ($92,274,688_d$)
0x20	0x04	Sector size	0x1000 (4096_d)
0x24	0x08	Type	0x00 (0_d)
0x42	0x10	Device UUID	0x3644...1EEA
0x52	0x10	FS UUID	0x2F72...7816

Once the DEV_ITEM has been processed the three CHUNK_ITEMs can be extracted. Listing 11.12 shows the contents of all three CHUNK_ITEMs and the commands used to extract them.

Table 11.24 shows the processed CHUNK_ITEMs. The CHUNK_TREE can be used to map logical addresses to physical addresses for the remaining structures in the file system.

```
1d07f9e: 0100 0000 0000 0000 0000 0020 0000 0000 ...........  ....
1d07fae: 0000 8005 0000 0000 0010 0000 0010 0000 ................
1d07fbe: 0010 0000 0000 0000 0000 0000 0000 0000 ................
1d07fce: 0000 0000 0000 0000 0000 0000 0000 0000 ................
1d07fde: 0000 3644 fd14 8918 449e a0c9 ed54 d791 ..6D....D....T..
1d07fee: 1eea 2f72 2027 c81b 4b8b bf6c b068 014b ../r '..K..l.h.K
1d07ffe: 7816                                     x.
```

Listing 11.11 The contents of the DEV_ITEM from the CHUNK_TREE.

```
$ xxd -s $((0x1D04000 + 0x65 + 0x3EE9)) -l $((0x50)) mnt/ewf1
1d07f4e: 0000 8000 0000 0000 0200 0000 0000 0000 ................
1d07f5e: 0000 0100 0000 0000 0100 0000 0000 0000 ................
1d07f6e: 0000 0100 0000 0100 0010 0000 0100 0100 ................
1d07f7e: 0100 0000 0000 0000 0000 d000 0000 0000 ................
1d07f8e: 3644 fd14 8918 449e a0c9 ed54 d791 1eea 6D....D....T....
$
$ xxd -s $((0x1D04000 + 0x65 + 0x3E79)) -l $((0x70)) mnt/ewf1
1d07ede: 0000 8000 0000 0000 0200 0000 0000 0000 ................
1d07eee: 0000 0100 0000 0000 2200 0000 0000 0000 ........".......
1d07efe: 0000 0100 0000 0100 0010 0000 0200 0100 ................
1d07f0e: 0100 0000 0000 0000 0000 5001 0000 0000 ..........P.....
1d07f1e: 3644 fd14 8918 449e a0c9 ed54 d791 1eea 6D....D....T....
1d07f2e: 0100 0000 0000 0000 0000 d001 0000 0000 ................
1d07f3e: 3644 fd14 8918 449e a0c9 ed54 d791 1eea 6D....D....T....
$
$ xxd -s $((0x1D04000 + 0x65 + 0x3E09)) -l $((0x70)) mnt/ewf1
1d07e6e: 0000 0002 0000 0000 0200 0000 0000 0000 ................
1d07e7e: 0000 0100 0000 0000 2400 0000 0000 0000 ........$.......
1d07e8e: 0000 0100 0000 0100 0010 0000 0200 0100 ................
1d07e9e: 0100 0000 0000 0000 0000 5002 0000 0000 ..........P.....
1d07eae: 3644 fd14 8918 449e a0c9 ed54 d791 1eea 6D....D....T....
1d07ebe: 0100 0000 0000 0000 0000 5004 0000 0000 ..........P.....
1d07ece: 3644 fd14 8918 449e a0c9 ed54 d791 1eea 6D....D....T....
```

Listing 11.12 Contents of the three CHUNK_ITEMS in the CHUNK_TREE root node.

11.2.4.5 Locate the Root Tree

At this stage the CHUNK_TREE has been obtained. The only other address available is that of the ROOT_TREE. This logical address is 0x1D58000. The CHUNK_ITEM with the nearest (but less than or equal to) key offset is CHUNK_ITEM 3 (Item 4 in the node) with key offset 0x1D00000. This contains two stripes, one beginning at 0x2500000 and one at 0x4500000.

The difference between the logical address and the key offset is:

$$0x1D58000 - 0x1D00000 = 0x58000.$$

The root node of the ROOT_TREE should therefore be located at:

$$0x58000 + 0x2500000$$

and

$$0x58000 + 0x4500000$$

Table 11.24 Partially processed CHUNK_ITEMs from the CHUNK_TREE root node.

Offset	Size	Desc.	CHUNK 1	CHUNK 2	CHUNK 3
0x00	0x08	Chunk Size	0x800000 ($8,388,608_d$)	0x800000 ($8,388,608_d$)	0x2000000 ($33,554,432_d$)
0x18	0x08	Type	0x01 (1_d)	0x22 (34_d)	0x24 (36_d)
0x2C	0x02	# Stripes	0x01 (1_d)	0x02 (2_d)	0x02 (2_d)
0x2E	0x02	Sub Stripes	0x01 (1_d)	0x01 (1_d)	0x01 (1_d)
			Stripe 1		
0x00	0x08	Device ID	0x01 (1_d)	0x01 (1_d)	0x01 (1_d)
0x08	0x08	Offset	0xD00000 ($13,631,488_d$)	0x1500000 ($22,020,096_d$)	0x2500000 ($38,797,312_d$)
			Stripe 2		
0x00	0x08	Device ID	N/A	0x01 (1_d)	0x01 (1_d)
0x08	0x08	Offset	N/A	0x1D00000 ($30,408,704_d$)	0x4500000 ($72,351,744_d$)

which are 0x2558000 and 0x4558000, respectively. 64_d bytes is extracted from each of these locations in Listing 11.13, in order to confirm that they are valid tree nodes.

```
$ xxd -s $((0x2558000)) -l 64 mnt/ewf1
2558000: 96af 641b 0000 0000 0000 0000 0000 0000 ..d.............
2558010: 0000 0000 0000 0000 0000 0000 0000 0000 ................
2558020: 2f72 2027 c81b 4b8b bf6c b068 014b 7816 /r '..K..l.h.Kx.
2558030: 0080 d501 0000 0000 0100 0000 0000 0001 ................
$
$ xxd -s $((0x4558000)) -l 64 mnt/ewf1
4558000: 96af 641b 0000 0000 0000 0000 0000 0000 ..d.............
4558010: 0000 0000 0000 0000 0000 0000 0000 0000 ................
4558020: 2f72 2027 c81b 4b8b bf6c b068 014b 7816 /r '..K..l.h.Kx.
4558030: 0080 d501 0000 0000 0100 0000 0000 0001 ................
```

Listing 11.13 First 64_d bytes of both copies of the ROOT_TREE's root node.

From this we see that the nodes are identical (checksums match) and that they are both referring to the correct file system (FS UUID) and represent the same logical address: 0x1D58000.

11.2.4.6 Locate the FS_TREE

The most interesting data structure in Btrfs for rebuilding the file system is the FS_TREE. In order to locate the FS_TREE it is necessary to process the ROOT_TREE to determine the location of the FS_TREE. The root tree's root node content is shown in Listing 11.14.

The node header (Listing 11.14) shows there are 0xA items in this node and that it is a leaf node. Alternate item pointers are highlighted. Processing of these is shown in Table 11.25.

The Object ID's in the keys show the trees for which information is present. In total there are seven distinct OID's present. These OID's represent the following objects: EXTENT_TREE (0x02); DEV_TREE (0x04); FS_TREE (0x05); ROOT_DIRECTORY (0x06); CSUM_TREE (0x07); UUID_TREE (0x09); and DATA_RELOC (-9_d)

```
4558000: 96af 641b 0000 0000 0000 0000 0000 0000 ..d.............
4558010: 0000 0000 0000 0000 0000 0000 0000 0000 ................
4558020: 2f72 2027 c81b 4b8b bf6c b068 014b 7816 /r '..K..l.h.Kx.
4558030: 0080 d501 0000 0000 0100 0000 0000 0001 ................
4558040: be4e 1e7a bae9 4f90 b7ea 8e3c 359f f328 .N.z..O....<5..(
4558050: 0a00 0000 0000 0000 0100 0000 0000 0000 ................
4558060: 0a00 0000 0002 0000 0000 0000 0084 0000 ................
4558070: 0000 0000 0000 e43d 0000 b701 0000 0400 .......=........
4558080: 0000 0000 0000 8400 0000 0000 0000 002d ...............-
4558090: 3c00 00b7 0100 0005 0000 0000 0000 000c <...............
45580a0: 0600 0000 0000 0000 1c3c 0000 1100 0000 .........<......
45580b0: 0500 0000 0000 0000 8400 0000 0000 0000 ................
45580c0: 0065 3a00 00b7 0100 0006 0000 0000 0000 .e:.............
45580d0: 0001 0000 0000 0000 0000 c539 0000 a000 ...........9....
45580e0: 0000 0600 0000 0000 0000 0c06 0000 0000 ................
45580f0: 0000 00b9 3900 000c 0000 0006 0000 0000 ....9...........
4558100: 0000 0054 d2c2 bf8d 0000 0000 9439 0000 ...T.........9..
4558110: 2500 0000 0700 0000 0000 0000 8400 0000 %...............
4558120: 0000 0000 00dd 3700 00b7 0100 0009 0000 ......7.........
4558130: 0000 0000 0084 0000 0000 0000 0000 2636 ..............&6
4558140: 0000 b701 0000 f7ff ffff ffff ffff 8400 ................
4558150: 0000 0000 0000 006f 3400 00b7 0100 0000 .......o4.......
```

Listing 11.14 Node header and item pointers from the root node of the ROOT_TREE of **BtrFS_V1.E01**.

Of the various trees present the one of most interest for forensic analysis is the FS_TREE[6] which is OID 0x05. There are two items associated with 0x05, which are an INODE_REF (0x0C) and a ROOT_ITEM (0x84). The ROOT_ITEM will contain the location of the tree. The contents of this are shown in Listing 11.15.

Highlighted is the logical address of the FS_TREE (0x1D48000). Converting this logical address to a physical address gives two locations: 0x2548000 and 0x4548000. The first 64_d bytes of each of these are shown in Listing 11.16. As can be seen these are identical (checksum) and represent the correct logical address (0x1D4C000).

As the FS_TREE has been located analysis continues by processing this tree. It is the processing of this tree that allows all files to be listed.

11.2.4.7 Processing the FS_TREE

The method used to analyse the FS_TREE is identical to that used to analyse the ROOT_TREE (and also the CHUNK_TREE). The common structure of all B-Trees in Btrfs means that the node header is first processed to determine the number of items and the node level (leaf or internal). If it is an internal node the other nodes are located in the tree and processed. In the case of a leaf node the data items are located in the node and each of these are processed. The contents of the FS_TREE's root node are given in Listing 11.17. Note that the first 0x60 bytes have been removed.

It is clear this is a leaf node with 0x1A items present. Alternate items are highlighted. Table 11.26 shows the interpretation of these items.

The FS_TREE contains information on all files/directories in the file system. From Table 11.26 there are six distinct OIDs in the table. These have different item types associated with them.

6 Processing the ROOT_DIRECTORY would also point to the FS_TREE.

Table 11.25 Processed item pointers from the root node in Listing 11.14.

Data	Item 1	Item 2	Item 3	Item 4
OID	0x02 (2_d)	0x04 (4_d)	0x05 (5_d)	0x05 (5_d)
Type	0x84	0x84	0x0C	0x84
Key Offset	0x00 (0_d)	0x00 (0_d)	0x06 (6_d)	0x00 (2_d)
Data Offset	0x3DE4	0x3C2D	0x3C1C	0x3A65
	($15,844_d$)	($15,405_d$)	($15,388_d$)	($14,949_d$)
Data Size	0x1B7 (439_d)	0x1B7 (439_d)	0x11 (17_d)	0x1B7 (439_d)
Data	**Item 5**	**Item 6**	**Item 7**	**Item 8**
OID	0x06(6_d)	0x06 (6_d)	0x06 (6_d)	0x07 (7_d)
Type	0x01	0x0C	0x54	0x84
Key Offset	0x00 (0_d)	0x06 (6_d)	0x8DBFC2D2	0x00 (0_d)
Data Offset	0x39C5	0x39B9	0x3994	0x37DD
	($14,789_d$)	($14,777_d$)	($14,740_d$)	($14,301_d$)
Data Size	0xA0 (160_d)	0x0C (12_d)	0x25 (37_d)	0x1B7 (439_d)
Data	**Item 9**	**Item 10**		
OID	0x09 (9_d)	-9_d		
Type	0x84	0x84		
Key Offset	0x00 (0_d)	0x00 (0_d)		
Data Offset	0x3626	0x346F		
	($13,862_d$)	($13,423_d$)		
Data Size	0x1B7 (439_d)	0x1B7 (439_d)		

Table 11.27 summarises the OIDs that have been discovered and the item types that are associated with each OID.

Previous knowledge of Btrfs item types implies that OIDs 0x100 and 0x101 are directories, as each contains DIR_ITEM and DIR_INDEX items, while the remaining OIDs are files, as each of these contain EXTENT_DATA items. All the items have INODE_ITEMs and INODE_REF items as both files and directories must have metadata associated with them (INODE_ITEM) and a name (INODE_REF).

11.2.4.8 Process Directories

OIDs 0x100 and 0x101 appear to be directories as both have items of type 0x54 (DIR_ITEM) and 0x60 (DIR_INDEX). The root directory always has OID 0x100 and processing begins with this directory. Initially its INODE_REF is processed in order to discover the name of the directory. The contents of the INODE_REF item for OID 0x100 are shown in Listing 11.18.

From this the name is .. commonly used for the root directory. Notice that the key offset in this item (2) shows the parent to be 0x100 – in other words the same directory. Next the DIR_ITEMs found in that OID are processed. Items 3, 4 and 5 above are DIR_ITEMs in 0x100 . Their contents are shown in Listing 11.19.

Table 11.26 Items discovered in the FS_TREE rcot node.

Data	Item 1	Item 2	Item 3	Item 4	Item 5	Item 6	Item 7	Item 8	Item 9
OID	0x100	0x100	0x100	0x100	0x100	0x100	0x100	0x100	0x101
Type	0x01	0x0C	0x54	0x54	0x54	0x60	0x60	0x60	0x01
Key Off.	0x00	0x100	0x33C3422A	0x409C1140	0x4DFAF554	0x02	0x03	0x04	0x00
Data Off.	0x3EFB	0x3EEF	0x3ECA	0x3EA4	0x3E81	0x3E5E	0x3E38	0x3E13	0x3D73
Data Size	0xA0	0x0C	0x25	0x26	0x23	0x23	0x26	0x25	0xA0
Data	**Item 10**	**Item 11**	**Item 12**	**Item 13**	**Item 14**	**Item 15**	**Item 16**	**Item 17**	**Item 18**
OID	0x101	0x101	0x101	0x101	0x101	0x102	0x102	0x102	0x103
Type	0x0C	0x54	0x54	0x60	0x60	0x01	0x0C	0x6C	0x01
Key Off.	0x100	0x1A9F0281	0x8C0E76C2	0x02	0x03	0x00	0x100	0x00	0x00
Data Off.	0x3D64	0x3D3D	0x3D15	0x3CEE	0x3CC6	0x3C26	0x3C14	0x3B59	0x3AB9
Data Size	0x0F	0x27	0x28	0x27	0x28	0xA0	0x12	0xBB	0xA0
Data	**Item 19**	**Item 20**	**Item 21**	**Item 22**	**Item 23**	**Item 24**	**Item 25**	**Item 26**	
OID	0x103	0x103	0x104	0x104	0x104	0x105	0x105	0x105	
Type	0x0C	0x6C	0x01	0x0C	0x6C	0x01	0x0C	0x6C	
Key Off.	0x101	0x00	0x00	0x101	0x00	0x00	0x100	0x00	
Data Off.	0x3AA6	0x3A71	0x39D1	0x39BD	0x397C	0x38DC	0x38CB	0x3896	
Data Size	0x13	0x35	0xA0	0x14	0x41	0xA0	0x11	0x35	

```
$ xxd -s $((0x4558000 + 0x65 + 0x3A65)) -l $((0x1B7)) mnt/ewf1
455baca: 0100 0000 0000 0000 0000 0000 0000 0000 ................
455bada: 0300 0000 0000 0000 0040 0000 0000 0000 .........@......
455baea: 0000 0000 0000 0000 0100 0000 0000 0000 ................
455bafa: 0000 0000 ed41 0000 0000 0000 0000 0000 .....A..........
455bb0a: 0000 0080 ffff ffff 0000 0000 0000 0000 ................
455bb1a: 0000 0000 0000 0000 0000 0000 0000 0000 ................
455bb2a: 0000 0000 0000 0000 0000 0000 0000 0000 ................
455bb3a: 0000 0000 0000 0000 0000 0000 0000 0000 ................
455bb4a: 0000 0000 0000 0000 0000 0000 0000 0000 ................
455bb5a: 0000 0000 0000 0000 0000 0000 0000 0000 ................
455bb6a: 0900 0000 0000 0000 0001 0000 0000 0000 ................
455bb7a: 0080 d401 0000 0000 0000 0000 0000 0000 ................
455bb8a: 0040 0000 0000 0000 0000 0000 0000 0000.@..............
455bb9a: 0000 0000 0000 0000 0100 0000 0000 0000 ................
455bbaa: 0000 0000 0000 0000 0000 0000 0000 0009 ................
455bbba: 0000 0000 0000 0083 cfd9 9fe6 b048 1093 .............H..
455bbca: aa4c e89f 1543 cd00 0000 0000 0000 0000 .L...C..........
455bbda: 0000 0000 0000 0000 0000 0000 0000 0000 ................
455bbea: 0000 0000 0000 0009 0000 0000 0000 0000 ................
455bbfa: 0000 0000 0000 0000 0000 0000 0000 0000 ................
455bc0a: 0000 0000 0000 00ae fd55 6500 0000 0041 .........Ue....A
455bc1a: 2a8f 1d8f d951 6500 0000 0000 0000 0000 *....Qe.........
455bc2a: 0000 0000 0000 0000 0000 0000 0000 0000 ................
455bc3a: 0000 0000 0000 0000 0000 0000 0000 0000 ................
455bc4a: 0000 0000 0000 0000 0000 0000 0000 0000 ................
455bc5a: 0000 0000 0000 0000 0000 0000 0000 0000 ................
455bc6a: 0000 0000 0000 0000 0000 0000 0000 0000 ................
455bc7a: 0000 0000 0000 00                        .......
```

Listing 11.15 The contents of the ROOT_ITEM item for the FS_TREE.

```
$ xxd -s $((0x2548000)) -l 64 mnt/ewf1
2548000: 6d3b 10e5 0000 0000 0000 0000 0000 0000 m;..............
2548010: 0000 0000 0000 0000 0000 0000 0000 0000 ................
2548020: 2f72 2027 c81b 4b8b bf6c b068 014b 7816 /r '..K..l.h.Kx.
2548030: 0080 d401 0000 0000 0100 0000 0000 0001 ................

$
$ xxd -s $((0x4548000)) -l 64 mnt/ewf1
4548000: 6d3b 10e5 0000 0000 0000 0000 0000 0000 m;..............
4548010: 0000 0000 0000 0000 0000 0000 0000 0000 ................
4548020: 2f72 2027 c81b 4b8b bf6c b068 014b 7816 /r '..K..l.h.Kx.
4548030: 0080 d401 0000 0000 0100 0000 0000 0001 ................
```

Listing 11.16 Excerpts from both copies of the FS_TREE root node.

```
4548060: 1a00 0000 0000 0100 0000 0000 0001 0000 ................
4548070: 0000 0000 0000 fb3e 0000 a000 0000 0001 .......>........
4548080: 0000 0000 0000 0c00 0100 0000 0000 00ef ................
4548090: 3e00 000c 0000 0000 0100 0000 0000 0054 >..............T
45480a0: 2a42 c333 0000 0000 ca3e 0000 2500 0000 *B.3.....>..%...
45480b0: 0001 0000 0000 0000 5440 119c 4000 0000 ........T@..@...
45480c0: 00a4 3e00 0026 0000 0000 0100 0000 0000 ..>..&..........
45480d0: 0054 54f5 fa4d 0000 0000 813e 0000 2300 .TT..M.....>..#.
45480e0: 0000 0001 0000 0000 0000 6002 0000 0000 ..........`.....
45480f0: 0000 005e 3e00 0023 0000 0000 0100 0000 ...^>..#........
4548100: 0000 0060 0300 0000 0000 0000 383e 0000 ...`........8>..
4548110: 2600 0000 0001 0000 0000 0000 6004 0000 &...........`...
4548120: 0000 0000 0013 3e00 0025 0000 0001 0100 ......>..%......
4548130: 0000 0000 0001 0000 0000 0000 0000 733d ..............s=
4548140: 0000 a000 0000 0101 0000 0000 0000 0c00 ................
4548150: 0100 0000 0000 0064 3d00 000f 0000 0001 .......d=.......
4548160: 0100 0000 0000 0054 8102 9f1a 0000 0000 .......T........
4548170: 3d3d 0000 2700 0000 0101 0000 0000 0000 ==..'...........
4548180: 54c2 760e 8c00 0000 0015 3d00 0028 0000 T.v.......=..(..
4548190: 0001 0100 0000 0000 0060 0200 0000 0000 .........`......
45481a0: 0000 ee3c 0000 2700 0000 0101 0000 0000 ...<..'.........
45481b0: 0000 6003 0000 0000 0000 00c6 3c00 0028 ..`.........<..(
45481c0: 0000 0002 0100 0000 0000 0001 0000 0000 ................
45481d0: 0000 0000 263c 0000 a000 0000 0201 0000 ....&<..........
45481e0: 0000 0000 0c00 0100 0000 0000 0014 3c00 ..............<.
45481f0: 0012 0000 0002 0100 0000 0000 006c 0000 .............l..
4548200: 0000 0000 0000 593b 0000 bb00 0000 0301 ......Y;........
4548210: 0000 0000 0000 0100 0000 0000 0000 00b9 ................
4548220: 3a00 00a0 0000 0003 0100 0000 0000 000c:...............
4548230: 0101 0000 0000 0000 a63a 0000 1300 0000 ........:.......
4548240: 0301 0000 0000 0000 6c00 0000 0000 0000 ........l.......
4548250: 0071 3a00 0035 0000 0004 0100 0000 0000 .q:..5..........
4548260: 0001 0000 0000 0000 0000 d139 0000 a000 ...........9....
4548270: 0000 0401 0000 0000 0000 0c01 0100 0000 ................
4548280: 0000 00bd 3900 0014 0000 0004 0100 0000 ....9...........
4548290: 0000 006c 0000 0000 0000 0000 7c39 0000 ...l........|9..
45482a0: 4100 0000 0501 0000 0000 0000 0100 0000 A...............
45482b0: 0000 0000 00dc 3800 00a0 0000 0005 0100 ......8.........
45482c0: 0000 0000 000c 0001 0000 0000 0000 cb38 ...............8
45482d0: 0000 1100 0000 0501 0000 0000 0000 6c00 ..............l.
45482e0: 0000 0000 0000 0096 3800 0035 0000 0000 ........8..5....
```

Listing 11.17 Contents of the FS_TREE root node, for presentation purposes the first 0x60 bytes have been removed.

```
$ xxd -s $((0x4548000 + 0x65 + 0x3EEF)) -l $((0x0C)) mnt/ewf1
0454bf54: 0000 0000 0000 0000 0200 2e2e         ............
```

Listing 11.18 Contents of the INODE_REF item associated with OID 0x100.

Table 11.27 OIDs and associated items in the FS_TREE.

OID	0x01 INODE ITEM	0x0C INODE REF	0x54 DIR ITEM	0x60 DIR INDEX	0x6C EXTENT DATA
0x100	1	1	3	3	
0x101	1	1	2	2	
0x102	1	1			1
0x103	1	1			1
0x104	1	1			1
0x105	1	1			1

```
Item # 3
$ xxd -s $((0x4548000 + 0x65 + 0x3ECA)) -l $((0x25)) mnt/ewf1
454bf2f: 0501 0000 0000 0000 0100 0000 0000 0000 ................
454bf3f: 0009 0000 0000 0000 0000 0007 0001 7365 ..............se
454bf4f: 612e 6a70 67                            a.jpg
$
Item # 4
$ xxd -s $((0x4548000 + 0x65 + 0x3EA4)) -l $((0x26)) mnt/ewf1
454bf09: 0201 0000 0000 0000 0100 0000 0000 0000 ................
454bf19: 0007 0000 0000 0000 0000 0008 0001 696e ..............in
454bf29: 666f 2e74 7874                          fo.txt
Item # 5
$ xxd -s $((0x4548000 + 0x65 + 0x3E81)) -l $((0x23)) mnt/ewf1
454bee6: 0101 0000 0000 0000 0100 0000 0000 0000 ................
454bef6: 0007 0000 0000 0000 0000 0005 0002 4669 ..............Fi
454bf06: 6c65 73                                 les
```

Listing 11.19 DIR_ITEMs found in OID 0x100 (the root directory).

Immediately what appear to be filenames (**sea.jpg**, **info.txt** and **Files**) are seen. These items are further processed as shown in Table 11.28.

The entry type in Table 11.28 provides the type of file that the entry refers to. The possible values are: 0x00 = unknown; 0x01 = regular file; 0x02 = directory; 0x03 = character device; 0x04 = block device; 0x05 = FIFO device; 0x06 = socket; and 0x07 = symbolic link. From Table 11.28 the root directory contains the following objects:

- OID: 0x101 (257_d); Directory; **Files**.
- OID: 0x102 (258_d); Regular File; **info.txt**.
- OID: 0x105 (261_d); Regular File; **sea.jpg**.

Recall the initial file listing performed after creating the device (Listing 11.5). Notice how the OIDs are used as the inode number in Btrfs. In order to list the remaining files, the contents of each sub-directory must be processed. In this case there is only one sub-directory, Files (OID: 0x101). This has two DIR_ITEM items (11 and 12). The contents of these are shown in Listing 11.20.

Again the filenames are clearly visible in ASCII. Processing the DIR_ITEMs in their entirety is shown in Table 11.29.

```
Item # 11
$ xxd -s $((0x4548000 + 0x65 + 0x3D3D)) -l $((0x27)) mnt/ewf1
454bda2: 0301 0000 0000 0000 0100 0000 0000 0000 ................
454bdb2: 0008 0000 0000 0000 0000 0009 0001 7269 ..............ri
454bdc2: 7665 722e 6a70 67                       ver.jpg
$
Item # 12
$ xxd -s $((0x4548000 + 0x65 + 0x3D15)) -l $((0x28)) mnt/ewf1
454bd7a: 0401 0000 0000 0000 0100 0000 0000 0000 ................
454bd8a: 0008 0000 0000 0000 0000 000a 0001 6465 ..............de
454bd9a: 6c65 7465 2e74 7874                     lete.txt
```

Listing 11.20 Contents of the two DIR_ITEMs for OID 0x101.

Table 11.28 Processing of DIR_ITEMs in the FS_TREE root node.

Offset	Size	Name	Item 3	Item 4	Item 5
0x00	0x11	Key	OID: 0x105 Type: 0x01 Offset: 0x00	OID: 0x102 Type: 0x01 Offset: 0x00	OID: 0x101 Type: 0x01 Offset: 0x00
0x11	0x08	Transid	0x09	0x07	0x07
0x19	0x02	Xattr Length	0x00	0x00	0x00
0x1B	0x02	Name Length (n)	0x07	0x08	0x05
0x1D	0x01	Entry Type	0x01	0x01	0x02
0x1E	(n)	File Name	sea.jpg	info.txt	Files

Table 11.29 Processing of DIR_ITEMs in the FS_TREE belonging to OID 0x101.

Offset	Size	Name	Item 11	Item 12
0x00	0x11	Key	OID: 0x103 Type: 0x01 Offset: 0x00	OID: 0x104 Type: 0x01 Offset: 0x00
0x11	0x08	Transid	0x08	0x08
0x19	0x02	Xattr Length	0x00	0x00
0x1B	0x02	Name Length (n)	0x09	0x0A
0x1D	0x01	Entry Type	0x01	0x01
0x1E	(n)	File name	river.jpg	delete.txt

This results in two files:

- OID: 0x103 (259_d); Regular File; **river.jpg**.
- OID: 0x104 (260_d); Regular File; **delete.txt**.

This process continues for any further directories discovered (there are none in this case) allowing all files to be listed.

11.2.4.9 Recovering Metadata

The next step in the process is to recover the metadata for a particular file or directory. This section examines **sea.jpg** (OID: 0x105) and attempts to recover metadata for this file. The INODE_ITEM for this file is item 24 (Table 11.26), the contents of which are provided in Listing 11.21. The processed INODE_ITEM appears in Table 11.30.

```
454b941: 0900 0000 0000 0000 0900 0000 0000 0000 ................
454b951: e47e 0400 0000 0000 0080 0400 0000 0000 .~..............
454b961: 0000 0000 0000 0000 0100 0000 0000 0000 ................
454b971: 0000 0000 e881 0000 0000 0000 0000 0000 ................
454b981: 0000 0000 0000 0000 0100 0000 0000 0000 ................
454b991: 0000 0000 0000 0000 0000 0000 0000 0000 ................
454b9a1: 0000 0000 0000 0000 0000 0000 0000 0000 ................
454b9b1: abfd 5565 0000 0000 4963 2830 abfd 5565 ..Ue....Ic(0..Ue
454b9c1: 0000 0000 4963 2830 abfd 5565 0000 0000 ....Ic(0..Ue....
454b9d1: 4963 2830 abfd 5565 0000 0000 4963 2830 Ic(0..Ue....Ic(0
```

Listing 11.21 The INODE_ITEM for OID 0x105 (**sea.jpg**). Alternate fields are highlighted.

The INODE_ITEM data shows information that is very similar to that found in ext. This is normal for Linux/Unix-based file systems as they all attempt to 'play nicely' with the **stat** command.

Table 11.30 Partially processed INODE_ITEM for OID 0x105 (**sea.jpg**).

Offset	Size	Description	Value
0x00	0x08	Generation	0x09 (9_d)
0x08	0x08	TransID	0x09 (9_d)
0x10	0x08	Size (actual)	0x47EE4 ($294,628_d$)
0x18	0x08	Size (allocated)	0x48000 ($294,912_d$)
0x28	0x04	# links	0x01 (1_d)
0x34	0x04	Mode	0x81E8 Regular File: -rwxr-x---
0x70	0x0C	Access time	Seconds: 0x6555FDAB 2023-11-16 11:31:55 UTC Nanoseconds: 0x30286349
0x7C	0x0C	Change time	Seconds: 0x6555FDAB 2023-11-16 11:31:55 UTC Nanoseconds: 0x30286349
0x88	0x0C	Modified time	Seconds: 0x6555FDAB 2023-11-16 11:31:55 UTC Nanoseconds: 0x30286349
0x94	0x0C	Created time	Seconds: 0x6555FDAB 2023-11-16 11:31:55 UTC Nanoseconds: 0x30286349

11.2.4.10 Recovering File Contents

The final step in processing a file in file system forensic analysis is to recover the actual contents of the file. In Btrfs file contents are stored either inline or in extents. Due to this, this section will recover the contents of two files, one inline and one stored in extents. Regardless of how the file contents are actually stored the information about the file content is stored in the EXTENT_DATA (0x6C) item. The two files chosen are **delete.txt** (OID: 0x104) and **sea.jpg** (OID: 0x105). The EXTENT_DATA item for Object 0x104 is item 23 (Table 11.26). The data contents of this item are shown in Listing 11.22. The complete processing of this data is shown in Table 11.31. The actual content is clearly visible in the EXTENT_DATA item.

```
$ xxd -s $((0x4548000 + 0x65 + 0x397C)) -l $((0x41)) mnt/ewf1
454b9e1: 0900 0000 0000 0000 2c00 0000 0000 0000 ........,.......
454b9f1: 0000 0000 0054 6869 7320 6669 6c65 2077 .....This file w
454ba01: 696c 6c20 6265 2064 656c 6574 6564 2061 ill be deleted a
454ba11: 7420 6120 6c61 7465 7220 7374 6167 652e t a later stage.
454ba21: 0a                                      .
```

Listing 11.22 Content of the EXTENT_DATA item for OID 0x104.

The key information first required from the EXTENT_DATA is how the data is stored. This is given by the type field in Table 11.31. For OID 0x104 the value for this field is 0x00, meaning the data is stored inline. In the case of inline data the size of the decoded data field informs how many content bytes are in the file (as long as no compression/encryption is being used). In this case, this value is 0x2C bytes meaning that the 0x2C bytes immediately following the EXTENT_DATA contain the actual file content. The contents in this case are: 'This file will be deleted at a later stage.\n'.

Moving to the next file, **sea.jpg** (OID: 0x105), the next task is to locate its content. The EXTENT_DATA for this file is contained in item 26. The contents of this item are shown in Listing 11.23.

The type of this EXTENT_DATA is 0x01, meaning that it is regular, in other words the contents are not stored inline but are contained in extent structures. The next 0x20 bytes contain information about the actual extent itself.[7] The processed values are shown in Table 11.32.

Table 11.31 Processed EXTENT_DATA for OID 0x104.

Offset	Size	Description	Value
0x00	0x08	Generation	0x09 (9_d)
0x08	0x08	Decoded extent size	0x2C (44_d)
0x10	0x01	Compression	0x00 – none
0x11	0x01	Encryption	0x00 – none
0x12	0x02	Other encoding	0x00 – none
0x14	0x01	Type	0x00 – inline

7 In the case of fragmented files there will be multiple EXTENT_DATA items each of which contains one single extent. The offset within the extent in the EXTENT_DATA structure indicates the position in the file content represented by this extent.

```
$ xxd -s $((0x4548000 + 0x65 + 0x3896)) -l $((0x35)) mnt/ewf1
454b8fb: 0900 0000 0000 0000 0080 0400 0000 0000 ................
454b90b: 0000 0000 0100 00d3 0000 0000 0000 8004 ................
454b91b: 0000 0000 0000 0000 0000 0000 0000 8004 ................
454b92b: 0000 0000 00                            .....
```

Listing 11.23 The EXTENT_DATA item for OID 0x105.

Table 11.32 The extent structure for the EXTENT_DATA item in OID 0x105.

Offset	Size	Description	Value
0x15	0x08	Logical address of extent	0xD30000 $(13,828,096_d)$
0x1D	0x08	Size of extent	0x48000 $(294,912_d)$
0x25	0x08	Offset within the extent	0x00
0x2D	0x08	Logical number of bytes in file	0x48000 $(294,912_d)$

The logical address (t_{log}) can be translated to a physical address using the CHUNK_TREE. The key offset for CHUNK_ITEM 1 is 0xD00000 (c_{log}), and the stripe for CHUNK_ITEM 1 is 0xD00000. Performing the calculation:

$$
\begin{aligned}
& (t_{log} - c_{log}) + c_{phy} \\
= \quad & \{Substitute\} \\
& (\text{0xD30000} - \text{0xD00000}) + \text{0xD00000} \\
= \quad & \{Calculate\} \\
& \text{0x30000} + \text{0xD00000} = \text{0xD30000}.
\end{aligned}
$$

The file size given in the EXTENT_DATA is the actual number of bytes allocated on the device, in this case 0x48000. However, the INODE_ITEM file size value was 0x47EE4 (it also listed the allocated size in bytes as 0x48000). Extracting 0x47EE4 bytes from 0xD30000 should provide the file contents as shown in Listing 11.24.

```
$ dd if=mnt/ewf1 of=sea.jpg bs=1 skip=$((0xD30000))
     count=$((0x47EE4))
294628+0 records in
294628+0 records out
294628 bytes (295 kB, 288 KiB) copied, 6.9254 s, 42.5 kB/s
$
$ file sea.jpg
sea.jpg: JPEG image data, JFIF standard 1.01, aspect ratio, ...
$
$ md5sum sea.jpg
752f037c544cd693424de0231f9c7a5a sea.jpg
```

Listing 11.24 Recovering the file contents for OID 0x101.

Figure 11.3 The recovered **sea.jpg** file.

The recovered picture is shown in Figure 11.3. The steps outlined in this section should be repeatable so the reader can now recover the files **info.txt** and **river.jpg** from the file system.

11.3 Btrfs Advanced Analysis

The file system that has been analysed is very simple. There are only a small number of files in the file system and there is very little historical data as this file system was created solely for the purposes of demonstrating basic file system forensics in Btrfs. In this section some advanced concepts present in Btrfs are examined. These topics include deleted files, internal nodes, simple RAID devices (RAID 1 – mirroring) and subvolumes and snapshots.

11.3.1 File Deletion

What happens when a file is deleted in Btrfs? In **BtrFS_V2.E01** there are two deleted files. In **BtrFS_V1.E01** the contents of OID 0x103 are located at 0xD00000. Listing 11.25 shows the contents at this point in both **BtrFS_V1.E01** (before deletion) and **BtrFS_V2.E01** (after deletion). From this the contents are identical both before and after deletion.

```
$ xxd -s $((0xD00000)) -l 16 mnt/ewf1
0d00000: ffd8 ffe0 0010 4a46 4946 0001 0100 0001 ......JFIF......
$
$ xxd -s $((0xD00000)) -l 16 mnt/ewf1
0d00000: ffd8 ffe0 0010 4a46 4946 0001 0100 0001 ......JFIF......
```

Listing 11.25 Contents at offset 0xD00000 both before and after deletion of OID 0x103.

The content of the file is still present but can it be recovered? To determine if it can be recovered processing of the file system (**BtrFS_V2.E01**) begins as it did previously. The first step is to process the superblock to determine the logical address of the ROOT_TREE and the CHUNK_TREE. The relevant information is highlighted in Listing 11.26.

```
0010000: 1c88 2757 0000 0000 0000 0000 0000 0000 ..'W............
0010010: 0000 0000 0000 0000 0000 0000 0000 0000 ................
0010020: 2f72 2027 c81b 4b8b bf6c b068 014b 7816 /r '..K..l.h.Kx.
0010030: 0000 0100 0000 0000 0100 0000 0000 0000 ................
0010040: 5f42 4852 6653 5f4d 0d00 0000 0000 0000 _BHRfS_M........
0010050: 00c0 d201 0000 0000 0040 5001 0000 0000 .........@P.....
0010060: 0000 0000 0000 0000 0000 0000 0000 0000 ................
0010070: 0000 0020 0000 0000 0080 0600 0000 0000 ... ............
0010080: 0600 0000 0000 0000 0100 0000 0000 0000 ................
0010090: 0010 0000 0040 0000 0040 0000 0010 0000 .....@...@......
00100a0: 8100 0000 0500 0000 0000 0000 0000 0000 ................
```

Listing 11.26 Contents of superblock in **BtrFS_V2.E01**. The logical addresses of the ROOT_TREE and CHUNK_TREE are highlighted.

The CHUNK_TREE address is the same as it was previously but the address of the ROOT_TREE has changed. The next step is to rebuild the CHUNK_TREE by processing the CHUNK_ARRAY and then locating the root of the CHUNK_TREE. The CHUNK_ARRAY is located at offset 0x32B and is 0x81 bytes in size (found at offset 0xA0 in the superblock). The contents of the CHUNK_ARRAY are shown in Listing 11.27.

```
001032b: 0001 0000 0000 0000 e400 0050 0100 0000 ...........P....
001033b: 0000 0080 0000 0000 0002 0000 0000 0000 ................
001034b: 0000 0001 0000 0000 0022 0000 0000 0000 .........".......
001035b: 0000 0001 0000 0001 0000 1000 0002 0001 ................
001036b: 0001 0000 0000 0000 0000 0050 0100 0000 ...........P....
001037b: 0036 44fd 1489 1844 9ea0 c9ed 54d7 911e .6D....D....T...
001038b: ea01 0000 0000 0000 0000 00d0 0100 0000 ................
001039b: 0036 44fd 1489 1844 9ea0 c9ed 54d7 911e .6D....D....T...
00103ab: ea                                       .
```

Listing 11.27 The contents of the CHUNK_ARRAY in **BtrFS_V2.E01**.

From this it is clear that there are two stripes with a key offset of 0x1500000, the stripes begin at 0x1500000 and 0x1D00000, meaning that the CHUNK_TREE itself can be found at the physical offsets 0x1504000 and 0x1D04000. The contents of these locations are shown in Listing 11.28.

Rebuilding the CHUNK_TREE leads to three chunks with a total of five stripes. This is shown in Table 11.33.

The next step is to locate the ROOT_TREE. The logical address of this is 0x1D2C000. Converting this to a physical address using the CHUNK_TREE (Table 11.33), gives two options: 0x252C000 or 0x452C000. The contents of these locations are shown in Listing 11.29, showing the same structure in both locations.

The OID for the FS_TREE is 0x05 and the ROOT_ITEM type is 0x84. Processing this item for the ROOT_TREE shows the logical address of the FS_TREE is 0x1D10000. This corresponds to the physical addresses: 0x2510000 and 0x4510000. When these locations are processed it is seen that there are only 16_d items in the FS_TREE, compared to 26_d items that were there previously (Table 11.26). There is no mention of items 0x103 and 0x104 in the current version of FS_TREE,

```
$ xxd -s $((0x1504000)) -l 64 mnt/ewf1
1504000: 2f66 96f7 0000 0000 0000 0000 0000 0000 /f..............
1504010: 0000 0000 0000 0000 0000 0000 0000 0000 ................
1504020: 2f72 2027 c81b 4b8b bf6c b068 014b 7816 /r '..K..l.h.Kx.
1504030: 0040 5001 0000 0000 0100 0000 0000 0001 .@P.............
$
$ xxd -s $((0x1D04000)) -l 64 mnt/ewf1
1d04000: 2f66 96f7 0000 0000 0000 0000 0000 0000 /f..............
1d04010: 0000 0000 0000 0000 0000 0000 0000 0000 ................
1d04020: 2f72 2027 c81b 4b8b bf6c b068 014b 7816 /r '..K..l.h.Kx.
1d04030: 0040 5001 0000 0000 0100 0000 0000 0001 .@P.............
```

Listing 11.28 The contents of both physical addresses for the CHUNK_TREE.

Table 11.33 Excerpts from the CHUNK_ITEMS in **BtrFS_V2.E01**. These excerpts provide sufficient information to map logical to physical addresses.

Field	CHUNK 1	CHUNK 2	CHUNK 3
OID	0x100 (256_d)	0x100 (256_d)	0x100 (256_d)
Type	0xE4	0xE4	0xE4
Key Offset	0x0xD00000	0x1500000	0x1D00000
	($13,631,488_d$)	($22,020,096_d$)	($30,408,704_d$)
Data Offset	0x3EE9 ($16,105_d$)	0x3E79 ($15,993_d$)	0x3E09 ($15,881_d$)
Data Size	0x50 (80_d)	0x70 (112_d)	0x70 (112_d)
# Stripes	0x01 (1_d)	0x02 (2_d)	0x02 (2_d)
Stripe 1	0xD00000	0x1500000	0x2500000
Offset	($13,631,488_d$)	($22,020,096_d$)	($38,797,312_d$)
Stripe 2	N/A	0x1D00000	0x4500000
Offset		($30,408,704_d$)	($72,351,744_d$)

these being the two items that were deleted. Hence the means of recovering the underlying data through the file system appears to be impossible.[8]

There is one way of recovering certain older file system information from Btrfs. This involves another area of the superblock called the super roots backup area. This area begins at offset 0xB2B and consists of 0x2A0 bytes. The area contains four *btrfs_root_backup* items the structure of which is shown in Table 11.34. Note that only the first 0x50 bytes of this structure are shown.

Each *btrfs_root_backup* is 0xA8 bytes in size (0x2A0/0x4). Listing 11.30 shows the second of these structures in the superblock from **BtrFS_V2.E01**.

In order to confirm the tree that resides at each location, the node header can be processed. Each tree node contains the ID of the tree that owns the node. This is also included in Table 11.35.

From Table 11.35 it is clear that there are older versions of a number of trees, including an older version of the FS_TREE (Generation 0x09). This is located at offset 0x2548000. The node header for this is shown in Listing 11.31. The checksum for this node is highlighted. This can be compared

8 Be aware that as long as the data is still present, as it is by default in Btrfs, it is still possible that data carving will be able to recover some or all of the deleted files.

```
$ xxd -s $((0x252C000)) -l 64 mnt/ewf1
252c000: fb2f 6f4f 0000 0000 0000 0000 0000 0000 ./oO............
252c010: 0000 0000 0000 0000 0000 0000 0000 0000 ................
252c020: 2f72 2027 c81b 4b8b bf6c b068 014b 7816 /r '..K..l.h.Kx.
252c030: 00c0 d201 0000 0000 0100 0000 0000 0001 ................
$
$ xxd -s $((0x452C000)) -l 64 mnt/ewf1
452c000: fb2f 6f4f 0000 0000 0000 0000 0000 0000 ./oO............
452c010: 0000 0000 0000 0000 0000 0000 0000 0000 ................
452c020: 2f72 2027 c81b 4b8b bf6c b068 014b 7816 /r '..K..l.h.Kx.
452c030: 00c0 d201 0000 0000 0100 0000 0000 0001 ................
```

Listing 11.29 Excerpts from the two copies of the ROOT_TREE's root node.

Table 11.34 btrfs_root_backup structure.

Offset	Size	Name	Description
0x00	0x08	Root Tree	The logical address of the root tree backup.
0x08	0x08	Root Tree Gen	The generation of the root tree backup.
0x10	0x08	Chunk Tree	The logical address of the chunk tree backup.
0x18	0x08	Chunk Tree Gen	The generation of the chunk tree backup.
0x20	0x08	Extent Tree	The logical address of the extent tree backup.
0x28	0x08	Extent Tree Gen	The generation of the extent tree backup.
0x30	0x08	FS Tree	The logical address of the FS tree backup.
0x38	0x08	FS Tree Gen	The generation of the FS tree backup.
0x40	0x08	Dev Tree	The logical address of the dev tree backup.
0x48	0x08	Dev Tree Gen	The generation of the dev tree backup.

Table 11.35 Logical and physical addresses from the second backup root structure.

Log. Addr.	Generation	Phys. Addr.	Tree OID
0x1D58000	0x0A	0x2558000	0x01 (ROOT_TREE)
0x1504000	0x05	0x1504000	0x03 (CHUNK_TREE)
0x1D5C000	0x0A	0x255C000	0x02 (EXTENT_TREE)
0x1D48000	0x09	0x2548000	0x05 (FS_TREE)
0x1D28000	0x06	0x2528000	0x04 (DEV_TREE)

to that found in the original FS_TREE root node (Listing 11.16). As these values are equal the node contents are equal. This means that the contents of both deleted files can be recovered from this backup structure.

This system of backups means that not much historical information is available through the file system but the information that is available is protected. While one of these backup trees links to the content of the file, the content will never be overwritten.

```
$ xxd -s $((0x10000 + 0xB2B + 0xA8)) -l $((0xA8)) mnt/ewf1
0010bd3: 0080 d501 0000 0000 0a00 0000 0000 0000 ................
0010be3: 0040 5001 0000 0000 0500 0000 0000 0000 .@P.............
0010bf3: 00c0 d501 0000 0000 0a00 0000 0000 0000 ................
0010c03: 0080 d401 0000 0000 0900 0000 0000 0000 ................
0010c13: 0080 d201 0000 0000 0600 0000 0000 0000 ................
0010c23: 00c0 d401 0000 0000 0900 0000 0000 0000 ................
0010c33: 0000 0020 0000 0000 0080 0900 0000 0000 ... ............
0010c43: 0100 0000 0000 0000 0000 0000 0000 0000 ................
0010c53: 0000 0000 0000 0000 0000 0000 0000 0000 ................
0010c63: 0000 0000 0000 0000 0000 0000 0000 0000 ................
0010c73: 0000 0000 0000 0000                     ........
```

Listing 11.30 The second btrfs_root_backup structure.

```
$ xxd -s $((0x2548000)) -l $((0x65)) mnt/ewf1
2548000: 6d3b 10e5 0000 0000 0000 0000 0000 0000 m;..............
2548010: 0000 0000 0000 0000 0000 0000 0000 0000 ................
2548020: 2f72 2027 c81b 4b8b bf6c b068 014b 7816 /r '..K..l.h.Kx.
2548030: 0080 d401 0000 0000 0100 0000 0000 0001 ................
2548040: be4e 1e7a bae9 4f90 b7ea 8e3c 359f f328 .N.z..O....<5..(
2548050: 0900 0000 0000 0000 0500 0000 0000 0000 ................
2548060: 1a00 0000 00                            .....
```

Listing 11.31 The contents of the FS_TREE addressed by the backup root structure in Listing 11.30. The checksum is highlighted, clearly showing the content of this node is identical to that shown in Listing 11.16 in which the deleted files were still allocated.

11.3.2 Analysis of Internal Nodes

The file system in **BtrFS_V3.E01** contains over 1000_d files. These are merely a collection of small text files but the sheer number of files is too large to be stored in one single FS_TREE node. Hence, internal nodes are required with pointers to other nodes. The physical address of the FS_TREE in this file system is 0x2528000. An excerpt from this node is shown in Listing 11.32.

```
2528000: 7d1b 16e2 0000 0000 0000 0000 0000 0000 }...............
2528010: 0000 0000 0000 0000 0000 0000 0000 0000 ................
2528020: 2f72 2027 c81b 4b8b bf6c b068 014b 7816 /r '..K..l.h.Kx.
2528030: 0080 d201 0000 0000 0100 0000 0000 0001 ................
2528040: be4e 1e7a bae9 4f90 b7ea 8e3c 359f f328 .N.z..O....<5..(
2528050: 0f00 0000 0000 0000 0500 0000 0000 0000 ................
2528060: 1c00 0000 0100 0100 0000 0000 0001 0000 ................
2528070: 0000 0000 0000 0040 d201 0000 0000 0f00 .......@........
2528080: 0000 0000 0000 0601 0000 0000 0000 5475 ..............Tu
2528090: acde 3200 0000 0000 c0d7 0100 0000 000f ..2.............
25280a0: 0000 0000 0000 0006 0100 0000 0000 0054 ...............T
25280b0: 9614 a35e 0000 0000 0080 d501 0000 0000 ...^............
25280c0: 0f00 0000 0000 0000                     ........
```

Listing 11.32 Excerpt from the FS_TREE root node in **BtrFS_V3.E01**. Only the first three pointers are shown.

Table 11.36 Values for the first three pointers in the FS_TREE root node.

	Pointer 1	Pointer 2	Pointer 3
OID	0x100	0x106	0x106
Type	0x01	0x54	0x54
Key Offset	0x00	0x32DEAC75	0x5EA31496
Block Number	0x1D24000	0x1D7C000	0x1D58000
Generation	0x0F	0x0F	0x0F

From Listing 11.32 it is clear that there are 0x1C items in this node and that the level is 1. Level 1 indicates that this is an internal node and as such the internal node structure (Figure 11.2 and Table 11.5) is required to process it. The processing of the first three elements in this node is shown in Table 11.36.

Each of the logical addresses discovered in the node is then translated to physical addresses and these are processed. In this case, each of these is a leaf node containing items. For instance the logical address of the first pointer is 0x1D24000. Mapping this to a physical address gives 0x2524000. At that offset a leaf node is found.

In the type field for the internal node pointer, the type appears to refer to the type of the first item on the subsequent page. For the three pointers presented in Table 11.36, the first item at the first pointer is type 0x01 and for the remaining two pointers, the first item in these nodes is type 0x54.

11.3.3 Multiple Device Configuration

One of the most exciting features of Btrfs is that RAID is built-in. The desired RAID level can be specified at creation. For the purposes of analysis a RAID 1 (mirrored) solution has been chosen. The creation of this is shown in Listing 11.33.

Btrfs RAID file systems can be mounted by providing any member device to the mount command. For instance, the file system created in Listing 11.33 could be mounted using the command **mount /dev/sdc1 mnt/**. When this file system is mounted the size is 'only' 256 M as seen in the output from **df** provided in Listing 11.34.

Notice that the size of this volume is given as 256 M, half the actual size used. This is due to the mirroring that RAID 1 introduces. The 512 M results in 256 M that is mirrored on both devices.

In order to analyse a single device file system the superblock is the starting point. It is the same for a multi-device file system but where is the superblock? On a single device file system the superblock is located at 0x10000 on the physical device, with backup copies throughout. On a multiple device RAID system the superblock (and copies) are located on every device. Hence we can examine the superblock on any of the devices. However, the superblocks are slightly different on each device as a superblock contains a DEV_ITEM structure for the device on which it resides. At the very least the device UUID in this will be different on different superblocks. Listing 11.35 shows an excerpt from the superblock of **BtrFS_Raid1_D1.E01**.

Listing 11.35 shows two devices in the file system and also the logical address of both the ROOT_TREE and the CHUNK_TREE. The file system UUID field can be used to confirm that the second device is part of the same file system. This UUID should match for all devices in the file system.

```
$ sudo mmkfs.btrfs -f -d raid1 -m raid1 -L "BtrFS-Raid"
       /dev/sdb1 /dev/sdc1
btrfs-progs v5.4.1
See http://btrfs.wiki.kernel.org for more information.

Label:                BtrFS-Raid
UUID:                 0876b354-2d32-4ea8-8975-dd9bda743b3a
Node size:            16384
Sector size:          4096
Filesystem size:      512.00MiB
Block group profiles:
  Data:               RAID1               64.00MiB
  Metadata:           RAID1               32.00MiB
  System:             RAID1                8.00MiB
SSD detected:         no
Incompat features:    extref, skinny-metadata
Checksum:             crc32c
Number of devices:               2
Devices:
   ID             SIZE            PATH
    1        256.00MiB            /dev/sdb1
    2        256.00MiB            /dev/sdc1
```

Listing 11.33 Output of the **mkfs.btrfs** command when creating a RAID 1 file system.

```
/dev/sdb1      256M      3.4M      215M      2% /home/fergus/BtrFS/mnt
```

Listing 11.34 Output for a RAID 1 Btrfs file system from the **df** command.

```
0010000: 2f52 3441 0000 0000 0000 0000 0000 0000 /R4A............
0010010: 0000 0000 0000 0000 0000 0000 0000 0000 ................
0010020: 0876 b354 2d32 4ea8 8975 dd9b da74 3b3a .v.T-2N..u...t;:
0010030: 0000 0100 0000 0000 0100 0000 0000 0000 ................
0010040: 5f42 4852 6653 5f4d 0b00 0000 0000 0000 _BHRfS_M........
0010050: 0080 d601 0000 0000 0040 5001 0000 0000 .........@P.....
0010060: 0000 0000 0000 0000 0000 0000 0000 0000 ................
0010070: 0000 0020 0000 0000 0080 0900 0000 0000 ... ............
0010080: 0600 0000 0000 0000 0200 0000 0000 0000 ................
0010090: 0010 0000 0040 0000 0040 0000 0010 0000 .....@...@......
00100a0: 8100 0000 0500 0000 0000 0000 0000 0000 ................
00100b0: 0000 0000 0000 0000 0000 0000 4101 0000 ............A...
00100c0: 0000 0000 0000 0000 0001 0000 0000 0000 ................
00100d0: 0000 0000 1000 0000 0000 0080 0600 0000 ................
00100e0: 0000 1000 0000 1000 0000 1000 0000 0000 ................
00100f0: 0000 0000 0000 0000 0000 0000 0000 0000 ................
0010100: 0000 0000 0000 0000 0000 0019 a107 1d10 ................
0010110: 704a 9389 31e1 211c 244b 8608 76b3 542d pJ..1.!.$K..v.T-
0010120: 324e a889 75dd 9bda 743b 3a42 7472 4653 2N..u...t;:BtrFS
0010130: 2d52 6169 6400 0000 0000 0000 0000 0000 -Raid...........
```

Listing 11.35 Excerpt from the superblock on **BtrFS_Raid1_D1.E01**, one device in a multiple device file system.

Table 11.37 Processed stripes from superblock CHUNK_ARRAY.

	Stripe 1	**Stripe 2**
Device ID	0x01 (1_d)	0x02 (2_d)
Offset	0x1500000	0x100000
	($22,020,096_d$)	($1,048,576_d$)
Device UUID	0x19A1...4B86	0x3E05...CC93

Step 2 in the analysis is to process the CHUNK_ARRAY. This is located at 0x32B in the superblock and in the above example is 0x81 bytes in size. The contents of this are provided in Listing 11.36 (the key is highlighted), while the remaining data is the CHUNK_ITEM itself. From the CHUNK_ITEM there are two stripes present in the item. The processed stripe values for this CHUNK_ITEM are shown in Table 11.37.

```
001032b: 0001 0000 0000 0000 e400 0050 0100 0000  ...........P....
001033b: 0000 0080 0000 0000 0002 0000 0000 0000  ................
001034b: 0000 0001 0000 0000 0012 0000 0000 0000  ................
001035b: 0000 0001 0000 0001 0000 1000 0002 0001  ................
001036b: 0001 0000 0000 0000 0000 0050 0100 0000  ...........P....
001037b: 0019 a107 1d10 704a 9389 31e1 211c 244b  ......pJ..1.!.$K
001038b: 8602 0000 0000 0000 0000 0010 0000 0000  ................
001039b: 003e 05a4 a0dd 994c da88 f497 2a73 a5cc  .>.....L....*s..
00103ab: 93                                       .
```

Listing 11.36 The CHUNK_ARRAY from the RAID 1 superblock.

Notice firstly that the two stripes are on different disks! Remember with RAID1 all data should be mirrored on both devices. However, the starting physical offset is different on both devices. We need to determine which device we are examining in order to know which stripe to use. Again, for bootstrapping purposes the superblock contains a DEV_ITEM structure relating to the device. This is located at 0xC9 and occupies 0x62 bytes. The content of this, from both devices in the RAID array, is shown in Listing 11.37. The values from these DEV_ITEMS are shown in Table 11.38.

The physical offset of the CHUNK_TREE in each disk can now be calculated. The logical address is 0x1504000, which is part of the recovered CHUNK (key offset: 0x1500000). Below the calculations for both stripes (i.e. both devices) are shown.

0x1504000 − 0x1500000 = 0x4000	
Device 1 (offset: 0x1500000)	Device 2 (offset: 0x100000)
0x4000 + 0x1500000	0x4000 + 0x100000
=	=
0x1504000	0x104000

```
$ xxd -s $((0x100C9)) -l $((0x62)) mnt/ewf1
00100c9: 0100 0000 0000 0000 0000 0010 0000 0000 ................
00100d9: 0000 8006 0000 0000 0010 0000 0010 0000 ................
00100e9: 0010 0000 0000 0000 0000 0000 0000 0000 ................
00100f9: 0000 0000 0000 0000 0000 0000 0000 0000 ................
0010109: 0000 19a1 071d 1070 4a93 8931 e121 1c24 .......pJ..1.!.$
0010119: 4b86 0876 b354 2d32 4ea8 8975 dd9b da74 K..v.T-2N..u...t
0010129: 3b3a                                    ;:
$
$ xxd -s $((0x100C9)) -l $((0x62)) mnt2/ewf1
00100c9: 0200 0000 0000 0000 0000 0010 0000 0000 ................
00100d9: 0000 8006 0000 0000 0010 0000 0010 0000 ................
00100e9: 0010 0000 0000 0000 0000 0000 0000 0000 ................
00100f9: 0000 0000 0000 0000 0000 0000 0000 0000 ................
0010109: 0000 3e05 a4a0 dd99 4cda 88f4 972a 73a5 ..>.....L....*s.
0010119: cc93 0876 b354 2d32 4ea8 8975 dd9b da74 ...v.T-2N..u...t
0010129: 3b3a                                    ;:
```

Listing 11.37 Contents of the DEV_ITEMs in superblocks from both RAID devices.

Table 11.38 Partially processed DEV_ITEMs from both superblocks.

Offset	Size	Description	Device 1	Device 2
0x00	0x08	Device ID	0x01 (1_d)	0x02 (1_d)
0x08	0x08	Total number of bytes	0x10000000 ($268,435,456_d$)	0x10000000 ($268,435,456_d$)
0x10	0x08	Number of used bytes	0x6800000 ($109,051,904_d$)	0x6800000 ($109,051,904_d$)
0x42	0x10	Device UUID	0x19A1...4B86	0x3E05...CC93
0x52	0x10	File system UUID	0x0876..3B3A	0x0876..3B3A

From the above result the CHUNK_TREE should be located at 0x1504000 on Device 1 and at 0x104000 on Device 2. Excerpts from these locations are provided in Listing 11.38.

It is now possible to rebuild the entire CHUNK_TREE structure. The CHUNK_TREE root node contains five items, two DEV_ITEMs (for the two devices in the file system) and three CHUNK_ITEMS. The CHUNK_ITEMS are provided in Listing 11.39 and processed in Table 11.39. The key offset is included with each one in Table 11.39.

Once the CHUNK_TREE is available, the remainder of the file system is processed normally, remembering to ensure that the correct device is being examined.

11.3.4 Subvolumes and Snapshots

Btrfs allows for the creation of subvolumes, separate file systems that are formed from part or all of the file system. By default every Btrfs file system has one subvolume, which is called default

Table 11.39 The processed CHUNK_TREE for the RAID 1 file system.

	CHUNK 1	CHUNK 2	CHUNK 3
Key Offset	0x1500000	0x1D00000	0x3D00000
	$(22,020,096_d)$	$(30,408,704_d)$	$(63,963,136_d)$
# Stripes	0x02 (2_d)	0x02 (2_d)	0x02 (2_d)
	Stripe 1		
Device ID	0x01 (1_d)	0x01 (1_d)	0x01 (1_d)
Offset	0x1500000	0x1D00000	0x3D00000
	$(22,020,096_d)$	$(30,408,704_d)$	$(63,963,136_d)$
Device UUID		0x19A1...4B86	
	Stripe 2		
Device ID	0x02 (2_d)	0x02 (2_d)	0x02 (2_d)
Offset	0x100000	0x900000	0x2900000
	$(1,048,576_d)$	$(9,437,184_d)$	$(42,991,616_d)$
Device UUID		0x3E05...CC93	

```
$ xxd -s $((0x1504000)) -l 64 mnt/ewf1
1504000: d5f8 36bd 0000 0000 0000 0000 0000 0000 ..6.............
1504010: 0000 0000 0000 0000 0000 0000 0000 0000 ................
1504020: 0876 b354 2d32 4ea8 8975 dd9b da74 3b3a .v.T-2N..u...t;:
1504030: 0040 5001 0000 0000 0100 0000 0000 0001 .@P.............
$
$ xxd -s $((0x104000)) -l 64 mnt2/ewf1
0104000: d5f8 36bd 0000 0000 0000 0000 0000 0000 ..6.............
0104010: 0000 0000 0000 0000 0000 0000 0000 0000 ................
0104020: 0876 b354 2d32 4ea8 8975 dd9b da74 3b3a .v.T-2N..u...t;:
0104030: 0040 5001 0000 0000 0100 0000 0000 0001 .@P.............
```

Listing 11.38 Excerpts from the mirrored CHUNK_TREE copies.

and is referenced by FS_TREE. Subvolumes can be mounted independently and with different options.

Btrfs also supports a special type of subvolume called a snapshot. Snapshots are created for a particular subvolume and record the state of that volume at a particular moment in time. Snapshots begin as references to existing trees but may be changed at a later point in time (unless created as read-only). In this section a subvolume and a snapshot are created on a Btrfs device and these are then analysed.

The image **BtrFS_V4.E01** consists of a number of files/directories. This file system also contains a sub-volume (**sub1**) and a snapshot of this subvolume (**sub1-snap**). After creating the snapshot some of the files in the subvolume were modified/deleted. However, from the snapshot it is still possible to recover these. Listing 11.40 contains the commands to create the subvolume. These commands must be executed in the root directory of the mounted Btrfs file system. After creating

```
$ xxd -s $((0x104000 + 0x65 + 0x3e67)) -l $((0x70)) mnt2/ewf1
0107ecc: 0000 8000 0000 0000 0200 0000 0000 0000 ................
0107edc: 0000 0100 0000 0000 1200 0000 0000 0000 ................
0107eec: 0000 0100 0000 0100 0010 0000 0200 0100 ................
0107efc: 0100 0000 0000 0000 0000 5001 0000 0000 ..........P.....
0107f0c: 19a1 071d 1070 4a93 8931 e121 1c24 4b86 .....pJ..1.!.$K.
0107f1c: 0200 0000 0000 0000 0000 1000 0000 0000 ................
0107f2c: 3e05 a4a0 dd99 4cda 88f4 972a 73a5 cc93 >.....L....*s...
$
$ xxd -s $((0x104000 + 0x65 + 0x3df7)) -l $((0x70)) mnt2/ewf1
0107e5c: 0000 0002 0000 0000 0200 0000 0000 0000 ................
0107e6c: 0000 0100 0000 0000 1400 0000 0000 0000 ................
0107e7c: 0000 0100 0000 0100 0010 0000 0200 0100 ................
0107e8c: 0100 0000 0000 0000 0000 d001 0000 0000 ................
0107e9c: 19a1 071d 1070 4a93 8931 e121 1c24 4b86 .....pJ..1.!.$K.
0107eac: 0200 0000 0000 0000 0000 9000 0000 0000 ................
0107ebc: 3e05 a4a0 dd99 4cda 88f4 972a 73a5 cc93 >.....L....*s...
$
$ xxd -s $((0x104000 + 0x65 + 0x3d87)) -l $((0x70)) mnt2/ewf1
0107dec: 0000 0004 0000 0000 0200 0000 0000 0000 ................
0107dfc: 0000 0100 0000 0000 1100 0000 0000 0000 ................
0107e0c: 0000 0100 0000 0100 0010 0000 0200 0100 ................
0107e1c: 0100 0000 0000 0000 0000 d003 0000 0000 ................
0107e2c: 19a1 071d 1070 4a93 8931 e121 1c24 4b86 .....pJ..1.!.$K.
0107e3c: 0200 0000 0000 0000 0000 9002 0000 0000 ................
0107e4c: 3e05 a4a0 dd99 4cda 88f4 972a 73a5 cc93 >.....L....*s...
```

Listing 11.39 Contents of the three CHUNK_ITEMs in the CHUNK_TREE.

the subvolume a number of files were added to both the default and newly created sub-volumes. A snapshot of **sub1** was then taken. The command to perform this task is given in Listing 11.41. Note that it is necessary to again execute this command from the root folder of the mounted file system.

```
$ sudo btrfs subvolume create sub1
Create subvolume 'subvols/sub1'
```

Listing 11.40 Creation of a subvolume (**sub1**) in the mounted root directory.

```
$ sudo btrfs subvolume snapshot sub1 sub1-snap
Create a snapshot of 'sub1' in './sub1-snap'
```

Listing 11.41 Creation of a snapshot (**sub1-snap**) in the mounted root directory.

Mounting the file system normally and listing files is shown in Listing 11.42. From this the sub-volume and snapshot are listed also. Note that the files in the subvolume (**sub1**) were deleted after this listing was created.

The subvolume can also be mounted independently as shown in Listing 11.43 (before trying this ensure the default subvolume has been unmounted).

```
$ mount /dev/sdb1 mnt/
$ ls -lihR mnt/
mnt/:
total 288K
257 -rwxr-x--- 1 root root 288K Nov 21 11:54 sea.jpg
256 drwxr-xr-x 1 root root   38 Nov 21 11:54 sub1
256 drwxr-xr-x 1 root root   38 Nov 21 11:54 sub1-snap

mnt/sub1:
total 196K
258 -rwxr-x--- 1 root root   44 Nov 21 11:54 delete.txt
257 -rwxr-x--- 1 root root 191K Nov 21 11:54 river.jpg

mnt/sub1-snap:
total 196K
258 -rwxr-x--- 1 root root   44 Nov 21 11:54 delete.txt
257 -rwxr-x--- 1 root root 191K Nov 21 11:54 river.jpg
```

Listing 11.42 Contents of the mounted Btrfs filesystem with subvolume (**sub1**) and snapshot (**sub1-snap**). Subvolume and snapshot files are visible.

```
$ mount -o subvol=sub1 /dev/sdb1 mnt/
root # ls -lihR mnt/
mnt/:
total 196K
258 -rwxr-x--- 1 root root   44 Nov 21 11:54 delete.txt
257 -rwxr-x--- 1 root root 191K Nov 21 11:54 river.jpg
```

Listing 11.43 Mounting the **sub1** subvolume. The parent contents are not visible.

The file **BtrFS_V4.E01** contains the image of the above setup. Locating the CHUNK_TREE in this allows the ROOT_TREE's physical address to be determined as 0x252C000. Examining that node in detail shows the expected items for the expected trees, but in addition it shows two items related to OID 0x100 and two for OID 0x101. In each case a ROOT_ITEM (0x84) and a ROOT_BACKREF (0x90) item are found. The ROOT_BACKREF contents for OID 0x100 are shown in Listing 11.44.

```
$ xxd -s $((0x252C000 + 0x65 + 0x3428)) -l $((0x16)) mnt/ewf1
252f48d: 0001 0000 0000 0000 0300 0000 0000 0000 ................
252f49d: 0400 7375 6231                          ..sub1
```

Listing 11.44 The contents of the ROOT_BACKREF item for OID 0x100.

From Listing 11.44 the name of the subvolume is evident. The complete processing of this item is shown in Table 11.40. Note the key offset contains the tree ID of the parent containing this tree. In this case this is 0x05, meaning that this is a child of the default FS_TREE.

The ROOT_ITEM for subvolumes can be processed to find the location of the root of the subvolume's file tree. This tree can then be processed in the same way that FS_TREE can be processed. Snapshots are processed in an identical manner. It is left as an exercise for the reader to process the snapshot and locate the deleted files (**river.jpg** and **delete.txt**).

Table 11.40 Values discovered in the ROOT_BACKREF item for **sub1**.

Offset	Size	Description	Value
0x00	0x08	Directory ID of the directory in the containing tree where this tree occurs	0x100 (256_d) root dir.
0x08	0x08	Sequence (index in the directory tree)	0x03 (3_d)
0x10	0x02	Size of name (n)	0x04 (4_d)
0x12	(n)	Name	sub1

11.4 Summary

This chapter introduced one of the many file systems available for the Linux operating system. Btrfs is seen as a viable replacement for the ext family of file systems in the Linux world and has become the default file system on some distributions. As such it is expected that it will be more frequently encountered over the coming years.

Btrfs is considered a modern file system and it provides much functionality which was not available in the ext family. This includes the use of copy-on-write (CoW) for updating content which leads to greater reliability, along with modern features such as pooling (e.g. RAID), snapshots and checksums. As with many modern file systems Btrfs uses a B-Tree structure for most storage, with almost everything represented as a tree structure. The only exception to this is the superblock structure which is not stored as a B-Tree.

Btrfs allows for snapshots and subvolumes which have some interesting forensic implications. The copy-on-write principle underlying the file system means that there is always the possibility of recovering older versions of the Btrfs file system structures.

Currently there are few tools which offer support for file system forensic analysis of Btrfs. With its growing popularity this may change in the near future but for now manual analysis of this file system is essential.

Exercises

For these exercises the file system in **BtrFS_V4.E01** is used.

1 There is a file in the default subvolume called **sea.jpg** (OID: 257_d). Recover this file.

2 In relation to the file **sea.jpg** (OID: 257_d) in the default subvolume answer the following questions:
a) When was this file created?
b) What size is the file?
c) What are the file's permissions?

3 List all files in the subvolume's snapshot.

4 A file called **river.jpg** (OID: 257_d) (MD5: 15ebaf1a1f34c57c8e89fae341cef8cd) was deleted from the subvolume. Recover this file using any valid means.
For the remaining exercises Mirrored RAID file system (**BtrFS-Raid1-D1.E01** and **BtrFS-Raid1-D2.E01**) is used.

5 What are the UUIDs for each individual device present in the RAID 1 array?

6 At what byte offset on both devices can the contents of **sea.jpg** (OID: 260_d) be found?

7 In relation to **info2.txt** (OID: 261_d) answer the following questions:
a) When was the file created?
b) What is the allocated file size?
c) Are the file's contents stored resident or non-resident?
d) What are the file's permissions?

8 List the contents of the **Files** (OID: 257_d) directory.

Bibliography

Bhat, W.A. and Wani, M.A. (2018). Forensic analysis of B-tree file system (Btrfs). *Digital Investigation* 27: 57–70.

BTRFS (2024a). BTRFS documentation [Internet]. btrfs.readthedocs.io. [cited 2024 April 2]. https://btrfs.readthedocs.io/en/latest/ (accessed 14 August 2024).

BTRFS (2024b). Data Structures - Btrfs Wiki [Internet]. archive.kernel.org. [cited 2024 April 2]. https://archive.kernel.org/oldwiki/btrfs.wiki.kernel.org/index.php/Data\LY1\textbackslash.Structures.html

BTRFS (2024c). On-disk Format - BTRFS documentation [Internet]. btrfs.readthedocs.io. [cited 2024 April 2]. https://btrfs.readthedocs.io/en/latest/dev/On-disk-format.html (accessed 14 August 2024).

Hartmann, A. (2022a). Working with Btrfs –General Concepts [Internet]. Fedora Magazine 2022 [cited 2024 Apr 2]. https://fedoramagazine.org/working-with-btrfs-general-concepts/ (accessed 14 August 2024).

Hartmann, A. (2022b). Working with Btrfs - Subvolumes [Internet]. Fedora Magazine 2022 [cited 2024 April 2]. https://fedoramagazine.org/working-with-btrfs-subvolumes/ (accessed 14 August 2024).

Hilgert, J.N., Lambertz, M., and Yang, S. (2018). Forensic analysis of multiple device BTRFS configurations using The Sleuth Kit. *Digital Investigation* 26: S21–S29.

Juch, A. (2014). Btrfs filesystem forensics. Dissertation. Technische Universität Wien. https://doi.org/10.34726/hss.2014.24504.

Kára, J. (2009). Ext4, btrfs, and the others. Proceeding of Linux-Kongress and OpenSolaris Developer Conference, pp. 99–111.

Mason, C. (2007). The Btrfs Filesystem, September 2007 [Internet]. [cited 2024 April 2]. https://giis.co.in/btrfs.pdf (accessed 14 August 2024).

Rodeh, O., Bacik, J., and Mason, C. (2013). BTRFS. *ACM Transactions on Storage* 9 (3): 1–32.

Son, D. (2018). btrForensics: Forensic Analysis Tool for Btrfs File System [Internet]. Penetration Testing [cited 2024 April 2]. https://securityonline.info/btrforensics/ (accessed 19 December 2024).

SUSE (2024). Storage Administration Guide –SLES 15 SP5 [Internet]. documentation.suse.com. [cited 2024 April 3]. https://documentation.suse.com/sles/15-SP5/html/SLES-all/book-storage.html (accessed 14 August 2024).

The Linux Kernel (n.d.). BTRFS - The Linux Kernel documentation [Internet]. docs.kernel.org. https://docs.kernel.org/filesystems/btrfs.html (accessed 14 August 2024).

Wani, M.A. and Bhat, W.A. (2018). Dataset for forensic analysis of B-tree file system. *Data in Brief* 18: 2013–2018.

Part IV

Apple File Systems

12

The HFS+ File System

For many years the Hierarchical File System (HFS) was the default on Apple systems. This file system utilised 16_d-bit addressing and as such was not suitable for the developments that occurred in storage technology, in particular the increased capacity that was available in newer storage devices. This led to the development of HFS+ which uses 32_d-bit addressing to cater for larger storage capacities. The HFS+ file system was introduced in 1998 and was the default file system on Apple devices for almost 20 years. In 2017, the HFS+ file system was replaced with APFS (Chapter 13).

The HFS+ file system is a journaled file system. All metadata operations are first written to a journal before being committed to disk. The journal provides a means of gathering more information about the file system than is present in the main body of the file system. As with many modern file systems, HFS+ storage is based on B-Trees. Table 12.1 shows some of the more common limits of the HFS+ file system.

One interesting point to note in relation to the analysis of HFS+ is that most data is stored in a big-endian format. This is similar to XFS (Chapter 10), but unlike the vast majority of file systems in common usage. Data in HFS+ is located through extents (similar to data runs in NTFS and extents in ext4).

Files are listed in the catalog file in which each file has a unique catalog node ID (CNID).[1] This is an identifying number that is incremented with each new file that is created. Once the supply of CNID values has been exhausted, then and only then is a CNID reused. This means that up to that point the CNID provides the order in which the files were created in the file system.[2]

The basic storage unit in HFS+ is referred to as the allocation block. Generally an allocation block is composed of a number of sectors. Sectors are generally 512_d bytes in size, although occasionally other sizes are encountered. The standard allocation block size is usually 4096_d bytes in size but this should be confirmed in the volume header. Allocation block numbering begins at 0_d and is used for logical addressing in HFS+.

12.1 On-Disk Structures

In this section some of the more important structures in the HFS+ file system are introduced. Knowledge of these structures is essential in order to fully understand the HFS+ file system and also for manual processing. These structures include:

1 Similar to the inode number in EXT and the MFT record number in NTFS.
2 The volume header structure will inform the analyst if the CNID values have been exhausted (and therefore reused).

File System Forensics, First Edition. Fergus Toolan.

Table 12.1 HFS+ file system limits.

Limit	Value
Max. Filename	255 unicode characters
Max. Volume Size	8 EiB
Max. File Size	8 EiB
Max. # Files	$2^{32} - 1$

- **Volume Header:** The volume header structure is similar in purpose to the superblocks found in Linux file systems and the volume boot records found in Windows file systems. It contains general information about the file system as a whole and allows other structures to be located.
- **Catalog File:** The catalog file contains information about all of the files/directories on the file system. It allows file content to be located and also provides all metadata related to every file. The catalog file's purpose is identical to that of the master file table (MFT) in the NTFS file system.
- **Extents Overflow File:** HFS+ uses extents to locate file content. The catalog file contains a number of extents, but in the case of heavily fragmented files the additional extents are found in the extents overflow file. This file is required only if there are more than 8_d extents needed to locate the file content.
- **Allocation File:** The allocation file contains information about the allocation status of each allocation block in the file system. It acts as a bitmap structure for the HFS+ file system.
- **Attributes File:** The attributes file is used to implement named forks. These allow for names to be associated with data, allowing for named attributes to be stored in this file.

Table 12.2 shows the reserved CNID values, each of which represents a special metadata file in HFS+. These include the files listed above, along with other files less commonly needed in digital forensics.

The above structures are described in this section along with some other structures that are required in order to effectively analyse HFS+. These structures include forks, which allow data to

Table 12.2 HFS+ reserved CNIDs.

CNID	Purpose
1	Root directory parent.
2	Root directory.
3	Extents overflow.
4	Catalog file.
5	Bad block file.
6	Allocation file.
7	Startup file.
8	Attributes file.
14	Repair catalog file.
15	Bogus extent file.
16	First user Catalog node. Usually journal.

be located in the file system, B-Trees which are used as the basic storage mechanism and the timestamp structure employed in HFS+. As HFS+ is a journaled file system, this section also introduces the journal structure.

12.1.1 Forks

HFS+ uses *forks* to store file data. Generally there are two types of fork available in HFS+, the data fork and the resource fork. Data forks are used to locate the actual content of the file, while a resource fork is used to store structured data related to the file's content. This might include icons, application code, etc. While there are standard resource fork types defined (such as for sounds, images and window definitions) it is possible to create a resource fork with any type of content (and provide it with any desired four-byte identifier).

The fork is an 80_d-byte structure shown in Table 12.3. Forks are generally found in the catalog file and in the volume header. The purpose of the fork is to locate the file's content, hence their presence in the catalog file. In the volume header, forks are used to locate the system files (including the Catalog file).

12.1.2 Time in HFS+

As always, time is a fundamental concept which must be understood in order to effectively analyse any file system. HFS+ stores a number of time values, both at a volume level (in the volume header structure) and also at the file/folder level (in the catalog file). The default date format in HFS+ is a

Table 12.3 HFS+ fork structure.

Offset	Size	Name	Description
0x00	0x08	Logical Size	Size in bytes of the fork contents.
0x08	0x04	Clump Size	When encountered in the fork this overwrites the default clump size in the volume header.
0x0C	0x04	Total Blocks	The total number of allocation blocks used by the contents of this fork.
0x10	0x08 × 8	Extents	This contains an array of 8_d extent descriptors. The structure of extent descriptors is shown in Table 12.4. In the case of a file requiring more than 8_d extent descriptors, these are stored in the extents overflow file.

Table 12.4 HFS+ extent descriptor structure.

Offset	Size	Name	Description
0x00	0x04	Starting Block	The first allocation block in the extent.
0x04	0x04	# Blocks	The number of allocation blocks in the extent.

32_d bit unsigned integer which represents the number of seconds since 1 January 1904. The HFS+ date value is stored in GMT.[3] The maximum representable date is 6 February 2040 at 06:28:15 GMT.

The easiest method to convert HFS+ time to a human-readable format is to first convert it to a Unix time. This is achieved by subtracting the number of seconds between 1 January 1970 and 1 January 1904 ($2{,}082{,}844{,}800_d$) from the HFS+ time. An example of this is shown in Listing 12.1 in which the HFS+ time value of 0xE17279B7 is shown.

```
$ date -ud @$(( 0xE17279B7 - 2082844800))
Thu 09 Nov 2023 11:57:43 UTC
```

Listing 12.1 Conversion of HFS+ time to a human-readable format.

12.1.3 Volume Header

The volume header is the first structure that is processed during analysis. It contains information about the file system as a whole and allows the location of other vital metadata components to be discovered. The HFS+ volume begins with 1024_d bytes of (generally) empty space. The volume header is found immediately after this. The structure is of such great importance to the HFS+ file system that a copy of the structure is maintained at the end of the file system. This is found in 1024_d bytes before the end of the file system. Tables 12.5 and 12.7 provide the structure of the volume header.

The volume header contains much of the information that is found using forensic tools such as **fsstat**. For instance one of the most important pieces of information contained in this structure is that of allocation block size. All addressing in HFS+ is performed through allocation block number making this value vital for all subsequent analysis. The volume header also provides information on the size of the file system (again in allocation blocks) and the number of blocks that are currently free. In addition to this information about the total number of files and directories in the file system is also provided. Similar to the ext family of file systems the volume header provides a number of time values including the creation date of the file system. This creation time is the only time in HFS+ that is stored in local time rather than UTC.

One of the most important functions of the volume header is to allow the main file system structures to be located. There are five files which are of particular interest. These are the catalog file, the extents overflow file, the allocation file (bitmap), the attributes file and the startup file. These files can appear anywhere between the primary and backup volume header structures. Hence these structures are located from the volume header. Each of these files is located through an 80_d-byte fork structure (Section 12.1.1). At the end of the volume header five of these structures appear which are used to locate the allocation file (Offset: 0x70), extents overflow file (Offset: 0xC0), catalog file (Offset: 0x110), attributes file (Offset: 0x160) and the startup file (Offset: 0x1B0), respectively. As with other forks, if the 8_d extents used in the fork structure are insufficient to locate the contents the extra extents are stored in the extents overflow file.

12.1.4 B-Trees

As with many modern file systems the metadata files in HFS+ are stored in B-Trees. A B-Tree is composed of a number of nodes, each of which contains multiple records. Figure 12.1 shows the structure of a HFS+ B-Tree.

3 One exception to this is the creation date in the HFS+ volume header. This value is stored in local time, rather than GMT.

Table 12.5 HFS+ volume header structure.

Offset	Size	Name	Description
0x00	0x02	Signature	This value is either H+ or HX.
0x02	0x02	Version	File system version number. If the signature is H+ this is 4_d. If the signature is HX this is 5_d.
0x04	0x04	Attributes	File-system-specific attributes (Table 12.6).
0x08	0x04	Last Mounted Version	Generally one of 8.10 (OS8.1 - 9.2.2), 10.0 in OS-X or HFSJ for Journaled file systems.
0x0C	0x04	Journal info blk	Block number of the journal information block.
0x10	0x04	Creation date	File system creation time (HFS+ time – Section 12.1.2).
0x14	0x04	Modification date	File system last modification time.
0x18	0x04	Backup date	File system last backup time.
0x1C	0x04	Checked date	File system last checked time.
0x20	0x04	File Count	Total number of files (ex. special files).
0x24	0x04	Folder count	Total number of folders excluding root.
0x28	0x04	Block size	The size of the allocation block in bytes.
0x2C	0x04	# Blocks	Total number of allocation blocks.
0x30	0x04	# Free Blocks	Number of free allocation blocks.
0x34	0x04	Next allocation	Next free allocation block.
0x38	0x04	Resource clump size	Clumps are groups of allocation blocks which are sometimes allocated to a file to avoid fragmentation.
0x3C	0x04	Data clump size	As previous but for data forks.
0x40	0x04	Next CNID	The next free CNID.

Table 12.6 HFS+ volume header attribute bit field values.

Bit	Value	Description
0–7	Reserved	Reserved.
8	Unmounted Correctly	Set if the volume was correctly unmounted. This should be the opposite of the inconsistent volume bit.
9	Bad Blocks	Set if there is an entry in the extents overflow file for bad blocks.
10	No Caching	Set if blocks should not be cached.
11	Inconsistent Volume	Set while the volume is mounted for writing and should be unset when a volume is unmounted. If set prior to mounting a consistency check should be performed.
12	CNID Reused	If set the last CNID has been used meaning older CNIDs can be reused.
13	Volume Journal	If set the volume has a journal.
14	Reserved	Reserved.
15	Write Protected	Set if the volume is write protected due to a software setting.
16–31	Reserved	Reserved.

Table 12.7 HFS+ volume header structure (continued).

Offset	Size	Name	Description
0x44	0x04	Write Count	The number of times the volume has been mounted.
0x48	0x08	Encodings Bitmap	A bitmap representing all text encodings used in the file system.
0x50	0x04	OS DIR ID	CNID of /System/Library/CoreServices.
0x54	0x04	Finder DIR ID	The CNID for boot.efi.
0x58	0x04	Mount Open Dir	Directory ID of the directory to be opened when the file system is mounted.
0x5C	0x04	OS8/9 Dir ID	Directory (in OS 8/9) that contains a bootable system.
0x60	0x04	Reserved	Reserved.
0x64	0x04	OS-X Dir ID	ID of /System/Library/CoreServices.
0x68	0x08	Volume ID	File system volume ID.

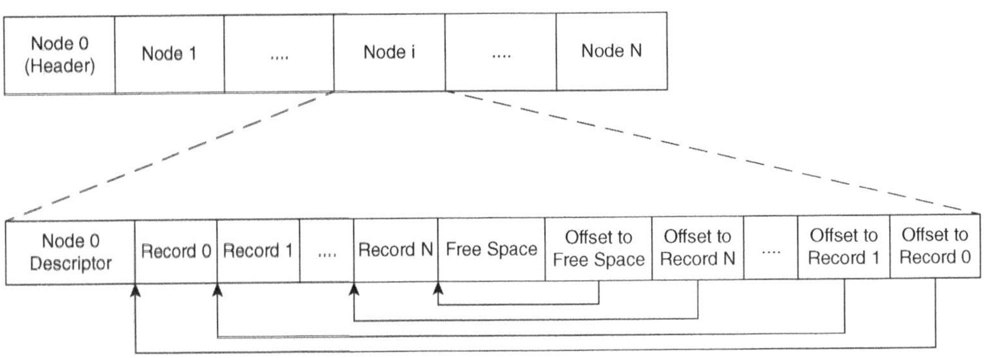

Figure 12.1 Structural overview of a HFS+ B-Tree.

Every metadata tree in HFS+ uses the structure shown in Figure 12.1. Every node begins with a node descriptor which contains information about that node's position in the tree as a whole. This structure is 14_d bytes in size. The structure of the node descriptor is given in Table 12.8.

The node descriptor provides information about the node itself and its position in the B-Tree. The forward and backward links are used to determine the position of the node in the tree as a whole, while the remaining fields provide information about the current node. This includes the node type and level. Certain node types are always at a particular level. For instance leaf nodes are level 1, while header nodes are level 0. Finally the node descriptor provides the total number of records in this node.

In total there are four node types in a HFS+ B-Tree. These are:

- **Header Node:** Each tree contains a single header node which provides the information required to find other nodes in the tree and information about the tree as a whole.
- **Map Nodes:** These nodes contain allocation data (bitmaps describing the free/allocated nodes in the tree). These nodes are used in the case in which the allocation mapping structure is larger than the space provided for it in the header node.

Table 12.8 HFS+ B-Tree node descriptor.

Offset	Size	Name	Description
0x00	0x04	Forward Link	The node number of the next node of this type or 0 if this is the last node.
0x04	0x04	Back Link	The node number of the previous node of this type, or 0 if this is the first node.
0x08	0x01	Node Type	This is a signed integer representing the node type. A leaf node has a value of 0xFF (-1_d), an internal node is 0_d, a header node is 1_d and a map node is 2_d.
0x09	0x01	Level	The level, or depth, of this node in the B-Tree hierarchy. Note that for the header node this is zero and for leaf nodes it is one. Internal nodes are one greater than the child they point to.
0x0A	0x02	# Records	The number of records contained in this node.
0x0C	0x02	Reserved	Reserved.

- **Index Nodes:** These nodes contain pointers to other nodes in the tree. The desired pointer is located by examining the keys in the index node.
- **Leaf Nodes:** These nodes contain data records. Data is associated with a particular key, each of which must be unique.

Examining the node structure in Figure 12.1 shows that the node is composed of a number of records. At the end of the node there exist a number of pointers to record offsets inside the node. Each of these offsets is 0x02 bytes in size. There is one more pointer in the node than the total number of records in the node. This final pointer points to the free space between the records and the pointers.

Every B-Tree begins with a header node. As with all nodes the header node begins with a 14_d-byte node descriptor. The header node contains information about the tree as a whole. The header node always contains three records. The first is the B-Tree header record, the second is the user data record (which is always 128_d bytes in length) and the final record is the map record which occupies the remaining space in the header node. The forward link value in the header node's node descriptor contains the node number of the map node (or 0_d if no map node is present). The backward link value is always set to 0_d.

The header node's header record contains information about the actual B-Tree structure. The structure of this record is shown in Table 12.9. This is always found immediately after the node descriptor (i.e. 14_d byte offset).

The header record is followed by the user data record. This structure is always 128_d bytes in size. It is used to store some information about the tree. In many trees this record is empty.

The remaining space in the header node is occupied by the map record. This is a bitmap structure that provides information about the allocation status of the various nodes in the tree. The node descriptor, header record and user record combined occupy 256_d bytes; hence, the map record size is node size less 256_d bytes. If this is not sufficiently large to store information about all the nodes in the tree then extra map nodes are also used. Map nodes consist of a node descriptor immediately followed by the continued map structure. The map node descriptor's forward link contains the node number of the previous node in the map structure. Map nodes can utilise up to node size less

Table 12.9 HFS+ B-Tree header node structure.

Offset	Size	Name	Description
0x00	0x02	Tree Depth	The current depth of the B-Tree.
0x02	0x04	Root Node	The node number of the root node for the tree. In the case of small trees the root node may be a leaf node.
0x06	0x04	Leaf records	The total number of records contained in all leaf nodes in the tree.
0x0A	0x04	First Leaf Node	Node number of the first leaf node.
0x0E	0x04	Last Leaf Node	Node number of the last leaf node.
0x12	0x02	Node Size	Node size in bytes.
0x14	0x02	Max. Key Length	The maximum key length.
0x16	0x04	Total Nodes	The total number of nodes in the B-Tree (both used and unused).
0x1A	0x04	Free Nodes	The number of unused nodes.
0x1E	0x02	Reserved	Reserved.
0x20	0x04	Clump Size	Generally unused. Sometimes set to the same value as the clump size in the volume header.
0x24	0x01	B-Tree Type	The B-Tree type 0_d is a control file, 128_d and higher are user trees and 255_d is reserved.
0x25	0x01	Key Compare	Defines if the volume is case sensitive or insensitive (0xBC and 0xCF, respectively).
0x26	0x04	Attributes	Attribute bit mask.
0x2A	0x04	Reserved	Reserved.

20_d bytes. The 20_d bytes are composed of the 14_d bytes for the node descriptor, two 2_d byte offset values and 2_d bytes of free space.

The remaining node types are index nodes and leaf nodes. These both use a common structure called keyed records. Each keyed record consists of a key length value, followed by a key and then the record data. The size of the key length and key values are determined by the type of keyed record in question. The data is dependent on the type of node, index or leaf and the type of data being stored in the leaf node's records.

In the case of an index node the record data contains pointer records. This data component of the keyed record merely contains a 4_d-byte node number. This is the node number of the child node in the current tree. In the case of a leaf node the record data contains the actual data associated with the key. The data is dependent on the type of tree in question, for instance catalog node data is different from extents overflow node data. Both leaf and index nodes will be processed later in this chapter.

12.1.5 Catalog File

The catalog file is analogous to the Master File Table in NTFS. It contains information about all the files/directories in the volume. This includes the metadata in relation to the file and also the location of the actual content.

The catalog file is structured as a B-Tree and hence contains a header node, along with index and leaf nodes (and map nodes where applicable). The catalog file is used to locate all files/folders on the volume. The information to locate the catalog file itself is found in the HFS+ Volume Header (Section 12.1.3).

Every entry (file or folder) in the catalog file is assigned a unique catalog node ID (CNID). This is a 4_d-byte value. The CNID value is automatically incremented as new files/folders are added to the volume. CNID values are not reused until the maximum value ($0xFFFFFFFF = 4,294,967,295_d$) is reached. The analyst can determine if these values have been reused based on the attributes field in the volume header (Tables 12.5 and 12.6). If this bit is unset the analyst can determine the order in which files/folders were created based on the CNID. The first 16_d CNID values are reserved (Table 12.2). Note that CNID 0 is never used as an actual CNID; instead, it serves as a *NULL* value.

As the catalog file is a B-Tree it is necessary to understand only the key format and the record data format in leaf nodes. Table 12.10 shows the catalog key structure.

The catalog file's leaf node record data structure is one of four types. These record types are:

1) **Folder Record:** This record contains information about a single folder on the HFS+ volume.
2) **File Record:** This record contains information about a single file on the HFS+ volume.
3) **Folder Thread Record:** This record provides a link between a folder and its parent folder.
4) **File Thread Record:** This record provides a link between a file and its parent folder.

Each data record begins with a record type value. These values are: folder record (0x0001); file record (0x0002); folder thread record (0x0003); and file thread record (0x0004). The particular value of the record type field determines how said data should be interpreted.

Folder records hold information about an individual folder in the HFS+ volume. The structure of these records is shown in Table 12.11

The catalog file record is used to hold information about files in the catalog file. This includes metadata information and also the data and resource forks, allowing for the recovery of file content. The structure of the file record is shown in Table 12.12.

File content is located through the data fork. In the case of all forks (both data and resource) the basic fork structure can hold up to eight extents. However, if the file requires more than 8_d extents (i.e. if the file is in 9_d or more fragments) further extents are found in the extents overflow file.

Thread records are required in HFS+ for all files and folders. These records link the file/folder to the parent folder in the file system. The structure of a thread record is shown in Table 12.13.

12.1.6 HFS+ Permissions

Similar to many of the Linux file systems, HFS+ maintains permissions as part of the file metadata structures. The HFS+ permission structure is provided in Table 12.14.

Table 12.10 Catalog file key structure.

Offset	Size	Name	Description
0x00	0x02	Key Length	The length of this structure in bytes.
0x02	0x04	Parent ID	The CNID of the containing folder (i.e. the parent folder).
0x06	0x02	Name Length	Name length (n) in unicode characters
0x08	(n)	Node Name	File/folder name (unicode).

Table 12.11 Structure of the folder record data item in the catalog file.

Offset	Size	Name	Description
0x00	0x02	Record Type	Record type (0x0001 for folder record).
0x02	0x02	Flags	Unused for folders.
0x04	0x04	Valence	Number of files/folders contained in this folder.
0x08	0x04	CNID	The CNID for this folder. Not to be confused with the parent CNID in the key.
0x0C	0x04	Creation Date	Folder creation time.
0x10	0x04	Modification Date	Folder content modification time.
0x14	0x04	Change Date	Folder metadata last modification time.
0x18	0x04	Access Date	Folder content last access time.
0x1C	0x04	Backup Date	Folder last backup time.
0x20	0x10	Permissions	File Permissions (Section 12.1.6).
0x30	0x10	Folder Info	Information used by finder – not part of the HFS+ structure.
0x40	0x10	Ext. Folder Info	Further information used by finder.
0x50	0x04	Text Encoding	Text Encoding (Section 12.1.7).
0x54	0x04	Reserved	Reserved.

Various owner and admin flags are provided in the BSD permission structure. The owner flags can be set by the owner or by the superuser. The various owner flags include:

- Bit 0 – No Dump: This file will not be backed up.
- Bit 1 – Immutable: The file may not be changed.
- Bit 2 – Append: Writes to this file can only append information, not overwrite it.
- Bit 3 – Opaque: The directory is opaque; in other words, it is hidden when multiple file systems are mounted as a single volume.

The admin flags can be set only by the superuser. These flags include:

- Bit 0 – Archived: This file has been archived.
- Bit 1 – Immutable: The file may not be changed.
- Bit 2 – Append: Writes to this file can only append information, not overwrite it.

The file mode value is identical to that found in Linux filesystems. This is a two-byte structure in which the nine least significant bits represent read, write and execute permissions for the owner, group and everyone, respectively. The most significant nibble represents the file type. The remaining three bits have special meanings. The least significant of these is the sticky bit. If this is set only the file owner can delete the file. Other users, even those with write permission to the file, are unable to delete this file. The remaining two bits are the set UID (most significant) and set GID (middle bit). If the setuid bit is set then the process will execute with the permissions of the owner, not the user who executed the file. The setgid bit has the same effect but for groups instead of users.

Table 12.12 Structure of the file record data item in the catalog file.

Offset	Size	Name	Description
0x00	0x02	Record Type	Record type (0x0002 for file record).
0x02	0x02	Flags	Flag values: Bit 0: File Locked; Bit 1: Thread Exists; Bit 2: Extended Attributes; Bit 3: Security Data; Bit 4: Folder Count; Bit 5: Hardlink;
0x04	0x04	Reserved	Reserved.
0x08	0x04	CNID	CNID for this folder not to be confused with the parent's CNID in the key.
0x0C	0x04	Creation Date	File creation time.
0x10	0x04	Modification Date	File content modification time.
0x14	0x04	Change Date	File metadata change time.
0x18	0x04	Access Date	File content last access time.
0x1C	0x04	Backup Date	File last backup time.
0x20	0x10	Permissions	File Permissions (Section 12.1.6).
0x30	0x10	Folder Info	Information used by finder.
0x40	0x10	Ext. Folder Info	Further information used by finder.
0x50	0x04	Text Encoding	Text encoding (Section 12.1.7).
0x54	0x04	Reserved	Reserved.
0x58	0x50	Data Fork	Data fork (Section 12.1.1).
0xA8	0x50	Resource Fork	Resource fork (Section 12.1.1).

12.1.7 Text Encoding

Earlier versions of the HFS file system did not use unicode characters in file names. Instead they used various text encodings. These values are still used in the HFS+ file system allowing for multiple encodings. The file/folder catalog records contain a text encoding field which describes how the text is encoded in the particular record. A bit field is also used in the volume header to list the encodings that are present on the device (bits remain set even if the last file using that encoding is deleted). The valid text encoding values are shown in Table 12.15.

12.1.8 Extents Overflow File

The extents overflow file is a B-Tree which contains extents that will not fit in the data/resource forks that are available in the catalog file itself. These are used in the case of heavily fragmented files.[4] As a B-Tree, the extents overflow file contains a header node followed by a number of nodes. As with all B-Trees each node begins with a node descriptor.

4 More than eight extents.

Table 12.13 Structure of the thread record data item in the catalog file.

Offset	Size	Name	Description
0x00	0x02	Record Type	Record type (0x0003 for folder thread record or 0x0004 for file thread record).
0x02	0x02	Reserved	Reserved.
0x04	0x04	Parent ID	CNID of the parent catalog record.
0x08	0x02	Name Length	The node's name length (n) in unicode characters.
0x0A	$n \times 2$	Node Name	The node name in unicode characters (max. 255 characters).

Table 12.14 HFS+ permission structure.

Offset	Size	Name	Description
0x00	0x04	UID	The owner's system user ID.
0x04	0x04	GID	The group ID of the group associated with the item.
0x08	0x01	Admin Flags	BSD flags that can be set only by the superuser.
0x09	0x01	Owner Flags	BSD flags that can be set by the file owner or the superuser.
0x0A	0x02	File Mode	The file mode/permissions analogous to those found in EXT (Section 8.1.3.1).
0x0C	0x04	Special	Unused for normal files and folders. This has different meanings for different object types. For instance for a hard link this contains the link reference number (inode number of the linked file), for indirect node files this contains the number of hard links that point to the file and for block and character devices this contains the raw device number.

Leaf node records contain a HFS extent key followed by eight extents. The structure of the extent key is given in Table 12.16.

In order to locate the relevant entries in the extents overflow file a search term is formed with the key length, fork type, padding and CNID values. The starting block is also added (in case there is more than one entry in the extents overflow file). The starting block is calculated based on the number of blocks that have already appeared in previous extents (i.e. those in the catalog file). Once the relevant entry is located in the tree the extents can then be processed. An example of this is shown in Section 12.3.3.

12.1.9 Allocation File

The allocation file is a bitmap structure describing the allocation status of every allocation block in the file system. The allocation file is located through the volume header structure. Each allocation block is represented by a single bit in the allocation file. A bit value of 1_b represents an allocation block that is currently in use, while a value of 0_b represents a free block.

Table 12.15 Text encoding values.

Encoding	Value	Encoding	Value	Encoding	Value
Roman	0_d	Tamil	14_d	Mongolian	27_d
Japanese	1_d	Telugu	15_d	Ethiopic	28_d
ChineseTrad	2_d	Kannada	16_d	CentralEur	29_d
Korean	3_d	Malayalam	17_d	Vietnamese	30_d
Arabic	4_d	Sinhalese	18_d	ExtArabic	31_d
Hebrew	5_d	Burmese	19_d	Symbol	33_d
Greek	6_d	Khmer	20_d	Dingbats	34_d
Cyrillic	7_d	Thai	21_d	Turkish	35_d
Devanagari	9_d	Laotian	22_d	Croatian	36_d
Gurmukhi	10_d	Georgian	23_d	Icelandic	37_d
Gujarati	11_d	Armenian	24_d	Romanian	38_d
Oriya	12_d	ChineseSimp	25_d	Farsi	140_d
Bengali	13_d	Tibetan	26_d	Ukrainian	152_d

Table 12.16 Extents overflow key structure.

Offset	Size	Name	Description
0x00	0x02	Key Length	The length of the key in bytes, excluding the key length itself. This is always 0x0A for extent keys.
0x02	0x01	Fork Type	The type of fork to which this record applies. This is either 0x00 (data fork) or 0xFF (resource fork).
0x03	0x01	Padding	0x00 padding byte.
0x04	0x04	CNID	The CNID to which the extents belong.
0x08	0x04	Start Block	The start block (in the file content) of the first extent in this file.

Each byte represents eight allocation blocks. The most significant bit represents the allocation block with the lowest block number. To locate the correct byte for a particular allocation block, the block number must be divided by 8_d. This will provide the byte offset to the entry in the allocation file. Consider block 61_d. To determine the correct byte this value is divided by 8_d which results in 7_d. Hence the contents of byte 7_d must be accessed. Byte seven contains information about blocks 56_d–63_d. Assuming that the value at that position is 0xFB (11111011_b) then block 61_d is unallocated. All other blocks represented by this byte are allocated.

12.1.10 HFS+ Journal

As with many modern file systems HFS+ contains a journal. The journal is used to ensure consistency of the file system in the event of a crash. The journal records metadata changes. Actual content changes are not journaled. Updates to HFS+ often require many metadata structures to be updated. For instance if a new file is added to the file system at a minimum the following changes are required:

- A file record is written to the catalog;
- a file thread record is written to the catalog;
- the catalog file is restructured (possibly even requiring a new node to be created);
- the allocation bitmap is updated;
- the volume header is updated;
- the extents overflow file is updated if the file is heavily fragmented.

If the system were to crash during these operations then the file system could become inconsistent. Hence the changes are first written to the journal. Only when marked complete there are they then written to disk. If a crash occurs now the changes can be rebuilt from the journal. If a crash occurs during the journal write the changes are ignored later. Either way the file system is left in a consistent state. Once the group of changes have been written to the disk they can be removed from the journal. The group of changes are called a transaction. The steps in a transaction are:

1) The transaction commences when the pending changes are written to the journal file;
2) the journal file is flushed to disk;
3) the transaction is recorded in the journal header;
4) the changes are performed on the actual file system structures; and
5) the journal header is updated to mark the transaction as complete.

Upon mounting a file system the journal structure is checked. Transactions may have failed at any stage in the above process. Those that fail before step 3 are lost, no record of them exists but the file system is still consistent. Those transactions that fail after step 3 have been successfully recorded in the journal and as such these transactions can be applied to the file system. In either case, the end result of the process is that the file system is consistent!

The journal file itself is a fixed-size contiguous file. Implementations of HFS+ must ensure that this is always the case. The file can never be resized or split. The journal file consists of a header which contains information about the journal and the current transactions in use and also a buffer. The journal buffer occupies the remainder of the journal file. The buffer is circular in nature. All transactions are written to the next available block in the journal buffer. This continues until the end is reached in which case the buffer 'wraps around' and begins to overwrite the first entry. No information is removed from the journal in any other way. This means that it is possible to use the journal to recover files that were deleted prior to the relevant block being overwritten.

The journal is located from the journal info block (which is itself located from the volume header). Table 12.17 shows the journal info block structure. The flags inform the analyst of the journal's location, either on the current device or on a separate device entirely. The journal itself is located using the offset and size values. The offset is a byte offset relative to the start of the volume, while the size value is the size of the journal in bytes.

Analysis of the journal proceeds through the analysis of the journal header. This structure is used to locate transactions in the journal itself. The structure of the journal header is provided in Table 12.18.

The start and end values provide some further information about the current state of the journal. In the case where the end value is less than the start value the journal buffer has wrapped and some transactions have been overwritten. In the case that these values are equal then there are no transactions that need to be replayed.

Table 12.17 HFS+ Journal info block structure.

Offset	Size	Name	Description
0x00	0x04	Flags	One-bit flags 0x01: Journal on filesystem; 0x02: Journal on other device; 0x04: Journal invalid.
0x04	0x20	Device Signature	Used when the journal is on another device.
0x24	0x08	Offset	Byte offset to the start of the journal relative to the start of the volume.
0x2C	0x08	Size	Size of journal in bytes.
0x34	0x40	Reserved	Reserved.

Table 12.18 The journal header structure.

Offset	Size	Name	Description
0x00	0x04	Magic	Magic value (0x4A4E4C78) used to verify journal integrity.
0x04	0x04	Endian	Endian magic value (0x12345678) also used to verify integrity.
0x08	0x08	Start	Byte offset to the first (oldest) transaction in the journal. This offset is relative to the start of the journal header structure.
0x10	0x08	End	Byte offset to the last (newest) transaction in the journal. This offset is relative to the start of the journal header structure.
0x18	0x08	Size	Journal size in bytes.
0x20	0x04	BL Header Size	Size of the block list header in bytes.
0x24	0x04	Checksum	Checksum for the journal header structure.
0x28	0x04	JH Size	Journal header size. This is generally equal to the sector size of the device.

12.2 Analysis of HFS+

This section examines the analysis method used in order to rebuild a HFS+ file system and to extract content and metadata from said file system. Section 12.3 will introduce some advanced topics in the analysis of HFS+.

12.2.1 Creating HFS+ File Systems

Support for HFS+ is included in all Linux distributions by default. Listing 12.2 shows the command to create a new HFS+ file system from the Linux terminal. HFS+ file systems can also be created from macOS; however, these are generally mounted automatically by macOS and many files are also created automatically during this process. Hence, for learning about the file system it is preferable to create these exemplars using Linux.

```
$ sudo mkfs.hfsplus -v "HFS-FS" /dev/sdc1
Initialized /dev/sdc1 as a 512 MB HFS Plus volume
```

Listing 12.2 Using Linux to create a HFS+ file system.

12.2.2 Supplied HFS+ Image Files

A number of HFS+ disk images are available from the book's website. These images are summarised in Table 12.19. The images consist of a basic HFS+ file system with a number of files and directories along with further file systems to demonstrate advanced concepts in HFS+. These concepts include deleted files; multi-level B-Trees; fragmented files; and links.

These images are used throughout this chapter to demonstrate the manual analysis of the HFS+ file system. Subsequent images are used to demonstrate some advanced topics in the HFS+ file system that may affect analysis.

12.2.3 HFS+ Manual Analysis

This section presents a method of manual analysis for the HFS+ file system. This method is as follows:

1) Process the volume header;
2) locate the catalog file;
3) process the catalog B-Tree;
4) gather metadata;
5) recover file content.

The following sections describe the method in detail using the **HFS_V1.E01** file system.

12.2.3.1 Process the Volume Header

As with all file systems the first step is to process the file system information structures. The HFS+ volume header is located at offset 1024_d bytes in a HFS+ disk image. Listing 12.3 shows the contents of the volume header in **HFS_V1.E01**.

Table 12.19 Supplied HFS+ disk images.

Filename	Description
HFS_V1.E01	Simple file system containing four files and a single directory.
HFS_V2.E01	This file system is created from the **HFS_V1.E01** file system by deleting two files (**delete.txt** and **foggy.jpg**).
HFS_V3.E01	This file system contains a directory with many files in order to demonstrate multi-level B-Trees.
HFS_V4.E01	This file system contains a heavily fragmented file.
HFS_V5.E01	This file system was created on MacOS and contains both hard and soft links.

```
0000400: 482b 0004 0000 0100 482b 4c78 0000 0000 H+......H+Lx....
0000410: e172 79b7 e172 7f8b 0000 0000 e172 79b7 .ry..r.......ry.
0000420: 0000 0004 0000 0002 0000 1000 0002 0000 ................
0000430: 0001 f791 0000 3005 0001 0000 0001 0000 ......0.........
0000440: 0000 0016 0000 0001 0000 0000 0000 0001 ................
0000450: 0000 0000 0000 0000 0000 0000 0000 0000 ................
0000460: 0000 0000 0000 0000 a03c e444 c73d a01b .........<.D.=..
0000470: 0000 0000 0000 4000 0000 4000 0000 0004 ......@...@.....
0000480: 0000 0001 0000 0004 0000 0000 0000 0000 ................
0000490: 0000 0000 0000 0000 0000 0000 0000 0000 ................
00004a0: 0000 0000 0000 0000 0000 0000 0000 0000 ................
00004b0: 0000 0000 0000 0000 0000 0000 0000 0000 ................
00004c0: 0000 0000 0040 0000 0040 0000 0000 0400 .....@...@......
00004d0: 0000 0005 0000 0400 0000 0000 0000 0000 ................
00004e0: 0000 0000 0000 0000 0000 0000 0000 0000 ................
00004f0: 0000 0000 0000 0000 0000 0000 0000 0000 ................
0000500: 0000 0000 0000 0000 0000 0000 0000 0000 ................
0000510: 0000 0000 0040 0000 0040 0000 0000 0400 .....@...@......
0000520: 0000 0405 0000 0400 0000 0000 0000 0000 ................
```

Listing 12.3 Excerpt from the volume header structure in **HFS_V1.E01**.

When processing a HFS+ file system there are some key items of interest in the volume header structure. Table 12.20 shows some of the items that are of particular interest and their associated values from Listing 12.3.

The combination of the signature (H+) and the version (4_d) informs that this is a HFS+ file system. In Table 12.20, the attribute value is determined to be 0x00000100 meaning that the eighth bit is set. This bit means that the file system was unmounted properly (Table 12.6). Note that the CNID reused bit is not set in this file system. This means that the order of file creation events can be inferred from the CNID values. Files with larger CNID values were created after files with smaller values.

The volume header structure in HFS+ provides four different time values. Note that the creation time is stored in local time while the others are stored as UTC. The creation time is often used as a device identifier and should not be affected by timezone/daylight savings changes. From Table 12.20 the creation and checked date/time values are 9 November 2023 at 11:57:43 UTC, while the last modified time is 9 November 2023 at 12:22:35 UTC.

The volume header also provides information on the volume usage. From Table 12.20 it is clear that there are only 4_d files and 2_d folders present on this device. The volume header provides information about the allocation blocks in the file system. Firstly, it provides the allocation block size, in this case 4096_d bytes. This piece of information is vital for all subsequent analyses as all addressing is done through block numbers rather than actual byte offsets. Finally the volume header provides information on the block usage statistics. Table 12.20 shows the total number of blocks to be $131,072_d$ of which $128,913_d$ blocks are currently available for use.

12.2.3.2 Locate the Catalog File

The catalog file provides information about all the files/folders in the volume. It is the single most important structure for file system forensics of HFS+ volumes. Directly after the volume header (offset 0x70 relative to the start of the volume header structure) are found five fork structures. These structures are each 0x50 bytes in size. These five structures refer to the locations of the allocation

Table 12.20 Processed volume header in **HFS_V1.E01**.

Offset	Size	Name	Value
0x00	0x02	Signature	H+
0x02	0x02	Version	0x04 (4_d)
0x04	0x04	Attributes	0x00000100
			(Unmounted properly)
0x10	0x04	Creation date	0xE17279B7
			09.11.2023 11:57:43
0x14	0x04	Modification date	0xE1727F8B
			09.11.2023 12:22:35
0x18	0x04	Backup date	0x00000000
0x1C	0x04	Checked date	0xE17279B7
			09.11.2023 11:57:43
0x20	0x04	File Count	0x04 (4_d)
0x24	0x04	Folder count	0x02 (2_d)
0x28	0x04	Block size	0x1000 (4096_d)
0x2C	0x04	# Blocks	0x20000 ($131,072_d$)
0x30	0x04	# Free Blocks	0x1F791 ($128,913_d$)

file, the extents overflow file, the catalog file, the attributes file and the startup file, respectively. This means that to find the catalog file location it is necessary to process the third fork after the volume header. This is located at offset 0x110 relative to the start of the volume header. The contents of this data fork are shown in Listing 12.4. The 'header' values are highlighted, while the remaining space is used to store extents.

```
0000510: 0000 0000 0040 0000 0040 0000 0000 0400  .....@...@......
0000520: 0000 0405 0000 0400 0000 0000 0000 0000  ................
0000530: 0000 0000 0000 0000 0000 0000 0000 0000  ................
0000540: 0000 0000 0000 0000 0000 0000 0000 0000  ................
0000550: 0000 0000 0000 0000 0000 0000 0000 0000  ................
```

Listing 12.4 Contents of the data fork for the catalog file in the volume header of **HFS_V1.E01**.

The contents of Listing 12.4 are processed in Table 12.21. In this case there is only one single extent present. The basic fork structure allows for up to 8_d extents to be stored for a single file. If any more are needed these are stored in the extents overflow file.

Table 12.21 shows that the catalog file is contiguous (only a single extent is used) and that it begins at block 0x405 (1029_d) and is 0x400 (1024_d) blocks in size. Listing 12.5 shows the command to extract the catalog file from the supplied image. The accuracy of this can be confirmed using Sleuth Kit to recover the catalog file and comparing the MD5 values!

Table 12.21 Processed values for the HFS+ catalog file fork in **HFS_V1.E01**.

Offset	Size	Name	Value
0x00	0x08	Logical Size	0x400000 $(4,194,304_d)$
0x08	0x04	Clump Size	0x400000 $(4,194,304_d)$
0x0C	0x04	Total Blocks	0x400 (1024_d)
0x10	0x04	Extent Start	0x405 (1029_d)
0x14	0x04	Extent Blocks	0x400 (1024_d)

Table 12.22 HFS+ Catalog file header node descriptor.

Offset	Size	Name	Value
0x00	0x04	Forward-Link	0x00 (0_d)
0x04	0x04	Back-Link	0x00 (0_d)
0x08	0x01	Node Type	0x01 (Header)
0x09	0x01	Level	0x00 (0_d)
0x0A	0x02	# Records	0x03 (3_d)
0x0C	0x02	Reserved	0x00 (0_d)

```
$ dd if=mnt/ewf1 of=catalog.dd bs=4096 skip=1029 count=1024
1024+0 records in
1024+0 records out
4194304 bytes (4.2 MB, 4.0 MiB) copied, 0.0494737 s, 84.8 MB/s
```

Listing 12.5 The **dd** command used to extract the catalog file from **HFS_V1.E01**.

12.2.3.3 Process the Catalog B-Tree

Once the catalog file has been located the next step is to process the content of this file. The catalog is a B-Tree and as such the first node is a header node. Listing 12.6 shows the node descriptor for the catalog's first node while Table 12.22 shows the processed values for the node descriptor.

```
00000000: 0000 0000 0000 0000 0100 0003 0000        ..............
```

Listing 12.6 Catalog file's header node descriptor from **HFS_V1.E01**.

As this is a header node most of the information is standard. The forward and backward link values are 0x00, the node type is 0x01 and the level is 0x00. The header node contains three records (the header information record, the user data record and the map record).

Table 12.23 HFS+ B-Tree header record for the catalog file's header node in **HFS_V1.E01**.

Offset	Size	Name	Description
0x00	0x02	Tree Depth	0x01 (1_d)
0x02	0x04	Root Node	0x01 (1_d)
0x06	0x04	Leaf records	0x0E (14_d)
0x0A	0x04	First Leaf Node	0x01 (1_d)
0x0E	0x04	Last Leaf Node	0x01 (1_d)
0x12	0x02	Node Size	0x1000 (4096_d)
0x14	0x02	Max. Key Length	0x204 (516_d)
0x16	0x04	Total Nodes	0x400 (1024_d)
0x1A	0x04	Free Nodes	0x3FE (1022_d)
0x1E	0x02	Reserved	0x00 (0_d)
0x20	0x04	Clump Size	0x400000 ($4,194,304_d$)
0x24	0x01	B-Tree Type	0x00 (0_d)
0x25	0x01	Key Compare Type	0xCF
0x26	0x04	Attributes	0x06
0x2A	0x04	Reserved	0x00 (0_d)

The node descriptor in the header node is immediately followed by the header record structure. This area is shown in Listing 12.7 and processed in Table 12.23.

```
000000e: 0001 0000 0001 0000 000e 0000 0001 0000 ................
000001e: 0001 1000 0204 0000 0400 0000 03fe 0000 ................
000002e: 0040 0000 00cf 0000 0006 0000 0000 0000 .@..............
```

Listing 12.7 Header record structure in the **HFS_V1.E01** catalog file.

Key information from the header record includes:

- The node size: The node size is used to find any node in the tree. The header node is node 0_d and the byte offset to a particular node number is found using *nodeNumber* × *nodeSize*.
- The root node: The root node is where tree processing begins. In the case of small trees the root node may also be a leaf node, in larger trees the root node will be an index node.

In addition to the above information the header record contains much more information about the structure of the tree. For instance in Table 12.23 it is clear that this tree contains 14_d (0x0E) leaf records. As the tree depth, first leaf node and last leaf node values are all one; it is clear that the tree only contains a single node (i.e. the root node is a leaf node).

Generally there is no need to process the user information record or the map record in the catalog tree. Analysis proceeds to the root node. From Table 12.23 the node size is 4096_d bytes and the root node is found in node 1_d. Listing 12.8 shows the node descriptor for this node with the processed values appearing in Table 12.24.

```
00001000: 0000 0000 0000 0000 ff01 000e 0000          ..............
```

Listing 12.8 Catalog file's root node descriptor from **HFS_V1.E01**.

Table 12.24 Catalog file's root node descriptor in **HFS_V1.E01**.

Offset	Size	Name	Value
0x00	0x04	Forward-Link	0x00 (0_d)
0x04	0x04	Back-Link	0x00 (0_d)
0x08	0x01	Node Type	0xFF (Leaf)
0x09	0x01	Level	0x01 (1_d)
0x0A	0x02	# Records	0x0E (14_d)
0x0C	0x02	Reserved	0x00 (0_d)

The root node's node descriptor shows that this is a leaf node (node type 0xFF) containing 14_d records. The pointers to the records are found at the end of the node. Each record pointer is two bytes in size. A pointer exists for each record in the node (14_d in this case) and also for the start of the free space area. Hence in this example there are 15_d pointers in total. These are shown in Listing 12.9.

```
0001fe0: 0000 06bc 0698 0674 0652 062c 051a 0406 .......t.R.,....
0001ff0: 03ea 03ae 0324 0214 0102 0098 007a 000e .....$.......z..
```

Listing 12.9 Pointers in the catalog file's root node in **HFS_V1.E01**.

The values for the pointers (in reverse order) are 0x0E, 0x7A, 0x98, 0x102, 0x214, 0x324, 0x3AE, 0x3EA, 0x406, 0x51A, 0x62C, 0x652, 0x674 and 0x698 with the free space area starting at 0x6BC. All of these offsets are relative to the start of the node.

Each record begins with a key structure (Table 12.10). Listing 12.10 shows the key structure at offset 0x51A from the root node in the catalog file.

```
000151a: 0018 0000 0011 0009 0066 006f 0067 0067 .........f.o.g.g
000152a: 0079 002e 006a 0070 0067                .y...j.p.g
```

Listing 12.10 Key structure for the catalog item at offset 0x51A in the root node of the catalog file in **HFS_V1.E01**.

From Listing 12.10 the key length is 0x18 bytes (excluding the key length field itself) meaning that the key occupies 0x1A bytes in total. The parent ID is 0x11, the name is 0x09 unicode characters long and the name itself is **foggy.jpg**. Table 12.25 shows all the processed keys for the 14_d items in the root node.

As described in Section 12.1.5 each of the catalog keys is followed immediately by one of four types of record. Each of these structures (folder, file, folder thread and file thread) begins with a two-byte record type value. These are also shown in Table 12.25.

Table 12.25 Processed keys in the **HFS_V1.E01** catalog file's root node. Offsets are relative to the start of the node.

	Item 1	Item 2	Item 3	Item 4
Offset	0x0E	0x7A	0x98	0x102
Key Length	0x12	0x06	0x10	0x18
Parent ID	0x01	0x02	0x02	0x02
Name Length	0x06	0x00	0x05	0x09
Name	HFS-FS	—	Files	hills.jpg
Type	0x01 (Folder)	0x03 (Folder Th.)	0x01 (Folder)	0x02 (File)

	Item 5	Item 6	Item 7	Item 8
Offset	0x214	0x324	0x3AE	0x3EA
Key Length	0x16	0x30	0x06	0x06
Parent ID	0x02	0x02	0x10	0x11
Name Length	0x08	0x15	0x00	0x00
Name	info.txt	HFS+ Private Data	—	—
Type	0x02 (File)	0x01 (Folder)	0x03 (Folder Th.)	0x03 (Folder Th.)

	Item 9	Item 10	Item 11	Item 12
Offset	0x406	0x51A	0x62C	0x652
Key Length	0x1A	0x18	0x06	0x06
Parent ID	0x11	0x11	0x12	0x13
Name Length	0x0A	0x09	0x00	0x00
Name	delete.txt	foggy.jpg	—	—
Type	0x02 (File)	0x02 (File)	0x04 (File Th.)	0x04 (File Th.)

	Item 13	Item 14
Offset	0x674	0x698
Key Length	0x06	0x06
Parent ID	0x14	0x15
Name Length	0x00	0x00
Name	—	—
Type	0x04 (File Th.)	0x04 (File Th.)

Table 12.25 shows the processed values from the Catalog file. From this it is clear that there are three folders (**HFS-FS,**[5] **Files** and **HFS+ Private Data**[6]) and four files present on the device (**hills.jpg**, **info.txt**, **delete.txt** and **foggy.jpg**). Listing 12.11 shows the output from the **fls** command when run upon **HFS_V1.E01**.

```
r/r 3: $ExtentsFile
r/r 4: $CatalogFile
r/r 5: $BadBlockFile
r/r 6: $AllocationFile
d/d 17: Files
+ r/r 18: delete.txt
+ r/r 21: foggy.jpg
r/r 20: hills.jpg
r/r 19: info.txt
d/d 16: ^^^^HFS+ Private Data
```

Listing 12.11 File listing from **HFS_V1.E01** using **fls -r**.

12.2.3.4 Gather Metadata

In order to gather metadata the analyst must process the file/folder records in the catalog file. Consider the file **foggy.jpg** in Table 12.25. The record type of this is given as 0x02 meaning this is a file record. The structure of the file record is given in Table 12.12. The file record appears immediately after the key. From Table 12.25 the offset to this item is 0x51A, with a key length of 0x18. This implies that the actual file record begins at offset 0x1A (the two bytes for the key length field are not included in the key length value). Listing 12.12 shows the contents of the catalog file at offset 0x534. The size of this structure is 0xF8 bytes. Table 12.26 shows the processed values of this file record structure.

From Table 12.26 the metadata in relation to **foggy.jpg** can be generated and the file's content can be recovered. In terms of metadata it is clear that the **foggy.jpg** file has CNID 0x15 (21_d). This can be compared to Listing 12.11 in which the **fls** output provides an identifying number for the **foggy.jpg** file of 21_d; in other words, **fls** is using the CNID for the file. The metadata includes five timestamps (although only four are specified in this example).

The permissions value is 0x81E8, which is interpreted in the same manner as in Linux file systems. This implies that this is a regular file with permissions rwxr-x---. The owner and group IDs are 0 meaning that the root user and group owns the file.

Table 12.26 can be compared with the output from the **istat** command for this file shown in Listing 12.13.

12.2.3.5 Recover File Content

The file content is also recovered through the catalog file record. The data fork (Section 12.1.1) contains the location of the file's content. The processed data fork for **foggy.jpg** is shown in Table 12.26.

5 This folder will not appear in the file listing. This folder is the actual root folder of the file system. The name is taken from the volume label assigned when the file system was created. If no volume label is provided this is generally called **untitled**.

6 The HFS+ Private Data folder's name actually begins with four null bytes. This is often written as ^ ^ ^ ^ HFS+ Private Data. This is a file-system-created folder (similar to **lost+found** in ext) which will not appear in a regular file listing.

```
0001534: 0002 0002 0000 0000 0000 0015 e172 7f85 .............r..
0001544: e172 7f85 e172 7f85 e172 7f85 0000 0000 .r...r...r......
0001554: 0000 0000 0000 0000 0000 81e8 0000 0001 ................
0001564: 3f3f 3f3f 3f3f 3f3f 0000 0000 0000 0000 ????????........
0001574: 0000 0000 0000 0000 0000 0000 0000 0000 ................
0001584: 0000 0000 0000 0000 0000 0000 0002 cc83 ................
0001594: 0000 0000 0000 002d 0000 0841 0000 002d .......-...A...-
00015a4: 0000 0000 0000 0000 0000 0000 0000 0000 ................
00015b4: 0000 0000 0000 0000 0000 0000 0000 0000 ................
00015c4: 0000 0000 0000 0000 0000 0000 0000 0000 ................
00015d4: 0000 0000 0000 0000 0000 0000 0000 0000 ................
00015e4: 0000 0000 0000 0000 0000 0000 0000 0000 ................
00015f4: 0000 0000 0000 0000 0000 0000 0000 0000 ................
0001604: 0000 0000 0000 0000 0000 0000 0000 0000 ................
0001614: 0000 0000 0000 0000 0000 0000 0000 0000 ................
0001624: 0000 0000 0000 0000                     ........
```

Listing 12.12 Contents of the file record structure for **foggy.jpg** in **HFS_V1.E01**.

```
File Path: /Files/foggy.jpg
Catalog Record: 21
Allocated
Type: File
Mode: rrwxr-x---
Size: 183427
uid / gid: 0 / 0
Link count: 1

File Name: foggy.jpg
Admin flags: 0
Owner flags: 0
File type: 3f3f3f3f ????
File creator: 3f3f3f3f ????
Text encoding: 0 = MacRoman
Resource fork size: 0

Times:
Created: 2023-11-09 12:22:29 (UTC)
Content Modified: 2023-11-09 12:22:29 (UTC)
Attributes Modified: 2023-11-09 12:22:29 (UTC)
Accessed: 2023-11-09 12:22:29 (UTC)
Backed Up: 0000-00-00 00:00:00 (UTC)

Data Fork Blocks:
2113-2157

Attributes:
Type: DATA (4352-0) Name: N/A Non-Resident size: 183427
                                       init_size: 183427
```

Listing 12.13 The output of the **istat** command when run on **foggy.jpg** (CNID: 21_d) in **HFS_V1.E01**.

Table 12.26 Partially processed catalog file record for the **foggy.jpg** file.

Offset	Size	Name	Value
0x00	0x02	Record Type	0x0002 (File)
0x08	0x04	CNID	0x15 (21_d)
0x0C	0x04	Creation Date	0xE1727F85 2023-11-09 12:22:29 (UTC)
0x10	0x04	Modification Date	0xE1727F85 2023-11-09 12:22:29 (UTC)
0x14	0x04	Change Date	0xE1727F85 2023-11-09 12:22:29 (UTC)
0x18	0x04	Access Date	0xE1727F85 2023-11-09 12:22:29 (UTC)
0x1C	0x04	Backup Date	0x00 (0_d)
0x20	0x10	Permissions	Mode/Permissions: 0x81E8 (rwxr-x---)
0x58	0x50	Data Fork	Logical Size: 0x2CC83 ($183,427_d$) Clump Size: 0x00 (0_d) Num. Blocks: 0x2D (45_d) Extent Start: 0x841 (2113_d) Extent Size: 0x2D (45_d)
0xA8	0x50	Resource Fork	Not present

The fork header shows the file size (0x2CC83 bytes) and the total number of blocks occupied by the file's contents (0x2D). In this case there is only a single extent structure, beginning at block 0x841 and occupying 0x2D blocks. The actual file size is 0x2CC83 bytes. Listing 12.14 shows the command to extract this file. The recovered file is shown in Figure 12.2.

```
$ dd if=mnt/ewf1 of=foggy.jpg bs=1 skip=$((0x1000 * 0x841))
     count=$((0x2CC83))
183427+0 records in
183427+0 records out
183427 bytes (183 kB, 179 KiB) copied, 4.71268 s, 38.9 kB/s
$
$ file foggy.jpg
foggy.jpg: JPEG image data, ...[snip]...
$
$ md5sum foggy.jpg
42e06f9ec4d17f440719ddaf7e9c4774 foggy.jpg
```

Listing 12.14 Recovering the contents of **foggy.jpg**.

Figure 12.2 The recovered **foggy.jpg** file.

12.3 HFS+ Advanced Analysis

This section examines some of the more complex topics involved in the analysis of HFS+ file systems. It begins with an analysis of deleted files and shows the changes that occur in the file system upon deletion rendering the file unrecoverable using traditional analysis techniques. To this point the encountered HFS+ B-Trees have been very simple, each requiring only a single leaf node. This section proceeds to examine more complex trees with more than one level. Finally this section examines fragmented files especially massively fragmented files in which the extents overflow file is required.

12.3.1 Deleted Files

Recovery of deleted files is generally not possible in HFS+ from the basic file system structures. Although the file content remains in place after deletion (Listing 12.15), the catalog entry is removed. This means that file recovery can be performed only by using the journal structures.

```
0841000: ffd8 ffdb 0043 0001 0101 0101 0101 0101 .....C..........
0841010: 0101 0101 0202 0302 0202 0202 0403 0302 ................
0841020: 0305 0405 0505 0404 0405 0607 0605 0507 ................
0841030: 0604 0406 0906 0708 0808 0808 0506 090a ................
...[snip]...
```

Listing 12.15 The contents of allocation block 0x841 in **HFS_V2.E01** clearly showing that the content from **foggy.jpg** is still present on disk.

Figure 12.3 shows a file about to be deleted (left). Once deletion occurs the catalog file is immediately restructured overwriting the deleted record. However, it is possible to discover older records in the slack space that is created after the restructuring process occurs. In the case of the **HFS_V2.E01** image there are older copies of the file thread records for both deleted files present but there is not sufficient information present to recover the file's content.

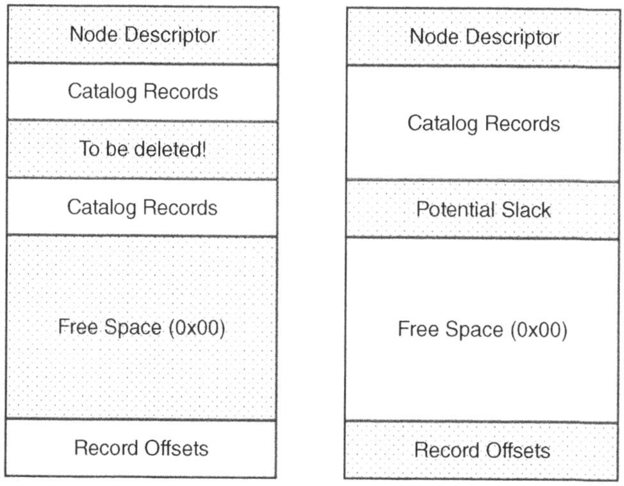

Figure 12.3 A HFS+ Catalog node before deletion (left) and after deletion (right).

12.3.2 Index Nodes

To this point all of the trees that have been examined have consisted of only a single level.[7] Generally file systems will be too complex for one single node to be sufficient to store all the required information. Hence index (or interior) nodes are normally found in trees.

Similar to leaf nodes, index nodes are another form of keyed record. While the keyed records in the catalog file's leaf nodes contain a key followed by the actual catalog record itself, in an index node the key is followed by a pointer to the relevant child node.

Figure 12.1 showed the overall structure of the B-Tree. The index nodes are searched based on the keys. In order to demonstrate this it is best to use an example. The file **HFS_V3.E01** contains a HFS+ disk image with many files. Hence the catalog file requires more than one node to store all information. Most of the file names (and content) in this image are randomly generated; however, there is a file called **hills.jpg** present in the disk image. This file is located in the file system root. The task is to locate the catalog record for this file.

The first step in locating the file is to build the key value for this file. The key consists of the CNID of the parent folder, followed by the name length, followed by the name itself. Listing 12.16 shows the key value (excluding the key length – 0x18).

```
0000 0002 0009 0068 0069 006c 006c 0073  .......h.i.l.l.s
002e 006a 0070 0067                      ...j.p.g
```

Listing 12.16 Desired key for **hills.jpg**.

As with all B-Trees in HFS+ the next step is to locate the root node of the tree. The header node (descriptor and header record) is shown in Listing 12.17 along with the header record interpretation in Table 12.27.

In this case the tree consists of two levels. This means that one index node must be processed before arriving at the leaf nodes and the desired catalog record. In this case the task is to search for the file **/hills.jpg**.

7 This means that the trees consist of two used nodes, the header node and a single leaf/root node.

```
0000000: 0000 0000 0000 0000 0100 0003 0000 0002 ................
0000010: 0000 0003 0000 0496 0000 0001 0000 0044 ...............D
0000020: 1000 0204 0000 0400 0000 03b6 0000 0040 ...............@
0000030: 0000 00cf 0000 0006 0000 0000 0000 0000 ................
```

Listing 12.17 Catalog header node from the Catalog file in **HFS_V3.E01**.

Table 12.27 Partially processed header record from the catalog file's header node in **HFS_V3.E01**.

Offset	Size	Name	Value
0x00	0x02	Tree Depth	0x02 (2_d)
0x02	0x04	Root Node	0x3 (3_d)
0x06	0x04	Leaf Records	0x496 (1174_d)
0x0A	0x04	First Leaf Node	0x01 (1_d)
0x0E	0x04	Last Leaf Node	0x44 (68_d)
0x12	0x02	Node Size	0x1000 (4096_d)
0x14	0x02	Max. Key Length	0x204 (516_d)
0x16	0x04	Total Nodes	0x400 (1024_d)
0x1A	0x04	Free Nodes	0x3B6 (950_d)

The search for the key begins from the root node (Node 0x3 – Table 12.27). Listing 12.18 shows the first two keys and their corresponding offsets in the root node of the catalog file. Table 12.28 shows the keys for each of these structures (parent ID and filename) along with the desired search key.

```
0003000: 0000 0000 0000 0000 0002 0048 0000 0012 ...........H....
0003010: 0000 0001 0006 0048 0046 0053 002d 0046 .......H.F.S.-.F
0003020: 0053 0000 0001 0018 0000 0016 0009 0061 .S.............a
0003030: 0031 0030 0032 0038 002e 0074 0078 0074 .1.0.2.8...t.x.t
0003040: 0000 002b 0018 0000 0016 0009 0061 0031 ...+.........a.1
...[snip]...
0003ff0: 00da 00bc 009e 0080 0062 0044 0026 000e .........b.D.&..
```

Listing 12.18 Keys and corresponding offsetsn the catalog file's root node.

The search operation begins with the parent ID field. The desired search term is 0x02. Key 1's parent ID is 0x01, which is smaller than the desired search term. Key 2's parent ID is 0x16 which is larger than the desired search term. Hence the desired file must be found by following key 1. The pointer in key 1 is 0x01. Hence the search must continue in node 0x01 (Listing 12.19).

Index nodes in all binary trees in HFS+ are searched in the same manner as the catalog file. The only difference is in exactly how the key structure is formed and the order in which these items are searched. The next section will show another key type found in the extents overflow file.

From Listing 12.19 the CNID of **hills.jpg** is seen to be 0x14 (20_d). This can be confirmed by running **fls** on the disk image.

Table 12.28 Keys from the two items in the root node with their pointer values in Listing 12.18 along with the desired search term.

Key	Parent ID	Name	Pointer
Key 1	0x01 (1_d)	HFS-FS	0x01 (1_d)
Key 2	0x16 (22_d)	a1028.txt	0x2B (43_d)
Search	0x02 (2_d)	hills.jpg	

```
000116a: 0018 0000 0002 0009 0068 0069 006c 006c .........h.i.l.l
000117a: 0073 002e 006a 0070 0067 0002 0002 0000 .s...j.p.g......
000118a: 0000 0000 0014 e172 7f80 e172 7f80 e172 .......r...r...r
000119a: 7f80 e172 7f80 0000 0000 0000 0000 0000 ...r............
00011aa: 0000 0000 81e8 0000 0001 3f3f 3f3f 3f3f ..........??????
00011ba: 3f3f 0000 0000 0000 0000 0000 0000 0000 ??..............
00011ca: 0000 0000 0000 0000 0000 0000 0000 0000 ................
00011da: 0000 0000 0000 0003 9ca7 0000 0000 0000 ................
00011ea: 003a 0000 0807 0000 003a 0000 0000 0000.:.......:......
00011fa: 0000 0000 0000 0000 0000 0000 0000 0000 ................
000120a: 0000 0000 0000 0000 0000 0000 0000 0000 ................
000121a: 0000 0000 0000 0000 0000 0000 0000 0000 ................
000122a: 0000 0000 0000 0000 0000 0000 0000 0000 ................
000123a: 0000 0000 0000 0000 0000 0000 0000 0000 ................
000124a: 0000 0000 0000 0000 0000 0000 0000 0000 ................
000125a: 0000 0000 0000 0000 0000 0000 0000 0000 ................
000126a: 0000 0000 0000 0000 0000 0000 0000 0000 ................
000127a: 0000 0016 0000 0002 0008 0069 006e 0066 ...........i.n.f
...[snip]...
0001ff0: 0416 038c 027c 016a 0100 0098 007a 000e ......j.....z..
```

Listing 12.19 An excerpt from node 0x01 in the catalog file showing part of the catalog record for **hills.jpg**. The listing begins with the key followed by the file record (underlined). The relevant offset (0x16A) is also shown.

12.3.3 Fragmented Files

Fragmented files in HFS+ can be stored in one of two ways. Due to the size of the data fork, files with up to eight extents require no extra storage as all information necessary to locate their content is found in the catalog file. Files which have more than eight extents will require the use of the extents overflow file. **HFS_V4.E01** contains a fragmented file called **hills.jpg** (CNID: $10,332_d$). The file information for this file is found at key index 0x284 in block 0x01 of the catalog file. This structure is shown in Listing 12.20. Note this listing begins after the catalog key structure.

In Listing 12.20 the general fork information is highlighted, while the eight extents follow this. The general fork information provides the file size (0x39CA7 bytes) and the total number of blocks (0x3A). Table 12.29 shows the processed extents.

```
000129e: 0002 0002 0000 0000 0000 285c e19c 8344 ..........(\...D
00012ae: e19c 8344 e19c 8344 e19c 8394 0000 0000 ...D...D........
00012be: 0000 0000 0000 0000 0000 81e8 0000 0001 ................
00012ce: 3f3f 3f3f 3f3f 3f3f 0000 0000 0000 0000 ????????........
00012de: 0000 0000 0000 0000 0000 0000 0000 0000 ................
00012ee: 0000 0000 0000 0000 0000 0000 0003 9ca7 ................
00012fe: 0000 0000 0000 003a 0000 02de 0000 0003 .......:........
000130e: 0000 030b 0000 0003 0000 0347 0000 0003 ...........G....
000131e: 0000 03a1 0000 0003 0000 03ce 0000 0003 ................
000132e: 0000 0458 0000 0003 0000 049d 0000 0003 ...X............
000133e: 0000 0557 0000 0003                     ...W............
```

Listing 12.20 The file record for **hills.jpg** in **HFS_V4.E01**. The key has been removed and the fork information is highlighted. This is followed by the extents.

From Table 12.29 it is clear that the start of the file's contents can be found in block 734_d. However, Table 12.29 provides information about a total of 24_d blocks of data, but the extent header shows that there should be 58_d blocks. Hence 34_d blocks have yet to be located.

The data fork contained in the catalog record contains eight extents. Any files that require less than eight fragments can be recovered from the catalog record itself. In the case that a file requires more than eight extents, the remaining extents are found in the extents overflow file. The extents overflow file is another B-Tree structure which can be located from the volume header (or recovered with Sleuth Kit). Listing 12.21 shows the header node of the extents overflow file. The node descriptor merely shows this to be a header node (type 0x01 and 0x03 records in the node). The processed header record is shown in Table 12.30.

```
0000000: 0000 0000 0000 0000 0100 0003 0000 0001 ................
0000010: 0000 0001 0000 0002 0000 0001 0000 0001 ................
0000020: 1000 000a 0000 0100 0000 00fe 0000 0010 ................
0000030: 0000 0000 0000 0002 0000 0000 0000 0000 ................
```

Listing 12.21 The node descriptor and header record (underlined) from the extents overflow file in **HFS_V4.E01**.

Table 12.29 Processed extents for **hills.jpg** (CNID: $10,332_d$) in **HFS_V4.E01**.

	Start Blk.	**# Blocks**
Extent 1	0x2DE (734_d)	0x03 (3_d)
Extent 2	0x30B (779_d)	0x03 (3_d)
Extent 3	0x347 (839_d)	0x03 (3_d)
Extent 4	0x3A1 (929_d)	0x03 (3_d)
Extent 5	0x3CE (974_d)	0x03 (3_d)
Extent 6	0x458 (1112_d)	0x03 (3_d)
Extent 7	0x49D (1181_d)	0x03 (3_d)
Extent 8	0x557 (1367_d)	0x03 (3_d)

Table 12.30 shows that this extents overflow file is very small. In total there are only two records in this file. These records occupy a single node (node 0x01). Before proceeding to analyse this node, it is first necessary to determine the structures that are found there. Table 12.31 shows the key structure used in the extents overflow file.

The desired key for searching for **hills.jpg** is therefore composed of the fork type (0x00 for a data fork), padding (0x00), the CNID (0x0000285C) and finally the block number in the file's content to which the extent refers. 24_d blocks were found in the catalog record's data fork, meaning that the desired key value should be looking for block 24_d which is 0x00000018.[8] Listing 12.22 shows the entire search key that will be used.

```
0000 0000 285C 0000 0018
```

Listing 12.22 Search key for the extents overflow file entries relating to **hills.jpg**.

Table 12.30 Partially processed header record from the extents overflow file's header node in Listing 12.21.

Offset	Size	Name	Value
0x00	0x02	Tree Depth	0x01 (1_d)
0x02	0x04	Root Node	0x01 (1_d)
0x06	0x04	Leaf Records	0x02 (2_d)
0x0A	0x04	First Leaf Node	0x01 (1_d)
0x0E	0x04	Last Leaf Node	0x01 (1_d)
0x12	0x02	Node Size	0x1000 (4096_d)
0x14	0x02	Max. Key Length	0x0A (10_d)
0x16	0x04	Total Nodes	0x100 (256_d)
0x1A	0x04	Free Nodes	0xFE (254_d)

Table 12.31 Extents overflow file's key structure.

Offset	Size	Name	Description
0x00	0x02	Key Length	Every key in HFS+ uses a key length field, which shows the length of the key in bytes (excluding the length field itself). In the case of the extents overflow file the key length is always 10_d bytes in size.
0x02	0x01	Fork Type	The fork type to which this extent record applies. The value 0x00 is used for a data fork, while 0xFF is used for a resource fork.
0x03	0x01	Padding	Padding.
0x04	0x04	CNID	The CNID to which this record applies.
0x08	0x04	Start Block	The starting block of the first extent described in this record.

8 Allocation block numbering begins at 0_d. 24_d blocks have been accounted for in the catalog record's data fork. These are blocks 0_d–23_d meaning that the next allocation block number is 24_d.

Listing 12.23 shows partial content of node 1 in the extents overflow file. This begins with the node descriptor and ends with the list of offsets to individual records. Both records in the extents overflow file refer to **hills.jpg** file.

```
0001000: 0000 0000 0000 0000 ff01 0002 0000 000a ................
0001010: 0000 0000 285c 0000 0018 0000 0581 0000 ....(\..........
0001020: 0003 0000 05b4 0000 0003 0000 05e7 0000 ................
0001030: 0003 0000 05ed 0000 0003 0000 064d 0000 .............M..
0001040: 0003 0000 068c 0000 0003 0000 06aa 0000 ................
0001050: 0003 0000 06cb 0000 0003 000a 0000 0000 ................
0001060: 285c 0000 0030 0000 06e9 0000 0003 0000 (\...0..........
0001070: 071f 0000 0003 0000 0725 0000 0003 0000 .........%......
0001080: 0737 0000 0001 0000 0000 0000 0000 0000 .7..............
0001090: 0000 0000 0000 0000 0000 0000 0000 0000 ................
00010a0: 0000 0000 0000 0000 0000 0000 0000 0000 ................
...[snip]...
0001ff0: 0000 0000 0000 0000 0000 00a6 005a 000e .............Z..
```

Listing 12.23 The relevant entries in the extents overflow file for CNID 0x285C in **HFS_V4.E01**. The keys are underlined.

The processed keys are shown in Table 12.32. The first key is followed by eight further extent structures with the second containing a further four extents. The processed values of these are shown in Table 12.33. Each extents overflow record can store up to eight extents. However, in this case the final three are not required.

Table 12.33 provides information on the remaining blocks in the file. Combining this with Table 12.29 shows that all 58_d allocation blocks are now accounted for. This highly fragmented file requires 20_d extents to record the locations of 58_d allocation blocks. Eight of the extents are found in the data fork of the catalog record, with the remaining extents found in two records in the extents overflow file. The result of this analysis can be confirmed using Sleuth Kit's **istat** command as shown in Listing 12.24.

The information discovered to date can be used to recover the contents of the file. The volume header shows the block size to be 4096_d bytes. This file occupies 57_d blocks in their entirety as shown in Listing 12.24. These account for $4096 \times 57 = 233,472$ bytes. However, the data fork in the catalog record (Listing 12.20) shows the file size to be 0x39CA7 ($236,711_d$) bytes. This means that the final 3239_d bytes are found in the final block, 1847_d. Listing 12.25 shows an excerpt from a sequence of commands to recover this file. The result of these commands is also compared to those of Sleuth Kit showing that the end result of the manual process is identical to that of the automated process.

Table 12.32 Processed extents overflow keys from Listing 12.23.

Offset	Size	Name	Key 1	Key 2
0x00	0x02	Key Length	0x0A (10_d)	0x0A (10_d)
0x02	0x01	Fork Type	0x00 (0_d)	0x00 (0_d)
0x03	0x01	Padding	0x00 (0_d)	0x00 (0_d)
0x04	0x04	CNID	0x285C ($10,332_d$)	0x285C ($10,332_d$)
0x04	0x04	Start Block	0x18 (24_d)	0x30 (48_d)

Table 12.33 Processed extents from the data forks in Listing 12.23.

Record 1		Record 2	
Start Blk.	**# Blocks**	**Start Blk.**	**# Blocks**
0x581 (1409_d)	0x03 (3_d)	0x6E9 (1769_d)	0x03 (3_d)
0x5B4 (1460_d)	0x03 (3_d)	0x71F (1823_d)	0x03 (3_d)
0x5E7 (1511_d)	0x03 (3_d)	0x725 (1829_d)	0x03 (3_d)
0x5ED (1517_d)	0x03 (3_d)	0x737 (1847_d)	0x01 (1_d)
0x64D (1613_d)	0x03 (3_d)		
0x68C (1676_d)	0x03 (3_d)		
0x6AA (1706_d)	0x03 (3_d)		
0x6CB (1739_d)	0x03 (3_d)		

```
File Path: /hills.jpg
Catalog Record: 10332
..[snip]..
Data Fork Blocks:
734-736 779-781 839-841 929-931
974-976 1112-1114 1181-1183 1367-1369
1409-1411 1460-1462 1511-1513 1517-1519
1613-1615 1676-1678 1706-1708 1739-1741
1769-1771 1823-1825 1829-1831 1847
..[snip]..
```

Listing 12.24 Output from the **istat** command confirming the results of the manual analysis shown in Tables 12.29 and 12.33.

12.3.4 Links

As with many file systems HFS+ allows links to be created in the file system. Both symbolic (soft) and hard links can be created in HFS+. For the purposes of this section, the disk image **HFS_V5.E01** is used. Note that this disk image was created on an Apple system and therefore has more information present than the other file systems examined to this point.

This section begins by examining the symbolic link structure in HFS+. Symbolic links store the path/file name of the link target file; hence, the link file is stored as an ordinary file. After recovery of the catalog file from **HFS_V5.E01**, Listing 12.26 shows the file record for the symbolic link named **softlink.jpg**.

Examining the catalog record for this symbolic link begins with the file mode value (0xA1ED). The most significant nibble of the Unix mode/permission value represents the file type. The value of 0xA represents a symbolic link file. Additionally in HFS+ the finder information structure begins with the ASCII values *slnk* representing a symbolic link. Note that this is always followed by the ASCII value *rhap*. Hence the combination of the mode (0xA) and the values *slnk* and *rhap* show that this file represents a symbolic link.

In order to determine the link target the data fork is processed. From the header it is clear that data size is 0x0C (12_d) bytes and occupies a single extent. The extent contains one single block

```
$ dd if=hfs_V3.raw bs=4096 count=3 skip=734 > hills.manual.jpg
$ dd if=hfs_V3.raw bs=4096 count=3 skip=779 >> hills.manual.jpg
$ dd if=hfs_V3.raw bs=4096 count=3 skip=839 >> hills.manual.jpg
...[snip]...
$ dd if=hfs_V3.raw bs=4096 count=1 skip=1829 >> hills.manual.jpg
$ dd if=hfs_V3.raw bs=1 count=3239
     skip=$((4096*1847)) >> hills.manual.jpg
$
$ icat mnt/ewf1 10332 > hills.tsk.jpg
$ md5sum hills.*
077b97d7b11d079d2ac47edaf25f9fc5 hills.manual.jpg
077b97d7b11d079d2ac47edaf25f9fc5 hills.tsk.jpg
```

Listing 12.25 Commands required to recover the contents of **hills.jpg** from **HFS_V4.E01**. Sleuth Kit is also used for automated recovery of the file. Some of the intermediate block recovery steps have been omitted.

```
$ xxd -s $((0x1000 + 0xC3E + 0x20)) -l $((0xF8)) catalog_V5.raw
0001c5e: 0002 0002 0000 0000 0000 001b e19c 90f2 ................
0001c6e: e19c 90f2 e19c 90f2 e19c 90f2 0000 0000 ................
0001c7e: 0000 0063 0000 0063 0000 a1ed 0000 0001 ...c...c........
0001c8e: 736c 6e6b 7268 6170 0000 0000 0000 0000 slnkrhap........
0001c9e: 0000 0000 0000 0000 0000 0000 0000 0000 ................
0001cae: 0000 0000 0000 0000 0000 0000 0000 000c ................
0001cbe: 0000 0000 0000 0001 0000 1f40 0000 0001 ...........@....
0001cce: 0000 0000 0000 0000 0000 0000 0000 0000 ................
...[snip]...
```

Listing 12.26 The **softlink.jpg** file's catalog record. The extent is highlighted along with the link signature and mode/permission values.

(only 12_d bytes are actually used) and begins at allocation block (0x1F40). Listing 12.27 shows the command to recover this file.

```
$ sudo dd if=mnt/ewf1 bs=1 skip=$((0x1F40 * 4096)) count=12
../hills.jpg
```

Listing 12.27 Command to recover the contents of the symbolic link.

This shows that the symbolic link file (**softlink.jpg**) contains a link to the file located one level higher in the directory hierarchy with the name **hills.jpg**. But what happens in the case of hard links. The file **hardlink.jpg** is also a link to the **hills.jpg** file found in **HFS_V5.E01** but in this case it is a hard link. The implementation of hard links in HFS+ is unusual. Firstly when a hard link is created the original file (target) content is copied to a file in the **HFS+ Private Data** directory. This can be seen in the output of **fls** on the **HFS_V5.E01** file system as shown in Listing 12.28. This clearly shows the new file **iNode23** in the **HFS+ Private Data** directory. Sleuth Kit shows the file to share a CNID number (23_d) with the original file **hills.jpg** and also with the link, **hardlink.jpg**. However, as will be seen later, this is merely a presentation convention used by Sleuth Kit.

```
...[snip]...
d/d 28:       Files
r/r 23:       hills.jpg
d/d 24:       Links
+ r/r 23:     hardlink.jpg
+ l/l 27:     softlink.jpg
d/d 18:       ^^^^HFS+ Private Data
+ r/r 23:     iNode23
```

Listing 12.28 The output of **fls** on **HFS_V5.E01**.

The original file, **hills.jpg**, initially had a CNID value of 0x17 (23_d). With the creation of a hard link this file became **iNode23** in the **HFS+ Private Data** directory. The current catalog record for **hills.jpg** is shown in Listing 12.29.

```
000157a: 0002 0022 0000 0000 0000 0019 e19c 9006 ..."............
000158a: e19c 9006 e19c 9006 e19c 9006 0000 0000 ................
000159a: 0000 001a 0000 0000 0002 8124 0000 0017 ...........$....
00015aa: 686c 6e6b 6866 732b 0100 0000 0000 0000 hlnkhfs+........
00015ba: 0000 0000 0000 0000 0000 0000 0000 0000 ................
00015ca: 0000 007e 0000 0000                     ...~............
...[snip]...
```

Listing 12.29 An excerpt from the catalog record for **hills.jpg** in **HFS_V5.E01**. Both the data and resource forks are empty and are not shown.

Examining this record shows that the CNID is 0x19 (25_d) and not 0x17 as had appeared previously. Directly after the permissions string is found the inode number (0x17). This can be added to the word iNode to get the target of the link.[9] Finally the Finder information structure will contain the ASCII values *hlnkhfs+* to denote that this catalog record refers to a hard link. The catalog record for the **hardlink.jpg** file itself is shown in Listing 12.30. This shows a similar pattern, the only difference being that the CNID of this record is 0x1A (26_d).

```
0001b46: 0002 0022 0000 0000 0000 001a e19c 9006 ..."............
0001b56: e19c 9006 e19c 9006 e19c 9006 0000 0000 ................
0001b66: 0000 0000 0000 0019 0002 8124 0000 0017 ...........$....
0001b76: 686c 6e6b 6866 732b 0100 0000 0000 0000 hlnkhfs+........
0001b86: 0000 0000 0000 0000 0000 0000 0000 0000 ................
0001b96: 0000 007e 0000 0000                     ...~............
...[snip]...
```

Listing 12.30 The catalog record for **hardlink.jpg** in **HFS_V5.E01**.

In order to recover the content of a hard link file, the catalog record for the newly created file should be examined. In this case the file is called **iNode23** and is found in the **HFS+ Private Data** directory. The catalog record for this file is shown in Listing 12.31.

9 In this example the content of the file with CNID 23_d was copied to a file called **iNode23**. The official documentation states that this number is random and is not the CNID number. Hence the number found here might not be the actual CNID for the target file; instead, it may be a random number.

```
0001812: 0002 00a6 0000 001a 0000 0017 e19c 90d3 ................
0001822: e19c 90d3 e19c 90e8 e19c 90d3 0000 0000 ................
0001832: 0000 0063 0000 0063 0000 81a4 0000 0002 ...c...c........
0001842: 0000 0000 0000 0000 0000 0000 0000 0000 ................
0001852: 0000 0000 6576 e053 0000 0000 0000 0002 ....ev.S........
0001862: 0000 0000 0000 0000 0000 0000 0003 9ca7 ................
0001872: 0000 0000 0000 003a 0000 1f06 0000 003a .......:.......:
0001882: 0000 0000 0000 0000 0000 0000 0000 0000 ................
0001892: 0000 0000 0000 0000 0000 0000 0000 0000 ................
00018a2: 0000 0000 0000 0000 0000 0000 0000 0000 ................
00018b2: 0000 0000 0000 0000                     ........
```

Listing 12.31 The partial catalog record for **iNode23** in **HFS_V5.E01**.

This record clearly shows the original CNID (0x17 – 23_d) along with a data fork that is used to locate the actual content (the extent is highlighted). Recall from Listing 12.28 that Sleuth Kit displays only a single CNID number for all three files (**hills.jpg**, **hardlink.jpg** and **iNode23**). This CNID is the one found in the **iNode23** file.

12.4 Summary

This chapter introduced the first of the Apple file systems, HFS+. This file system was the standard in all Apple devices for many years. In its day it was an advanced file system allowing for 32_d-bit addressing and fast searching through the use of B-Trees. It has not kept pace with modern storage devices and as such is less frequently encountered now.

The HFS+ file system utilises a number of structures that are key for file system forensic analysis. One of the first HFS+ structures analysed by file system forensic tools for macOS is that of the volume header. This structure is analogous to the volume boot sector found in Windows file systems (and also the superblocks found in Linux file systems). It contains much information about the file system and is the area of disk that forensic tools such as **fsstat** mainly query.

In order to recover file content and metadata the catalog file is required. This structure, similar to the MFT in NTFS, contains information about all files and directories in the file system. It contains a wealth of information about the contents of the file system. This structure is used to gather all metadata related to files in the file system and also to locate the content of the file. In HFS+, file content is located through the use of data forks. Each fork can store information on up to eight extent structures. In the event that more than eight extents are required, the extents overflow file is used to store more extents. Theoretically there is no limit to the number of extents that can be stored in relation to a single file.

As storage technology advanced HFS+ began to show its age. The use of 32_d-bit CNID values leads to a limit on the number of files that can be used ($2^{32} \approx 4$ billion). This, combined with 32_d-bit block addresses, meant that the file system was unable to scale to larger devices. In 2017 Apple began to deploy HFS+'s replacement, APFS. The APFS file system is examined in the next chapter.

Exercises

The following questions should be answered in relation to **HFS_V3.E01**.

1 Answer the following questions in relation to this file system:
   a) When was the file system created?
   b) How many files/directories are present in the file system?
   c) How many free blocks are present on the file system?
   d) What size are the allocation blocks?

2 Locate the file records in the catalog file for the following files:
   a) **hills.jpg** located in the root directory
   b) **foggy.jpg** located in the Files directory (CNID: 17_d)

3 In relation to the file **foggy.jpg** answer the following questions:
   a) What is the file size?
   b) When was the file last modified?
   c) What are the file permissions?
   d) Which text encoding is used in this file?

4 Manually recover the contents of **foggy.jpg**.

Bibliography

Altheide, C. and Carvey, H.A. (2011). *Digital Forensics with Open Source Tools: Using Open Source Platform Tools for Performing Computer Forensics on Target Systems: Windows, Mac, Linux, UNIX, etc.* Rockland, MA: Syngress; Oxford.

Apple Developer (2004). Technical Note TN1150: HFS Plus Volume Format [Internet]. developer.apple .com.https://developer.apple.com/library/archive/technotes/tn/tn1150.html (accessed 14 August 2024).

Burghardt, A. and Feldman, A.J. (2008). Using the HFS+ journal for deleted file recovery. *Digital Investigation* 5: S76–S82.

Craiger, P. and Burke, P. (2005). *Mac Forensics: Mac OS X and the HFS+ File System*. Department of Engineering Technology University of Central Florida.

Craiger, P. and Burke, P. (2006). Mac OS X forensics. In: *Advances in Digital Forensics II*, vol. 2006, 159–170. Orlando, FL; New York: Springer.

Fortuna, A. (2020). iOS Forensics: HFS+ file system, partitions and relevant evidences –Andrea Fortuna [Internet]. https://www.andreafortuna.org/2020/08/31/ios-forensics-hfs-file-system-partitions-and-relevant-evidences/

Garijo, J.M. (2015). Mac OS X Forensics. Technical Report, RHUL-*MA-2015-8*.

Maes, B. (2012). Comparison of contemporary file systems [Internet]. https://citeseerx.ist.psu.edu/document?repid=rep1type=pdfdoi=cdf3d691255bbe069492f3b430067037e2f3ade0 (accessed 14 August 2024).

Metz, J. (2024). libfshfs/documentation/Hierarchical File System (HFS).asciidoc at main. libyal/libfshfs [Internet]. GitHub. 2024 [cited 2024 April 2]. https://github.com/libyal/libfshfs/blob/main/documentation/Hierarchical (accessed 14 August 2024).

Schneider, J., Eichhorn, M., and Freiling, F. (2022). Ambiguous file system partitions. *Forensic Science International: Digital Investigation* 42: 301399.

Su, L.J., Wu, S.X., and Cao, D. (2011). Windows-based analysis for HFS+ file system. *Advanced Materials Research* 179-180: 538–543.

Ware, S. (2012). Hfs plus file system exposition and forensics. M.S. Dissertation. Florida: University of Central Florida, 145p.

Wikipedia (2024). HFS - Sleuth KitWiki [Internet]. wiki.sleuthkit.org. [cited 2024 April 2]. https://wiki.sleuthkit.org/index.php?title=HFS (accessed 14 August 2024).

13

The APFS File System

Apple File System (APFS) was developed by Apple as a replacement for the HFS+ file system. It was first released, in beta form, in macOS 10.12.4 in 2017 and quickly became standard on all Apple products. It is now the default file system on all new Apple devices, and many devices that have been updated to newer versions of Apple operating systems also have the file system updated to APFS in the background.

HFS+ was originally released in the late 1990s and by the mid-2010s was showing its age. During that time many changes occurred in storage technology. One of the most obvious changes was in the capacity of storage devices. The great increase in capacity meant that HFS+ was struggling to support modern devices in their entirety. Another major change was the prevalence of SSDs over traditional HDDs. The SSD has some features which can be exploited by file systems, but older systems such as HFS+ were unable to do this. Hence the need for a new APFS.

APFS allows for a number of advanced features which allow it to outperform HFS+ in terms of both functionality and efficiency. These features include:

- **64_d-bit Inodes:** Inodes are now represented using 64_d-bit addresses (although only 60_d bits are used for the inode number, the remaining four bits are used to describe the type of object). This allows for a vast increase in the number of possible files on an APFS volume when compared to the 32_d-bit CNIDs used in HFS+.
- **Encryption:** APFS provides for encryption at the file system level. This can be achieved at whole disk or single file level. Potentially this makes APFS more difficult to analyse than the HFS+ file system in which encryption had to be added at a higher level.
- **Snapshots:** APFS supports snapshot creation. In particular 'read-only' snapshots can be created for backup purposes with very little overhead. This also has implications for the forensic process as there is potential to recover older versions of the file system through these snapshots.
- **Sparse Files:** APFS provides sparse file support, in which blocks of zeros in file content are not stored on disk. This feature results in more efficient use of space in APFS when compared with HFS+.
- **Space Sharing:** APFS containers consist of a number of volumes (see Section 13.1.4). Every volume in the container shares space in the container.
- **Checksums:** All APFS structures support checksums in order to provide improved reliability.
- **Crash Protection:** APFS does not update metadata; instead, it uses copy-on-write (CoW) to create a new instance of the metadata structure, updates that and changes the pointer. This ensures the file system will never be left in an inconsistent state.
- **Checkpoints:** APFS creates a number of automatic checkpoints. This allows for historical views of the file system to be obtained. However, these checkpoints are overwritten quickly and may not be of great use to an investigator.

File System Forensics, First Edition. Fergus Toolan.

The use of checkpoints and snapshots in APFS means that potentially, from a file system forensics perspective, there is more chance to recover previous file system states. Consider the case of HFS+ (and other systems using B-Tree structures), in which tree balancing means that metadata structures are overwritten. This means that older information is quickly lost. However, in APFS, the checkpoints and snapshots protect older information from deletion. While no longer available in the current file system, the automated checkpoints (of which there are many in APFS) will often protect historical information. Both metadata and content can be protected in this way.

13.1 On-Disk Structures

The general layout of an APFS container is shown in Figure 13.1. The container superblock (CSB) exists in sector 0_d on the device and contains information about the container as a whole. This CSB should theoretically be the latest version of the CSB, but other CSBs are also found on the device.These are found in the checkpoint area in the container which follows immediately after the primary CSB. The CSB in block 0_d is generally used only to locate the latest CSB in the checkpoint area. This is the CSB that is used to mount the file system.

Following the checkpoint area the container contains the space manager. The purpose of the space manager is to manage the allocation of blocks throughout the entire container. There is a single space manager area in the container which has responsibility for all space. Due to the possibilities for multiple volumes in a single APFS container, the space manager might be responsible for allocation of blocks in more than one volume. All other information in APFS (volumes, file content, metadata etc.) can appear anywhere following the space manager area.

This section examines some of those structures vital for the analysis of the APFS file system. Unless otherwise noted all values in the APFS file system are stored in little-endian format.

13.1.1 Time in APFS

APFS uses a 64_d-bit unsigned timestamp value which records the number of nanosecond intervals (10^{-9} s) since the Unix epoch (1 January 1970). This provides for much better granularity than that provided for in HFS+ (and indeed by Unix time itself) and also provides for a better range of time values. The final representable time value in this system occurs in July 2554 as opposed to February 2106 for unsigned 32_d-bit Unix time.[1] Timestamps in APFS are stored in UTC.

13.1.2 Objects

Almost all items in the APFS file system, except for the bitmap structure, are stored as objects. Every object is identified by an object identifier (OID). There are three types of OID reflecting three different object storage/addressing mechanisms. These are physical, virtual and ephemeral.

In the case of physical OIDs, these objects are stored at a known block address on disk. It is this block address that is used as the object's OID. These objects are the easiest to locate in the file system, merely requiring access to the block number that corresponds to the object's OID. However, physical OIDs are not constant across an object's lifetime. When a change is made to a physical object in APFS, the use of copy-on-write (CoW) means that a new copy of the object is created.

1 And only January 2038 for 32_d-bit signed Unix time.

Figure 13.1 APFS container structure.

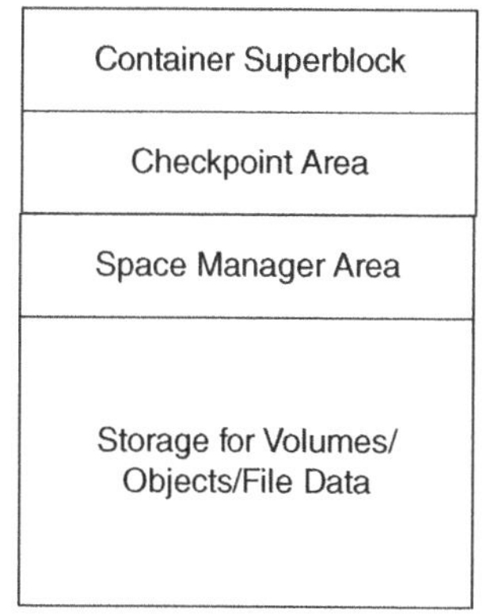

This will reside at a different physical address and as such it will have a different OID to that of the original. Hence every change made to a physical object results in a new OID for that object.

Objects with a virtual OID are also found on disk. The OIDs of these objects do not correspond to a physical location. In order to locate an object from a virtual OID the OID must be translated to a physical block address. This is done through an object map structure. Each APFS container will have multiple object map structures each with different scope. Every container will have a container object map and at least one object map for every volume in the container. When a modification occurs to an object with a virtual OID a copy of the object is created (again due to CoW) but in this case the OID remains constant (as it is virtual). Instead the XID (transaction identifier) is updated. This value is used to locate the desired version of the OID in question. After the modification is complete, and the object's copy is created, the relevant object map structure is updated to show the new physical location of the virtual object.

The third type of object is an ephemeral object. These are not stored on-disk as are objects with physical and virtual OIDs. Instead they are stored in memory for a mounted container. When the container is unmounted these objects will be written to the checkpoint data area. These objects are modified in-place, in other words they don't use CoW. This is because they reside in main memory and are only stored in checkpoints on disk. During traditional digital forensic analysis ephemeral objects will be found only in the checkpoint area. However, these objects may be encountered during memory forensics as they exist in RAM.

All objects, regardless of purpose or type, consist of a 32_d-byte header followed by the object itself. The structure of this object header is shown in Table 13.1.

The object header describes the type/subtype of the object in question. The subtype is used in the case of a structure which can hold many different types. For instance a B-Tree is used in APFS to store both object maps and file systems (along with other data). In both cases the object type will be 0x02 (for the root node) or 0x03 (for non-root nodes). This alone does not allow these structures to be distinguished. Hence in these cases the subtype is also used. The object map will have a subtype of 0x0B (object map) while the file system B-Tree's subtype will be 0x0E (file system B-Tree).

The flags in the object header are used to determine how the object is stored. The value shows whether they are physical, virtual or ephemeral. Flags can also provide other information. For instance the flag 0x8800 represents a non-persistent ephemeral object. This object is never written to disk, even in a checkpoint. This flag should never be encountered in traditional digital forensics. A flag value of 0x1000 means that the object is encrypted, while 0x2000 means the object has no header. This no header flag will obviously not be encountered in the object header structure, but it

Table 13.1 APFS object header structure.

Offset	Size	Name	Description
0x00	0x08	Checksum	A variant of Fletcher's checksum calculated over the block's contents (less these 8_d bytes).
0x08	0x08	OID	The object's identifier.
0x10	0x08	XID	The transaction ID (XID) is the version number of the object which is incremented when the object is updated.
0x18	0x02	Type	The object type. There are 33_d object types (see Apple File System Reference). Some of the more important types for digital forensics include: **0x01:** Container superblock; **0x02:** B-Tree; **0x03:** B-Tree node; **0x0B:** Object map; **0x0C:** Checkpoint map; **0x0D:** Volume superblock; **0x0E:** File system B-Tree.
0x1A	0x02	Flags	Flags are used in the object header to provide additional information about the current object. The values for the flags are: **0x0000:** Virtual OID; **0x4000:** Physical OID; **0x8000:** Ephemeral OID; **0x2000:** No header; **0x1000:** Encrypted; **0x0800:** Non-persistent.
0x1C	0x02	Subtype	The object's subtype. These values are the same as those in the object-type field.
0x1E	0x02	Padding	Padding values (0x00).

can be encountered in other areas (for instance information about bitmaps will generally have this flag set!).

13.1.3 B-Trees

As with many modern file systems APFS uses B-Tree structures to store much of the file system information. B-Trees are balanced trees that store information in an ordered form and allow for quick searching for desired information. The basic structure of a B-Tree is shown in Figure 13.2.

There are three types of node in APFS B-Trees. These are:

- **Root Nodes:** There will always exist a single root node in every B-Tree. This node exists at the highest level of the tree (level 2 in Figure 13.2). Depending on the size of the B-Tree the root node will also serve as either an index or leaf node.

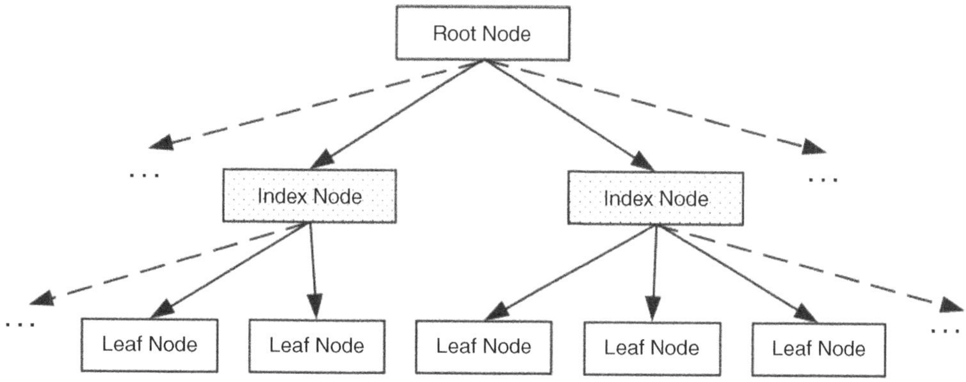

Figure 13.2 APFS B-Tree structure.

Figure 13.3 APFS B-Tree (root) node structure. ToC is the node's table of contents.

- **Index Nodes:** Index nodes contain pointers to other nodes in the tree. As with all B-Trees the keys in APFS index nodes (and indeed all nodes) are sorted which allows quick location of the desired child node and hence location of the content of interest.
- **Leaf Nodes:** Leaf nodes contain the actual data in the tree. The type of data depends on the B-Tree's purpose. For instance the file system tree (subtype: 0x0E) will contain inode and extent structures, while the object map tree (subtype: 0x0B) will contain mappings from virtual OIDs to physical locations on disk.

Almost all nodes, regardless of type, share a common structure shown in Figure 13.3. This shows a B-Tree root node. Non-root nodes are identical to this structure, except that they do not include the B-Tree info structure at the node's tail.

The various areas present in the B-Tree node include:

- **Node Header:** This area provides information about the structure of the node. The structure of the node header is shown in Table 13.2.
- **Table of Contents:** The table of contents (ToC) provides the locations for the keys and values that are present in the tree node. It allows the association of keys and values and also access to the actual data.
- **Keys:** The keys are used for sorting the tree. It is this area that is searched if a particular file is sought. The ordering of keys in a B-Tree allows for very efficient searching (although inserts can be much slower). Keys are stored directly after the ToC.
- **Values:** Values are stored at the end of the node. In the case of root node the values are located immediately before the B-Tree info structure. In non-root nodes values are located at the very end of the node block.
- **Free Space:** Keys fill from the beginning of the node and values fill from the end of the node. Generally there exists free space between these two areas.
- **B-Tree Info:** This structure is found only in root nodes and contains information about the tree as a whole.

Table 13.2 APFS B-Tree node header structure.

Offset	Size	Name	Description
0x00	0x20	Object Header	The generic object header structure (see Table 13.1).
0x20	0x02	Flags	Flag values: **0x0001:** Root node; **0x0002:** Leaf node; **0x0004:** Fixed key-value size; **0x0008:** Hashed; **0x0010:** No header; **0x8000:** Transient.
0x22	0x02	Level	The number of child levels below this node. For a leaf node this value is 0x00. Referring to Figure 13.2 the root node would be level 0x02, the index nodes 0x01 and the leaves 0x00.
0x24	0x04	Num. Keys	The number of keys in this node.
0x28	0x02	ToC Offset	The byte offset to the table of contents structure. This value is relative to the end of the node header (0x38 bytes).
0x2A	0x02	ToC Length	The length of the table of contents in bytes.
0x2C	0x02	Free Space Offset	The byte offset to the free space area relative to the end of the node header.
0x2E	0x02	Free Space Length	The length of the free space area in bytes.
0x30	0x02	Free Key List Offset	The byte offset to the free key list relative to the end of the node header.
0x32	0x02	Free Key List Length	The length of the free key list in bytes.
0x34	0x02	Free Value List Offset	The byte offset to the free value list relative to the end of the node header.
0x36	0x02	Free Value List Length	The length of the free value list in bytes.

When a B-Tree node is encountered during analysis processing begins at the node header. The structure of the node header is shown in Table 13.2.

The information provided by the node header will allow for all the structures in the node to be located. This means that each area in Figure 13.3 can be identified. The free key and free value lists provide the offsets to the next free space (for keys and values, respectively). These are used when new key value pairs are added to the node.

In the case of a root node the final 40_d bytes of the node form the B-Tree info structure. This structure contains information about the B-Tree as a whole. The structure of this is provided in Table 13.3.

The next step in processing the node is to get the locations of the keys and values. This is done by processing the Table of Contents (ToC) structure. Before doing this it is necessary to determine the type of keys/values being used. Referring to the flags in the node header (Table 13.2), a flag value of 0x0004 means that keys and values are of fixed length. In this case the B-Tree info structure (Table 13.3) is used to determine the key/value sizes. In the case of fixed key value sizes the ToC entries are structured as key offset/value offset pairs. This structure is given in Table 13.4. In the

Table 13.3 B-Tree info structure.

Offset	Size	Name	Description
0x00	0x04	Flags	Flags related to this B-Tree. The values include: **0x01:** Optimised comparisons; **0x02:** Sequential insert; **0x04:** Allow ghosts; **0x08:** Ephemeral OIDs for children; **0x10:** Physical OIDs for children; **0x20:** B-Tree does not persist; **0x40:** Unaligned key values; **0x80:** Index nodes store hashes; **0x100:** No object header.
0x04	0x04	Node Size	The size of each node in bytes.
0x08	0x04	Key Size	The size of keys in this B-Tree. A value of 0x00 means that keys are variable sized.
0x0C	0x04	Value Size	The size of values in this B-Tree. A value of 0x00 means that values are variable sized.
0x10	0x04	Longest Key	The byte length of the longest key that has ever been stored in this B-Tree.
0x14	0x04	Longest Value	The byte length of the longest value that has ever been stored in this B-Tree.
0x18	0x08	Key Count	The number of keys in this B-Tree.
0x20	0x08	Node Count	The number of nodes in this B-Tree.

Table 13.4 ToC entry structure for fixed length key value pairs.

Offset	Size	Name	Description
0x00	0x02	Key Offset	The byte offset to the key. This offset is relative to the end of the table of contents.
0x02	0x02	Value Offset	The byte offset to the value. This offset is relative to the start of the B-Tree info structure (for root nodes) or to the end of the node (for non-root nodes). This offset is *subtracted* from the designated point!

case where the key/value lengths are not fixed, the structure is slightly more complex as the key and value lengths must be included. This is given in Table 13.5.

The processing of the ToC allows the keys and values to be located. The key/value structure is dependent on the type of tree that is being used. These structures will be covered later in this chapter.

13.1.4 Containers and Volumes

APFS introduces a new concept to file systems, that of the container. When an APFS file system is created (Section 13.2.1) it is actually a top-level container that is being created. This container

Table 13.5 ToC entry structure when handling variable length keys and values.

Offset	Size	Name	Description
0x00	0x02	Key Offset	The byte offset to the key. This offset is relative to the end of the table of contents.
0x02	0x02	Key Length	The length of the key in bytes.
0x04	0x02	Value Offset	The byte offset to the value. This offset is relative to the start of the B-Tree info structure (for root nodes) or to the end of the node (for non-root nodes). This offset is *subtracted* from the designated point!
0x06	0x02	Value Length	The length of the value in bytes.

can contain multiple volumes, which can be used to store files. Volumes in the same container share space in that container. The container stores all information about the volume locations and also stores information about all structures that are common to all volumes. Each container has a superblock object found at block 0_d in the container (Section 13.1.5). Data blocks in the container are shared between all the volumes present in the container.

13.1.5 Container Superblock

All analysis begins at the CSB which is found in block 0 of the container. This object contains information about the entire APFS container such as block size, number of blocks and checkpoint information. The CSB is an APFS object and as such the first 0x20 bytes consist of an object header (Table 13.1). The type code that should be found in the CSB object header is 0x01. Table 13.6 provides the structure of the CSB itself.

In order to analyse an APFS container the CSB is the first structure processed. This structure provides much information that is required in order to analyse the file system. Some of the information that must be recovered includes the following:

- **Object Header:** This is required to confirm that the structure is a container superblock (Type: 0x01).
- **Magic Value:** This is used along with the object's type to confirm it is a container superblock. The value should be NXSB.
- **Block Size:** The size in bytes of each block. Physical addresses are given in terms of block number; hence, the size of a block is required to get to the correct location in the container.
- **UUID:** From an investigative point of view the UUID may be used to determine if a device was attached to a particular computer.
- **Checkpoint Descriptor and Data Area locations:** There are a number of fields which allow the checkpoint descriptor and data areas to be located. These include descriptor blocks and descriptor base and data blocks and database.
- **OMAP OID:** This is the OID for the object map structure. This is a physical OID. The object map is used to map virtual to physical addresses.
- **Max File Systems:** The maximum number of file systems informs the size of the FS_OID array. All locations in this array should be tested to see if they contain a FS_OID item. If so (i.e. the value is non zero) there is a volume present.
- **FS_OID[]:** The virtual OIDs of the volume roots.

Table 13.6 APFS container superblock structure.

Offset	Size	Name	Description
0x00	0x20	Object Header	An object header structure (Table 13.1).
0x20	0x04	Signature	Four character signature value (NXSB).
0x24	0x04	Block Size	The size of each block in bytes.
0x28	0x08	Block Count	The total number of blocks in the container.
0x30	0x08	Features	A bit field representing the optional container features in use. Containers can still be mounted even if the implementation does not support these features.
0x38	0x08	RO Compat. Features	Read-only compatible features in use in this volume. Containers can be mounted read-only if the implementation does not support these features.
0x40	0x08	Incompat. Features	Incompatible features bit field. If the implementation doesn't support one of these features then the volume cannot be mounted.
0x48	0x10	UUID	The universally unique identifier for this container.
0x58	0x08	Next OID	The next object identifier to be used for a virtual or ephemeral object. Physical objects' OIDs are given by the actual physical address in which the object is located.
0x60	0x08	Next XID	The next transaction identifier to be used.
0x68	0x04	Desc. Blocks	The number of blocks used in the checkpoint descriptor area. The most significant bit should be ignored for calculating the number of blocks. This bit is used as a flag. If the bit is zero the checkpoint descriptor is contiguous and the descriptor base value points to the start of the area. Otherwise the area is fragmented and descriptor base gives the physical OID of a B-Tree whose values are physical size and block numbers.
0x6C	0x04	Data Blocks	The number of blocks in the checkpoint data area. The most significant bit is used as a flag (meaning as in the descriptor blocks field).
0x70	0x08	Desc. Base	Block address of the first block in the checkpoint descriptor area. If the most significant bit is set this is the physical OID for a B-Tree.
0x78	0x08	Data Base	Block address of the first block in the checkpoint data area. If the most significant bit is set this is the physical OID for a B-Tree.
0x80	0x04	Desc. Next	The next index used in the checkpoint descriptor area.
0x84	0x04	Data Next	The next index used in the checkpoint data area.
0x88	0x04	Desc. Index	The index of the first valid item in the checkpoint descriptor area.
0x8C	0x04	Desc. Length	The number of blocks in the checkpoint descriptor area used by the checkpoint this superblock points to.
0x90	0x04	Data Index	The index of the first valid item in the checkpoint data area.
0x94	0x04	Data Length	The number of blocks in the checkpoint data area used by the checkpoint that this superblock belongs to.

(Continued)

Table 13.6 (Continued)

Offset	Size	Name	Description
0x98	0x08	Spaceman OID	The ephemeral OID for the space manager.
0xA0	0x08	Object Map OID	The physical OID for the container's object map structure.
0xA8	0x08	Reaper OID	The ephemeral OID for the reaper.
0xB0	0x04	Unused	This should always be zero. Officially it can be used for testing purposes but Apple implementations never use it!
0xB4	0x04	Max. Volumes (n)	The maximum number of volumes that can be stored in this container. This is calculated by dividing the container size by 512 MiB and then rounding up. However, this value can never exceed the NX_MAX_FILE_SYSTEMS value which is generally 100_d.
0xB8	0x08 * n	Volume OID	An array of virtual OIDs for volumes. The size of this structure is determined by the maximum volumes value. The objects represent volume superblocks.

When analysing an APFS container the next step is to process the container object map structure. This will allow all the volume root structures to be located. Hence the object map OID is a physical OID, as it is necessary to locate this structure without using the object map itself. The file system OIDs (FS_OID[]) are virtual OIDs. This is why the object map must be processed in order to map these virtual OIDs to physical block addresses.

13.1.6 Volume Superblock

Every APFS volume contains a volume superblock structure which provides information relating to a particular volume. The first step in processing a volume is to process the volume superblock (VSB) structure itself. The structure of the VSB is given in Table 13.7.

The following information is generally required when processing the volume superblock:

- **Object Header:** This provides information about the object as a whole and is used to confirm it is a volume superblock (Type: 0x0D).
- **Magic:** This is also used, along with the object header type, to confirm this is a volume superblock. This value should be APSB.
- **OMap OID:** In order to map virtual OIDs to physical blocks it is necessary to process the object map tree. This value is the physical OID of this structure. Note this object map is different to the container's object map structure. Every volume will have its own object map structure.
- **Root Tree OID:** This value is the root node of the file system B-Tree and is where file recovery will commence. This is a virtual OID which can be mapped to a physical OID using the object map.

The volume superblock contains further information which might be helpful for an investigation:

- **Unmount Time:** This is the time at which the device was last unmounted. Assuming this is accurate it gives some indication of when the device was last used. However, it is dependent on the file system driver's implementation whether it is updated correctly or not!

Table 13.7 APFS volume superblock structure.

Offset	Size	Name	Description
0x00	0x20	Object Header	An object header structure.
0x20	0x04	Magic	Signature value (APSB).
0x24	0x04	FS Index	Volume index in the CSB's FS_OID array.
0x28	0x08	Features	The optional features in use in this volume. The volume can still be mounted even if the implementation does not support these.
0x30	0x08	RO Compat. Features	A bit field of features that are read-only compatible. If the implementation does not support one or more of these the volume should be mounted read only.
0x38	0x08	Incompat. Features	A bit field of incompatible features. If the implementation does not support one or more of these the volume should not be mounted.
0x40	0x08	Unmount Time	The time the volume was last unmounted.
0x48	0x08	Reserved Block Count	The number of blocks reserved for this volume to allocate.
0x50	0x08	Quota Block Count	The maximum number of blocks that this volume can allocate.
0x58	0x08	Allocated Count	The number of blocks that are currently allocated to this volume.
0x60	0x14	Crypto	Information about encryption.
0x74	0x04	Root Tree Type	The root tree type.
0x78	0x04	Extent Tree Type	The extent tree type.
0x7C	0x04	Snapshot Tree Type	The snapshot tree type.
0x80	0x08	OMAP OID	Physical OID of volume object map.
0x88	0x08	Root Tree OID	Virtual OID of file system tree root node.
0x90	0x08	Extent Tree OID	Physical OID of extent reference tree.
0x98	0x08	Snapshot Tree OID	Virtual OID of snapshot metadata tree.
0xA0	0x08	Revert to XID	The transaction ID (XID) of a snapshot that this volume reverts to.
0xA8	0x08	Revert to OID	The physical OID of the volume superblock that the volume reverts to.
0xB0	0x08	Next OID	The next OID that will be assigned to a file system object in this volume.
0xB8	0x08	Num. Files	The number of regular files in this volume.
0xC0	0x08	Num. Directories	The number of directories in this volume.
0xC8	0x08	Num. Symlinks	The number of symbolic links in this volume.
0xD0	0x08	Num. Other FS Objects	The number of other files in this volume. This includes anything that is not a regular file, directory or symbolic link. This might include sockets, character/block devices, etc.
0xD8	0x08	Num. Snapshots	The number of snapshots in this volume.
0xE0	0x08	Total Blocks Allocated	The total number of blocks that have been allocated by this volume. This number does not decrease when blocks are freed.

(Continued)

Table 13.7 (Continued)

Offset	Size	Name	Description
0xE8	0x08	Total Blocks Freed	The total number of blocks that have been freed by this volume.
0xF0	0x10	Volume UUID	The universally unique identifier for this volume.
0x100	0x08	Last Modified Time	The time at which the volume was last modified.
0x108	0x08	FS Flags	The Volume's flags (see the Apple File System Reference document for a list of flags).
0x110	0x30	Formatted By	Information about the software that was used to create this volume. This field contains a 0x20 byte string that provides the name of the software. An 0x08 byte timestamp of when the software last modified the device and an 0x08 byte XID which is the last transaction identifier of this program's modifications.
0x140	0x30 * 8	Modified By	Information about the software that has modified this volume. There is space for eight items in this (each is 0x30 bytes in size and has the same structure as the formatted by field). The newest instance is stored in position zero of the array – older instances are shifted upwards.
0x2C0	0x100	Volume Name	The volume name. This is stored as a NULL (0x00) terminated UTF-8 string.
0x3C0	0x04	Next Doc. ID	Used with the document ID extended attribute.
0x3C4	0x02	Role	See below.

Note there are other items in the VSB structure but they are of little importance for forensic analysis. For the complete structure see the Apple File System Reference document.

- **FS Statistics:** Information about the number of files, number of directories, etc. may be of interest to the investigation. It can also be used as a means of ensuring that all files have been recovered from the device.
- **Volume UUID:** As with the container UUID this value may appear in logs showing usage of this structure.
- **Last Modified Time:** This value can again show usage of the file system.
- **Formatted by and Modified by:** These values can show what software was used to create the device initially and also any software used to modify the device. Software version numbers might be helpful in linking the device to a certain OS/computer – although of course there will be multiple instances of the same version number.
- **Volume Name:** The name of the volume as given when the volume was created.
- **Role:** This might show if it was a specific system volume. This could lead to prioritising the device based on the likelihood of finding evidence in this file system.

13.1.7 Object Maps

Object map structures provide a means of converting a virtual OID into a physical address of the content block. They are essential in the analysis of APFS. There are a number of object maps in existence. Firstly there is an object map at the container level. It is this object map that is used to map the virtual FS_OID values to physical addresses; in other words, it is used to find the volume superblocks. However, there is also an object map in every volume. This is used for volume-level virtual OIDs.

Object maps store information in a B-Tree. The first block of an object map stores information about the object map itself, including the physical OID for the object map tree's root node. The structure of this block is shown in Table 13.8. In this B-Tree structure keys consist of a combination of OID and XID, while the values contain the 8_d-byte physical addresses (i.e. block offsets) along with some further information (the structure of these values is given in Table 13.9).

When analysing the object map information block the following information is vital:

- **Object Header:** Used to ensure this is an object map information block.
- **Tree OID:** The physical OID for the actual object map tree itself. It is here that the actual mappings will be found.

Processing continues by processing the actual object map B-Tree itself. The tree is a standard APFS B-Tree (Section 13.1.3) where the keys are 16_d bytes consisting of an 8_d-byte OID and 8_d-byte XID. Object map B-Tree values are 16_d bytes in size. The structure of these is shown in Table 13.9.

The object mapping is constructed by combining the keys and values. The key OID is the virtual OID for the object. The value's physical address field contains the physical block at which the key's virtual OID is located.

13.1.8 File-Related Structures

Each APFS volume has a file system tree. The virtual OID of this tree is found in the volume superblock. This can then be mapped to a physical block address using the volume object map.

Table 13.8 The object map structure.

Offset	Size	Name	Description
0x00	0x20	Object Header	An object header structure (Table 13.1).
0x20	0x04	Flags	Flag values: **0x01:** No snapshots; **0x02:** Encrypting; **0x04:** Decrypting; **0x08:** Keyrolling (encryption); **0x10:** Crypto generation.
0x24	0x04	Snapshot Count	The number of snapshots present in this object map.
0x28	0x04	Tree Type	The type of tree used for the object map.
0x2C	0x04	Snapshot Tree Type	The type of tree used for snapshots.
0x30	0x08	Tree OID	Physical OID of object map B-Tree.
0x38	0x08	Snapshot Tree OID	Physical OID of snapshot B-Tree.
0x40	0x08	Most Recent Snapshot	Transaction ID (XID) of the most recent snapshot stored in this object map.
0x48	0x08	Pending Revert Min.	Smallest XID for an in-progress event.
0x50	0x08	Pending Revert Max.	Largest XID for an in-progress event.

Table 13.9 Structure of the object map B-Tree values.

Offset	Size	Name	Description
0x00	0x04	Flags	Flags describing the particular mapping. These are the same as those for the object map structure itself (Table 13.8).
0x04	0x04	Size	The allocated size of the object in bytes. This is always a multiple of the block size (found in the CSB).
0x08	0x08	Physical Address	Physical block address of the object.

APFS uses a B-Tree structure to store file related information. This includes inodes (containing file metadata), directory records (showing the files present in a directory) and extents (allowing data content to be located) along with a number of other records. This section examines some of these structures.

Processing of the file system tree is the fundamental task in file system forensics. This structure allows files to be listed and also allows for metadata and content recovery. Hence, knowledge of this structure is vital for all digital forensic analysts.

13.1.8.1 File System Keys

As the file system information is stored in a tree, it consists of key-value pairs. Most file related structures have a similar key structure. This section presents the key structure most commonly encountered in the file system tree. Deviations from this generic file system key structure are provided when appropriate.

The default key is a simple 8_d byte structure which contains a bit field representing the Object type and OID (O_{TID}). In order to access the actual type and OID, minor calculations are performed on the 8_d-byte value. The Apple File System Reference document defines two constants that are used in these calculations. These are:

- **OBJ_ID_MASK (O_{ID_m}):** This mask has a value of 0x0FFFFFFFFFFFFFFF and is used to determine the OID from the complex structure.
- **OBJ_TYPE_MASK (O_{T_m}):** This mask has a value of 0xF000000000000000 and is used to determine the object type from the complex structure.

The following formulae show how these are used in calculation. Equation 13.1 shows the calculation of the OID (O_{ID}) from the complex value. This is achieved by performing a binary AND operation using the OBJ_ID_MASK value. The result of this provides the OID. Similarly Equation 13.2 shows the calculation of the object-type value (O_T). This involves a binary AND operation with the OBJ_TYPE_MASK value, the result of which is then right-shifted 60_d positions. The meaning of the object-type values is given in Table 13.10.

$$O_{ID} = O_{TID} \ \& \ O_{ID_m} \tag{13.1}$$

$$O_T = (O_{TID} \ \& \ O_{T_m}) >> 60 \tag{13.2}$$

When listing files in an APFS volume the object ID shown here is the actual inode number used by the file system.

Table 13.10 Object-type codes for file system tree keys.

Code	Type	Code	Type
0x0	Any: A record of any type. Only used for testing.	0x8	File Extent: A physical extent record for a file. This allows the file's content to be located.
0x1	Snapshot metadata.	0x9	Directory Record: A directory entry recording information on the file's presence in a directory.
0x2	Extent: A physical extent record.	0xA	Directory Statistics: Information about a directory.
0x3	Inode record: This structure allows for metadata recovery.	0xB	Snapshot name.
0x4	XAttr: An extended attribute.	0xC	Sibling Map: A mapping from a hard link to a target.
0x5	Sibling Link: A mapping from an inode to hard links of which the inode is the target.	0xD	File Info: Additional information about a file.
0x6	DStream: A data stream object.	0xF	Invalid: An invalid object type.
0x7	Crypto State: Information about file encryption.		

13.1.8.2 Inode

Inodes are one of the most important structures in performing file system forensics. The inode structure contains all the metadata about a file. This includes time information, file size, owners, etc. The inode structure in APFS uses the generic file system key shown in the previous section. The inode value structure is provided in Table 13.11.

Table 13.11 is not the sole provider of metadata. It is also necessary to process the file mode and extended fields. The file mode is identical to that encountered in EXT file systems. For details on processing this structure see Section 8.1.3.1.

Extended fields are used for extra data associated with the inode. Both inodes and directory records may contain extended fields. To determine if a record contains an extended field the file system tree node's table of contents is consulted. If the value length of an inode is greater than 0x5C bytes the record contains extended fields. Similarly if the value length of a directory record in the table of contents is greater than 0x12 bytes the entry contains extended fields.

The structure of the extended fields is shown in Figure 13.4. The extended field area is composed of three parts. The first of these is the extended field information structure. This provides information about all the extended fields present in this area. The structure of this is provided in Table 13.12. This is followed by an array of items providing information about each individual extended field. The number of elements in this array is the total number of extended fields present in the record. The structure of these entries is provided in Table 13.12. Finally the extended field area contains the data array. Again this area contains one entry per extended field in the record. The structure of this data is dependent on the type of record in question. The various extended field type values are shown in Table 13.13.

Table 13.11 APFS inode structure.

Offset	Size	Name	Description
0x00	0x08	Parent ID	Parent directory inode.
0x08	0x08	Private ID	Unique ID used by file's data stream.
0x10	0x08	Creation Time	File's creation time.
0x18	0x08	Modification Time	File's modification time.
0x20	0x08	Change Time	File's metadata change time.
0x28	0x08	Access Time	File's last accessed time.
0x30	0x08	Flags	Flags representing this particular inode. Values can be found in the Apple File System Reference Documentation.
0x38	0x04	Num Children/Links	This field's content is dependent on the file type. For directory inodes this is the number of children. For file inodes this is the number of hard links.
0x3C	0x04	Protection Class	The default protection class.
0x40	0x04	Write Gen. Count	Counter that is incremented every time this inode or its data is modified. Note that this value can wrap!
0x44	0x04	BSD Flags	BSD Flags.
0x48	0x04	Owner	The Owner ID of the file's owner (UID).
0x4C	0x04	Group	The group ID (GID) owning the file.
0x50	0x02	Mode	The file mode (Linux permissions).
0x52	0x02	Padding	Reserved.
0x54	0x08	Size	The uncompressed size of the file. This is zero if the file is compressed.
0x5C	???	Extended Fields	This area contains the inode's extended fields.

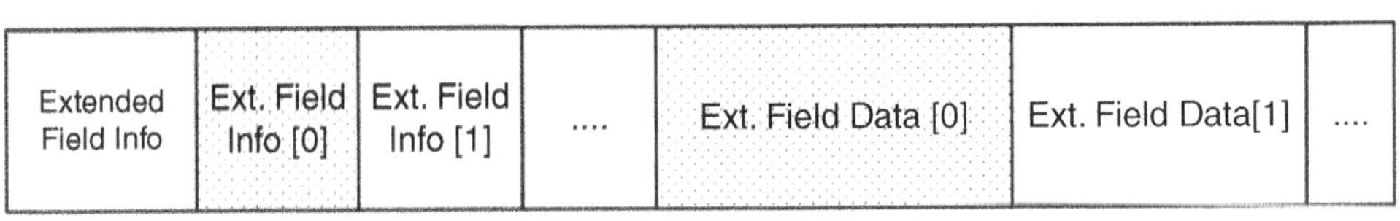

Figure 13.4 Extended field structure.

The two most commonly encountered extended fields in inodes are that of filename (type 0x4) and data stream (type 0x8). The filename structure is trivial, it is merely a null (0x00) terminated UTF-8 string. The data stream structure is more complex and is shown in Table 13.14. The data stream allows for the actual file size, along with other information, to be obtained.

The inode structure, along with its extended fields, allows all metadata to be recovered. This includes the various timestamps associated with the file, along with the filename (in the file name extended field), the file size (in the data stream extended field), owner and group information.

13.1.8.3 Directory Record

Directory records store information about the file's that are present in a directory (and also the time that they were added to the directory). The directory record key is formed from the OID followed

Table 13.12 Extended field information structure.

Offset	Size	Name	Description
0x00	0x01	Type	The extended field's data type (Table 13.13).
0x01	0x01	Flags	Extended field's flags. Values for these can be found in the Apple File System Reference document.
0x02	0x02	Size	The size in bytes of the stored data in the extended field. Note that as attributes are aligned to 8_d-byte boundaries, the next field may not start immediately after the preceding field.

Table 13.13 Extended field data-type values.

Value	Type	Value	Type
0x1	Sibling ID if found in a directory record. Snapshot ID if found in an inode.	0x9	Reserved.
0x2	Virtual OID of the snapshot extent delta list.	0xA	Directory statistics.
0x3	The file's document identifier.	0xB	Reserved.
0x4	File Name. The data is a null (0x00) terminated UTF-8 encoded string.	0xC	Reserved.
0x5	Previous file size.	0xD	Sparse Bytes: The number of sparse bytes in the data stream.
0x6	Reserved.	0xE	RDev: Device identifier for a block or character device.
0x7	Finder info.	0xF	Reserved.
0x8	Data stream.	0x10	Synchronisation root.

Table 13.14 Extended field data stream structure.

Offset	Size	Name	Description
0x00	0x08	Size (Actual)	Size (in bytes) of the data.
0x08	0x08	Size (Allocated)	Allocated size (in bytes) of the data.
0x10	0x08	Crypto ID	Default encryption key used.
0x18	0x08	Total Bytes Written	Total number of bytes written to this data stream.
0x20	0x08	Total Bytes Read	Total number of bytes read from the data stream.

by a four-byte name length and hash value.[2] This structure uses the least significant 10_d bits as the length and the remaining 22_d bits as a hash value. This is followed by the null-terminated file name. The directory record value structure is given in Table 13.15.

2 The hash value is calculated over the normalised UTF-32 name (including the null terminator) using complemented CRC-32. Only the lower 22_d bits are maintained.

Table 13.15 Directory record structure.

Offset	Size	Name	Description
0x00	0x08	File ID	The inode of the file that this record represents.
0x08	0x08	Date Added	The time that this directory record was added to the directory.
0x10	0x02	Flags	Directory Entry Flags: These provide the file type. The following values are possible: **0x00:** Unknown; **0x01:** FIFO; **0x02:** Character device; **0x04:** Directory; **0x06:** Block device; **0x08:** Regular file; **0x0A:** Link; **0x0C:** Socket; **s0x0E:** WHT.
0x12	???	Extended Fields	Identical to the extended fields found in the inode structure.

Notice that the directory record structure provides further temporal information in relation to files. The timestamp located in the directory record is the time at which the record was added to the directory; in other words, the time at which the file was created in this directory. This time might represent file creation or a copy/move operation.

13.1.8.4 Extent

The final piece of information that is required is the file's content. The file system B-Tree contains file extent records. These are used to locate the file's contents. Extents are commonly used in many modern file systems. The extent gives a starting block and a number of blocks. Multiple extents are encountered if a file is fragmented.

The key for the file extent record consists of the OID and the logical starting point in the file. Consider the case in which three keys are present for a file (Inode Number 0x15). The keys are:

- Inode: 0x15 AND Logical Address 0x00;
- Inode: 0x15 AND Logical Address 0x20;
- Inode: 0x15 AND Logical Address 0x30.

The first key points to the extent which contains the first 0x20 blocks of the data starting at logical block 0x00. The number of blocks can be determined by checking the logical address in the subsequent key. The second points to the value that contains the next 0x10 blocks of data, and the final key points to the extent value which contains the remaining data. Notice that the sorting order will mean extents appear in the B-Tree in the order they need to be processed!

The file extent value structure is provided in Table 13.16.

13.1.9 Checkpoints

Checkpoints are used extensively in APFS to ensure file system integrity and implement copy-on-write updating. This means that it is possible to find older versions of structures in APFS

Table 13.16 File extent value structure.

Offset	Size	Name	Description
0x00	0x08	Length/Flags	Length and Flags Bitfield: Currently there are no flags defined for this value so the entire value can be used as the length in bytes! Strictly speaking the value should be AND'd with 0x00FFFFFFFFFFFFFF to get the length and AND'd with 0xFF00000000000000 and right-shifted 56 places to get the flags. The length is given in bytes but is always a multiple of the block size.
0x08	0x08	Physical Block Num.	The physical block number at which the extent starts.
0x10	0x08	Crypto ID	Encryption key information.

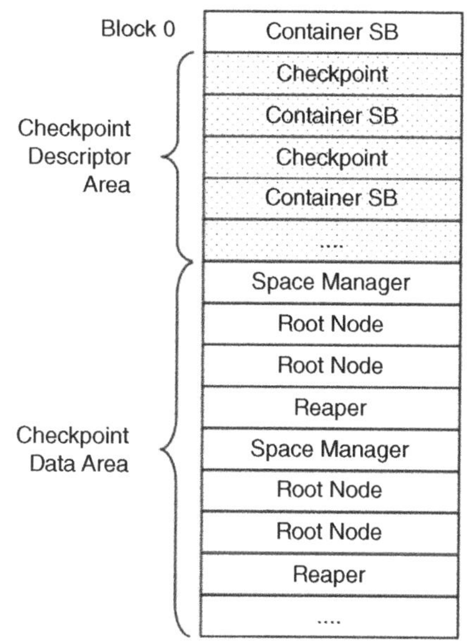

Figure 13.5 APFS container structure showing the checkpoint descriptor and data areas.

file systems. The container superblock is immediately followed by a checkpoint descriptor area and a checkpoint data area. The starting locations and size of these are determined from the container superblock. Figure 13.5 shows the general layout of this area.

The locations of the data area are found in the container superblock itself. The checkpoint descriptor area contains a checkpoint mapping structure (which maps ephemeral objects to their place in the checkpoint data area) and a container superblock. The checkpoint mapping block begins with two four byte fields immediately after the object header. These are the flags and the number of checkpoint mappings in the block. Note the checkpoint map may contain more than one single block. The only valid flag is 0x01. If this is set the current block is the last block in the checkpoint map. If this is not set then the next block contains more checkpoint maps.

This is followed by an array of checkpoint maps each of which follows the structure shown in Table 13.17.

The combination of copy-on-write and checkpointing means that much information can be found from older versions of file systems. For instance, consider a volume's file system tree. If

Table 13.17 Checkpoint mapping structure.

Offset	Size	Name	Description
0x00	0x04	Type/Flags	The object type – the low 16 bits indicate the type and the high 16 bits represent the flags (see Section 13.1.2).
0x04	0x04	Subtype	The object subtype (see Section 13.1.2).
0x08	0x04	Size	The object size in bytes.
0x0C	0x04	Padding	Reserved.
0x10	0x08	FS OID	Virtual OID of the volume the object is associated with.
0x18	0x08	OID	Ephemeral OID for this object.
0x20	0x08	Physical Address	The physical address in the checkpoint data area where this object is stored.

a change is made to that structure a new, modified copy will be created (copy-on-write) but the old copy is still present. Checkpointing means that checkpoints are routinely created during the system, so not only is the older version of the file system tree present on disk, it is also still allocated as it is part of a checkpoint! This means that older versions of the file system can be recovered in APFS. The recovery of these checkpoints will be discussed further in Section 13.3.2.

13.1.10 Other APFS Structures

There are a number of other APFS artefacts that are of interest but generally less relevant to digital forensics. This section briefly introduces some of these artefacts including the space manager and the reaper.

The space manager is responsible for maintaining the allocation status of blocks in the file system. It can also be used to pre-allocate blocks for certain files. The space manager keeps track of the allocation status of all blocks in the file system.

The reaper allows large objects to be deleted over multiple transactions. This improves efficiency in the file system. The deletion of a large object will not affect other file operations in the file system.

13.2 Analysis of APFS

This section examines the analysis methods that are required for the successful analysis of the APFS file system. Unlike other file systems APFS is not supported by Sleuth Kit, and as such it is not possible to verify findings. This section begins with an overview of the creation of APFS file systems on macOS and then introduces some of the supplied file systems. Section 13.2.3 introduces the manual analysis of APFS from the gathering of container and volume information to file and metadata recovery.

13.2.1 Creating APFS File Systems

In order to create an APFS file system macOS is generally used. At the time of writing there is no write support for APFS on Linux.[3] Listing 13.1 shows the command to create an APFS container on **/dev/disk5** in macOS. Note that the disk utility app can also be used.

3 Read-only support is provided through the **apfs-fuse** module.

```
diskutil partitionDisk disk5 GPT \
         apfs APFS-FS 512M \
         free temp R
```

Listing 13.1 Using **diskutil** to create an APFS container on macOS.

The **diskutil** command is used to perform many operations on physical devices in macOS. The command is provided a verb, in this case **partitionDisk**, which partitions the disk and creates a file system. In order to use APFS the GPT partitioning scheme must be specified. APFS will not function with MBR or other partitioning schemes. The second line in the command provided in Listing 13.1 relates to the partition/file system itself. In this case the file system type is provided, **apfs**, followed by the file system name, **APFS-FS**. Finally the size of the file system is given as 512M. The final line is provided to ensure that the remaining space on the device is kept free. This is achieved through creating a *dummy* partition/file system. During initial file system creation failure to do this resulted in a file system which occupied the entire device, not just the 512M provided to the command.

13.2.2 Supplied APFS Image Files

Table 13.18 shows the supplied disk images in this lesson. Analysis will commence with the **APFS_V1.E01** image file. This contains a simple APFS volume which was created on macOS 12.6. A single volume (**APFS-FS**) was created in this container to which a single user directory and four files were added. The initial manual analysis of APFS will analyse this image and attempt to recover a file along with its associated metadata.

The subsequent images are used to demonstrate some advanced topics in the analysis of APFS. In **APFS_V2.E01** two files have been deleted from the original **APFS_V1.E01** file system. The file system in **APFS_V3.E01** contains many files which require the use of multi-layer B-Trees for metadata storage and is used to demonstrate searching the file system tree for particular entries. **APFS_V4.E01** contains two volumes to show the method of processing multi-volume containers. Finally, **APFS_V5.E01** contains a hard and soft link.

13.2.3 APFS Manual Analysis

This section presents a method to manually analyse an APFS container. There are a number of steps that need to be performed during analysis in order to recover files and metadata. This process involves:

Table 13.18 Supplied APFS container images.

Filename	Description
APFS_V1.E01	A simple APFS container with one volume containing a single user-created directory and four files. There are also a number of macOS system files on the device.
APFS_V2.E01	Two files were deleted (and trash emptied) from **APFS_V1.E01** to create this disk image.
APFS_V3.E01	This contains many files meaning that multi-layer B-Trees are required for storage of all metadata.
APFS_V4.E01	This image contains an APFS container with two volumes.
APFS_V5.E01	An APFS file system with hard and soft links.

1) **Process the Container Superblock:** The container superblock provides general information about the container as a whole. Additionally it provides the locations of the various volume roots, but these OIDs are virtual. The CSB is also required to locate the container object map.
2) **Process the Container Object Map:** The container object map provides a means of mapping virtual OIDs to physical block addresses in order to locate the volume roots. Processing the container object map (indeed processing of all object maps) is a two-step process. The object map is used to locate the object map B-Tree which is then processed to determine the mappings from OID to physical address.
3) **Process the Volume Superblock:** For each volume located in the container superblock the volume superblock is then processed. This structure provides the virtual OID of the file system tree. In order to map this to a physical address it is also necessary to determine the physical OID of the volume's object map structure.
4) **Process the Volume Object Map:** This is identical to step 2 for the container-level object map structure. It allows the root of the file system tree to be located.
5) **Process the file system tree:** The task of processing the file system tree involves listing all files and recovering metadata and content.

The remainder of this section will look at each of these steps in more detail using **APFS_V1.E01** as an exemplar.

13.2.3.1 Process the Container Superblock

Listing 13.2 shows an excerpt from the container superblock structure of **APFS_V1.E01**. This listing contains the object header also (first 0x20 bytes). Alternate fields are highlighted. Table 13.19 shows some of the processed values.

```
0000000: 14e9 d704 8603 52dc 0100 0000 0000 0000  ......R.........
0000010: 0800 0000 0000 0000 0100 0080 0000 0000  ................
0000020: 4e58 5342 0010 0000 48e8 0100 0000 0000  NXSB....H.......
0000030: 0000 0000 0000 0000 0000 0000 0000 0000  ................
0000040: 0200 0000 0000 0000 5b66 8f13 3d52 47b2  ........[f..=RG.
0000050: 9410 bd4a 265f 8300 0804 0000 0000 0000  ...J&_..........
0000060: 0900 0000 0000 0000 0800 0000 8001 0000  ................
0000070: 0100 0000 0000 0000 0900 0000 0000 0000  ................
0000080: 0000 0000 1e00 0000 0600 0000 0200 0000  ................
0000090: 1a00 0000 0400 0000 0004 0000 0000 0000  ................
00000a0: 7e02 0000 0000 0000 0104 0000 0000 0000  ~...............
00000b0: 0000 0000 0100 0000 0204 0000 0000 0000  ................
00000c0: 0000 0000 0000 0000 0000 0000 0000 0000  ................
```

Listing 13.2 An excerpt from the container superblock of **APFS_V1.E01**

The first pieces of key information are required to confirm that this is a container superblock. This is discovered from two sources: the object header's type value of 0x01 (Offset: 0x18) and the CSB's magic signature value of *NXSB* (Offset: 0x20). The combination of these values along with the OID of 0x01 (Offset: 0x08) confirm that this structure is indeed the container superblock.

Following the confirmation of the container superblock it is now possible to process the CSB in its entirety. Table 13.19 shows the required information from the CSB in order to perform file system forensic analysis. However, as shown in Table 13.6 there is much more information present.

Table 13.19 Partially processed container superblock from **APFS_V1.dd**.

Offset	Size	Name	Value
0x08	0x08	OID	0x01 (1_d)
0x10	0x08	XID	0x08 (8_d)
0x18	0x02	Type	0x01 (1_d – CSB)
0x1A	0x02	Flags	0x8000 (Ephemeral)
0x20	0x04	Magic	NXSB
0x24	0x04	Block Size	0x1000 (4096_d)
0xA0	0x08	Obj. Map OID	0x27E (638_d)
0xB4	0x04	Max. Volumes	$0x1_d$
0xB8	0x08	FS_OID[0]	0x402 (1026_d)

Block size is a vital item for continued processing. All physical addresses in APFS are provided in terms of block offsets. Hence to jump to the exact position it is necessary to know the size of each block in the file system. The block size is located at offset 0x24 and has a value of 0x1000 (4096_d) bytes in Listing 13.2.

The next step is to determine how many volumes are present in the container and where these are. The maximum number of volumes is found to be 0x01. The volume roots are located in an array at offset 0xB8. Each entry in this array is 0x08 bytes in size with one entry per file system max. value. In the case in Listing 13.2 only a single element in this array has a value. This volume's superblock has a virtual OID of 0x402 (1026_d). As this is virtual it must be located in the container's object map structure so that the physical location on disk can be determined. The physical OID of the object map is also located in the CSB. In the case of Listing 13.2 this value is 0x27E (638_d). This means that the object map structure is located at byte offset 0x27E × 0x1000.

13.2.3.2 Process the Container Object Map

Having located the container object map from the CSB the next step is to process this structure in order to determine the location of each volume. Listing 13.3 shows the contents of the object map structure itself. These values are processed in Table 13.20.

```
027e000: 74c7 ebff 7533 1440 7e02 0000 0000 0000 t...u3.@~.......
027e010: 0800 0000 0000 0000 0b00 0040 0000 0000 ...........@....
027e020: 0100 0000 0000 0000 0200 0040 0200 0040 ...........@...@
027e030: 7f02 0000 0000 0000 0000 0000 0000 0000 ................
027e040: 0000 0000 0000 0000 0000 0000 0000 0000 ................
```

Listing 13.3 The container object map structure from **APFS_V1.E01**.

The object map structure is used to locate the root of the object map B-Tree. This value, Tree OID, is a physical OID which in this case has the value 0x27F (639_d). Listing 13.4 shows the object and node headers for this root tree node. Table 13.21 shows the processed values from this.

The object header informs the analyst that this object is a root node (type 0x02) of an object map tree (subtype 0x0B). The node header flag value is 0x07 – this is 0x01 + 0x02 + 0x04. This means

Table 13.20 Partially processed container object from Listing 13.3.

Offset	Size	Name	Value
0x08	0x08	OID	0x27E (638_d)
0x10	0x08	XID	0x08 (8_d)
0x18	0x02	Type	0x0B (B-Tree)
0x1A	0x02	Flags	0x4000 (Physical)
0x30	0x08	Tree OID	0x27F (639_d)

```
027f000: 4724 511e 729f ec91 7f02 0000 0000 0000 G$Q.r...........
027f010: 0800 0000 0000 0000 0200 0040 0b00 0000 ...........@....
027f020: 0700 0000 0100 0000 0000 c001 2000 a00d ............ ...
027f030: 1000 1000 2000 1000                     .... ...
```

Listing 13.4 Object and node headers of the root node from the container object map.

Table 13.21 Partially processed object and node headers of the object map B-Tree root node (Listing 13.4).

Offset	Size	Name	Value
0x08	0x08	OID	0x27F (639_d)
0x10	0x08	XID	0x08 (8_d)
0x18	0x02	Type	0x02 (Root Node)
0x1A	0x02	OH Flags	0x4000 (Physical)
0x1C	0x04	Subtype	0x0B (Object Map)
0x20	0x02	NH Flags	0x07 (0x04 + 0x02 + 0x01) 0x04: Fixed key-value size 0x02: Leaf node 0x01: Root node.
0x22	0x02	Level	0x00 (0_d)
0x24	0x04	Num. Keys	0x01 (1_d)
0x28	0x02	ToC Offset	0x00 (0_d)
0x2A	0x02	ToC Length	0x1C0 (448_d)

that this node is a root node (0x01), a leaf node (0x02) and that this node contains fixed key value lengths (0x04). As expected the level of this node is 0x00 (it has to be as it is a leaf node!). The node contains only a single key.

The final task is to locate the table of contents for this node. This occurs at offset 0x00. This offset is relative to the end of the node header (0x38); hence, the table of contents is found immediately after the node header, 0x38 bytes into the node itself. The table of contents is 0x1C0 bytes in length. When, at a later stage, the key offsets are located, these key offsets will be relative to this point.

Table 13.22 Partially processed B-Tree information area from Listing 13.5.

Offset	Size	Name	Value
0x00	0x04	Flags	0x12 Sequential Insert; Physical OIDs for children.
0x04	0x04	Node Size	0x1000 (4096_d)
0x08	0x04	Key Size	0x10 (16_d)
0x0C	0x04	Value Size	0x10 (16_d)
0x18	0x08	Key Count	0x01 (1_d)
0x20	0x08	Node Count	0x01 (1_d)

As this is a root node, the final 0x28 bytes contain a B-Tree information structure. The raw data from this area is shown in Listing 13.5 along with the command used to extract it. The processed values are shown in Table 13.22.

```
$ xxd -s $((0x280 * 0x1000 - 0x28)) -l $((0x28)) mnt/ewf1
027ffd8: 1200 0000 0010 0000 1000 0000 1000 0000 ................
027ffe8: 1000 0000 1000 0000 0100 0000 0000 0000 ................
027fff8: 0100 0000 0000 0000                     ........
```

Listing 13.5 The B-Tree information structure in the container object map B-Tree root node in **APFS_V1.E01**.

The most important information in the B-Tree information area in the case of a node with fixed key value sizes are actual key and value sizes. Table 13.22 shows that both keys and values are of 0x10 bytes in size.

From the node header it was determined that the table of contents starts immediately after the node header (Offset: 0x00). This means that the table of contents begins at 0x38. The node header also informs the analyst of the number of keys in this particular node (0x01). As the keys and values have a fixed size, each table of contents entry merely consists of a two-byte key offset and a two-byte value offset. The entire table of contents (and the command used to extract it) is shown in Listing 13.6.

```
$ xxd -s $((0x27F * 0x1000 + 0x38)) -l 4 mnt/ewf1
0027f038: 0000 1000                              ....
```

Listing 13.6 The table of contents from the container object map's B-Tree root node.

This means that the key can be found at offset 0x00 relative to the end of the table of contents, and the value can be found at offset 0x10, relative to the start of the B-Tree information structure. Remember this value offset must be subtracted from the starting point! Hence the offset to the key is given by adding the size of the object header (0x20), the size of the node header (0x18), the offset to the table of contents (0x00) and the length of the table of contents (0x1C0). From the B-Tree information structure the key length is 0x10 bytes and from Listing 13.6 the offset to the start of the key is known to be 0x00.

Similarly the value offset (0x10) is relative to the end of the node (or the start of the B-Tree information structure in this case). The easiest way to calculate this value is to take the byte offset to the start of the next block (0x280 * 0x1000 in this case) and subtract 0x28 (it is a root node) and then subtract the value offset (0x10). Again the value size is fixed at 0x10 bytes. Listing 13.7 shows the key and value being extracted from the disk image.

```
$ xxd -s $((0x27F * 0x1000 + 0x1F8)) -l $((0x10)) mnt/ewf1
027f1f8: 0204 0000 0000 0000 0800 0000 0000 0000 ................
$
$ xxd -s $((0x280 * 0x1000 - 0x28 - 0x10)) -l $((0x10)) mnt/ewf1
027ffc8: 0000 0000 0010 0000 7d02 0000 0000 0000 ........}.......
```

Listing 13.7 Extraction of the object map B-Tree key and value.

Object map keys are composed of an 8_d-byte virtual OID and an 8_d-byte transaction ID (XID). Examining the key in Listing 13.7 shows that this represents the virtual OID 0x402 and XID 0x08. Returning to the container superblock the virtual OID of the volume present in this container was 0x402 – hence, the entry for this virtual OID has been found!

The value consists of a four-byte flag, followed by a four-byte size. The final 8_d bytes in the value represents the physical address, in this case 0x27D. Hence the object map structure allows the virtual OID 0x402 to be translated to a physical OID of 0x27D. At this stage the processing of the volume itself can begin.

13.2.3.3 Process the Volume Superblock

The container superblock shows that there is a single volume present in this container with a virtual OID of 0x402. The container's object map shows that this virtual OID maps to a physical block address of 0x27D. The next step is to process the volume superblock (VSB) found at this location. The contents of the VSB are shown in Listing 13.8, and the interpretation of some of this data is shown in Table 13.23. The aim of this exercise is to locate the file system tree for which the volume object map will need to be processed.

Processing of the VSB shows that the root node of the file system tree has a virtual OID of 0x404. As this is virtual it must be found in the volume object map. This structure has the physical OID of 0x278. The next step is to process the volume object map.

13.2.3.4 Process the Volume Object Map

The structure of the volume object map is identical to that of the container object map. Processing of this structure is left as an exercise for the reader.

The object map structure itself (block 0x278) shows that the object map B-Tree is found at block 0x279. When processing this the flags show that this node is both a root and a leaf and that it has fixed size keys and values. Processing of this tree results in three object mappings. Virtual OID 0x404 maps to a physical address of 0x26F, virtual OID 0x406 maps to a physical address of 0x272 and virtual OID 0x407 maps to a physical address of 0x277. From processing the volume superblock structure the root of the file system tree is found at a virtual address of 0x404 which corresponds to

```
027d000: 227a 10bc a8fb 1ce5 0204 0000 0000 0000 "z..............
027d010: 0800 0000 0000 0000 0d00 0000 0000 0000 ................
027d020: 4150 5342 0000 0000 0200 0000 0000 0000 APSB............
027d030: 0000 0000 0000 0000 0100 0000 0000 0000 ................
027d040: f8e4 2c2e 08d1 a617 0000 0000 0000 0000..,.............
027d050: 0000 0000 0000 0000 af00 0000 0000 0000 ................
027d060: 0500 0000 0000 0000 0600 0000 7300 4715 ............s.G.
027d070: 0100 0000 0200 0000 0200 0040 0200 0040 ...........@...@
027d080: 7802 0000 0000 0000 0404 0000 0000 0000 x...............
027d090: 6d02 0000 0000 0000 ad01 0000 0000 0000 m...............
027d0a0: 0000 0000 0000 0000 0000 0000 0000 0000 ................
027d0b0: 1700 0000 0000 0000 0500 0000 0000 0000 ................
027d0c0: 0200 0000 0000 0000 0000 0000 0000 0000 ................
027d0d0: 0000 0000 0000 0000 0000 0000 0000 0000 ................
027d0e0: a800 0000 0000 0000 0000 0000 0000 0000 ................
027d0f0: b798 8546 ed3b 43d9 9c4c 04dc a472 623c ...F.;C..L...rb<
027d100: d13b 232e 08d1 a617 0100 0000 0000 0000.;#.............
027d110: 6e65 7766 735f 6170 6673 2028 3139 3334 newfs_apfs (1934
027d120: 2e31 3431 2e32 2900 0000 0000 0000 0000.141.2).........
027d130: 705c 73b4 ecd0 a617 0200 0000 0000 0000 p\s.............
...[snip]...
027d2c0: 4150 4653 2d46 5300 0000 0000 0000 0000 APFS-FS.........
```

Listing 13.8 Contents of the VSB in **APFS_V1.E01**. Note that some information has been removed.

the physical block 0x26F. Hence the root of the file system tree will be found in block 0x26F. The next step in file recovery is to process the file system tree.

13.2.3.5 Process the File System Tree

Listing 13.9 shows the contents of the object and node headers of the volume's file system tree (Block: 0x26F). A selection of the processed values is shown in Table 13.24.

```
026f000: 4d6c f1d4 4b13 c078 0404 0000 0000 0000 Ml..K..x........
026f010: 0600 0000 0000 0000 0200 0000 0e00 0000 ................
026f020: 0100 0100 0200 0000 0000 4000 6600 ea0e ..........@.f...
026f030: 1800 1f00 ffff 0000                     ........
```

Listing 13.9 The object and node headers in the file system tree's root node.

This tree consists of multiple levels as the node-type value is 0x01 meaning this is a root node. The level of this node is 0x01. This implies that at the next layer down leaf nodes will be encountered. Another interesting item from the type value is that it informs that analyst that this node does not have fixed key and value sizes.

The table of contents is located immediately after the node header (offset 0x00 relative to the end of the node header). This structure contains information about 0x02 keys which are located in the 0x40 bytes of the table of contents. Due to variable length keys and values used in the file system

Table 13.23 Partially processed VSB from Listing 13.8.

Offset	Size	Name	Value
0x08	0x08	OID	0x402 (1026_d)
0x10	0x08	XID	0x08 (8_d)
0x18	0x02	Type	0x0D (VSB)
0x1A	0x02	Flags	0x00 (Virtual)
0x20	0x04	Magic	APSB
0x80	0x08	Object Map OID	0x278 (632_d)
0x88	0x08	Root Tree OID	0x404 (1028_d)
0xB8	0x08	Num. Files	0x05 (5_d)
0xC0	0x08	Num. Directories	0x02 (2_d)
0x2C0	0x100	Volume Name	APFS-FS

Table 13.24 Partially processed object and node headers from Listing 13.9.

Offset	Size	Name	Value
0x08	0x08	OID	0x404 (1028_d)
0x10	0x08	XID	0x06 (6_d)
0x18	0x02	Type	0x02 (Root Node)
0x1A	0x02	OH Flags	0x00 (Virtual)
0x1C	0x04	Subtype	0x0E (Files)
0x20	0x02	NH Flags	0x01 – 0x01 (Root)
0x22	0x02	Level	0x01 (1_d)
0x24	0x04	Num. Keys	0x02 (2_d)
0x28	0x02	ToC Offset	0x00 (0_d)
0x2A	0x02	ToC Length	0x40 (64_d)

tree the table of contents must be processed using the structure in Table 13.5 which consists of two bytes for the key offset, two bytes for the key length, two bytes for the value offset and two bytes for the value length. Note that as this node does not have fixed key and value sizes it is not necessary to process the B-Tree information structure. Listing 13.10 shows the contents of the 0x40 byte table of contents. These key/value offsets and lengths are shown in Table 13.25.

```
026f038: 0000 1800 0800 0800 3700 2f00 1000 0800  ........7./.....
026f048: 0000 0000 0000 0000 0000 0000 0000 0000  ................
026f058: 0000 0000 0000 0000 0000 0000 0000 0000  ................
026f068: 0000 0000 0000 0000 0000 0000 0000 0000  ................
```

Listing 13.10 Contents of the table of contents of the file system tree's root node.

Table 13.25 Processed ToC entries from Listing 13.10.

	Key		Value	
ToC Entry	**Offset**	**Size**	**Offset**	**Size**
1	0x00 (0_d)	0x18 (24_d)	0x08 (8_d)	0x08 (8_d)
2	0x37 (55_d)	0x2F (47_d)	0x10 (16_d)	0x08 (8_d)

The contents of the first key are shown in Listing 13.11. All file system keys begin with an 8_d-byte OID and type value (see Section 13.1.8). The value of this is 0x9000000000000001. Following the calculation presented earlier the inode number is 0x01 and the type is 0x9. Hence this record refers to the directory record for inode 0x01 (1_d).

```
$ xxd -s $((0x26F * 0x1000 + 0x78)) -l $((0x18)) mnt/ewf1
026f078: 0100 0000 0000 0090 0c8c a6ac 7072 6976 ............priv
026f088: 6174 652d 6469 7200                     ate-dir.
```

Listing 13.11 Contents of key 1 in file system tree's root node.

The value contains the virtual block address of the block containing the contents related to this key. The contents of the first value are shown in Listing 13.12. This has the value 0x407. Referring to the volume object map informs the analyst that the corresponding physical address of this is 0x277.

```
$ xxd -s $((0x270 * 0x1000 - 0x28 -0x8)) -l $((0x8)) mnt/ewf1
0026ffd0: 0704 0000 0000 0000                    ........
```

Listing 13.12 Contents value 1 in the file system tree's root node.

Processing of the node header in block 0x277 shows it to be a leaf node with variable length keys and values. Listing 13.13 shows the table of contents from this node. The highlighted entries all refer to the same file (OID 0x14) and will be processed in the remainder of this section. The two unhighlighted entries between the first and second highlighted entries also refer to the same file but are not necessary for basic analysis and will be processed later.

ToC Entry 1

Listing 13.14 shows the key for ToC Entry 1. This is found at offset 0x131 relative to the end of the table of contents (0x38 + 0x100 = 0x138). The length of this key is 0x08 bytes.

All file system keys begin with an 8_d-byte OID and type value (see Section 13.1.8. The value of this is 0x3000000000000014. Following the calculation presented earlier the inode number is 0x14 and the type is 0x3. Hence this record refers to the inode record for inode 0x14 (20_d).

The value (i.e. the inode in this case) is located at offset 0x470 relative to the end of the tree node.[4] The length of this value is 0xA0 bytes; however, initially only 0x5C bytes are extracted. This is the size of the basic inode structure. The remaining 0xA0 – 0x5C = 0x44 bytes contain extended

4 Remember that this is a non-root node and as such there is no B-Tree Information structure at the end of the node. In the event that this was both a root and leaf node the 0x28 B-Tree information structure must be allowed for also.

```
0277038: 0000 1800 1200 1200 1800 1100 2400 1200 ............$...
0277048: 2900 0800 9000 6c00 3100 2000 9800 0800 ).....l.1. .....
0277058: 5100 1900 aa00 1200 6a00 1500 bc00 1200 Q.......j.......
0277068: 7f00 1700 ce00 1200 9600 1200 e000 1200 ................
0277078: a800 0800 5401 7400 b000 0800 c801 7400 ....T.t.......t.
0277088: b800 1b00 da01 1200 d300 0800 7a02 a000 ............z...
0277098: db00 0800 7e02 0400 e300 1000 9602 1800 ....~...........
02770a8: f300 0800 0203 6c00 fb00 1600 1403 1200 ......l.........
02770b8: a701 1700 940a 1200 1101 0800 b403 a000 ................
02770c8: 1901 0800 b803 0400 2101 1000 d003 1800 ........!.......
02770d8: 3101 0800 7004 a000 3901 2f00 7109 0105 1...p...9./.q...
02770e8: 6801 1f00 ae09 3d00 8701 0800 b209 0400 h.....=.........
02770f8: 8f01 1000 ca09 1800 9f01 0800 820a a000 ................
```

Listing 13.13 Table of contents of block 0x277.

```
$ xxd -s $((0x277 * 0x1000 + 0x138 + 0x131)) -l $((0x08)) mnt/ewf1
00277269: 1400 0000 0000 0030                    .......0
```

Listing 13.14 The key content for ToC entry 1.

attributes which will be processed later. Listing 13.15 shows the content of the first 0x5C bytes of the inode. Processed values for this structure are found in Table 13.26.

```
$ xxd -s $((0x278 * 0x1000 -0x470)) -l $((0x5C)) mnt/ewf1
0277b90: 0200 0000 0000 0000 1400 0000 0000 0000 ................
0277ba0: f34d cc85 ffd0 a617 c608 d385 ffd0 a617 .M..............
0277bb0: 130e d785 ffd0 a617 f34d cc85 ffd0 a617 .........M......
0277bc0: 0080 0000 0000 0000 0100 0000 0000 0000 ................
0277bd0: 0200 0000 0000 0000 6300 0000 6300 0000 ........c...c...
0277be0: a481 0000 0000 0000 0000 0000            ............
```

Listing 13.15 Contents of the inode structure for inode 0x14 in **APFS_V1.E01**.

The inode structure provides most of the metadata information. From Table 13.26 the file's timestamps are available along with permission information. The owner id (UID) and group ID (GID) of the file are accessible. Note that in this case these values are both 99_d which represents the macOS Unknown account. This is a special account that is generally used for removable media. Hence these are common values to see for these fields in removable media.

The inode also provides information about this file's location in the file hierarchy. In this case the parent ID is given as 2_d. This means that this file is found in the directory with inode 2_d (the root directory!).

There is some expected information that is absent. In most file systems the metadata information would provide the file size and often the filename. Neither of these have been discovered to this point. This is due to the use of optional extended attributes in the inode. The basic inode size is 0x5C bytes; however, this inode's table of content entry provided a size value of 0xA0. The remaining 0x44 bytes form the extended attributes. This data is shown in Listing 13.16.

As shown in Section 13.1.8 the extended attributes comprised three sections. The first shows the number of extended attributes present (0x2) and the length of the extended attribute data (0x38

Table 13.26 Processed inode from Listing 13.15.

Offset	Size	Name	Value
0x00	0x08	Parent ID	0x02 (2_d)
0x08	0x08	Private ID	0x14 (20_d)
0x10	0x08	Creation Time	0x17A6D0FF85CC4DF3 2024-01-03 10:55:04.886308339
0x18	0x08	Modification Time	0x17A6D0FF85D308C6 2024-01-03 10:55:04.886749382
0x20	0x08	Change Time	0x17A6D0FF85D70E13 2024-01-03 10:55:04.887012883
0x28	0x08	Access Time	0x17A6D0FF85CC4DF3 2024-01-03 10:55:04.886308339
0x38	0x04	Num. Links	0x01 (1_d)
0x48	0x04	Owner	0x63 (99_d)
0x4C	0x04	Group	0x63 (99_d)
0x50	0x02	Mode	0x81A4 (rw-r--r--)

```
$ xxd -s $((0x278 * 0x1000 -0x470)) -l $((0xA0)) mnt/ewf1
...[snip]...
0277be0: a481 0000 0000 0000 0000 0000 0200 3800 ..............8.
0277bf0: 0402 0d00 0820 2800 4865 6164 6c61 6e64 ..... (.Headland
0277c13: 2e6a 7067 0000 0000 9482 0400 0000 0000 .jpg............
0277c10: 0090 0400 0000 0000 0000 0000 0000 0000 ................
0277c20: 9482 0400 0000 0000 0000 0000 0000 0000 ................
```

Listing 13.16 The contents of the extended attributes in inode 0x14.

bytes). The second area contains an array of structures providing information about each of the extended attributes present. In this case there are 2_d extended attributes. The first of these (underlined) is of type file name (0x04) with a flag value of 0x02 and whose data component is 0x0D bytes in length. The data in this attribute is the null-terminated filename, **Headland.jpg**.

The second extended attribute is a data stream (0x08) with flags of 0x20 and is 0x28 bytes in size. The corresponding data elements are highlighted in the same manner as the array entry. Note that data elements start on 8_d-byte boundaries. The processed data stream attribute is shown in Table 13.27.

ToC Entry 2

Listing 13.17 shows the key for ToC Entry 2. This is found at offset 0x187 relative to the end of the table of contents (0x38 + 0x100 = 0x138). The length of this key is 0x08 bytes.

```
$ xxd -s $((0x277 * 0x1000 + 0x138 + 0x187)) -l $((0x08)) mnt/ewf1
002772bf: 1400 0000 0000 0060                    .......`
```

Listing 13.17 The key content for ToC entry 2.

Table 13.27 Processed data stream extended attribute from Listing 13.16.

Offset	Size	Name	Description	Value
0x00	0x08	Size	The size in bytes of the data.	0x48294 ($295{,}572_d$)
0x08	0x08	Alloc. Size	The allocated size on disk in bytes.	0x49000 ($299{,}008_d$)
0x10	0x08	Crypto ID	The default encryption key used in this data stream.	0x00 (0_d)
0x18	0x08	Bytes Written	The total number of bytes that have been written to this data stream.	0x48294 ($295{,}572_d$)
0x20	0x08	Bytes Read	The total number of bytes that have been read from this data stream.	0x00 (0_d)

The key shows this to be related to inode (0x14 – 20_d) and be of type 0x06. Referring to Table 13.10 shows this to be a data stream item. Listing 13.18 shows the value associated with this key along with the command used to extract it.

```
$ xxd -s $((0x278 * 0x1000 -0x9B2)) -l $((0x4)) mnt/ewf1
0027764e: 0100 0000                                ....
```

Listing 13.18 The data stream value.

The value of this data stream is 1_d. This value is referred to as the reference count, the record may be deleted when this value reaches zero.

ToC Entry 3

Listing 13.19 shows the key for ToC Entry 3. This is found at offset 0x18F relative to the end of the table of contents (0x38 + 0x100 = 0x138). The length of this key is 0x10 bytes.

```
$ xxd -s $((0x277 * 0x1000 + 0x138 + 0x18F)) -l $((0x10)) mnt/ewf1
02772c7: 1400 0000 0000 0080 0000 0000 0000 0000 ................
```

Listing 13.19 The key content for ToC entry 3.

This key again refers to inode 0x14 with a type of 0x8. This represents the file extent. In other words the value associated with this key allows file content to be located. The final eight bytes in this key refer to the starting logical block to which the extent refers. In this case there is only a single extent so the key refers to logical block 0_d. Listing 13.20 shows the value corresponding to this key.

```
$ xxd -s $((0x278 * 0x1000 -0x9CA)) -l $((0x18)) mnt/ewf1
0277636: 0090 0400 0000 0000 c201 0000 0000 0000 ................
0277646: 0000 0000 0000 0000                     ........
```

Listing 13.20 The file extent value.

The extent value provides the allocated size of the extent in bytes (0x49000) and the starting physical block of this extent (0x1C2). The final step in the analysis is to recover the file content

Figure 13.6 The recovered **Headland.jpg** file.

itself. Based on the extent in Listing 13.20 this is achieved by recovery of 0x49 (73_d) blocks (the block size is 0x1000 so 0x49000 bytes is the equivalent of 0x49 blocks. Of course from the data stream in the inode it is known that the file is actually 0x48294 bytes in size). The command to recover this file is shown in Listing 13.21 along with the recovered file in Figure 13.6.

```
$ dd if=mnt/ewf1 of=Headland.jpg bs=1 skip=$((0x1C2 × 0x1000))
    count=$((0x48294))

$ md5sum Headland.jpg
40e0d95be96cc0a9faff22829a58b81 Headland.jpg
```

Listing 13.21 Recovery of **Headland.jpg** from **APFS_V1.E01**.

Hence, the combination of the inode and the file extent keys in the file system B-Tree allow metadata and file content to be recovered from APFS.

13.3 APFS Advanced Analysis

So far this chapter has focused on the basic recovery of live files. In this section some advanced topics in APFS are introduced. These include deleted file recovery, multi-level B-Trees, multiple volumes and checkpoints. Many of these have implications for file system forensics and can be of vital importance in the processing of APFS file systems.

13.3.1 Deleted Files

The next question to ask is what occurs when a file is deleted in APFS? The image **APFS_V2.E01** was created from **APFS_V1.E01** but with two files **Headland.jpg** and **Files/delete.txt** deleted from the disk image. Previously **Headland.jpg** had been recovered. Listing 13.22 shows the contents of block 0x1C2 in **APFS_V2.E01** clearly showing that the file content is still present. Indeed

```
$ xxd -s $((0x1C2 * 0x1000)) -l 64 mnt/ewf1
01c2000: ffd8 ffdb 0043 0002 0202 0202 0102 0202 .....C..........
01c2010: 0203 0202 0303 0604 0303 0303 0705 0504 ................
01c2020: 0608 0709 0808 0708 0809 0a0d 0b09 0a0c ................
01c2030: 0a08 080b 0f0b 0c0d 0e0e 0f0e 090b 1011 ................
...[snip]...
```

Listing 13.22 Contents of block 0x1C2 after deletion of **Headland.jpg**.

the command shown in Listing 13.21 can still be executed on **APFS_V2.E01** to recover the file's content. Clearly file deletion in APFS does not overwrite the file's content immediately.

Next recovery is attempted to determine if the file can be recovered using file system structures as was done previously. This involves the same method shown in the previous section. The CSB is processed and the object map tree is located. This is then processed to determine the physical address of the VSB the object map of which is then used to determine the physical address of the file system tree itself. It is left as an exercise for the reader to attempt this recovery process. Upon successful completion of this process the file system tree is discovered at block 0x294. However, processing this returns no reference to the deleted file. Hence it is not possible to recover deleted files in APFS using existing structures.

13.3.2 Checkpoint Recovery

Due to the use of CoW in APFS it should be possible to find older versions of structures in the file system. This is due to the nature of CoW in which data to be updated is copied and changes are made to the copies. Hence it should be possible to discover older versions of file system structures (including the file system tree) still present in the file system.

APFS manages this process through checkpoints. The container superblock is immediately followed by a checkpoint descriptor area and a checkpoint data area. The starting locations and size of these are determined from the container superblock. Figure 13.5 shows the general layout of this area.

The checkpoint descriptor area contains a series of checkpoint mapping structures followed by the container superblock associated with that checkpoint. The checkpoint mapping structure allows related structures to be located in the checkpoint data area. For file system forensics the older copies of the container superblock are often sufficient for analysis purposes.

Based on the general structure of the checkpoint descriptor area every second block will contain a CSB structure. From the CSB this file system contains 8_d blocks in the checkpoint descriptor area. Table 13.28 summarises the transaction ID values for each of the five CSB blocks located in **APFS_V2.E01**.

Recall from the manual recovery of the **Headland.jpg** file that the transaction ID in the CSB was 0x06. The latest version of this file system does not contain that transaction ID in a checkpoint, so the nearest one is chosen. The checkpoint CSB with the nearest XID (0x09) is located in block 2_d in **APFS_V2.E01**. Using this as the CSB for the start of analysis allows the **Headland.jpg** file to be recovered from the checkpoint, even though the content has now been deleted and it was not possible to recover it through current structures. The complete recovery of this file is left as an exercise for the reader.

Table 13.28 The XID values in each of the container superblocks located in the checkpoint descriptor area.

Block #	XID	Block #	XID
0_d (Master)	0x0C (12_d)	2_d	0x09 (9_d)
4_d	0x0A (10_d)	6_d	0x0B (11_d)
8_d	0x0C (12_d)		

13.3.3 Multi-Level B-Trees

The file system tree in **APFS_V1.E01** contained three nodes over two levels. However, during the recovery of **Headland.jpg** the location of the relevant information was not shown. In this section the file system contained in **APFS_V3.E01** is used which contains 400_d random-user-created files.[5] On this device exists a file called **Headland.jpg** which has the Object ID of 0xDC (220_d). This section shows how this file can be located.

Processing begins as normal with the volume located using the CSB and the container object map. Then the file system root is located using the VSB and the volume object map. The virtual OID for the file system root is 0x404. The volume object map contains a large number of mappings. These are provided in Table 13.29. Checking the validity of these is left as an exercise for the reader.

The volume superblock informs the analyst that the file system root is located at virtual OID 0x404. Consulting Table 13.29 shows the physical location of this to be 0xBE2. Listing 13.23 shows the object and node header for this block.

Table 13.29 Contents of the volume object map located in block 0xC00 in **APFS_V3.E01**.

Virt. OID	Phys. Addr.	Virt. OID	Phys. Addr.	Virt. OID	Phys. Addr.
0x404	0xBE2	0x406	0x6B9	0x407	0xBFE
0x408	0xBE1	0x409	0x6BC	0x40A	0x6BD
0x40B	0xBE9	0x40C	0xBED	0x40D	0xBF1
0x40E	0xBF3	0x40F	0xBDE	0x410	0xBE5
0x411	0x6C4	0x412	0xBF7	0x413	0x6C6
0x414	0x6C7	0x415	0x6C8	0x416	0xBE3
0x417	0xBE6	0x418	0xBE7	0x419	0xBE8
0x41A	0xBEA	0x41B	0xBEB	0x41C	0xBEC
0x41D	0xBEE	0x41E	0xBEF	0x41F	0xBF0
0x420	0xBF2	0x421	0xBF4	0x422	0xBF5
0x423	0xBF6	0x424	0xBF8	0x425	0xBF9
0x426	0xBFA				

5 There are also a number of system-generated files present on the device.

```
0be2000: e7f8 381c b898 d511 0404 0000 0000 0000..8.............
0be2010: 0500 0000 0000 0000 0200 0000 0e00 0000 ................
0be2020: 0100 0100 2100 0000 0000 4001 7401 e40b ....!.....@.t...
0be2030: ffff 0000 ffff 0000                     ........
```

Listing 13.23 The object and node header for the file system tree's root node in **APFS_V3.E01**

Table 13.30 Interpreted key/value pairs from Listing 13.25. Note that keys have been left in little-endian format for comparison reasons.

Highlighting	Key	Value
Underlined	0xDB00 0000 0000 0030	0x416 (1046_d)
Bold	0xEB00 0000 0000 0030	0x417 (1047_d)

The root node of this file system tree contains 0x21 (33_d) keys. Before commencing analysis it is necessary to analyse the B-Tree information structure located at the end of the node. Listing 13.24 shows the contents of the B-Tree information structure.

```
0be2fd8: 4200 0000 0010 0000 0000 0000 0000 0000 B...............
0be2fe8: 2000 0000 b800 0000 4306 0000 0000 0000  .......C.......
0be2ff8: 2200 0000 0000 0000                     ".......
```

Listing 13.24 The contents of the B-Tree information structure in the file system tree in **APFS_V3.E01**.

From the B-Tree information structure it is clear that this tree needs more than a single node. The total number of nodes in this tree is 0x22 (34_d) with 0x643 (1603_d) keys. In order to determine the location of a particular key, the B-Tree is sorted based on the OID value. The OID for the desired file **Headland.jpg** is 0xDC (220_d). The keys are processed in the root node to find the key that is less than or equal to the desired key. Listing 13.25 shows an excerpt from the root node's table of contents, key and value areas. Corresponding entries are highlighted. The key value pairs are shown in Table 13.30.

Comparing the keys in Table 13.30 to the target OID (0xDC) shows it to be greater than the first key (underlined) but less than the second key (bold font). As such the desired file will appear in the first key value pair, as this key has the closest, but smaller, value to the target key. The desired node to follow for this information has a virtual OID of 0x416. Referring to Table 13.29 the physical address of this virtual ID is 0xBE3. Listing 13.26 shows an excerpt from this node showing the inode for this file. This is the fourth ToC entry in the node. The key value is found at offset 0x20 (relative to the end of the ToC) and is 0x08 bytes in size. The key is 0xDC00000000000030, meaning this is an inode (type: 0x03) for OID 0xDC, the desired target. The value is located at offset 0x15C and is 0xA0 bytes in size. Remember that the offset for the value is relative to the end of the node. Also this is a leaf node, not a root node, so there is no B-Tree information structure present.

This section has shown how a particular record can be located in a multi-layer B-Tree in APFS. It is left as an exercise for the reader to discover the other entries in this node related to the target file.

```
Table of Contents
...[snip]...
0be20c8: ac00 0800 7800 0800 9400 0800 8000 0800 ....x...........
0be20d8: bc00 0800 8800 0800 c400 0800 9000 0800 ................
0be20e8: b400 0800 9800 0800 a400 0800 a000 0800 ................
...[snip]...

Keys
...[snip]...
0be2220: 0000 0030 bb00 0000 0000 0030 fb00 0000 ...0.......0....
0be2230: 0000 0030 db00 0000 0000 0030 eb00 0000 ...0.......0....
0be2240: 0000 0030 1200 0000 0000 0090 0af4 27c2 ...0..........'.
0be2250: 6731 3136 342e 7478 7400 1b01 0000 0000 g1164.txt.......
...[snip]...

Values
...[snip]...
0be2f40: 1804 0000 0000 0000 1704 0000 0000 0000 ................
0be2f50: 1604 0000 0000 0000 1504 0000 0000 0000 ................
0be2f60: 1404 0000 0000 0000 1304 0000 0000 0000 ................
...[snip]...
```

Listing 13.25 Excerpts from the FS tree's root node in **APFS_V3.E01** showing selected ToC entries along with corresponding keys and values.

13.3.4 Multiple Volumes

One of the unusual features about APFS is that a container can contain multiple volumes, each of which shares free space. Locating (and processing) multiple volumes is a relatively straightforward process. Processing begins as normal at the CSB. Listing 13.27 shows the CSB from **APFS_V4.E01**. This container contains two volumes.

```
0be3ea4: 0200 0000 0000 0000 dc00 0000 0000 0000 ................
0be3eb4: 821f 4843 6f73 a717 38a8 4e43 6f73 a717 ..HCos..8.NCos..
0be3ec4: 965c 5043 6f73 a717 821f 4843 6f73 a717 .\PCos....HCos..
0be3ed4: 0080 0000 0000 0000 0100 0000 0000 0000 ................
0be3ee4: 0200 0000 0000 0000 6300 0000 6300 0000 ........c...c...
0be3ef4: e881 0000 0000 0000 0000 0000 0200 3800 ..............8.
0be3f04: 0402 0d00 0820 2800 4865 6164 6c61 6e64 ..... (.Headland
0be3f14: 2e6a 7067 0000 0000 9482 0400 0000 0000 .jpg............
0be3f24: 0090 0400 0000 0000 0000 0000 0000 0000 ................
0be3f34: 9482 0400 0000 0000 0000 0000 0000 0000 ................
```

Listing 13.26 The inode for the desired target file **Headland.jpg**.

The CSB shows that there can be a maximum of four volumes in this container. The array of file system roots contains two instantiated elements. These show the virtual OIDs for the two volumes. These values are 0x402 and 0x406, respectively. These virtual OIDs must be translated to physical addresses using the object map structure. This is located at the physical block 0x8B5. Processing the object map tree (Block: 0x8B6) shows that the virtual OIDs 0x402 and 0x406 map to 0x8AB and

```
0000000: c8a5 6c10 e7aa 53f8 0100 0000 0000 0000..l...S.........
0000010: 0b00 0000 0000 0000 0100 0080 0000 0000 ................
0000020: 4e58 5342 0010 0000 7681 0700 0000 0000 NXSB....v.......
0000030: 0000 0000 0000 0000 0000 0000 0000 0000 ................
0000040: 0200 0000 0000 0000 39ca 46aa f93c 48b8 ........9.F..<H.
0000050: a76b 94b0 79a7 57d6 0804 0000 0000 0000.k..y.W.........
0000060: 0c13 0000 0000 0000 1800 0000 7407 0000 ............t...
0000070: 0100 0000 0000 0000 1900 0000 0000 0000 ................
0000080: 1600 0000 2a00 0000 1400 0000 0200 0000 ....*...........
0000090: 2600 0000 0400 0000 0004 0000 0000 0000 &...............
00000a0: b508 0000 0000 0000 0104 0000 0000 0000 ................
00000b0: 0000 0000 0400 0000 0204 0000 0000 0000 ................
00000c0: 0604 0000 0000 0000 0000 0000 0000 0000 ................
00000d0: 0000 0000 0000 0000 0000 0000 0000 0000 ................
```

Listing 13.27 Excerpt from the CSB of **APFS_V4.E01** showing two file system roots.

0x8B4, respectively. VSB structures are found at these locations. These can be processed as normal to recover all files in each of the volumes.

13.3.5 Extended Attributes

APFS also provides support for extended attributes which are used in a manner similar to alternate data streams in NTFS. Recall the manual analysis of **APFS_V1.E01**, only three keys from the table of contents related to the **Headland.jpg** file were actually analysed (Listing 13.13), there were two other records that were not examined. These are at key offsets 0x139 and 0x168, respectively. Listing 13.28 shows the key and value associated with key offset 0x139. In this case the name of this extended attribute is com.apple.metadata:kMDItemWhereFroms, which is a standard attribute used to show where a file was obtained from (URL, email, etc.).

```
$ xxd -s $((0x277 * 0x1000 + 0x138 + 0x139)) -l $((0x2F)) mnt/ewf1
0277271: 1400 0000 0000 0040 2500 636f 6d2e 6170 .......@%.com.ap
0277281: 706c 652e 6d65 7461 6461 7461 3a6b 4d44 ple.metadata:kMD
0277291: 4974 656d 5768 6572 6546 726f 6d73 00   ItemWhereFroms.
$
$ xxd -s $((0x278 * 0x1000 - 0x971)) -l $((0x501)) mnt/ewf1
027768f: 0200 fd04 6270 6c69 7374 3030 a201 025f ....bplist00..._
027769f: 1104 ad68 7474 7073 3a2f 2f6d 6169 6c2d ...https://mail-
02776af: 6174 7461 6368 6d65 6e74 2e67 6f6f 676c attachment.googl
...[snip]...
```

Listing 13.28 The key value pair for the first extended attribute for OID 0x12 in **APFS_V1.E01**.

The value is composed of a two-byte flag value (0x02) followed by a two-byte data length value (0x4FD). This is then followed by the actual data itself. The possible flag values are:

- 0x0001: The extended attribute data is stored in a data stream;
- 0x0002: The extended attribute data is stored in the record itself; and
- 0x0004: The extended attribute record is owned by the file system. One example of this is found in symbolic links which are covered later.

In Listing 13.28 the flag is 0x0002 meaning that the data is stored in the record. In other words the data is found directly after the data length value. The processing of the remaining extended attribute is left as an exercise for the reader.

13.3.6 Links

As with most modern file systems APFS implements links (both hard and soft) in the file system structures themselves. Listing 13.29 shows the table of contents for the file system root node in **APFS_V5.E01**. All of the highlighted entries refer to OID 0x12 (**Headland.jpg**).

```
082c038: 1900 1800 9000 1200 0000 1100 1200 1200 ................
082c048: 1100 0800 7e00 6c00 9300 2000 3802 0800 ....~.l....8...
082c058: b300 1900 4c03 2200 3900 1700 1601 1200 ....L.".9.......
082c068: 3501 1900 e201 1200 0401 1900 1303 2200 5.............".
082c078: 3100 0800 0401 7400 5000 0800 8a01 7400 1.....t.P.....t.
082c088: 5800 1b00 9c01 1200 7300 0800 d802 a000 X.......s.......
082c098: 7b00 0800 1402 0400 8300 1000 2c02 1800 {...........,...
082c0a8: cc00 0800 0404 a000 ec00 1000 2a03 1700 ............*...
082c0b8: 1d01 1000 f102 1700 d400 0800 fe01 0400 ................
082c0c8: dc00 1000 fa01 1800 fc00 0800 1002 0800 ................
082c0d8: 2d01 0800 0802 0800 4e01 0800 7804 7400 -.......N...x.t.
082c0e8: 5601 1f00 d001 1100 0000 0000 0000 0000 V...............
```

Listing 13.29 Table of contents for the root node in the file system tree in **APFS_V5.E01**.

The first highlighted entry provides the inode itself for this file. The contents of this inode value are shown in Listing 13.30. The highlighted value provides the number of links to this inode (0x02). The file name is still found in the extended attributes as before.

```
082cbd4: 0200 0000 0000 0000 1200 0000 0000 0000 ................
082cbe4: 3f45 73aa 9355 a817 9aff 7aaa 9355 a817 ?Es..U....z..U..
082cbf4: f468 6f56 9755 a817 3f45 73aa 9355 a817 .hoV.U..?Es..U..
082cc04: 0080 0000 0000 0000 0200 0000 0000 0000 ................
082cc14: 0200 0000 0000 0000 6300 0000 6300 0000 ........c...c...
082cc24: e881 0000 0000 0000 0000 0000 0200 3800 ..............8.
082cc34: 0402 0d00 0820 2800 4865 6164 6c61 6e64 ..... (.Headland
082cc44: 2e6a 7067 0000 0000 9482 0400 0000 0000 .jpg............
082cc54: 0090 0400 0000 0000 0000 0000 0000 0000 ................
082cc64: 9482 0400 0000 0000 0000 0000 0000 0000 ................
```

Listing 13.30 The inode value for OID 0x12 in **APFS_V5.E01** showing that two links exist to this file.

The basic inode structure provides no information on the names of the hard link. The next two table of content entries represent the sibling link types (0x5). The keys and values of these are shown in Listing 13.31. The key structure contains the standard first 8_d byte OID/Type value. In each of these cases the type value is 0x5 showing this to be a sibling link entry. The remaining 8_d bytes contains the sibling ID which is the OID for the sibling map record. In this case these values

```
Key Offset: 0xEC
082c1e4: 1200 0000 0000 0050 1300 0000 0000 0000 .......P........
Value Offset: 0x32A
082ccae: 0200 0000 0000 0000 0d00 4865 6164 6c61 ..........Headla
082ccbe: 6e64 2e6a 7067 00                        nd.jpg.
-------------------------------------------------------------------
Key Offset: 0x11D
082c215: 1200 0000 0000 0050 1400 0000 0000 0000 .......P........
Value Offset: 0x2F1
082cce7: 0200 0000 0000 0000 0d00 6861 7264 6c69 ..........hardli
082ccf7: 6e6b 2e6a 7067 00                        nk.jpg.
```

Listing 13.31 The sibling keys for OID 0x12 in **APFS_V5.E01**

Table 13.31 The structure of the sibling link record with values from Listing 13.31.

Offset	Size	Name	Value 1	Value 2
0x00	0x08	Parent Folder OID	0x02 (2_d)	0x02 (2_d)
0x08	0x02	Name Length (n)	0x0D (13_d)	0x0D (13_d)
0x0A	(n)	Filename	Headland.jpg	hardlink.jpg

are 0x13 and 0x14. This means that OID's 0x13 and 0x14 contain sibling map records for this file. These will be examined later in this section.

The values of the sibling link entries are also shown in Listing 13.31. These contain the name of the link. The structure of these (with the interpretation of the values in Listing 13.31) is found in Table 13.31.

At this stage the sibling OIDs have been identified (0x13 and 0x14). These are now sought in the table of contents in order to locate their sibling map records. Referring to the table of contents (Listing 13.29) the relevant key entries are found at offset 0xFC and 0x12D. These keys and corresponding values are shown in Listing 13.32. The keys contain only the OID and the type value (0xC0). The value is composed of a single 8_d-byte OID for the target of the link. In this case, both show the same OID 0x12.

```
Key Offset: 0xFC
0082c1f4: 1300 0000 0000 00c0                    ........
Value Offset: 0x210
0082cdc8: 1200 0000 0000 0000                    ........
-------------------------------------------------------------
Key Offset: 0x12D
0082c225: 1400 0000 0000 00c0                    ........
Value Offset: 0x208
0082cdd0: 1200 0000 0000 0000                    ........
```

Listing 13.32 The sibling map keys for OID 0x13 and 0x14 in **APFS_V5.E01**

The implementation of hard links in APFS differs slightly from that of other file systems. The original inode (0x12 in this case) contains a reference to the original file and the created hard link through the sibling map records. Even the original file, **Headland.jpg**, gets its own sibling map record (and a new OID number), along with the hard link as would be expected.

The file system in **APFS_V5.E01** also contains a symbolic link (OID: 0x15). The symbolic link is a separate file with its own OID and inode information. The symbolic link file also contains an extended attribute. Listing 13.33 shows the extended attribute for OID 0x15 in **APFS_V5.E01**.

```
ToC Entry: 5601 1f00 d001 1100
Key
$ xxd -s $((0x82C * 0x1000 + 0xF8 + 0x156)) -l $((0x1F)) mnt/ewf1
082c24e: 1500 0000 0000 0040 1500 636f 6d2e 6170 .......@..com.ap
082c25e: 706c 652e 6673 2e73 796d 6c69 6e6b 00   ple.fs.symlink.
Value
$ xxd -s $((0x82D * 0x1000 - 0x28 - 0x1D0)) -l $((0x11)) mnt/ewf1
082ce08: 0600 0d00 4865 6164 6c61 6e64 2e6a 7067 ....Headland.jpg
082ce18: 00                                       .
```

Listing 13.33 The extended attribute key/value pair for the symbolic link file (OID 0x15) in **APFS_V5.E01**. The ToC entry is also provided.

The name of this extended attribute is found to be com.apple.fs.symlink, which signifies that this is a symbolic link. The value flags (0x06) show the data is stored in the record itself and that this is a system-owned extended attribute. The data length is given as 0x0D and the data is found to be **Headland.jpg**. Hence OID 0x15 in **APFS_V5.E01** is a symbolic link to the file **Headland.jpg** in the same directory as the link.

13.4 Summary

This chapter examined the APFS file system, the default file system on all Apple devices since 2017. This is a modern file system which can be challenging to analyse due in part to its complexity but also to its (current) novelty.

As with many modern file systems APFS uses B-Tree structures to store metadata along with the use of CoW for updating said structures. While information remains on the file system after deletion, the file system B-Tree is generally restructured meaning that the file content can't be located through traditional means. However, the use of CoW (along with checkpointing) means that older versions of the file system are sometimes still present. From these older file system trees deleted content may be recoverable. It should be noted that these structures are updated frequently and there is only a limited amount of storage space for checkpoint structures. This means that deleted file recovery may not be possible.

Support for APFS amongst commercial (and open source) tools will improve in the coming years; however, knowledge of the inner workings of the file system will always be important!

Exercises

1 The file system contained in **APFS_V2.E01** contains a file called **Abbey.jpg** (OID: 0x15). In relation to this file answer the following questions:
   a) When was the file last modified?

b) What is the file size in bytes?
c) Who is the user ID of the file's owner?
d) What is the name of the directory in which this file is contained?
e) What is the MD5 for this file?

2 A file, **delete.txt** (OID: 0x16), was previously deleted from **APFS_V2.E01**. Can this file be recovered?

3 **APFS_V3.E01** contains a file with OID 416_d. Locate all file system entries for this file. In doing so answer the following questions:
a) When was the file created?
b) What is the file size in bytes?
c) What is the MD5 sum of this file?

Bibliography

APFS Overview - NTFS.com [Internet] (n.d.). www.ntfs.com [cited 2024 April 3]. https://www.ntfs.com/apfs-intro.htm.

APFS Structure - NTFS.com [Internet] (n.d.). www.ntfs.com [cited 2024 April 3]. https://www.ntfs.com/apfs-structure.htm.

Apple File System Reference Developer Contents [Internet] (2020). [cited 2024 April 3]. https://developer.apple.com/support/downloads/Apple-File-System-Reference.pdf.

Cho, G.S. (2022). Design and implementation of APFS object identification tool for digital forensics. *International Journal of Internet, Broadcasting and Communication* 14 (1): 10–18.

Dewald, A. and Plum, J. (2024). APFS Internals for Forensic Analysis [Internet]. ERNW White Paper [cited 2024 April 3]. https://static.ernw.de/whitepaper/ERNW_Whitepaper65_APFS-forensics_signed.pdf.

Göbel, T., Türr, J., and Baier, H. (2019). Revisiting data hiding techniques for apple file system. *Proceedings of the 14th International Conference on Availability, Reliability and Security 2019*, 1–10.

Hansen, K.H. and Toolan, F. (2017). Decoding the APFS file system. *Digital Investigation* 22: 107–132.

Nordvik, R. (2022). APFS. In: *Mobile Forensics–The File Format Handbook: Common File Formats and File Systems Used in Mobile Devices 2022 (eds. Hummert, C. and Pawlaszczyk, D.)*, 3–39. Cham: Springer International Publishing.

Oakley, H. (2023). APFS Hard Links, Symlinks, Aliases and Clone Files: A Summary [Internet]. The Eclectic Light Company [cited 2024 April 3]. https://eclecticlight.co/2023/04/28/apfs-hard-links-symlinks-aliases-and-clone-files-a-summary/.

Part V

The Future

14

Future Challenges in Digital Forensics

But what about the future? What changes will occur in the digital and file system forensic areas in the years ahead? How will practitioners maintain their currency in the field? This chapter examines a number of challenges that are facing the file system forensic and larger digital forensic communities in the coming years and discusses possible means to alleviate some of these potential issues. It should be noted that many of these challenges are not new. They have been known about for many years, but have not been suitably addressed to date.

14.1 Challenges in Digital Forensics

For many years digital forensics was required only in a tiny minority of cases. That situation has changed. In 2018 the EU estimated that digital evidence was necessary in 85% of criminal investigations[1] which has led to one of the single largest challenges in digital forensics, that of data volume. More and more data must be analysed in every case than ever before and more cases involve digital evidence than before.

New technologies arrive almost every day meaning that new challenges exist in terms of how to analyse these artefacts. For instance the combined total number of apps available between Google's Play Store and Apple's App Store is over 5.5 million.[2] Each of these potentially involves new forensic challenges.

Many new technologies are utilising encryption at both hardware and software levels. Some of this software-level encryption is found in the file system itself. For instance from this book ext4 and APFS can provide encryption at the file system level. NTFS can be combined with the Encrypting File System (EFS) to provide encryption for Windows machines.

Traditionally digital forensics operated under a single standard method. Power off the device in question, acquire an image and analyse said image. With the advent of encryption (and cloud storage technologies) the risks associated with this strategy increased. Powering off the machine could lose some or all potential evidence on the device. This, along with new devices such as IoT, drones and smart phones, led to the need for new methods of operation, none of which have yet been standardised.

It has often been recognised that with all these advances in technology criminals are often *early adopters* of new technologies. This means that law enforcement will see these new technologies at an early stage and need to be conversant with their functionality and analysis. This is often hindered

1 https://ec.europa.eu/commission/presscorner/detail/en/MEMO_18_3345.
2 Figure correct as of May 2022. Source https://www.statista.com/statistics/276623/number-of-apps-available-in-leading-app-stores/.

File System Forensics, First Edition. Fergus Toolan.

by the lack of knowledge and skills in handling this new form of technology. An example of this is the use of cryptocurrencies in criminal markets. Bitcoin, the *de facto* standard in cryptocurrencies was first used in 2009 and by 2011 began to regularly record over 1000 transactions per day. According to the Drug Enforcement Agency approximately 90% of transactions in bitcoin were related to criminal activity in 2013.[3] For many years law enforcement was behind the criminals in this area. Now there are numerous courses available for law enforcement in blockchain analysis.[4]

Another challenge faced by digital forensics is that of the scientific basis of the discipline. From the definition of digital forensics (Chapter 1) it is based on scientific principles but these are sometimes lacking. Digital forensic tools are often not validated and as such it is difficult to be confident exactly how these tools perform. There are a number of reasons for this: the lack of maturity in the discipline, the lack of standardised testing methods/datasets, etc. For scientific and technical evidence to be admissible in court it should conform to the Daubert standards.[5] One of the Daubert requirements is that the technique must have a known error rate. Without testing it is impossible to determine the accuracy of the tool and therefore impossible to determine an error rate.

Historically the challenges in digital forensics have focused on technical and sometimes legal issues. There is, however, a third aspect of these challenges, the human being. Human factors, in particular bias, have been recently identified as having an effect on the digital forensic process something which does not occur in more established forensic disciplines. Improved standardisation of working practices is one means suggested to overcome this problem.

The remainder of this chapter focuses on these challenges in digital forensics, specifically in terms of file system forensics and proposes some possible solutions to these issues.

14.1.1 Data Volume

One of the largest problems facing digital forensics, and by extension file system forensics, is that of data volume. This refers to the volume of data which must be analysed in every case. Consider modern society where the majority of people have more than one digital device (computers, laptops, phones, tablets, games consoles, etc.) capable of storing information. Additionally people have online personae (social media) that may also be of interest. In the early days of digital forensics digital evidence was relevant only in a small minority of cases. This has changed in recent years. Current estimates suggest that digital evidence is relevant in 85–90% of investigations. This has increased the number of devices that must be analysed.

At the case level the volume has also increased. Consider a modern computer system. Most hard disk drives are between 512 GiB and 1 TiB in size. The largest commercially available hard drive in 2024 could store over 30 TiB of data. In 2002 the largest hard drive in existence was approximately 128 GiB. In 2020 Seagate estimated the average hard drive size to be just over 2 TiB. Removable media have also increased the problem. Removable media originally meant floppy disks! These had a storage capacity of a mere 1.44 MiB! Now removable media mean many things, USBs, CDs, DVDs, External HDDs. Many external HDDs are in the terabyte capacity. Hence the amount of data that can be stored on each device has increased over the years.

---

3 The level of criminal activity associated with cryptocurrencies has fallen over the years, but the early adopters were often criminals.

4 The blockchain is the underlying cryptographic structure that maintains the integrity and anonymity of the Bitcoin network.

5 This is a requirement only in the US legal system. However, following the Daubert standard guidelines will improve the quality of the evidence presented in digital forensics regardless of the jurisdiction in which the tools are being used.

The final issue in terms of data volume in digital forensic analysis is the number of devices. Traditionally a single device might have been involved in an investigation. Consider your own home. How many digital devices are there in that home? Remember you need to include phones, tablets, laptops, computers, external storage devices, games consoles, smart devices, IoT devices, vehicles, etc.

The combination of digital evidence being relevant in more cases, more devices requiring analysis in each case, and the fact that these devices are much larger than they were previously means that the volume of data that must be processed has reached enormous proportions. This problem will only grow in the years to come. Storage technology will improve leading to a further increase in capacity. This will be combined with increased numbers of devices used by people and digital evidence therefore being relevant in even more cases in the future. All these factors will combine to further exacerbate the data volume problem.

One of the reasons that the data volume problem is so prevalent is that many law enforcement agencies lack the necessary resources to process all the devices recovered (see Section 14.1.6 for a more detailed view of this). Even with added resources it is not guaranteed that this problem would improve. Some possible solutions to this problem that have been suggested include the use of automation (and AI) and the use of triage techniques.

Triage is most commonly associated with medicine (in particular emergency room medicine) in which incoming patients are assessed and the order of treatment is decided upon based on this assessment. This can be utilised in the digital forensic domain also. Incoming devices can be triaged and the likely relevance of the device can be estimated from this process. This can decide the priority which can be assigned to a device. The triage process is a *quick* scan which does of course risk missing something of importance but it can streamline the digital forensic process and ensure greater efficiency.

Recently researchers have begun to examine the possibility of automation of digital forensics through the use of artificial intelligence (AI) techniques. To the author's knowledge AI-based systems have yet to be successfully deployed in real-case environments.

14.1.2 Multi-Source Correlation

One of the reasons for the increasing data volume in digital forensics is the increasing number of potential digital evidence sources to which people have access. This includes local sources (i.e. sources that are in their possession) such as computers, laptops, phones and TVs. and also remote sources such as cloud storage systems and social media profiles. Along with the increasing data volume to which this leads, it also introduces a further complication which is the correlation of evidence across multiple sources.

Information obtained from multiple sources in a single investigation must be correlated both logically (ensuring that it makes sense as a whole) and also temporally (ensuring that the correct timeline of actions is generated). Generally this is a manual task for the investigator but it requires much effort on the part of the investigator and therefore is prone to error.

Temporal correlation of computing devices provides a number of issues that were rarely present in non-digital evidence sources. While we now have more access to temporal information (for instance the MFT record in NTFS stores eight timestamps about each file) and this information is more accurate than ever before (NTFS timestamp granularity is 100 ns) the difficulties in correlating this information are vast. Hence one of the fundamental questions that we ask in digital forensics is to try to establish the time settings on every device. In addition to the amount of time information present the investigator must also consider the timezone information. For instance the author works in Norway (UTC+1) and lives in Ireland (UTC+0). The author's computers are set to the Irish timezone even when in Norway. Hence there is a potential one hour discrepancy between the author's computer and sources of digital evidence seized in Norway.

Mitigation of this multi-source correlation problem is challenging. Certainly, as with most of the challenges in this chapter, training and education can help prepare the investigator for correlation of disparate sources but it is still a manual task. Another potential solution is the use of AI and machine learning (ML) to automate the process.

14.1.3 New File Systems

When new file systems are created they cause a major issue for file system forensics. Our standard tools no longer support all of the common file systems. For instance when APFS was first introduced none of the forensic tools were able to support this. The file system required reverse engineering (as little was published officially). This process requires great skill and knowledge and is very time consuming. The process is also subject to error.

Even in the case when a new open source file system is created in which all of the source code/-documentation is available it is still a great challenge to interpret this. The analyst must examine the system manually or develop tools internally to process the file system. New file systems do not appear very often (or gain popularity very quickly). In the last 15 years only ext4 and APFS have been created and gained popularity sufficiently quickly to cause regular problems for analysts. Other modern file systems such as BtrFS and XFS are rarely encountered during investigation and as such are less problematic for analysts.

In terms of solving this problem, again training and education will help. Knowledge of how existing file systems function will provide insight into how new file systems will be structured. For instance every file system that has been examined in this book contains some form of volume boot record/superblock structure. This is a common structure found in all file systems which will contain information about the file system as a whole. Many file systems use extent-based storage which are all processed in a similar manner. All file systems will store time values. Knowledge of these common features will help analysts in handling new file systems.

Additionally file systems are increasingly complex. Consider the changes between ext3 and ext4 in which ext4 used more than mere block pointers for data storage. Ext4 could use block pointers but could also use extents (and extent trees), inline storage and symbolic links. These features 'broke' most digital forensic tools at the time and as such required manual analysis.

Another possible means of mitigation of this issue is through information and resource sharing. From a law enforcement perspective this might take place through organisations such as Interpol and Europol or at a federal level inside a state. Rather than many people attempting to analyse a new file system independently effective information sharing could simplify the task for all.

14.1.4 Encryption

More and more modern devices are encrypted by default. Breaking modern encryption schemes through brute force is almost impossible. Certainly to have any hope of doing so requires vast computing resources, more so than most organisations can afford. As such, encryption is viewed by many as being one of the most challenging trends in modern computing, not just in terms of file system forensics but in terms of digital investigation as a whole.

However, there are no easy solutions to this problem. Realistically brute force attacks are not feasible, as such a number of stop-gap measures have been proposed. One of the most reliable occurs at the crime scene where traditional wisdom would say to pull the plug. This is now changing. Instead it is recommended to analyse the running machine and acquire as much information as possible from that. Although this changes information on the device (and as a consequence breaks the ACPO principles) it will allow for encrypted data to be acquired in a manner in which it can be analysed. If the plug were pulled this information would be lost.

A potential legal solution to the encryption challenge is through the use of key escrow systems. In this, the keys required to decrypt data are held by a trusted third party. In certain circumstances these keys can be released to relevant authorised authorities (i.e. law enforcement) to allow for the decryption of data. Of course the drawback to an escrow system is that the keys must be submitted and maintained by the users. Most likely the criminal element would not provide the correct key to this system making it untenable.

Certain governments have requested manufacturer support in gaining access to encrypted data. This would generally be achieved through the creation of a back-door into the system which would bypass the encryption. However, manufacturers and the general public are against this feature in modern computing devices and it is assumed that it will not happen at any large scale.

14.1.5 Cloud Storage

One of the largest single changes in data storage in recent years has been the advent of the cloud. Previously the majority of data in criminal investigation was held on physical devices owned by the suspect. This included all documents, pictures, emails, etc. Now times are different. The majority of people use cloud storage (although they may not be aware of the fact); however, cloud storage in itself raises some potentially serious challenges for digital investigation.

The cloud introduces a range of problems from acquisition (how are forensically sound copies of data acquired remotely), to management challenges (the dependence on cloud service providers to co-operate), leading to jurisdictional challenges (where is the data located and does the warrant cover acquisition of said data).

Mitigation of these challenges is a complex task in itself. There are no clear solutions to these issues. Some will certainly require global legal agreements to allow for the acquisition of data from geographically remote cloud services and to compel corporate entities in other jurisdictions to cooperate with the investigation.

In many jurisdictions it is possible to legally acquire cloud-based material if it is accessible from a device for which a warrant has been obtained. This means that the use of live data forensics (LDF) techniques will allow for (at least) logical acquisition of data. However, LDF introduces risks of its own and must be carefully considered in each case as to whether the risk outweighs the reward.

14.1.6 Lack of Resources

File system forensic analysis is a resource-intensive process. The task requires hardware, software and human resources in order to succeed. This section examines the resourcing issues under these three headings and proposes potential solutions to the issues in resourcing.

14.1.6.1 Human Resources

The human is one of the most vital components in the file system forensic analysis process. No matter how good technology becomes there will always be a need for experienced analysts to ensure the accuracy of the file system forensic process.

However, the human resource is not necessarily suitable to the task at hand. One of the main reasons is the lack of knowledge that many analysts have. There are many people who can 'push the button' during the file system forensic analysis process. For the vast majority of cases this is sufficient. The suspect is using standard technologies in a standard manner and has made no serious attempts to hide potential digital evidence. Hence, an analyst with basic training should be able to recover the potential evidence.

Now consider the case in which the suspect is actively trying to thwart the file system forensic process. The suspect might employ encryption (Section 14.1.4), or use remote storage (Section 14.1.5) or they might employ obscure technologies such as file systems that are unsupported by file system forensic tools (Section 14.1.3). In this cases the 'push button' approach is no longer suitable and further expertise is required.

From a legal perspective the increase in digital forensic knowledge and skill in the general population (and most particularly in the IT world) increases the possibilities of cross examination of digital evidence. Questions such as 'how did your forensic tool recover this file?' may not be answerable by the general file system forensic analyst. The inability to answer the question might lead to sufficient doubt to invalidate the results of the forensic process, at least in the eyes of the court.

Another human resource issue is found in the numbers of people working in the area. This is a general issue in the cybersecurity field with many industries desperately short of qualified staff. This problem is only exacerbated for law enforcement (LE) agencies as government salaries generally are not comparable to industry salaries and as such there are more recruitment issues in LE than the private sector.

One of the main solutions to the human resource issue is to increase the training/educational opportunities for people in this area. Educational opportunities are becoming more commonly available as many universities now offer digital forensics/cybersecurity programs at degree and master's level. Most commercial tool vendors and some independent training companies also offer training on particular products.

14.1.6.2 Software Resources

Another required resource for file system forensics is that of software. Generally commercial softwares are used by most digital forensic units. One of the main driving forces for this is that these are familiar to the court system and therefore generally accepted by the courts. However, from a resourcing perspective the issue with these commercial solutions is cost. These products are not cheap. The products are generally licensed on a per user basis, so the larger the unit, the larger the cost of the software. This means that it quickly becomes infeasible to increase the size of a unit as it is not only personnel costs (i.e. salary) but also the software (and hardware) that must also be provided for each analyst.

A possible solution to this issue is to move away from closed-source commercial software, or at least to augment this software with other cheaper/free alternatives. This allows for more software resources to be used in a case and has other benefits also. For instance the use of open-source software in conjunction with closed-source software will act as a form of validation of results (Section 14.1.7) from commercial tools. The open-source nature of the software allows for much greater disclosure in the court system, thereby strengthening the worth of any digital evidence presented to the course.

14.1.6.3 Hardware Resources

The final aspect of the resource triad is that of hardware. Even with sufficient numbers of suitably trained people with access to all software resources that they require, the unit still requires hardware resources. The increase in potential sources of digital evidence (Section 14.1.1) coupled with the growth in device size in recent years has led to more processing required in each case. This means that digital forensic units require highly efficient hardware which has associated costs. These hardware solutions must also be scalable – as the data volume increases so must the data analysis capabilities.

There are a number of potential solutions available to units in this area. Generally it is cheaper to get high-end workstations by building them on-site. Individual components are purchased and assembled by the purchaser.

Another mitigating factor is to utilise triage approaches. Anecdotally it is clear that the majority of devices analysed during an investigation contain little or no evidence. It is assumed that the suspect will keep 'interesting' activity limited to a small number of devices in their possession but every device must be analysed. Triage is the process of evaluating the device for potential digital evidence and deciding on the analysis path based on this evaluation. One means of performing triage is to use bootable live Linux distributions to conduct a preliminary analysis. This uses the suspect's hardware to run (thereby removing the need for any hardware resources for this case[6]) and uses open source software (no software costs) to analyse the device. Based on the triage results the plan for further analysis can be developed.

A final solution to the hardware resource issue might be to virtualise the workstations. This generally involves using a third-party service provider who provides virtualised workstations. This approach is still costly (although generally less so than purchasing the same physical computing power) but has the advantage of scalability. Virtual hardware can be upgraded more easily than physical hardware.

14.1.7 Tool Validation/Datasets

We don't know what digital forensic tools are doing! The community of file system forensic analysts knows at an abstract level what a file system forensic tool does but they don't understand this at the raw level. Generally the tools that are being used are not validated by any independent body. Errors can exist in computer software which fit one of a number of categories. These might be coding bugs (an error in implementation of the algorithm), algorithmic bugs (an error in the algorithm itself) and unimplemented features (as I discovered when writing this book certain forensic tools do not appear to support extent trees in ext4!). New versions of software are created either to fix bugs or to add new functionality. However, these new versions of software will often introduce more bugs to the system.

Tools and techniques that are relied upon in court should, at the very least, be validated. However, in the area of digital forensics this is a non-trivial task. This is due to a number of reasons including:

- **Lack of Expertise:** Validation of tools is a challenge in itself and this expertise is not necessarily present amongst digital forensic analysts.
- **Lack of Resources:** Validation is also a complex task and as such the resources (especially time) may not be present.
- **Lack of Standard Data:** There are limited standardised datasets by which a tool can be evaluated. Hence it is difficult to validate data.
- **Lack of Realistic Datasets:** In order to validate tools datasets should be realistic. However, file system forensic tools are often tested/validated on small disk images (such as a USB key).[7]

6 This is not strictly true, the live Linux distribution must be available on removable/network media for booting. However, the costs associated with this solution are minimal compared to the cost of forensic workstations.

7 And yes, the author is aware of the irony in this statement as all datasets used in this book were created on small USB devices!

- **Lack of Standardised Tests:** It is impossible to compare tools with a standardised test methodology (along with standardised data sets).

There are some potential solutions to the lack of tool validation but all are complex. For instance simple procedures such as dual tool verification could be used. In this, two independent tools are used to analyse the same data and the results are compared. The analyst can have more confidence in results that are obtained using two distinct tools – these are more likely to be correct. This is another use of open-source tools as budgetary constraints will often not permit the purchase of a second tool solely for validation purposes. Hence the open source tool might be used for validation.

Standardised testing methods and datasets can be used. There have been some attempts at this such as the Computer Forensic Tool Testing (CFTT) project in NIST[8] but, as yet, nothing has been supported globally. Section 14.1.9 will further elaborate on this topic as digital evidence can also be considered scientific evidence and as such more stringent requirements also apply. These requirements will help to further define the standardisation requirements necessary for tool validation.

14.1.8 Lack of Standardisation

As yet there are no universal standards in digital forensics. As with many areas in the digital forensic discipline certain units/countries operate internal standards but there are no national/international standards. Both techniques and qualifications of personnel may require standardisation in the future.

Work has begun in many organisations in terms of the lack of standardisation in digital investigation. For instance in terms of the development of standard operating procedures the Council of Europe developed the Electronic Evidence Guide which attempted to standardise certain procedures.

In terms of the investigator a European partnership involving Europol, The European Union Agency for Law Enforcement Training (CEPOL), Eurojust, The European Judicial Training Network (EJTN) and The European Cybercrime Training and Education Group (ECTEG) has recently begun the process of standardising the requirements for all persons involved in the digital investigation process. This framework identifies the main stakeholders in the process from law enforcement management to first responders and attempts to formalise the knowledge/skills that each require. However, as yet there is no formal process for evaluating the person's ability in each area of desired expertise.

14.1.9 Legal/Scientific Challenges

Related to the lack of tool validation are the legal challenges to the scientific nature of digital evidence. The domain of digital forensics is a new domain in terms of admissibility of evidence in court proceedings. To date this evidence has been generally accepted but this might change in the future. Even court systems which accept digital evidence from certain standard tools might not accept evidence from any other sources. In that case what happens with a new, unsupported file system?

Many states in the US legal system (along with Federal courts) utilise the Daubert standard[9] in relation to the admissibility of evidence. This set of five guidelines can be used by judges to decide upon admissibility. While this standard is a legal requirement only in the United States, it

---

8 https://www.nist.gov/itl/ssd/software-quality-group/computer-forensics-tool-testing-program-cftt.

9 *Daubert v. Merrell Dow Pharms., Inc., 509 U.S. 579, 595 (1993).*

is beneficial for all digital analysts to consider the Daubert standard as the use of techniques that satisfy the Daubert criteria will greatly strengthen the admissibility of said evidence.

The Daubert criteria are:

- **Testing:** Has the technique been independently tested? Note that this is related to tool validation (Section 14.1.7) as testing forms a major part of the validation process. The key is that this testing should be conducted by an independent party (although in-house testing is better than no testing!).
- **Peer Review:** Has the technique been published and subject to peer review? Theoretically this is simple to achieve, the technique merely needs to be published in order to pass this criterion. Considering the area of file system forensics there are many publications in the area that could help with this requirement; however, there is one issue with this. LE do not always wish to publish techniques that are being used as this might provide the criminal with insight in how to disrupt the LE process (i.e. conduct anti-forensics).
- **Known Error Rate:** Does the technique have a known error rate? This knowledge is important so that the judge can evaluate the worth of the evidence obtained through this technique. Again this is related to testing and tool validation. This criterion is probably the most difficult to implement. It requires access to standard datasets (and standard testing methods) neither of which exist at this moment. As such most tool testing (and by extension error rate calculation) is performed on small single-use datasets and are therefore potentially suspect.
- **Standards:** Are there standards governing the use of the technique in actual investigation? While there are often standard operating procedures at the unit level, these do not often translate to national (or international) level. Also as discussed in Section 14.1.8 the person is part of the execution of the technique along with the technique itself. As such any standard must inform the court of who is permitted to perform the technique (i.e. what skills/training are required).
- **General Acceptance:** Is the technique generally accepted in the relevant scientific community? This is the most abstract of all but also the one that is often easiest to show. General acceptance is often evaluated by the courts as how often the technique is seen before the courts. Hence commercial file system forensic tools are often accepted (as they are used many times) whereas open-source tools may be challenged more often!

As it currently stands LE are weak in their implementation of the Daubert criteria; however, there are means of improving this. Many of the solutions to the challenge of lack of tool validation (Section 14.1.7) and the lack of standardisation (Section 14.1.8) will also aid in this particular challenge. For instance the creation of standard datasets and validation of tools will immediately address Daubert's testing criteria, and in doing so bring law enforcement closer to calculation of the known error rate. The creation of standardised processes and qualification frameworks directly addresses one of the criteria. Publishing knowledge about law enforcement techniques (in peer-reviewed publications) will address the peer-review (and general acceptance) criteria.

14.1.10 Presentation of Evidence

Presentation of evidence is an umbrella term that covers many forms of presentation with many different audiences. Most people will immediately think of presentation in the court room, as the expert provides testimony to the court. This is indeed a crucial aspect of presentation. However, there is more to this than just presentation in the court room. It also includes report writing, both of the final report and also intermediary reports. For instance the person who seizes a device will generally write a report about this stage in the process, before handing the device (and the report) to the analyst for further processing. Internal team briefings are another form of presentation. In these the analyst presents the results to date to other members of the investigative team.

Presentation of digital evidence has a number of complexities associated with it, which provide many challenges to the analyst. First and foremost digital evidence is highly technical in nature and this evidence must be presented to a non-technical audience in as clear a manner as possible. This in itself is a non-trivial task. It requires great understanding of the evidence in question and the methods used to obtain the evidence and also requires excellent communication skills.

Generally the presentation of results from certain tools is relatively straightforward. For instance the courts will generally accept the results from commercial file system forensic tools when run on traditional file systems. However, consider the case in which the evidence is obtained from technologies that are unsupported by current tools. This will increase the difficulty in communicating the information to a non-technical audience as the analyst generally needs to work at a lower level which introduces further complexities to the task and by extension to the presentation of said evidence.

There are a number of potential mitigation strategies possible in this area. First and foremost training/education are vitally important. The required training is both technical (as the analyst must better understand the results that they are presenting and also how these results were obtained) and also non-technical such as in relation to communication skills.[10] Communication skills might refer to report writing and/or court room presentation.

Another potential means of simplifying the presentation aspects is to use a common reporting template. The use of such a template will make it easier for the audience to interpret the results correctly. Generally there is a standard template for most police forces; however, each template is individual. With the advent of cybercrime (and other transnational crimes) communication occurs more frequently between police forces and therefore a standard might be beneficial at an international level also. Numerous guides to reporting exist (some of which are specifically geared toward digital evidence) but none are, as yet, accepted as standards.

The tool development process could be improved in such a way that the tools in the area are more reliable. Software development is an inherently buggy area but there are techniques that can be used to improve the quality of the final product. These can be combined with standardised operating procedures (Section 14.1.8) and development that is driven with the Daubert tests in mind (Section 14.1.9). The combination of these would lead to more reliable software and consequently less need to explain the intricacies of the results during presentation of evidence.

Some argue that presentation of evidence may be less of an issue in the future as the average technical ability of society as a whole is increasing. However, this is coupled with an increase in the complexity of digital systems which, in the author's opinion, means that the gap in technical complexity and societal knowledge will remain. This means that presentation of evidence will always be an area of concern for law enforcement.

14.1.11 Human Error/Bias

Within forensic science as a whole there has been an increasing realisation that both cognitive and human factors can lead to error. This has led to the conclusion that forensic experts are

---

10 Many years ago the author taught a series of 'train the trainer' courses for law enforcement and was surprised at how popular it was. The majority of students did not wish to become trainers but wished to improve presentation skills in court. One student described the court as similar to a classroom: the audience has limited knowledge and the expert must explain complex data to this audience.

subject to bias when making certain decisions. The lack of standardised approaches and validation procedures in digital forensics when compared with other forensic disciplines means that the analyst must make more interpretation of data that is discovered. This provides more potential for human error and bias.

There are a number of possible mitigations that could be implemented to avoid cognitive bias. One, as with many other challenges, is to train analysts more directly in terms of this. It is vital that the analyst is aware of the possibility of bias so that they can more readily avoid it. Remember that while some of this would be part of basic police education, many digital forensic analysts come from civilian backgrounds and have only limited (if any) investigative training/experience.

The creation of standard operating procedures with the awareness of bias/error would help to alleviate the issue in the future. Following the same, well-tested steps where possible would help ensure that bias/error is reduced. Ensuring that techniques are reproducible (where possible) also allows independent reviews to be conducted. This provides greater oversight on the analyst thus reducing the risk of bias/error.

The standard operating procedure might also include peer review of cases (or a certain number of cases). This peer review could be anything from proof-reading of the report all the way through to complete, independent reanalysis of all digital evidence sources. This of course is a resource-intensive task in an area in which resources are already an issue (Section 14.1.6).

14.2 Where Do We Go from Here?

When the challenges presented in the previous section are examined, and more importantly their possible mitigation strategies, a number of common items are identified. These are summarised in Table 14.1.

The potential solutions in this table apply to more than one challenge in each case. The remainder of this chapter describes each of these potential solutions in their current state in more detail.

Table 14.1 Identified current and future challenges in file system forensics and possible mitigation strategies.

	Training	FOSS	AI	Triage	Legal	LDF	Datasets	Testing	Standards	Info. Sharing	Virtualisation
Data Volume		✓	✓	✓							✓
Source Correl.	✓		✓								
New FS	✓									✓	
Encryption					✓	✓					
Cloud	✓				✓	✓					
Resources	✓	✓	✓	✓							✓
Validation	✓	✓					✓	✓			
Standards					✓		✓		✓	✓	
Legal/Sci.	✓	✓			✓		✓	✓	✓	✓	
Presentation	✓								✓		
Bias	✓								✓		

14.2.1 Training/Education

Training and education is one of the most important aspects when addressing challenges in digital forensics. It is directly relevant to almost all the challenges that are presented in this chapter. Before describing some of the current options in this category it is worth describing the difference between training and education. Training is generally accepted as the process of learning something with the aim of performing a specific skill or behaviour. In the realm of file system forensics this might include learning how to use a particular tool effectively. Education is the process of learning something with the goal of acquiring knowledge. Both approaches are necessary in digital forensics.

Training will create more effective analysts in that the result of training will increase the skills that they have. These skills are generally applicable in certain specialised cases and as such may not be sufficiently broad when the analyst is faced with non-standard challenges. The knowledge acquired through education will allow the analyst to not only handle the standard cases but to take the knowledge and apply it more effectively in other scenarios.

Training and education do not need to be only technical. There are many soft skills that are required by analysts that are often overlooked when describing necessary training for this group. For instance as shown in Section 14.1.10, communication (both written and verbal) skills are essential. Evidence by itself is worthless unless it is communicated effectively to the relevant people in order to successfully conclude the investigation.

The key question for digital forensic management is what level of training/education is required by their analysts. Should all receive a minimum level of basic training and then some select few receive education (with potential for academic qualifications) or do all require this education in addition to training?

14.2.2 Free Open-Source Software (FOSS)

As discussed in Chapter 2 open-source software is 'software with source code that anyone can inspect, modify and enhance'. While not always the case, open-source software is often free of charge. This can greatly alleviate software resource issues that exist in digital forensics today. Rather than purchasing a commercial tool a free open-source solution can be utilised instead. The addition of further resources for analysis will also address the data volume challenge.

From a scientific perspective (i.e. Daubert and rules of admissibility) open-source software should be more favoured than commercial closed-source tools. With closed-source software the analyst relies upon the software developers doing their job correctly. They rely upon the fact that the tool performs as expected. However, with open-source software (and the necessary knowledge of computer programming) it is possible for the analyst to inspect the source code and determine exactly what it does. This allows for greater weight to be associated with the open source solution.[11] There are many open source file system forensic packages available for use, from large-scale software projects such as the Sleuthkit and Autopsy (the GUI frontend) to smaller tools used to analyse a single file system or file system structure (e.g. *analyzeMFT*).[12]

There are a number of potential drawbacks to the use of open source software. One of the main ones is that they are often not immediately accepted in court. Another commonly cited drawback

11 In reality the situation is directly opposite this. Generally closed-source software is accepted in courts as, through common usage, it is considered acceptable. Open-source tools need to be accepted by the court prior to their use. However, in the event of many analysts using open-source tools they would, over time, also become generally accepted in the court.
12 A list of tools (both open and closed source) is available from https://www.dftoolscatalogue.eu/.

is that they are more difficult to use than commercial products. However, with proper validation of methods and the creation of standard operating procedures these issues can be addressed.

14.2.3 Triage

Another potential solution in relation to data volume and also the lack of resources in law enforcement agencies is through the use of triage techniques. Triage is a medical term which the Oxford English Dictionary defines as 'the assignment of degrees of urgency to wounds or illnesses to decide the order of treatment of a large number of patients or casualties'. In the domain of file system forensics triage refers to the prioritisation of different devices in a case in relation to the chances of finding relevant information.

One of the main benefits of triage is that it can be performed using live Linux distributions, distros that can be used to boot the suspect machine allowing access to all information on the hard drive (assuming there is no encryption present) without changing any of the content. All of the specialist forensic distros provide this feature (and also provide all the tools that the analyst might require!).

Triage techniques will allow the analyst to quickly get an indication of the worth of a particular device to the investigation, allowing the analyst to remove those devices which contain no relevant information from the investigation. This reduces the total number of devices that need to be processed in the case, thereby alleviating the data volume problem.

From a resource perspective, triage requires only an external storage medium (CD/DVD, USB or even a network storage device) which can be used to boot the system using the live Linux distribution. The hardware that is required to run this distribution is the hardware under investigation. Therefore triage techniques require only a minimal outlay in expenses (storage media) in order to provide much processing power to the unit.

14.2.4 Artificial Intelligence (AI)

AI and ML are seen by many as being the next step forward in digital forensics, and more generally in digital investigation. There are a number of proposed and prototype AI systems that may be applied to digital forensics but very few, if any, have been used in court.

AI involves the study of intelligent agents, software that reacts to the environment to achieve a specific goal. In the case of digital forensics this goal might be to locate relevant evidence that either strengthens or weakens the investigative hypotheses. These systems can be viewed as being driven by the data (the input) rather than explicitly by code. To provide an example of this, file system forensic tools are (currently) driven by code. The analyst pushes a specific button in the system and a certain set of actions are executed. Now consider fragmented files in which no metadata is available. File system forensic tools require metadata in order to locate file content. However, there are a certain subset of tools which perform carving. These tools can search for key indicators of files and recover the content from this. However, in the case of fragmented files this may prove impossible due to fragmentation. AI has shown some success in carving heavily fragmented files by using ML techniques to classify fragments of data as to their file type (e.g. Word and Excel). These sets of various fragments can be further analysed to recreate the original file.

Another proposed use of AI is in the area of triage. Triage prioritises devices for analysis based on their likelihood of containing evidence relevant to the case. Initial results in this area have been promising but much more remains to be done. There are many other proposed AI solutions which have the potential to defeat encryption, to correlate across devices, to detect relevant objects, etc.

While AI and ML have the potential to reduce the data backlog in digital forensics and to improve correlation between devices, these techniques also suffer from certain issues. One of the most pressing issues in AI is the lack of datasets that are available. Many AI algorithms require training in order to operate effectively. Training is achieved through providing the algorithm with pre-classified data and then the algorithm determines why it was classified this way. This rule generation phase cannot occur without the training data. As one of the biggest issues in tool validation in file system forensics is the lack of available datasets, it will always be difficult to train AI systems in the digital forensic domain.

Another issue with the use of AI is the explanation of results. In court it is not enough to merely recover evidence, the analyst must also show how that evidence got there and how it was recovered. Due to the nature of AI it is often difficult to understand the reasoning employed by these algorithms and hence it is difficult to explain to the courts how the evidence was recovered. This may prove problematic for the large-scale deployment of AI solutions.

14.2.5 Live Data Forensics

With the increased use of encryption and cloud-based storage solutions, the traditional *pull-the-plug* approach to running computers at the crime scene is no longer recommended. In the worst-case scenario, in which the drive is encrypted and it is impossible to recover the key, no information is recoverable from the device in question. LDF is the 'forensic acquisition and/or analysis of the data from a running (live) digital system for use in a court of law'. LDF has great potential for ensuring that all evidential data is recovered from a suspect (or victim) system. Certain information such as active network connections and volatile data (such as RAM) is impossible to recover through post mortem forensics. In certain cases of malware investigation no information is ever placed on disk, all is maintained in memory and as such is only accessible from the running computer.

LDF however has many risks associated with the process. The first *rule* of evidence is that investigators make no changes to any evidence that will later be relied upon in court. This is impossible to realise in LDF. Every action taken by the investigator alters evidence on the running system. Even the simplest of actions, such as moving the mouse on a running Windows computer, will alter information on the device. LDF practitioners must be aware that evidence is changing and as such must ensure that the processes they use make minimal changes to the running system and are well documented.

Certain tasks performed in the course of LDF have the potential to cause system crashes. A common task during LDF is to acquire a copy of RAM. This action is directly accessing the memory of the computer system which is not desirable. As such it might cause the system to crash, potentially losing all access to remaining information.

Due to the risks LDF is often used as a form of triage. The on-scene analyst will perform LDF on the running computer system with the aim of discovering if it is safe to shut the computer down. This involves looking for processes which might cause loss of information for traditional dead-box forensics. Common tasks at this stage are to search the suspect system for evidence of encryption or remote storage. If none of these are discovered it is often safer to *pull-the-plug* and perform a traditional forensic examination of the system. If, on the other hand, evidence of these processes is discovered accessible data can be gathered live from the system. This might include copying files that are stored in encrypted or remote locations to a collection drive for later analysis or even acquiring the computer's RAM.

Another issue with LDF is that the process is never repeatable. With traditional forensics using an acquired disk image, the analyst can document the commands used to recover evidence from the image file. Anyone else with access to the commands and the image file will be able to generate the exact same evidence. In LDF, the simple act of performing LDF changes the underlying system meaning that it might be impossible to recreate the evidence recovered. This means that documentation (the ACPO audit trail) is even more important in LDF than in traditional digital forensics.

Overall LDF is a vital part of modern digital forensics. It can help investigators to overcome technical limitations of dead-box forensics by allowing access to information that would be otherwise inaccessible through traditional approaches. It can also reduce the data volume problem if used as a form of triage. However, the risks associated with the practice are many and as such it should be used with caution. In the event that the investigator is uncertain how to proceed expert advice should be sought immediately!

14.2.6 Legal Solutions

File system forensics operates in the legal domain and as such a number of challenges may be addressed through legal channels. An obvious potential use of legal initiatives to address these problems is in the area of encryption. Generally encryption algorithms function through use of a key. As long as the key is secure access to the data is practically impossible. In some jurisdictions key escrow is considered a solution to the encryption challenge. In this a trusted third party stores all keys for all citizens in the state. This trusted third party can, on receipt of an application from an authorised party (such as law enforcement/court), provide this key to the authorised party. This system of key escrow would allow legal access to all encrypted data. Most countries do not currently legislate for this and as such to be effective it would need some additional legislation.

However, there are drawbacks to escrow. Encryption is often implemented through software which can be downloaded from many sources, including international sources. This software may not enforce key escrow, allowing criminals to bypass the system entirely. Consider the current case of firearms. In most jurisdictions firearm ownership must be registered with the governmental authorities. However, criminals often bypass this system and carry unregistered weapons. The same might apply in key escrow in which the criminal bypasses the system therefore providing law enforcement with the same challenges that exist currently as no key will be available for decryption.

The nature of modern storage and in particular the greater prevalence of cloud-based storage solutions has led to new challenges in file system forensics (and digital investigation in general). Often with cloud-based storage systems the best outcome that can be hoped for is that of logical acquisition of data. However, depending on the scope of the warrant this may not even be legal. Depending on the jurisdiction in which an investigation takes place the allowable actions are different. In some cases a warrant (from an authorised party) allows investigators to acquire information that is accessible from the device in question. This means that data stored in the cloud is accessible to the investigator. In certain jurisdictions the warrant covers only the data stored locally. The creation of universal legislation to address this would ensure greater access to potential evidence and also greater clarity in what tasks are permitted for law enforcement.

Improved legislation can also be used to address the lack of standards in digital investigation and, on a related note, the admissibility of technical evidence to the courts. Evidence admissibility is often left to the presiding judge in a particular court case to decide. However, judges are experts in law, not in digital evidence. Legislation to codify the exact tests that need to be passed in order for digital evidence to be admitted to the court would greatly ease the admissibility decisions. This legislation would also improve on the current system by enforcing certain standards on tools/techniques which would greatly increase the reliability of evidence and lead to a situation in which evidence would no longer be accepted merely because this type of evidence had been accepted previously.

14.2.7 Data Set Development/Tool Testing

The file system forensic community is facing a myriad of challenges in the coming years. Many of these could be aided through the development of standardised corpora for tool testing. Currently there are a number of available datasets for this area; however, there is no agreed standard. The development of standardised datasets would alleviate many of the challenges in the area. Firstly, and most importantly, standardised corpora would allow for the testing of current file system forensic tools. The ability to test (and validate) the performance of tools would greatly increase their acceptance in the courts. This would lead to increased confidence in the investigation as a whole.

From an investigative view point these corpora would not only allow for performance to be evaluated but also for tool performance to be compared. There are a number of potential tools available for file system forensics. Both open- and closed-source tools are available, some of which are general (i.e. support many file systems) while others are specialised to a single (or a small number of) file system(s). While many of the community have their favourite tools (along with anecdotal evidence as to why they are the best), the development of standardised corpora would allow a comparison to be made. This means that the best tool could be used for a particular task!

Running hand-in-hand with dataset development is the topic of tool testing. The reason these are so closely bound is that tool testing can never be performed without access to standardised corpora. The results of tool testing can be used to enhance the admissibility of digital evidence in the courts. Consider again the Daubert standards for evidence admissibility. Previously it was stated that one of the most difficult facts to establish about a tool/technique in this area is the error rate. The development of datasets will allow these rates to be calculated (and therefore allow performance of different tools to be compared) greatly improving the confidence in tool results.

It should be noted that the areas of dataset development and tool testing are not without their own particular challenges. It has long been agreed that the development of realistic datasets is a difficult task. Consider the sample data presented throughout this book. In each case the device was first zero'd (thereby removing all older information that might interfere with the analysis of the file system) and then a new file system was created. To this were added the exact (small) number of files to demonstrate the desired aspects of the file system. Only those actions deemed essential for the book's contents were performed on these file systems. Now consider a realistic scenario. A computer is seized with a 1TiB disk. This computer has been in use for multiple years. Numerous files have been created/deleted on the device. The operating system is modifying many files in the background. This is a more realistic case in which countless actions are performed on file systems prior to analysis. It is difficult to build these *noisy* actions into any manufactured dataset. A solution to this is to use actual devices. However, this introduces privacy concerns and also the realistic noise means that it is impossible to say with any certainty what actions were performed and therefore what data should be present (and recoverable) on the device.

14.2.8 Standardisation

Standard operating procedures are often found in digital investigation units for particular tasks but these procedures are often specific to the unit. With modern investigations there is more chance of the involvement of a number of agencies/units and the possibility of multiple countries being involved in an investigation. The current lack of standard approaches makes it more difficult to ensure consistency and correct interpretation from all relevant parties.

The creation of standards for multiple organisations/countries would benefit the investigative process in its entirety. Following standardised procedures would reduce the effects of human error/bias on investigation and also allow for transfer of human resources between units/countries during an investigation. These would greatly improve the quality of digital investigation.

Additionally standardising the reporting of digital evidence would ease the interpretative process of all recipients of the report. This may be achieved through standardised reporting templates and the use of the same standard operating procedures in all cases.

14.2.9 Information Sharing

The rapid development in technology requires that vast resources are dedicated to research in the area of digital investigation. While the academic community in this area has grown dramatically in recent years, there is still much work done *behind the scenes* by technical investigators. This work is often not shared amongst other practitioners. This leads to duplicated efforts in solving similar problems.

Consider the case in which a new file system is released. Multiple investigative agencies would work on this independently with little knowledge of what other groups/individuals are doing. A more structured approach to information sharing could aid in the analysis of new artefacts (be they file system or others) and might avoid the duplication of work by multiple entities.

Information is already shared amongst many entities related to crime investigation (generally through organisations such as Interpol and Europol). The next step in this information sharing is to share information on the tools/techniques that are developed by individuals in the area. Few domains progress as rapidly as that of digital evidence and as such this area would be a great exemplar to demonstrate the effectiveness of information sharing.

14.2.10 Virtualisation

One of the challenges identified previously was the lack of resources that are available to investigators. This includes human, software and hardware resources. One potential solution to the hardware resource issue is that of virtualisation.

Basic virtualisation can be used to create multiple independent computers, while only needing one hardware instance. These virtual machines can run on individual cases. Also these virtual machines can be destroyed upon completion of a case, with a new machine created. This ensures that there is no previous information from other cases which might cause an issue in the current case. Also, in the case of malware-related investigations (and indeed the analysis of any potentially infected device), the single-use nature of these virtual machines protects other case work from any malware-related effects.

The ultimate in virtualisation is the realisation of forensics as a service (FAAS). With this approach forensic analysis is conducted remotely. This allows for multiple organisations to pool resources to create a single large-scale digital forensic solution which is accessible by all members. FAAS is a specific example of software as a service (SAAS), in which the software that is served is that of digital forensic software. The use of FAAS could potentially reduce the resource challenge and with it reduce the data backlog suffered by many digital forensic practitioners.

14.3 Summary

This chapter summarised some of the future challenges in the area of file system forensics and in more general digital investigation. The increasing data volume has led to a more challenging environment for digital investigation and file system forensics. The increasing number of devices requiring analysis also highlights the lack of resources in this area. Sufficient human, software and hardware resources are beyond the budgets of many players in this area. The data volume and resourcing challenges go hand-in-hand to form a vicious cycle, in which the lack of resources adds to the data volume problem.

The data volume leads to further challenges in the area. For instance most cases involve multiple devices, meaning there is a need for correlation across these devices in order to rebuild the entire sequence of events. This correlation can be challenging for investigators based on a number of reasons such as time settings and lack of expertise. The correlation task can be very time consuming further exacerbating the data volume/backlog challenge.

New technologies have also introduced new challenges to the area. The increasing adoption of encryption at both hardware and software levels has increased the difficulties of the digital investigation task. The increased use of cloud-based storage technologies has also affected the efficiency and quality of digital investigation.

Other challenges such as the lack of validated tools and the lack of standardised corpora have introduced their own challenges as they lead to potential doubt in digital investigation results. Currently results are generally accepted because the tools/techniques used to gather results have been previously accepted in the courts although the scientific backing of these is still under review.

However, it is not all doom and gloom. There are a number of promising avenues that are available (and are being actively studied) that will alleviate, if not remove, some of these challenges. The creation of standardised corpora will lead to more potential for tool/technique validation and therefore provide more weight to the evidence obtained from these tools. Increased training and education in the area will lead to an increase in human resources and also an increase in the general skill level of the investigative population. This in turn leads to more experts in the court's eyes allowing for more weight to be associated with evidence provided. The increased training and education will also allow practitioners to go beyond the tools and to analyse novel artefacts for which tools may not yet exist.

Techniques such as live data forensics and triage have the potential to reduce the data backlog by reducing the number of devices that require full examination. These techniques can be used to gather all the required evidence in certain cases and may remove other potential sources from further consideration. In either case, it represents one less device in the backlog.

Bibliography

Al Fahdi, M., Clarke, N.L., and Furnell, S.M. (2013). Challenges to digital forensics: a survey of researchers & practitioners attitudes and opinions. *2013 Information Security for South Africa 2013*, 1–8. IEEE.

Andreassen, L.E. and Andresen, G. (2019). Live data forensics: a quantitative study of the Norwegian Police University College students LDF examinations during their first year of practice [dissertation]. Dublin: University College Dublin.

Arshad, H., Jantan, A.B., and Abiodun, O.I. (2018). Digital forensics: review of issues in scientific validation of digital evidence. *Journal of Information Processing Systems* 14 (2): 346–376.

Butler, S. (2019). Criminal use of cryptocurrencies: a great new threat or is cash still king? *Journal of Cyber Policy* 4 (3): 326–345.

Carrier, B. (2005). *File System Forensic Analysis*. Boston, MA, London: Addison-Wesley.

Casino, F., Dasaklis, T.K., Spathoulas, G.P. et al. (2022). Research trends, challenges, and emerging topics in digital forensics: a review of reviews. *IEEE Access* 10: 25464–25493.

Cervantes Mori, M.D., Kävrestad, J., and Nohlberg, M. (2021). Success factors and challenges in digital forensics for law enforcement in Sweden. *7th International Workshop on Socio-Technical Perspective in IS Development (STPIS 2021), virtual conference in Trento*, Italy (11–12 October 2021), 100–116. CEUR-WS.

Clipper, S.M. (2017). Meets Apple vs. FBI–A comparison of the cryptography discourses from 1993 and 2016. *Media and Communication* 5 (1): 54.

Cybercrime Training Competency Framework –Homepage [Internet] (2024). www.ecteg.eu. [cited 2024 June 4]. https://www.ecteg.eu/tcf/co/TCF.html.

Difference between Training and Education - The Peak Performance Center [Internet] (2024). thepeakperformancecenter.com [cited 2024 April 2]. https://thepeakperformancecenter.com/business/learning/business-training/difference-between-training-and-education/.

Du, X., Hargreaves, C., Sheppard, J. et al. (2020). SoK: Exploring the state of the art and the future potential of artificial intelligence in digital forensic investigation. *Proceedings of the 15th International Conference on Availability, Reliability and Security 2020*, 1–10.

Garfinkel, S.L. (2010). Digital forensics research: the next 10 years. *Digital Investigation* 7 (7): S64–S73.

Garrie, D.B. (2014). Digital forensic evidence in the courtroom: understanding content and quality. *Northwestern Journal of Technology and Intellectual Property* 12: 121.

Gaskell, A. (2024). The Pressing Need To Grow The Cyber Workforce [Internet]. Forbes. [cited 2024 June 4]. https://www.forbes.com/sites/adigaskell/2022/05/19/the-pressing-need-to-grow-the-cyber-workforce/?sh=227c7c521441.

Hansen, K.H. and Toolan, F. (2017). Decoding the APFS file system. *Digital Investigation* 22: 107–132.

Horsman, G. (2019). Tool testing and reliability issues in the field of digital forensics. *Digital Investigation* 28 (28): 163–175.

Horsman, G. and Sunde, N. (2020). Part 1: The need for peer review in digital forensics. *Forensic Science International: Digital Investigation* 35: 301062.

Humphries, G., Nordvik, R., Manifavas, H. et al. (2021). Law enforcement educational challenges for mobile forensics. *Forensic Science International: Digital Investigation* 38: 301129.

Irons, A. and Ophoff, J. (2016). Aspects of digital forensics in South Africa. *Interdisciplinary Journal of Information, Knowledge, and Management* 11: 273–283.

Lillis, D., Becker, B., O'Sullivan, T., and Scanlon, M. (2016). Current challenges and future research areas for digital forensic investigation. arXiv preprint arXiv:1604.03850.

Mitchell, F. (2010). The use of Artificial Intelligence in digital forensics: an introduction. *Digital Evidence and Electronic Signature Law Review* 7: 35–41.

National Police Chief's Council (2020). Digital Forensic Science Strategy [Internet]. [cited 2024 April 3]. https://www.npcc.police.uk/SysSiteAssets/media/downloads/publications/publications-log/2020/national-digital-forensic-science-strategy.pdf.

Page, H., Horsman, G., Sarna, A., and Foster, J. (2019). A review of quality procedures in the UK forensic sciences: what can the field of digital forensics learn? *Science & Justice* 59 (1): 83–92.

Pandey, A.K., Tripathi, A.K., Kapil, G. et al. (2020). Current challenges of digital forensics in cyber security. In Critical Concepts, Standards, and Techniques in Cyber Forensics, edited by Mohammad Shahid Husain and Mohammad Zunnun Khan, 31–46. Hershey, PA: IGI Global, 2020. https://doi.org/10.4018/978-1-7998-1558-7.ch003.

Qadir, A.M. and Varol, A. (2020). The role of machine learning in digital forensics. *2020 8th International Symposium on Digital Forensics and Security (ISDFS)*, 1–5. IEEE.
Rafique, M. and Khan, M.N. (2013). Exploring static and live digital forensics: methods, practices and tools. *International Journal of Scientific and Engineering Research* 4 (10): 1048–1056.
Reedy, P. (2020). Interpol review of digital evidence 2016–2019. *Forensic Science International: Synergy* 1 (2): 489–520.
Roussev, V., Quates, C., and Martell, R. (2013). Real-time digital forensics and triage. *Digital Investigation* 10 (2): 158–167.
Rughani, P.H. (2017). Artificial intelligence based digital forensics framework. *International Journal of Advanced Research in Computer Science* 8 (8): 10–14.
Shaw, A. and Browne, A. (2013). A practical and robust approach to coping with large volumes of data submitted for digital forensic examination. *Digital Investigation* 10 (2): 116–128.
Sunde, N. and Dror, I.E. (2019). Cognitive and human factors in digital forensics: problems, challenges, and the way forward. *Digital Investigation* 29: 101–108.
Vincze, E.A. (2016). Challenges in digital forensics. *Police Practice and Research* 17 (2): 183–194.
Wu, T., Breitinger, F., and O'Shaughnessy, S. (2020). Digital forensic tools: recent advances and enhancing the status quo. Forensic Science International. *Digital Investigation* 34: 300999.

Index

a

ACPO principles 5–10, 88, 441, 451
acquisition 7–9, 69, 88–92, 441
- cloud 441
- dc3dd 90
- dcfldd 90
- dd 89, 90
- ewf 90, 91
- guymager 91
- live data forensics 450
- logical 88
- physical 88

admissibility 438, 444, 445, 448, 451, 452
allocation map 85
- APFS 412
- ExFAT 127, 128, 134
- ext 201, 209
- FAT 104, 105
- HFS+ 356
- NTFS 152, 165, 166, 187
- XFS 265, 283–285

APFS 393
- analysis 413
- B-tree 396–399, 427–429
- checkpoint 393, 410–412, 426
- checkpoint area 394, 411
- container 399, 400
- container superblock 399–402, 414, 415
- content recovery 423–425
- copy on write 394, 395, 410, 411, 426
- creation 412, 413
- deletion 425, 426
- directory record 408–410
- ephemeral object 394, 395
- extended attribute 407–409, 423, 430, 431
- extent 410, 411
- file system key 406, 421, 422
- file system tree 414, 419
- fragmentation 410
- inode 393, 407, 408, 422, 423, 431
- layout 394, 395
- link 431–433
- metadata recovery 420–422
- object 394–396
- object header 396
- object map 404, 405, 414–418, 427
- OBJ_ID_MASK 406
- OBJ_TYPE_MASK 406
- physical object 394, 395
- reaper 412
- sibling link entry 432
- snapshot 393
- space manager 394, 412
- time 394
- virtual object 394, 395
- volume 399, 429, 430
- volume superblock 399, 402–404, 414, 418–420

artificial intelligence 439, 449, 450
ASCII 40, 56, 57
- decoding 56, 57
- limitations 57, 59

b

bias 438, 446, 447, 453
binary 45–49
- bc 52
- conversion 49, 50
- fixed point 54
- floating point 54, 55

binary (*contd.*)
group names 46
negative number (*see* twos complement)
place-value system 49
repeated division 51
twos complement 53
bitmap. *see* allocation map
block 83
B-tree. *see* trees
B+-tree. *see* trees
BtrFS 303
addressing 315–317, 323, 326
analysis 318–349
backup roots area 320, 340–342
B-tree 303, 305, 342, 343
btrfs_root_backup 340–342
btrfstools 317
checksum 304
CHUNK_ARRAY 306, 319, 321–323, 339
CHUNK_ITEM 313, 314, 321–323
CHUNK_TREE 307, 319, 322–325, 339
content recovery 319, 336–338
copy on write 303, 304, 321
creation 317
CSUM_TREE 307
deletion 338
DEV_ITEM 313, 314, 325, 326
DEV_TREE 307, 320
directory 319, 329
DIR_INDEX 311, 329
DIR_ITEM 311, 329
extent 304
EXTENT_CSUM 311
EXTENT_DATA 311, 319, 336, 337
EXTENT_TREE 307
FS_TREE 307, 319, 327–334, 339
inline storage 311, 313, 336
INODE_ITEM 310, 319, 335
INODE_REF 311, 329
item 305, 310
key 305, 309
layout 304, 305
metadata recovery 319, 335
node 307–309
RAID 303, 343–346
ROOT_BACKREF 313
root directory 307
ROOT_ITEM 313, 328
ROOT_REF 313
ROOT_TREE 307, 319, 326
snapshot 304, 346–350
STRING_ITEM 315
subvolume 304, 346–350
superblock 305, 306, 318, 320, 321
time 315

c

carving 70, 96, 97
artificial intelligence 449
foremost 97
photorec 97
scalpel 97
signature 96
cloud storage 441
cluster 72, 83, 84
copy on write 85
APFS 394, 395, 410, 411, 426
BtrFS 303, 304, 321
XFS 273

d

datasets, standardised 443, 444
data volume 437–439, 443, 447–449
Daubert standard 21, 438, 444–446, 448, 452
decimal 48
bc 52
conversion 51
place-value system 49
deletion 84
APFS 425, 426
BtrFS 338
ExFAT 140, 141
ext 225, 249–252
FAT 116, 117
HFS+ 380, 381
NTFS 187–189
XFS 289, 290
digital forensics 4
definitions 4, 5
methodologies 7–10
principles, ACPO 5, 6, 441, 451

e

education. *see* training/education
encryption 437, 440, 441
endianness 64–66
  APFS 394
  big-endian 64, 65
  BtrFS 305
  ext 203
  ext journal 235
  FAT 101
  HFS+ 355
  interpreting 65, 66
  little-endian 64–66
  mixed-endian 81, 82
  XFS 263
  XFS journal 295
ExFAT 121
  allocation bitmap 125, 127, 128, 134
  analysis 132–142
  backup VBR 122
  cluster 122, 133, 134
  content recovery 137–139
  creation 132
  data area 122
  deleted files 140, 141
  directory entry 125–132
  directory entry, primary 126
  directory entry, secondary 126
  FAT chain 123, 124, 141
  file 125, 129, 130, 135, 137
  file allocation table 123–125, 141
  filename extension 131, 135, 139, 140
  fragmented files 141, 142
  fsstat 122, 123, 133, 134
  layout 121, 122
  long file names 139, 140
  metadata recovery 137, 138
  root directory 133–136
  stream extension 130, 131, 137, 138, 141
  time 129, 130, 142, 143
  timezone 130, 143
  up-case table 125, 128
  volume boot record 122, 123, 133
  volume GUID 125, 130
  volume label 125, 128, 129
expert witness format 90
  ewfacquire 90–92
  ewfexport 91
  ewfinfo 90
  ewfmount 91–93
  ewf-tools 90
  ewfverify 91
ext2. *see* extX
ext3. *see* extX
ext4. *see* extX
extent 84
  APFS 410, 411
  BtrFS 307, 311, 319, 336, 337
  ext4 244–248, 251, 252
  HFS+, fork 357, 379, 384
  NTFS, runlist 154, 183, 184
  XFS 274
extX 199
  analysis 211–226
  bitmap 201, 209
  block group 200, 201, 204, 211, 213–216
  block group descriptor table 204–206, 213–216, 255, 256
  block pointer 208, 209, 219–223, 225
  comparison 200
  content recovery 211, 219–221
  creation 210
  data bitmap 201, 209
  deletion 225, 226, 249–252
  directory entry 201, 218, 219, 238, 239
  extended attribute 252–255
  extent 244–246, 251, 252
  extent tree 246–248, 251, 252
  flexible block group 255–258
  fragmentation 222, 223
  fsstat 203, 212, 214, 215, 231, 255
  htree directory 230, 237–240
  inline storage 248–250, 440
  inode 201, 205–207, 211, 216, 217, 219, 225, 241
  inode bitmap 201, 209
  inode flags 208
  inode location 209, 210
  inode table 205–207, 222
  journal 229–237
  journaling level 230, 231
  layout 200
  links 223–225, 248, 249, 251
  lost+found 219

extX (*contd.*)
metadata recovery 211, 220
mode 207
permissions 207, 208
reserved area 200
root directory 211, 216–219
sparse_superblock 203
superblock 200–204, 211–213
time 241–243

f

File Allocation Table (FAT) 101
access time 105–107
analysis 110–117
cluster 109
content recovery 113–115
creation 109, 110
data area 102
deletion 116, 117
directory entry 105–108
FAT chain 104, 105
file allocation table 104, 105
filename 101
fragmentation 105
FSINFO 102–104
fsstat 102, 111
layout 102
long filenames 107, 108
metadata recovery 113, 114
reserved area 102
root directory 110, 112–114
time 47, 48, 108, 109
volume boot sector 102–104, 110–112
volume label 117
fragmentation 84
APFS 410
ExFAT 141, 142
ext 221, 222
FAT 105
HFS+ 383, 384
NTFS 187, 189, 190
XFS 274

h

hashing 36–38
collisions 38
crc32 38, 81, 270
md5 37, 38
pigeon hole principle 38
purpose 37, 90
sha family 37, 38
HFS+ 355
allocation block 355
allocation file 356, 366, 367
analysis 369–390
attributes file 356
B-tree 358, 360–362, 381–383
catalog file 356, 362–365, 371–377
CNID 355, 363
CNID, reserved 356
content recovery 377–380
creation 369, 370
deletion 380, 381
endianess 355
extent (*see* fork)
extents overflow file 356, 365–367, 384–387
file record 363, 365, 375–379, 387
file thread record 363, 366, 375, 376
folder record 363, 364, 375–377
folder thread record 363, 366, 375, 376
fork 357, 379, 384
fragmentation 383, 384
fsstat 358
journal 367–369
layout 355, 356
link, hard 388–390
link, symbolic 387, 388
metadata recovery 377
permissions 363, 364, 366
text encoding 365, 367
time 357, 358
volume header 356, 358–360, 370–373

i

imaging. *see* acquisition
inline storage 84
BtrFS 311, 313, 336
ext 248–250, 440
NTFS 151–154, 182
XFS 274
inode 205
APFS 393, 407, 408, 422, 423, 431
BtrFS 310, 319, 335

ExFAT, file directory entry 125, 129, 130, 135, 137
ext 205–207, 211, 216, 217, 219, 225, 241
XFS 265, 271–273, 289, 290, 292

j

journal 85
ext 229–237
HFS+ 367–369
NTFS 146
XFS 292–300

k

key escrow 441, 451

l

LDF 6, 8, 450, 451
ACPO 6
acquisition 88, 441
primary storage 70
links 223
APFS 431–433
BtrFS 333
ext 223–225, 248, 249, 251
HFS+ 387–390
NTFS 152, 166, 167
XFS 291, 292
linux 17
application 22
description 21, 22
distributions 27, 28
file system management 24
file system support 24, 25
GNU utilities 22, 25, 26
GUI 22, 26
history 28, 29
kernel 22–25
structure 22–27
use of 29
user accounts 30
linux commands 32
attr 290
bzip 39
cat 35
cd 33, 35
date 64
dc3dd 90
dcfldd 90
dd 89, 90
df 77
dmesg 74
egrep (*see* grep)
fdisk 74
file 40
gdisk 74
grep 41, 42
guymager 91, 92
gzip 39
head 35
less 35
ls 32, 33
lsblk 74
man 34
mkdir 35
mkfs 77
mkfs.btrfs 316, 317, 344
mkfs.exfat 132
mkfs.ext2 210
mkfs.hfsplus 370
mkfs.ntfs 168
mkfs.vfat 110
mkfs.xfs 275
more 35
mount 77
pipe 35, 36
pwd 32, 33
redirection 35, 36
strings 40, 41
sudo 31, 32
tail 35
tar 39
whoami 31, 32
xxd 38, 39
zip 39
live data forensics. *see* LDF

m

metadata 84
mounting 77
ewfmount 92, 93
mount 77

n

NTFS 145
 alternate data stream 145, 190–193
 analysis 167–193
 $AttrDef 186, 187
 attribute 151, 152, 155
 $ATTRIBUTE_LIST 151, 156, 191, 192
 $BITMAP 152, 165, 166, 187
 $Boot 146, 148, 168–171
 B-tree (*see* index)
 content recovery 182–184
 creation 168
 $DATA 152, 163, 172, 173, 182
 deletion 187–189
 directory 173–177
 $EA 152, 167
 $EA_INFORMATION 152, 167
 extent (*see* runlist)
 $FILENAME 151, 156–158, 175
 fixup array 149, 150, 177, 180, 183
 fragmentation 187, 189, 190
 fsstat 169, 170, 185, 186
 index 145–149
 $INDEX_ALLOCATION 152, 165, 173–177
 $INDEX_ROOT 152, 163–165, 173
 layout 146
 $Logfile 146
 master file table (*see* $MFT)
 metadata recovery 177, 179–182
 $MFT 151–154, 168, 171–173
 non-resident 151–154, 182–184
 $OBJECT_ID 152, 157–159
 $REPARSE_POINT 152, 166, 167
 resident 151–154, 182
 runlist 154, 183, 184
 $SECURITY_DESCRIPTOR 152, 159–162
 $STANDARD_INFORMATION 152, 155, 156
 time 150, 151
 update sequence array (*see* fixup array)
 $VOLUME_INFORMATION 152, 163, 164, 185
 $VOLUME_NAME 152, 162, 185
number representation 48
 fixed point numbers 54
 floating point numbers 53–56
 IEEE 754 55, 56
 integers 49–51
 negative numbers 53
 ones complement 53
 twos complement 53
number systems 48
 binary 49
 bit 45, 46
 bit field 47
 byte 45–48
 conversion 51
 conversion, bash 51–53
 decimal 48, 49
 hexadecimal 50, 51
 repeated division 51

o

open source 17
 advantages 19, 20
 copyleft 19
 cost 20, 448
 definition 19, 448
 digital forensics, in 20, 21
 disclosure 21, 448
 FOSS 20, 448, 449

p

partition 74
 creating 74, 75
 extended boot record 79
 extended partition 79
 fdisk 74
 gdisk 74
 GUID partition table 80–83
 master boot record 78–80
 protective MBR 80
 UUID 82

r

RAID 86

s

sector 83
slack space 9, 84, 85, 88
 ext directory entry 218
 HFS+ index 381
 MFT record 151
sleuth kit, the 92–96
 blkls 96

fls 94, 95
fsstat 93
icat 95
istat 95
jcat 233, 234
jls 233, 234
mactime 95, 96
mmls 93
tsk_recover 96
snapshot 85
APFS 393
BtrFS 304, 346–350
standardisation 444, 452
storage media 69
categorisation 70
cloud 441
flash memory 73
HDD 71, 72
offline 71
optical media 72
primary 70
RAM 70
ROM 70
secondary 70
SSD 73
tertiary 70, 71
superblock. *see* volume boot record

t

textual representation 56
ASCII 56, 57
ISO-8859 57–59
Unicode 59–62
UTF-8 60, 61
UTF-16 61, 62
time 62
date command 64
epoch based 62, 63
FAT time 47, 48, 108, 109
unix time 63
training. *see* training/education
training/education 8, 440, 442, 444, 446–448
trees 84
APFS 396–399, 427–429
BtrFS 303, 305, 342, 343
ext 230, 237–240
HFS+ 358, 360–362, 381–383
NTFS 145–149
XFS 264, 267, 268
triage 439, 443, 449

u

unallocated space 9, 84, 88, 93, 96

v

validation 442–444, 452
virtualisation 453
volume boot record 85
APFS, container superblock 399–402, 414, 415
APFS, volume superblock 399, 402–404, 414, 418–420
BtrFS, superblock 305, 306, 318, 320, 321
ExFAT 122, 123, 133
ext, superblock 200–204, 211–213
FAT 102–104, 110–112
HFS+, volume header 356, 358–360, 370–373
NTFS 146, 148, 168–171
XFS, superblock 264, 265, 268–271, 276, 277
volume header. *see* volume boot record

x

XFS 263
allocation group 264, 265, 283
analysis 264
block addressing 266
b+-tree 264, 267, 268
content recovery 276, 281, 282
copy on write 273
creation 275
deletion 289, 290
directory 273, 274, 276, 279
directory entry 265, 273, 274, 279, 280, 289
endianness 263
extended attribute 290, 291
extent 274
fragmentation 274
free block info 265, 283, 284
free list 265, 285, 286
free space b+-tree 265, 283–285
inline storage 274
inode 265, 271–273, 289, 290, 292
inode addressing 266, 267, 278
inode B+-tree 265, 287, 288

XFS (*contd.*)
inode B+-tree info 265, 286, 287
internal free list 265
journal 292–300
layout 263–265
links 291, 292
metadata recovery 276, 281, 282
root directory 276–281
signature 264, 271
superblock 264, 265, 268–271, 276, 277
time 264, 275
xfsprogs 275

Printed and bound by CPI Group (UK) Ltd, Croydon, CR0 4YY
17/09/2026
14964336-0002